THE FLETCHER JONES FOUNDATION
HUMANITIES IMPRINT

The Fletcher Jones Foundation has endowed this imprint to foster innovative and enduring scholarship in the humanities.

The publisher gratefully acknowledges the generous support of the Fletcher Jones Foundation Humanities Endowment Fund of the University of California Press Foundation.

IRVING THALBERG

Mark A. Vieira · IRVING THALBERG

Boy Wonder to Producer Prince

University of California Press

Berkeley   Los Angeles   London

University of California Press, one of the most distinguished university presses in the United States,
enriches lives around the world by advancing scholarship in the humanities, social sciences, and natural
sciences. Its activities are supported by the UC Press
Foundation and by philanthropic contributions from
individuals and institutions. For more information,
visit www.ucpress.edu.

University of California Press
Berkeley and Los Angeles, California

University of California Press, Ltd.
London, England

Library of Congress Cataloging-in-Publication Data

Vieira, Mark A., 1950–.
    Irving Thalberg : boy wonder to producer prince /
Mark A. Vieira.
        p.   cm.
    Includes bibliographical references and index.
    ISBN 978-0-520-26048-1 (cloth : alk. paper)
    1. Thalberg, Irving G., 1899–1936.   2. Motion
picture producers and directors—United States—
Biography.   I. Title.

PN1998.3.T467V547   2009

791.4302'32092—dc22   2009011534
[B]

Manufactured in the United States of America

18   17   16   15   14   13   12   11   10
10   9   8   7   6   5   4   3   2   1

This book is printed on Cascades Enviro 100, a 100%
postconsumer waste, recycled, de-inked fiber. FSC
recycled certified and processed chlorine free. It is
acid free, Ecologo certified, and manufactured by
BioGas energy.

To the memory of my parents

"Nothing exists except that which is imagined."

ANATOLE FRANCE, *The Crime of Sylvestre Bonnard*, 1897

CONTENTS

PREFACE

The awards ceremony of the Academy of Motion Picture Arts and Sciences takes place once a year. One award, however, is not presented yearly. The Irving G. Thalberg Memorial Award is presented only when the Academy's Board of Directors wishes to honor a special producer, one whose work reflects "a consistently high quality of motion picture production." Past recipients of this prestigious award include Walt Disney, Jack L. Warner, Alfred Hitchcock, Billy Wilder, and Warren Beatty. The Thalberg award was first presented on March 10, 1938, to Darryl F. Zanuck, so current viewers of the awards may ask about its namesake. If Irving Thalberg could be magically conjured up on Oscar night, those viewers would be surprised at his attractiveness, his modesty, and his wisdom. More than seventy years after his premature death, the "Boy Wonder" continues to influence the industry to which he gave his life, yet his name is not a household word like Disney or Warner.

Viewers of Turner Classic Movies (TCM) know that David O. Selznick produced *Gone with the Wind* and that Cecil B. DeMille produced *The Sign of the Cross;* their names are in the credits. Look at the credits of *Ben-Hur, The Big Parade, Grand Hotel, Mutiny on the Bounty,* and hundreds of other Metro-Goldwyn-Mayer films made between 1924 and 1936. These films survive—a vibrant component of American culture, respected, beloved, and enjoyed. Irving Thalberg supervised all of them and personally produced scores of them, but unless you know Hollywood history, you might think they were made by Leo the Lion. Thalberg declined to affix his name to any film, simply saying: "Credit you give yourself isn't worth having."

This is not to say that Thalberg has been overlooked by film historians. Numerous books have been devoted to him or have dealt with him, including Bob Thomas's *Thalberg: Life and Legend,* Samuel Marx's *Mayer and Thalberg,* and Scott Eyman's *Lion of Hollywood.* These books have done well by their subject, and why not? Thalberg's story is as romantic and improbable as a silent-movie plot.

Irving Grant Thalberg, born in Brooklyn in 1899, survived a series of childhood illnesses only to be told that his damaged heart would not sustain him past the age of thirty. He coped with this death sentence as he had coped with illness—lying in his sickbed, reading the classics, seeing the characters from these books dance like dreams on his bedroom walls. Urged on by his ambitious mother, Thalberg pushed himself into the fledgling film industry. Beginning with *The Hunchback of Notre Dame,* Thalberg brought the characters on the walls of his room to America's screens. In 1924 he and Louis B. Mayer founded M-G-M. In 1927 Thalberg married Norma Shearer, one of the stars he and Mayer had launched, and guided her to superstardom.

Then as now, Hollywood was given to self-congratulation, but even without hyperbole, Thalberg's achievements were impressive. Within three years, his partnership with Mayer had made M-G-M the most successful studio in Hollywood. For twelve years, virtually no M-G-M film was made without Thalberg's imprint. His drive, discernment, and resourcefulness were balanced by an almost mystical understanding of his colleagues. He was respected—indeed, loved—by employees at every level of the corporation. He introduced the horror film and coauthored the Production Code. He innovated story conferences, sneak previews, and extensive retakes. He strove to achieve a synthesis of theater and film. He made stars of Lon Chaney, Ramon Novarro, John Gilbert, Joan Crawford, Clark Gable, Jean Harlow, Robert Montgomery, Marie Dressler, Wallace Beery, and Greta Garbo. To his everlasting credit (or disgrace), he established the producer—not the director—as the author of the Hollywood film.

Every well-constructed suspense film has a ticking time bomb. Thalberg's time bomb was his health. Knowing that he was on borrowed time, he pushed himself to the limit, working sixteen hours a day on forty films a year, determined that motion pictures should be accorded the same respect as literature and drama. By age thirty-seven he was acknowledged the greatest producer in Hollywood, his films a rare blend of commercialism and taste, ratified by box office and honored with awards. Then, as he stood poised to lead the film community to new horizons,

Thalberg suddenly died, leaving a widow, two children, and a host of unfinished projects. The story of his race with the time bomb—and what he accomplished before it exploded on a sunny morning in 1936—is the one I want to tell.

In previous books I have told stories of George Hurrell, Boris Karloff, and Greta Garbo in strict chronology and detailed narrative. In each case, my archival discoveries brought a new understanding of these legendary figures. In some ways, Thalberg is as mysterious as Garbo, whose persona he did so much to create. Like her, he created fantasies while appearing detached, almost unemotional. His legend stands in equally bold relief, and his persona lends itself to hagiography, as his biographers have noted. Many interviews conducted by Thomas and Marx began with the word "genius," and some stopped just short of calling Thalberg a saint. A few dismissed him as an opaque, icy autocrat. The human being behind the legend has eluded most historians. How did he accomplish all he did in his short lifetime? Who was he?

I believe that by combining a revised chronology, the recollections of his colleagues, and newly uncovered archival documents, I can answer these questions and find the human being behind the legend. If you were to be transported from 2010 to 1930, what would you experience as you walked the studio streets leading to Thalberg's office? What insight would you gain about his production methods if you could go from the purchase of a play all the way to the premiere of the film he made from it? What would you learn by sitting next to him in a story conference? With this book, you will go not only from conception to execution but also into Thalberg's confidence, hearing in his own words what he wanted to do, how he planned to do it, and most important, how he felt when he reached his goals—or did not.

I have written another book about Thalberg. *Hollywood Dreams Made Real: Irving Thalberg and the Rise of M-G-M* was published by Harry N. Abrams in October 2008. It is a visual survey of the Thalberg era with highlights of his achievements. It was not meant to be a conventional biography, but a companion volume to a more comprehensive work, as well as a guide to the Thalberg films shown on TCM and released by Warner Home Video. Irving Thalberg deserves a full-scale biography, one that details previously unexamined aspects of his professional, political, and personal lives. Foolish and sometimes hostile apocrypha have formed around his legend. Otherwise intelligent critics such as Pauline Kael have perpetuated the myth of an obsessed executive foisting an untalented wife on an unwilling public. The archival documents that form the basis of this book tell a different tale.

In my research I was fortunate to have access to most of Thalberg's films, both from TCM and Warners. I also had access to the interviews Bob Thomas conducted for *Thalberg: Life and Legend*. His generosity made it possible for me to study documents that began with notations such as: "William Haines, 446 South Canon Drive, 10/31/67" or "Joan Crawford, 1/24/68, Cock and Bull [Restaurant, West Hollywood]." Unfortunately, Mr. Thomas was not granted an interview by Thalberg's most intimate colleague, Norma Shearer. After her retirement from films in 1942, Shearer granted almost no interviews. When she did, for Bosley Crowther's books on M-G-M in the mid-1950s, she asked not to be quoted. Inasmuch as I considered her thoughts on Thalberg essential to this project, I hoped and prayed for some archival record of them. My prayers were answered by the discovery of an unpublished document.

In 1955 Shearer felt that the time had come to tell the story of her work and her life with Thalberg. She was brought up short when the first draft of her dictated memoirs was rejected by Random House's Bennett Cerf. He called it "bland and romanticized." Between bouts of debilitating illness, Shearer spent the next twenty years reworking her manuscript. She never completed it. In its final form it portrayed M-G-M as a plantation populated by contented celebrities. Shearer wrote honestly about her childhood, her struggles to enter the movies in New York, and about the early days of M-G-M, but she refused to visit the painful memories of Thalberg's estrangement from Mayer, her husband's tragic death, or her own problems with Mayer during the making of her favorite film, *Marie Antoinette*. In 1976 MGM vice president Howard Strickling tried to tell her as gently as possible that her manuscript was unpublishable. Shearer was too ill to care. For the next thirty years, the manuscript was believed to have been destroyed. Fortunately, one copy survived—and made its way to me.

Shearer's memoirs are indeed romanticized. In the decades following Thalberg's death, she became obsessively protective of his memory and fought to keep him from being misrepresented. She took great pains, for instance, to see that Robert Evans was cast as Thalberg in the 1957 biography of Lon Chaney, *The Man of a Thousand Faces*. As much as she tried to sugarcoat history, her memoirs have immediacy. They relate episodes crucial to any Thalberg biography: her first meeting with Thalberg, her early problems with Mayer, the transition to the big company after the merger, her first encounter with Joan Crawford, and details of studio life that appear nowhere else and from no one else. Most important, Shearer's memoirs tell how she felt about her career, about M-G-M, and about Thalberg.

Interweaving Shearer's stories with those of other M-G-M veterans, with transcriptions of Thalberg's previously unpublished letters, speeches, and interviews, and with transcriptions of his conversations found in archival documents, I have learned how he made his films. I have gone beyond the legend of Thalberg to find the human being. To do this, I had to look at him from perspectives that even I found difficult. I had to know what pushed him to defy doctors, ignore bureaucrats, and overcome treachery as he worked to refine and uplift the product manufactured by America's sixth-largest industry. I have turned away from the image of the Boy Wonder and looked at his life as I looked at those of Hurrell, Karloff, and Garbo—week by week, film by film, and story by story. After "living with" Irving Thalberg for five years, I can tell the story of the self-educated boy who so vitally influenced our culture.

PART ONE • THE MERGER

In the waning years of the nineteenth century, William and Henrietta Thalberg were living at 19 Woodbine Street in Brooklyn, New York, a narrow brownstone wedged into a middle-class German-Jewish neighborhood. The young couple could not afford to rent the entire home, so they contented themselves with a multiroom attic. William was an importer of lace, a small, passive man. Henrietta was petite, too, but powerful. Years later, family friend Irene Mayer Selznick described Henrietta's eyes as "dark and menacing." Like her family, the owners of the Heyman & Heyman department store, Henrietta was ambitious. She expected her husband's business to improve her station in life. When it did not, she turned to motherhood, hoping to mold a son into the man of vision that William would never be. According to Irene Selznick, "Henrietta got revenge against an ineffectual husband—against life—through this boy."

Irving Grant Thalberg was born at home on May 30, 1899. Henrietta's hopes for her child were nearly dashed when he was diagnosed with a congenital heart defect. Born a "blue baby" because of a faulty supply of oxygen to his blood, Irving had a sickly color and arms like matchsticks. He was given a poor prognosis by the family doctor and by the specialists who were brought in later. The child might live to twenty, or if he was lucky, to thirty.

A daughter, Sylvia, was born a year later, but Henrietta spent her energies on Irving. To prove the doctors wrong, she conducted a seven-year regimen: sponge baths, rubdowns, hot water bottles, enemas, and forced rest periods. If Irving had lived his life in quarantine, he would have escaped the usual childhood illnesses. When he started school, he was hit first by bronchial infections and then by diphtheria. When he could attend classes, he was an eager, inquisitive student. He excelled in English and social studies at Brooklyn Boys' High School, but lagged in mathematics. Henrietta drilled him until he improved, and one day he brought home a silver award. His mother looked at it. "What does that mean?" she asked.

"Second," answered Irving quietly.

Henrietta socked him in the arm. "Next time, you bring home the gold award." The harshness of this blow was softened by the nurturing that followed, but its message was imprinted in Irving's mind more indelibly than the drills. He was expected not merely to achieve, but to surpass.

Irving did achieve the gold medal and he did surpass his fellow students, but he was distracted by chest pains, dizziness, and fatigue. In the fall of 1916, rheumatic fever dealt the coup de grace to his academic career, putting him in bed for a year. He could not graduate from high school. Henrietta tried to keep him from losing ground. She brought homework, books, and teachers to his sickroom. She tried to make him ignore the tantalizing sounds of children playing outside his window. She had to motivate him without giving unrealistic expectations. To accomplish this, she had to impose her will. The Thalbergs became a matriarchy with one goal: keeping its crown prince alive.

Irving enjoyed reading, which was fortunate; there was little else to entertain him. Prevented from learning about life on the streets of New York, he learned about it in books. He began to devour popular novels, classics, plays, and biographies. He took a lively interest in philosophy, studying and comparing the works of Schopenhauer, Kant, and Hegel. He was taken with William James's philosophy of pragmatism, which held that a philosopher "turns away from abstraction and insufficiency, from verbal solutions, from bad *a priori* reasons, from fixed principles, closed systems, and pretended absolutes and . . . turns towards concreteness and adequacy, towards facts, towards action and towards power." In time, Irving distilled these philosophies into five rules:

Never hold an "unassailable" opinion.

The clearness with which I see my goal determines my speed in reaching it.

Expect help from no one.

Pride goeth before a fall, and the height of the pride determines the severity of the bump.

Never take any one man's opinion as final.

For all his mental agility, Irving was losing contact with the world. The literary characters who inhabited his bedroom were more real to him than his former playmates. There was no action in his existence, let alone power. Henrietta feared that this isolation would lead to emotional illness. "You've been sick long enough," she said to him one day in 1916. "I want you to make something of yourself." With this imperative ringing in his ears, the thin, precocious boy ventured into Manhattan.

He had by this time been informed of his expected life span. Children who endure grave illness often acquire maturity before their peers. If this was true of the seventeen-year-old, he would need all the wisdom he had gained to face his limited prospects. Due to years of seclusion, he had missed his adolescence. He had few social skills. His ability to relate with people on a simple human level was impaired. He was quiet, but he was considered reserved rather than shy. When included in conversation, however, he was honest and incisive. He barely had a high school education, but this was a moot point. He lacked the stamina he would need for the rigors of college, for all-night sessions writing term papers and cramming for exams. He was spindly, so a blue-collar job was out of the question. Of necessity Irving chose a moderate course. He worked part-time as a clerk with his maternal grandfather while taking evening classes at New York University and various business schools. He became expert at typing, shorthand, and Spanish. After a few office jobs, a chance encounter brought the first work that truly stimulated him.

In June 1918 he was staying at his grandmother's vacation cottage at Edgemere, Long Island. Sensing a job prospect, Henrietta urged Irving to introduce himself to one of her mother's neighbors, a genial businessman named Carl Laemmle. The fifty-one-year-old Laemmle was unabashedly wealthy, the founder of the Universal Film Manufacturing Company. At five foot one, the elfish Laemmle had to look up at Irving, who was five foot six. Laemmle asked the young man's opinion of the moving pictures that he projected on a bedsheet on his front porch. Irving's comments were articulate and well received, but Laemmle did not offer him a job. When Laemmle next saw Irving, the boy was working in Laemmle's own office at 1600 Broadway in New York as a $35-a-week secretary to his assistant, D. B. Lederman. Unlike many of Laemmle's employees, Irving had secured the job by applying for it, not by virtue of nepotism. Irving made a practice of writing memos to suggest improvements, both in office management and in the films he screened with Lederman. These memos so impressed Laemmle that he told Lederman to find another secretary. Irving became Laemmle's secretary, earning $60 a week.

Among Irving's duties was transcribing Laemmle's comments during screenings of the latest Universal product. It was the mogul's habit to review practically every new release. He began asking Irving's opinion. Irving was not a sycophant. If he thought a film could be improved, he said so. Laemmle took umbrage when Irving criticized a film starring world-famous prizefighter James J. Corbett. Irving thought it was poor.

"But it has Corbett!" Laemmle corrected him. Irving had to concede the point.

While working in Laemmle's office, Irving made the acquaintance of another well-read youth. Eighteen-year-old Samuel Marx was working in the company's export department and enjoyed passing time with Irving at the cafeteria downstairs. Their conversations revolved around the film industry. Irving was committed to it. "It changes so fast that it offers unlimited opportunities," said Irving. He admitted that Universal's films were second-rate, even if they were profitable. "The people have to take what we give them," he told Marx over a dinner tray one night. "It seems to me that they deserve better." Both boys knew why audiences were getting mediocre films. Uncle Carl had a penchant for hiring relatives; his California studio was a nepotistic nest. Irving looked into the dark-paneled expanses of Thompson's Cafeteria and wished he could get to the fellows who were grinding out films for Universal. "I'd make them do it my way," he said, "so they'd never know if their way was better."

Like most film companies, Universal had corporate headquarters in New York and production facilities in California. Laemmle had founded "Universal City" in 1915 on 230 mountainous acres in the San Fernando Valley, just up the Cahuenga Pass from the unincorporated part of Los Angeles called Hollywood. A mere three years after feature films had been introduced in America (with 1912's *Oliver Twist*), Universal City was a town devoted to their manufacture. Universal maintained a schedule of nearly two hundred films a year—melodramas, comedies, westerns, and serials—made quickly and cheaply. Because Universal did not own a theater chain, it relied on independent theaters, many of which were outside the big cities. Its middlebrow product appealed to rural audiences.

Mismanagement and bickering were slowing Universal's release schedule. Studio managers came and went. Since opening the plant, Laemmle had hired (and fired) sixteen. The studio was currently being run by Isadore Bernstein, Laemmle's brother-in-law; by Maurice Fleckles, a Laemmle cousin, who was after Bernstein's job; and by novelist Tarkington Baker. Julius Stern was in charge of comedies. When a manager questioned their quality, Stern snapped at him: "Our comedies are not to be laughed at!"

In the fall of 1919, Laemmle made one of his periodic trips to California. Just before he left, he told Irving that he needed him to come too. This would be Irving's first time away from New York—and his mother—but he was more excited than anxious. Henrietta packed a hot water bottle in his luggage and made sure he was wearing woolen underwear under his suit. She had no idea what California would do to her son. She burst into tears at Grand Central Station.

Irving found California stimulating and the studio awe-inspiring. Robert H. Cochrane, one of the few Universal executives not related to Laemmle, watched Thalberg with interest. "When Laemmle brought Thalberg to the Coast, he would accompany the boss around the lot, sit in on conferences and such. He was a keen observer and would make suggestions that were helpful and valuable. He had a good business mind as well as an artist's mind." Laemmle let Irving get the lay of the land while trying to find out who was slacking.

Frances Marion was already known as the most prolific writer of original scenarios (and the highest paid) when she visited Universal. "While I was sitting in Mr. Laemmle's outer office, patiently waiting like a milkman's horse," she later wrote,

> I whiled away the hours talking to his secretary, a young lad with a sensitive face, the dark searching restless eyes of the ambitious, and a frail body. He seemed so knowledgeable when he discussed any subject, from movies to art to philosophy, that assessing his future, I knew he would not remain a secretary for long. The upshot of this visit was that on my next appointment at Universal I brought him an armful of the books I had used during one of my summer courses at the University of Southern California.

At the end of 1919, Laemmle demoted two of the three current studio managers. He then announced that he was returning to New York, but without Irving. "I need someone to keep an eye on things for me," said Laemmle. Surprisingly, he mandated that Irving work on an equal basis with Stern, Bernstein, and another executive, Samuel Van Runkle.

On January 2, 1920, Laemmle left for New York. He had neglected to tell Irving the extent of his authority. As Stern, Bernstein, and Van Runkle soon discovered, Irving did not need to be told. "It was one of those periods when people were getting fired right and left," Irving said later. "I took charge because there was no one left to take charge." The young man who had spent years chafing under the restrictions of ill health could now assert the confidence that Henrietta had burned into him. It was time to go after the "facts, action, and power" of William James. "In a business where no one had the courage of his own convictions," said Irving, "I knew I was right that I should make them do it my way."

In February, after receiving telegrams from angry executives, Laemmle sent Pat Powers, one of his partners, to see what Thalberg was doing. The report was positive. Laemmle returned to Universal City in March, and Irving told him point-blank: "The first thing you should do is establish a new job of studio manager and give him the responsibility of watching day-to-day operations."

"All right," said Laemmle. "You're it."

"I'm what?"

"I would like that you should stay here," Laemmle answered. "You are completely in charge of the studio." On April 30 Laemmle departed for Europe with an entourage of relatives. Thalberg was left with nine productions to oversee, three times as many scenarios to develop, and a shortage of funds.

"Irving fought his way through this tangled mess," recalled Norma Shearer, "but to get the wheels really turning, he needed money. There was none in the till and banks were adamantly against any further loans." Because Laemmle would be gone until November, Irving had to go alone to meet the Bank of Italy president, A. H. "Doc" Giannini. "In spite of the man's resistance," said Shearer, "Irving made a splendid presentation—he was a persuasive speaker—and he gained his objective. The president presented papers for him to sign, as he was now general manager of Universal. Irving said politely: 'I am sorry, sir, but my signature won't do you any good. I'm not twenty-one yet.'"

When Irving G. Thalberg turned twenty-one—on May 30, 1920—he was earning $450 a week as general manager of Universal City. Before long, journalistic wags were calling him the "Boy Wonder of Hollywood." Henrietta was not surprised at his ascendance. When she asked him what he was going to do next, she did not have to speak the obvious. They both knew his time was limited.

.   .   .

Most of the "film folk" working in Hollywood in 1920 had come from the East Coast. The warm heaviness of the air, the scent of winter-blooming jasmine, and the dusty streets that meandered into orange groves were a shock to their systems. "In those days it took a long time to travel to Hollywood," recalled actor Conrad Nagel. "It took five days by train and then that long, ridiculous layover in Chicago. And when I got there, I hated it. Oh, gosh, did I hate Hollywood. You see, we came out of the bitter cold of New York into the terrific warmth of California, and it was all I could do to stay awake. I'd get on the set, and if I stood still for two minutes, I'd doze off." Actress Marion Davies had a similar reaction. "When I first arrived in Hollywood, I didn't like it," she wrote. "I couldn't understand the big wide spaces. I was a city girl, and I was afraid of everything. After a while I learned to like California, so that when I went back east, I didn't like New York any more. I got to feeling crowded in, crushed." Buster Keaton, who was both directing and acting in his own films, adjusted quickly. "We were all young," he remembered. "The air in California was like wine. Our business was also young—and growing like nothing ever seen before."

How did Irving Thalberg, a short, slight easterner with little education and less experience, learn to handle himself in the wilds of Hollywood? After a day of story conferences and casting, screening, and editing, the young studio manager would partake of the seductive climate. His friend Sam Marx later wrote: "Thalberg liked to stand in the doorway of his office to steal a few moments of contemplation, with the leaves of the tall red eucalyptus trees on the near hill rustling tremulously and the late sun throwing an orange glow over the sets and stages at Universal City."

Anyone encountering Thalberg at twilight might wonder if he was really an adult. He weighed 122 pounds, and his shallow chest cavity and thin limbs made him look undernourished. In striking contrast to the spareness of his body were the thickness of his black hair, the expressiveness of his eyes, and the symmetry of his features. In a town full of "pretty" men, he had an unselfconscious beauty. Novelist Edna Ferber wrote: "I had fancied motion-picture producers as large gentlemen smoking oversized cigars. But this young man whose word seemed so final at Universal City turned out to be a wisp of a boy, twenty-one, so slight as to appear actually frail. Something about this boy impressed me deeply." When journalist Louella Parsons interviewed Thalberg for the first time, she was surprised at his youth, but decided that "it was no boy's mind that was being asked to cope with the intricate politics of Universal City."

When fledgling screenwriter Lenore Coffee first visited Thalberg's office, she stared at him. "Although I had seen photographs of him," she wrote, "I was not prepared for the slender body, the delicately boned and strikingly Italianate face. I thought immediately of how he would look as a Renaissance prince, for he had a princely air." In his first years in the industry, Thalberg had learned to compensate for his appearance by carrying himself with authority. "When you were shown into his office," wrote Coffee, "he was invariably standing behind his desk, looking at a letter or fiddling with various objects with an abstracted air, as if he were quite unconscious of your presence. After a good moment he would look up as if startled to find you there. On leaving the studio, I kept thinking back what a remarkable young man he was. Although barely twenty-one, he had enormous dignity. I couldn't imagine anyone taking a liberty with him, either in business or in his personal life."

Thalberg never questioned himself, and woe to anyone who did. The director of a film called *The Flirt* had shot so many angles that the editor did not know where to begin. "Cut it all from the point of view of the father," Thalberg instructed him, "and it will come down to the proper length."

"It worked!" exclaimed the editor a few days later.

"What did you expect it to do?" asked Thalberg, to whom being right was becoming a way of life. Since his production methods were new to Hollywood, no one dared ask if he was performing them correctly. They followed orders, learning all the while. Thalberg started with scripts, which were often cliché-ridden yarns without suspense or surprises. He had to make them good enough to shoot—and better than the competition. Cochrane later asked Laemmle how Thalberg was able to assimilate filmmaking techniques so readily. "Irving was that way from the first," replied Laemmle.

"He understood stories," said Shearer. "He had read so much. He got the wheels turning by first revising the scripts and then putting more pictures to work, by assigning directors and casts, by contending tactfully with conflicting authority when he could, and by overruling when he couldn't. He would just make up his mind and bear the consequences." Predictably, there were Universal employees (and Laemmle relatives) who resented Thalberg's manner. A number of actors and directors, including Harry Carey, Mae Murray, and Robert Z. Leonard, went to studios where they would not be supervised so closely. For the most part, though, Thalberg won over his staff.

Carl Laemmle had two children. Rosabelle was eighteen. Carl Jr. (born Julius) was thirteen. Their mother had died of influenza in January 1919, so Rosabelle ran the home at 465 West End Avenue in New York. Thalberg had encountered her at the Broadway office, where she had made it clear that she was not interested in friendship with a secretary. He watched the self-assured girl come and go, and then spent dinners with Sam Marx talking about her. By the spring of 1921 Thalberg's authority had thawed Miss Laemmle. She came to California and began to spend time in the editing room, watching patiently as he edited and re-edited a Priscilla Dean vehicle called *Reputation*. He moved scenes around, pulled them, and then replaced them, trying to give the mediocre film some dramatic power. He hoped that Laemmle would find it worthy of a special release. When Thalberg finished, Rosabelle felt that her father should make a special trip from New York to see the results. Thalberg and Rosabelle were understandably nervous as Laemmle watched the film one night in a chilly screening room. The film had no accompaniment but the chatter of sprockets in the projector gate. When Thalberg turned to check Laemmle's reaction, he was disappointed to see the older man's head tilted back, resting on the frame of his chair. When the lights came up, Laemmle got up, stretched, and then walked out.

"Your father fell asleep," said Thalberg.

"No," replied Rosabelle. "He always tilts his head back when he doesn't want to cry."

Thalberg did not believe her. He was so downcast that he slept in a chair in his office that night. The next morning he received a telegram sent by Laemmle from the train station. "Please thank all connected with the finest picture ever to carry my name."

Before long, the general manager and the boss's daughter were seeing each other regularly. Henrietta had met Rosabelle in New York and was less than thrilled. Her son was too young to be serious about any girl, and he could do better than this stuck-up child with the pointed chin. (Rosabelle had at one point tried to become a film actress, but screen tests showed that she was not photogenic.) Henrietta made her feelings known, but Thalberg and Rosabelle continued with an involvement that was sincere if not passionate. He devoted most of his energy to work, and he was not given to displays of affection, either in public or in private. He became known for his dislike of physical contact; it was as if he might break if someone touched him. In the parlance of the time, he was a "cool customer." This coolness could be mistaken for coldness, and would be a component of his success.

After living in a series of modest hotel rooms, Thalberg missed his family. He moved them from 1303 Bushwick Avenue in Brooklyn to 446 South Norton Avenue in Los Angeles. After settling in the attractive two-story home, Henrietta resumed her role as matriarch, guardian, and nurse. This made it easier for her to drive a wedge between her son and his imperious girlfriend. The romance continued, but after seeing Rosabelle through his mother's eyes, Thalberg began to have doubts.

In late 1921, after two years at Universal City, Thalberg tried collaborating on a scenario. He would not put his name on it, however. He was not satisfied with its story. *The Dangerous Little Demon* was credited to "I. R. Irving." This was the first and last time that he allowed any part of his name in the credits of a film. The incident also marked the beginning of both his insecurity about writing and his ambivalence toward writers.

In November, Julius Stern was elected second vice president and installed as Laemmle's personal representative in Universal City. The move was made, in part to stop rumors that a boy was single-handedly running the studio, and in part to release Thalberg from tiresome duties. "I am freeing him from the details of business administration," said Stern, "in order that he may devote his entire time to production." He wisely left Thalberg alone.

The only real resistance Thalberg encountered was from Erich von Stroheim, the headstrong Austrian director who had joined Universal when Thalberg was still in New York. Stroheim had been an out-of-work actor known for playing German villains in World War I epics when he convinced Laemmle to let him write, direct, and star in a low-budget film. In *Blind Husbands*, Stroheim portrayed a bullet-headed, monocle-wearing, heel-clicking officer who seduces married women vacationing in the Alps. In the process of creating this decadent milieu, Stroheim ignored his $25,000 budget and worked his company day and night, shooting hours of morbidly sharp images. By the time *Blind Husbands* premiered, it cost $250,000. Happily for Universal, the cynical film grossed almost half a million and made the thirty-three-year-old Stroheim a star. For the first time, the little studio had a film that was both profitable and prestigious, an insightful work in the tradition of Arthur Schnitzler.

Emboldened by this success, "*Mr.* von Stroheim" began to snap his riding crop at anyone who questioned him. He cultivated the image of a Viennese officer; like the "von" in his name, it was a fiction. He was a middle-class Austrian Jew with no authentic connection to the Hapsburgs. But this was Hollywood, where everyone was self-invented. "Von" Stroheim was an "artiste," and if his cynical vision of Alt Wien made money, his eccentricities could be excused. In June 1920 Stroheim commenced his third film, *Foolish Wives*, and set tongues wagging with a full-size reproduction of the plaza at Monte Carlo. A year later, Thalberg was shocked to discover that the film was still shooting. He called the director to his office. "I have seen all the film and you have all you need for the picture," said Thalberg. "I want you to stop shooting."

"I have not finished as yet," said Stroheim, who stood flanked by a retinue of assistants.

"Yes, you have," said Thalberg. "You have spent all the money this company can afford. I cannot allow you to spend any more." Thalberg picked up a contract and read the clause that said, "The Director agrees that he will direct as ordered by the Producer."

"You will have to fire me first if you want to give me orders," laughed Stroheim. "If you remove me as the director of this picture, you also remove me as star. How will you finish it then?" Stroheim and Thalberg were about the same height, but Stroheim was stocky and muscular. "If you were not my superior," said Stroheim, "I would smash you in the face."

"Don't let that stop you," said Thalberg, unflinching.

Stroheim glared at him for an instant, then thought better of it. He strode off, muttering, "Since when does a child instruct a genius?"

Thalberg said nothing, and Stroheim continued filming night scenes at Lake Forest, California. William Daniels, a twenty-five-year-old cameraman who was working on both his first Stroheim film and his first feature film, reported to the set at dusk and found the cameras missing. "I got a car and went after the cameras," recalled Daniels. "I was told that Thalberg had removed them permanently. By the time I got back, he had taken the lights away too."

Foolish Wives premiered a few months later, and it created an even greater sensation than *Blind Husbands*. It made more money, too, but as Thalberg pointed out, most of that money paid for footage that Stroheim had shot but not used. The two men reconciled in time to attend the New York premiere of *Foolish Wives*. While there, Thalberg began a practice that would serve him throughout his career—seeing Broadway plays to sniff out potential properties. On this trip, Stroheim went with him to watch Richard Bennett play the pathetic clown in Leonid Andreyev's *He Who Gets Slapped*. On the train back to California, Thalberg noted Stroheim's preoccupation. "Got an idea?" asked Thalberg.

"Half an idea," replied Stroheim, recalling the carnival setting of Andreyev's play and that of Ferenc Molnar's *Liliom*. Back at Universal, Stroheim and Thalberg spent two months thrashing out a script for Stroheim's next project, *Merry-Go-Round*. Stroheim promised Thalberg that he would adhere to the script, the schedule, and the budget. On the set in late August, Stroheim promptly forgot his promise; it was absurd to think that Thalberg or anyone else could control him. According to Shearer, Thalberg "watched Mr. von Stroheim use up 83,000 feet of film just for the first few scenes. Wise words quietly spoken failed to check this extravagance." One of these scenes was scripted as a banquet but shot as a drunken orgy. "Stroheim served real champagne by the bucketful and whisky as well," recalled Daniels. "All the extras got loaded. A girl stepped naked out of a punchbowl. It was during a shot when I irised in on her that von Stroheim passed out cold." In late September Thalberg called Stroheim to his office to warn him that he was on the verge of being fired.

"That is impossible," replied Stroheim. "*Merry-Go-Round* is my picture. I conceived it, and I will see it through to the end. No one can take von Stroheim off a von Stroheim picture."

"Perhaps that was impossible in the past," said Thalberg quietly, "because you appeared in your other films. But you are not acting in *Merry-Go-Round*. And so you can be replaced."

On October 6, 1922, Thalberg wrote Stroheim: "You have time and again demonstrated your disloyalty to our company, encouraged and fostered discontent, distrust, and disrespect for us in the minds of your fellow employees, and have attempted to create an organization loyal to yourself, rather than to the company you were employed to serve." Thalberg had also seen the rushes of the banquet scene. "Among other difficulties with which we have had to contend," wrote Thalberg, "has been your flagrant disregard for the principles of censorship and your repeated and insistent attempts to include scenes photographed by you, situations and incidents so reprehensible that they could not by any reasonable possibility be expected to meet with the approval of the censorship boards." Thalberg ended his letter by telling Stroheim: "You are discharged from our employ, your discharge to take effect as of this date." Shock waves were immediately felt in Hollywood.

"This was the first time a director had been fired," said producer David O. Selznick in 1964. "It took guts and courage. Thalberg was only twenty-two. Remember that a matter of hundreds of thousands of dollars in those days could wreck a company, particularly a company which was not that strong." With this bold act, Thalberg established the precedent of the omnipotent producer. In a few years it would change the structure of Hollywood filmmaking, shifting power from directors such as Stroheim, D. W. Griffith, and Rex Ingram to producers such as B. P. Schulberg, Darryl Zanuck, and Sol Wurtzel. For the time being, though, its significance was that of a David-and-Goliath story. A frail, untutored youth had bested a powerful, worldly man. It was incredible that Thalberg should dare to do this, let alone succeed. Where did he get the will, the courage? Only a handful of people in Los Angeles knew the wellspring of his ambition. It was his inescapable realization that time was running out. After staring down death for years, he would not be cowed by a strutting poseur.

The money Thalberg saved Universal on *Merry-Go-Round* went in part to a pet project. Lon Chaney, a miraculously clever character actor, had suggested to

Thalberg that Universal produce *The Hunchback of Notre Dame* with Chaney himself as star. Thalberg was in favor of the idea, having read the book in his sickbed years earlier. Universal was doing well enough to afford an epic production, one that could open at the newly completed Astor Theatre in New York. Laemmle approved the project, which included the construction of a full-size façade of the Cathedral of Notre Dame, a sprawling town square, nineteen acres of sets, and a cast of two thousand. While Laemmle was in Europe, Thalberg authorized additional crowd scenes. By the fall of 1922, it appeared that Thalberg would have a masterpiece in his portfolio, not to mention a new star. But Thalberg was not happy at the "Big U."

Henrietta had given her son a sense of self—his poise, his impatience with mediocrity, his need to achieve success in a limited time. She pondered the question of his marrying. Doctors told her that his heart was strong enough to sustain the exertions associated with sexual intercourse. If his heart was overtaxed by long work hours and corporate struggles, however, there might be danger. Henrietta saw it at Universal, which took for granted the improvements her son had effected. She also saw it in Rosabelle. If her son married the boss's daughter, he would be tied to Universal. Henrietta was happy for his accomplishments there, but it was not the most admired company in the industry. There was one maxim he had not read in William James, pragmatic though it was: "Never remain in a job after you have gotten all you can from it." Would Laemmle let him make more films like *The Hunchback of Notre Dame*, or would he have to content himself with middlebrow material?

When Laemmle returned from Europe, he was gravely concerned about the money that Thalberg had spent on the Victor Hugo epic. After he reviewed the rough cut, however, he did an about-face and ordered a lavish publicity campaign and a special release program. Thalberg thought this an opportune time to ask for a raise. He had, after all, been earning $450 a week for nearly three years. He was stung when Laemmle refused, citing operation expenses. Thalberg accepted Laemmle's decision without argument but conjectured that economy was not the real reason. The romance between Thalberg and Rosabelle had lost its blush, and he did not want to marry her. Henrietta had warned him that he could never run the Fox Film Corporation or First National if he married into the Laemmle family. By the same token, he was refused a raise because he was not part of the family.

Even so, Laemmle's refusal made no sense. He allowed his relatives and even Stroheim to squander money, yet he was unwilling to share it with Thalberg, whose value to the company had increased demonstrably. Thalberg became quietly resentful and then asked Laemmle's attorney Edwin Loeb for advice. Loeb suggested that Thalberg call on Cecil B. DeMille and Jesse Lasky at their studio on Vine Street in Hollywood. When Thalberg asked them for $550 a week, Lasky took DeMille aside. "We can't do it, Cecil."

"But Jesse, this boy is a genius. I can see it. I know it."

"Geniuses we have all we need, Cecil. Tell him no."

Thalberg next approached Pathé; then comedy producer Hal Roach, who agreed to take him on at $550 a week, but then reneged at the last minute. Loeb suggested that Thalberg meet with an independent producer whose studio was located—of all places—in an East Los Angeles zoo. Thalberg had recently had an unnerving encounter with a lion at Universal's zoo, so he asked if he could meet this man in Loeb's home. When he did, he met a producer who was a lion in his own right.

Louis Burt Mayer was born Lazar Meher in the Ukraine in July 1884. He was never sure about the date because record keeping for Jews was haphazard in the reign of the anti-Semitic Alexander III. (Mayer later chose July 4, 1885, as his birthday, a salute to his adopted country.) To escape the czar's persecution, Mayer's family immigrated in 1887 to St. John, New Brunswick. By the time Mayer was in his teens, his father, Jacob, was a prosperous scrap-iron dealer and his mother, Sarah, was running a dry goods store. Mayer idolized his mother but had little use for his selfish, tyrannical father, especially when he found that he could surpass him. Among Mayer's many gifts were a rich, rumbling voice, a theatrical flair, and a knack for galvanizing talent. He also had a flexible set of scruples. If he failed to get his way by blathering, blustering, or blubbering, he used his fists. While still a teenager, he pulled shiftless youths from the streets and organized them into a productive company. He spent eight strenuous years in the world of salvage, even donning a diving suit to retrieve sunken scrap. He changed his name from Lazar to Louis; influenced by the French-speaking population of St. John, he pronounced it "Lou-ee." He married a girl named Margaret, moved to Massachusetts, and had two daughters, Edith and Irene. When a nickelodeon owner gave Mayer a glimpse of show business, he saw that there were better things to sell than junk.

In 1907 the Gem Theatre in Haverhill, Massachusetts, was a run-down burlesque house sneeringly called the Germ. Movie theaters were springing up around it, offering the prospect of quick and easy profits to anyone with a little venture capital. Fascinated by this show-business milieu, Mayer bought the Gem, scrubbed it down, spruced it up, and renamed it the Orpheum. There he proudly presented family fare, leading his audience in sing-alongs before films. The Orpheum became Mayer's entrée into the world of entertainment. He parlayed one house into a string of theaters, and those into a film exchange.

In 1915 the well-connected Mayer joined the newly formed Metro Pictures Corporation in New York, became its secretary, and made the beneficial acquaintance of an attorney named J. Robert Rubin. At the same time Mayer formed a syndicate on the side to snap up the second-run franchise to D. W. Griffith's *The Birth of a Nation*. The film earned a fortune on the Eastern Seaboard, and Mayer used his share to launch Louis B. Mayer Productions. As he saw it, the future of moving pictures lay not in exhibiting films but in making them—and in making them "great." To Lois Weber, one of the first directors he hired, Mayer proclaimed: "My unchanging policy will be great star, great director, great play, great cast. You are authorized to get these without stint or limit. Spare nothing, neither expense, time, nor effort. Results only are what I'm after."

Mayer got his first real results by snatching Anita Stewart from Vitagraph Pictures and showcasing the star in an expensive literary property, George Loane Tucker's *Virtuous Wives*. Richard Rowland, the self-important president of Metro, wanted too much money to distribute *Virtuous Wives*, so Mayer left Metro and let First National handle his distribution. Mayer was so fretful about the presentation of his first film that he began working on poster displays outside the Strand Theatre two months before the premiere. It was there—on Armistice Day—that Irving Thalberg first saw him, a purposeful figure with the build of a wrestler, oblivious to the crazed celebration dashing past him. Heralded by a strategically placed advertising campaign, *Virtuous Wives* opened on December 29, 1918. "Not a picture that would set the world on fire," Frances Marion later wrote, "but it had the quality of freshness, movement, and heart interest."

Mayer instructed his directors and writers to give his films an unabashedly emotional appeal. "If a story makes me cry," he told one writer, "it's good." He also required that his films be wholesome. "Louis B. is more puritanical about sex than my Quaker relatives," said actress Hedda Hopper, who acted in *Virtuous Wives*. Every writer he hired got the same speech. "I will make only pictures that I won't be ashamed to have my children see," said Mayer. "I'm determined that my little Edie and my little Irene will never be embarrassed. And they won't be if all my pictures are moral and clean."

In early 1919, Mayer moved his company to 3800 Mission Road in East Los

Angeles, renting space from a fading studio called Selig Polyscope, located on the same lot as Colonel William Selig's Zoo, the largest private collection of exotic animals in the country. "Louis B. chose the Selig Zoo because it was the cheapest place in town," Hedda Hopper wrote years later. "That was a funny lot, with wild animals roaming around just like the actors." Mayer's office was in a warehouse not far from the lion cages. It was nothing more than a clapboard lean-to stuck in a corner, but from it he supervised five Anita Stewart hits a year. When novice film editor Margaret Booth came to Mayer from D. W. Griffith's company in Hollywood, the remoteness of the strange little studio frightened her. She found out too late that Mission Road streetcars did not run regularly. After her first day in East Los Angeles, she made a tearful journey back to Seventeenth Street in Los Angeles and then telephoned head editor Billy Shea. "My mother doesn't want me to work with you because I can't get home!" blurted Booth. Only when Shea promised to drive her both ways did she agree to return.

With the success of his Stewart vehicles, Mayer began to attract talented directors such as John Stahl and Reginald Barker. "I will go down on my knees to talent," Mayer would say during an interview with a prospective employee, and then he would excuse the sound of lions bellowing. "These are only temporary quarters, you understand. I'll not be here long." Few people saw the self-doubt that Mayer hid behind the mask of bravado. His secretary Florence Browning sometimes had to reassure him when a bill collector came to call; she would find Mayer weeping in his office, give him a pep talk, and then watch him score another victory. Years later, she described him as "a funny little man riding around in a Ford, telling everyone confidently that he was going to be the greatest man in the picture-making business. He seemed to have absolutely no reticence, no inhibitions, no sense of embarrassment at his evident manifestations of conceit." Mayer's complexity was a mystery to everyone who knew him. To Irving Thalberg, it was oddly appealing.

Thalberg met Mayer at Edwin Loeb's home at 815 South Kingsley Drive, in the Wilshire district of Los Angeles, in November 1922. Mayer shot through the front door, gave Thalberg a perfunctory greeting, and then directed his attention to Loeb, asking his advice about a troublesome film project called *Pleasure Mad*. Mayer said that its director planned to film naked women cavorting in artists' lofts. Mayer was troubled by this, but the film was already cast and in progress. Mayer wanted to shut it down. Loeb said that could cost him a great deal.

"So it costs!" Mayer exclaimed. "Am I some kind of monster? What will people say about Louis B. Mayer if he puts his name on a picture that he's ashamed to let his family see?" Suddenly Mayer turned to Thalberg, for whose benefit he had been airing his laundry. Although Thalberg had seen Mayer in front of his theater years earlier, they had not met. Thalberg was pleased—but not surprised—to be acknowledged. "You, Thalberg," said Mayer. "Tell me. What would you do? I've got Mrs. Mayer and my Edith and Irene to think about. And you have your mother."

"And father," Thalberg said quickly. He then addressed Mayer's problem by citing the system at Universal, in which directors were required to respect the script, which was an extension of the producer's authority. Thalberg explained that he had instituted a procedure in which the script went through a series of "story conferences" until it was approved by the producer. Only then did it go before the cameras. Mayer was impressed by Thalberg's acumen.

On the way to his car, Mayer said to Loeb: "He's a good boy. I like him. You see how he thought of his father?" This was a curious statement since neither Mayer nor Thalberg had much rapport with his own father. On the other hand, Mayer worshiped the memory of his mother, who had died nine years earlier, and Thalberg was still beholden to his. He was living with her, his father, and his sister, and was supporting them.

In subsequent meetings, Mayer was smart enough to let Thalberg do the talking. Thalberg told him how he had upgraded Universal. Loeb chimed in that Carl Laemmle did not appreciate Thalberg. "For God's sake, Eddie," Laemmle had said. "Do me a favor, will you? Take that young man off my hands." Loeb had then proposed Thalberg to First National's Joseph Schenck. "I'll pick the people to make pictures," Schenck had said. "You stick to the law." Mayer was incredulous. "If he comes to work for me," he told Loeb privately, "I'll look after him like he's my own son." Mayer at first considered giving Thalberg a subsidiary producing company and 20 percent of the profits, but Mayer's releasing contracts with both First National and Metro Pictures precluded it.

On February 15, 1923, Louis B. Mayer Productions hired Irving Thalberg as vice president in charge of production at a salary of $500 a week. "This is one of the proudest moments in my life," Mayer told Frances Marion. "So Irving Thalberg joined our family," recalled Irene Mayer Selznick. "My father got a son without having to raise one—wise, loving, filial." Henrietta Thalberg was part of the bargain, and she became Mayer's ally, working with him to ensure that Thalberg did not overextend himself. "The doctors had warned my father that [Irving] could go at any time, and that there was no chance of his living beyond the age of thirty," wrote Selznick. "By making Henrietta's life easier, we made Irving's life easier. She only appeared to be an overprotective mother; in truth, he needed her badly and depended on her."

Mayer's favorite refrain was "Find your way around. A man must crawl before he walks, walk before he runs." At whatever pace, Mayer and Thalberg needed more than one star. Anita Stewart was leaving. Mayer's last two films, *Hearts Aflame* and *The Dangerous Age*, featured Frank Keenan, Anna Q. Nilsson, and Lewis Stone, who were good, dependable actors but not star material. Mayer and Thalberg shut down *Pleasure Mad* and took time out to scout for talent.

Thalberg suggested a twenty-year-old Canadian girl named Norma Shearer. She had been making films in New York for three years (in spite of being told by both D. W. Griffith and Florenz Ziegfeld that she looked too odd to photograph). While at Universal, Thalberg had been urged by his friend Sam Marx in the New York office to screen two of her films, *The Stealers* and *Channing of the Northwest*. Though far from skilled, Shearer was versatile, and with her pale blue eyes and chiseled profile, she had the prerequisite of stardom. She was watchable. Shearer's agent, Edward Small, had declined Universal's offers, not only because they were modest but also because Universal's representative had made advances to her. Thalberg now offered Small a five-year contract for Shearer with options every six months. Shearer asked that her mother, Edith, accompany her, a demand that sat favorably with both Mayer and Thalberg. They ratified her contract.

In the first week of March 1923, Norma Shearer and her mother arrived at the train station in downtown Los Angeles. "No one met us but a taxi driver," recalled Shearer. "He said he'd better take us to Hollywood. He thought we should live there—not Los Angeles—if we were going to be movie stars. 'The Hollywood Hotel is the place for you,' he told us. 'They all go there.' He was right. It harbored some of the best stars in Hollywood—and some of the best mice."

The mice should have prepared Shearer for the Selig Zoo. A *zoo?* "This sounded ominous," she said, "but away we went in another taxi, back to Los Angeles." The trip to the zoo did nothing to encourage Shearer and her mother. Riding out Mission Road was like traveling to a foreign country. Budd Schulberg, whose father, B. P. Schulberg, was renting space from Mayer, later wrote: "Mission Road was still what its name implied, a narrow, winding rural road that led from the little Spanish church in the Plaza to the mission in the open fields." To get to 3800 Mission Road, Shearer had to pass Lincoln Park (formerly Eastlake Park), a cluster of half-timbered buildings reflected in a lovely little lake. Mayer's new offices had been built in the style of the château of Chenonceaux. Inside the fanciful structure, Shearer and her mother wondered what was coming next.

We were sitting in the reception room waiting to see whomever we were supposed to see when a very polite and modest young office boy came through a small swinging gate. He held it open for us, smiled, and said nothing. In we went. He followed us and opened a door down the hall. We found ourselves in Mr. Mayer's office, which was large and luxurious. To our amazement the young man went around the big desk and sat down behind it. I thought to myself, He'd better get out of that chair before someone comes in! Then he started pressing buttons on that big, shiny desk. Now he's playing games, I thought. He'd better stop fooling around or Mr. Mayer will come in and fire him. He looked so handsome. I didn't want that to happen.

Just then Mr. Mayer did come in. The young man stood up calmly and introduced us to him. Then two other gentlemen came in, moving-picture directors named John Stahl and Fred Niblo. Their names were vaguely familiar. They bowed, shook hands with us, and went out. We soon suspected that the young man who had greeted us could not be an office boy. And indeed we soon learned that he was Irving G. Thalberg, Hollywood's so-called "Boy Wonder." We also began to see that he was running Mr. Mayer's studio—with his permission, of course.

And when we left the studio, Mother asked me, "Did you see those eyes?"

"I should say I did. What eyes!"

Later that day it occurred to me that I had seen the most beautiful face on a young man that I would ever see. Mother told me that he was a Jew and perhaps that was why he was so beautiful. "Wouldn't it be wonderful if you married that nice young man!" she said.

As starry-eyed as the women were that day, they were no more quixotic than Mayer or Thalberg. The young men in the small studio fully expected to compete with large companies like Fox Film, which owned a theater chain. On quiet Sunday mornings, Mayer would drive Irene by the Metro Studio in Hollywood, pointing at its tall white columns and cheerful green trim. "I bet you'd be surprised if I became the head of a studio like this some day," he said. Irene could not picture it. "Just wait a year or two," he would tell her. "Just wait." The man who counseled others to crawl, then walk, then run was wise enough to heed his own advice, but in less time than even he expected, he would be sprinting.

CHAPTER 3 · Three Shaky Little Stars

The Metro Pictures studio at 1325 Eleanor Avenue in Hollywood was eight miles from Louis B. Mayer's Mission Road château. Thirteen miles from Mission Road, on Washington Boulevard in Culver City, was an even bigger studio, the Goldwyn Pictures Corporation. Behind its Corinthian-columned, eight-hundred-foot façade was a forty-six-acre facility comprising six glass-walled stages, dozens of outdoor sets, a swimming pool, a three-story administration building, writers' offices, editing rooms, screening rooms, dressing rooms, carpentry shops, lumber sheds, paint shops, and a restaurant. Goldwyn was located in Culver City and not in Hollywood because the city father, a real-estate developer named Harry Culver, had in 1915 offered free land to any filmmaker who wanted to set up shop there. Thomas Ince accepted Culver's offer and, with D. W. Griffith and Mack Sennett, founded Triangle Films on sixteen acres of land. Triangle made two stars, William S. Hart and Douglas Fairbanks. When its stars departed, it was abandoned.

In the summer of 1918 an East Coast producer named Samuel Goldwyn leased space at the idle studio. The aggressive, fractious Goldwyn was trying to reestablish himself after having been bought out of his partnership in Famous Players–Lasky by Adolph Zukor. Goldwyn grew to like the Triangle property, and in early 1919 he bought it for $325,000. He then hired a Columbia University graduate named Howard Dietz as publicist. Dietz's first job was to come up with a logo. Universal had gotten its name from a passing delivery truck in New York. Metro had gotten its name from a lithography shop. Dietz thought about the lion on the masthead of his college newspaper. Sam Goldwyn's studio was soon bearing the proud profile of a lion in repose and the legend *Ars Gratia Artis,* which was loosely translated as "Art for Art's Sake."

On the infrequent occasions when Mayer had time to motor by the Metro and Goldwyn studios in 1923, both companies were feeling the recent slump in box-office revenues. Metro, through whom Mayer released some of his films, had a fine distribution system but few stars. Alla Nazimova had blazed briefly, and Rex Ingram's *The Four Horsemen of the Apocalypse* had made Rudolph Valentino a star, but the studio mishandled and lost him. Mayer knew that Metro was owned by the New York theater magnate Marcus Loew, who had built a theater chain from vaudeville houses and storefront nickelodeons. Loew had bought Metro for $3 million in 1920 with the expectation that it would provide movies for his 111 theaters, but Metro had yet to deliver enough product. Its facility was small and its management shortsighted. Metro's 1923 production schedule included hits such as *The Three Ages* with Buster Keaton and *Where the Pavement Ends* with Ramon Novarro, but sixteen films were not enough to feed Loew's theaters, so Metro added Mae Murray vehicles made by Tiffany Productions to its release schedule.

Mayer knew that the Goldwyn Company was also in trouble; in fact, it was no longer being run by Sam Goldwyn. After spending $50,000 to buy thirty more acres, establishing a superb physical plant, and contracting a series of "Eminent Authors" to write his films, Goldwyn had been forced out of his own company by board members Abraham Lehr and Frank Godsol. The company retained Sam Goldwyn's name, and while he made films elsewhere, Godsol tried to generate enough income to support the massive facility and its excellent staff. This included plant manager J. J. Cohn, directors Marshall Neilan, King Vidor, Charles Brabin, Victor Seastrom, and Irving Thalberg's nemesis Erich von Stroheim. There were also cameraman William Daniels and art director Cedric Gibbons. In front of the camera were performers such as Blanche Sweet, Conrad Nagel, Aileen Pringle, Renée Adorée, and William Haines. In February 1923 the Goldwyn Company signed a deal with publisher William Randolph Hearst to release films made by his company, Cosmopolitan Productions. Besides getting Hearst's handsomely mounted movies (many of which starred his mistress, Marion Davies), Goldwyn also got the benefit of publicity in the Hearst press. This alliance and Goldwyn's array of talent were still not enough to keep it out of the red.

To Mayer, Metro and Goldwyn looked like an army and a fortress without a general, and more than once he imagined what he could do with their resources.

Back at Mission Road, he was working with Thalberg on modest vehicles for Marie Prevost and Barbara LaMarr. Prevost was a former bathing beauty whom Thalberg had brought from Universal. He found her easy to work with and even spent some time with her on weekends. LaMarr, a dusky, exotic beauty dubbed "The Girl Who Is Too Beautiful" by journalist Adela Rogers St. Johns, had made hit films for both Metro and Goldwyn but had to be watched; she had a penchant for drinking, drugs, and debauchery. "I take lovers like roses," said LaMarr. "By the dozen." Screenwriter Paul Bern was besotted with her, but LaMarr was interested only in friendship with the pudgy older man. "He has a Magdalene complex," actor John Gilbert explained to Thalberg. "Paul does crazy things for whores." On one occasion, the craziness was nearly fatal.

According to St. Johns, it started when Bern implored LaMarr to marry him. There was a drawback to his proposal. "Paul has no right to marry any woman. This I *know*," LaMarr told St. Johns. (Ten years would pass before St. Johns—and Thalberg—would learn the full implication of her statement.) LaMarr refused Bern, but he would not give up. LaMarr preferred the virile cowboy star Jack Dougherty, so Bern proposed a compromise. "We will have a beautiful spiritual life together," he told LaMarr. "You and Mr. Jack Dougherty can have the occasional affair."

"Dear," the heavy-lidded LaMarr said to Bern, "it will work better if I sleep with Mr. Dougherty and have the occasional spiritual affair with you."

Bern lived with writer Carey Wilson on Chula Vista Avenue in the Hollywood Hills, next to St. Johns. When Thalberg and Gilbert visited them, they brought out bootleg liquor and cranked up the gramophone. "We fought all the time," recalled St. Johns, "because they played records all night. I had three children and two shepherd dogs and no one of us could sleep." One night St. Johns heard odd sounds coming from the bachelors' house. She pushed her way into it and found Wilson, Gilbert, and Thalberg in the bathroom, huddled over Bern. "Paul had put his head in the toilet to drown himself," St. Johns recalled. "When it didn't work, he couldn't get out of the bowl. Thalberg took a screwdriver and got him out of the bowl. But the seat was still around Paul's neck."

After a night like that, it was easy for Thalberg to appear unflappable at the studio, even when confronted by a brazen new talent. Having made seven films in New York, Norma Shearer thought herself a professional moving-picture actress. When informed that she would have to submit to a screen test, she went directly to Thalberg. "Mr. Thalberg," she said, glaring at him from across his desk, "I didn't have to come out and work for this studio, you know. This was only one of many offers I had. Universal wanted to sign me up a year ago for two hundred dollars a week, but I was too tied up with work in New York."

An awkward silence followed. Thalberg did not respond, but sat quietly looking at her, a quizzical expression on his face. Then he began to smile, a slow, knowing smile. "I know about that offer," he said.

"You know?"

"Yes," he said, still smiling. "And it wasn't for two hundred dollars. It was for considerably less. I approved it, as well as the other offers. You apparently don't know that I was in charge of the studio at the time."

Shearer immediately regretted her cheekiness. "I knew it was a horrible mistake," she recalled. "I could have slit my throat! I saw in that smile of his the entire story. I knew then that he had seen me in those awful little pictures, and that *he* had been the one, the only one, to make all those offers."

A few days later, Shearer arrived promptly at 8 A.M. in her shiny new Chevrolet roadster and was surprised to hear that her screen test with director John Stahl was scheduled for 8 that night. Instead of driving back to the Hollywood Hotel, she rambled down Mission Road to downtown Los Angeles, where department stores like Bullock's could tempt her. "I found an elaborate beaded tunic like the kind mother used to wear to balls and a pair of dazzling earrings to wear with it." Arrayed in her newfound finery, Shearer made her 8 P.M. entrance: "When Stahl caught sight of me with my hair piled high and those long rhinestone earrings, he said in the tone a doctor uses when he has to tell you he must operate, 'My dear, why are you trying so hard to be what you aren't?'"

Shearer dissolved into tears. Stahl took time to calm her. "He succeeded in stemming the tide," Shearer said, "and soon had me smiling and even laughing for the camera. With this accomplished, he then said, 'My dear, I would now like you to cry. Do you think you can do this for me?' I tried, but—horrors! I had shed all my tears already. Now I couldn't squeeze out a drop."

Stahl was drawing on reserves of patience, for he was known as a director who was skilled with actresses, but his unidentified cameraman had no aesthetic investment in the test. When Shearer viewed it the next day, she saw a pale apparition on the screen; she looked as if she had been photographed for a police lineup. "The custom then," she said, "when a cameraman was in a hurry, was to use flat lighting—to throw a great deal of light from all directions, in order to kill all shadows that might be caused by wrinkles or blemishes. But strong lights placed on each side of my face made my blue eyes look almost white, and by nearly eliminating my nose, made me look cross-eyed." Louis B. Mayer told Shearer that, based on what he had seen, he did not think that he and Mr. Thalberg would be able to use her. Shearer was crestfallen. She was about to learn a lesson about the science and art of motion pictures; it would be a lesson for Mayer and Thalberg, too.

When she left Mayer's office, nearly in tears, she encountered a cameraman named Ernest Palmer. He saw that she was agitated and he introduced himself, hoping to calm the pretty youngster. Shearer told him her name and that everyone hated her test. Later that day, when Palmer took the time to run it, he saw that he could improve on it and asked Mayer if he could reshoot it. Mayer did not want to throw good money after bad, but Palmer persisted.

Once on the stage, Palmer took the time to light Shearer in various ways. He discovered that Shearer did have an eye problem. Due to a weakness in her right eye muscle, that eye tended to wander inward if she looked in a certain direction. Working carefully with her, Palmer captured a series of appealing close-ups. The results taught Mayer and Thalberg a lesson: the artist behind the camera was as valuable as the talent in front of it.

Thalberg then cast Shearer as the leading lady of Stahl's film *The Wanters*, only to have Stahl replace Shearer with Marie Prevost. Shearer was demoted to a supporting role, but she made the most of it. On the basis of this performance, Thalberg cast her in the lead of *Pleasure Mad*. He had replaced its offensive plot with one by novelist Blanche Upright, whose name he liked. "You can hardly be more wholesome than that, Mr. Mayer," Thalberg said, then smiled at Mayer, who realized that he was being kidded by the usually serious Thalberg. The two partners were getting along well in their first year together. Mayer's daughter, Irene, observed them at family dinners as they "exchanged opinions and ideas, exploring each other's reactions. The growing bond between them was evident. There was confidence, enthusiasm, and affection—all of it mutual." This unanimity was illustrated in their approach to Shearer's next crisis.

In *Pleasure Mad*, Shearer was playing a sensitive girl torn between her divorcing parents. Director Reginald Barker had made twelve films in four years and had little patience with Shearer. "[Barker] didn't like me," she said. "No doubt he resented having to handle an amateur in such a role. I sensed this, which made me miserable. The more critical he was, the more incompetent I became. I lost what little confidence I had. I was tied up in knots. I felt like crying, but this time I didn't." Finally Barker blew up. "You don't seem to know what it's all about!" he yelled at her in front of the entire company and then left the set. The next thing she knew, she was in Mayer's office, and he was telling her quietly that she was about to be replaced. Shearer attempted to explain and Mayer suddenly pounded the table. "The trouble is you're yellow!" he snarled at her. "Here you are, given a great chance, the chance of your life, and what do you do? You throw it away because you don't like the director or something! I'm through with you!"

Shearer was stunned. Her eyes widened, filled with tears, and then she drew herself up to her full five foot three and advanced toward Mayer. "I am NOT yellow!" she said through her tears. "I'll fight it out! I'll show you! I can do it! Give me another chance!"

Mayer blinked and agreed to let her return to the film. Later that day, he confided to Thalberg that Shearer had given a "magnificent" performance in his office. Could she do it in front of the camera? In her dressing room, Shearer asked herself the same thing. Before she could find out, Thalberg shut down *Pleasure Mad*. He was unhappy with the camera work. Although his initial approach to a film was to craft a plausible story, he knew full well that the story had to be told visually, and (as he had learned from Shearer's tests) if the actors and sets did not look their best, the audience would subconsciously mistrust the characters. Shearer had not seen a filmmaker so concerned with quality. "This young man believed that if a picture was worth making at all it was worth making well," said Shearer. The interruption gave her a week to marshal her resources. "Here was my second chance with this heaven-sent part," she said. "I decided to show Mr. Barker that I wasn't afraid of him, that I could act along with the rest of the pros. I made up my mind to be as brave as the lions in the zoo next door. I could hear them roaring through the walls of my dressing room. I decided to roar too—as loud as they did. This time I let go. I gave it all I had. I took that scene—lock, stock, and barrel, fur, fins, and feathers!"

Mayer and Thalberg were pleased with the new Shearer footage, and she completed the film without further incident. After this, she was wary of Mayer, yet grateful for his patronage. She was awestruck by Thalberg. "I seldom saw the little boss on those busy days," said Shearer, "except to say 'Good morning, Mr. Thalberg,' as I passed him crossing the lot. He usually had his eyes cast downward in a shy manner. He was mysterious. He seemed to do more thinking than talking. He had a quiet authority, but he wore it with grace and with a gentle humor." Thalberg's value was not lost on his new partner, according to Irene Mayer Selznick. "My father's pride and delight in Irving were overwhelming. That was an aspect of him we never saw before or after. At times he bore him an aching love." The ache came from the inescapable fact that Thalberg was living on borrowed time. "If only he were healthy," Mayer sighed to his wife and daughters.

Mayer and Thalberg began loaning Shearer to other studios, a practice that netted them a profit on her fees and gave her experience that a small production schedule could not. It frustrated Mayer to see stages and talent sitting idle while Thalberg painstakingly prepared each vehicle. A larger facility could be shooting numerous scripts at the same time. Fewer than ten Mayer films reached the public in Thalberg's first year there, and while their healthy box-office returns confirmed the efficiency of the Mayer-Thalberg system, Mayer knew that he and Thalberg could handle a bigger studio. "Think big," Mayer would often say, as much for himself as for Thalberg. "That's the path of the future." J. Robert Rubin, the attorney who had been Mayer's friend since the Metro founding eight years earlier, agreed with him, and in his new position as counsel to Loew's, Inc., he was in a position to help.

Metro was performing so poorly that Marcus Loew was ready to close it down, but that would waste a superior distribution setup. While vacationing in Palm Beach to rest his ailing heart, Loew was approached by Frank Godsol of the Goldwyn Company, who had also been ordered to take time off from the rigors of motion picture management. Whether an idea occurred to them singly or simultaneously or was the brainstorm of the theatrical impresario Lee Shubert, who had arranged the meeting and was an investor in both companies, is not known. The idea was this: instead of closing or selling Metro, why not merge it with the Goldwyn Company?

This plan was overwhelming in its implications. Metro had what Goldwyn lacked, a pipeline to the Loew's theaters. Goldwyn had what Metro lacked, a huge physical plant full of proven directors, writers, and players—and the publicity tie-in with the Hearst press. Yet Godsol had been unable to compete with Hollywood's "Big Two," Famous Players–Lasky and First National. Now he thought how pleasant it would be to have a forty-six-acre load lifted from his shoulders. Loew, who had recently opened the Loew's State Theatre at 1540 Broadway, thought how nice it would be to own the Capitol Theatre at 1645 Broadway; the 5,300-seat theater was the world's largest, and Goldwyn had part ownership in it. This was what Adolph Zukor of Famous Players–Lasky had pioneered—a vertical monopoly comprising film production, distribution, and exhibition. With better management, the company created by this merger could take on the Big Two. Competent management was what Metro and Goldwyn lacked; Metro's Richard Rowland was a theatrical personality more than a manager and "In Godsol We Trust" was a Culver City joke. Who was qualified to run the superstudio this merger promised?

PART TWO · THE PERFECTION
OF SILENCE

CHAPTER 4 · A Studio Style

The merger of the Metro, Goldwyn, and Louis B. Mayer companies became official on May 10, 1924, but long before the contract was signed, long before the dedication ceremonies, Irving Thalberg had been visiting the Goldwyn lot and cultivating its plant manager Joseph "J.J." Cohn. "Unbeknownst to anyone out here," recalled Cohn seventy years later, "I was making a deal with Irving Thalberg about leasing, about them coming in and renting space on a yearly basis. At the same time, back east, they were talking about the amalgamation, which no one knew anything about." Louis B. Mayer had also been at Goldwyn before the merger, having maintained an office there since the first week of January. Once the merger took place, Mayer huddled with Thalberg and Cohn. "I went over the payroll with them," recalled Cohn. "Would we use the man from Metro? Would we use the man from the Mayer studio? Would we use the man from the Goldwyn studio? We went through it and we picked the best people of the three organizations." Populating dozens of departments was a formidable task, but there was a lot of deadwood.

Prominent executives were gotten rid of as quickly as lesser ones. Metro boss Joe Engel and Goldwyn studio boss Abraham Lehr were among the first to be dismissed. "They were just paid off," said Cohn. "Strangely enough," wrote Irene Selznick, "out-and-out enemies were not fired—not if they were talented." Frank Godsol was allowed to join the new board of directors but soon left of his own volition. The headstrong Goldwyn director Marshall Neilan was retained, though he had been a thorn in Mayer's side since he directed Mayer's first film, *In Old Kentucky*. Erich von Stroheim, who had been welcomed at Goldwyn after being fired from Universal, was also invited to join Metro-Goldwyn. The few actors who demanded higher salaries because of the merger were shown the door. Edith Shearer advised Norma to agree to a modest salary of a thousand dollars a week as long as her contract included a yearly increase of a thousand dollars a week. Mayer doubted that Norma would be with the company more than a year, so he approved the contract. "I'm telling you! Mother was no fool!" said Norma's brother Douglas fifty years later.

The Metro plant yielded Rex Ingram's discovery Ramon Novarro and the stalwart leading man Lewis Stone, as well as several glass stages, which were cut into sections and trucked across town. Ingram, who valued his autonomy, began looking at European studios. One of the first Metro projects reviewed by Thalberg was Albert Lewin's scenario *Bread*. Lewin was a five-foot-tall, five-year veteran of Hollywood, having worked as a script clerk for both King Vidor and Victor Seastrom. Lewin's credentials intimidated some studio employees; he had a master's degree in English from Harvard. This intrigued Thalberg, who called him to his new office. Lewin found Thalberg equally intriguing, a far cry from the aging poseurs who had run Metro. "I just got back from the merger signing in New York," Thalberg told Lewin. "I took a lot of scripts to read on the train. One of them was *Bread*." Thalberg thought Lewin's script well written but wanted him to change one scene to make it more dramatic. Lewin refused.

"You can't lie about ideas," he said, and then waited for Thalberg to pull rank and make him comply.

"It's your picture," said Thalberg. "Go ahead with it the way you want it." When Lewin completed the film on July 1, the green-shuttered Metro studio was quietly dismantled.

Two of Norma Shearer's loan-out films from the Mayer studio had been made at the Warner Bros. studio on Sunset Boulevard in Hollywood. The producer of these films (and of the profitable Rin Tin Tin series) was a vaudeville veteran and talent manager named Harry Rapf. Thalberg noted the care that Rapf took with Shearer and hired him for Mission Road. The first weeks after the merger saw Rapf readying talent, Mayer working with Cohn to organize the physical plant, and Thalberg preparing scripts. The first film to start shooting on the new Metro-Goldwyn lot after the dedication was a Goldwyn project, Hobart Henley's *Sinners in Silk*. The historic date was Wednesday, April 30. The mood at the new studio was upbeat, except for some minor confusion. Robert Z. Leonard, who was directing his wife, Mae Murray, in *Circe the Enchantress*, saw the *Sinners in Silk* lighting equipment sitting unattended during a lunch break. Instead of waiting for his own equipment to be delivered, Leonard moved *Sinners'* to his own stage; it was retrieved after lunch.

The employee roster already topped 350, and four—count 'em, four!—companies were shooting. Title writer Katharine Hilliker saw "enthusiasm everywhere" on the new lot, which she described as "a modern version of Sleeping Beauty's Court coming to life." Lenore Coffee remembered that "everything was very exciting during that time. We all lived in a state of euphoria." She attended Saturday morning meetings with Thalberg and his executives "in a poky little ground floor room. All the offices were small and shabby. No energy was wasted on that sort of thing. 'Anyone can buy equipment,' Irving said at our very first meeting, 'but you can't photograph it.' Talent, stories, ideas were what counted. There were discussions of what films we'd seen during the week. Which ones were doing good business? Why? Which films were not? Why? Much good came out of these informal meetings." As Irene Selznick recalled, "Thalberg was at first concerned with the mastery of a single sequence in each film." He eventually became known for the maxim "Every great film must have one great scene." In these early Metro-Goldwyn films, he was pleased if his scenarist and director could come up with something that played, yet Thalberg knew his limits. "I could make a movie out of *Mrs. Rorer's Cookbook*," he said whimsically. "But no one would come to see it."

Thalberg's stable of writers included novelists Elinor Glyn, Alice D. G. Miller, and Adela Rogers St. Johns; tried-and-true scenarists Waldemar Young, Bess Meredyth, and Agnes Christine Johnson; and the imported talents of Hungarian Bela Sekely and Jewish-Irish Benjamin Glazer. *Los Angeles Times* columnist Harry Carr described this stable as "the most imposing array of writing talent that any studio has ever gathered together." Thalberg was respectful of this talent. "I don't want to impose too many of my ideas on you writers," he said. "I merely want to help clarify and build up your own ideas. You're the creators, not I."

One of the few Goldwyn films making money for the new company was *Three Weeks*, a florid romance based on the book by Madame Elinor Glyn. After titillating her readers with a succession of sexy novels set in mythical kingdoms, the eccentric British writer had become a supervisor of Goldwyn films based on her books. Audiences thrilled to the scene in *Three Weeks* in which Conrad Nagel makes love to Aileen Pringle on a bed of roses. A popular refrain asked: "Would you care to sin / Like Elinor Glyn / On a tiger skin / Or would you prefer / To err / on some other fur?" When director King Vidor visited Glyn's suite at the Ambassador Hotel, he found her reclining on a tiger skin. "When she saw the shock on our faces," wrote Vidor, "she quickly explained that the tiger skin was a wonderful cloth imitation and if we needed any for pictures (or otherwise) she would be most happy to tell us where it could be purchased." With *Three Weeks*, Glyn became Hollywood's arbiter of glamour and sex, coining the term "It" to describe sexual magnetism.

Norma Shearer remembered Glyn as a "high priestess of the art of love [who] looked much too austere to be hopping into bed or even taking off her elegant clothes. In these you felt she'd been born and had no intention of removing them, even in a romantic crisis. That shiny braid that crowned her bronze hair and chalky face seemed like a permanent fixture, too." Sophisticated screenwriters like Frances Marion had read Glyn's racy books while growing up but now found her slightly ridiculous, a sixtyish woman traipsing around Hollywood in veils and turbans. "Miss Glyn was quite weird," recalled Vidor. "Her dress, her talk, and her appearance were altogether strange. She had false gums that startled you by turning purple under the copper-hued vapor lights whenever she smiled."

Metro-Goldwyn was fortunate to own another Glyn novel, *His Hour*, a project that Thalberg could begin immediately if Glyn approved. Her contract with Goldwyn, which was still in force, gave her approval of director and casting. Thalberg assigned Vidor to start *His Hour* on May 14, which meant that Thalberg and the handsome young director from Galveston, Texas, had to visit Glyn at the Ambassador. They also had to bring a young actor whom Thalberg had recruited from the Fox Film Corporation. When Glyn cast her eyes on the raven-haired John Gilbert, she exclaimed: "Ahhh, behold the black stallion!" For his part the moody Gilbert remembered meeting Glyn with both "self-consciousness and scorn." After the meeting he told Thalberg that Glyn's book was trash. "Of course it's trash," replied Thalberg, "but it's what the public wants. Do this role and you'll get some of the best exposure of your career. Afterward, we'll see if we can find something more interesting for you." Gilbert and Vidor became part of Thalberg's social scene, sometimes accompanying him and his family to Catalina Island. On these excursions, according to Vidor, Thalberg "acted like the little boy he could never be at the studio."

In Hollywood, Thalberg tried to act his age with three colleagues who were named John but nicknamed Jack. "The Three Jacks" were actor John Gilbert, director Jack Conway, and playwright John Colton. Writer Victor Heerman was at the Culver City studio picking up a manuscript one Sunday morning when he spied Gilbert sauntering down a deserted street. "What are you doing here?" asked Heerman. "Don't you take Sundays off like the rest of us?"

"I just can't stay away from this place, Victor," replied Gilbert. "It's so great to be a part of anything like this. I just can't believe I'm really here."

Jack Gilbert's insecurity was the result of a grim childhood. Deserted by his itinerant actor father, he was grudgingly raised by his actress mother—after she tried to give her newborn infant away. Gilbert grew up in touring companies, learning to love show business and hate his mother. She died when he was fourteen. His stepfather pulled him out of school, handed him ten dollars, and pushed him onto the streets of San Francisco. Twelve years later, Gilbert had eighty films to his credit, some of which he had written and directed. He was on the verge of stardom, but even though he was married to actress Leatrice Joy, he still felt that he belonged nowhere and to no one. The newborn studio—and his friendship with Thalberg—gave him his first sense of family.

Jack Conway had been working in films for fifteen years, first as an actor and then, beginning as an assistant director on D. W. Griffith's *Intolerance*, behind the camera. Thalberg had met Conway at Universal. Like Cedric Gibbons, Conway was known as a "cocksman." Jack Colton was also notorious, not only for his hit play *Rain* (an adaptation of W. Somerset Maugham's *Miss Thompson*) but also for his nocturnal visits to the seamy side of Los Angeles. Gilbert and Conway enjoyed titillating Thalberg by plying Colton with gin so that he would tell what exotic young men he had recently picked up—and what he had done with them in bed.

Hearing of these shenanigans, Mayer told Gilbert: "You've got a beautiful wife. Why don't you leave Irving alone and stay home with her and keep your nose clean? You're gonna be a star, and you gotta have dignity." Gilbert ignored Mayer and kept Thalberg up until all hours, nightclubbing and carousing with the two other Jacks, as well as with director Howard Hawks and his brother Kenneth. Diversion was also provided by Harry Rapf, whose Ambassador Hotel party for *Cosmopolitan* editor Ray Long slid into a row of bungalows one night. "I was cold sober," recalled screenwriter Frederica Sagor, "but I was curious about what was going on in those bungalows. Several drunken men tried to entice me there, but I shook them off. I finally got to where the action was and saw more than I had bargained for. Undressed, tousled men chased naked women, shrieking with laughter. Included in this orgy were Ray Long, Harry Rapf, and even the immaculate Irving Thalberg—all drunk, drunk, drunk."

"These bums!" exclaimed Henrietta when rousing her son one morning. "They're killing my golden boy!"

In this corrupting company, Thalberg met the notorious gold digger Peggy Hopkins Joyce, with whom he carried on his first adult affair, much to Henrietta's dismay. At the same time, Edith Shearer was powerless to prevent her daughter from being seduced by director Victor Fleming while on location filming *Empty Hands*. Thalberg's affair with Joyce was of short duration, primarily because he was not wealthy enough for her. After some uneventful dates with actresses Bessie Love and Marie Prevost, Thalberg fell—and fell hard—for a star at another studio.

First National's Constance Talmadge was related by marriage to Metro-Goldwyn. Her sister, movie star Norma Talmadge, was married to producer Joseph Schenck, whose brother Nicholas was second-in-command at Loew's. If Thalberg needed to increase the budget of a film in Culver City, he had to call Nick Schenck in the New York office. Constance was something new for Thalberg, a witty, worldly, well-traveled young woman who had her own production company. While the spoiled Rosabelle Laemmle expected preferential treatment, the bubbly "Dutch" Talmadge laughed at propriety, finding entertainment with gay actor William Haines in boozy nocturnal gambols. "She scintillated," recalled Irene Selznick. "She was not only the toast of New York, but also the only movie star who moved in the better circles of Europe and London." When Thalberg was with Connie, his grave, purposeful airs vanished and he became whimsical and boyish.

"Constance brought out in him an even more charming personality than we had heretofore seen," wrote Selznick. "Seeing him like this, one forgot there was any possible shadow over him." Henrietta Thalberg thought Constance a little too ebullient. "She's frivolous," said Henrietta. "She's not concerned with his health, with his future." In truth, Constance found Thalberg too slow. She craved excitement, and, having witnessed her sister's union with a stodgy executive, she was not interested in a Hollywood marriage. "Often Irving would leave his studio at a late hour to park his car in front of the Talmadge home in Beverly Hills," wrote screenwriter Anita Loos. "He'd wait in the dark until Dutch got back from some party. Only after her bedroom light went out would Irving give up his vigil over the one girl in Hollywood he could never impress." To Henrietta's relief, Constance broke off the romance. Thalberg was crestfallen but not heartbroken. He was learning about real life with the Three Jacks and applying it to "reel" life at Metro-Goldwyn.

In the second week of June, Marcus Loew released a progress report on his new studio. "There are twenty-two companies now at work. We are way ahead of our schedule. By the first of September, there will be prints of twenty-five productions in our exchanges." This was a slight exaggeration. Only five directors were shooting on the lot, and these were still projects inherited from Metro or Goldwyn. Pending releases were either in the same category or were films made by Buster Keaton, Inspiration Pictures, or Cosmopolitan. It remained for Thalberg to produce the first true Metro-Goldwyn film, one that was planned, filmed, *and* released by the company.

Since its earliest days, the Goldwyn company had maintained a production slate. As a script was approved for production, it was assigned a number and an account to which all production costs could be charged. The Goldwyn company's final production had been Number 191, *Nellie the Beautiful Cloak Model*. In April 1924 Mayer, Thalberg, and Rapf put Number 192 on the schedule. *He Who Gets Slapped* became Metro-Goldwyn's first production. This was the strange play that Thalberg had enjoyed in New York two years earlier. He saw it as a way to trumpet new players—and the new company—in a November engagement at New York's Capitol Theatre. *He Who Gets Slapped* was an odd choice for the company's inaugural project, but it showed Thalberg's fascination with offbeat love tales.

He Who Gets Slapped tells the story of a circus clown known only as "HE," a former scientist whose renowned act is a masochistic reenactment of the brutal slaps he received when his mentor stole both his invention and his wife. The pathos of this story called for a special director. Goldwyn's last 1924 hit, *Name the Man*, had been cowritten and directed by Victor Sjöström, a forty-five-year-old Swedish director who had made more than forty films since 1913—simple, moving tales like *The Outlaw and His Wife*. (In America he worked under the name of Victor Seastrom.) "There is that something about him—a subdued majesty—that commands mingled awe and respect," wrote the "hobo journalist" Jim Tully. "An oak in a forest of pines, he is one of the very few big men that the cinema world has produced." Mayer was in awe of Seastrom, and actors found him sympathetic. "Besides being a master of mood and sensitivity," said Shearer, "Mr. Seastrom was also a fine actor, so it was natural for me to develop hero worship for this soft-spoken man who seemed to carry the sadness of the world in his tired blue eyes." Thalberg assigned the play script of *He Who Gets Slapped* to Seastrom, who wrote his scenario in Swedish. After it was translated, it was polished by Carey Wilson, who had just written Shearer's *Empty Hands* for Paramount. (Wilson would become a pillar of the writers' department by doing last-minute rewrites of other writers' scripts—and attaching his name to their credits.)

Shearer was still being loaned out to other studios, but this did not keep her out of Thalberg's new office. According to Mayer's secretary, Florence Browning, there was more to it than just career advancement. "Norma Shearer was determined to get Irving from the first day she walked into our studio on Mission Road and saw him," recalled Browning in 1953. "She used to sit in my office, pretending to talk to me but actually waiting to see him—and be seen by him—when he came in." At one point, Shearer's mother became suspicious of her long hours at the studio. "Mr. Thalberg," Edith said over the telephone, "will you please see that my daughter gets home a little earlier at night so she won't always have to eat a cold dinner?"

"Mrs. Shearer," Thalberg answered, "will you please see that your daughter's dinner is kept hot for her?" Lenore Coffee sensed Thalberg's attraction to Shearer, but he denied it. "She makes me feel paternal," said the baby-faced mogul.

There was no shortage of leading ladies at the new studio—Renée Adorée, Eleanor Boardman, Mae Busch, Aileen Pringle, and Viola Dana—but Shearer's propinquity led Thalberg to cast her as the leading lady in *He Who Gets Slapped*. She would play Consuelo, the bareback rider whom HE secretly loves. For Consuelo's riding partner, Thalberg wanted John Gilbert, but Gilbert wanted no part of a film in which he had only twenty scenes. After reading the script, he stormed into Thalberg's office, his eyes burning with tears. "Look here," he blurted to the startled but impassive Thalberg. "If you want to get rid of me, you don't have to give me rotten parts to do it. I'll leave today and it won't cost you a penny!"

"Are you stark staring mad?" asked Thalberg calmly. "This part—as small as it is—will do you more good than anything you have ever done." Fortunately, Gilbert listened to reason.

To play the tragic clown HE, Thalberg called upon Lon Chaney, who was riding high from the fanfare being accorded *The Hunchback of Notre Dame*, but still working as a freelance artist. Thalberg offered him the lead in *He Who Gets Slapped*—and the possibility of a contract. The film went into production on June 17, and Seastrom immediately found a rapport with Thalberg's people. "It was like making a picture back home in Sweden," said Seastrom. "I wrote the script without any interference, and the actual shooting went quickly and without complications." The hitch came when Thalberg saw the rough cut of the film.

According to Jim Tully, "When Thalberg saw *He Who Gets Slapped* in the projection room, he walked out in despair." The overt masochism of Chaney's character and the pervasive sadness of the film made it a dubious candidate for the Capitol's fifth-anniversary gala in November. The film had already cost two times more than the average Metro-Goldwyn film. By the fall of 1924, there were seventeen of them in release and they were doing well, but *He Who Gets Slapped* was in a different category. Thalberg set his jaw, and according to studio publicist Frank Whitbeck, "he disappeared into the cutting room and didn't come out for two days and a night." When he did, he felt that *He Who Gets Slapped* was ready for the Capitol. Its manager, Samuel "Roxy" Rothapfel, staged an especially lavish premiere, which was only fitting; Marcus Loew was his new boss. On November 15, Helen Klumph of the *Los Angeles Times* reported: "This immense theater is literally jammed at every performance, with standing room only at even the opening and dinner-hour shows. It will surely play a second week." It did more than that; it became Metro-Goldwyn's first smash hit.

At 10 P.M. on Christmas Eve 1924, Shearer had just finished a long day on Lot Two with director Monta Bell, making a film called *Two Worlds* (later retitled *Lady of the Night*). When she emerged from her portable dressing room, she found that the bus had left for Lot One without her, so she had a half-mile walk to her dressing room. When she arrived at the two-story wood-frame actors' building, the only Christmas cheer she found was her maid's thermos of hot chocolate. It was past 11 when her telephone rang. "Norma, this is Irving Thalberg."

"Good evening," she answered warily.

"I heard you worked late tonight," he said with slightly less reserve than usual. "I just wanted to call and wish you a Merry Christmas." Shearer looked out her window, and, yes, the light was on in his office. Thalberg signed off without further ado, but the unexpected call cheered her more than the chocolate and the good reviews she was getting for *He Who Gets Slapped*. After working nearly two years with the inscrutable young boss, she was finally doing well enough to merit his attention. And perhaps this attention would not be strictly business.

CHAPTER 5 · Wicked Stepchildren

Metro-Goldwyn's first year saw only two films in serious trouble: Erich von Stroheim's *Greed* and Charles Brabin's *Ben-Hur.* Curiously, each had been adopted from Goldwyn, and each was the brainchild of scenarist June Mathis, the plump, petite powerhouse who had urged Rex Ingram to cast Rudolph Valentino in Metro's *The Four Horsemen of the Apocalypse.* The combination of her writing and Ingram's direction had turned Valentino's burnished physicality into gold. When Metro foolishly let Mathis go, Goldwyn grabbed her. When Thalberg fired Stroheim from Universal, Mathis told Abe Lehr to grab him, and the Goldwyn company seduced Stroheim, not with money but with artistic freedom. "The author and the play are the thing" was the company's new slogan.

To the relief of Goldwyn's executives, Stroheim was not interested in a large canvas; his first film would be an American morality tale. On December 15, 1922, Lehr and Frank Godsol drew up a contract that allowed Stroheim freedom, but within limits. He had to deliver three films within a year, and none of them could be longer than 8,500 feet (ninety-five minutes). For each completed film he would receive $30,000. He announced that his first would be based on the 1899 Frank Norris novel *McTeague,* the naturalistic story of a San Francisco dentist whose lovely young wife turns into a phobic miser. To assure the company of his good intentions, Stroheim announced that he would film *McTeague* in the locations in which the author had set his story, thereby eliminating the need for expensive sets. "I had graduated from the D. W. Griffith school of film making," he later wrote, "and I intended to go the Master one better as regards film realism. In real cities, not corners of them designed by [art directors] Cedric Gibbons or Richard Day, but in real tree-bordered boulevards, with real streetcars, buses and automobiles, through real winding alleys, with real dirt and foulness, in the gutters as well as in real castles and palaces."

Three months after signing his contract, Stroheim was in San Francisco, converting a building at 601 Laguna Street into a Polk Street rooming house of forty years earlier. To steep his actors in the film's raw ambience, Stroheim moved them into the building. He suddenly decided that Norris's book had insufficient exposition, so he began writing dozens of additional scenes and hiring hundreds of extras to populate them. By March 13, 1923, when he finally started shooting, he had changed the title of the film to *Greed,* and his budget had ballooned from $174,000 to $347,000; no one was surprised when he collapsed from nervous exhaustion a few days later. He then subjected his cast to worse treatment than any of his previous had experienced. He caused Jean Hersholt to be knocked unconscious in a fight scene, the elderly Cesare Gravina to leap into the frigid San Francisco Bay, and Zasu Pitts to be grazed by an Oakland train.

Visiting journalist Edwin Schallert described the "movie set" on which Stroheim was directing Gibson Gowland (as McTeague) and Pitts (as his wife, Trina): "The room into which they were crowded was miserable beyond belief," wrote Schallert. "Lights looked glaringly down on the players' faces and the sweating atmosphere literally stifled them as they fought their way through rehearsal after rehearsal and scene after scene. And the rehearsals were many and the scenes few, for they were driven, as few players ever have been driven, by the unflagging zeal of the director's militaristic will."

Stroheim also exposed his cast to the rigors of a Gold Country location, but nothing compared with the hellish stint in Death Valley. "There were no roads and no hotels as there are today," Stroheim later wrote. "We were the only white people (forty-one men and one woman) who had penetrated into the lowest point on earth (below sea level) since the days of the pioneers. We worked in 142 degrees Fahrenheit in the shade, and there was no shade." Stroheim's colleagues brought back harrowing stories. "The paint on the cars curled up and fell off," recalled cameraman Paul Ivano. "You couldn't touch a piece of metal. One of the cooks on the company died—I think he had high blood pressure, and the heat didn't help."

The climax of *Greed* has McTeague confronted in Death Valley by another covetous character, the churlish Marcus (Jean Hersholt). Hersholt recalled:

Every day Gibson Gowland and I would crawl across those miles of sunbaked salt—bare to the waist, unshaven, blackened and blistered and bleeding, while Stroheim dragged every bit of realism out of us. The day that we staged our death fight I barely recollect at all. Stroheim had made our hot, tired brains grasp that this scene was to be the finish. The blisters on my body, instead of breaking outwards, had burst inwards. The pain was intense. Gowland and I crawled over the crusted earth. I reached him, dragged him to his feet. With real bloodlust in our hearts we fought and rolled and slugged each other. Stroheim yelled at us, "Fight, fight! Try to hate each other as you both hate me!"

Hersholt finally had to be hospitalized for heatstroke.

Stroheim finished shooting *Greed* on October 6. He had exposed 446,103 feet of film and spent nearly half a million dollars. Having exceeded both schedule and budget, he was taken off salary by Goldwyn. In order to underwrite the editing process, Stroheim mortgaged his house and sold his automobile.

On January 12, 1924, Stroheim held the first screening of *Greed* at the Goldwyn studios. Mayer and Thalberg were already in evidence on the lot but were not invited. Mayer's daughter, Irene, managed to wangle an invitation. About ten of Stroheim's friends were present, including Idwal Jones, drama critic of the *San Francisco Daily News*. The private screening commenced at 10 A.M. "The picture was like the book; not a single detail omitted," wrote Jones. "It is evident that von Stroheim, sitting motionless in a straight chair, cane in hand and staring right ahead, as if boring through the screen, worships realism like an abstract ideal; worships it more, and suffers more in its achievement, than other men do for wealth or fame." Stroheim was not the only one suffering that day. *Greed* was an unheard-of forty-two reels in length—more than seven hours. "We went to the studio early [that] morning to see it," wrote Irene Mayer Selznick, "and sat through till evening of a very, very hot day, made no cooler by the final hours of endless footage shot in the blazing sun of Death Valley."

Acting on his own initiative, Stroheim began to edit *Greed*. "When I arrived at twenty-four reels I could not, to save my soul, cut another foot," he wrote. "During the time I was cutting the film, the Goldwyn Company became Metro-Goldwyn. With Irving Thalberg as the new General Manager, their slogan became 'The producer is the thing.' I soon realized that the change boded no good for me, as Thalberg and I had often crossed swords at Universal." This was the new company's quandary: what to do with a four-hour film called *Greed*. "Mayer and Thalberg insisted on cutting it down to what they described as a 'commercial length,'" said Stroheim. "Mayer, in fact, made it his business to impress upon me that I was only a small employee in a very large pants factory."

A 130-minute version of *Greed* premiered at William Randolph Hearst's Cosmopolitan Theatre on December 4, 1924, and *New York Times* critic Mordaunt Hall described a premiere where "spectators laughed, and laughed heartily, at the audacity of the director." Hall acknowledged brilliant performances by Hersholt, Pitts, and Gowland but deplored two hours of grit. "Irving Thalberg and Harry Rapf, two expert producers, clipped this production as much as they dared and still have a dramatic story. They are to be congratulated on their efforts, and the only pity is that they did not use the scissors more generously."

In Thalberg's opinion, the editing (accomplished by director Howard Hawks and title writer Joe Farnham) had not destroyed the film. For years, only Stroheim's side was heard, but Thalberg did speak his mind on *Greed*. "This whole story is of greed—a progressive greed," Thalberg told the *Los Angeles Times*. "It is the story of the way greed grew in Trina's heart until it obsessed her. I found that the junk dealer's greed [the subplot of Zerkow, played by Cesare Gravina] was so much greater than hers that it almost destroyed this theme. His intense greed drowned out Trina's greed just as a steam whistle drowns out a small street noise. Instead of hurting the picture, throwing out this junk dealer's story made the picture stronger." Stroheim considered Thalberg's cutting of *Greed* arbitrary and heartless, but Thalberg had gone to considerable trouble. "We took no chances in cutting it," he said. "We took it around to different theaters in the suburbs, ran it at its enormous length, and then we took note of the places at which interest seemed to droop." According to Martin Quigley, editor of the trade paper *Harrison's Reports*, Thalberg had labored in vain.

> If a contest were to be held to determine which has been the filthiest, vilest, most putrid picture in the history of the motion picture business, I am sure that *Greed* would walk away with the honors. In my seven-year career as a reviewer and in my five-year one as an exhibitor, I do not remember ever having seen a picture in which an attempt was made to pass as entertainment dead rats, sewers, filth, rotten meat, persons with frightful looking teeth, characters picking their noses, people holding bones in their hands and eating like street dogs or gorging on other food like pigs, a hero murdering his wife and then shown with hands dripping with blood.

Only a tiny minority found something to praise in Stroheim's shortened film. Richard Watts Jr. of the *New York Herald Tribune* named it "the most impor. int picture yet produced in America. . . . When the 'movies' can produce a *Greed* they can no longer be sneered at." An uncredited review in *Exceptional Photoplays* magazine stated that "Mr. von Stroheim has always been the realist as Rex Ingram is the romanticist and Griffith the sentimentalist of the screen, and in *Greed* he has given us an example of realism at its starkest. Like the novel from which the plot was taken, *Greed* is a terrible and wonderful thing." *Greed* cost $665,603 and grossed $247,000. Since Goldwyn had bankrolled the film, Metro-Goldwyn had to bear only the cost of prints and advertising. The lesson of *Greed* was not lost on Thalberg. He would never again let a director go so far afield. Yet he spent much of 1924 wrestling with another Goldwyn project.

Ben-Hur: A Tale of the Christ was both a literary and theatrical phenomenon when Goldwyn acquired its rights in 1922. The story of a Jewish prince who loses his position to Roman tyranny and his family to a leper pit before Christ converts him was written in 1867 by a Confederate general, Lew Wallace. Published in 1880, the novel became a blockbuster; by the end of the century, only the Bible was selling more copies. Wallace sold theatrical rights to Broadway impresarios Abraham Erlanger and Marc Klaw, and the property's success again exceeded expectations, running consistently into the 1920s. It was then that Erlanger and his investors offered *Ben-Hur* to Hollywood for an unheard-of $1 million. In 1922 Goldwyn's Godsol stepped in with a proposal based on his cash-poor status. If Erlanger would "entrust" him with the property, he would pay for the entire production and give him an unprecedented 50 percent of the profits. "It is a contract I do not want to claim credit for," Marcus Loew later said.

Once the astonishing contract was signed, June Mathis ingratiated herself with Erlanger and took over the project. Valentino was not available to play Judah Ben-Hur, so she cast the second-tier actor George Walsh, and then announced that second-string director Charles Brabin was to film her *Ben-Hur* scenario in Italy. Goldwyn executives said yes to Mathis, just as they had to Stroheim. What Mayer, Thalberg, and Rapf found in their corporate lap after the merger was, according to Norma Shearer, "a baby, in its teething stage, and causing a lot of trouble. The company was faced with the difficulty and expense of supervising a production in Italy. It was no easy task to re-create—at long range—a saga of ancient feuds in a country in the midst of Fascist conflicts. Labor disputes and the language barrier were also slowing things." Worse than that, *Ben-Hur* had exceeded its $1.25 million–dollar budget in less than two months. "I could make the whole thing right here for $800,000," said Thalberg.

Since several large sets had already been completed in Italy, including the Joppa

Gate, the Circus Maximus, and a fleet of Roman galleys, Mayer and Thalberg decided to let the shooting finish there. They fired June Mathis, Charles Brabin, and George Walsh. Fred Niblo would take over direction, with a new script by Carey Wilson and Bess Meredyth. Walsh's replacement remained a secret until Sunday, June 8, 1924, when Ramon Novarro received an unexpected telephone call at the Gramercy Place mansion he shared with his mother, father, and siblings. "That Sunday noon," recalled Novarro, "Thalberg called me up and he wanted me to come see him at the studio right away. And I thought, Well, this is a funny thing. So I went right away."

"Would you like to play Ben-Hur?" Thalberg asked him.

"Well, I'm not crazy! Of course I would!"

"Well, we want to make a test of you," Thalberg said.

"Nothing doing," replied Novarro. "You'll make a test in a hurry, without the right costumes, without the right photography, and I won't have a chance. If you want to look at my legs, look at them in [the 1923 film] *Where the Pavement Ends*. In fact, the upper part looks better now since I've been exercising.'"

"Well, it's a wonderful role," Thalberg said as he signed Novarro.

Thalberg was less cheerful when he saw Brabin's footage. "It is almost beyond my conception," Thalberg wrote Niblo, "that such stuff could have been passed by people of even moderate intelligence, that June Mathis, in fact anyone over there could have tolerated for one single day the ill-fitting costumes, the incongruous action, the almost silly and typically European movements of the people. Not in my wildest imagination could I have pictured anything that broad." Niblo's direction improved on Brabin's, but no one could make headway with the Italian bureaucracy, which kept sets unfinished and tempers on edge.

By January 1925, the footage Niblo was sending back had Thalberg worried. It was undistinguished. Even the chariot race lacked excitement, though a stunt driver had been killed while making it. The film had already cost nearly $3 million. If it flopped, it could jeopardize the very existence of Metro-Goldwyn. Thalberg had to whip *Ben-Hur* into shape. He brought the entire company back to Culver City, rewrote scenes, and had the film back in production by February 18. He also got $300,000 from Marcus Loew to reshoot the chariot race.

To create a credible Circus Maximus, art director Cedric Gibbons designed a set that would combine an outdoor stadium with a hanging miniature in which tiny toga-clad spectators waved their arms. The blueprints were impressive but Thalberg was worried. "The audience is going to think the set is a fake unless we prove to them that it isn't," he said. "What we need are some statues, huge statues we can place the extras beside so the audience will get a sense of the scale." Gibbons added twenty-foot-tall male figures crouching at each end of the racetrack, and began construction in a vacant lot at the intersection of Venice Boulevard and Brice Road (later La Cienega Boulevard). Eight hundred workers took four months to complete the immense structure.

On the morning of Saturday, October 3, 1925, the celebrated of Hollywood— stars such as Harold Lloyd, Douglas Fairbanks, and Mary Pickford—joined throngs of extras in the Circus set. "Everyone in the picture business was there," recalled Shearer. "There were forty-two cameras and thousands of extras and little cardboard dummies in the top rows in the distance fluttering their little paper hands as twelve chariots and forty-eight fine horses came thundering by." The thunder did not commence on time, though. At 10 A.M. Thalberg was looking up at the crowd of extras in the stadium. "How many people have you got?" he asked studio manager Joe Cohn.

"Thirty-nine hundred," Cohn answered.

"Not enough." Thalberg shook his head. "Get some more."

"But where? How can we find them at this hour?"

"I don't care. Pull them in off the street. The set needs more people."

Four hundred were recruited from the streets of Culver City, West Los Angeles, and Skid Row, but at 11:30, filming still could not begin. A heavy fog had settled over the set, rendering useless the miniature that hung in front of the camera; its verticals would not line up with the blurred columns in the foggy distance. It was near noon when the sun finally broke through. Niblo wanted to break for lunch, but Cohn risked his job and impulsively started the race, braving the possibility that four thousand spectators might riot. "So it'll look like they're cheering the race," said Cohn.

There was much to cheer. Reaves "Breezy" Eason, a director of westerns, motivated his twelve stunt drivers by offering a prize of $150 to the winner. The drivers roared around the track, inspired in their emulation of ancient charioteers. It soon became obvious that the competition was real. Extras and spectators alike screamed with enthusiasm. Then, in the sixth lap, a chariot wheel caught on the edge of the track. The chariot swerved out of control and crashed into another. Assistant Director Henry Hathaway ran out to wave down the oncoming chariots. He was too late. Three chariots crashed into the wreckage, throwing men and horses in all directions. Miraculously, no driver was injured, but seven horses had to be euthanized. Representatives of the Society for the Prevention of Cruelty to Animals (SPCA) were angry when Cohn asked them, "What about the people?"

Because Loew's, Inc., had insisted on booking *Ben-Hur* for a Christmas holiday premiere, Thalberg was faced with the task of completing and editing the chariot race, plus dozens of other scenes by mid-December—while supervising the twenty other films Metro-Goldwyn was making in the fall of 1925. *Ben-Hur*'s production costs were approaching $4 million, and although Thalberg stood atop a pyramid of assistants, he was ultimately responsible for the most expensive film yet made in Hollywood. As his workdays lengthened and his workweeks melted one into the other, few of his intimates saw how much stress his unstable constitution was fielding. All they saw was a year-old company making hits faster than any other studio in the world.

If 1924 was the year in which Irving G. Thalberg and Louis B. Mayer grabbed the brass ring, 1925 was the year in which they turned brass into gold. Their Mission Road origins were soon forgotten as Thalberg's filmmaking and Mayer's management pushed Metro-Goldwyn into the front ranks of the film industry. By the company's first anniversary, ten of its films were in 1924's top-grossing forty. "The average theater patron," said Mayer, "now shops for screen entertainment instead of following the old habit of dropping into whatever theater is closest to home or most accessible in the downtown section. This practice means a greater appreciation of the worthwhile product, making better pictures possible." Yet Mayer knew that a "worthwhile" film such as *Bread* could not compete with a film that had a star in it.

Paramount, the most prosperous studio in town, had Gloria Swanson, Rudolph Valentino, and Pola Negri. United Artists had Norma Talmadge, Mary Pickford, Charlie Chaplin, and Douglas Fairbanks. First National had Colleen Moore and Constance Talmadge. Metro-Goldwyn had contract players Aileen Pringle, Conrad Nagel, Eleanor Boardman, John Gilbert, Renee Adorée, Ramon Novarro, and Norma Shearer; they were popular, but they were hardly stars of the first magnitude. Its biggest draws were Marion Davies, Mae Murray, Buster Keaton, and Jackie Coogan, independent entities who only released their films through it.

There were three ways in which Mayer and Thalberg would catch up to the other studios: Thalberg would buy literary properties for the talent he had, making stars of contract players such as Shearer and Gilbert. Mayer and Thalberg would assimilate the stars who released through the company—Coogan, Davies, Murray, and Keaton. Or Mayer would scout for new talent, recruiting both stars like Lillian Gish and unknowns like Greta Garbo.

Mayer's trip to Europe in the fall of 1924 had yielded Mauritz Stiller, a Swedish director recommended to him by Seastrom. Mayer had also signed Stiller's protégée. "Mr. Mayer has put under contract one of the most popular of continental stars," wrote the *Times*'s Helen Klumph. "He will not divulge her name until she arrives in this country but he says that she has the beauty and ability of Corinne Griffith or Norma Talmadge." Mayer's unusual reticence was due to his discomfort with the actress's name, Greta Garbo. He thought Garbo sounded like "garbage."

Harry Rapf was in New York in December when the studio's East Coast publicist Howard Dietz told him about a vivacious chorus girl named Lucille LeSueur. Rapf joined Dietz at the Winter Garden Theatre to see the girl. "[Harry] agreed she was a natural for pictures," wrote Dietz. "Her personality knocked you over." Rapf signed LeSueur, and she arrived in Culver City on New Year's Day. For the next nine months she posed for hundreds of still photographs and played bit parts. Then Rapf changed her name to Joan Crawford. He thought LeSueur sounded like "sewer."

To elevate contract players to stardom, the level at which they became household words, Thalberg had to match the right actor to the right property. June Mathis had done this with Valentino in *The Four Horsemen of the Apocalypse* and *The Sheik*. "Irving felt that the actor was a very special human being," wrote Norma Shearer in 1958. "'This is a business of personalities,' he told me. 'Nothing can change that.'" In 1925 these personalities captured Thalberg's imagination, tapped his ingenuity, and burned his energy.

Metro-Goldwyn's first "season" had ended in April 1925 with a total of twenty-six releases. As the next season promised forty, Thalberg's hours lengthened and his home life suffered. He was sharing a rented house on Fountain Avenue in Hollywood with writer Nat Ross, but still spent time with his family in Los Angeles. Producer Lucien Hubbard, who had been a pal of Thalberg's since Universal, recalled family excursions to Catalina Island and Palm Springs—and the pecking order in the household. "Henrietta always entered the dining room first," said Hubbard in 1967. "William was a nice German Jew—immaculate, dapper, and a thorough gentleman. He was proud of Irving but he never interfered with Henrietta. There was a weak quality about William. Henrietta ran things. She knew all the backstage gossip from the studio. When Irving visited her, they talked all night. He sat on the sofa listening and would absentmindedly pull feathers out of the cushions."

Thalberg's schedule permitted a trip to New York in early 1925. The *Los Angeles Times* reported: "Mr. Thalberg writes the studio that he is looking at all the new plays and shopping for novels to turn into pictures." In Los Angeles, his schedule also allowed for Sunday afternoon parties given by the Rapfs or by Marion Davies, who had recently moved to Metro-Goldwyn with William Randolph Hearst's Cosmopolitan Productions. These parties were sedate affairs, marked by nothing more scandalous than the new Charleston craze. Thalberg could be seen practicing the dance at more than one party, and just as often making deals for new films. "Irving loved parties," recalled Marion Davies. "They were his way of relaxing. And everybody loved him." For the most part, though, Thalberg had little time for Hollywood society or for family visits. His office was more than a home away from home; the studio *was* his home, and its 1,100 employees were his responsibility.

Besides acting as story editor for every M-G-M production, Thalberg personally supervised seventeen of the thirty-three films released in 1925. When Mayer welcomed Hearst's Cosmopolitan Pictures to the lot, Thalberg added the first Davies production, *Lights of Old Broadway,* to his schedule. He was also supervising the completion of the massive *Ben-Hur.* Visitors to Thalberg's office sensed the pressure. Journalist Harry Carr interviewed Thalberg early that year. "I always feel a fine ironical disdain underneath," wrote Carr. "In talking to him I always feel that I am on the other side of the fence. I have the uncomfortable feeling of being looked over and catalogued." Hearst newspaper columnist Arthur Brisbane enjoyed both Thalberg and Mayer but deplored their insularity. "They are so frightfully wrapped up in themselves," he wrote Hearst, "in their own great responsibilities, the fact that their work is killing them, etc., etc., etc., that it is hard for them to think of anything else. These gentlemen can stand everything but prosperity."

Conrad Nagel, who besides acting in seven 1925 films also coached Mayer in elocution, recalled Thalberg's calm in the midst of turmoil. "Mayer would sometimes get hot and abusive," said Nagel. "Thalberg would sit with him and calm him down by saying, 'Now, Louis.'" One of Mayer's pet peeves was the fractious John Gilbert. "That Gilbert is a bad apple!" Mayer yelled one day after his sensibilities had been wounded by one of Gilbert's childhood anecdotes. Gilbert was carrying the train of his mother's dress during a performance one night when he tripped. "I lost my grip on the dress and she fell forward on her face," he laughed. "Her train flew up in the air and she wasn't wearing any drawers. That was the last time I saw my mother's ass!"

"No decent man would speak that way about his mother!" Mayer said to Thalberg.

"Now, Louis," said Thalberg. "We can't afford to throw away talent because we don't like the personality that goes with it. I work with a lot of people who rub me the wrong way. Every new star means millions to the company."

"It's no use," growled Mayer. "I hate the bastard. He doesn't love his mother."

Mayer also hated the director of Gilbert's current film. "Irving was not one to underestimate the extraordinary talent of Erich von Stroheim," recalled Shearer, "and so he brought his nemesis back to direct Jack Gilbert as the dashing Danilo in *The Merry Widow*." Gilbert suffered under Stroheim's direction. "Stroheim would watch the actor go through the scene," wrote Harry Carr, "then leap up from his chair and walk up and down, muttering, 'My God! My God! My God!' Then he would turn to the abashed actor and almost scream: 'Won't you please stop acting and just be natural? Won't you please?'" Gilbert put up with Stroheim, but Mae Murray did not. When Stroheim told Murray (a former Ziegfeld dancer) that her "Merry Widow Waltz" was "rotten" in front of two hundred extras, she responded by calling him "a dirty Hun," at which he walked off the film. Thalberg was in New York, so Louis B. Mayer stepped in. "I called them both to my office and gave them hell," he told the *Los Angeles Times*. "They are now on the set as if nothing had happened."

Murray then went to Thalberg and complained that Stroheim was shooting pornographic scenes. "This is filth," she told Thalberg. "Kissing people's bottoms and kissing feet, and an old man behaving obscenely with a closet full of shoes!"

"You'll never see eye to eye with von Stroheim," Thalberg answered. "The man's a genius. He's giving the picture dimension." When Thalberg finally saw the almost interminable rushes, he questioned Stroheim.

"The old man is a degenerate," said Stroheim. "He has a foot fetish."

"And *you*, sir," snapped Thalberg, "have a *footage* fetish!" *The Merry Widow* was shaping up as a major hit, but Stroheim's inability to contain his coverage was once more jeopardizing a film's potential. This time he and Thalberg agreed to abrogate his contract.

Thalberg's days could have been less stressful, or at least shorter, but, like Stroheim, he was temperamentally unable to restrain himself. "No matter how late you left the studio," recalled Nagel, "the light was still on in Irving's office." Albert Lewin recalled conferences dragging on because Thalberg could not break away. "Irving loved to debate," said Lewin in 1967. "He was obviously in a position to command, but he loved those debates. He took endless time to argue, and he was very convincing and creative in his arguments. Even though you knew he had the authority, he never arbitrarily imposed his will on you as other producers did."

King Vidor had been directing at the studio since before the merger, and felt he could do better than Elinor Glyn vehicles. "I was weary of making ephemeral films," recalled Vidor. Thalberg asked what really interested him. "Steel, wheat, or war," replied Vidor. Thalberg gave Vidor the freedom to create a new type of war story, one that would not glamorize war. "I wanted it to be the story of a young American who was neither overpatriotic nor a pacifist," said Vidor, "but who went to war and reacted normally to all the things that happened to him." Vidor's concept grew to become *The Big Parade*. He wrote it with Thalberg and playwright Laurence Stallings while traveling cross-country in a train compartment that was so hot they worked in their underwear.

By September, the long days of writing and the late nights of editing were taking a toll on Thalberg. He fell ill around Labor Day but bounced back in time for more weekend parties and the October chariot race. By November, there was some question as to whether *Ben-Hur* would be completed in time for its December premiere, and other films needed reworking. In the course of pushing his associates, Thalberg pushed himself. In late November he pushed too hard. One day just before the Thanksgiving weekend, the twenty-six-year-old executive began to feel nauseated and short of breath. He experienced stabbing chest pains and fell to the floor. He had been stricken with a heart attack.

While Thalberg lay in a hospital bed, Mayer sat in his office, weeping and casting about for a solution. Specialists at the hospital gave the young man a 50 percent chance of survival. Mayer was frightened and the company was demoralized. Its phenomenal success was due to its executive team. Without Thalberg, what would happen? A call finally came from the hospital. Mayer was surprised to hear that Thalberg had improved dramatically. Within a short time, Thalberg's determination to return to his company proved a healing agent. He resisted his mother's demands that he move to her home, preferring to recuperate at the Crenshaw Boulevard home of supervisor Bernie Fineman and his wife, actress Evelyn Brent. The reason was that the "sickroom" there had the ideal dimensions for the projection of movies onto the ceiling over the bed. "Irving was still too weak to sit up," recalled Lucien Hubbard. "He had to lie on his back and look at the rushes of *Ben-Hur* on the ceiling."

Marion Davies heard about this and had to see for herself. "The cutter was there and they were working like mad," she recalled in 1951.

"Sit down for a minute," Thalberg said to her from his bed. "I'm sort of working." He spoke to the film editor: "Cut this here and cut that there and two inches here and . . ." This went on until they came to the end of the reel. "All right," he turned to Davies, "what's griping you?"

"Nothing," she replied. "I just wanted to come over and see how a sick person acts. And I've learned plenty."

Ben-Hur premiered in New York on December 30, but Thalberg was not allowed to attend. Nick Schenck cabled him the next day: "Well, kid, you were repaid last night for all the hard work you put in on *Ben-Hur*. It was the most magnificent opening I ever witnessed. There was continuous applause right through the picture. The only time I remember getting as big a thrill as I did during the chariot race was at the Dempsey-Firpo fight." This encouraged Thalberg to cable Fred Niblo, who was also at the opening. "I cannot tell you how happy I am over our success," wrote Thalberg. "It has done more than all the doctors to make me feel better." Norma Shearer visited Thalberg to cheer him up. "That glorious night found him sitting in a wheelchair," she wrote. "He was tired and pale, wishing he could see the sights, hear the applause and the shouts. His great moment was lost. His eyes said this. His mother was there, watching him. He said nothing, just kept looking at me sadly."

Another factor may have contributed to Thalberg's illness. He felt that he was not being sufficiently compensated. He expressed his resentment to Mayer, saying: "Others are ready to pay me what I want."

"I'll see about getting you more money," said Mayer. "But don't go about it this way. Look." Mayer closed his fist as if to strike someone. "When you do this, nothing goes out. True." He opened his fist, and then closed it again. "But nothing goes in either."

Perhaps as an acknowledgment of Thalberg's dedication, and surely in recognition of the studio's extraordinary progress, Loew's, Inc., agreed to a new contract. This contract increased Thalberg's weekly salary from $650 to $2,000. Mayer's rose from $1,500 to $2,500, and Robert Rubin's from $600 to $1,000. The Mayer group would also share in profits from Loew's theaters as well as from its own films, and was guaranteed a minimum annual bonus of $500,000. In return, the Mayer group was expected to produce forty-four films a year. Capital would not be a problem. By the end of 1925, the studio had made a profit of $4,708,631, outdistancing every Hollywood studio except Paramount, which grossed only a million more. "The Lasky forces at Paramount seem to be hanging over the fence gazing at Metro-Goldwyn in terrified awe," wrote Hollywood columnist Herbert Howe. "In fact, the Metro-Goldwyn lion has them all worried. They meander around their lots wishing they could borrow Novarro or Gilbert or Norma Shearer or Monta Bell or King Vidor. Bother that! They'd have to borrow Irving Thalberg to know what to do with them."

CHAPTER 7 · Top of the Heap

In early 1926, a roaring logo began to precede every Metro-Goldwyn film, but Leo the Lion, like the movies, was still silent. "Leo, our gentle friend, had not yet learned to roar," recalled Norma Shearer. The lion's real name was Jackie, and he resided at Gay's Lion Farm in El Monte. Just as audiences began to connect him with the two-name studio, it acquired a third name. Louis B. Mayer's surname was added—both to the producing company's name and to the distributing company's. The Culver City studio became "Metro-Goldwyn-Mayer." It was also called M.G.M. Eventually "M-G-M" became the more popular style. Employees called it Metro. Whatever it was called, Irving Thalberg's name was not on it. Yet the part he played in its progress was indisputable. By the end of 1926—less than three years after its founding—M-G-M was the most lucrative studio in Hollywood, running $6,388,200 in the black.

Thalberg looked around Hollywood and saw the awe with which he was regarded. The *New York Times* referred to him as the "old head on young shoulders." Though only a year had passed since his last raise, Thalberg decided to ask for a still bigger piece of the pie. Marcus Loew was ill with his own heart ailment, so negotiations with Nicholas Schenck were conducted in a suite at the Ambassador Hotel in Los Angeles by Mayer and J. Robert Rubin. When they emerged, the Mayer group's percentage had been reapportioned. Mayer received 53 percent, Rubin 27 percent, and Thalberg 20. In addition, their profit shares would come not from the studio's profits but from those of Loew's itself. Last but not least, Thalberg's salary was raised to $4,000 a week with a guaranteed yearly salary of $400,000. With characteristic understatement, Thalberg admitted that he was pleased with the contract, which would not expire until 1932.

Much of M-G-M's revenue came from domestic comedies like *There You Are!*, *Mike*, and *The Boy Friend*. They featured appealing (and inexpensive) players like Lew Cody, Sally O'Neil, and Conrad Nagel. These films were typically made for $150,000 (which was liberal but not extravagant) and grossed twice that. What really brought M-G-M to the top of the heap were well-written, tastefully mounted, stirringly directed films showcasing Hollywood's largest group of stars—Mae Murray, Lon Chaney, Marion Davies, Buster Keaton, Lillian Gish, Ramon Novarro, Norma Shearer, and John Gilbert. Topping this was income from *Ben-Hur* and *The Big Parade*, which played limited-release engagements in key cities, the prestigious road shows. These blockbusters were more than great entertainments. They were proof that specially crafted films could break out of the standard exhibition pattern.

"Most films," recalled King Vidor, "would just come to town, play the big theater downtown for one week, and then be gone." Films usually showed a profit in a week's time in the big-city theaters (New York, Chicago, Philadelphia, Los Angeles, and San Francisco), but there was the occasional flop, as the *Los Angeles Times* reported: "The Capitol, which averages about $50,000 weekly, played to the starvation receipts of $39,000 with *Time, the Comedian*, a bad break in the splendid record made at that house by Metro-Goldwyn-Mayer." One week at the Capitol was not enough for Vidor. "I thought about how hard we worked, how careful we were, and then somebody would go in . . . see it, say, 'Oh, it's pretty good,' and then it would be forgotten." There had been road shows such as *The Covered Wagon* and *The Ten Commandments*, but Vidor was more ambitious. When he told Thalberg in early 1925 that he wanted to make a film that would run on Broadway for a long, long time, Thalberg said: "Well, you'd better start looking for stories." The result, of course, was *The Big Parade*, which ran for an unprecedented ninety-six weeks at the Astor Theatre—and made John Gilbert a star. *The Big Parade* also played in other Loew's theaters; thanks to the acquisitive Marcus Loew, they numbered 144. M-G-M was keeping them supplied, and though Loew still regarded films as assembly-line products, Thalberg imbued every M-G-M film with quality. Scenarist Dorothy Farnum called Thalberg "the skilled surgeon who cuts to heal."

Mindful of his recent health crisis, Thalberg carried a bottle of nitroglycerine tablets in his coat pocket, but he reduced the number of films he personally produced by only two, from seventeen in 1925 to fifteen in 1926. There was no *Ben-Hur* to harry him, but his mother tried to make him cut his hours at the studio. For a time she succeeded. Most of the time, though, Henrietta's boy could be found in a conference room or a screening room. He rarely visited sets, and preferred viewing the rough cut of a film to the rushes.

In a *New York Times* interview, Thalberg described the process of creating a film, beginning with its literary source. "The purchase of a book or a play," said Thalberg, "is made for characterization, or for a situation, for a well-recognized title, for a background (when the story is old but its situation unusual), or simply for its merit, as it stands; that is, for its straight story value." He then asked the all-important question: "What star—or director—will it suit best?"

After the question was answered and the property purchased, its first test was the "treatment," a breakdown of the plot into four or five thousand words by a professional reader. Thalberg sometimes used the term "ditch digging" to describe this part of the process; analyzing characters and putting plot elements into a dramatic structure. "This is where the novel or play begins to be constructed—or 'perverted'—for the screen," said Thalberg, showing a bit more humor than usual, and then explaining that this was the junction where most writers went wrong. "Persons may see a situation in a flash, build a picture on it, and find out afterward that the situation really wasn't strong enough to make the foundation for a successful picture."

The most important element in a motion picture script was what Thalberg called "audience values," something difficult to define but "without which, no picture has audience appeal—or greatness. I might say that almost without exception every great picture has had definite audience values. And the few cases where great pictures have not been financial successes have been because some fundamental by-issue has been overlooked. I might cite [F. W. Murnau's] *The Last Laugh* in this connection, where all interest concentrated in an old man [Emil Jannings] with no romantic element at all." This brought him to the necessity of tailoring the story to the star. "The audience expects certain things of the star, and those elements are worked in if they are not there originally. . . . John Gilbert is expected to be a lover. Chaplin must be a clown and the victim of a cruel world."

Surprisingly, Thalberg also spoke of the necessity of casting a director properly, even though his system did not give the director the final say, as Marshall Neilan and Erich von Stroheim could attest. Yet Thalberg acknowledged his directors. "John Stahl is very clever at showing men and women as they are, at portraying humanity; Victor Seastrom is remarkable for his characterizations; King Vidor has amazing breadth." Thalberg related how Vidor had worked on the script of *The Big Parade* not only with Laurence Stallings but also with John Gilbert and Renée Adorée.

"Now the novel or play goes into production," Thalberg continued. "It has lost its identity as a novel or play; it is now a screen vehicle. The director begins to put it on the screen. He has been close to it and a part of it from the beginning because he must be able to see and feel every part of it as real. Otherwise there can be no truth on the screen. I might say that no big picture is made today that is not as much an outgrowth of the director's knowledge as it is of the property itself. Sometimes, just as a picture is going into production, I find that some individual thing that was most attractive in the original has been lost. That element must be worked back in."

Thalberg closed by saying that when a film based on a popular property was screened, he often heard the question "The picture is so different from the play (or story). Why did you buy it?" He answered that if Rachmaninoff and Gershwin were each commissioned to write a piece based on *The Last Supper*, the results would be very different. "So," concluded Thalberg, "a picture for Lon Chaney is prepared very differently from a picture for John Gilbert." The one ingredient Thalberg had failed to mention was the supervisor, the Hunt Stromberg, Bernie Hyman, Harry Rapf, Paul Bern, or Albert Lewin who exercised a degree of control over each project—and each director—not seen at other studios. Thalberg also omitted his own part in the process. The judgment that stabilized the entire sequence resided with him, as did the personality of every M-G-M film.

Thalberg's office was in the long structure that sat behind the fluted columns on Washington Boulevard. To reach his office, employees climbed a tired wooden staircase or rode a groaning, cagelike elevator. A waiting room usually held eight frustrated people. Once admitted, the interviewee walked through a Dutch door, past three secretaries, and down a wood-paneled corridor. Thalberg's office was small and unassuming, a simple setting for a complex process. Grooming a star involved more than finding a talented unknown with a camera-proof face. It required constant perusal of novels, plays, and original scenarios by a staff of readers. A discerning story editor named Kate Corbaley prepared stacks of scripts and readers' reports for Thalberg to carry home with him. His coworkers marveled at his ability to discuss each with total recall at a story conference days later. "I have a compartmentalized mind," he said. If anyone was skeptical, he would locate a scene instantly. "I also remember page numbers, you know." While absentmindedly flipping a twenty-dollar gold piece, he would suggest the proper writer to develop the idea into a script, shift gears to mention the contractual status of a certain actor, and then return to the story to propose a scene that would make it a vehicle for that actor.

Thalberg's involvement in the process did not end when the film went into production, but continued up to the premiere. The sneak preview was not a Thalberg innovation, but to preview virtually *every* film at a neighborhood theater was unusual. Thalberg would sit—or more often, stand—in a dark corner in the front of the theater, gauging audience response. Speaking for Thalberg, Rapf said: "When a production is finished, I want to take it just as far away from technical men as possible [and] get out where just plain audiences will tell me how they like it. I don't care about what they say in words so much as the way they act during its presentation. . . . Ocean Park, Pasadena, Glendale, Santa Monica, Monrovia—all have told me what they thought of our productions."

If a preview was unfavorable, Thalberg returned to the studio, sat down with a writer, and dreamed up new scenes, which then, too, had to be previewed and approved. "We were always previewing," said Margaret Booth. "You'd preview two, three, four times until you got it right." Getting it right meant calling back directors, actors, and technicians who were working on a new film to have them revisit a scene they had left a month earlier. This was difficult, time-consuming, and expensive, but it usually worked. "Sometimes three or four days of retakes would improve a picture enormously," said Albert Lewin. "Irving never hesitated to spend the extra money. He would push and push to get the very last bit of excellence into a production."

Thalberg was philosophical about his process. "The difference between something good and something bad is great," he said, "but the difference between something good and something superior is often very small." Spending $15,000 to reshoot a scene could convert a $50,000 loss into a $100,000 profit. "Movies aren't made," said Thalberg. "They're *re*-made." The best example of this was *The Big Parade*. It started as a "John Gilbert Special," but after an exhibitor praised the preview to Thalberg, he and Mayer convinced Loew's to underwrite battle scenes that would make it the first war epic. Not even Thalberg could have predicted that it would gross ten times its cost.

In January 1926 Thalberg was sufficiently recovered from his heart attack to resume socializing. He began by attending a much-publicized "dansant" at the Beverly Hills home of actress Patsy Ruth Miller. He was seen dancing the Charleston and indulging the latest addition to his very short list of vices, card playing. He did so in resistance to his mother's domination. "Henrietta was a battle-ax," said Irene Selznick in 1953, "and the Thalberg family home was a dull and tasteless place."

By March, Thalberg was well enough to travel to New York, where he rekindled his romance with Rosabelle Laemmle. On his return he was greeted by Norma Shearer, who became his escort for a few months. "When Rosabelle or Constance are away, or if someone stands him up, I'm always available," she told Irene. "I'll break a date any time to be with him." She referred to herself as "Irving's spare tire," a double-edged quip; one of her New York modeling assignments had been as "Miss Lotta Miles" in the ad campaign for Kelly-Springfield Tires. She stepped aside in June, when Rosabelle came to Los Angeles, but the hiatus was short-lived. Thalberg and Rosabelle had a date to go to a party one night. Thalberg became engrossed in a story conference and asked her to meet him at the party. "That won't do," Rosabelle angrily replied by way of a secretary. Thalberg turned red, but controlled himself long enough to adjourn the conference and pick up Rosabelle. The awkward, silent date was their last.

By September, Thalberg was dating Shearer again, which pleased Henrietta. Shearer would never keep Thalberg out late on a work night. "Norma told me that she got Irving by watching Rosabelle and avoiding the things that Rosabelle did wrong," recalled Mayer's secretary, Florence Browning. In truth, Shearer was genuinely solicitous of Thalberg—and she owed him a great deal. He had cast her as the drab character in *His Secretary,* and the film had made her a star. "This ugly duckling was a long way from the bareback rider on the big white horse, but I made the leap," recalled Shearer. "Suddenly I found my name up in lights, and from now on, it would be above the title of the picture instead of below. And it would be above those hot and cold pavements I had grown to know so well while looking for work. It had taken five years, almost six, but now that it had happened, I was a little frightened. It was such a great responsibility. Why should people go to the theatre just to see me?"

Once reports of profits came in, Shearer became more confident, and dates with Thalberg became more frequent. "They just seem to be going about together all the time," gushed the *Los Angeles Times* social column in August. At a Harry Rapf party that month, two hundred guests laughed at a specially made gag film in which Thalberg was shown in serious contemplation of "the perfect film story." A reverse angle revealed the screen of his projection room. On it was a series of closeups from various Shearer films. In November, Monta Bell proposed to Shearer. She turned him down, saying, "I'm going to marry Irving Thalberg."

Not long after, a cheeky journalist said to Shearer: "Tell me if and when you are going to marry Irving Thalberg."

"Oh, never," replied Shearer. "I hope no one springs a question like that on poor Irving. I am not going to marry anyone for ever so long. I am going to work and make lots of money, and, maybe after I have marked time in another jolly ordinary little picture or two, I may rise to the distinction of playing, say, Jenny Lind or Juliet." If "poor Irving" read the article, he may have chuckled. The task of finding the next role—however fanciful—for his girlfriend was only a fraction of his workload.

Lillian Gish was the first established Hollywood star to be signed by Mayer and Thalberg. "Metro-Goldwyn-Mayer welcomed me with great banners strung across the streets of Culver City," wrote Gish in 1969, "proclaiming that Lillian Gish was now an M-G-M star. Looking at them, I said a silent prayer that they would be equally warm in farewell." To engage this star of D. W. Griffith's epics, M-G-M offered a handsome six-film contract. It included approval of story, director, costar, and cameraman. Gish wanted to play Joan of Arc or Juliet in her first M-G-M film, but the studio declined Joan as too costly, and more than half of American exhibitors said that they would not buy a film based on Shakespeare.

Gish had definite ideas about filmmaking and was not afraid to impose them. "We frequently found ourselves subjected to Lillian's will," recalled Vidor. Gish insisted on rehearsing the entire script in the open air without props. She refused Erté's costume designs as extravagant but required silk in even the simplest gowns. She told Thalberg that the cameraman should change from orthochromatic film stock (which accounted for the heavy makeup of the period) to the new panchromatic. She even tried to force her notion of romance on M-G-M.

"Where are the love scenes?" Thalberg asked after seeing the first cut of *La Bohème*.

"It seemed to me that if we avoided showing the lovers in a physical embrace," Gish explained, "the scenes would build up suppressed emotion and be much more effective." Thalberg ordered retakes. "Oh, dear, I've got to go through another day of kissing John Gilbert," Gish complained to her secretary, Phyllis Moir, who knew that both Gilbert and Vidor were smitten with Gish.

"Jack Gilbert fell in love with her," wrote Marion Davies, who saw him waiting at the stairs to the women's dressing rooms with a bunch of violets in his hand. Gish was upstairs, trying to take possession of Davies's dressing room, which had been promised to Gish in error. "I took her things and moved them out and

I stayed there," said Davies. "I wouldn't leave, not even to go to the set. Well, Lillian got furious and wouldn't leave either. She said to me: 'Yughh.' Now for a nice, sweet little girl she was very nasty. But finally she thumped out and I locked the door." Gish lost few contests in her first year at M-G-M. *La Bohème* became the studio's biggest hit of 1926, and the *New York Post* wrote: "The Gish can do no wrong."

Gish wanted to film Nathaniel Hawthorne's *The Scarlet Letter*, but Mayer worried that rural audiences might be offended by a story of Puritan adultery. Gish countered that the book was taught in English classes across the nation. After several contract writers failed to produce an acceptable treatment, Thalberg thought of Frances Marion, who had befriended him outside Carl Laemmle's office five years earlier. She was riding high on the success of recent work for Sam Goldwyn and the Fox Film Corporation. Sure enough, she found an intelligent approach to *The Scarlet Letter*. Thalberg wisely signed the prestigious writer to a contract on August 24, 1926. "I consider the acquisition of Miss Marion one of the most important affiliations for M-G-M in months," Thalberg told the *Los Angeles Times*. "Miss Marion has proven a tremendously important factor in the success of any picture with which she has been associated." Marion would prove equally important to Thalberg's system.

"Irving asked me which director I would like for *The Scarlet Letter*," wrote Gish. "I suggested Victor Seastrom. It seemed to me that he had Mr. Griffith's sensitivity to atmosphere. I have always believed that the Scandinavians are closer in feeling to New England Puritans than are present-day Americans. I found Victor Seastrom's direction an education in itself. The Italian school of acting was one of elaboration; the Swedish was one of repression."

With *The Scarlet Letter*, M-G-M had another film that played longer than a week. It became the studio's second-biggest moneymaker of 1926. Thalberg's newest star was praised by no less a critic than playwright Robert Sherwood. "Miss Gish reveals substantial dramatic power," wrote Sherwood. "She proves here that her Dresden china fragility is backed by Bessemer steel strength."

While Gish was filming *The Scarlet Letter* in February, a young actress watched from the sidelines. Greta Garbo had finished her first M-G-M film, *The Torrent*, and was beginning her second, *The Temptress*. The shy, withdrawn twenty-year-old was happy that she would be directed by her mentor, Mauritz Stiller, whom Mayer had engaged because of his renown in Europe. After seeing the rushes of *The Temptress*, Thalberg sensed that Stiller was deviating from the script. He asked Lars Hanson, who had worked with Stiller in Sweden: "Is the man mad?

Has he ever been behind a camera before?" Hanson attempted to explain Stiller's approach. "He had his own particular way of making a picture," recalled Hanson. "He shot scenes as he wished, not necessarily in sequence and not necessarily the ones he intended to use. He liked to shoot everything, and then make the film what he wanted it to be by cutting." Having been through this with Erich von Stroheim, Thalberg was not receptive. He began monitoring Stiller, which made the high-strung director more erratic. Mayer was caught between them.

"My father was tortured by the Stiller situation," recalled Irene Mayer Selznick. "It was heartbreaking." She heard her father plead with Thalberg: "Give him another chance." Thalberg agreed and tried to communicate with Stiller through Hanson, but Stiller knew only one way to make a film. "They brought me here to direct because they liked my methods," he told Hanson. "They say they are something special. Then they won't let me use my methods. Instead they try to teach me how to direct."

After *The Temptress* had been shooting for a month, Thalberg again called Stiller to his office. The meeting took place on an evening in late April. Albert Lewin happened to be walking in the alley below Thalberg's office. He could see Thalberg and Stiller in the brightly lit window above. "I couldn't hear what was being said, of course, but it was plain that a very lively discussion was in progress," recalled Lewin. "It was a curious sight, a kind of dumb show. As I stood there, I saw Garbo walking up and down the asphalt street alongside the old wardrobe building. She would look up into the office where Irving and Stiller were talking, watch the characters inside for a moment, and then walk away again." The meeting ended with Stiller's dismissal.

Thalberg replaced Stiller with Fred Niblo, who had saved *Ben-Hur* from disaster. Reshooting *The Temptress* was an expensive proposition, but Thalberg's judgment was vindicated. Within a few weeks of its release, *The Temptress* was playing fourteen theaters in Los Angeles, an unheard-of number. It became one of the top-grossing films of the 1926–27 season, with nearly $1 million in receipts, and it gave M-G-M another star, Greta Garbo.

CHAPTER 8 · "More Stars Than There Are in Heaven"

As Metro-Goldwyn-Mayer entered its fourth year, it inspired both admiration and envy. Paramount, struggling to regain first place, had no affection for the Culver City studio. Paramount's production chief, B. P. Schulberg, "hated M-G-M and was jealous of its success," recalled David O. Selznick. "He was eager to tell me and the rest of Hollywood that Paramount had more respect for independent opinion than did M-G-M." When Schulberg said "M-G-M," he meant Irving Thalberg, who was flanked by a brainy corps of executives. Films were no longer being supervised by Thalberg and Harry Rapf alone. There was a smoothly functioning team atop the corporate pyramid, but it did not comprise yes-men. "The last thing I need is flattery," Thalberg warned his lieutenants. He seldom needed to remind them.

Albert Lewin, in addition to advising Thalberg on literary matters, was writing scenarios. Paul Bern was under contract as Thalberg's assistant after a short stint as a director for Paramount. Hunt Stromberg, a Norwegian American who had started as a St. Louis sportswriter before becoming a Hollywood publicist, was supervising action and adventure films. Bernard Hyman, whom Thalberg had brought to Mission Road from Universal, supervised bread-and-butter comedies starring the teams of Aileen Pringle and Lew Cody or Karl Dane and George K. Arthur. Harry Rapf oversaw Norma Shearer comedies and Lon Chaney thrillers. Thalberg managed prestige projects such as the Marion Davies vehicles. In truth, though, no one handled only one kind of film. Everyone made comedies and melodramas, and even Thalberg made horror films and Westerns.

The studio's 1926–27 product sampler promised exhibitors an ambitious sixty titles. To turn out this many films required six-day workweeks and a team as dedicated as Thalberg. They worked on Saturday and sometimes on Sunday, but the work paid off. The sampler proudly announced that M-G-M had "More Stars Than There Are in Heaven." These included Marion Davies, Lillian Gish, Ramon Novarro, Mae Murray, John Gilbert, Buster Keaton, Lon Chaney, and Norma Shearer. In less than three years, Louis B. Mayer and Irving Thalberg had done the impossible. They had groomed eight stars, the largest stable in Hollywood.

Much of this was the result of trial and error. A newly recruited player such as Joan Crawford was put into a variety of roles until fan mail indicated the right match. Then Thalberg would put that player in a similar role, hoping for a hit. If the hit occurred, the tricky part was finding the formula that would continue the star's ascent. A case in point was Greta Garbo. Even after her success in *The Torrent* and the promising previews of *The Temptress*, the studio still had doubts, so Thalberg cast her as a destructive siren in Clarence Brown's *Flesh and the Devil*. She was billed under John Gilbert and Lars Hanson, but when the film was released in January 1927 (concurrently with *The Temptress*), audiences were mesmerized by her beauty and titillated by her love scenes with Gilbert. She was a sensation.

"At first Gilbert didn't know whether he wanted to work with her," recalled Brown in 1975. Gilbert's initial impression of Garbo had been unpleasant. When he passed her on the lot in the summer of 1926, she repeatedly looked through him. He thought she was snubbing him. In truth, her English was so poor that she spoke only through an interpreter. Gilbert's formal introduction to Garbo came on August 17, when they filmed their first scene together. It was a simple one. He had to encounter her in a train station and then stare at her, dumbstruck by her beauty. His performance was heartfelt. "I introduced them," said Brown, "and that was the beginning of the romance. It started on the set. It started when they looked at each other."

Their next scene took place under an arbor, romantically lit by William Daniels. "It was the damnedest thing you ever saw," recalled Brown. "It was the sort of thing Elinor Glyn used to write about. When they got into that first love scene, well, nobody else was even there. Those two were alone in a world of their own." Brown called "Cut," but Garbo and Gilbert continued kissing, more and more passionately. "I don't know where they went that night!" he said.

Before long, Garbo was living at Gilbert's glamorous estate at 1400 Tower Grove Road. At Gilbert's Sunday parties, Garbo mingled with King Vidor, his wife, Eleanor Boardman, scenarists Carey Wilson and Benjamin Glazer, and even with Shearer and Thalberg. "Jack lived like a prince of the realm," recalled Shearer, "with his great Spanish mansion in the mountains above Beverly Hills. With his tennis courts, swimming pool, and tropical gardens, he was the master of all he surveyed—all but the elusive Miss Garbo. She came and went like an amusing child, sometimes swimming and playing tennis with us, but just as often hiding in her rooms." Hiding would become a way of life for Garbo—and a weapon. Thalberg wanted her to follow *Flesh and the Devil* with another seductive role. Garbo read *Diamond Handcuffs*, the story of a kept woman, and thought otherwise, according to Shearer:

> Miss Garbo at first didn't like playing the exotic, the sophisticate, the woman of the world. She used to complain: "Mr. Thalberg, I am just a young gur-rl!" Irving tossed it off with a laugh. With those elegant pictures he was creating the Garbo image. The true essence of glamour is mystery. Garbo already had, even at her age, an aloofness and sophistication, but she also had a teasing quality that made her endearing, and, yes, she had a subtle humor. But most of all she had a sensuousness that was both elegant and touching. For her, sex didn't seem evil. In those days this was a welcome thought and something new.

Thalberg was trying to find the right vehicle for this unusual new talent, and beyond that, the right formula for a new star. Garbo did not give him the chance to experiment. In October 1926 she went into hiding, forcing him to cast Pauline Starke in her place. Garbo's uniqueness was further demonstrated by her indifference. When Mayer threatened to end her career, she replied quietly: "I think I will go home."

"She could hop a boat to Sweden!" Mayer exclaimed to Thalberg.

"In that case, I intend to let her," Thalberg replied.

After four months, it became apparent that Garbo did not care about Hollywood. She had neither come to the studio nor appeared in public since October 13, 1926. There were rumors that her protracted absence was due to pregnancy or domestic violence. For whatever reason, a Hollywood star had literally vanished. Not even Thalberg could locate her. Indeed, he was surprised to discover irregularities in the studio's handling of her so-called salary strike. On February 21 he ordered an accounting. The report showed that Garbo had been suspended for only six and one-sixth weeks, and on "Lay-Off" for seven weeks. Yet she had been paid $1,400 for eight and one-third weeks of "Idle Time." This was crazy;

Garbo had refused to work. When Mayer would not explain, Thalberg deduced that Garbo's strike was a smokescreen. Mayer was colluding with Garbo, Gilbert, and Harry Edington (manager for both stars) to cover up something. It may have been pregnancy. Garbo may have gotten an abortion. Gilbert admitted to pushing Garbo down the side of his mountain, and then Gilbert was hospitalized under mysterious circumstances. Gilbert kept firearms. Garbo may have shot him. That Mayer would handle a crisis of this magnitude without consulting Thalberg was troubling, a portent of things to come. The questions occasioned by Garbo's disappearance were never answered.*

Only when Mayer raised Garbo's salary and Thalberg gave her an acceptable script did she return. Thalberg was then able to use her fourth film, *Love*, to crystallize her formula. This succinctly renamed version of Tolstoy's *Anna Karenina*—with Garbo as Anna and John Gilbert as Vronsky—confirmed what *Flesh and the Devil* had suggested, that Garbo worked best as the passive point of the eternal triangle. *Love* was a sensation, establishing Garbo as a star and adding, if possible, to John Gilbert's universal popularity. The film grossed $1.67 million, which made it M-G-M's biggest draw since *Ben-Hur* ($9.39 million), *The Big Parade* ($6.13 million), and *The Merry Widow* ($1.93 million).

Thalberg decreed that henceforth Garbo would play a young but worldly-wise woman who is married to (or kept by) an older man. She discovers love for the first time with an inexperienced younger man, and for him she must give up everything, perhaps even her life. In the same way, Thalberg evolved a formula for Lon Chaney. The many-faced actor was popular for his monstrous characterizations but did not reach stardom until Thalberg decided that he should be redeemed in the last reel. Casting Chaney as a Marine sergeant looked risky, but *Tell It to the Marines* became Chaney's most profitable M-G-M film.

In the year since Frances Marion had scripted *The Scarlet Letter*, she had developed a warm working relationship with Thalberg. He called her into his office and proposed that she craft a story for Chaney based on the life of General John J. Pershing. As Marion prepared a story about the Mexican War, Chaney received fan mail asking for another "scary" film. "I guess we'll have to turn him into a freak again," Thalberg said to Marion, and canceled her Pershing script.

Thalberg was aware of the female quotient of his audiences and he cultivated women writers such as Marion, Lenore Coffee, and Bess Meredyth. Marion felt

*For a complete treatment of this episode, see the author's 2005 book *Greta Garbo: A Cinematic Legacy*, published by Harry N. Abrams.

that she could also offer casting advice. Marie Dressler was a fifty-nine-year-old vaudeville star who had fallen on hard times. In her glory days she had given a young San Francisco reporter an exclusive interview. Years later the reporter wanted to repay the favor, so she tailored a role for her. The scenario of *The Callahans and the Murphys* featured an Irish-American matron given to punching, nose thumbing, and beer swilling. "Any special actresses in mind?" asked Thalberg. When Marion suggested Dressler, she was relieved to hear him speak respectfully of her. "My theory," said Thalberg, "is that anybody who once hits the bull's-eye—it doesn't matter in what profession—has the brains and stamina to stage a comeback. So I figure that a woman who held the spotlight for so many years has been the victim of bad writing—and probably a lot of bad advice."

Thalberg agreed to give Dressler $1,500 a week, and instead of doing a sneak preview in a neighborhood theater, he gave *The Callahans and the Murphys* an industry preview. "That hard-boiled audience!" recalled Dressler. "How kind they were! How generous! Many of them were too young ever to have heard of me." Alas, Marion had painted the Hibernians a bit too vividly. The film was criticized for its stereotypes, riots broke out in some theaters, and Denis Cardinal Dougherty of Philadelphia sermonized against it. M-G-M was forced to cancel the film's exhibition contracts.

Thalberg still felt that breaking the template of the "Good Guys Wear White" was necessary, as he told Edwin Schallert of the *Los Angeles Times:*

> Films are more accurate today in the portrayal of settings than they have ever been. The same is true of characterizations. These are more accurate. We are going further afield than we have ever gone in our quest for types. We do not choose simply those personalities that are known, but those which most closely fit a character interpretation. When I select a star for a picture, I don't ask if she is 'so-and-so,' but does she seem like the character she is going to portray. Thought registers in closeups on the screen.

On September 5 Marcus Loew died of progressive heart disease. He was fifty-seven. Nicholas Schenck acceded to the presidency of Loew's, Inc. The film industry was experiencing a slump, attributed by some to the popularity of radio. Paramount was regaining its lead over M-G-M because of a new star, Clara Bow. Still, Schenck saw no reason to modify Thalberg and Mayer's system. Despite eight flops, M-G-M would finish the year with $6.7 million in profits. Six of 1927's top-grossing films were Thalberg productions. The wunderkind was looking more "wunder-ful" than ever, and his legend continued to grow. Agnes Christine Johnson, who worked for Thalberg as a scenarist, told an interviewer: "He's so marvelous that no one who doesn't know him can believe it. Seeing him sitting in with all the important people, looking such a boy, and deferred to by everybody, you'd think that either they were crazy or you were. But if you stayed and listened, you'd understand. He has a mind like a whip. Snap! He has an idea—the right idea—the only idea!"

Among the many witnesses to Thalberg's sagacity was Conrad Nagel, who worked almost as many hours as his boss. In addition to Nagel's four screen appearances in 1927, he was working with Thalberg and Mayer to obtain a state charter for an Academy of Motion Picture Arts and Sciences. "This was the country's sixth largest industry," recalled Nagel in 1967, "but it was the only industry where a bad product could make a profit. We had to do something." The Academy was inaugurated on May 11, 1927.

Nagel also joined Thalberg to confer with Will Hays, president of the Motion Picture Producers and Distributors Association (MPPDA) about a growing problem. State censor boards were subjecting expensive release prints to arbitrary and injurious cuts. Both *Ben-Hur* and *The Big Parade* had been cut in some states; the former for nudity and the latter for the intertitle "God damn them all!" It was thought that the MPPDA should establish an office in Hollywood to regulate the content of both scripts and finished films. There were complaints not only from grassroots organizations but also from industry insiders. Thalberg's former Universal Pictures colleague R.H. Cochrane found it necessary to warn Hays against the bigger studios. "Unless Paramount can curb the natural lasciviousness of Bennie Schulberg," wrote Cochrane, "and unless Metro can tone down Irving Thalberg (who, though fine in other respects, has a leaning toward the suggestive because of his showmanship) there is *[sic]* going to be a lot of dirty pictures during the coming season." Rumblings in Washington, D.C., indicated that federal censorship was a possibility, so Thalberg collaborated with Sol Wurtzel of the Fox Film Corporation and E.H. Allen of Paramount on a document called "The Don'ts and the Be Carefuls." This set of guidelines for reviewing both scenarios and finished films was adopted by the MPPDA in September 1927 and administered by Colonel Jason S. Joy and the Studio Relations Committee (SRC) from an office on Hollywood Boulevard.

As a liaison between these parties and agencies, Nagel was uniquely qualified to describe his vice president. "Thalberg never raised his voice," said Nagel. "He just looked into your eyes, spoke softly, and after a few minutes he cast a spell on you." Edwin Loeb recalled Thalberg's wisdom. "The real foundation of Irving's success," said Loeb, "was his ability to look at life through the eyes of any given person. He had a gift of empathy, an almost complete perspective." Director Hobart Henley felt that this empathy also extended to his creative partners. "He wants pictures with the ideas of the people who are paid for them," said Henley. "He wants me, for instance, to give him the best stuff I have—mine, not a rehash of his. But if something that read well [in a conference] turns out not so good on the screen, I go to him and, like that"—Henley snapped his fingers—"he has a remedy. He's brilliant. But he wasn't only born that way. He's on the job every second of every hour."

Another aspect of Thalberg's legend was his ability to work late without showing signs of fatigue, sometimes after only five hours of sleep. "Most people sleep too much," said Thalberg. "They think they must have eight or nine or ten hours' sleep, and if they don't get it, they think they ought to be tired. 'I didn't get to bed till midnight last night, and it's almost two now. I'll be worn out tomorrow,' they say, and instead of going to sleep, they worry—and drag themselves out of bed completely exhausted." Thalberg had a practical attitude. He believed that as long as his mind was engaged by his work and as long as he was not bored, he would not feel tired. Since he was never bored, he was never tired. Even between conferences he kept his mind revved up, dipping into his favorite books—Bacon, Epictetus, and Kant. "They stimulate me," he said modestly. "I'd drop out of sight in no time if I didn't read and keep up with current thought—and the philosophers are brain sharpeners." He also kept up with current authors. "[Theodore] Dreiser is a greater writer than [Jakob] Wasserman—not so superficial. I can't see the young highbrows," he commented on flippant novelists such as Carl Van Vechten. "What have they got that other people haven't—except a feeling of superiority?" When Van Vechten visited Hollywood, both Thalberg and Garbo avoided him.

Having come so far in such a short time, Thalberg was aware that his privilege was not shared by everyone of his background. When Shearer told him that she thought Irving was the most beautiful name in the whole world, he replied, "You wouldn't think so if you came from Brooklyn." And when a fan magazine writer tried to bait him with some subtle anti-Semitism, he rose to the occasion. "Mr. Thalberg," said the writer, "I realize that you are of the new order in films—a young man with ideals."

"Just a minute," he interrupted, perhaps thinking of Marcus Loew. "If you mean that I think I'm superior to the so-called cloak and shoe and glove manufacturers who have really given their lives and their pocketbooks to this business in order to allow us something to build on—why then, you are wrong. I respect them very much. They had ideals also."

With items like this appearing in fan magazines and dailies, *Vanity Fair* magazine decided it was time for journalist Jim Tully to do a piece on Thalberg. "In the cinema world the word genius is more common than a threadbare plot," Tully began in his typically mordant tone. "Thalberg has piled one piece of clay upon another until he has succeeded in building a hill for the commonality. Upon this hill his co-workers, being lesser people than himself, and more near-sighted, see a mirage which they call genius. It often takes the form of a young man with a sad expression, leading sheep to a withered pasture." After lamenting Thalberg's triumph over Erich von Stroheim, "the first man of genuine and original talent to break his heart against the stone wall of cinema imbecility," Tully granted that Thalberg was more than a manager of frustrated artists:

> Thalberg is boyish, kindly, and intuitive. He has a quick mentality that runs in narrow grooves. If it were deeper and vaster and more profound, he would be a financial failure in the business of films. To Thalberg all life is a soda fountain. He knows how to mix ingredients that will please the herd on a picnic. It is doubtful if such an attribute can be listed among the great talents. It was possessed by Barnum and Bailey. . . . When I asked him why it was possible for a young woman in his employ who is ten years old mentally to receive forty thousand dollars a year as a "writer," he replied, instantly and decisively, "Because she reflects what the people want." When I asked him for a success slogan he said, "I just guess." Irving Thalberg is too modest. There are many who claim that he does not guess. He possibly has more flashes of good guessing than any man in pictures.

Tully ended his left-handed tribute with an ambiguous comment: "Thalberg has essentially the beginnings of the artist in his make-up. But as a corporation official, he must give to money the first and last consideration." It was not only as an official that Thalberg had to give money his consideration but also as an employee of a corporation. In February, four months after Schenck had agreed to Thalberg's new contract, Thalberg had not yet received papers to sign. Thalberg made an irate transcontinental call. Nick Schenck assured him that the papers were in the mail. Weeks later they still had not arrived. Thalberg berated Schenck to Eddie Mannix, the former Palisades Park bouncer whom Schenck had hired as Mayer's assistant. Mannix tried to reason with Thalberg. "You're the only producer in Hollywood who never has interference from his home office," said Mannix.

"I'm the only producer in Hollywood who doesn't need any," snapped Thalberg, who was equally defensive about his personal affairs. In early June he was upset by rumors of a secret marriage with Shearer. She and Thalberg had been seen together often, but only she knew the truth. One morning, after a night of dancing at the Cocoanut Grove, she received a bouquet of roses and a card with two words written on it in "scrawly" handwriting. "'Yes, sir!' was all it said," wrote Shearer. "Bright little me couldn't figure it out until later that day, when I found myself humming that tune we had danced to the night before. 'Yes, sir, we've decided / No, sir, we won't hide it / Yes, sir, that's my baby now!' For three years I had been watching that pale, grave face, and if those wise brown eyes had ever cast me a sly glance, they seemed to say 'You're a little too young.' Now they were saying 'You're my baby.'"

In early August, Shearer's mother caused a flurry of excitement by telling the press: "There is no question in my mind but that [Norma and Irving] are in love with each other and that some day they will marry." The pressure was on Thalberg to consider what day that might be. Less than two weeks later, he was at the Cocoanut Grove with Shearer. They were sitting at a candle-lit table under a metal palm tree that had a stuffed monkey hanging from it. Thalberg had turned twenty-eight on May 30. Shearer, who wanted people to think she was younger than she was, had turned twenty-five on August 10. Thalberg looked at her and said: "Well, don't you think it's about time we were married?"

"I laughed and looked up at the monkey and pretended I hadn't heard," recalled Shearer. "I was sure that this was the first foolish remark that Irving Thalberg had ever made. If this was a proposal I was sure he would regret it. After all, everything was coming his way. Why should he want me?"

Samuel Goldwyn's wife, Frances, wondered the same thing when Thalberg told her about his proposal. "But you told me that you were in love with Peggy Hopkins Joyce," said Frances.

"That was sex," replied Thalberg. "This is love."

Shearer's friends were equally skeptical. Scenarist Frederica Sagor had a friendship of sorts with the single-minded Shearer; they shared hiking trips in the Santa Monica Mountains. She was one of the few who knew that Shearer and her mother had moved out of their cozy little house at 2004 Vine not for the glamorous setting of the Garden of Allah on Sunset but because Shearer's sister, Athole, was suffering from hallucinations and needed a live-in nurse. "I had been privileged to be one of Norma's confidantes," wrote Frederica Sagor Maas in 1999, "but as happy as I was for her, because I knew how much she was in love, I could not help but be apprehensive about this strange alliance. Here was this young actress with a Protestant background, closely tied to her mother, sister, and brother, marrying this Jewish wunderkind who was closely tied to his Orthodox mother and neurotic sister. He was a mama's boy, the result of being a sickly child. Two different cultures. How would it work out? I tried desperately to warn Norma of what she was going into, but she was too much in love to listen."

A few days later, Shearer was called to Thalberg's office. She was not made to wait in the anteroom. When she entered the office, she saw Thalberg standing over his desk, inspecting a tray of diamond rings. He looked up at her, gave her his enigmatic smile, and said: "Why don't you pick out the one you're going to wear?" Shearer decided on a large blue marquis-cut diamond.

"Irving's decided to marry her!" Mayer announced to his family that night. "There's no risk. Everything will go on as it was. Henrietta's accepted the situation." Mayer's secretary, Florence Browning, had watched Shearer's campaign since Mission Road. "Irving never knew he was being caught," said Browning. "After he was married, he said to me, 'Well, Florence, you never thought I'd get her, did you?'"

The wedding took place on September 29, 1927, in the garden of the Pauline Frederick mansion (which the Thalberg family was now renting) at 503 Sunset Boulevard in Beverly Hills.* As Henrietta helped her son put on his cutaway, he insisted on conducting a story conference with Laurence Stallings. "I want to talk to you about those scripts we've been discussing," said Thalberg as his mother tried to push the studs through his dress shirt.

"Now?" asked Stallings.

"Yes, now!" replied Thalberg with such vehemence that one of the studs flew off the shirt. "I'll find it," he assured his mother.

"No, no!" she gasped. "And crease your trousers? I will find it!" It was Stallings who spied the stud behind the leg of the dresser, but because of his artificial limb, he could not get down on his hands and knees to retrieve it. Henrietta had to do it.

Rabbi Edgar F. Magnin officiated at the ceremony. Shearer's brother, Douglas, a radio engineer, gave the bride away. Louis B. Mayer was best man. At the wedding banquet, Douglas Shearer's remarks about talking pictures were drowned out by the sounds of merrymaking. That evening, Mr. and Mrs. Irving Thalberg drove up the coast to the Del Monte Lodge in Monterey. The only mishap in their short honeymoon took place when neither of them could figure out how to unclasp

*503 Sunset was later renumbered as 9419 Sunset.

the shockingly expensive Cartier bracelets given Norma by Joseph Schenck, Marion Davies, and William Randolph Hearst. "Finally we decided to give up the struggle," recalled Shearer. "Doubled up with laughter, we rolled unceremoniously into our conjugal bed."

While still on his honeymoon, Thalberg was approached by reporters for his opinion of talking pictures. On October 6 in New York, Warner Bros. had premiered the first feature film using synchronized sound to convey dialogue. It was called *The Jazz Singer*. Thalberg had seen Fox Movietone newsreels and Vitaphone shorts, but he believed that in spite of a slump, the silent drama was invincible. "Novelty is always welcome," he told the reporter, "but talking pictures are just a passing fad."

PART THREE · THE TALKIES

CHAPTER 9 · The Golden Silents

Nineteen twenty-eight greeted Irving G. Thalberg with the prospect of new projects and new profits. Before the year was over, the onslaught of the "new" would have him scrambling to keep up. He would face challenges not to his executive ability or his creative perception but to the cultural framework within which he worked. Three months after the premiere of *The Jazz Singer*, the film industry was still talking about the talking picture. Warners producer Hal Wallis had been there that night. "After the first musical number," he reported, "the audience sprang to its feet and cheered. Every successive number got a standing ovation." One number had Al Jolson speak a snatch of dialogue before going into his song. "When Jolson ad libbed the first line of dialogue [ever heard] in a motion picture, the audience literally became hysterical," recalled Doris Warner Vidor, daughter of Harry Warner. "You could hear the crowd roar down several city blocks," said Wallis.

Although newspapers said skeptics "refused to believe that Al Jolson was not hidden behind the screen during the Vitaphone sequences in which he sings and talks from the screen," the more typical reaction was awe. "*The Jazz Singer* is credited with having been the biggest box office success released in 1927," asserted one article. "The film coined money," averred another. "At the time it was released, there were but 400 theaters wired for sound. It went into every one of them and broke record after record." Without providing data, another article stated: "Theater records were broken by *The Jazz Singer*. Towns where a release was doing excellent business if it ran for three days held a print for weeks." Reports like these did not address the reality of how few theaters in the country could accommodate a Vitaphone film. Furthermore, *The Jazz Singer* was doing strong but not overwhelming business in New York; silent films such as *Don Juan*, *Seventh Heaven*, and *Love* were doing better. The authors of these articles may have been influenced by press releases from the only two companies with an investment in sound (Warner Bros. and the Fox Film Corporation) or by bribes from companies who owned sound patents (Western Electric and American Telephone and Telegraph), or they may simply have enjoyed scaring people. In any case, the hyperbole had an effect. Describing talking pictures as a fait accompli hastened their advent.

In early 1928, Thalberg had a production slate of fifty-six films and was preparing for a European honeymoon, so he limited his involvement in talking-picture debates to terse statements. "The talking motion picture has its place," he told the press, "as has color photography, but I do not believe that it will replace the silent drama any more than I believe color photography will replace entirely the present black and white." Louis B. Mayer was similarly unimpressed. "It was certainly the opinion of Mayer that this was all a fad," recalled William Haines. As Thalberg looked toward his February departure, he was a bit concerned about Mayer. Since hiring Herbert Hoover's former secretary Ida Koverman as his personal assistant, Mayer had thrown himself into Republican politics and was preparing for the national convention in June, hoping it would nominate Hoover. Thalberg did not expect Mayer to watch over production for him. Paul Bern, Hunt Stromberg, Harry Rapf, and Albert Lewin would manage that, just as Henrietta managed his home.

"Knowing that Irving was devoted to his mother and sister," wrote Norma Shearer, "I thought it would make him happy to live with them until he got used to the idea of living with me." This was a gesture more practical than heartfelt, as her colleagues noted. "Norma became a live-in wife without many prerogatives," said Irene Selznick. "It remained Henrietta's house. She sat at the head of the table; at the other end sat William, a pale man with pale blue eyes and a pale personality. Guests were invited by Henrietta, and she was the hostess who was thanked." Frederica Sagor liked Shearer's mother, sister, and brother, but liked nothing about her in-laws. "Not the kind of people you'd want to talk to twice," wrote Sagor. Henrietta had no time for small talk. Her son's health was her priority, whether that meant keeping his dinner warm until midnight or banishing Shearer to a separate bedroom at the end of a very long hallway. "It's my duty to protect his life," said Henrietta defensively. Shearer did her best to adjust. "This hardly held the privacy that a bride and groom would desire," she later wrote, "but after five months Irving and I were able to enjoy our delayed honeymoon."

Before Thalberg left, he had to oil several squeaky wheels. The first was Buster Keaton, whom he brought to M-G-M with the help of Nick Schenck, whose brother Joseph held Keaton's contract at United Artists. Keaton was uncertain about the move, but the Schencks had told him that M-G-M would offer him greater resources and artistic license. How could he lose? "Don't do it," Charles Chaplin warned him. "They'll ruin you by 'helping' you. They'll warp your judgment. You'll get tired of arguing for things you know are right." Keaton was not worried. Thalberg had promised him autonomy. He believed him. Then he attended a story conference. "Thalberg was in charge," recalled Keaton, "and he wanted—oh, I wasn't in enough trouble trying to manipulate a camera—he wanted me involved with gangsters, in trouble with this one and that one. *That* was my fight—to eliminate those extra things." After a few days filming street scenes for *The Cameraman* in New York City, Keaton felt constrained by the script and bothered by gaping crowds. He called Thalberg and said: "For God's sake authorize me to throw this cockeyed script in the ashcan and shoot from the cuff."

"Well, okay," Thalberg answered. "God knows what the front office will say, but go ahead." Eddie Mannix was the executive who called director Edward Sedgwick on the carpet about *The Cameraman*. Sedgwick tried to explain. "Often a situation arises that has comedy potential," he said, "and Buster likes to milk it for all it's worth." Mannix responded that he couldn't budget the film if Keaton didn't follow the script.

In spite of interference, Keaton made *The Cameraman* both accomplished and profitable, but the system was taking its toll. One night in front of Louise Brooks and Buster Collier, Keaton picked up a baseball bat and wordlessly smashed every pane of glass in his well-appointed studio bungalow. "Buster had his own fun factory when he was on his own," said Collier, "but at M-G-M he was just another employee. Expensive, yes, but still an employee."

David O. Selznick, son of Mayer's old rival Lewis J. Selznick, was working with Hunt Stromberg on a series of profitable Tim McCoy westerns when he saw an opportunity for advancement. "I was madly in love with *White Shadows in the South Seas*, Frederick O'Brien's book on the destruction of the Polynesian race by the white man," wrote Selznick. "I was delighted to be told that I was to produce the picture, which had been in the hands of Stromberg, who at one time had been publicity director for my father." Selznick's delight evaporated when Stromberg informed him that he planned a very different type of film. "The only reason he was making the picture," wrote Selznick, "was because it presented an opportunity to show women's breasts." Stromberg was later quoted as saying "Tits and sand sell tickets!" and "Let's fill the screen with tits!"

Perhaps injudiciously, Selznick stormed into the executive dining room and found Thalberg sitting with Stromberg and a group of supervisors. "I told Thalberg in the rather strong language of youth that Stromberg didn't know what he was talking about," recalled Selznick.

"If you don't apologize to him, you're going to have to leave," snapped Thalberg. "We must have authority here."

"I've already cleared out my desk," replied Selznick.

Thalberg took into account Selznick's bitterness over his father's fall from grace. "Thalberg gave me a chance to apologize for having disagreed with him," said Selznick, "which I refused to do, and I was out of a job."

At about the same time, Joan Crawford came to Thalberg's office in high dudgeon. "Why do you save all the good roles for your darling Norma?" Joan demanded. "Don't you think I deserve some consideration?"

"Joan, your career is coming along nicely," Thalberg answered. "You still have much to learn. If you tried something too ambitious, it might be disastrous. You wouldn't want to be laughed at, would you?" Thalberg assigned her to a Tim McCoy western, which was not her idea of a step up. "I'm going to enjoy working with you and your cowboys if it kills me," she told McCoy, but stardom was closer than she realized.

William Randolph Hearst tested stories by publishing them in his weekly magazines. Joan Crawford read the serialized *Our Dancing Daughters* and then found out that he planned to make it for M-G-M. "I stole the script, went to producer Hunt Stromberg, begged for it, and was given it," wrote Crawford. "As Diana," wrote Crawford, "I was the flapper, wild on the surface, a girl who shakes her windblown bob and dances herself into a frenzy while the saxes shriek and the trombones wail, a girl drunk on her own youth and vitality. *Our Dancing Daughters* opened at the Capitol in October to a $40,000 weekend." When these figures got to Culver City, Thalberg told Mayer: "We've got ourselves another star."

With an itinerary planned by the globe-trotting Douglas Fairbanks, Mr. and Mrs. Irving G. Thalberg departed Los Angeles on February 15, 1928, bound for Gibraltar, Algiers, the French Riviera, Naples, Rome, Pompeii, Berlin, Heidelberg, Paris, and London. The most important aspect of the trip for both Thalberg and

Shearer was that they had never seen each other outside Hollywood. It was enlightening for Shearer to wander the streets of a foreign city with Thalberg and to see how he reacted to surprises. In Algiers, for example, a wily guide ushered the well-dressed young couple into a brothel. "We were greeted by a very fat lady who clasped us to her ample bosom," recalled Shearer. "Inside there were girls wearing nothing but black silk stockings, red satin garters, and gaucho hats. The girls were evidently proud of what they were exposing between their extremities. A couple of them came over and sat down beside us as though they were completely dressed, and started chattering in French. I don't think it mattered to them what sex we were because the one beside me kept saying very sweetly: 'Nize ladee. Nize ladee.' I found them charming but Irving did manage to get me out of there before anything took place."

More typical was their encounter with the headliner at the Folies-Bergère in Paris. Thalberg went backstage to offer Maurice Chevalier a screen test. The performer was polite but noncommittal, so Thalberg and Shearer returned to the theater. A short time later, Chevalier had them escorted to his dressing room so that he could apologize. "You see, I did not believe you," he explained. "I say to myself that this cannot be the big boss from Hollywood. He looks like a baby! Now I know you really are Mr. Thalberg. I will take the test for you! For no one else!" Chevalier made a silent screen test, but when it arrived in Culver City, Mayer wanted to know why money had been wasted on this unattractive man. Jesse Lasky, who had seen the dynamic Chevalier perform, stepped in and signed him for Paramount.

The Thalbergs returned to New York on May 13. While Shearer shopped and sat for portrait photographers such as Alfred Cheney Johnston and Nickolas Muray, Thalberg gave interviews. "He is now generally known around Hollywood as 'the little genius,'" wrote the *New York Times*. "He is a somewhat nervous young man, with a trick of toying with pencils as he talks and a habit of putting his feet on the nearest desk. When he registers surprise or pleasure, his right eyebrow goes up more than his left, giving a severe appearance—which is belied by his generally soft-spoken manner."

Thalberg was quoted on film production in Europe; after seeing no less than forty films there (including Fritz Lang's *Spies*, Vsevolod Pudovkin's *Mother*, and Jacques Feyder's *Thérèse Raquin*), he thought that American films were being unfairly derided. "The time has come when the ridicule of motion pictures must stop," he said. "If a picture can move audiences, it must be praised. The motion picture is a new art in America, and there is need that it be respected here. No matter how many bad ones are made, the important thing is to point out the good ones." Back in Los Angeles, he criticized the European quota system. "Motion pictures are not shoes, wheat, or tobacco. One cannot consider them as a purely economic proposition. They represent a highly creative form of art, and for that reason must be unrestricted and worldwide in their appeal and their development." Thalberg's contention that motion pictures were art was not hucksterism. He believed that even if the projects did not succeed, he and his colleagues could learn from them, and in the face of studio opposition, he launched three dubious projects: *The Wind*, *The Trail of '98*, and *The Crowd*.

The Wind was Thalberg's attempt to find a formula for Lillian Gish after the flop of *Annie Laurie* in 1927. When he asked her to reduce her salary, she wrote her attorney: "Has Metro reached the point where they think they would be better off without me? I cannot help but think that this is the real motive in back of all the trouble they are giving." Gish agreed to a reduction and Thalberg agreed to film two stories she suggested. The first was *The Wind*, a grim novel by Dorothy Scarborough. "It's pretty gloomy," said Thalberg to Frances Marion, "but I think the public welcomes a strong melodrama now and then." Clarence Brown was assigned to direct the film. "I worked on the script," he recalled, "but then got cold feet. People don't *like* wind." Thalberg gave the film to Gish's favorite, Victor Seastrom, who took her and his crew to the Mojave Desert, where the heat was 120 degrees. "I don't mind the heat so much," Gish told the *New York Times*, "but working before the wind machines all the time is nerve-wracking. It isn't very hard for me to enter the state of mind of the character I'm playing, I can assure you. You see, out here the wind blows the sand all the time, but they didn't think that was quite enough, so they added sawdust." After enacting the scene in which she buries her rapist in a blinding sandstorm, only to have the wind uncover his corpse, Gish swore: "Never again! Not for any amount of money!"

While *The Wind* was being edited, Thalberg had Fred Niblo direct Gish in an antiwar story called *The Enemy*. Thalberg told Gish that it would be one of her most successful pictures. *The Enemy* made less than a routine comedy. Then *The Wind* was previewed. "All of us, including Thalberg, thought it was the best film we had ever done," recalled Gish. Yet the studio was unsure how to sell it and shelved it for almost a year. The delay hurt the film. Audiences hungry for talking pictures had no patience for a silent film, no matter how powerful. "Miss Gish, in some of her most dramatic moments," reported *Variety*, "drew laughter instead of tears from a Sunday afternoon audience composed mainly of New Yorkers." Gish took the disappointment in stride but made a decision. "I hardly think I will continue at Metro," she wrote the Moscow Art Theatre. "Theirs is such a large organization that I feel they haven't the room or the time for me." Thus departed the performer whom Max Reinhardt dubbed "the supreme emotional actress of the screen."

The Trail of '98 was Thalberg's attempt to meld a historical epic from the writings of Robert W. Service and newspaper accounts of the Klondike Gold Rush. Location filming outside Denver (at 11,600 feet and sixty below zero) pushed the film's budget higher than expected; worse yet, a river sequence drowned two stunt men and an avalanche crushed three extras. "It was a tough picture," recalled director Clarence Brown forty years later. "Oh, God, it was tough." Film editor Margaret Booth remembered Thalberg sitting nervously at the preview. "People just didn't care for the picture," said Booth. "We were all very disappointed." Brown wrote it off as "just one of those conglomerates." Its star Harry Carey referred to it as "The Smell of the Yukon." *The Trail of '98* was premiered (as were Paramount's *Wings* and *Old Ironsides*) with an enlarged-screen presentation, and people did go to see it, but its cost made a profit impossible.

King Vidor conceived of *The Crowd* as his "Big Parade of Peace." "It's the story of one of the crowd," said Vidor. "The protagonist does nothing unusual, nothing that everyone can't understand. Birth, youth, school, love, business struggles, married life, always against the background of the crowd." At first glance, the no-star project looked uncommercial, but Thalberg took an unusual stance. "I can certainly afford to make a few experimental projects," he told Vidor. "It will do something for the studio. It will do something for the whole industry."

If Thalberg had shared the attitude that films were solely merchandise, he would never have initiated these projects. He would never have made films without stars *(White Shadows in the South Seas)*, without glamour *(West of Zanzibar)*, or with stars in offbeat roles *(The Masks of the Devil)*. When he purchased the popular novels *Trader Horn* and *The Bridge of San Luis Rey*, he conceded that their episodic structure posed problems. "Just as these stories are very different from the field of literature," he said, "so, too, must their picturizations be different; in fact, so radically different that they may establish far-reaching reforms in the field of silent drama." In the four years since the merger, he had done much to advance both the content and the style of the silent film. Upon returning to M-G-M, he saw this nearly perfected art form threatened by the thing that most often threatens the status quo in America—commercially motivated technology.

In early July 1928, after testing the waters with talking short subjects and several part-talkers, Warner Bros. released an "All-Talking Vitaphone Picture,"

The Lights of New York. "This 100 percent talkie is 100 percent crude," sneered *Variety*, but the film was a bigger hit than *The Jazz Singer*. Warners and Fox immediately accelerated the wiring of theaters for sound. This was the job that cowed Loew's, Inc.; its chain comprised more than 140 theaters. In addition, M-G-M had contracts with 13,000 independent theaters. Yet it was likely that Warners and Fox would be wiring more than 1,000 houses for sound by the end of 1928. Fifteen American sound stages were under construction. Warners was already grossing 500 percent more than it had in 1927.

Thalberg convened a number of emergency meetings, but Mayer was preoccupied with the Republican National Convention. Before he left for Kansas City, Missouri, he authorized the construction of two sound stages and the addition of music and sound effects to the uncompleted *White Shadows in the South Seas*. When the film premiered in late July, Leo the Lion was heard for the first time; his roars were dubbed onto silent footage of the "Lion Head Logo." *White Shadows in the South Seas* soared to number two of the studio's 1928 grosses. Thalberg continued to watch and wait.

King Vidor had been on vacation in Europe. When he returned, he saw panic. Directors, writers, and especially actors were terrified that sound would ruin them. Few filmmakers had worked as hard as Vidor to give the silent screen its own unique parlance. "The screen appeared—after a long and bitter struggle—to be coming into its own," said Vidor. "Now everyone is thinking of the new development, and rushing to get in on it. I ask why they want to start something else when they have just learned straight pictures."

While Mayer continued his politicking, Thalberg prepared a slate of silent films large enough to carry the studio into 1929, while hedging his bets on sound. When Mayer returned, a joint decision was made. The executives turned to Norma Shearer's brother, Douglas, who was working in special effects and had experience in radio. "Suddenly I was asked to be a one-man sound department," recalled "Doug." "Irving didn't give you a job, you know. He gave you an order. But I was happy to accept. Irving had a broad editorial personality. He was very enthusiastic about sound. He saw sound as the completion of the medium. He believed it would bring reality to film." Doug was sent to the Bell Laboratories to study sound and hire a staff. Thalberg told him not to be afraid to make mistakes. "After all, Doug, we know as much about sound as anyone does."

All-Talking, All-Singing,
All Profitable

The decade known as the Roaring Twenties was coming to an end. "It was the flaming youth period, the jazz era," wrote Joan Crawford. "We weren't supposed to have problems. We didn't rationalize that as an aftermath to war, old standards had broken down, that ours was a freedom our parents had never had. . . . We only knew that we were free and we wanted to try everything, do everything, have everything." This attitude had set in motion the giddy cycles of consumerism, ballyhoo, and faddism that defined the "Era of Wonderful Nonsense." By 1929, the genteel conversation of church socials had been drowned out by the buzzing of radios, talkies, and electrocutions; and the lemonade on the veranda was spiked with bootleg gin.

Irving Thalberg had spent much of the 1920s watching other people get drunk, partly because of his fragile health and partly because he preferred the intoxication of work, but there was one habit he did acquire. Along with millions of Americans, he was playing the stock market. And why not, after hearing about the elevator operator, the cattleman, and the nurse who had followed secret tips to find fortunes in the Big Bull Market? In 1929, a decade of speculation pushed stocks to unseen highs and the volume of trading to a spectacular 5 million shares daily. It was a boom with no bust in sight, and no one believed it would end. No one saw the fine cracks in the golden monolith, the stress of overvalued stocks and a corrupt banking system. In *Only Yesterday*, the definitive chronicle of the period, Frederick Lewis Allen wrote: "The gigantic edifice of prices, honeycombed with speculative credit, was breaking under its own weight."

When Thalberg prepared his income tax returns for 1928, he listed two dubious deductions: gifts of stock to his mother and the screenwriting salary of his sister, Sylvia, who had married supervisor Lawrence Weingarten on June 2, 1928. Thalberg was also buying property in outlying areas through his father's real estate company in downtown Los Angeles. None of these matters concerned Thalberg. He was preoccupied with the transition to talking pictures, so he delegated financial matters to accountants he thought competent. His biggest worry in early 1929 was that M-G-M had slipped to third place. The main reason for this was his resistance to sound. Through a combination of arrogance and incredulity, he had waited too long. Paramount had rushed ahead and, as a result, showed a 1928 profit of $8.7 million, compared to M-G-M's $8.5 million. Both studios were trailing Warner Bros., which jumped from zero profit in 1927 to $2 million in 1928, and was heading for an unreal $17 million in 1929. M-G-M needed to catch up, but in January 1929 Thalberg had only one talking picture in the works, a modest experiment.

A year earlier, when Thalberg had visited New York's Capitol Theatre, its manager, Major Edward Bowes, had urged him to make a talking picture with songs, something akin to a musical comedy or a Broadway revue. This film could open a season at the Capitol and establish M-G-M's dominance in the sound market. Thalberg knew what music could do for film. "There never was a silent film," said Thalberg. "We'd finish a picture, show it in one of our projection rooms and come out shattered. It would be awful. Then we'd show it in a theater with a girl pounding away at a piano and there would be all the difference in the world." After pondering Bowes's suggestion, Thalberg remembered the quicksilver talents of Edmund Goulding. He assigned Goulding and Weingarten to develop an all-talking film.

"Eddie was terribly inventive and full of ideas," recalled Weingarten, "but one of his peculiarities was that he could tell a story in the morning and forget everything about it by afternoon. Knowing that, I had Irving's secretary, Vivian Newcom, take down every suggestion that Eddie rattled off." Goulding had spent as much time on the stage as he had behind a camera. "I knew Broadway," said Goulding. "In my story I tried to combine the attributes of the musical comedy, the play, and the moving picture. Just a musical comedy put on the screen would be trite. I wanted music and life. So I went backstage." He employed the plot device of two sisters in love with the same song-and-dance man and called it *Whoopee*.

"The girls were easy to cast," said Weingarten. "We had Bessie Love and Anita Page under contract. They weren't great singers or dancers but they weren't supposed to be." Weingarten's memory in 1974 was faulty; Bessie Love was not under contract. Thalberg's onetime girlfriend was playing vaudeville, her film career ended. "Somebody at M-G-M, Thalberg possibly, wanted me to do a test," remembered Love. "My agent and I both refused. I had done enough films for them to know my work, and if they wanted to hear me they could see me in the variety show. Still, Metro insisted on the test, and while I was against it, my agent wisely booked me into Grauman's Egyptian Theatre for a week, and they saw me there." The strategy worked and Thalberg hired Love.

Goulding could have written music for *Whoopee*, but he had commitments elsewhere. Thalberg turned to the songwriting team of Fred Fisher and Billy Rose, but their songs were unappealing. Title writer Ralph Spence recommended the team of Freed and Brown. Arthur Freed (one of Bessie Love's beaus after Thalberg) wrote lyrics to melodies composed by the wealthy realtor Nacio Herb Brown. While Rose had hired an orchestra for his audition, Freed and Brown used only a piano to audition "The Broadway Melody" and "You Were Meant for Me." Thalberg was not known for any great musical sympathy; he could barely carry a tune. He listened respectfully to Freed and Brown, then called Rose. "I don't want to decide between you and them," said Thalberg, "until I hear their songs with an orchestra, too." Thalberg and Shearer went to radio station KFI to hear Freed and Brown backed by the Earle C. Anthony studio orchestra. After the performance, Freed was worried that his shaky baritone had ruined his chances. Thalberg strode up to him and said: "I like your songs better than Rose's." When Thalberg learned that Goulding's title *Whoopee* was already taken by a Ziegfeld show, he renamed his project *The Broadway Melody*.

"This is an experiment," Thalberg told Weingarten. "We don't know whether the audience will accept a musical on film. So we'll have to shoot it as fast and as cheaply as we can. I want quality, but I don't want to spend too much money." For its director, he chose Harry Beaumont, who had done *Our Dancing Daughters* and *Our Modern Maidens*. "Musical comedy will prove the best bet in sound pictures," Beaumont said hopefully. "A sound picture must be a combination of the best things of the silent picture and the best of the stage. It must reveal a new, separate art, not be just a record of a stage play." The new art needed new components, but Douglas Shearer could not find them at the studio. "We have a lot of problems," Doug told Thalberg at the end of a long recording session. "There's no system here. Every time we need some music, we have to go out and hire musicians!"

"You're talking to me as if I were an office boy," said Thalberg, bridling.

"And *you're* talking to me like *I* was an office boy!" Doug shot back at him.

"You're right," sighed Thalberg. "What do you suggest?" Doug had the idea that Major Bowes could supply all the resources they needed: not only his music library but also an arranger, a music librarian, and a conductor. The next day, Thalberg called New York and requisitioned an entire music department.

Making a talking picture presented challenges at every step. Microphones had to be positioned to pick up the actors but not be seen by the camera. "We were on stepladders holding the microphones over their heads while they talked," recalled Freed. "The tough thing was that we had cameras that were not quiet. So they were put into a box. And you couldn't move the camera or even pan it." Studio employees saw their routine change daily, both technically and aesthetically. "Word had come down to us that Thalberg and Mr. Mayer had seen the rushes and were very pleased with the film," said Love. "The first rushes we saw were of a scene where I opened an envelope with a card inside, and after reading it, ripped it in half. When we heard the sound of the card being torn, we were surprised and excited. It was still such a novelty, hearing noises one made from the screen."

The musical numbers were shot with the orchestra on the soundstage, which allowed for a certain amount of improvisation. "We just went along day by day and tried what we thought was right for the story," said Freed. "We didn't see too much of Irving because he was doing so much all over the studio, and you couldn't ever get to see him, at least not when you wanted to, but whenever there was a major decision to make, he made it." When Thalberg saw the rushes of the finale number, "The Wedding of the Painted Doll," he was not pleased. The scene had been shot straight-on, proscenium-arch style.

"That's not a motion picture," Thalberg barked. "It's not a movie at all! It's a stage presentation!" Thalberg calmed down and started to think. The scene would have to be reshot, possibly with large, motorized sets. "This time arrange the cameras so we can get some different angles," said Thalberg, "instead of making the audience look at it from the front, as if they were in a legitimate theater." Thalberg was planning retakes when Doug voiced a thought. "We've got a perfectly good recording of the music. Why not just play the record and have the dancers go through the number? Then we can combine the film and the sound track in the lab."

"Can you do that?" asked Thalberg.

"I see no reason why we can't," said Doug.

"Okay. Do it." Thalberg thus initiated the technique of shooting musical numbers with actors "lip-syncing" to playback. As an added touch, he authorized the use of the "two-color" Technicolor process for "The Wedding of the Painted Doll."

The Broadway Melody had a splashy premiere at Grauman's Chinese Theatre on February 6, 1929. Bessie Love was there. "When the picture turns out to be good—just right—the way you meant it to be—and this elephantine cinema in 'the town where they made 'em' comes to life from cellar to rafters, with everyone applauding and shouting their appreciation in the *middle* of the film, it's something, I tell you. It really is."

After all this, the film did not play Major Bowes's Capitol, which would have commenced a regular release. Thalberg decided to open it as a road show at the slightly smaller but more prestigious Astor. *Variety*'s "Bid" confirmed the rightness of his decision. Calling the film "the initial onscreen musical," the review praised the "quality of the interpolated numbers," and "the theatrical license" of an unseen orchestra introducing a song for the first time in talking pictures. The review also hailed the film's integration of image and sound. "Its technique is strictly a punch formula," wrote Bid, "generally ending dramatic situations with a giggle. Arnold has moved his camera all over the place, constantly ranging from closeups, to mediums, to full length. It's pretty near a classic in how to take a talker and then cut it to keep it moving." The review also praised Love's acting. The scene in which she gives up her man to her sister "had some of the women in the house still crying when they left the theatre. And when women cry, that's box office." *The Broadway Melody* played a road-show engagement for fifty-three weeks and eventually grossed over $4.3 million, which made it M-G-M's highest-grossing film of 1929, and, after *Ben-Hur* and *The Big Parade*, the studio's most profitable to date.

Thalberg's newfound interest in the musical idiom led to another million-dollar hit, *The Hollywood Revue of 1929*. This film's format was that of a vaudeville show, with every M-G-M star (except Ramon Novarro, Lon Chaney, and Greta Garbo) doing some sort of skit. This time Thalberg allowed the numbers to be shot mostly straight on. Although Freed and Brown supplied only one song, "Singin' in the Rain," Freed had Thalberg's ear. "When I started out at Metro, I had a lot of talks with Thalberg," recalled Freed. "Irving and I got pretty close." Freed's only problem was to find Thalberg. "He was the hardest man to see," said Freed. "If he made a date with you for 2:00, you were lucky to see him at 5:30. Or 7:00. Because he was doing so much." Few M-G-M employees suspected how much Thalberg was doing—or why.

In mid-1928 Paul Bern, Thalberg's most trusted adviser, had gone to Pathé to become a producer. The reason for his abrupt leave-taking was the atmosphere in the M-G-M offices. The amity of the early years had given way to a brusque civility. Thalberg and Mayer were frequently at odds, and Rubin was siding with Thalberg. "I learned of the Mayer-Rubin-Thalberg rift from Paul Bern," recalled Florence Browning. "Thalberg and Rubin were of a mind that they didn't need Mayer any longer." Simply put, Thalberg resented Mayer's running off to play politics and leaving him with the problem of sound. He felt that Mayer, having ingratiated himself with the paternalistic William Randolph Hearst, was now indulging in sycophantic hero worship of Herbert Hoover. This was unfair to Mayer.

As manager of the most successful company in America's sixth-largest-industry, Mayer had to cultivate both the press and the government. It was true, however, that Mayer was neglecting Culver City duties while getting the lion's share of profits from both M-G-M films and Loew's theaters. He could have delegated some of his politicking. Instead he went off to the convention (which he underwrote) and left Thalberg in charge of the studio—where Thalberg was already approving fifty scenarios and producing fifteen films a year. In truth, Mayer enjoyed the limelight, not to mention getting a president elected. Thalberg's health continued to be stable, but a workload of this magnitude could compromise it.

From all accounts, though, it was not the threat of a heart attack that consumed Thalberg; it was the unfairness of the situation. He was doing the work of two executives while second in command and third in salary. Worse, in mid-1928 Mayer brought Cecil B. DeMille onto the lot, gave him his own bungalow, and made him the only producer who was not subject to Thalberg. In late 1928 Thalberg's confidence was further shaken when he saw Nick Schenck negotiate John Gilbert's new contract—simply because Mayer refused to talk to Gilbert, whom he detested. As a result, Gilbert had to make only two films a year for three years, but would be paid an outrageous $250,000 for each. This would never have occurred if Mayer had made himself available.

Thalberg began to hold secret meetings with J. Robert Rubin. Before long they were discussing the possibility of an ouster. "Mayer adored Rubin," said Browning. "Rubin was everything that Mayer was not—educated, handsome, elegant. Mayer looked up to him and respected him. It was a terrible shock when he realized that his partners contemplated ditching him." For nearly six years, Mayer had not made a decision without Thalberg. The turning point of any meeting in Mayer's office was the moment when he reached for the intercom and said, "Wait a minute—I'll see what Irving thinks." Now executives like Bern found themselves identified as either Thalberg men or Mayer men. When the two camps began to polarize, Bern decamped to Pathé.

Fred Wilcox, brother of Schenck's new wife, Pansy, was one of the few M-G-M employees who knew that Mayer suspected his partners. One night in early 1929 Thalberg left for a San Bernardino preview with his supervisors. Wilcox was surprised to see that Mayer had not gone with them. Mayer offered Wilcox a ride home. In the car, Mayer was at first silent, then morose. Then he began to cry, and ended up sobbing. "Mr. Mayer, what's the matter?" asked Wilcox. "Is there anything I can do?"

"They all went off and left me!" wept Mayer, taking Wilcox's hand. "They didn't ask me to go along!"

Wilcox naturally told Schenck about this, and the Culver City schism played right into his hands. Mayer was too busy with politics and Thalberg too busy with talkies to notice that Schenck was in constant communication with the Marcus Loew estate and the lawyers of a certain film company.

One afternoon in late February, Florence Browning received a call at Loew's in New York. On the line was an agitated Ed Hatrick, Hearst's publicist. "Florence," yelled Hatrick, "they're over at the bank right now, signing the papers to sell your company to Fox!"

"I was flabbergasted," recalled Browning. "I called Mayer in Washington and told him. He was stunned. Then, after a long pause, he said, 'Well, Schenck is president of the company. He can do what he wants with it.'"

On the same day, Thalberg was in his office preparing for an evening of bridge with Jack Conway, Hunt Stromberg, and agent Phil Berg. Vivian Newcom announced a long-distance call from Rubin. Thalberg went into the next room to take it. His associates were shocked to hear him shouting into the telephone. He slammed down the receiver, and then came in and told them that Nick Schenck had just sold their studio to Fox Film. The bridge game was canceled.

A few days later, on Sunday, March 3, 1929, publicist Glendon Allvine called a press conference for William Fox, founder and president of the Fox Film Corporation. Pandemonium broke out when Fox disclosed that he had just purchased a controlling interest in Loew's, Inc., M-G-M's parent company.

The fuse to this bomb had been lit a week earlier at the Park Ambassador Hotel in New York, when Allvine was summoned to a secret meeting between Fox, his vice-president, Winfield Sheehan—and Nick Schenck. As an incredulous Allvine watched, Fox and Sheehan handed checks to Schenck's lawyers. The checks were supposed to total $50 million, but were $20 million short. The fifty-year-old Fox was momentarily flustered. He looked in every pocket, which was difficult because he could use only his right arm. His left arm hung limp, crippled by a childhood accident that had healed improperly because his parents could not afford medical care. "Then in the small watch pocket of his trousers," wrote Allvine, "Fox found the folded, crumpled certified check for twenty million dollars, and the deal was closed."

The "deal" was the purchase of 400,000 shares of stock belonging to Marcus Loew's widow. Without consulting the Mayer group, Schenck had sold the controlling interest in Loew's to the predaceous Fox.

The head of Fox Film had come a long way since the days when he was Wilhelm Fried, textile manufacturer and nickelodeon owner. "I always bragged of the fact that no second of those contained in the twenty-four hours ever passed but that the name of William Fox was on the screen, being exhibited in some theater in some part of the world," said Fox. Indeed, he owned ten times as many theaters as Loew's, had a larger studio than M-G-M, and owned the Movietone sound-on-film patent. "Now Fox had Leo the Lion's tail in his firm 53-percent grip," wrote Allvine. "More stars than there are in heaven—and Irving Thalberg, too! When Schenck and the lawyers left, I shook the hand that ruled the motion picture industry."

Mayer attended Hoover's inauguration the next day, after which he was a guest in the White House. He then joined Thalberg and Rubin in New York. "No one knew what was going to happen," recalled Browning. "Everything could have fallen apart right then. They met in Rubin's offices. Mayer and Rubin shook hands. Mayer told me later: 'When Bob held out his hand to me, it was like the clouds had broken and the sun was shining again.'" The reunited Mayer group then went to Schenck's offices. The meeting was for the most part polite. Schenck explained that Fox's requirement of secrecy had prevented him from notifying anyone, but assured them that he had looked out for their interests. Thalberg found this hard to swallow and called Schenck's actions "an unprincipled sell-out." Fox had made remarks about consolidating Fox Film and M-G-M, and that Sheehan would like to look over the Culver City facilities. Thalberg brought this up and promised to bring legal action if his authority was usurped.

"My good friend Irving," said Schenck, "Mr. William Fox considers your contract one of our most important assets."

Irving Thalberg, though a few months short of thirty, was used to having power and accustomed to using it. He did not like the prospect of becoming a chess piece. He managed to suppress his anger and his fear. Mayer spoke quietly to him: "Go back to your job. Let me handle this." After Thalberg left the meeting, Mayer faced down Schenck, who had made $2 million on the Fox deal. "You haven't heard the last of this," said Mayer. "I have friends in Washington. They don't like the idea of big corporations swallowing up other ones. They might like to look into this particular deal." Schenck informed Mayer that Fox had foreseen this contingency and gotten a nod from Washington. Mayer and Rubin left the meeting in low spirits.

Back in Culver City, Thalberg engrossed himself in the conversion to sound. "The integrity of the Metro-Goldwyn-Mayer organization will be preserved," he said, referring obliquely to Fox's takeover. "The 1929–30 season will be our biggest. We completed plans at our conference for fifty talking pictures, with complete silent versions." This was because fewer than eight thousand domestic theaters (out of nineteen thousand) had been wired for sound. "Where a story lends itself to silent treatment, we will produce a complete silent adaptation," he added. "This applies particularly to films having a foreign locale and an exotic atmosphere." Thus, unwired theaters could expect silent versions of talkies, plus silent films starring Ramon Novarro, Greta Garbo, and Lon Chaney, since none of them had yet committed to speaking on screen. Their reluctance was not foolish. In spite of the huge grosses of *The Broadway Melody*, the "speakers," as some called them, were not perfected and not universally popular. The transition was awkward. After a month of acting in a silent film, actors would have to film two more scenes—or an entire talking version—with a new technique. Years later Norma Shearer wrote: "People ask me: 'Did you have lines to speak in silent pictures or did you just say anything you felt like saying?' Some ask if we spoke at all, if it wasn't all pantomime. The answer, of course, is that we did speak. We had lines in the script that were necessary to the meaning of the scene, and we had to memorize them. They were usually short speeches. Too much movement of the lips was thought to look unattractive or even comical."

In early 1929, silent films were still being made and still being seen. "The talking picture is still regarded as a novelty," wrote *Photoplay* editor James R. Quirk in March. "Nine out of ten [letter writers] say they would rather have a first-rate silent picture than a second-rate talking picture. They complain of the mediocre photography and static quality of the acting in talking films." M-G-M silent films now had sound tracks so that they could be advertised as "sound films," but their music-and-effect tracks were often jarring. Released in March, *The Duke Steps Out* suffered in comparison with all-talking films. "The synchronization gives signs of having been hastily and clumsily done," wrote Philip K. Scheuer in the *Los Angeles Times*, "never rising above the level of an old phonograph in travail."

In spite of holdouts such as Chaney, total conversion looked likely by late spring. Many actors tried to disguise apprehension with disdain. "If they want me to talk, I'll talk," said Garbo. "I'd love to act in a talking picture when they are better, but the ones I have seen are awful." Her countryman Nils Asther, questioned about his accent, replied: "Sounds are sounds, and you can learn to make them. I can learn lines phonetically." By the late summer, people were speaking of silent films in the past tense. "In the silent movies we achieved certain beautiful things," Lillian Gish told *Film Daily*. "I mean that there were moments of beauty in pantomime and beauty in photography. Much of what we did was poor, but if the silent movies had had more time to develop, we might have made a really great and individual art in them." M-G-M director Jack Conway, who was having a hard time with the new sound technology, told the press that he deplored "the passing of the inaudible drama, because with it went the myriad nuances, the directorial and pantomimic touches which made subtlety in the cinema a fine art."

Thalberg hoped that silents and talkies could coexist. "The great quality that made motion pictures a success was realism," he told the *Los Angeles Times*.

> One had a feeling of going into people's houses, of looking into their eyes and seeing their thoughts, of gazing into their hearts and of understanding their emotions. Now voice has been added to pictures, making them just that much more intimate and real. . . . The talkie is absolutely the nearest thing to life, the greatest form of expression yet.
>
> Of course, not all pictures should be talkies. It is ridiculous to thrust dialogue into certain subjects that are better done in pantomime. Certain productions which have great variety of movement and pictorial appeal are definitely for the silent form. I would always want to make pictures like *Wild Orchids* and *Our Dancing Daughters* silently. There is nothing the people in those stories say that they cannot express without words. On the other hand, *The Trial of Mary Dugan* would be deadly dull as a silent film.

The last-mentioned title was a sensational Broadway hit starring Ann Harding. This story of a showgirl tried for murder had been written by Bayard Veiller. In short order, Thalberg invited the portly playwright to direct M-G-M's second all-talking film. "I talked with Thalberg over the telephone about what he wanted," wrote Veiller, "and that was to place on the screen, as nearly as possible, an exact replica of the play. . . . I was to minimize the fact that Mary Dugan had been the mistress of a man, but aside from that we felt that for this experiment we could disregard most of the censorship rules." Thalberg was confident that he could circumvent the increasingly vocal groups that were criticizing racy films. Censored or not, *Mary Dugan* was a plum role; both Crawford and Shearer began eyeing it. Thalberg tried to discourage his wife. "Irving said that the change from the light comedies I had been doing to heavy drama was too drastic," said Shearer. "And besides, I had no stage experience. The microphone might frighten me." Veiller, meanwhile, was approached by Crawford. "She was coming along pretty rapidly," wrote Veiller, "but didn't appeal to me very much."

In early 1929, almost all of M-G-M's players were taking voice tests. "During these sessions," wrote Shearer, "we were told to stand in front of a microphone and say 'What am I doing?' as many ways as possible—'What *am* I doing?' and then 'What am *I* doing?' and so on. Suddenly a voice blasted back at us through a loudspeaker: 'Making a damned fool of yourself!' Irving invented this bit of nonsense. It was supposed to leave us shrieking with laughter, and then we were supposed to be relaxed and ready to take the real test." William Haines was frozen with fear as he stood waiting for the sound technician to set a level for his test. In the midst of the dead silence, someone sneezed. Haines jumped a foot and lost his breath. A first playback invariably caused surprise. According to Shearer, "Every one of us said: 'But that's not *me!*'" When Crawford heard her test, she said: "That's a *man!*"

"I was scared to death when I got a call that I had to make a sound test at M-G-M," wrote Marion Davies, who had no stage experience—and a severe stammer. "I'd had a little sherry, and you'd think I knew what I was talking about. . . . I started a routine. I said, 'This is a dinner party where we are eating ersters. From Brooklyn . . . *ersters.*' And I went on from there, and I wouldn't stop. I said to George K. Arthur: 'Sit down.'"

"There's no chair," said Arthur.

"Well, fall down. What's the difference?"

"That's it. That's the end," came Doug Shearer's voice from a sound booth high above the stage. Davies was sure she had flunked. She went home and crawled into bed, telling her family: "Go away from me. Don't talk to me, please. I don't care for this idea at all. I'm going to sleep and I hope I never wake up." The next day she got a call from Thalberg telling her to report to the studio. "I can't," said Davies. "I'm not feeling well."

"Look," said Thalberg. "I want to talk to you. I have some news for you which you're not going to like." Davies roused herself and went to M-G-M. Thalberg saw her immediately. "What did you do?" he asked her. "You made a test last night. What did you do?"

"I didn't do anything."

"Well, whatever you did, you stunned the other people," said Thalberg. "Who wrote your dialogue?"

The next step was to go into training with one of the "vocal culturists" who were descending on Hollywood like loquacious locusts. Accredited coaches included Dr. P. M. Marafioti, who had trained Enrico Caruso, and Oliver Hinsdell, a Texas regional theater veteran. "Irving believed in training for your craft," recalled Shearer, "so a drama coach tried to show me how to breathe and what gestures to make. She almost drove me crazy. Luckily I didn't develop any phobias or pick up any affectations from crackpots posing as voice authorities. I left the pear-shaped tones to others."

Shearer felt confident enough to audition for *Mary Dugan*'s author. "I couldn't wait to use my voice," she said. "I felt that this would be an advantage, not a hazard." Thalberg was not so sure. "If you want her to play it, you can have her," he told Veiller. "That's up to you." When Veiller saw "that funny little twisted grin," he booked Stage 23 for the audition, but when Shearer stepped onto the empty stage, which was 80 feet wide and 180 feet long, her confidence wilted. "In the center of this awful arena of emptiness," wrote Veiller, "was a kitchen table and two kitchen chairs. And there we sat. I've seen a good many frightened actresses in my day, but Norma was very frightened." After five minutes, Veiller and Shearer made a silent trek back to Thalberg's office.

"Irving, it isn't fair," began Shearer. "I haven't had a fair chance with Bayard—just one speech, that's all he'd let me say. I think I ought to have another chance at it."

"Don't you like her?" Thalberg asked Veiller. "You don't have to have her, you know. I told you that."

"Irving, somebody's gone stark, raving crazy and it isn't me. Norma has given me exactly what I wanted. I don't know any moving-picture actress who can approach her in this part."

"Well, I'll be damned!" said Norma. "I thought you didn't like me."

Veiller may have been satisfied, but Thalberg was not. After two weeks of rehearsals, he made Shearer perform *The Trial of Mary Dugan* with the entire cast before an audience on a stage. "They'll be the jury," he said. "I'll be the judge."

Shearer's real test came on a newly completed soundstage. Gone were the familiar sounds of hammering, conversation, and catcalls. Conspicuously absent were the musicians who had played mood music during the shooting of each scene. Now there was a grim silence. "King Mike" picked up every noise, including the rumble of trucks on Washington Boulevard. "Even the whir of the camera's wheels had to be muffled," wrote Bayard Veiller. "The camera was set up in a cabinet of its own—a thing about eight by ten feet square, made soundproof, on rollers." This camera booth varied slightly from studio to studio, but it was essentially the same for every camera operator—an airless cell. With the temperature on the soundstage at 120 degrees, the operator was drenched in sweat when he emerged from the booth. Some operators fainted inside. "It took eight men to move it," said Veiller. "When we took a few shots at a distance of eight or ten feet, and then wanted to come up for a close-up, it took two hours to change the camera angle." Actors who were accustomed to a freestanding camera found the booth intimidating—or hypnotic. "The inside of the booth was so black that the plate-glass window in front of the camera reflected as a mirror," said Shearer. "Once I became so engrossed in watching my reflection that I stopped acting right in the middle of an important scene and fully expected my reflection to go on acting for me."

When *The Trial of Mary Dugan* premiered in April, acting was the issue. "For Norma Shearer this picture is a vindication and a triumph," wrote Norbert Lusk in the *New York Times*, "the former because it validates her claim to stardom in the minds of some of us for the first time, and the latter because in her first talking picture she skillfully combines the techniques of both stage and screen and emerges as a compelling actress of greater individuality than she ever revealed in silent pictures."

Shearer's success was particularly timely. She was feeling embattled at home, where Henrietta continued to hold court. In November 1928 the stress of that environment had overwhelmed her. Shearer discovered that Thalberg had sent flowers to Bessie Love on the set of *The Broadway Melody*, something he had not done for any other performer. Shearer knew that he had dated Love some years earlier. Thalberg came home one night to discover that Shearer had moved to her mother's house. After a few days of negotiations, she returned to the Thalberg mansion, but only with the assurance that this living arrangement was temporary. Thalberg promised that in July they would rent the Santa Monica house belonging to Bebe Daniels and Ben Lyon.

While Thalberg sweated out the talkies and waited to hear what Fox planned to do, he was hit by another broadside. The Internal Revenue Service had found inconsistencies in his income tax deductions and audited him. In June he was accused of tax evasion. His lawyers tried to blame the discrepancies on his accountants, but the government would not be mollified. According to Samuel Marx, "Irving was informed that if he was judged guilty, it would result in a jail sentence." On July 5, he wrote to the commissioner of internal revenue, explaining that he had taken the allegedly illegal deductions in good faith. "The first few years of my connection with the motion-picture industry brought hard work and small pay," he claimed. His family had underwritten his career, and he felt the need to repay them, as well as to benefit by their business acumen. The "outright gift" of stock to his mother, he maintained, was within his rights because of her age. "I have attempted to show that this transfer was made for the purpose of providing for funds which would protect her from the hazards of speculation and accumulate for her future security. This purpose was uppermost in my mind, not the question of how it could be done for income-tax purposes."

Thalberg would have to go to New York at the end of the year to attend a hearing. Mayer had been corresponding with the Hoover administration about the possibility of an antitrust suit. He also secured an audience with Hoover to speak on Thalberg's behalf. "Mr. President, the boy did wrong," said Mayer. "He admits it. But he didn't mean to. Putting him in prison would mean endless shame for his beautiful family. . . . I beg of you, Mr. President, to spare this boy. He is willing to pay all the penalties the government demands. And by sparing him you will assure him a productive life for himself and M-G-M and the entire industry."

On May 30, 1929, Thalberg turned thirty. For years he had been living with the fear that he might not reach this milestone. Lenore Coffee recalled a day in 1924 when she walked into his office just as an insurance examiner was completing a physical. Thalberg rolled down his shirt sleeve, gave her a wry smile, and said: "I'm twenty-five, and I have to pay the premium of a man forty years old." In spite of the pressures of 1929, he had reached thirty. He even looked hale and hearty. He and Shearer continued to attend social functions. The most lavish of these was the Bal Masque held at the Beverly Hills Hotel in May to celebrate the third wedding anniversary of Ouida Bergere and Basil Rathbone. John Gilbert attended with his latest flame, Broadway star Ina Claire. Garbo came dressed as Hamlet, albeit masked. Thalberg and Shearer came as West Point cadets. William Haines took advantage of their androgyny to sneak up behind Thalberg and goose him. Thalberg turned angrily on him, but Haines defused his anger with a flick of the wrist and a silly giggle. "Oh, excuse me, Irving!" said Haines. "I thought you were Norma." Haines was confident of his star status, or he would not have attempted such insolence. "It was the height of my career," he recalled. "Anything I made they came to see." His gesture was more than arrogant and worse than disrespectful; it was a denial of the unspoken rule that except for the officially sanctioned horseplay of athletics and family parties, Thalberg was never to be touched. Shearer was known for a decisive handclasp, but Thalberg eschewed physical contact.

Haines was the first M-G-M star to make a successful sound debut. He was followed by Shearer, Davies, Novarro, Crawford, Buster Keaton, and the numerous contract players who made cameo appearances in *The Hollywood Revue of 1929.* The studio's one casualty was the least likely, its most expensive star, the bigger-than-life John Gilbert. Director Clarence Brown had anticipated Gilbert's problems during the making of the silent *A Woman of Affairs* in September 1928. "The talkies had already arrived," said Brown, "and John Gilbert went completely ham in the middle of shooting, demonstrating what he was going to do in his first sound film. He began speaking titles with great flamboyance." Gilbert's acting style had always been grand; his denunciation scene two years earlier in *Flesh and the Devil* had caused comment. "The audience fairly howled with laughter," reported the *New York Sun,* "at what was supposed to be his heaviest, most dramatic scene. Healthy American lads like Mr. Gilbert can't get away with such tactics."

Since the advent of talking pictures, the pitch of love scenes had become difficult to gauge. "Seems the only type of love stuff received as intended since the advent of the talkies is the comedy love scene," said one critic. "The screen comics are becoming the heavy lovers and the heavy lovers, comedians. The normal kiss, delivered with the usual smack, sounds like an explosion. For that reason, kiss scenes have them rolling in the aisles." At a time when cinematic restraint was essential, Thalberg inexplicably assigned the direction of several important films to Lionel Barrymore. The least flamboyant member of the "Royal Family of Broadway" had defected from the stage to become a ubiquitous supporting player in M-G-M films.

"As an old and experienced hand to whom nobody has paid any attention these many years, let me explain," Barrymore told Thalberg. "Sound won't make quite as much difference as you fearfully expect. Action will remain the chief ingredient of these cultural dramas of ours." Barrymore's first assignment was *Madame X,* but he put no action in it, just a series of dialogues shot straight on. Ruth Chatterton's forceful performance made *Madame X* the studio's third-biggest film of the year. Barrymore's next assignment was to do retakes on Gilbert's first talkie, *Redemption.* For some reason Fred Niblo's rough cut looked lifeless. When Thalberg reviewed the Barrymore cut with Gilbert, it still looked bad—so bad that Gilbert asked Thalberg to shelve the film. Thalberg agreed but then assigned Barrymore to direct Gilbert's next film, *Olympia,* a Ferenc Molnar farce. Thalberg did not know that Barrymore was suffering from chronic joint pain and was using narcotics to dull it.

"I watched Jack Gilbert being destroyed on the soundstage by one man, Lionel Barrymore," wrote Hedda Hopper. "Talking pictures had to be approached cautiously. Lionel had plenty of experience on the stage; Gilbert had none. By the time sound came in, 'love' was a comedy word. Use it too freely and you got a belly laugh. Whether by diabolical intent or careless accident I'll never know, but Jack's very first speech was 'I love you, I love you, I love you.'"

Renamed *His Glorious Night*, the film opened on September 28 at the Capitol, while Gilbert was honeymooning in Europe with Ina Claire. Most reviewers tried to distance themselves from the giggling of first-night audiences. The usually diplomatic Edwin Schallert of the *Los Angeles Times* had to report that "Gilbert has not as yet hit quite the perfect note of intonation for the microphone but, barring a certain over-resonant delivery of lines, his enunciation is crisp and fine." He blamed the film, not Gilbert, when the audience "chose not to take its love scenes too seriously."

The damning review came from *Variety*. "A few more talker productions like this, and John Gilbert will be able to change places with [comedian] Harry Langdon. His prowess at love making, which has held the stenoes breathless, takes on a comedy aspect that gets the gum chewers tittering at first and then laughing outright at the very false ring of the couple of dozen 'I love you' phrases." A report from London was, if possible, worse. "White-hot love speeches brought only snickers from the first-run audience at Loew's here," wrote the *Film Spectator*. "Snickers, too, which threatened more than once to become a gale of laughter. Quite obviously they were at a loss to know what had happened to their idol and most of them seemed a little ashamed of themselves for laughing. But they laughed, and all the talking pictures in the world, all the fine salary, all the publicity puffs, all the paid reviews, can never undo that laugh." According to Irene Selznick, Mayer came home carrying these reviews. He dropped them onto a table and said: "That should take care of *Mr.* Gilbert."

Mayer's remarkable luck, which had brought him from a ghetto in Russia to the upper reaches of American industry, contrived to deliver a deus ex machina when he needed it most. It assumed the form of an automobile hurtling toward an intersection on Long Island. On July 17 William Fox was on his way to meet Nick Schenck for a golf game. An inattentive driver smashed into Fox's limousine. The vehicle was upended. His chauffeur was killed. Fox was seriously injured, losing a third of his blood at the scene. His protracted recovery kept him away from his office at a crucial time. By mid-September, the unprecedented volume of stock trading was alarming market veterans. Many began to sell their holdings.

Fox's advisers urged the mogul to sell his Loew's stock. His judgment blurred by morphine and hubris, Fox refused.

Of the fifty M-G-M films released in 1929, all but five showed a profit. To Thalberg, the most disappointing flop was King Vidor's *Hallelujah!* It was the first major studio film to be cast exclusively with African Americans. When Vidor proposed the idea to Thalberg in 1928, he was honest about its prospects. "I doubt that it will make a dollar at the box office."

"Don't worry about that," Thalberg replied. "I've told you that M-G-M can afford an occasional experiment."

Mayer tried to dissuade him. "Let the other fellows make this kind of movie," he said. "If they're good, then we'll step in and do them better."

"It's not practical," warned Schenck. "A picture like that will attract too many Negroes to the theaters, and the whites will stay away." When Thalberg began to waver, Vidor made a put-up-or-shut-up proposition to Schenck. "I'll put my salary into the picture's cost, dollar for dollar with everything you spend. I'm willing to gamble my money with yours." Another attractive element was that the studio did not have to purchase a literary property or pay Vidor for a scenario. Schenck gave Thalberg the go-ahead. "It took me longer to see Thalberg about it than it did to write it," said Vidor.

Vidor then took a film company to the swamps of Arkansas and the woods of Tennessee. While he was on location, Thalberg cabled him about the rushes, in particular about the "very outstanding hairline on [the] upper lip" on the female lead. "Terribly disappointed in Honey Brown," wrote Thalberg. "She has lots of pep but very little, if any, sex. Great for first part with comedy scenes but afraid audiences would laugh at the sex scenes and question whether they would believe sincerity of the story, which is the strong sex attraction between the two [principals]." Vidor replaced Brown with Nina Mae McKinney, whom he had seen in the chorus of *Blackbirds of 1928* in Harlem. McKinney's bouncy charm more than compensated for her lack of film experience. "Nina was full of life, full of expression, and just a joy to work with," recalled Vidor. Her costar, Daniel Haynes, had been an understudy in a road company of *Show Boat.* When Vidor had to finish his all-black film as a talkie, these talents made the film totally authentic. "All the incidents in *Hallelujah!* derived from my youth and childhood in Texas," said Vidor. "My father owned sawmills and lumber mills, and we frequently used to witness religious meetings and mass baptisms." Vidor recreated these episodes on location and then shot talking sequences in Culver City.

Hallelujah! hit the pitfalls that Schenck had predicted. "The big Chicago theater owners refused to show the film," said Vidor, "so a fellow in a small side-street theatre booked it, gave a dinner-jacket-and-black-tie opening; after that the theater was sold out. Only then did Balaban and Katz, operators of the large movie houses, agree to show *Hallelujah!* We always had to break the barrier like that." *Hallelujah!* cost a nominal $320,000, but it was not only racism that made it a losing proposition. It was the idea of an M-G-M film without stars. "There is nothing in it to attract the flappers or superficial lunch-goers who flock to a matinee after a morning's shopping in town," wrote a New York reviewer. "This element, wanting only a box of chocolates and a little light diversion, will take a rather indignant leave, as did several of its number at Monday's crowded matinee."

Thalberg was right on another count. Even in a year packed with innovations, *Hallelujah!* brought the studio prestige. "Vidor has poured himself into this picture, designed as an epic of the Negro," one reviewer wrote. "He has packed in glamour and action and humanity. This picture is ammunition with which to meet those who say 'They never try anything new in the film industry.'" *Hallelujah!* and Cecil B. DeMille's *Dynamite* were the best examples of what the sound film could do when not subjugated to a recording engineer. Most of Thalberg's talkies were static recordings of stage plays, as *Variety* noted in its *Mary Dugan* review: "We guess it's a moving picture because it comes in cans and unwinds through a projector to reach the screen." Although *Mary Dugan* opened with impressionist zoom-lens shots, the rest of it was strictly "canned theater." *Hallelujah!* and *Dynamite* were *moving* pictures, making liberal use of a mobile camera, quick-cut editing, and contrapuntal sound. They were almost as cinematic as the silent films they were replacing. Silents were scarce in the summer, but a few still appeared here and there. Suddenly, there were none. M-G-M released the last silent version of a talkie in September with *The Unholy Night*, and the studio released its last silent film in late November. *The Kiss*, besides being M-G-M's, and Garbo's, last silent, turned out to be Hollywood's last silent. Before anyone could say "Okay for sound," an era had ended. No one at M-G-M was complaining. The year ended with a profit of $12 million. Did the year end with M-G-M working for Fox?

On October 12, the still-recovering William Fox held a press conference to confirm the merger. On October 29, henceforth to be known as "Black Tuesday," the stock market crashed. In one cataclysmic day, 16,410,030 shares were dumped and $14 billion of wealth simply evaporated. In M-G-M offices, executives and low-level employees alike yelled into telephones. There were lines outside phone booths. In stockbrokers' offices across the country, the scene was the same. "One saw men looking defeat in the face," wrote Frederick Lewis Allen. "One of them was slowly walking up and down, mechanically tearing a piece of paper into tiny and still tinier fragments. Another was grinning shamefacedly, as a small boy giggles at a funeral. Another was abjectly beseeching a clerk for the latest news of American & Foreign Power. And still another was sitting motionless, as if stunned, his eyes fixed blindly upon the moving figures on the screen, those innocent-looking figures that meant the smash-up of years of hopes."

Thalberg had hoped to make restitution to the Treasury Department using stock sale proceeds. The stock market dashed that hope, and his December appointment loomed before him. He soon learned that the crash had also hurt Fox. Both the Fox stocks and the precious Loew's shares had dropped precipitously. Fox found himself unable to pay the bankers who had financed his deal. He began to cast about for help, and tried to unload assets. As Mayer and Thalberg watched quietly, the predator became the prey. On November 27 Fox was served with an antitrust suit by the Justice Department. In short order, both his bankers and his executives turned on him. In December, Fox was ordered to surrender control of the Fox Film Corporation and the Fox theater chain to his creditors. When it appeared that Mayer's Washington connections had saved M-G-M, the Mayer group confronted Schenck.

Thalberg told Schenck that after the events of the past year, he deserved another salary raise. Schenck declined, so Mayer offered to adjust his own profit percentage, reducing it from 53 percent to 43 percent so that Thalberg's could increase from 20 percent to 30 percent; Rubin's remained the same. With his tax problems unresolved, Thalberg continued to press Schenck, reminding him that even though Fox was now powerless, Schenck still had his fat percentage. "L.B. was sure the Fox deal had to fall apart," recalled Eddie Mannix. "Irving could make Nick pay for his actions." Mannix expected Thalberg to share part of his bonus with him, Albert Lewin, Hunt Stromberg, and the recently returned Paul Bern. "We were all burned in the Crash," said Mannix. "The thought of making Nick pay seemed to cheer up Irving. He left for New York saying, 'Whatever I get, I'll split with you fellows.'" As Irene Selznick heard it, "Irving locked horns with Nick and got an enormous bonus, but only after a terrible fight." Thalberg's bonus was $250,000, of which $100,000 would go to the government. Mayer's appeal to Hoover had worked. What Thalberg got from the IRS was the equivalent of a rap on the knuckles. When he returned to M-G-M, though, he said nothing about sharing his bonus. "He got a quarter of a million," said Mannix, "but we never saw a dime." None of Thalberg's executives dared remind him of his promise. "What would that accomplish?" Mannix asked Samuel Marx later.

"After all, it wasn't something that would simply slip his mind. Irving was a sweet guy, but he could piss ice water."

"His only weakness was love of money," Mayer later said of Thalberg. It was at this time, at the end of their seventh year together, after surviving a minor estrangement and a hostile takeover, that the two men's interests diverged and Thalberg's relationship with Mayer changed. "[Irving] wanted as much as L.B. was getting," said Mannix. "That touched off a rivalry between them. Irving was after the big money, and L.B. began to think of the day he would produce the pictures. It changed them both, and it never should have happened." Irene Selznick looked at it differently. "I found Irving's demands understandable," she wrote. "No one else was a saint about money; there was no reason for him to be. He had a growing family, his life span was limited, but, above all, his value was incalculable."

Thalberg's relationship with his wife also changed in 1929. To outsiders such as Doug, Thalberg and Shearer were well matched. "Their marriage worked," he said many years later. "Oh, a great pair! Gosh, they were like that! Wonderful." Others saw a cold, pensive husband and a restless, ambitious wife. Still others saw an executive whose wife's projects came first and an actress who ordered her schedule around the medical prerogatives established by her mother-in-law. Anyone who saw the Thalbergs arrive at a premiere saw a beautiful young couple who also happened to be rich and famous. Yet in spite of their social position, something was missing. The move to Santa Monica helped, but with Thalberg fighting battles on several fronts and Shearer making three talkies in a row, there was little time for passion, even in the privacy of a rented home. What renewed Thalberg's passion was Shearer's professional drive, which was in turn accelerated by a threat.

Thalberg had authorized the purchase of Ursula Parrott's *Ex-Wife*, a scandalous novel about a career woman who refuses to let her philandering husband ruin her life. "I knew that M-G-M owned the story," said Shearer, "and that the studio was considering borrowing someone from another lot to play it. I was there on the lot, under contract, and I felt in my heart that I could do it." Possible stars included Ruth Chatterton, Ann Harding, and Constance Bennett. Joan Crawford was also a contender. "I was the one person made a star in 1929 without a talking picture," said Crawford, who was more than just a new star. When she appeared in two hugely popular sound films and married Douglas Fairbanks Jr., she became the rage of '29. Shearer began to look over her shoulder.

This was the girl whose first job at Metro was doubling for Shearer when she played a dual role in 1925's *Lady of the Night*. "My first appearance before the moving camera was anonymous," wrote Crawford in 1959. "While Norma played the Tough Girl (full front, close-up), I played the Lady (with my back to the camera); when she did the Lady, I was the Tough Girl (with my back to the camera)." Shearer, who had been tutored by veterans like Hedda Hopper and Mae Busch, saw Crawford's potential. "I found myself sitting in a car," wrote Shearer in 1955, "and in the other corner was a girl with the most beautiful eyes. They were the biggest eyes I had ever seen. But they didn't trust me. I could see that. They never have."

Shearer recalled their next encounter. "I saw her crying up on the balcony outside the dressing rooms. I stopped and asked her what was troubling her. She told me that she didn't like the dress the wardrobe department had given her. I tried to console by telling her it looked lovely." For a time, Crawford idolized Shearer. "I tried to watch everything Norma did," wrote Crawford. "She dated Irving Thalberg, who was in charge of studio production. Thalberg would come by the set occasionally, a cool-looking, dark young man who tossed a gold coin in the air, tossed it and tossed it, with such concentration that you never dared speak to him." She never dared speak to him—because Shearer was dating him. Thus was born a rivalry that would worry M-G-M for the next fifteen years.

"They were complete opposites," wrote Frederica Maas. "As warm and outgoing as Norma was, Joan was cold and reserved. Norma was generous in spirit; Joan was calculating. She remained envious of Norma Shearer as their careers progressed." Irene Selznick viewed Crawford from her father's vantage point. "She blamed her overwhelming sense of rivalry on the preferred position Norma Shearer came to hold as Irving's wife. She overlooked the fact that Norma had been with the company since Mission Road and had traveled a long way." Forty years later, Crawford had not changed her mind. "Certainly Norma had an advantage," Crawford told Bob Thomas. "Any time an actress sleeps with the producer, she is bound to have an advantage. Sex is a very potent weapon."

Sex or no sex, Shearer had no claim on *Ex-Wife*. "Irving laughed at me when I told him I thought I could do [it]," said Shearer. "It was so utterly different from the type of thing with which I'd been associated." Shearer's maid, Ursula, heard the title *Ex-Wife* and said, "Oh, Miss Shearer, you don't want to play a part like that. She's almost a bad woman!" That was the point. Her last film, *Their Own Desire*, required no more from her than the portrayal of a naïve teenager; and she had turned twenty-seven on August 10. Said Shearer: "I had to prove to Irving that I could look sexy if it were necessary for the role." Crawford, who looked like she was dancing the Charleston even when she was walking, had no trouble looking sexy.

While Shearer was making *Their Own Desire*, Ramon Novarro visited the set to show her a portfolio of portraits he had recently commissioned. "Why, Ramon," exclaimed Shearer, "you've never been photographed like *this* before!" The images were obviously not the work of chief studio portraitist Ruth Harriet Louise. The stamped credit read: "George E. Hurrell, 672 South La Fayette Park Place, Los Angeles." It transpired that Novarro had gone to an atelier in the arty Westlake district to circumvent the studio publicists who printed photos he disliked. Shearer contemplated the Hurrell photos and started to strategize. "Norma planned her campaign carefully," said Thalberg. "She bought herself just about the goldest and most brocaded negligée she could find. Then she had portraits made wearing this gorgeous thing."

When Shearer arrived at Hurrell's studio in her canary-yellow Rolls-Royce, the photographer saw "a tough little gal, fighting in her own way to get the part." She sat Hurrell down on the boudoir furniture she had brought with her. "I loved your photographs of Mr. Novarro," she told the photographer. "Now there is a part in my husband's new picture that I must have. Can you turn me into a siren?"

"I'll try," said Hurrell, with a modesty that belied his firecracker personality. "A great deal depended on the results of that sitting," recalled Hurrell, "but if Norma was nervous, there was nothing to indicate it. She spent the better part of the day being photographed, and I remember that I used more than sixty plates . . . the height of lavishness."

Shearer could not keep her secret from Thalberg. "She was like an excited child as she waited for the proofs," said Thalberg. Indeed, she was so excited that she brought the special "red proofs" to a jaunt on Joseph Schenck's yacht *Invader*, where sunlight quickly faded them. Hurrell rushed out a second set, which Shearer presented to Thalberg in his office. He was duly impressed. "Why, I believe you *can* play that role!" he beamed. When Hurrell delivered the finished prints, Thalberg knew he was looking at the work of an extraordinary artist. Shearer had sat for some distinguished photographers, but none of them had seen the sensual young woman Thalberg knew—or thought he knew. He instructed publicity director Howard Strickling to offer Hurrell the post of chief portrait photographer, since Louise was retiring on December 31. When Hurrell accepted, Thalberg had a new marketing tool. He spent the end of 1929 reacquainting himself with his wife, trying to find the person Hurrell had captured in those remarkable images. Before the year ended, Thalberg had another surprise from Shearer; he was going to be a father.

After the distractions, stress, and tumult of 1929, Irving Thalberg returned to his Culver City routine. Ahead of him lay a new year and a new decade. He had a child on the way and two years left to his Loew's contract, yet he could not dismiss thoughts of mortality. "I'd settle for another ten years," he confided to Albert Lewin in a reflective moment, and then, as usual, turned to the business at hand. He had to. Louis B. Mayer was spending a great deal of time away from the studio. In the spring of 1930 his daughter Edith married William Goetz, his daughter Irene married David Selznick, and his father died. These milestones did not distract him as much as his infatuation with politics; in the fall he was appointed vice-chairman of the Republican State Central Committee. More often than not, Thalberg found himself doing Mayer's work, negotiating contracts and welcoming talent.

There was George Hurrell, acceding to the position of head portrait photographer. There was the father-and-son writing-and-acting team of J. C. Nugent and Elliott Nugent. And there was Samuel Marx, Thalberg's friend from his early days at Universal's New York office; he had rediscovered him in a chance encounter on a New York street in December 1929. Thalberg was rushing from the Treasury Department to Loew's, and Marx was rushing to review a play for *Amusements*, a free periodical he edited. Although Thalberg was respectful of Marx's enterprise, he could not resist offering him something better. "Why don't you try screenwriting?" he asked Marx. "Get a leave of absence from your paper and come to the

Coast." Marx was hesitant about leaving his new wife, but Thalberg insisted. "I'll give you the same money you're getting now and if it works out I'll give you a raise. At least you'll have a vacation with pay." Marx gave Thalberg a tentative yes, and Thalberg proceeded to 1540 Broadway, where Nick Schenck was crowing about matinee audiences at both the Astor and the Capitol. "They'll go see anything!" laughed Schenck. "We can make money showing blank film!"

Skeptics could have pointed out that M-G-M was trailing Warners, but in the big-city theaters, Leo the Lion was as loud as Vitaphone. Thanks to the talkies, every studio was doing record business. Weekly attendance was 90 million—in a country with a population of 122 million. The average movie ticket was fifteen cents. Estimates claimed that movies accounted for 75 percent of America's entertainment spending. This was the rosy picture in early 1930. A closer look would reveal somber strokes. The stock market crash had been followed by a series of smaller crashes. Instead of regaining its former strength or leveling out, the market kept sliding. By mid-1930, more than five hundred banks had closed, business was 20 per cent below normal, and factories were closing. Breadlines were beginning to form on city streets. As Frederick Lewis Allen wrote a year later, "Each employee thrown out of work decreased the potential buying power of the country." Talk of a depression began to circulate. For the moment, Hollywood was insulated from these realities, and although M-G-M was raking in the cash, Thalberg was discovering just how costly it was to make sound films—at every stage of the process. A sound film took twice as long to shoot as a silent did, and almost that long to write and edit. He would spend most of 1930 trying to speed up the assembly line, only to learn that haste makes waste.

On Monday mornings, Thalberg could be found on the second floor of the executive building, the three-story structure facing Washington Boulevard. "Irving had French doors in his office," recalled publicist Howard Dietz. "He could look through the glass and see all the approaches to Metro." Thalberg knew who was coming through the studio gates below, on the way to a story conference with him. While he waited, he reviewed the stack of scripts that he had taken home over the weekend and tried to ignore the mail on his desk. "If I leave it there long enough," he said to his secretary, "I don't have to answer it." On one morning in early 1930 he dropped his reserve long enough to give a warm welcome to a group of writers who had been with him since the merger—Dorothy Farnum, Waldemar Young, Joe Farnham, John Colton, and Frances Marion—his tried-and-true scenarists.

"How'd you like to turn out some original stories?" Thalberg asked his writers.

This would give newly contracted playwrights some competition. One veteran wanted to know if he would be writing for an established studio star or for a new contractee. Did Irving want a vehicle for Ramon Novarro or for Lawrence Tibbett, the Metropolitan Opera star? "You'll decide that when your story is finished," answered Thalberg.

"Comedy, melodrama, or tearjerker?" asked another writer.

"Choose your own weapon," said Thalberg, "and go to work."

Of all the writers in his office that day, only Frances Marion came up with an original, *The Big House*. Cameraman-turned-director George Hill had written a short treatment for a prison story. Marion took it over, went to San Quentin to do firsthand research, and submitted a first draft. "Don't go ahead with a finished script," Thalberg told her. "Right now, with everything in flux, we had better see what catches the public's eye." Two prison riots changed his mind. Hill ultimately directed Marion's script for *The Big House*.

After Hill directed Marion's *Min and Bill* (which made full-fledged stars of Wallace Beery and Marie Dressler), Marion decided to marry him. Thalberg rarely involved himself in his employees' lives, but this time he made an exception. "Irving was the only one who opposed the marriage," wrote Marion, "and he talked to me frankly. George was a fine man, but he was also temperamental, exceedingly high-strung, and easily upset if everything did not run smoothly. He would walk off, leave us in the lurch, then return, contrite, to try and pick up the tangled skein where he'd left it." Marion reminded Thalberg that the film business was full of personalities with "tempers and temperaments," but felt sure that Hill would be a good match. What Thalberg sensed but did not tell her was that Hill was prone to alcoholic rages. Marion married Hill, and his daily drinking doomed the marriage.

Thalberg enjoyed the company of writers, and though he could relate a story and make a compelling pitch, he doubted his own ability to sit down and compose. Curiously enough, this is what he was asked to do in early 1930. The document he had cowritten in 1927, "The Don'ts and Be Carefuls," had proven powerless to hush the adult tone of the talkies. One reason was that many of them were adapted from plays; there was no censorship on Broadway. Another reason was that most films used the Vitaphone sound-on-disc process; there was no way a censor could cut a line of dialogue from a sixteen-inch acetate disc. As a result, the rough language and risqué situations that had been confined to Broadway were being loosed upon an entire nation. One outspoken critic was Daniel Lord, S.J., a drama professor at St. Louis University and editor of the Catholic youth magazine *The*

Queen's Work. "Plots had narrowed down to seduction and murder and illegitimate children and immoral women and rapacious men," wrote Lord. "Even Hollywood, clamoring for authors, grew alarmed over the authors who came and the material they began to inject into their films. Silent smut had been bad. Vocal smut cried to the censors for vengeance."

Church leaders and clubwomen were the most outspoken critics of the talkies, but Martin Quigley, Catholic publisher of the trade paper the *Exhibitor's Herald*, was also sounding a tocsin. If Will Hays and the MPPDA did not take action against low-minded films, he warned, Congress would enact federal censorship, and Hollywood's waterfall of profits would dry up. It was in this charged atmosphere that Hays urged Thalberg to collaborate with Jason Joy of the Studio Relations Committee on an updated code. They called their first draft "General Principles to Govern the Preparation of a Revised Code of Ethics for Talking Pictures." Quigley, meanwhile, enlisted the aid of Father Lord, and together they drafted "The Reasons Supporting the Code." With input from Fox Film, Paramount, and Warners, Thalberg and Joy completed the "General Principles" in January 1930. Their document began, "No picture shall be produced which will lower the moral standards of those who see it."

To join the two documents into a cohesive code required meetings and debates. It was obvious to the Hollywood phalanx that Lord, Quigley, and the "Midwest Catholics" wanted nothing less than to arbitrate the "morality of entertainment," forcing the studios to present a fantasy world in which there was neither sin nor conflict. Drama without conflict would not be entertainment. "We do not create these types of entertainment," Thalberg explained in a debate on February 10. "We merely present them. The motion picture does not present the audience with tastes and manners and views and morals; it reflects those they already have. . . . The motion picture is literally bound to the mental and moral level of its vast audience."

Father Lord, not about to let Thalberg get away with this rationalization, insisted that scenes of wickedness could be shown on the screen only if the film offered "compensating moral values." When Thalberg and Lord could not agree on how to implement this loophole, Hays adjourned the meeting and sent Lord and Quigley to work out a solution. Their "Code to Govern the Making of Silent, Synchronized and Talking Motion Pictures" was accepted by Thalberg and his peers on February 17 and ratified by the New York Board of the MPPDA on March 31. An editorial in the *New York World* chuckled, "That the Code will actually be applied in any sincere and thorough way, we have not the slightest belief." In truth,

Thalberg had been cooperating with Joy and the SRC, but he saw no reason that this document should hinder his high-priced scribes.

The Broadway invasion did not begin with talkies. Herman Mankiewicz had deserted the Algonquin Round Table in 1926 to write *The Road to Mandalay* for Thalberg and dozens of films for Jesse Lasky, pausing long enough to send Ben Hecht the much-quoted telegram: "Will you accept three hundred per week to work for Paramount Pictures? All expenses paid. Millions are to be grabbed out here and your only competition is idiots. Don't let this get around." The talkies' dependence on dialogue led to Broadway, and Thalberg summoned Broadway's best. Among those who answered his call was playwright John Howard Lawson, whose first assignment was a talking sequence for Greta Garbo and John Gilbert. The dreamlike scene (intended for *A Woman of Affairs*) was never filmed, but writing it gave Lawson an insight. "Thalberg read every word slowly," recalled Lawson, "and then spoke with genuine surprise: 'There's an *idea* in it.'" Lawson later saw his idea expanded into a transitional sequence in *The Trial of Mary Dugan* (among other films). The zoom lens had been in use at the studio since the 1927 Norma Shearer film *After Midnight,* but Lawson's surrealist template gave it a context; while images dissolved in and out, the lens compressed perspective in its unnatural way and audiences felt Mary Dugan's fear at entering the courtroom for the first time.

Thalberg was determined to compress time, too. He needed to catch up with both Warners and Paramount; the obvious way was to accelerate production. John Arnold, head of the camera department, had gotten the camera out of its sound-proof box by designing a streamlined silver "camera blimp," an insulated metal case that could be fitted around the whirring Mitchell camera. The combo was then placed on a tripod that had wheels large enough to minimize vibration during moving shots. This breakthrough should have enabled every M-G-M director to return to the mobility of the silent screen, but Thalberg had another imperative. He decided that instead of capturing a scene from various angles (wide shot, two-shot, over-the-shoulder, tracking shot in or out of the scene), the director must record every dialogue scene with two (and often three) blimped cameras—one for the wide angle and the others for closer views of the actors. This would give the film editor the "coverage" he or she required without spending time—and, consequently, money—on additional angles.

Multiple-camera angles had to allow for movement during the scene, so a traditional over-the-shoulder reaction shot was impossible. Awkward three-quarter angles were now the norm, replacing the powerful, plot-propelling closeups that had distinguished M-G-M silents. Paramount's films used traditional one-camera setups and were, as a result, more cinematic, even if they were also shooting "canned theater." Watching an M-G-M film, the viewer felt a subliminal urge to step in front of the actor. This annoying practice caused more problems than it solved. Seventeen out of forty-nine M-G-M films released in 1930 failed to make a profit.

Among the casualties were eight musicals, two of which were personally produced by Thalberg. He and Mayer had high hopes for Metropolitan Opera stars Grace Moore and Lawrence Tibbett. Moore, the celebrated soprano from Jellico, Tennessee, was nervous about playing Jenny Lind in *A Lady's Morals*. Thalberg attempted to bolster Moore's confidence by comparing her latest footage to her first screen test. "Look!" he said. "What a difference!" He fell into his own trap when it became obvious that Moore had gained more weight than acting experience.

"It's the lighting," she explained.

Thalberg pointed to his private bathroom. "Come and see my scale." He had similar problems with Tibbett. "Mr. Tibbett announced his arrival as a film star by breaking all the valves with his full-throated singing," reported Doug Shearer. When Tibbett's first film, *The Rogue Song*, opened, a *Variety* critic wrote: "A lot of people are going to find it hard to reconcile that huge physique and terrific voice with Tibbett's round and rather pudgy face." Neither Tibbett nor Moore had a hit at M-G-M.

Part of the problem was that the public was tired of musical films. Cecil B. DeMille, the only M-G-M director who did not report to Thalberg, made a colossal film called *Madam Satan*, but even the autocratic DeMille had to bow to convention. "Nothing would do but that it should be a musical," DeMille ruefully recalled. "The characters had to burst into song at frequent intervals." *Madam Satan* did not need tuneless songs to tell the story of a woman who masquerades as a vamp to win back her husband. It had a spectacular finale set on a doomed zeppelin. True to form, DeMille had the zeppelin crash, spilling weirdly costumed partygoers into incongruous settings; the vampy Lillian Roth crashes through the skylight of a men's locker room. Thalberg shook his head at the film, saying: "It contains no semblance of reality." *Madam Satan* flopped, but Thalberg was in no position to criticize.

In March former president Calvin Coolidge visited the studio and watched the filming of *The March of Time*, a two-color Technicolor musical. After viewing several costly but lifeless sequences, Thalberg halted production. "Why spend money trying to turn a lemon into a lime?" he asked. In September he and Hearst decided on the same action when a Marion Davies musical called *Rosalie* sent disappointing footage from its West Point location. (He had also stopped a Davies film, *The Five O'Clock Girl*, in 1928 because Hearst was displeased with it.)

In late September, Joan Crawford returned from shooting in New Orleans and told Thalberg that she could not finish the musical *Great Day*. He felt that he could improve it, but Crawford was adamant. She went to Mayer, who had just returned from Washington, and pleaded with him. "Well, I'm dreadful, Mr. Mayer," she said. "Southern drawl I can do but I just can't talk baby talk." Mayer looked at the *Great Day* rushes and saw Crawford being forced to play a spiritless ingénue. He halted production and then spoke to Thalberg about the surprising number of aborted films. "You control the artistic side," Mayer said. "I'm only a businessman. But that makes it my job to decide if a picture can make money."

"Musicals are a special type," sighed Thalberg. "And I haven't found the right approach." Part of the problem was that Thalberg could not muster the feeling for notes that he could for words. "When it came to musicals, Irving was basically for the operetta," recalled Arthur Freed. "He never did understand what we call musical comedy." When Freed saw the musical vogue wane, he expected to be let go. Thalberg surprised him: "Arthur, you can be here as long as I'm here."

Musical or not, Thalberg's search for screen material continued. One of his few concessions to life outside the studio (other than a token involvement in the Mayfair Club) was a busman's holiday. He attended legitimate theater productions in Los Angeles, where touring companies played recent hits such as *Strange Interlude*. Excited by the greatness he saw in live performances, he would return to M-G-M and become frustrated with his writers' plodding output. "Why are there so many writers and so few ideas?" he asked sixty employees in a meeting on a soundstage. "Perhaps you don't *care* about your work. You must realize that this studio cannot live without ideas." The story department comprised five units: secretarial, research, story acquisition, readers, and writers. The ideas that Thalberg needed so badly had to come through this department, which was currently headed by an aspiring writer named Robert Harris. In May 1930 Samuel Marx arrived unannounced at the front gates of M-G-M, and only his special place in Thalberg's personal history got him past the guards. "What brings you to California?" Thalberg asked him.

"Pardon me while I collapse," answered Marx. "I thought I was going to work for you."

Thalberg smiled as he recalled the sidewalk conversation in New York six months earlier and then buzzed for an assistant to take Marx to his new office. "I was wondering where I'd find someone to take this job," said Thalberg. "I think you can handle it. If you'd shown up yesterday I'd have given you an assignment and forgotten you. If you'd arrived tomorrow the position would have been filled." Marx was settling into his office before it occurred to him to ask what the job was. It was Robert Harris's job—story editor. Thalberg's loyalty to Marx was rewarded. After ten years on Broadway, Marx knew American letters. "Thalberg wanted superior writing," wrote Marx. "Several times during my first days on the job he reminded me to be on the lookout for important literary talent and to go after it at whatever cost." Within a few months, Marx had begun the recruitment of some major American talent.

Already in residence at M-G-M was playwright Charles MacArthur, one half of Hecht and MacArthur, the authors of the wild—and wildly successful—play *The Front Page*. "Irving Thalberg was a fine boss for MacArthur," wrote Ben Hecht. "The soft-eyed, skimpy-limbed genius of Metro saw quickly into Charlie's talent. Unlike his assistant, Bernie Hyman, Irving's delight in the new Metro employee included a respect for his carefully created sentences." MacArthur's first assignment was a William Haines movie, *The Girl Said No*. The more-than-accomplished dramatist cheerfully turned in his first draft to Hyman, only to be told: "I know less about writing than you do. But so does the audience. My tastes are exactly those of the audience. What I didn't like, the audience won't like." Hyman cut pages of MacArthur's best work. Thalberg restored them.

Other Broadway recruits included Willard Mack, whose initial success with *Voice of the City* and *Madame X* made him a scenario workhorse, turning out eight movies in less than two years. The equally prolific Al Boasberg specialized in comedies and often collaborated with Robert ("Hoppy") Hopkins, who could not construct a plot to save his job but was never at a loss for a one-liner—or an insult. "What's all this crap about heroes?" Hopkins asked in the privacy of the writers' building one day. "Who needs heroes in this fucking business? I can make a snake a hero. The villain grabs the girl's tits and the snake stings him in the ass. Audience cheers. Snake's a hero. Get it? Only business in the world that can make a fucking snake a hero."

A more reserved writer was Sidney Howard, whom Thalberg hired to turn his Pulitzer Prize–winning play *They Knew What They Wanted* into an M-G-M opus called *A Lady to Love*. Howard did his work quickly and quietly, and then returned to his Massachusetts farm to write more plays. Thalberg hoped *A Lady to Love* would restore silent star Vilma Banky (who had been dropped by Samuel Goldwyn because of her Hungarian accent) and make a star of Edward G. Robinson (who had impressed Thalberg with his portrayal of a gangster in Bartlett Cormack's play *The Racket*). To direct the film, Thalberg chose Victor Seastrom, the artist who had given M-G-M its first success. Confronted with multiple cameras and pages of dialogue, Seastrom began to wish he was in Sweden. Robinson was at first intimidated. "I was ready to read the play and rehearse," wrote Robinson. "But there was no reading and no rehearsal. We plunged into the middle of the film, and it did not take long to realize that Miss Banky was seriously out of her depth. My heart went out to her, and I tried to help. Mr. Seastrom didn't seem to try at all. He was as frightened as Miss Banky." After the film was completed, both Banky and Seastrom turned their backs on Hollywood. Robinson's robust portrayal of a middle-aged Italian winegrower caught the public's fancy, however, and he found himself in Thalberg's office, discussing a six-film, million-dollar contract.

"Look, Mr. Thalberg," said Robinson, "I'm essentially a stage actor. That's where my loyalties are. Couldn't we settle for a six-month contract? You see, I don't want to be away from the theater any longer than that."

"We don't operate that way at M-G-M," said Thalberg patiently. "If we're going to build you into a star, we want to enjoy the cumulative benefits. And I might add that the benefits to you will be considerable, too." Robinson saw Thalberg's cordiality giving way to disdain. Robinson had only recently become a Broadway name—yet he was questioning Thalberg's judgment. "He assured me," wrote Robinson, "that he well understood my devotion to the theater (he himself was a theater buff) but I should realize that it was, if not a dying art, certainly one soon to be replaced by the talking film. . . . I compromised on some minor points, certainly demonstrating some good will. Thalberg compromised on nothing. He sat there, stern and immovable—the godhead. I disliked him thoroughly. His eyes showed me that an actor was beneath contempt." Then Robinson did the unthinkable. He turned down the million-dollar contract. "My agent and I abruptly left Thalberg's office. Then, trying to hide myself from the extras and executives in front of his building, I vomited."

The resistance Thalberg got from Robinson was nothing compared to the fool-hardy hostility of Charles Bickford, another newly famous stage actor. Bickford was invited to meet Thalberg, Mayer, and Harry Rapf in the executive dining room; his performance in DeMille's *Dynamite* was being discussed. The burly red-head strode into the room with DeMille and eyeballed his hosts. "Irving Thalberg seemed a bit out of place in this company," wrote Bickford. "He impressed me as a personable young man who had somehow fallen in with bad companions. Frail, unhealthy-looking (his skin had a bluish tinge), his eyes revealed intelligence and sensitivity. I liked him on sight and tabbed him as someone I could probably talk to on my own level."

Mayer praised Bickford and offered him the male lead in *Anna Christie*, Greta Garbo's talkie debut and the most anticipated film of 1930. Incredibly, Bickford griped about the size of the role. Thalberg took Bickford aside. "Thalberg said that the picture would expose me to millions of Garbo fans throughout the world," wrote Bickford, "and create the following necessary to make me a motion-picture star." Thalberg was also getting resistance from Garbo, who had reservations about Eugene O'Neill's play. "She says it portrays Swedes as low characters," said Harry Edington, her manager.

"You don't suppose we'll end up having to make them Americans?" asked Frances Marion, who was writing the script.

"They're American citizens," said Thalberg.

"What if Miss Garbo refuses to make the picture?" asked Edington.

"I try not to take people off salary," replied Thalberg, "but if she turns down this role, I will stop her paycheck."

Both Garbo and Bickford cooperated; the filming of *Anna Christie* went smoothly. Garbo's voice recorded well (according to the sound engineer), Bickford's blustering fit the character of Matt, and director Clarence Brown even managed to include some closeups, lovingly lit by William Daniels. Bickford expected better things to follow; instead, Thalberg decided to loan him to Universal for a low-budget film. "It's bad enough to play second fiddle to Garbo," snarled Bickford. "I didn't come to Hollywood to be a stooge. I won't do it."

"Where do you get off coming in here and telling me what you will or will not do?" asked Thalberg. "You're under contract to this studio and you'll do as you're told!"

Bickford growled and groused, but he went to Universal. Thalberg next put him in a couple of films that Bickford considered "lousy," William Demille's *Passion Flower* (a hit) and Wesley Ruggles's *The Sea Bat*. "With blood in my eye," wrote Bickford, "I crashed into Thalberg's office, only to be immediately disarmed by his appearance. In the two-month interval since I had seen him, he had lost considerable weight, his color was ghastly, and he looked very tired. My anger melted into concern. I apologized for adding my comparably petty troubles to his already top-heavy burden of responsibilities. With a wan smile he brushed away my concern." Thalberg's tone changed when Bickford challenged his authority. "Don't get sarcastic with me, Charlie," said Thalberg. "I only work here, too, you know." When Bickford started for the door, Thalberg shouted at him. "Will you, for Christ's sake, stop acting like a spoiled child and listen to me? There's nothing I can do about *The Sea Bat*. It's been sold on next year's program and we have to make it."

Bickford was summoned to Mayer's office, where he made the mistake of cursing out the most powerful man in Hollywood. Having surpassed Marshall Neilan, Erich von Stroheim, and John Gilbert in defiance, the unrepentant Bickford left M-G-M. He could not find work at any studio for two years.

Robinson, who had angered Thalberg but not Mayer, shot to stardom in Warner Bros.' *Little Caesar*, but was never requested for a loan-out by Thalberg's M-G-M. Both cases were regrettable, if only because the talkies had revealed M-G-M's lack of male star power. Although they were still popular, John Gilbert, William Haines, Ramon Novarro, and Nils Asther were limited in the roles they could play. The studio's biggest male star had not yet made a talkie. Part of Lon Chaney's delay was due to illness, and part was due to a sincere reluctance. "I don't want to talk and spoil any illusion," he explained to Thalberg.

"You've done all kinds of dialect and character stuff on the stage," Thalberg reasoned. "Just use a couple of voices and let 'em guess."

Chaney had to negotiate his contract with Mayer. The sticking point was a bonus of $75,000, which Mayer insisted would be a loan, not a bonus. Chaney refused to sign. Thalberg invited him to his office and persuaded him to accept a $50,000 bonus. Chaney agreed, and Thalberg chose to remake *The Unholy Three* as Chaney's sound debut. Supervisor Hyman hired the Nugents to write the script, but soon decided that they should base it on Tod Browning's silent version. As Elliott Nugent recalled in 1976, "Hyman kept talking about 'In the silent we did this; in the silent we did that,' so we had a moviola put in our office, and we would run the silent. We wrote the screenplay with the same continuity. Then they were satisfied!" Filming commenced on April 1, just as *Redemption*, which had been shot a year earlier as John Gilbert's first talkie, was finally being released.

"Dull, sluggish, agonizing," wrote a *Variety* critic. "Hardly a redeeming aspect. Even the photography, editing and other taken-for-granted items are under standard.... *Redemption* is unworthy of first runs, regardless of John Gilbert." The film had opened at the Capitol but did not last long, even in the second-run houses. The question was why the film was released at all. If the studio had hoped to redeem Gilbert, this was not the vehicle. His voice, in spite of journalistic jibes, was not high-pitched. It did not have the roundness of Conrad Nagel's, who was also in *Redemption*, but it certainly was not "several tones higher than most men's," as a fan magazine claimed, quoting (of course) an unnamed source.

Gilbert's real problem, something that could have been easily corrected after viewing the first rushes, was an excess of gesture. When he flailed his arms and flexed his back, when he punctuated each line of dialogue with a dancing eyebrow, he looked as if he were doing a parody of the most overripe performance of 1910. Even more damaging was his insistence on pronouncing every consonant with grisly vividness. Most scenes showed him declaiming his guilt and contemplating either a gun or a glass of vodka, all in a desperate, humorless pitch and with the same absurd diction. Per the new strictures, the film had no closeups, so the magic of his flashing eyes and mile-wide smile could not help him. *Redemption* confirmed what the fan magazines had been saying, that the Great Lover of the Silent Screen was the Big Joke of the Talkies.

Sam Marx was collared by Thalberg and instructed to find a literary property to restore Gilbert. He came up with a rough-and-tumble novel about the merchant marine, *Way for a Sailor*. While Gilbert stayed idle, a stationary target for the press, Thalberg inexplicably allowed four writers (including Laurence Stallings and Charles MacArthur) to spend six long months turning a colorful novel into an execrable script. With Thalberg producing, the usually competent Sam Wood made a grimy, tiresome film. "This can't be considered complete ruination for Gilbert," said one charitable critic. "His voice isn't at all bad. His diction merely doesn't suit a hard-boiled sailor character." *Way for a Sailor* lost $670,000, the second-highest loss since the merger; a goodly portion of it was due to Gilbert's salary. "Just before Gilbert did his first talkie," P. G. Wodehouse wrote to a friend, "they signed him up for six more at $250,000 a picture, and the thought of having to pay those smackers gashes them like a knife. The rumor goes that in order to avoid this, they are straining every nerve to ensure that his next picture will be such a flop that he will consent to a brokenhearted settlement."

Thalberg had been Gilbert's friend and advocate from the beginning, but as in the case of Bickford, Thalberg could not overrule Mayer—if Mayer really wanted to destroy Gilbert. On the other hand, why would a corporation want to destroy a valuable asset? Thalberg believed in the resilience of great talents. "Once a star, always a star," he told Marx. "Actors aren't athletes. When you've been a champion in this business, you're always a champion." Gilbert had certainly been that. Surely five years of triumphs could not be erased by three flops. Unhappily for Gilbert, these simplistic equations did not allow for the random factors of show business. A fickle audience and an overworked executive could forget the accomplishments of an artist if his excesses were as grandiose as his acting style. Even at his most charming, Gilbert was hard on the nerves. He could not contain his performances, and he could not (or would not) cope with shifting fortunes. The Great Lover became the Great Drinker, thrashing about in black moods, brandishing a gun, marrying and divorcing with all the bad publicity he could attract. Even casual friendships became settings for his private melodrama.

After a party at Charles MacArthur's one night, Grace Moore innocently (and foolishly) agreed to go to Gilbert's home to hear his opera records. After setting a stack on the phonograph, he disappeared from the living room. "The records kept going," wrote Moore. "The time was flying without the host himself. Suddenly he reappeared. My eyes popped in amazement. Mr. Gilbert was virtually naked." Moore tried to maintain the composure of a New York prima donna as she watched Gilbert take a seat, pick up his glass of wine, and nonchalantly continue the conversation; he had gone swimming, it seemed. "Suddenly, having talked himself out, he leaned his head back on the couch and fell fast asleep. I tiptoed out for fear I should disturb him, such was his power to wake concern in a woman's heart. . . . Next day in my dressing room appeared twelve dozen American Beauty roses with a card inscribed, 'Why didn't you nudge me?'"

Gilbert's moodiness worsened after the dismal *Way for a Sailor*. He showed up at Thalberg's office drunk and argumentative. Thalberg attempted to placate him with the prospect of a better project; there were scripts in progress that could put him back on top, Wodehouse's play *Candlelight* and the novel *Susan Lenox*. Gilbert calmed down. Thalberg sensed that gangster films were going to be the next cycle, so he told Marx to find a gangster story for Gilbert, who had no choice but to wait.

After the misfires of Gilbert, Moore, Tibbett, Bickford, and Robinson, Thalberg found two stars without even looking. Once again, it happened because of Frances Marion's well-intentioned meddling. She knew that the forty-four-year-old screenwriter Lorna Moon was dying of tuberculosis. The publication of Moon's novel, *Dark Star*, would not generate enough money to pay her sanitarium expenses, and M-G-M would never buy the story of an abused Scottish girl who jumps off a cliff. Nevertheless Marion pitched the book to Thalberg. He remembered Moon but had not heard of *Dark Star*. "This is a rip-roaring comedy," Marion enthused, "laid right here in San Pedro, where the tuna fleet is anchored. We can change the title and find one that fits the rowdy main characters, Min and Bill, who live on Cannery Row." Marion's ploy worked. M-G-M paid Moon $7,500 for *Dark Star*, and she was able to move to a sanitarium in Arizona. She died there in May 1930, before the film was even cast.

Dark Star became *Min and Bill*, and its lead players, Marie Dressler and Wallace

Beery, became M-G-M's newest stars. "It was not until Frances wrote *Min and Bill* that I got a part after my own heart," wrote Dressler. "The moment I read the script, I knew that here was the role I had been waiting for all my life. . . . Min was the keeper of a wretched dump of a hotel on the water front. Bill was her man." The salty chemistry between sixty-year-one-old Dressler and forty-five-year-old Beery made *Min and Bill* the most profitable M-G-M film of the year. "The best tunes are played on an old violin," mused Dressler.

Thalberg had seen what Broadway did for its female stars—Helen Hayes, Katharine Cornell, Lynn Fontanne. The uniquely stirring moment when a star made her entrance left an impression on him as indelible as the first page of a classic had when he was sixteen years old, lying in his bed on Woodbine Street. Now that pictures could talk, it might be possible to bring that magic to the screen. And if he could not lure these grand personalities to Hollywood, he could groom his own stars in similar roles, giving them scenes with the same glamour. "The play was a showcase for the woman star," recalled Lawrence Weingarten. "Mr. Thalberg believed that. That's how we built the female stars, the Garbos and Shearers and Crawfords."

Turning Garbo into a talking-film star involved more than just recording her voice correctly, so Thalberg involved himself in the publicity for *Anna Christie*. He requested that ad art be made up from Clarence Bull's portraits of Garbo from her last film, *The Kiss*. Frank Whitbeck, a Fox West Coast Theaters advertising executive, brought large mounted prints to Thalberg's office and set them up on chairs along the walls so that Thalberg could stroll past them and visualize them as billboards. With his fingers knit tightly behind him, he walked the length of the display, quietly inspecting each mockup. Whitbeck waited for some sign of approval. Thalberg was inscrutable. After a ponderous silence, he finally spoke: "It's a good campaign, Frank, but it's just not what I want. And I can't even tell you what it is I *do* want!"

Two hours passed and Thalberg had not solved the problem. The glowing soft-focus images were marvelous but did not convey the excitement that was Thalberg's connection to the theater. The moment that was going to electrify audiences—he hoped—was Garbo's entrance and her first words emanating from the screen. But how to get that into an ad campaign? Whitbeck strode over to Thalberg's desk, grabbed a used manila envelope, and attacked it with a pencil. A picture came into being, a massive billboard, large enough for a 24-sheet. On the billboard were two words: GARBO TALKS.

"That's it!" cried Thalberg, whacking Whitbeck's back. "Now get the hell out of here."

Variety agreed with Thalberg: "'Garbo Talks' is, beyond quarrel, an event of major box-office significance." Released in February 1930, *Anna Christie* became the highest-grossing Hollywood film of 1930, but because of Garbo's salary, it was not as profitable as *Min and Bill*. M-G-M's next most lucrative star was Norma Shearer. It was not her determination to play the scandalous *Ex-Wife* that moved Thalberg to push the film through the Hays Office before the new Production Code went into effect; it was the film's box-office potential. Indeed, Thalberg was not totally convinced that his wife should play the promiscuous Jerry. "She had to fight all the studio heads—including myself—to put her idea over," Thalberg told the SRC's Jason Joy. "Norma is a very . . . *strong-minded* girl. She knows what she wants. And she usually gets it. And she's usually right." Thalberg went on to stress that his script "presents divorce in the light of the growing evil it is looked upon to be, but . . . with less suspicion than that with which it was looked upon before." He had consulted with Father Sullivan, president of Loyola College, who agreed that "a picture based on this treatment will do a tremendous amount of good in the deterrence of divorces." The Montana-born Joy, a former Red Cross executive, was the least contentious of censors. He usually tried to find a way to rework objectionable material without compromising the plot. He approved the filming of *Ex-Wife*, provided that Thalberg change its title to *The Divorcee* and refrain from mentioning the novel in advertising.

Aided by Robert Z. Leonard, Shearer threw herself into the controversial role of a working woman whose husband's infidelity tests her own code; learning that he has betrayed her, she impulsively sleeps with his best friend. On April 3, Shearer and Thalberg took a break from editing their film to attend the second Academy Awards ceremony. He was roundly applauded when his *Broadway Melody* won the Best Picture Award. After *The Divorcee*, Thalberg rushed his pregnant wife into a film that was a variation on its theme. In *Let Us Be Gay*, she portrayed Kitty, a mousy, no-makeup mother of two with a wandering husband. When she finds out he has a girlfriend, Kitty divorces him and transforms herself into a woman of the world. Unlike *The Divorcee*, this makeover parable was played for laughs, with Marie Dressler as Kitty's grumpy duenna. "We had lots of fun making this one," recalled Shearer. "Miss Dressler was always forgetting her lines and making up clever new ones. I was definitely, as the French say, 'in bloom.' I became clever, too, hiding myself behind sequined fans, pieces of furniture, and even behind Miss Dressler."

Costume designer Gilbert Adrian, who had come to M-G-M two years earlier with Cecil B. DeMille, used various tricks to disguise Shearer's condition, but her new weight was not unattractive; she looked voluptuous. "I'm having a baby to get Irving away from Henrietta," she confided to a select few. Thalberg was highly solicitous of her health, and other than working on this film, Shearer was cautious in the extreme. "She allowed nothing to interfere with the regimen her doctor had laid down for her," said Dressler. "She wouldn't eat a mouthful of anything unless it was on that diet." Shearer could not disguise her nervousness and had to ask for numerous retakes. After completing *Let Us Be Gay*, Shearer went into seclusion and awaited the arrival of her baby—and the premiere of *The Divorcee*.

"She affects a laugh that is used too frequently to be effective," carped one review of *The Divorcee*, but most critics praised Shearer's performance and commented on her daring new image. "It was a tremendous gamble," she later admitted, "but it was a lucky one." Indeed, *The Divorcee*'s opening week broke attendance records at the twelve-hundred-seat Fox Criterion Theatre and became a nationwide sensation.

As Shearer moved into the final term of her pregnancy, she had a tête-à-tête with her mother-in-law. "Alas," said Norma to Henrietta, "we just can't live here any more. With a little one, we will be too many. Isn't that a pity?" Shearer took pains to assure Henrietta that Irving's health would be as closely monitored as ever. Henrietta accepted the inevitable gracefully but not happily; for once, there was nothing she could do. Shearer waited until she was gone before breathing a sigh of relief. "It was the only way I could get out of there!" she later told Irene Selznick. Thalberg consulted with architect John Byers, and plans were drawn up for a home on the beach in Santa Monica.

Shearer's pregnancy made her surrender a plum role. The script was *Paid*, a talkie version of Bayard Veiller's 1912 play *Within the Law*. Thalberg assigned the lead, not to Ruth Chatterton or Kay Johnson, but to Joan Crawford, who had been begging for a strong dramatic part. "If I have to do any more three-girl dancing daughter stories, I'll kick somebody," said Crawford. "A role like that is like holding a handful of sand. I need something to mold. I like the 'drab.' I want to play a human being in the gutter. But when I express my idea of such a story, everybody goes 'Ugh!'" In *Paid*, she played a shopgirl, unjustly sent to prison by a department store magnate, who learns enough legal loopholes in the prison library to exact revenge through his playboy son. After two years of stardom, Crawford proved that she, too, could tackle a tough assignment. Her three 1930 films were right behind Shearer's in profitability. What M-G-M was losing in male star power (Keaton, Haines, and Novarro notwithstanding) it was making up with Dressler, Garbo, Shearer, and Crawford.

On August 24, Shearer gave birth to a son, Irving Thalberg Jr., in Good Samaritan Hospital. Thalberg was overjoyed as a crowd of producers and department heads greeted him at the studio gates. He emerged from his car, raised his hands to quiet their cheers, and announced: "My son has the intelligence of a three-week-old!" When he reached his office, there was a sobering message on his desk. Lon Chaney was in St. Vincent's Hospital in grave condition. The stubborn ailment that had been dogging the actor for a year had finally been diagnosed as carcinoma of the bronchus. Chaney was forty-seven. His talking-picture debut a month earlier in *The Unholy Three* had been an unqualified success. In two days he was dead.

Thalberg delivered the eulogy at Chaney's funeral, using the word "great" to describe the unique artist with whom he had forged the American horror film. "Great not only because of his God-given talent," said Thalberg, "but also because he used that talent to illuminate certain dark corners of the human spirit. He showed the world the souls of those people who were born different than us."

Chaney's funeral was the second Thalberg attended in 1930. The first was Mabel Normand's in March. He had rushed to the mortuary from a *Billy the Kid* story conference with King Vidor and Laurence Stallings, not telling them where he was taking them. They tried to shift gears as best they could, but Thalberg did not bother. As the priest chanted *"Dies irae"* at the altar, Thalberg whispered: "Too many murders."

"Was Mabel murdered?" asked Vidor, thinking of her alleged involvement in the 1922 William Desmond Taylor murder.

"No," said Thalberg. "Billy the Kid. Too many killings. The public won't accept it." When the priest suddenly stopped speaking, Thalberg's voice carried to nearby pews: "Why not kill him before he gets to the hotel?"

"In that silence, he sounded titanic," recalled Stallings. Lew Cody, Normand's widower, was not amused.

Shearer was tending to her newborn son in a rented house in Santa Monica when she achieved one more triumph. On November 5, at the third Academy Awards ceremony, she was announced Best Actress for her performance in *The Divorcee*. In 1930, endorsed by Hollywood and guided by Thalberg, she transcended stardom and became a regal entity. She had first call on the best plays, novels, and original stories. "Norma Shearer was Big Queen then," Grace Moore wrote years later. "She landed at her dressing room in the shiny yellow Thalberg Rolls-Royce while the gentry bowed and scraped. But Norma, in spite of the Hollywoodian grandeur, was a very simple, hospitable woman. She and Thalberg complemented each other perfectly. They were very happy and very much in love. They entertained well and surrounded themselves with all that was rich and satisfying in their position. They had the capacity—which is more than many have—of savoring all the joy of their good fortune."

In truth, Shearer's only competition came from people like Moore, stars whom Thalberg was importing from Broadway. The theater was feeling the effects of a worsening depression, yet M-G-M finished the year with an astonishing profit of $15 million. Thalberg felt justified in making a handsome offer to any Broadway star who was interested. Ignoring unemployment, breadlines, and the Production Code, he was molding a new type of entertainment.

PART FOUR • "HIS BRAIN IS
THE CAMERA"

Irving Thalberg and Norma Shearer each began 1931 with a head cold. To most people, this would signify a psychogenic reaction to stress. To Shearer, Thalberg's illness signaled something deeper. "After abusing his health outrageously," Shearer recalled, "Irving would suddenly become worried. This was amusing—somewhat. After a grueling week, he would get conscience-stricken and crawl into bed. Then he would start feeling his pulse and reach for a pill. The doctor supplied Irving with a new kind and color of pill whenever he had a little ache or pain." With Thalberg safely tucked into bed for the holidays, Shearer went to her own doctor to prevent the onset of laryngitis, the last thing she needed on the eve of a new film, *Strangers May Kiss*. "We haven't been allowed to hold baby Irving or even go near him," Shearer lamented to Louella Parsons. "My only glimpse of him has been from the door." In 1931, with new directions in career and home life, Shearer and Thalberg would see more of their son.

For the first time since the merger, Thalberg was reducing his workload. Instead of personally supervising a dozen films a year, he was now doing only two—a Greta Garbo film called *Inspiration* and a Shearer film based on Noël Coward's play *Private Lives*. His other personal projects were divided among his supervisors, who now numbered eight since the recruitment of Bernard Fineman. In truth, Thalberg was still shepherding every film.

Enchanted by Broadway, Thalberg had begun to pursue his vision of a new entertainment, a synthesis of cinema and theater. Nineteen thirty had been highly profitable for M-G-M. Thalberg could afford not only playwrights but also stage stars, so he started at the top. Ethel Barrymore, the "First Lady of Broadway," responded with a polite no. So did Katharine Cornell, the "Great Lady of the Stage." Tallulah Bankhead, the "Bad Girl of Broadway," was already in films. Helen Hayes had no title yet, but she had been a stage star for nearly a decade. She was married to M-G-M screenwriter Charles MacArthur, so Thalberg had an advantage. He instructed J. Robert Rubin to approach her in New York. Hayes found Rubin pushy. "No," she told her husband in a transcontinental call. "I won't go to the Coast." Thalberg called Hayes himself.

"Disregard your dealings with Loew's," he said. "I'll handle your contract personally." As soon as Hayes signed with him, she was flattered with offers from other studios; she agreed to make *A Farewell to Arms* for Jesse Lasky and *Arrowsmith* for Samuel Goldwyn—once she finished her first M-G-M film. When Hayes arrived in Culver City, she was optimistic. "Charlie and Irving had hit it off and become fast friends," wrote Hayes. "Irving treated him—and all writers—with respect, an unusual attitude when most studio executives tended to put writers at the bottom of the totem pole." MacArthur expected Thalberg to find a worthwhile property for Hayes's debut, and he bribed typist Nellie Farrell to let him look at the script. He was at first incredulous, then furious; it was a mawkish tale of a self-sacrificing mother.

"God damn it, Irving!" MacArthur exploded in Thalberg's office. "You can't do this to Helen!"

"What's the matter?"

"I've violated a studio rule. I know that. But by God! This script! You know what it is? It's Knoblock's *Lullaby*. It was rancid when Florence Reed played it years ago. You want Helen to play it *now?* You wouldn't ask Norma to do it! It would sink Garbo!"

"You don't like it?" Thalberg smiled. "Fine. You're a writer. You fix it."

With Hayes and MacArthur under control, Thalberg next approached the American theater's "First Couple," Alfred Lunt and Lynn Fontanne. Knowing Thalberg's reputation, the Lunts considered his offer. It was tempting—$60,000 for a single film. To further tantalize them, Thalberg bought the rights to Eugene O'Neill's *Strange Interlude*, which Fontanne had opened in 1928.

At this point, M-G-M's stars began to wonder what Thalberg was thinking. The big moneymakers of the last few months were Marie Dressler, Greta Garbo, Norma Shearer, and Joan Crawford. The studio did not need new female stars; it needed vehicles for Wallace Beery, John Gilbert, Ramon Novarro, Buster Keaton, and William Haines. Thalberg's interest in Broadway did not bode well for them, and his preoccupation with Shearer vexed his female stars. He had three expensive projects planned for her, in spite of his stance on overexposure. Yet if anyone was tempted to question his judgment, it was hard to question a profit of $15 million, especially when Paramount's had fallen to $8 million.

Fifteen months after the stock market crash, the film industry was feeling the effects of the depression. Six million Americans were unemployed. Some desperate jobless were selling apples on street corners. Breadlines were forming outside newly opened missions, and riots were occurring outside newly closed banks. On December 11, 1930, the secretary of the Hollywood Guaranty Savings and Loan announced that he had lost $7 million in the stock market, and then closed his doors; a thousand banks failed in 1930. When a down-and-out man saw a line of people snaking down the street from a theater showing Charles Chaplin's *City Lights*, he quipped: "Is that a breadline or a bank folding?"

Weekly movie attendance, which had risen from 60 million to 90 million with the advent of sound, had slid back to 60 million in 1930. As box office dwindled, the studios tried to reassure themselves. One example of this was the February celebration of Carl Laemmle's fifteen years in Hollywood. Thalberg attended (along with a group of Universal veterans that included Erich von Stroheim), and he spoke warmly of "Uncle Carl" for the newsreel camera. Laemmle's jollity was short-lived; in March he was forced to lay off fifteen hundred employees. A nervous Nick Schenck called Louis B. Mayer. "Make lots of pictures," said Schenck. "There's nothing wrong with this business that a good picture won't cure." Mayer and Thalberg began making foreign-language versions of films that had performed well. *Let Us Be Gay* was remade with a French-speaking cast as *Soyons gais* for release in France and French-speaking territories. Thalberg also stepped up production of the short subjects made by former publicist Pete Smith, and contracted with independent producer Hal Roach to release the comedies he produced with Stan Laurel, Oliver Hardy, Thelma Todd, and Charley Chase. Ultimately, though, it was up to Thalberg to make the "good" pictures that Schenck needed. At lunch in the executive bungalow, Thalberg told his supervisors, "Now, more than ever, we have to give the public its money's worth." How would he reconcile this goal with his new priority?

The first film to answer this question was *Trader Horn*. Thalberg had snapped up the 1927 best seller by Ethelreda Lewis shortly after its publication. Then, fired by its tale of a white goddess in the Dark Continent, he did what he had not done since *Ben-Hur*: he sent a film company on location with an incomplete script and an open-ended budget. "The front office wanted to shoot in Africa," recalled J.J. Cohn, "so we never even tried to work out a budget. Who knows what's going to happen when you're shooting in Africa?" Thalberg nodded to economy by cutting salaries. He wanted Harry Carey to portray the hirsute Horn for $600 a week. "You know damned well I got $2,500 for *The Trail of '98*!" Carey exclaimed. He was still recovering from Colorado, and he was not going to wear a Santa Claus beard in Africa for that kind of money.

"That's as high as I can go," said Thalberg. "This is going to be an expensive picture, and we've got to hold down expenses wherever possible. Why don't you talk it over with Olive and let me know?"

Carey spoke with his wife, Olive Golden, who then conferred with Will Rogers and his wife at a speakeasy. They saw *Trader Horn* as a prestige project and advised Carey to accept, if Thalberg would cast Golden as a missionary and forget about the long white beard. The deal was made. Casting the white goddess "Nina" was another matter. The book described her as the missionary's child who was kidnapped and raised by an African tribe to be a "fetish in a Joss house." There was no one under contract who could play such a role. Director Woodbridge Strong ("W. S.") Van Dyke tested nearly two hundred actresses, and then, when he had given up, found his Nina in twenty-five-year-old Constance Woodruff, a Mormon girl from Provo, Utah. The unflappable Van Dyke was taken aback when Woodruff (who was working as an extra under the name of Edwina Booth) upbraided him because he had not paid her for publicity work connected with his Nina search. The contrast between her placid blonde beauty and her violent temper won her the part. After scraping by as an extra, she felt lucky to be offered $75 a week. A handsome contract player named Duncan Renaldo was paid $600 a week to play the young Peruvian who helps Horn rescue Nina from murderous natives.

In April 1929, Van Dyke led an expedition of 35 whites, 192 Africans, and ninety tons of equipment into the African interior. The only women in the company were a script girl, a hairdresser, Golden, and Edwina Booth. Nothing that Van Dyke had seen in Tahiti while making *White Shadows in the South Seas* prepared him—or anyone in the company—for the rigors of Africa. In spite of inoculations, most of them contracted malaria immediately. "Oh, it was tough," recalled Golden. "You had to fight bugs all the time." Booth was suffering more than the rest of the company, since she had to wear a skimpy costume. "I learned about 'doo-doos,' insects which bite you, crawl upon you and into your soup," Booth told a reporter. Golden corroborated this. "She was always ripped to pieces. . . .

The bugs and ticks would be all over her. I pinched ticks as big as the end of my finger out of that girl's body." Said Renaldo: "We had insects in our eyebrows and in our hair."

After filming for a short time, Van Dyke was told to convert to sound. "They decided they would send over a sound truck," said Golden. "They started to unload it from the boat and dropped it overboard, so that was another three or four weeks' delay." While waiting, Van Dyke used a silent Akeley camera to shoot scenes of wildlife, animal attacks, and natives, and drank gin to further immunize himself. Other company members drank three fingers of whisky in the morning and at night. Booth's religious beliefs precluded this. Renaldo thought her naïve as she tried to find poetry in the hostile setting. "Africa just pours into one," she said. "Throbbing with life of every sort—animal, insect, black man—it drifts lazily, sleepily, rhythmically into your veins, until it is pulsating all about you, through you, saturating you with its feeling of eternal movement." Renaldo was more frank. "In order to live in Africa," he said, "everything has to eat something else, and you hear this agony going on night and day." In seven months of filming, one African crew member was eaten by a crocodile, and another was smashed by a rhinoceros. Carey was knocked down by a crocodile's tail, and even though Booth took her turn shoving a lighted torch down the crocodile's throat, neither she nor any of the Americans were injured. But Africa did find its way into Booth, in the form of a parasite.

When Van Dyke and his company returned to Culver City, he had set numerous records for location filming: crossing the equator eighteen times in seven months; filming fifteen tribes in four colonies (Tanganyika, Kenya, Uganda, and the Congo); traversing more than nine thousand miles; and, of most interest to Thalberg, spending $1 million and exposing 4 *million* feet of film. Of lesser importance were Booth's dysentery and sunstroke. When Thalberg and Mayer sat down to watch Van Dyke's footage, they too began to feel faint. There was no continuity, no connection between the shots of animals and actors running around the veldt. "What are we going to do with this?" demanded Mayer. "Cut it into travelogues?"

"We'll just have to fix it," replied Thalberg, who then ordered Sam Marx to put several writers onto the project. Bernard Hyman was the unhappy supervisor saddled with *Trader Horn*. By mid-1930 he was telling Mayer that it might be best to shelve the film. Renaldo informed William Randolph Hearst, who had been publicizing it. "The picture must go on as intended," Hearst thundered. "That is all."

"We're not getting anywhere," said Thalberg after looking at six drafts.

"Did you ever think to open the book?" Carey asked him. His wife was with him. "I remember Irving calling for his secretary," she said, "and do you know they didn't have a copy on the lot? They sent over to a bookshop—and the dialogue was mostly there—the old man talking."

At this point Marx asked Cyril Hume, a novelist who was being dropped from the staff, to look at the footage and scripts with Hyman. When Marx looked in on them later, he stared in disbelief. "Hyman and Hume were weeping like babies," Marx wrote. "The writer had written a connecting scene that was so right for it that the supervisor burst into tears. Seeing that, Hume, too, started to cry."

Van Dyke spent the rest of 1930 shooting connecting scenes for *Trader Horn* in Culver City. Cameraman Clyde DeVinna's new footage was so skillfully matched to his African scenes that no one could tell the difference. Booth and Renaldo made their retakes for the same pay. Shortly before his death, Lon Chaney told Carey to hold out for more. "Listen, Carey, you got 'em over a barrel," Chaney said. "They fired you, now they need you. Sock 'em for all you can get."

"No," Carey shook his head. "I set out to make it for six hundred and I'll finish it at six hundred."

Golden was not so agreeable after Hyman replaced her with Marjorie Rambeau. *Min and Bill* had made Rambeau a bigger name, but her shots did not match Golden's, so Thalberg offered Golden $300 a day to rejoin the cast. "How much were you paying Rambeau?" asked Golden. Thalberg refused to tell her. "I found out," she said. "It was a thousand dollars a day. That's what I want."

"I won't pay that," said Thalberg.

"Oh, yes, you will," said Golden, heading for the door.

Golden got $1,000 a day for five days but never worked for Thalberg again. Van Dyke had anticipated retakes, so he brought the Masai tribesman who played Horn's gun bearer with him from Africa. Mutia Oomooloo was over six feet tall, with a shaved head, a ring in his nose, and a will as strong as his body. His requirements for completing the film included having a Wakamba tribesman, Riano Lindami, accompany him, having a hut built for them on Lot Three's jungle set, and being supplied with wild animals that they could slaughter and cook according to Muslim custom. Interviewers were tickled by Mutia's assessment of Hollywood: Greta Garbo was too thin, Leo the Lion was too fat, and material wealth was immaterial. "We can't use it in Africa," Mutia sneered in Swahili.

Mutia's disdain for America did not extend to its women. "In their village in Africa," explained a translator, "Mutia has eight wives and Riano has six. So they have—how would you say—the habit of women. But they have had no women since they left Africa. They are getting very . . . restless. Maybe soon they will get difficult." Thalberg immediately contacted his African American chauffeur, Harold Garrison, who was better known as "Kid Slickem, the studio shoeshine boy." Garrison procured two prostitutes from Central Avenue. After dallying with them, Mutia and Riano followed them back to their brothel, where a party proceeded until Mutia realized that his new watch was missing. When no one admitted to stealing it, he picked up a woman and swung her around by her ankles, knocking the other girls into the walls and furniture.

The studio hushed up the incident, but Mutia soon found himself in a Culver City hospital with a case of venereal disease. When he grew bored, he escaped and started walking down Washington Boulevard toward M-G-M, dressed in a hospital gown that did not cover him sufficiently. After his recovery, he began to suspect that his new woman was sharing her favors with Garrison. Mutia left the backlot and crept onto Lot One, working his way through the shrubs between the executive building and the commissary. In perhaps the most unusual encounter between labor and management in M-G-M history, Mutia Oomooloo sprang from the bushes as Irving Thalberg strode down a path, lost in thought. Thalberg stopped in his tracks. Towering over him was Mutia. The warrior put a hand on Thalberg's shoulder and a knife to his throat. "Boss keep Slickem away from my woman," rumbled Mutia. Before Thalberg could reply, Mutia disappeared into the shrubbery. Thalberg paged Garrison, and a tragedy was averted.

Trader Horn became M-G-M's most profitable film of 1931, but was sullied by bad publicity. Renaldo's wife sued Booth for alienation of affection. Mrs. Renaldo was declared unbalanced and the case was thrown out of court. Renaldo was arrested for having illegally entered the country years earlier. He served time. Booth grew increasingly ill. When a full recovery was declared unlikely, she sued M-G-M for $1 million. The suit claimed that Thalberg had withheld medical treatment because it would have delayed departure from Africa and subjected the studio to huge penalties. M-G-M settled out of court for $35,000, the smallest of several judgments the studio would pay during Thalberg's tenure. Resentment of Thalberg was not limited to *Trader Horn*'s cast.*

*The most complete account of Edwina Booth's sad encounter with fame has been written by Utah journalist D. Robert Carter. His series of articles in 2006 for the *Daily Herald* finally answers the oft-asked question "Didn't Edwina Booth die from the tropical disease she caught while making *Trader Horn?*"

A number of stars had been with M-G-M since the merger, so in early 1931 it was time to renew their seven-year contracts. Shearer signed a three-picture deal for $100,000. The contract Thalberg offered William Haines was not as generous; it cut his salary from $1,750 a week to $1,500. Haines asked Thalberg for a meeting, but when Thalberg finally made time to see him, Haines slumped in his chair with his arms folded and would not come to the point. "Take the nipple out of your mouth and tell me what's wrong," said Thalberg. Haines straightened up and said he wanted more money. Thalberg refused the amount he asked but gave him a $10,000 bonus. "Don't spend it," Thalberg advised. "This is a time to save." Haines would have done better to complain about the properties Thalberg was assigning him; they still used the formula of the smart aleck who learns humility. Haines was too mature for such roles, as indicated by snide reviews and dwindling box office, but he preferred Thalberg's benign neglect to Mayer's lectures on his personal life. While Thalberg was aware of Haines's homosexual lifestyle, he never censured him. Forty years later, Haines revered Thalberg. "He was a great, great fellow," Haines recalled. "I was blind when it came to him. It was just the opposite with Mayer. I remember everything nasty about that one and everything good about the other."

Ramon Novarro was not so easily pacified. He felt that Thalberg was handing him "baby roles and salacious parts." In *Son of India,* he played a prince who must renounce his love for a white girl; in Arthur Schnitzler's *Daybreak,* he played the seducer of an immature music teacher. Thalberg thought that the inventive director Jacques Feyder would keep Novarro's image fresh in these films, but since the advent of sound no one was sure what this image was. Like Haines, he was homosexual, unwilling to marry for the sake of appearances, and aging. Neither man sounded particularly effeminate in the talkies; he simply did not have the youthful glamour of his silent films. Talkies were a tricky medium; a stage play that looked good downtown did not necessarily fit an M-G-M star. Besides feeling ill-served by Thalberg's literary tastes, Novarro became irritated when a promised vacation failed to materialize. When it was renewal time, he declined a three-year contract in favor of a one-picture contract for *Mata Hari;* for the time being, it was a wise decision.

In spite of their misgivings, both Novarro and Haines continued to attend Thalberg parties. John Gilbert stayed home and brooded. "The Story of Hollywood's Unhappiest Man," an August 1931 *Los Angeles Times* piece by Harry Carr, called Gilbert a "self-appointed pariah, so miserable that he never comes to the studio if he can possibly avoid it. When he has to come, he walks in with his hat pulled down over his eyes, avoiding everyone, speaking to no one." What this article had in common with every other in 1931 was the foregone conclusion that Gilbert's voice had ended his career two years earlier. "It is an open secret that the producers would like to wriggle out of Gilbert's contract," wrote Carr. "They are signed up to pay him $250,000 a picture, make two pictures a year, and his contract still has eighteen months to run." Though Gilbert had languished through most of 1930 without an assignment, in 1931 Thalberg gave him three.

Gentleman's Fate was a gangster story directed by Mervyn LeRoy, who was soon to do *Little Caesar* for Warner Bros. Leroy could make a star of Edward G. Robinson but could do nothing for Gilbert, mainly because the script had him lose every fight and die in the end. Ironically, most reviews praised his voice. The film's failure was underscored by his personal turmoil. His wife, Ina Claire, returned from a trip to find herself locked out of their hilltop home. Gilbert refused to see her. "I'm going to miss you terribly," he explained in a letter, "but I'm not fit company now." Reporters clamored for a reconciliation. "He is a great actor," Claire told them. "We shall always be friends. But as a husband he is a 'fade-out.' Reunited? Don't be silly. There will be no 'Came the dawn' in this story."

At the divorce hearing in August, Paul Bern testified: "Jack was very much distressed by his stock losses and dissatisfied with his pictures, [and so distraught that] he would suddenly turn away from us in the middle of a conversation and leave the room." According to screenwriter Gene Markey, "Jack had a good friend in Paul Bern. He was intent on getting a good vehicle for Jack." Bern persuaded Thalberg to purchase *Cheri-Bibi*, based on a novel by Gaston Leroux, author of *The Phantom of the Opera*. In *The Phantom of Paris*, Gilbert had the most dashing role since his silent films, performing Houdini-like escapes and impersonating the look-alike adversary played by Ian Keith. "When anyone can stir a Baltimore audience to applause, he must be great," a Gilbert fan wrote *Photoplay* magazine. "They forgot *The Phantom of Paris* was just a picture and applauded with such vigor as has not been shown here since *The Big Parade*."

Unfortunately for Gilbert, the film was a case of too little, too late. His next, *West of Broadway*, was a sad affair that had him playing an alcoholic. "Jack told me that the studio put him in this picture hoping he'd refuse it and break his contract," recalled fellow actor Ralph Bellamy. "I'll do anything," Gilbert told him. "I'll clean spittoons if those bastards tell me to, until this contract is up." After the film's preview, a trade paper wrote: "If it was the purpose of M-G-M to lead John Gilbert to the guillotine and end the waning popularity of one of the most popular stars the silver screen has ever known, then *West of Broadway* is a great success."

Thalberg ordered retakes; the film still flopped. Was this the best he could do for the actor whom he had brought to M-G-M? For his friend?

Twenty-five years later, Norma Shearer was still trying to answer this question. "People—just people—put the stamp of disapproval on Jack Gilbert's voice," she wrote. "When the fan magazines wrote that he was doomed, Jack began to believe that he was. I wonder now why Irving could not help him. Irving was known for salvaging careers. The renaissance of personalities was his specialty. He held out his frail hand to many, and many found strength in it, but not Jack Gilbert. He became difficult and even belligerent." Gilbert stormed into Thalberg's office, obviously intoxicated, to demand better scripts. Thalberg told him to calm down and then described a play he had just bought. It was about a group of characters in a Berlin hotel. "There's a part in it that's made to order for you," said Thalberg. "A gambler who has an affair with a ballet dancer." Gilbert was momentarily soothed, and he resumed contact with the Thalbergs.

Buster Keaton also felt ill-used by Thalberg. It had been three years since a nepotistic sleight of hand had moved his contract from United Artists' Joseph Schenck to Loew's Nick Schenck. In that time, Keaton had lost his creative freedom. "Look, Buster," Thalberg had said, "you don't need a producer. But we have to go through the motions to satisfy the front office. I'm assigning you Larry Weingarten. A nice boy. Just married my sister. But I'll look out for you. You're my pet." Before long, Weingarten and Keaton were arguing. Thalberg usually ruled in Keaton's favor. When sound came in, Thalberg swung to Weingarten.

"There was only one thing that I wanted—that you talk in the most natural way," said Keaton. "Don't give me puns. Don't give me jokes. No wisecracks." Keaton also needed dialogue breaks in which to slip his sight gags, those moments of acrobatic legerdemain unique to his screen persona. Weingarten begrudged him this, even after the success of *Doughboys*, for which Thalberg had granted Keaton more control. Now Keaton had to sit outside Thalberg's office for hours, waiting to appeal his case. "Thalberg, as well as being a fine judge of light comedy and farce, appreciated slapstick," wrote Keaton in 1960. "Nevertheless, he lacked the true low-comedy mind. Like any man who must concern himself with mass production, he was seeking a pattern, a format. Slapstick comedy has a format, but it is hard to detect in its early stages unless you are one of those who can create it. . . . Brilliant though he was, Irving Thalberg could not accept the way a comedian like me built his stories."

Thalberg relied on Weingarten, but the supervisor had no more feeling for the idiom than he did, and finding the next vehicle became a nuisance. "We were desperate," recalled Weingarten. "We didn't know what to do. Sedgwick [the director] and I were riding down Hollywood Boulevard by the old El Capitan Theater [and we] saw a matinee, an old Avery Hopwood play, *Parlor, Bedroom, and Bath*." Weingarten decided the play was good enough and snapped it up for a nominal $6,000. Keaton was not impressed. "It's a farce," the Great Stone Face told Thalberg. "Not my kind of story."

Thalberg stared at him with the same expression.

"But we'll make a good pic," Keaton hastily added. Keaton did not expect the subsequent increase in both writers and story conferences. "There were too many cooks," said Keaton. "Everybody at Metro was in my gag department, including Irving Thalberg. They'd laugh their heads off at dialogue written by all the new writers." Keaton tried to find spots in which to interpolate physical comedy, but they were scarce—and hard won. "You just kept fighting," he recalled. "When I found out that they could write stories and material better than I could, what was the use of fighting?"

What really upset Keaton was that in spite of its mediocrity, *Parlor, Bedroom, and Bath* made money. If it had flopped, he could have argued for a return to his silent technique; there was little hope of that now. His next 1931 project was *The Sidewalks of New York*, in which he was expected to play a rich man who befriends slum kids. He was appalled. "Larry likes it," responded Thalberg. "Everyone in the studio likes the story. *You* are the only one who doesn't." Keaton tried to argue with Thalberg, but found his powers of logic running a sad second to the genius behind the desk. "In the end," said Keaton, "I gave up like a fool and said 'What the hell?'" To his amazement, this film also made money, in spite of his opinion that it was "such a complete stinker, such an unbelievable bomb." Much as Keaton hated to admit it, giving in to Thalberg was making him wealthy. Unlike Gilbert, he could not claim that Thalberg was selling him down the river. Yet he could no longer call his soul his own. Like Gilbert, he began to drink, heavily and conspicuously.

Lenore Coffee recalled in 1968 how Thalberg would assign a property to his stars. "They would be given a script, and told: 'This is your next picture, Miss X.' They would read it with varying reactions—some of them stormy—but the picture was made ninety percent as originally written. They had no choice whatsoever in what parts they played, not even Mrs. Thalberg." This was true, but Coffee was not aware how greatly Shearer was influencing—if not manipulating—Thalberg's choice of properties. When they saw a play in Los Angeles, she would tell him to buy it. If they could not attend a play in New York, he would arrange to have a film made of a private performance. Then they would watch it in his private screening room to decide if she should do it.

In the end, though, even the First Lady of M-G-M had to defer to the Little Boss. In one interview, he admitted that he was more sympathetic to actors now that he was married to one. In truth, Thalberg regarded actors as capricious beings who did not know what was best for them. "Actors are like children," he told Frances Marion. "No matter how many gifts are under the Christmas tree, they always want the ornament on top." This statement was hypocritical, considering that he had Shearer, Crawford, and Garbo under contract, yet was reaching for Hayes, Fontanne, and Cornell.

If Thalberg's actors thought him patronizing, his writers found him lordly. Coffee had watched his progress since Universal, when he praised her for declining a job with him in order to learn her craft from Bayard Veiller. At Mission Road she had single-handedly saved *The Dangerous Age* for Thalberg by rewriting all its titles, one of which became a Jazz Age aphorism: "When a man of forty courts a girl of twenty, it isn't her youth he is seeking, but his own." She had helped M-G-M through its transition to sound with the surprise hit *The Bishop Murder Case*. Of equal importance was her willingness to review and polish scripts at a moment's notice and without credit. "Irving would always give a script to Lenore Coffee or Bess Meredyth or me to read before he shot it," said Frances Marion. "He valued the woman's angle." The *Exhibitors Herald-World* reported in 1931 that the average film audience was 75 percent women, and perhaps more at matinees. "Wives and shopgirls can always get their men to the movies they want to see," said Thalberg, "but a man can never get a woman to see one that doesn't interest her." It was odd, then, that he was eliminating women writers, most of whom had been (or still were) novelists. His East Coast imports were mostly playwrights—and all male. "A silent film was like writing a novel," said Coffee, "and a [talkie] script was like writing a play. That's why women dropped out." As holdouts, both Coffee and Marion found themselves sparring with Thalberg.

When Thalberg learned that Warner Bros. had Mervyn LeRoy's *Little Caesar* and William Wellman's *The Public Enemy* primed for release in early 1931, he asked Warners production head Darryl F. Zanuck for a preview of *Public Enemy*. "That's not a motion picture," Thalberg said to Zanuck after the preview. "That's beyond a motion picture." In fact, Thalberg had already sent Frances Marion to Chicago to research his own gangster film. *The Secret Six* would star Wallace Beery as a bestial gangster and Johnny Mack Brown as a muckraking reporter. As Thalberg had predicted, Marion's marriage to George Hill was on the rocks (Hill had grown violent), but Thalberg assigned them to work together on *The Secret Six*. In spite of this tension, the project grew into a finely realized film, a cohesive match of words and images. Hill ignored Thalberg's multiple-camera requirement and used one well-placed camera to make shots that built logically one upon the other. M-G-M was returning to real filmmaking.

Marion ran afoul of Thalberg when she insisted on refining the part played by a new contractee named Clark Gable. "Irving was giving Johnny Mack Brown a big buildup," recalled Marion. "I knew it wouldn't work." Marion preferred Gable. Six months earlier, Lionel Barrymore, who knew Gable from the stage, had dressed him as a South Seas native for a screen test, thinking to cast him in *Never the Twain Shall Meet*. Thalberg had made some remark about Gable's "bat ears" and vetoed him. Gable had nevertheless been cast as Constance Bennett's brother-in-law in *The Easiest Way*. After the December preview at the Alexander Theatre in Glendale, Thalberg stood outside the box office to ask female audience members, "How did you like the fellow who played the brother-in-law, the laundryman?" He was surprised by the enthusiastic replies he heard. "What's going on?" he asked Howard Strickling when loads of fan mail began to arrive for Gable. Casting director Benjamin Thau opposed signing Gable, saying that he looked like a villain. "No more than Chester Morris," replied Thalberg, who did sign Gable but resisted when Marion wanted to give Gable more scenes in *The Secret Six*. "I tried to interest Irving in Gable," said Marion, "but he couldn't see it. He said he wasn't good looking, that his ears were too big, and so on. But I knew Gable had that something that appealed to a woman." Thalberg grudgingly accepted the scenes, and when Gable got raves, he apologized. "You were right and I was wrong," he told Marion.

After Marion's two hits with Beery, Thalberg hoped for a third. "I'd like to star Beery in an old-fashioned Western," he said. "Drive down to the Mexican border and sop up some atmosphere." One night shortly thereafter, Marion was strolling along a saloon-lined street in what was then called Tia Juana when she saw an imposing man stumble out of a bar. Not surprisingly, he was drunk. What was surprising was the bravado of the boy at his side. "Git outa the way, you sons o' bitches!" the small boy hollered at the crowd. "Can't you see the Champ needs air?" As the screenwriter watched the grim scene, she imagined a story. She hurried back to Culver City and began writing. "Did you finish the Western?" Thalberg asked her in his office a few days later.

"No," Marion answered. "I fell in love with a drunken ex–prize fighter and his kid."

"Women have the most perverse minds," said Thalberg. "I commission you to do a Western and you come back with—what?" Marion wrote a script called *The Champ*, which became a bigger hit than Beery's two previous.

Thalberg's chauvinism was not atypical of his era, but Lenore Coffee saw something else as she watched him from across the room at the studio's 1930 Christmas party.

> He sat on a short, carpeted stairway, a step or two up. He was extremely affable and charming, but anyone who had known him as long as I had would have had the strong feeling that he would rather be somewhere else. I don't think he liked this overlapping of his professional and social life. He had an enormous sense of guarding a kind of inner privacy, even from his friends. I wonder if Norma herself ever knew him completely. . . . When he married I believe it was because he fell truly in love and became a devoted husband and father. But I don't believe he ever had a woman friend in the whole of his life. Although we did not know the term in those days, he had what is now called a "love-hate" feeling towards women. And he had precisely the same thing towards writers, for, *au fond*, he was himself a frustrated writer. He knew he needed writers, and that very need irritated him.

"Irritated" is a weak word for the emotion Thalberg felt when a woman, a writer, or worst of all, a woman writer overstepped her position. Mercedes de Acosta met with Thalberg at the behest of Greta Garbo, who had taken an interest in her writing career (but not in her, much to Acosta's frustration). "Thalberg sat in a large chair behind a large desk, which was elevated on a platform," wrote Acosta. "In front of it were several extremely low and soft armchairs. Instead of sinking into my chair and allowing him to play the Emperor, I sat straight and as high up on the arm of it as I could, bringing myself almost on a level with him." Rather than offend Garbo, Thalberg put up with Acosta—for the time being.

Coffee had the misfortune to provoke Thalberg when she was vulnerable. She had been seriously hurt by the stock market crash and was expecting her first child. (She was married to director William J. Cowen.) She had also been writing for Cecil B. DeMille on the M-G-M lot, which was another strike against her. When Thalberg hired her in early 1930, it was with an option. "We are picking up your option, although the date has been passed," Thalberg told her. "There was an error in the accountancy department." Coffee then made her own error. Instead of *asking* Thalberg to "let it go," she *told* him to, arguing that they could give each other a mutual thirty-day closing notice. His face turned red but his voice stayed cool. "Well . . . why not?" he shrugged.

Some weeks later, Coffee received a call. Thalberg was letting her go. "You can't do that," she protested. "We have a thirty-day mutual closing notice." She assumed that when he had called her back in less than ten days' time, the closing notice had been canceled and a fresh thirty days started. Thalberg refused to acknowledge this—and Coffee had nothing in writing. "You can find other work," he told her.

"I can't very well look for work at a time like this," replied the very pregnant Coffee.

"I don't see why not."

"If you don't see why not, Mr. Thalberg, then no one could possibly explain it to you."

According to Coffee's theory, the next time Thalberg needed her services, his resentment was doubled. He wanted her to adapt a play called *Mirage* into a Crawford vehicle and was in a hurry to sign her because he was about to leave for Europe. "Of course I want to come back to work here," Coffee assured him. "I write very good scripts. I write very good dialogue. And there's no use writing good dialogue for actors and actresses who can't speak it. M-G-M has the best of them tied up."

"What's all this business of being a writer anyway?" Thalberg asked her. "It's just putting one word after another."

"Pardon me, Mr. Thalberg—it's putting one *right* word after another."

"I see. Would you take an office in the studio or insist on working at home?"

"Whichever you wish."

"So you've become organization-minded."

"If that's what you wish to call it."

"You know," he told her, "I can't possibly pay you a thousand dollars a week, and carry you between pictures." Coffee asked that he not cut her salary too drastically. "Leave that to me," said Thalberg with a smile. Coffee took this in good faith, expecting to get $800 a week.

A few days after Thalberg's departure, Coffee was shocked to find that he had cut her salary in half. Several of his associates were also surprised. "This doesn't sound like Irving at all," came the chorus from Harry Edington, Cecil B. DeMille, Bayard Veiller, and agent Phil Berg. When Coffee's script later became the hit film *Possessed*, Thalberg raised her salary to $650 and give her a nominal bonus, neither of which comforted her when she learned that he was telling other studios that he could not loan her out because of her contract. There was no contract. DeMille, who was leaving M-G-M after three flops in a row, belied his reputation for cold-heartedness by taking Coffee with him. When she returned to M-G-M several years later, her agent got her $1,000 a week. She never worked for Thalberg again, although she maintained her friendship with Shearer.

Thalberg's treatment of Coffee was in some measure repaid by the defection of a prized writer. The British humorist P. G. Wodehouse had been ceremoniously welcomed to M-G-M in 1930 and then assigned to spruce up the very British dialogue spoken by Reginald Denny in *Those Three French Girls*. Director Harry Beaumont could not make sense of Wodehouse's "What, ho!" parlance. "It reads funny but it doesn't play," he told Thalberg. Wodehouse refused to do his revisions in the tar-roofed, airless writers' building. He carried his typewriter to a deserted set on the backlot or stayed by the pool at his rented house in Laurel Canyon. Most of the time, he sat idle, waiting for assignments that did not come, and, although he wanted more work, he was unwilling to sit outside Thalberg's office. To pass the time, Wodehouse made notes for stories satirizing Hollywood life. When his contract ran out on May 9, 1931, he granted a scandalous interview.

"The motion-picture business dazes me," he sniffed to a *Los Angeles Times* reporter. "They paid me $2,000 a week—$104,000—and I cannot see what they engaged me for. After all, I have the Jeeves novels, a score of successful plays, and countless magazine stories to my credit. I was led to believe that there was a field for my work in pictures, but I was told that my stuff was 'too light.' They seem to have such a passion for sex stuff. I wonder if they really know the tastes of their audiences." The reporter commented on the glistening palm trees and sparkling pool at Wodehouse's home. "It is what every Englishman dreams about on a muggy day at home," agreed Wodehouse. Recalling the few lines he had contributed to scripts that were never filmed, Wodehouse smiled and said: "That about sums up what I was called upon to do for my $104,000. They were extremely nice to me—oh, extremely—but I feel as if I have cheated them. If it's only 'names' they want, it seems such an expensive way to get them."

When the interview was printed, Thalberg's telephone rang off the hook. "You silly boys out there!" Schenck snorted through the receiver. "You throw away our money!"

"If you know how to make pictures without writers, tell me!" Thalberg fired back.

Shearer often heard Thalberg defending his writers. "Irving had a most practical awareness of their problems," she wrote. "Perhaps he thought solitude would lead Mr. Wodehouse to inspiration. The more likely story is that even the most resourceful brain can lose the creative impulse when faced with a blank page at nine o'clock in the morning."

Mayer looked askance at Thalberg's staff. "Oh, these writers!" Mayer groused. "Some of them are getting drunk, and they have three-hour lunches in the [Brown] Derby [restaurant]. I ought to put my foot down. Jack Warner over there runs a tight ship!"

"Now, Louis, they're signed for fifty-two weeks," sighed Thalberg. "If I get forty-two weeks a year out of them, that's fine with me. It's worth it. Let them alone. They're doing fine." Thalberg was usually game for a debate but was unequivocal about his writers. "If it isn't for the writing," he said, "we've got nothing."

Thalberg would truly have nothing if his health should be impaired. In the first four months of 1931, he had endured a score of sneak previews, dozens of story conferences, two Shearer films, and the occasional all-night poker game with Sam Goldwyn, Joe Schenck, and Constance Bennett. Henrietta and Norma were both convinced that he needed a rest, so he agreed to take a vacation. On the eve of his departure, his associates gave him a farewell luncheon in the executive bungalow. "He had the gift of inspiring great friendship among men," observed Coffee. "He had men friends who really and truly loved him, and for whom I think he himself had great affection." Sam Marx was surprised to hear Thalberg make an announcement to his eight subordinates. "Supervisor has become an old-fashioned word," he said. "You fellows are rightfully producers now." The new title implied that screen credit might be allowed. Paul Bern asked Thalberg if he planned to put his name on his own productions. Thalberg shook his head. Bern turned to Lewin, Stromberg, and the rest of his colleagues. One by one, they agreed that the time for screen credit had not yet arrived. Marx saw Mayer observe this display of loyalty, both impressed and envious.

Thalberg, Shearer, and Irving Jr., left Los Angeles on April 23 and then stopped at a Chicago hotel for an appearance at a Loew's sales convention. This allowed for an early-morning meeting with Alfred Lunt and Lynn Fontanne, who were touring in Maxwell Anderson's *Elizabeth the Queen*. "My dear, I have something to tell you," Fontanne said to Shearer. "I saw you in *Let Us Be Gay*. I would like to give you some advice. You must not laugh at your own lines after you deliver them." A properly respectful Shearer thanked Fontanne, who then turned her imperious gaze on Thalberg and said: "Alfred and I will not do any swimming, high-diving, fast horseback riding or any of the other things you do out there in the films."

"Miss Fontanne," said Thalberg, "I can assure you that motion pictures have progressed beyond such things. We will give you a nice dignified picture, something quiet and artistic. You will find making pictures a more peaceful experience than acting on the stage." At that instant, the door of the hotel room was flung open, and Leo the Lion came through it—on a leash, but nonetheless in person. The Lunts were startled. Thalberg was nonchalant. "Oh, they're having a sales convention here," he explained. "The lion is part of it. Don't give it a thought." After Leo was removed, Thalberg offered the Lunts $75,000 to make one film of their choice; they signed.

On May 1 Thalberg boarded the *Europa* with his wife and son and called Culver City for a last consultation. Bernie Hyman made a point of asking if Thalberg had warm clothing for the Atlantic crossing. After Hyman hung up, the writer Bertram Bloch asked him: "Why was that?"

"Because as long as Irving lives, we're all great men."

On May 6 the Thalberg family checked into the Dorchester Hotel, where Shearer gave one of the few indications of the stress under which she lived. A male secretary was attempting to drill her on the fine points of court protocol. After two hours, she turned on him and screamed: "Not another thing until tomorrow!" Then she did something that caused the secretary to run out of the room. "Mr. Thalberg! Mr. Thalberg!" he shouted. "Mrs. Thalberg has gone mad!" Thalberg attempted to laugh it off, but in view of the nervous breakdowns suffered by Shearer's sister, this outburst was worrisome. "Norma has disciplined herself to an amazing degree," said Thalberg, "but even she has her breaking point. When she does get angry, she tears off her clothes."

Shearer's anxiety was due to a star-studded schedule that included a visit to the House of Commons to meet Lloyd George and Winston Churchill; tea at 10 Downing Street with Prime Minister Stanley Baldwin; and a formal dinner at Londonderry House, where Shearer was seated next to the duke of York. She had met the duke at a Hollywood party a few years earlier, but he had danced twice with Greta Garbo and not at all with her. She now told him that he looked like his father, the king, to which he replied, "Yes, we all have those tired fish eyes." His wife stopped Shearer in the powder room and gave the girl from Montreal something to tell the folks back home. "Imagine the future queen of England asking me what it was like to be a movie star!" recalled Shearer. In such company she deferred to her husband. "Irving behaved like visiting royalty," she recalled. "I was in over my head in such company. But I hid under a cloak of confidence. I was married to Irving Thalberg and I was a movie star."

One less publicized purpose of the trip was an appointment with the renowned cardiologist Dr. Franz M. Groedel, whose spa at Bad Nauheim, Germany, specialized in the hydrotherapeutic treatment of heart disease. "Dr. Groedel told Irving that if he did things in moderation," wrote Shearer, "he could live to be a hundred, which Irving didn't really want. It wasn't how *long* he lived that interested Irving—it was how *well*." While in Germany, the Thalbergs spent rare hours in each other's company. "We left the baby at the Schwarzwald Hotel with my maid Ursula and we walked hand in hand on paths in the Black Forest, pushing our feet through the moss and bark, feeling a little like babes in the woods. But we weren't lost. We had each other."

At the Hotel Crillon in Paris, Shearer awoke from a nightmare in the middle of the night. In the dream, their new house, now under construction, had gone wrong. She woke up Irving and they talked, looking at the ceiling. Soon they became obsessed with it. How high was it? "We reached for Irving's favorite cane," said Shearer. "It was made of ebony with an ivory tip joined by a gold band, and measured exactly three feet. We climbed on furniture and measured the ceiling: fifteen feet. In the morning we called Cedric Gibbons in Santa Monica and woke him from a sound sleep. He told us our half-finished house had eight-foot ceilings."

"Okay, Cedric," said Thalberg, "see if you can raise the roof. Have them make all the ceilings higher if it isn't too late. Also discuss the possibility of air conditioning. Consult with Carrier Air. What? They've never put it in a residence? They can experiment with ours. Oh, by the way . . . how are you? I'm afraid I sound crazy asking these things—but I'm used to your miracles." To apologize for waking Gibbons, the Thalbergs bought his wife, Dolores Del Rio, a pair of diamond-and-ruby earrings at Van Cleef and Arpels the next day.

On June 6 the Thalbergs received a sad call from Douglas Shearer in Los Angeles. Since his success as head of the sound department, he had been spending less time with his Canadian wife, Marion, at their cottage in Santa Monica Canyon. "Douglas had fallen hopelessly in love with a rather exotic, dark-haired young studio writer called Ann Cunningham," wrote Shearer. "Doug decided to tell Marion the truth, hoping she would offer him his freedom. Instead she used a kind of stoic strength to seek her own." According to the *Los Angeles Times*, a shooting gallery attendant at the Venice Pier observed Marion Shearer "acting strangely."

"She fired three rounds and won some dolls," said the attendant. "Then suddenly she aimed the pistol between her eyes, pulled the trigger, and fell dead."

The Thalbergs' homecoming on July 22 was a somber one. After they settled in the Santa Monica summer home of Ben Lyon and Bebe Daniels, Thalberg grew eager to return to M-G-M. While Shearer observed the completion of their new home at 707 Ocean Front, Thalberg went to M-G-M to see what films needed his help. Charles MacArthur had just endured two dismal previews of his wife's film *Lullaby*. "Helen has been a star for fifteen years," he cried, "and I've ruined her in an hour and a half!"

"Helen is fine," Thalberg assured him. "Edgar [Selwyn, the director] didn't give her the protection she needs. She is a stage actress, not a motion picture actress, and she must be directed with care."

"What about the picture?" asked MacArthur. "Can anything be done with it?" Both Rapf and Mayer had told him that the maudlin film should be shelved.

"I see more than two thirds of a picture here," said Thalberg. "All we have to do is supply the other third." That other third needed motivation. As the story stood, the jailed Madelon Claudet has no reason to prostitute herself to raise a child she barely knows. Thalberg told MacArthur that they needed to show a bond forming between the unwed Madelon and the newborn son she has just wished dead. "Irving had Charlie write a scene," said Hayes in 1967, "in which Madelon comes to love her child so much that she will fight destiny, God, or the devil to make life good for that child." The new scene had Madelon's friend Rosalie (Marie Prevost) bring the newborn to her bed. Madelon, exhausted from childbirth, moans and says, "Take it away!" Rosalie insists on placing the infant on the pillow next to Madelon. There is a moment of silence. Madelon slowly turns her head to look into the infant's face, then closes her eyes, weeps, and pulls him to her.

MacArthur rewrote the rest of the film with uncredited help from Ben Hecht. Thalberg was not keen on Hecht's participation, rightly suspecting that the two were as likely to get into alcoholic mischief as they were to complete the assignment. Thalberg had MacArthur trick Hecht into leaving Los Angeles in the company of a doctor. Hecht was at the Chicago train station before he realized that MacArthur was not meeting him. As a result of this episode, he held a long-standing grudge against Thalberg. "He lived two thirds of his time in the projection room," Hecht said of Thalberg in 1959. "He saw only movies. He never saw life. He had never noticed life. He was a hermit. He hadn't the faintest idea what human beings did—but he knew what their shadows should do."

The next time Hayes and MacArthur saw *Lullaby*, it was called *The Sin of Madelon Claudet*. To see it, they had to sneak into the packed Capitol Theatre after the film had started. As they watched the new scenes, they could not help whispering comments. Patrons on either side of them began shifting and sighing. Finally a man reached from behind and tapped MacArthur on his arm. "Say, mister," the man said, "if you don't like this picture, we do! You and your lady keep your mouths shut or I'll call an usher and get him to put you out of here!" Hayes and MacArthur quieted down, but could not bear to finish the film. *Variety* predicted success: "In the scene following the birth of the child, Miss Hayes takes up her option on the audience's tear ducts." *The Sin of Madelon Claudet* was indeed a hit. What was more important to Thalberg was that one film made a Broadway star an M-G-M star and won her an Academy Award.

Thalberg had equally high hopes for the Lunts, who had just completed *The Guardsman* when he returned from Europe. In reprising the play that had made them the toast of Broadway in 1924, the Lunts had to adjust to Hollywood—and vice versa. Frances Marion thought it marvelous that these Theatre Guild stars were gracing M-G-M with their presence, but most of her colleagues were horrified that Thalberg would waste film on unknown actors who were over forty. The Lunts demanded full rehearsals but were anxious when Sidney Franklin had them face the camera for the first time. "Don't be nervous," said a veteran electrician after their first take. "I think you're good." They thanked him, but could not bear to look at the rushes.

After three days, Fontanne steeled herself and sat through a few minutes' worth of shots. Lunt was sitting in their modest 1927 Ford sedan when Fontanne came out, blinking in the sunlight. "Well?" he asked.

"Oh, you're good," said Fontanne, "but you need a little more makeup to define your mouth. You look as if you have no lips. But, oh, Alfred, I am *dreadful*. I look scared to death—very plain and haggard with awful lines under my eyes, and no shine in my hair. I look as if I'd been buried and dug up again. I look as if—" Suddenly it occurred to Fontanne that Lunt was not listening. She turned and looked at him. He was staring into space.

"No lips, eh?" he asked softly.

Fontanne may not have liked her rushes, but according to assistant film editor Chester Schaeffer, the editing staff did. Cameraman Norbert Brodine had carefully framed a shot of her naked back in a mirror as she prepared to enter the bathtub. When the doorbell sounded, Fontanne turned to the camera. "Cut! Cut!" yelled Franklin. "We can't use that, Lynn! You can't turn toward the camera when you have nothing on!"

"But the bell sounded from that direction," said Fontanne. "Naturally I would turn in the direction from which it came." The shot was remade with her turning only her head, but the outtake made the rounds of the editing department for some time.

After completing the film, the Lunts found themselves waiting in Franklin's office for a summons from Thalberg. After waiting for an hour and a half, Fontanne had had enough. "He said he wanted to see us, so we'll just go up to his office."

"You can't do that with Irving," Franklin said. "You have to wait until he's ready for you."

"Nonsense," said Fontanne, as she climbed the stairs and strode past several benches full of stars, right into Thalberg's office. Franklin expected him to be angry, but he maintained his reserve and began to discuss the previous night's San Bernardino preview. Fontanne and Lunt listened as he read from the cards. Comments on the characters' implied adultery ranged from mildly disapproving to downright hateful. Fontanne raised her hand. "Don't read any more if they're all as moronic as those," she said. "They sound like children."

"They are children," said Thalberg, indicating some scrawled comments.

"Then why are you bothering to read them to us?"

"Because this is our audience," Thalberg stated.

"Then I don't want to hear their opinions," said Fontanne. "This film, in sophistication and maturity, is way outside their world. It is a subtle, brilliant comedy, and you will find an audience for it, but it won't be made up of people like the ones who wrote those nasty, vulgar cards."

Thalberg felt that the film could reach a wider audience if a scene was made in which Lunt was shown to be less egotistical. "But that's entirely out of keeping with the character," Lunt said. Nevertheless, Thalberg required that the scene be made, and at nine that night. Lunt dutifully played it, but when Thalberg saw it, he was angered to see that one of Lunt's eyes was doing what Shearer's tended to do—it was wandering. The film was unusable. Thalberg called Lunt. "You did that on purpose—to ruin the retakes!"

"I assure you that I could not make my eye roll out if I wanted it to," Lunt defended himself. "It only happens when I am fatigued." The Lunts were fatigued in general. Thalberg, on the other hand, was so pleased with *The Guardsman* that he wanted them to stay. Fontanne refused. "Your wife will get all my stage roles," she told him, "and I'll get the B pictures." Thalberg insisted that the Lunts would have first choice of properties and went as far as to offer them $925,000 for seven films. "Thalberg was, in his way, a clever man," recalled Fontanne, "and he had taste and intelligence. He seriously wanted to make good movies, we both felt. But he wanted slaves, not actors, and we could not be any person's slaves. We had worked too hard for our independence." *The Guardsman* had the distinction of garnering excellent reviews, "enjoying the just reward of packed houses at the Astor" (according to the *New York Times*) and then faltering in the provinces, which made it Thalberg's first "prestige picture." He was satisfied. As long as a prestige picture did well in the big cities, the company could write off its Midwest losses and boast of stage stars in its stable.

Thalberg was obsessed with the idea that movies were looked on with condescension and treated like the poor relation of literature and drama. He made several statements in 1931 asking for critical respect. "Now and again," he told a London reporter, "a little softer judgment should be exercised by the critics. This business is entertaining millions of people all over the world. It would benefit by a sense of loyalty." In another interview, he explained his practice of retakes. "The 'lowly' movies are often likened to an art," he told a Los Angeles journalist. "This is the best argument in the world in favor of reshooting sequences. Sometimes we shoot a promising script, and then we are not satisfied with the result. So we reshoot it, adding a scene here, cutting out one there, until it is reasonably satisfactory. What do we accomplish by that? I'll tell you. We are safeguarding the exhibitor, the public and ourselves. In other words, we are guaranteeing a certain standard in our product."

In a meeting with Jason Joy, Thalberg proposed that each studio contribute to the industry's image by making a quota of "ten important pictures a year, in none of which should appear the common sex and crime angles. Each of these pictures should be expertly and expensively exploited for the purpose of catching the eye of organized groups. Some radical and expensive activity such as this is necessary to 'shock' the public into a demand for the kind of stories which are not now profitable." He was perhaps thinking of Mordaunt Hall's review of *The Guardsman*, which said that if Hollywood could do more stage plays, "this medium of entertainment would be on a far higher plane." Yet, as Joy could attest, Thalberg's idea of a higher plane involved adult themes.

M-G-M's big moneymakers were family-oriented comedies with Marie Dressler and Polly Moran. Highbrow critics might sneer at *Politics* and *Reducing,* but they were as well crafted as the prestige films, with sympathetic characters, hilarious gags, and tightly built stories, and they were as daring in their own way as *The Divorcee* or *Strangers May Kiss,* because they showed middle-aged wives stepping out of their kitchens and running their towns. Thalberg's M-G-M was never thought of as a fun factory, but when these films were advertised as "Laff Riots," there was truth in advertising. Still, he hated admitting to a formula. "Studios are accused of imitation because they so often move in cycles," he told the *Los Angeles Times.* "Yet imitation is not their purpose. It is simply that a new field has been opened to them. The success of *An American Tragedy,* for instance, has called their

attention to Theodore Dreiser's works—and they are eager to develop that field."
Joy repeatedly found himself in the awkward position of helping Thalberg adapt
banned works like *Ex-Wife*, only to have them inspire troublesome cycles: divorce
films, horror films, gangster films, jungle films, and now, "kept women" films like
The Easiest Way and "fallen women" films like *Susan Lenox* and *Possessed*. Said
Thalberg:

> The vital, pioneering films have always come from the major companies.
> The very fact that they are forced into mass production compels them to
> be continuously on the *qui vive*—lest they be outstripped by a competitor.
> Anybody can make a picture. There is no monopoly on that. But he must have
> the initiative, the material, and then make a profit. There, I think, is the flaw in
> the whole plan. We will grant a certain amount of idealism, high aims, to start
> with. The producer beating a new path for himself through the wilderness is
> going to do the thing "differently," of course. But after a while, he looks about
> him. The territory is unfamiliar, the forest ahead forbidding. Just how "differ-
> ent" dare he be? He looks at his resources, and then at the established successes
> of the past. He suddenly realizes he must play safe, be sure. The unknown is a
> gamble; the known isn't—at least comparatively. The safest plan, obviously,
> is to follow the trailblazers. So he produces an imitation of one of the current
> successes. Usually it is a mediocre imitation.

That Thalberg managed to avoid this dreaded mediocrity, even when hopping on
someone else's cycle (Garbo's *Mata Hari* followed Marlene Dietrich's *Dishonored*),
was a credit to his insight. What was remarkable was how many cycles he initiated
while ostensibly creating star vehicles. Examples of this were the end-of-the-year
hits enjoyed by Shearer, Crawford, and Garbo.

With *Strangers May Kiss*, Shearer revisited the Ursula Parrott school of sexual
emancipation, but took it one lesson further; instead of playing a married woman
who tests society's limits, Shearer played a woman who dared to sidestep marriage.
The SRC had judged the novel "wholly objectionable under the Code [because]
unconventional love is the accepted condition," so Thalberg invited Joy to his
home on a Sunday afternoon and kept him there until he approved the treatment.
"Thalberg was inconsiderate," recalled Howard Dietz. "He would talk to you
until your dinner grew cold." Shearer recalled Thalberg smiling and saying,
"Only small minds tick with the clock." Likewise he reasoned that only small
minds would resist his ideas. He bought a risqué play for Marion Davies called *It's
a Wise Child*. Hearst thought it indecent, and Marion Davies found herself stuck

between him and Thalberg. "Is this entirely your thought?" Thalberg asked about her refusal to make the film.

"Yes," Davies said coyly. "In a way."

"You don't understand what I'm trying to do," said Thalberg. "I'm trying to get you away from those namby-pamby pictures. Mr. Hearst doesn't want you to do anything the slightest bit off-color. I have no intention of doing that. I just want to strike a happy medium. I want you to do something that isn't entirely gutless, something that means something. And I don't want to be told about these things by another person. Don't you have confidence in me?"

As Davies summed it up, "Irving could talk me into anything, and he knew damned well he could. I just wanted him to know that I respected his opinion, which I did. And who didn't?"

In this case, Thalberg was proved wrong, although *It's a Wise Child* didn't flop because it was risqué; it flopped because audiences were losing interest in Davies. *Strangers May Kiss* was a hit because of Shearer's new image. "Audiences like to see me as the girl who doesn't wither under a blow," said Shearer. "They like to see me go to hell, but they want me to come back. Women have been smarting for years under the passive role they were called on to play, and at last they are getting the courage to fight back. I don't mean that every woman should carry the rebellion as far as Miss Parrott's heroines, but it gives them satisfaction to see me do it."

Shearer's next film exemplified Thalberg's belief in "oblique casting," that is, not to put a star in the same type of role two times in a row, but rather to go off at an angle from her image. "Typecasting is slow death for actors," Thalberg told Sam Marx, who alerted him to *A Free Soul*, a play by Adela Rogers St. Johns. The autobiographical story of a bibulous criminal lawyer and his quirky daughter could give Shearer's persona another facet, if Thalberg and St. Johns could come to terms.

"How much do you want for it?" he asked.

"Forty thousand dollars."

"That's ridiculous!" said Thalberg. "I can't pay you half that."

"I'll have to think it over," said St. Johns. A day later, her banker, Irving Hellman, called to tell her that Thalberg had inquired as to her balance. She asked Hellman what it was. She was surprised to learn that it was $10.85. Back in Thalberg's office, she was resolute, even when he proffered a check for $25,000.

"Now, Adela, don't be ridiculous!" he said. She was obdurate. He shook his head, opened his desk drawer, and extracted a check for $40,000. Unlike Lenore Coffee, St. Johns was able to square herself. She later gave Thalberg a straightforward appraisal of a worthless script. For ten pages of analysis, she got a check for six weeks' salary. "You deserve this," he wrote her. "You could have taken the script and worked on it for weeks. Then I would have made the picture, but it still would have been wrong. You saved me several hundred thousand dollars by telling me what you did." The other reason that Thalberg did not send St. Johns to Siberia was that Shearer wanted *A Free Soul*. She was not the only one.

"There were several roles I wanted very badly," recalled Joan Crawford. "One was *A Free Soul*. I was dying to do it. And Adela wanted me to. But Norma got it anyway."

"Norma was the Queen," said George Hurrell, "and what she wanted, she got. No expense was spared." Thalberg invited St. Johns to watch Norbert Brodine's camera tests of Shearer for *A Free Soul*. "She looked like her own grandmother," recalled St. Johns. "She bawled [Irving] out in language I wouldn't tolerate from anyone." Thalberg made sure that William Daniels was assigned to the film; Brodine was given to Lynn Fontanne.

Thalberg went against the current by casting the passé Lionel Barrymore as Shearer's father. "I bit like a carp at the bait," wrote Barrymore, whose directing career was over. Shearer wanted Clark Gable for the film; she had met him three months earlier in a test for *Strangers May Kiss*. "He was shy and ill at ease," wrote Shearer. "Perhaps he was being deferential and polite. He had just signed a contract with the company, so perhaps he was nervous acting with the boss's wife. The Gable arrogance and authority weren't there that day, so the Little Boss cast the former Arrow Collar Man [Neil Hamilton] in *Strangers May Kiss*."

Cast as a sexually menacing gangster in *A Free Soul*, Gable gained confidence, and his first scene with Shearer sizzled. "When I looked up and I saw that slow, ingratiating grin," wrote Shearer, "I knew that he was on his way to one of the most spectacular careers in Hollywood history." Preview audiences who thought Shearer's last three films had gone as far as the Production Code would allow were electrified by the chemistry between her and Gable. "A stirring scene finds me in a plush penthouse atop his gambling lair," said Shearer. "As I let my ermine cape slip from my body, the camera reveals that I am clad in a white satin sheath. The eternal game begins, this time between a gangster and a lady. The lady gives her body but not her soul, and therein lies the problem of the play." When the gangster decides to take possession of the lady's soul, she reminds him of his status and starts to walk out. He shoves her into a chair, snarling: "Sit down! Take it and like it!" More than any other scene in *A Free Soul*, this one shocked audiences. No leading man had ever treated a lady in such a fashion on screen. Shearer's emancipation had its drawbacks; controversy had few. Gable was declared a star, and both Shearer and Barrymore received Academy Award nominations. Barrymore won the award.

Crawford's three 1931 films did not garner nominations, but they made twice as much money as Shearer's; Gable was in all three. In *Possessed*, Thalberg cast him as a lawyer. "Will they accept me as this Harvard guy?" he asked Coffee.

"Yes," she answered, "if you accept yourself."

Crawford had no trouble playing an ambitious shopgirl. "The only trouble is," chuckled Thalberg several years later, "she's been playing it ever since." After years of dancing-daughter parts, though, it was a startling change, a little too startling for the SRC. Censor Lamar Trotti took issue with the means by which Crawford improved her status. "I fear that we have another *Strangers May Kiss* on our hands," he wrote Joy, who was having ever more frequent confrontations with Thalberg; a telegram from Trotti to Joy captured the tenor of the relationship:

> I had a long and pleasant discussion with Thalberg regarding *Possessed* [and I] conveyed to him my worry at another "kept woman" picture. . . . He appreciates our fears and admits that he is also somewhat worried but insists that because his picture has been handled in such good taste, without sex scenes, that it does not violate the Code, which is a matter of opinion. I am sure that it does. He holds that his company had a perfect right to use such material and thinks our office expects too much on that score, but you are doubtless familiar with that argument.

Thalberg was able to have the film released as shot, but he had to deal with hostile women's clubs, cuts made by local censor boards, and even rival companies. Jack Warner accused the SRC of favoritism, claiming that one scene in *Possessed* showed Crawford disrobing in front of Gable; a screening of the scene proved him wrong.

Thalberg also had to deal with a potentially scandalous romance between Crawford and Gable, who were both married. "In the picture," wrote Crawford, "we were madly in love. When the scenes ended, the emotion didn't. We were playing characters very close to our own. It was a love bounded by the flats on the set." This was one problem that Thalberg let Mayer handle. The big boss told Crawford and Gable to end the affair—or else. "He would have ended my career in fifteen minutes," recalled Gable. "And I had no interest in becoming a waiter." After chastising Gable, Mayer asked Thalberg why he had cast Gable opposite

Shearer, Crawford, and Garbo. "If you were ever here, L.B., you'd know these things," replied Thalberg, referring to Mayer's numerous trips.

"Wherever I am, Irving, I am the head of this studio."

"Don't I know it?" said Thalberg, reddening. "Isn't that why Nick pays you a million dollars a year?"

Mayer backed down, and instead of waiting to talk with Thalberg when he was in a better mood, he turned to the person whom he had vowed never to trust again. Nick Schenck was coming to California with the rest of the Loew's executives for a late-autumn conclave; Mayer hoped he would intervene. It was sadly obvious that the friendship of Mayer and Thalberg had ended.

Thalberg's sudden flashes of anger alerted his associates that something was wrong. In spite of his vacation, or perhaps because of it, he was again resentful—not of the Loew's group, but of the profit-sharing setup within the Mayer group. In late November, Schenck, Rubin, publicity director Howard Dietz, and head of sales Felix Feist arrived for an anti-depression powwow. After observing a few social niceties, Thalberg sat Schenck down and confronted him. He felt that there was a gross inequity. Mayer was getting more money, recognition, and time off while he, Irving, was working fourteen-hour days. "I'm being shortchanged," said Thalberg.

Schenck answered that he was powerless to increase anyone's profit percentage because of the contractual setup of the group's profit sharing. Thalberg was adamant, and a heated argument ensued. Schenck called Mayer in to calm Thalberg. Mayer, seeing that Thalberg would not yield, offered to reduce his percentage by 5½ percent so that he and Thalberg would have an even 37½ percent each. Thalberg was still not satisfied. He demanded a three-month yearly vacation such as Mayer was getting, as well as stock options. Schenck quickly approved the vacation and, after getting approval from the Loew's board of directors, approved the stocks. Thalberg's new terms would take effect on April 7, 1932.

Mayer and Schenck could shake their heads at Thalberg, but by the end of the year it was patently obvious that Thalberg was worth the money. Every M-G-M star (except Marion Davies) had at least one hit; most had two, and the triumvirate of silent stars turned talkie stars—Shearer, Crawford, and Garbo—had three big hits each. Garbo was in her own category, of course—a cultural phenomenon, the only silent film star who became more popular in talkies—yet it was Thalberg's formula that had made her a star and kept her one. In no year was his magic touch more evident than in 1931, when he transformed three muddled scripts into spectacularly profitable releases. *Inspiration, Susan Lenox,* and *Mata Hari* were all problem productions saved by previews and retakes. That *Mata Hari* made a *profit* of $1 million in the grim Christmas season of 1931 was due to many factors—casting, timing, the creation of a fantasy world—but the key factor was Thalberg's ability to find a story, refine the story, and tell that story. One example of his work was the polishing of a single line of dialogue. It could have been a throwaway, as it was spoken by a supporting character to a bit player, but by improving it, setting it up, and staging it properly, it became a much-quoted distillation of the story, the character, and the era.

In John Colton's first-draft script, the detective Dubois, who is obsessed with capturing Mata Hari, commands the early-morning execution of a young soldier who has betrayed France for a night with the alluring spy. After the firing squad has done its work, Dubois tells his attaché, Lafarge, that he will be attending a party at which Mata Hari will be performing her erotic dance to the Lord Shiva. Lafarge cynically says, "Some must die . . . others dance." Thalberg had playwright Leon Gordon rewrite the scene so that Lafarge now says, "Some dance and some—die." Then Dubois snaps, "And some do both." In Bayard Veiller's rewrite, Lafarge says, "Oh, well. Some dance, some die." Dubois answers, "And some will do both." The final version, which Thalberg dictated to Bernard Fineman in a story conference, had a nasty, ominous cadence that, when combined with the image of rifle smoke drifting over the dead traitor and followed by the shadow of a biplane heading to its doom, was powerful and succinct.

> DUBOIS: (bitterly and ironically)
> Tonight I'm to see your Mata Hari dance. A soiree at Le
> Marchand's. It's to be smart and *very* private. After all,
> there *is* a war going on.
>
> LAFARGE: (tolerantly)
> Oh well, some dance—and some die . . .
>
> DUBOIS: (with unpleasant emphasis, menacingly)
> And some—will do both.

Mata Hari premiered on December 31, the same night that Thalberg and Shearer attended a New Year's Eve party given by Marion Davies at the palatial beach house Hearst had built for her. The party was so lavish that George Hurrell was hired to take pictures of the guests, all of whom wore "kiddie" attire. Thalberg did not want to show his skinny legs, so he wore a sailor suit. As usual, he enjoyed the party in his own formal way, but his mind was at M-G-M, on the next project. In this case it was *Grand Hotel*, a Garbo vehicle that he hoped to make into something even bigger. Even though M-G-M finished 1931 with a profit of $12 million, and his new profit sharing was making him wealthier than he already was, he could not relax. "The wheels were always going around in Irving's head," remembered Shearer. "No matter how late I left the studio, the light was always on in Irving's office," recalled Conrad Nagel. Within a year Thalberg would learn how long that light could shine.

Irving Thalberg's career soared in an unbroken arc over Hollywood in 1932, even as the Great Depression grounded his competitors. Warner Bros. began the year $8 million in the red; RKO Radio Pictures, $5 million; Fox Film, a mere $3 million, thanks to its vast theater chain. Universal managed to stay in the black by periodically shutting down production. Paramount showed a profit, though it fell from $18 million in 1930 to $6 million in 1931. In a desperate attempt to cut overhead, Paramount began selling its heavily mortgaged theaters. This left fewer outlets for its product, which was a moot point. In a mere two years, weekly movie attendance had fallen from 90 million to 50 million. Twelve million Americans were unemployed. Many of them simply could not afford a movie. In 1932 the United States was depressed, both fiscally and psychologically. "The fog of despair hung over the land," wrote historian Arthur Schlesinger Jr. "One out of every four American workers lacked a job. Factories that had once darkened the skies with smoke stood ghostly and silent, like extinct volcanoes. Families slept in tarpaper shacks and scavenged like dogs for food in the city dump."

During the unseasonably warm Christmas season of 1931–32, Hollywood carried on with its usual social events, trying to ignore the grim vignettes around it. "Those who had survived the transition to the talkies," wrote Frances Marion, "formed a little green island in a sea of tears. All about us was misery, the backwash of the depression. Only the picture colony seemed to thrive, where blinds were pulled down so that none of the prosperous would have to see the sorrow and destruction around them." The climate of Los Angeles was less hostile to depression victims than that of other cities, but even if they were basking in sunlight, they could not be dismissed, as Ethel Barrymore discovered when attending her first Hollywood premiere. "The onlookers on the sidewalks were silent and sullen as people wearing furs and jewels rode by them in big cars," wrote Barrymore. "It was a very uncomfortable experience."

Neither Nick Schenck nor Louis B. Mayer had imposed any austerity measures on Thalberg, so he proceeded with thirty-eight films, expecting their originality and glamour to carry M-G-M through the crisis. He crafted each film in the usual manner: a battery of big-name writers working simultaneously to create one script; a series of story conferences to distill the best of each draft; negotiations with the SRC to satisfy the censors; a producer to tailor the material to its star; a preview to test the film's effectiveness; and retakes to fix whatever was wrong. Other studios were adopting his methods. In October 1931, RKO Radio installed David Selznick as a vice president in charge of production. "I had long believed that the whole system of assembly-line production was absurd," wrote Selznick, "and that the business had to be broken into small producing units." It was understood, however, that like Thalberg, Selznick would exercise artistic control. At Paramount, B. P. Schulberg also emulated Thalberg, overseeing every film. Paramount had the best directors in Hollywood—Josef von Sternberg, Rouben Mamoulian, and Ernst Lubitsch—but could not overtake M-G-M, because the rest of its films were poor. At a Paramount sales convention, exhibitors were delighted to hear that M-G-M might lend them Clark Gable. "But will they lend us Thalberg?" came a plaintive voice from the back of the auditorium. The crowd burst into laughter, but the point was well taken. M-G-M's solvency was due as much to Thalberg as to its seventeen stars. Years later, Paramount executive D. A. Doran said: "We were making pictures for people to see. He was making pictures for people to feel."

Samuel Goldwyn produced films under his own banner but had no equivalent of Thalberg working for him, so he began showing up at Norma Shearer's soirees to buttonhole Thalberg. Mayer, who held Sunday luncheons down the street from Thalberg, rarely attended Thalberg's parties; when he did, he was angered by Goldwyn's presumptuousness. One Monday morning Howard Strickling received an urgent phone call from Thalberg. "Get to Hillcrest right away!" The publicity chief raced to the all-Jewish country club in West Los Angeles to find that Mayer and Goldwyn had gotten into a fistfight in the locker room after Mayer had told Goldwyn to stop pumping Thalberg for production secrets. Mayer's suspicions were unfounded. Thalberg was imparting nothing of value to Goldwyn. The ingredients of Thalberg's success could not be communicated at a cocktail party, nor would he confide them to a rival. He rarely confided in his peers, as F. Scott Fitzgerald observed during a January 1927 visit to the studio. Only esteem for the author of *The Great Gatsby* made Thalberg lean across a dining room table and reveal something of himself:

> Scottie, supposing there's got to be a road through a mountain—a railroad, and two or three surveyors and people come to you and you believe some of them and some of them you don't believe, but all in all, there seem to be half a dozen possible roads through those mountains, each one of which, so far as you can determine, is as good as the other. Now suppose you happen to be the top man. There's a point where you don't exercise the faculty of judgment in the ordinary way, but simply the faculty of arbitrary decision. You say, "Well, I think we will put the road there," and you trace it with your finger and you know in your secret heart, and no one else knows, that you have no reason for putting the road there rather than in several other different courses, but you're the only person that knows that you don't know why you're doing it and you've got to stick to that and you've got to pretend that you know and that you did it for specific reasons, even though you're utterly assailed by doubts at times as to the wisdom of your decision, because all these other possible decisions keep echoing in your ear. But when you're planning a new enterprise on a grand scale, the people under you mustn't ever know or guess that you're in any doubt, because they've all got to have something to look up to and they mustn't ever dream that you're in doubt about any decision.

Thalberg's unshakable self-possession would make 1932 his most accomplished year, but not without casualties, among them Fitzgerald.

In mid-1931 Sam Marx's endless search for story material had brought him to the Philadelphia offices of the *Saturday Evening Post*, which was publishing Fitzgerald's short stories, including *Babylon Revisited*. While there, Marx found something equally intriguing, an unfinished serial called *Red-Headed Woman*. Thalberg authorized Marx to purchase the Katharine Brush story and to offer Fitzgerald a six-week contract (at $1,200 a week) to adapt it. Fitzgerald was grateful for the opportunity. His daughter Scottie was attending an expensive school and his wife, Zelda, was recovering from a series of breakdowns. Fitzgerald started at M-G-M in November, working on the script with producer Paul Bern and Marcel de Sano, a director of foreign-language versions. The novelist found Hollywood "much more polite" than he had in 1927. "Everyone is more courteous," he told an interviewer. "There is not so much 'Whoop! And off we go!' Workmen seem to be respected. People listen to other people's opinions. There is not so much of the know-it-all spirit as there was."

Fitzgerald's courteous colleagues included two New York friends recently hired by M-G-M: Dwight Taylor, a promising young playwright, and Anita Loos, who was famed for her 1925 novel, *Gentlemen Prefer Blondes*. They found Fitzgerald deferential. "Poor Scott had quit drinking," wrote Loos, "and had taken on that apologetic humility which is characteristic of reformed drunks." When he visited Loos's cubicle in the writers' building, he would hesitate at the door, and ask: "You don't really have time for me, do you?" Loos found it depressing to see meekness in "the man who had ripped up the Riviera while he was roaring drunk." Fitzgerald's reformation was far from complete, however, as Marx and King Vidor found out. When they met him for dinner at the Hollywood Roosevelt Hotel, Fitzgerald was more interested in drinks. "Almost at the first sip," wrote Marx, "his tongue slurred and skidded over simple words. He was unable to go on to dinner."

Back at the studio, Fitzgerald was on his best behavior and eager to learn. "He was worried about camera angles," wrote Taylor. "I pointed out that it was his dialogue and characterization that they were after, and if he could manage to get his story down, he could be sure that they would photograph it." The problem was getting the story down. Fitzgerald did not like working in collaboration, and de Sano was more of a con artist than a film artist. Furthermore, Fitzgerald could not justify the need to tell a story visually, especially at the expense of his beloved prose. Thalberg was aware of this pitfall. He told an interviewer: "Novelists and playwrights without picture experience—especially those who don't see cinema and who have never visited a studio—will be inclined to sacrifice action to dialogue." Thalberg did not know the full extent of Fitzgerald's resistance. "There was a rankling indignity," Fitzgerald later wrote, "that to me had become almost an obsession, in seeing the written word subordinated to another power, a more glittering, a grosser power." Worse than this, Fitzgerald had no sympathy for his subject.

Red-Headed Woman was the tawdry saga of Lil Andrews, a secretary who seduces her boss, and then his boss, and then that boss's chauffeur. "I want to show Hays and the SRC that M-G-M can make sex entertaining, not offensive," said Thalberg, who was also making a film called *New Morals for Old*. It was not a coincidence; most of the films he planned for release in 1932 reflected his impatience with SRC rules and Hollywood formulas. "I have never seen a film made outside this lot that had a convincing story," he said to Bern one day. Thalberg's adult-themed projects included *Strange Interlude, Grand Hotel, Unashamed, Kongo,* and *Freaks.*

"Irving was a realist," wrote Shearer. "He knew what lay behind man's weakness. He was fascinated by the unusual, the colorful—even the decadent and evil. He loved the impact of horror, but not merely for the sake of horror. These elements had to possess a reality, a logic, a meaning. There had to be sound ideas behind these ugly images to lend a story reason, to give the audience hope, and to impart some beauty—even if it was a sad beauty—to these visions of life. In spite of his sophistication, his detachment, and his ironic humor, Irving was also an idealist, and, luckily for me, a romantic." He also appreciated the picaresque side of life, according to producer Walter Wanger, who joined M-G-M in late 1932 after butting heads with Schulberg at Paramount for five years. "Irving was tough and discerning," said Wanger, "but he had humor and he understood sex. After all, the bachelor dinner the night before his wedding took place at Madam [Lee] Francis's house of joy on Sunset Boulevard." Donald Ogden Stewart later saw Thalberg sitting in the lobby of the same brothel, reading a script while waiting for another executive to come downstairs.

On reading Fitzgerald's first draft of *Red-Headed Woman*, a disappointed Thalberg told Marx to have Fitzgerald try again. "I couldn't get him to grasp the idea that Thalberg wanted the audience to laugh *with* Lil Andrews, not *at* her," recalled Marx. Fitzgerald continued to revise his script, but he was swimming against the current. "Far from approaching it too confidently, I was far too humble," he later wrote. "I ran afoul of a bastard named de Sano . . . and let myself be gypped out of command. I wrote the picture, and he changed as I wrote. I tried to get at Thalberg but was erroneously warned against it as 'bad taste.' Result—a bad script."

On a Sunday afternoon in December 1931, Fitzgerald accompanied Taylor to a party at the Thalbergs' home. "We found ourselves standing at one of those huge white doors which guard the portals of the curious monoliths along the sand," wrote Taylor. "After a long walk across the patio to the doors of the house, we were shown into a huge living room, and I could see at once that we had landed on our feet. Everybody who was anybody in the picture colony was there. . . . Pretty faces which had gazed with bland enticement from a thousand billboards were now animate." Taylor resolved to keep Fitzgerald sober and did his best to watch him but was soon distracted by the dazzling array of celebrities. The party was one of the "take-a-chance affairs" that Shearer occasionally hosted. "She likes to throw varied personalities together to see how they jell," Thalberg later admitted.

"Sometimes this results in very nice parties, sometimes in failures." When Robert Montgomery arrived from a polo match still dressed in a riding outfit and asked Taylor for an introduction, he could not find Fitzgerald. Then Fitzgerald suddenly reappeared, gin martini in hand. Taylor made introductions, but Fitzgerald stared at Montgomery and asked dully, "Why didn't you bring your horse in too?" Montgomery was not amused. He turned on his heel and walked off.

Before Taylor could collect Fitzgerald and escape the party, the inebriated novelist called for attention and announced that he was going to sing. The group of rich and famous guests, piqued at being upstaged on their own turf, "gathered in a half-circle near the piano but not too near, their faces devoid of expression, like people gathered at the scene of an accident." Shearer tactfully placed her dog in Fitzgerald's arms, with which he launched into a nonsensical song about "man's best friend." After three identical verses, John Gilbert and Lupe Velez began hissing. "I could see," wrote Taylor, "the figure of Thalberg at the far end of the room, his hands plunged deep into his trouser pockets, his shoulders hunched slightly in that characteristic posture which seemed to be both a withdrawal and a rejection. There was a slight, not unkind smile on his lips as he looked toward the piano. But he did not move." It was incumbent upon Taylor to unfreeze the ghastly tableau.

"Come on, Scott. We're going home."

The next day Taylor was surprised to see Fitzgerald at the door of his cubicle. "Nice party," ventured Fitzgerald. "I hope I didn't make too much of a jackass of myself. This job means a lot to me." Later that same day, Fitzgerald received a telegram from Shearer. It read: "I thought you were one of the most agreeable persons at our tea."

A few days afterward, Fitzgerald met with Bern, who praised his script and told him that he could return to Alabama early. In truth, Thalberg was afraid that Fitzgerald would go on a binge if he learned what he really thought of the script. "Scott tried to turn the silly story into a prose poem," said Thalberg, who contrived for Fitzgerald to leave Hollywood none the wiser. "I don't want a word of this to reach him." Thalberg's plan might have worked—but Fitzgerald ran into de Sano. "You've been tricked," de Sano told him. "They've thrown out your work. Anita Loos is starting over from the beginning." De Sano was fired for betraying a confidence, but that did not stop Fitzgerald from going on a three-week binge.

Other talents who failed to fit the Thalberg template were John Gilbert and Buster Keaton, both of whom had been cast in M-G-M's most ambitious project yet. For fifteen years the star system had driven Hollywood, and a Hollywood film was by definition a vehicle for one star. Thalberg saw good films with great stars failing because of the depression and reasoned that M-G-M could afford to put more than one star in a film. At first, his idea was thought wasteful; he dug in his heels.

"Under the law of averages one will always make mistakes," he once said. "I can take a long time and still be wrong. If I take a short time to make the decision, I am not costing the studio a lot of money while I'm making up my mind." *Mata Hari* showed that a two-star film could be a hit, but Thalberg envisioned an "all-star" film. He had a specific property in mind for this experiment, a Broadway play that had—not coincidentally—been backed by M-G-M. *Grand Hotel* was a dramatization of the Vicki Baum novel about the mingled destinies of five guests in a Berlin luxury hotel. Fascinated by a scandal involving an industrialist and a call girl, the German writer had researched her story by working as a chambermaid. When Thalberg saw the play in New York, he told an interviewer: "The swift-moving, episodic character of [this] play will probably serve as a pattern for many films. . . . The general idea will be that of drama induced by the chance meeting of a group of conflicting and interesting personalities." The idea that the five personalities could all be played by stars was unheard of, but Thalberg thought it could work—with the right stars. Greta Garbo would play Grusinskaya, a fading, unloved ballerina who attempts suicide in the hotel. Joan Crawford would play Flaemmchen, a stenographer who sells herself to a client. The three male roles were dramatically different: Preysing, a crude middle-aged industrialist who hires the stenographer; Baron von Gaigern, a glamorous nobleman who is also a jewel thief, loved by the stenographer and in love with the ballerina; and Kringelein, a mousy, mortally ill accountant, spending his life savings on a last spree in the big hotel, who also loves the baron.

Thalberg announced in October 1931 that Clark Gable would play Preysing, John Gilbert the Baron, and Buster Keaton Kringelein. Circumstances changed his plans. Gable's sudden leap to stardom made the part of Preysing undesirable, and Wallace Beery was revealing himself as an actor of greater range and power than anyone had guessed, so Beery, despite his protests, replaced Gable. Gilbert had the world-weariness of the Baron but was losing his verve. "His confidence had been eaten away," wrote his daughter, Leatrice Gilbert Fountain. "And he was ill. His troublesome stomach had developed bleeding ulcers. Any amount of drinking made him sick. . . . But still he drank, because the Scotch seemed to help keep away the night. His insomnia had worsened, and with it his private fears." When Gilbert began to brandish a gun, dinner invitations ceased.

In November 1931 Marx heard Thalberg talking with Bern about the magic of the first double-Barrymore film, *Arsene Lupin*, then in production. To add John and Lionel Barrymore to Garbo and Crawford in *Grand Hotel* would be newsworthy casting. John could play the Baron, and Lionel could do Kringelein. Director Edmund Goulding had sounded out Keaton for Kringelein; Keaton was tremendously enthusiastic. When Lionel Barrymore was cast as Kringelein, no one bothered to tell Keaton. He read it in *Variety*, and his drinking accelerated to the point of orgiastic bouts. A prostitute used an incident at a party in Keaton's studio bungalow to frame him for rape, and Mayer sacked him. Thalberg interceded, saying, "I can't make stars as fast as you can fire them."

"Go ahead," Mayer challenged Thalberg. "Argue with me. Show me where I'm wrong!"

Thalberg told Mayer that Keaton's wife, Natalie (the sister of Thalberg's old flame Constance Talmadge), had been making Keaton's life miserable, that he had repeatedly asked Thalberg for his own production unit, and that Thalberg had repeatedly refused him because he would not conform. Mayer relented. Keaton's response to the news was a bitter one: "You studio people warp my character."

Gilbert was another headache; he would not be happy to hear that he had lost *Grand Hotel* to John Barrymore. "Thalberg decided that he had no choice and broke the news to Gilbert personally," wrote Marx. "They would continue to communicate thereafter—it was necessary in order to do business—but their friendship was finished." Yet Thalberg was best man at Gilbert's August 10 wedding to Virginia Bruce.

William Haines remained friendly with Thalberg after being demoted from star to featured player in early 1932. Haines was not merely being a good sport; he was starting an interior decoration business and wanted the Thalbergs as clients. Similarly, Ramon Novarro accepted the dubious role of a football-playing college student in a film called *Huddle* because Thalberg had let him direct Spanish-language versions of two of his films. Even so, it was obvious that Thalberg had lost interest in the male stars of his silent films.

Signing John Barrymore to a contract was the latest outpost in Thalberg's campaign to legitimize film. He was resentful that movies, despite their worldwide influence, were accorded less respect than the legitimate stage—or sports. "People go to the movies more than they go to baseball games," he said, pointing to the *Los Angeles Times* sports section, "but look what the papers give sports—page after page. Look at how little space they give us. Why don't they give us the same coverage as sports?" Thalberg hoped that enticing a film star like Tallulah Bankhead or a stage star like Ethel Barrymore made as good publicity as signing

Babe Ruth. But it was not borrowed glamour that made 1932 Thalberg's greatest year. It was adventurous filmmaking—the most diverse catalogue of entertainment in Hollywood's history.

Each project began with a fresh concept. As often as not, this concept originated with Thalberg. An all-star film. Two Barrymores in one film. All three Barrymores in one film. Norma Shearer in an old-fashioned romance. A horror film more horrible than *Dracula* and *Frankenstein* combined. A jungle film like *Trader Horn*, directed by Woody Van Dyke, but shot in California.

Yes. And why not from an Edgar Rice Burroughs novel? Thalberg authorized Marx to go as high as $100,000 to get *Tarzan of the Apes* from Burroughs, but told him to start low. "Don't lose it," said Thalberg when other studios began bidding. Burroughs wanted $100,000. Marx countered with $15,000. Burroughs refused. Marx went to $25,000. Burroughs asked $75,000. Only after a price of $40,000 had been signed on did Burroughs's agent admit, "We were so anxious to have M-G-M make this picture that if you had held out long enough you would have got it for nothing."

"If you had held out long enough you would have got your hundred thousand," Marx said coolly.

In fact, neither party could have held out forever, because of competition, casting, and climate. Burroughs eventually sold Tarzan stories elsewhere (to Paramount and independent producer Sol Lesser). M-G-M rushed to test actors (including Johnny Mack Brown and Charles Bickford) because Thalberg wanted W. S. Van Dyke to shoot the outdoor film before the rains started.

After a concept crystallized into a project, Thalberg assigned writers to it, often writers who found the assignment off-putting. "It's good discipline for writers to work on stories that are foreign to them," said Thalberg. Thus he assigned British playwright (and matinee idol) Ivor Novello and *Trader Horn* adapter Cyril Hume to craft a plausible story from Burroughs's tales of a young British lord raised in the African jungle by apes. In addition to defining the romantic primitive of the story, they had to decide the character of Jane Parker, the young woman whom Tarzan kidnaps from an expedition. "I think it would be very nice to establish the sophistication of the girl, even with all her sweetness," said Van Dyke. "I don't know, though. This is a kid's picture."

"I think it's for everybody," said Novello.

Thalberg did not feel the same way, according to J. J. Cohn, who submitted a budget of $700,000. "Joe, we can't spend that much money," said Thalberg. "We have got to get it down." Cohn worked with producer Bernard Hyman to cut costs and returned, still frustrated. "Irving, the least we'll make this picture for is six fifty," said Cohn. "But . . . we would really like it to be seven fifty."

"Joe, I've argued with Bernie as much as I want to," laughed Thalberg. "Do the best you can." The film was made for $660,000 plus $60,000 overhead, and its mass appeal made it M-G-M's second-most profitable film of 1932. Although budgets were officially Mayer's responsibility, his continuing absences left Thalberg free to dictate that a submarine film called *Pig Boats* could not spend more than $30,000 on sets but that the Barrymore film *Rasputin* could spend over $100,000. "A successful picture may gross $3 million at the box office," explained Thalberg to a colleague. "An unsuccessful one may gross one tenth of that. If the difference between those two is fifty thousand dollars in production, why not chance it?" Whether Thalberg's decision was creative or financial, it was final.

"This man looks almost frail," a Los Angeles journalist wrote of Thalberg. "His nerves are always keyed to a high tension, yet always under control. He is usually seen in a blue serge suit, walking up and down restlessly while figuring out a problem. He toys with a fountain pen or draws little figures while discussing a contract with an actor. An agreement is reached. Thalberg jots down a memorandum on a pad, and with a laconic 'Sign here,' the matter is settled."

"I'd get sore because Irving was reading mail while I tried to talk to him about a script," recalled Lawrence Weingarten. "'Go on,' he said. I did and he could correct me as I recited—while he continued to read his mail." His habit of flipping a twenty-dollar gold piece in the air was known throughout the industry. One day he flipped the coin so high it lodged in a chandelier. Another day he began bouncing the coin on the glass top of his desk. Within a few days, he was startled to see all his associates bouncing coins on his desk. He took it with good humor, but as Lewin recalled, "Irving was invariably impersonal about personal matters." He was also overawed by formal education—and a little envious. John Lee Mahin came to M-G-M from a Chicago advertising firm via the redoubtable duo of Hecht and MacArthur. When Thalberg learned that Mahin was a Harvard man, he grew reserved. "You're asking four hundred a week," said Thalberg. "We're not all millionaires out here, you know. Did Charlie tell you to ask that much? How much have you been getting?"

"Two hundred a week, sir."

"Well, you can start there," said Thalberg. Mahin made good with *The Beast of the City* and *The Wet Parade*, and Thalberg raised his salary to $500.

"I had a master's degree from Harvard," said Lewin, "and I sensed that even though Irving was more widely read than most college graduates, he felt insecure.

Like many of those who hadn't gone, he overestimated the importance of higher education. He had better taste in music, decor, and writing than most so-called intellectuals. But he insisted on having me correct his speeches."

Lewin and the erudite Bern were the only M-G-M executives who knew of Thalberg's insecurity. To most of Hollywood, Thalberg was still the Boy Wonder. On May 30, 1932, he turned thirty-three but continued to look boyish. If anything, his personal magnetism had increased in direct proportion to his wealth and power. "He was an amazingly attractive man," wrote Wanger. "He had terrific eyes. You thought that you were talking to an Indian savant. He could cast a spell on anybody. There has never been anybody like him, and more wonderment because nobody in his family had the magic of personality that he had. His very appearance was impressive. Although he was quite slight, he carried himself in a most effective manner. It was amazing what he got people to do for him."

Thalberg's other insecurity was about his health. Lewin and Bern occasionally had the impression that Thalberg was holding his breath in disbelief as time passed. Hadn't the doctors predicted that he would not live past thirty? And yet here he was, working sixteen-hour days with no ill effects; at least no discernible ill effects. In truth, Thalberg constantly watched for signs of illness. He kept apples and dates on his desk top. He carried multicolored pills in his coat pocket and nitroglycerine tablets in his vest pocket, ready to pop two under his tongue should he feel chest pains. Henrietta sometimes irritated Shearer by showing up at 707 Ocean Front unannounced "to look in on Irving." Shearer could not question Henrietta's intentions when she herself had learned to use a hypodermic syringe, "just in case."

Thalberg had maintained a childhood friendship with David Perla, a distinguished doctor who also had a weak heart. Perla's wife, Jessie Marmorston, was a cardiologist who sometimes treated Thalberg. The Perlas were fond of Thalberg and had given him a first edition of Sigmund Freud's collected writings for his thirty-second birthday. "Freud has helped me to understand myself and given me courage to confront my particular future, which in the past I had tried to block out," Thalberg wrote in a letter to Perla. Even minor symptoms were a reminder of his "particular" future. "His head would vibrate at night," recalled Frances Goldwyn. "You could feel his heart throbbing in the palms of his hands. In spite of all that, he was handsome in a unique way."

Anita Loos was also ambivalent about Thalberg. "Irving was still a rather pathetic figure," wrote Loos. "His natural pallor was intensified by long hours in offices and projection rooms, shut away from the California sunshine. I was enormously touched that the shoulders of Irving's jacket were too obviously padded, in order to make him seem more grown-up and robust."

Myrna Loy was signed by M-G-M in late 1931 but did not meet Thalberg until late 1932, after she had endured what she thought were six pointless assignments, films like *The Mask of Fu Manchu*. Thalberg sent for her, which meant waiting for hours on a bench outside his office. Karen Morley had gotten so impatient one day that she sat on the floor in front of his door. Her ploy worked; he cast her in *Arsene Lupin*. Loy was too reserved not to wait. When she was finally ushered into Thalberg's office, she began to study him. "Although his shoulders hunched forward slightly," she wrote later, "he was an attractive man, really beautiful, I thought, with a great face and deep, penetrating eyes." He turned away from her and began looking out at Washington Boulevard. Loy rose and started for the door. Thalberg turned around. "Thank you," she said, surprised at her own nerve. "I was brought up to look at people when I talk to them."

"Myrna," he said without commenting on her behavior, "you're terribly shy. There's no reason why you should be. It's hurting you, putting a veil between you and the audience. You've got to cut through that veil and take hold of the audience. It's there, but they like you. You're beautiful enough for the movies, and you're making good progress here, so make it work for you." What he did not tell her was that he had not yet found a writer to craft a role for her. For Thalberg, writers were the mysterious link between stars and the camera. As intuitive as he was, he could not divine the source of their brilliance. "I can keep tabs on everyone else in the studio and see whether or not they're doing their jobs," Thalberg told Loos, "but I never can tell what's going on in those so-called brains of yours."

"I wrote *Red-Headed Woman* for and *with* Thalberg," recalled Loos in 1964. "I say that because one always wrote *with* him. You would take your material in and go over it with him, and his suggestions became part of your script." Donald Ogden Stewart came to M-G-M as a celebrated novelist and playwright. In short order he realized that he had a lot to learn. Thalberg assigned him to rewrite a scene for *Smilin' Through*, the film that would take Shearer away from "sophisticated" roles. The film had been shooting for two weeks, and Thalberg was unhappy with a scene between Shearer and Fredric March, who was due to return to Paramount. "I somewhat condescendingly agreed to help Irving," wrote Stewart, "especially as he needed the scene for the next day's shooting. When I confidently handed it in, pleased that I had made the deadline, I got the shock of my life. I had never heard such contempt for anything that I had written."

After four years at M-G-M, Bayard Veiller was also learning from (and about)

Thalberg. "He had an endless capacity for work, and his demands on the people who were working with him were brutal, but they were fair," wrote Veiller. "I've written for a good many producers of pictures, but Thalberg was fairer than any of the others. I don't mean he slopped over with praise, because he never praised. Anyway, he never praised me, and I wrote four or five pictures for him, and messed up with four or five more that everybody was writing." Veiller was one of the eighteen writers trying to make sense of *Susan Lenox*. During a conference in Thalberg's office, Veiller handed him a new scene. Thalberg rose to go to his private bathroom, pages in hand. "Oh, Irving," said Veiller, "not in *there!*"

"Don't worry," said Thalberg with his usual poker face. "I'll bring it all back."

Veiller's scenes did not make the final cut of *Susan Lenox*, but he was called upon to rewrite a scene for *Arsene Lupin*. "You have three days to fix it up," Thalberg told him.

"What's the matter with it?" Veiller asked.

"It reads as if it's been written for Universal," Thalberg grinned.

Veiller might—or might not—ask Thalberg what he meant. "Sometimes he couldn't express what he meant, or he didn't know what he meant and was uneasy about it," wrote Veiller. "There was a feeling of unrest, perhaps dissatisfaction. Sometimes he would express his meaning with a gesture—a wave of the hand, a shrug of the shoulders—and you'd say 'yes,' hoping blindly that something of this would seep into your mind."

More often, Thalberg would extemporize a plot during a morning story conference at the studio, complete with twists, turns, and characters. "Irving was a natural-born storyteller," said Ben Hecht. "He had a flair for telling movie stories, and he knew about the medium—more than most writers knew. He was like a man who hadn't learned to write, who hadn't even learned to think, because he hadn't the faintest idea what was going on anywhere in the world except in his office. But he had a flair for telling stories like comedians have for telling jokes. He had an *Arabian Nights* storytelling flair. It was a fantasy-ridden head he had, and it was good." By 1932 Thalberg's twists and turns had become so convoluted that he was having his conferences transcribed. In this way, it was possible for his writers to go backward several steps in the process if necessary. With Thalberg talking off the top of his head and several executives interjecting ideas, it was easy to lose track of the characters, let alone the plot.

Thalberg purchased Luigi Pirandello's play *As You Desire Me* as a possible Garbo vehicle. In it, "The Strange Lady," an amnesiac victim of World War I atrocities, passes her mindless existence as a Berlin nightclub dancer in the company of drunken young men and a jealous, sadistic novelist: "Wine, wine—dance and shout—they're all curled up together, naked—no natural law any more—nothing but the obscene madness that comes from not being able to find any satisfaction—anywhere." In a conference with writer Gene Markey, Thalberg expounded on the gap between the property and the proposed vehicle. "The girl in the play was a sordid, beastly slob," said Thalberg. "You felt sorry for her. Just as when you walk into a party and you see a nice woman who has degenerated, who is drunk and slobbery. You don't dislike her. You just pity her. But Garbo doesn't give you that feeling. Garbo has a quality of beauty and charm that to a certain extent robs her of the proper characterization of a role of this kind." His solution was to invest the character with enough dignity for Garbo to play her. The three men should be admirers, not bedmates, and her only involvement should be with the novelist. "Her playing with the three men is innocent," he suggested.

A story conference for the Marion Davies film *Blondie of the Follies* included Thalberg, Paul Bern, Anita Loos, Frances Marion, and director Edmund Goulding. Marion had tried to write a realistic story of a showgirl and yet satisfy William Randolph Hearst's requirement that every Davies character be romanticized. "I put into my original story some of the dramatic and some of the slightly unpleasant episodes that had taken place during the early Twenties to counterbalance the sugary ones," wrote Marion, "but Mr. Hearst penciled them out. His verdict was: 'There must be neither spice nor sadness in yesterday's dream.'" Thalberg had the worldly Loos do the next draft, basing it on conferences between herself, Goulding, and Marion. Then Goulding added a colorful backstage atmosphere, complete with an oil magnate (Douglas Dumbrille) who plans to turn the innocent Blondie (Davies) into a kept woman. "I want to soft-pedal it if we can," Goulding told Thalberg during a conference. "But you do know she is [going to be] kept. Murchison is after Blondie. He's a climber. He's a Joe Kennedy. She's a chicken. He's definitely after her."

"You've disrobed the story of all its simplicity and honesty," complained Bern.

"Then I should just go and take tickets somewhere," said Goulding in mock irritation.

"Well, *I* know what the story's about," said Thalberg, "but I think you *have* lost something, Eddie." Thalberg saw the story as a parable of two slum girls whose friendship is destroyed by their rivalry for a young millionaire. In the latest draft, Blondie's father rails at her for getting involved with the rake. "All that drama of the father's [outrage] is so false," said Thalberg. "He's just a beast. You can't make a great drama of a father's love for a daughter who's going to pieces if she really isn't going to pieces. Not in 1932. To me, the original story had a certain simplicity. The story you told me today was about a family girl who goes out and gets everything she wants, but her father is mistaken. He thinks that she has given up her virginity. It's too simple now. It hasn't the feeling of life. You see my point, don't you?"

"I'm just beginning to," answered Goulding.

Thalberg proposed showing Blondie's friend Lurline ending up in the gutter because she becomes a kept woman. "Lurline is slipping, slipping, going with cheaper men. Show me any of these girls that ever last—unless they are fortunate enough to find a man that really loves them. The rest of them go to hell. They go from rich men to prizefighters. From prizefighters to bootleggers. And so on down the line."

The story conferences for *Grand Hotel* were especially strenuous. Thalberg was determined to preserve the excitement of the New York presentation while translating five unique characters into star turns. Bern, who was producing, recommended the momentarily out-of-favor Goulding as director. "People around here treat failure like it's a form of leprosy," said Bern. "My dear Irving, you and I know that isn't right."

Goulding preferred Baum's novel to William A. Drake's play script and based his adaptation on that. "To me the play was far better, Eddie," said Thalberg. "In my humble opinion." On November 17, 1931, in the first official *Grand Hotel* story conference, Thalberg explained what he was after.

> The scene in the Yellow Room [the cabaret on the ground floor of the Grand Hotel], my feeling about that, if I can recapture the excitement, is this: I felt a certain something in this play, which may or may not be important, but I think it's lacking in your treatment. In the play there was this mood. A group of men and women having problems: Preysing and his lie about the merger, the Baron not able to steal the ballerina's pearls, etc. Then we come down to a music-filled room in which these [four] characters are enjoying life. They make light of their problems. The Baron, who has a terrific problem, makes a joke of it. He is amused by Kringelein, but is kind to him. He takes the time to be nice to him, in spite of his own problems. He dances with Flaemmchen, tells her he's found love with the ballerina, and to be nice to his little friend Kringelein. She dances with him. In the background is Preysing. They laugh at him. Kringelein tries to be nice to him. Preysing rebuffs him. Kringelein after so many years [of enduring his tyranny at the provincial factory], tells Preysing what the

hell he thinks of him, tells him where to get off, in the best way he can. You get that marvelous feeling of underdogs defying overlords. We fade out on that high point, but we see that in spite of all that Kringelein said, Preysing will get Flaemmchen to go with him. In the last analysis, Flaemmchen has to have clothes and a living. She has to accede to Preysing. And the Baron can't postpone his own business any longer. He'll get his money. One of the most desperate men in the world is a man who will gamble to get money. Here you get the profound philosophy of the lower classes. No matter how they fight against the assurances of life as they see it, in the end they have to succumb to money, and they do. This is in the play.

In the next story conference, on December 9, Thalberg discussed Goulding's latest draft. "I miss the increasing tempo in these damn scenes," said Thalberg. "I'm a great believer in curtain lines. Work it up to that point. Bang! Fade out before the audience is on to you, while they're still wondering: 'What did he mean?' Fade out!"

"I don't think you should fade out unless you have to," said Goulding. "Let the story tell itself."

"I feel the lack of certain punch lines that were in the play."

"The camera tells you what you want to see. It has eyes and ears. It goes to the most interesting spots in a play. You could show it in one long shot."

"Yes," said Thalberg, "but you have to underline those things for an audience. If you were able to put that across by showing a lot of extras walking out of the scene carrying golf bags, pictures would cost us about twenty-five thousand dollars apiece to make. The thing that is most important is this: that audiences love our characters. They must say: 'Aha! This is like my life. It's not a bit important to the night clerk that somebody was killed upstairs.' To me this was a lousy play that succeeded only because it was lousy. But it's full of life, a painted carpet upon which figures walk. Audiences love those damn things if they're properly done."

Shooting was scheduled to commence on December 30, but as late as December 26, Thalberg and Goulding were conferring on how to open *Grand Hotel*—with the characters in phone booth vignettes or with an uninterrupted tracking shot of soup being carried from the kitchen, scalding a woman, and then rolling into the dining room, where the pompous Preysing complains that it is cold. Star power won out over cinematic art, and the film began at the booths. But how long should the vignettes be?

"I think Kringelein's speech can be cut," said Thalberg. "If Lionel plays this, it will take six reels."

"When an actor has to think of his lines," agreed Goulding, "you get sixty percent groping and forty percent acting."

"Barrymore would have to take six months off for this speech alone," sniggered Bern, referring to the actor's drawl.

Thalberg read certain speeches aloud to cut length and improve cadence. Thus Flaemmchen's line "Caviar for me? No, it tastes like herring" became "Have caviar if you like, but it tastes like herring to me." He was also enthusiastic about introducing the heavy with a string of self-righteous statements. "I'm an honest businessman, a good husband and a father," says the devious Preysing. Thalberg felt that Preysing's hypocrisy was only obvious because of dialogue. "Let me explain," he said to Goulding and Bern. "This is going to be one of the few pictures made in the new style. I'll tell you what I'm getting in the pictures I'm making now. I've come to the realization that you have to endow a character with greater complexity than you ever had to in silent pictures. There's nothing new about a man trying to make a girl. But if he starts by pretending that he's a family man, then that's something else again. And that's what talking pictures have given us."

In addition to sitting in exhaustive (and exhausting) story conferences, Thalberg also had to meet with and secure the approval of the SRC. Since the uproar over *Strangers May Kiss* and *Possessed*, Will Hays had mandated that every script be submitted and approved before a film could go before the cameras. Usually the producer could negotiate changes with an SRC officer by mail, but a troublesome film sometimes required that Thalberg go to the SRC to plead his case in person. *Red-Headed Woman* was a problem film from the outset. F. Scott Fitzgerald had not gone quietly. "How could you do this to me?" he wrote to Lewin upon learning that his script was being rewritten by Loos. "If there's anything I know, it's the sound of how my generation has spoken. I've listened to its dialogue for twenty years. I've done little else with my life than listen to it speak. How can you throw me away in this fashion?" Loos later commented: "Scott should have gone on drinking. What he wrote when he was sober was dull."

When Thalberg turned *Red-Headed Woman* over to Loos, he told her to make fun of its sex element just as she had in *Gentlemen Prefer Blondes*. Loos had no compunction about the sex, but she wondered why anyone would care about such unlovable characters. She watched Thalberg flip his coin over and over. This was how he got his brain going, she thought. "Let's first of all decide about the love affair in this story," he announced to her and Lewin. A few more flips of the coin and he had decided. "I think I know what the love story can be. Our heroine will be deeply in love with herself."

"I'd call that pretty unsympathetic," said Lewin.

"But why? The poor girl has the flashy type of looks that would frighten off any man with the qualities of a hero. Who else is there for her to love, when she attracts only fools?"

With the premise decided, Loos was off and running, and Thalberg began to look for an actress to play the eponymous Lil Andrews. Clara Bow turned him down, and he turned down real-life redheads Jeanette MacDonald and Joan Crawford, but made tests of blonde Dorothy Mackaill. There was another possibility—Jean Harlow, the twenty-year-old "platinum blonde" who was under contract to Howard Hughes. Lewin had lunch with Bern every other day and knew of his interest in Harlow. Bern was convinced that she should star in *Red-Headed Woman;* Thalberg was frankly skeptical. Bern convinced Mayer to buy her contract from Hughes, who had made her a star in his aviation epic *Hell's Angels* and then lost interest in her career. Bern kept after Thalberg, and he finally agreed to an interview. "Do you think you can make an audience laugh?" Thalberg asked Harlow in front of Bern, Lewin, and Loos.

"With me or at me?"

"At you."

"Why not?" asked Harlow. "People have been laughing at me all my life." When Harlow walked out of Thalberg's office, Loos noted that she paused at the door and gave a smiling nod of farewell; it would be incorporated into the script.

"I don't think we need worry about Miss Harlow's sense of humor," Thalberg commented, but it was apparent to Loos that he was uncomfortable with Harlow. Thalberg was no stranger to the female sexuality displayed in Hollywood, but he had never seen a woman so unselfconscious about it. He assigned Jack Conway to direct her, hoping he could get a better performance out of her than her last five directors had. "You can say what you want, Irving, but people are not going to laugh at this," warned Conway. "I know. I've been in situations like this, and it's no laughing matter. This girl busts up a family!"

"Look at the family," said Loos. "They deserve to be busted up."

"Shoot it as is," said Thalberg. "Anita will stand by if you need some funny lines."

Conway almost got off the hook when SRC staffer Lamar Trotti blew the whistle on *Red-Headed Woman,* calling it "utterly impossible" and threatening to bring in Will Hays. "Thalberg agreed that major changes were necessary and a new script is being written," Trotti wrote his bosses in New York. "If they get into it a feeling of satire, and make the girl a gold digger rather than an out-and-out strumpet, it may be all right, but right now it is the worst ever."

"It was not any particular scene that the censors objected to," recalled Loos. "It was the fact that a naughty girl came out victorious at the end of the picture." The film was scheduled to start shooting on April 28, 1932. On April 27 Trotti sent Thalberg a special-delivery letter demanding that he make changes or halt production. "This is in my mind the most awful script I have ever read," Trotti cabled his boss that night. "On receipt of our letter, Mr. Thalberg telephoned. While he insisted that he disagreed 100 percent with our opinion and argued that there was nothing offensive in the story, he suggested many vital changes. Apparently the picture won't go into production immediately." Three days later, Thalberg and Shearer stopped at the SRC office in Hollywood as Trotti and his wife were closing up for the night. "He and I went into a session which lasted literally far into the night while my wife and his wife sat outside in the anteroom and starved," Trotti reported to Hays. "Thalberg, of course, is a man of persuasive powers and he used the usual high pressure salesmanship methods on me. His contention is that they are playing it as a broad burlesque and that the audience will laugh at the situations as broad comedy."

After more rewrites, *Red-Headed Woman* went into production, where Harlow's mere presence was as provocative as Loos's dialogue. Crew members from adjacent sound stages crept onto the catwalks to watch Harlow perform. Her unique blend of humor, innocence, and sexuality became the talk of the studio. "The newspapers have got a nerve calling me a sexpot!" Harlow complained to Frances Marion. "Where'd they ever get such a crazy idea?" Crazy or not, the idea stuck with *Red-Headed Woman*, the most frankly sexual film Thalberg had yet made.

Thalberg's determination to make adult fare reflected his taste in literature. "He had a fanatic fondness for good writing," recalled Bayard Veiller. "He even liked to read books for his own amusement. Picture people do not. They read books looking for material to put on the screen. But Thalberg read all kinds—books on science, books on religion." At a party, Frances Goldwyn asked Thalberg about his philosophy; the next day he sent her a copy of William James's *What Is Pragmatism?* Thalberg was equally conversant with Freud's *Civilization and Its Discontents* and Richard Kraft-Ebbing's *Psychopathia Sexualis;* his purchases favored explorations of human nature and abnormal psychology. He bought *Limpy,* the story of a crippled boy, for Jackie Cooper (released as *When a Feller*

Needs a Friend) and bought an original story by John Gilbert about a woman-izing chauffeur (released as *Downstairs*). As offbeat as these subjects may have appeared, they had a common denominator. "To Irving Thalberg every film had to be a love story," wrote Loos. Not long after the merger, he had given his writers a mandate. "I want the audience to see when the boy and girl discover they love each other," said Thalberg, "or I won't make the picture." By 1932 the nature of the love story had changed. "It wasn't at all necessary for the affair to concern people of the opposite sex," said Loos. "One of Irving's most poignant romances was *The Champ*, in which the relationship between Jackie Cooper and Wallace Beery held all the rapture of a love affair. In *The Sin of Madelon Claudet*, the love affair involved the aging prostitute and her upstanding son. . . . Irving could spot the sublimated sex in any human relationship."

An excellent indicator of Thalberg's connection to his audience was the fan mail that his product occasioned. Many of these letters were published in the thirty-odd fan magazines that served the film industry. *Photoplay, Modern Screen*, and *Movie Mirror* strove for impartiality, printing both sides of an argument. "Why should producers be hobbled with various forms of censorship?" asked an Indianapolis woman. "Books on all subjects are placed within the reach of young people. Why pick on the movies?" "Connie Bennett and Lil Tashman are the best-dressed women in pictures," wrote a woman in Troy, Ohio. "Jean Harlow and Norma Shearer are the best *un*dressed!" Letters such as these gave Thalberg a feeling for his audience, but there was a more exact gauge.

The sneak preview was like a play's out-of-town tryout. Once a week, Thalberg and his staff took a trolley ride to a theater in an outlying Southern California town. Depending on the weather and the type of film, the town might be Glendale, Santa Ana, Pomona, Riverside, San Bernardino, or Huntington Park. "Thalberg said that Huntington Park was the crossroads of the world," recalled Chester Schaeffer, who carried the rough cut of *Tarzan the Ape Man* into the projection booth there early in the year. "What he meant was that it was a cross-section of the population. It was mostly working class, but there were USC students living there, too. It gave him a fair sampling."

By 1932 the sneak preview had become ritualized. At 6 P.M. on the day of the preview, a large trolley would be sitting at the edge of Lot One with its shades pulled down. "The snub-nosed Interurban was familiarly known throughout Southern California as 'Big Red,'" wrote Marx. "It traversed tracks of the Pacific Electric System and cost $400 a night. It was ordered so often that Pacific Electric laid a spur directly onto the lot." Thalberg's staff waited for him outside the car.

When he arrived, they boarded and settled down to dinner and card games in the car's lounge.

The Big Red hummed and lurched its way across town, going thirty miles an hour at most. Its destination was recognizable by a revolving orange beacon that signaled a studio preview to savvy movie patrons. "Thalberg was first to swing off the car," wrote Marx, "hurrying through the lobby, offering a light salute to the obsequious manager, who waved him past the ticket taker. The others followed and took seats in rows especially roped off for them. Thalberg moved further front, to find a single seat for himself, a silent observer." Schaeffer recalled that Thalberg moved around during the screening to better see audience reactions. "Sometimes he would be right up there by the proscenium arch, looking straight out at the people," said Schaeffer. "He would see if they started shifting in their seats during a scene that ran too slow or if they would all let out a sigh and slump down after a tense scene."

Red-Headed Woman was previewed at the Alexander Theatre in Glendale. Harlow was still an unknown quantity to Thalberg. "Well, you know," he said to Lewin after the preview, "that girl's so bad, she might just be good." The audience was similarly undecided, uncertain whether to take the film seriously. So was SRC boss, Jason Joy, who was seeing it for the second time. "My feeling is that this picture is either very good or very bad," wrote Joy, "dependent on the point of view of the spectator who sees it either as farce or as heavy sex. When we saw the picture with an audience, we got a definite impression that the audience was laughing *at* the girl and that the sympathy was wholly with the wife. As a matter of fact, when the wife turned on the girl, the audience applauded. Such a reaction is lost in the cold projection room." Thalberg called Loos to his office the next day. "I'd like you to contrive a prologue which will tip the audience off that the movie is a comedy," he said. She quickly wrote a new opening sequence, a montage of self-mocking wickedness: "Can you see through this [dress]?" asks Lil. "Good. I'll wear it. So gentlemen prefer blondes, do they?" And Lil keeps a picture of her intended victim in her garter. "That did it!" wrote Loos. "Laughs began at once and never ceased."

Sometimes preview revelations told a little too much. Thalberg had adapted the Mildred Cram novel *Tinfoil* and borrowed Tallulah Bankhead from Paramount to make the story of a spoiled rich girl humbled by the depression. In one scene she scorns advertising executive Robert Montgomery's salary of $20,000 a year, saying she could not possibly live on it. This line of dialogue drew derisive laughter from a San Bernardino preview audience. Most of the M-G-M personnel were puzzled, including the writer, Charles MacArthur. Standing outside the theater, Thalberg gave them a dose of reality. "They laughed because she said that fellow had an 'average income' of twenty thousand a year." He glared at MacArthur. "Twenty thousand a year! Charlie thinks that's what everybody makes."

"When I run this country," said MacArthur, "we'll pay twenty thousand a year for coolie labor."

"The trouble with us," said Thalberg, "is that we don't know we're in a depression."

For all his insularity, both moral and economic, Thalberg could appease censors and please viewers. "Thalberg's idea was that the script was a blueprint," wrote Wanger. "You were never finished with a picture. You could always improve it." Sets were kept standing on soundstages longer than at other studios in case they were needed for reshooting. "Thalberg caused M-G-M to be called 'Retake Valley,'" recalled Howard Strickling. "He was the first to do extensive retakes. It paid off. And he never criticized a script without giving a suggestion about how to improve it."

Nor was he particular about the source of the suggestions. "He didn't go to previews just to get cards to show to exhibitors," recalled Wanger. "His purpose was to find out what the hell was wrong with the picture and then make it right. And he would call everybody in the next day—secretaries, writers, other producers, even gag men—to look at the picture." Even writers at other studios, big names like Nunnally Johnson, heard about Thalberg's practices. "You work for Thalberg," he said. "You come back from a sneak preview. You're driving back with him in the car. Thalberg begins plying you with questions—about everything. 'Did you think that came through? Did you think that was clear? Did you think that was effective?'" Sometimes the verdict was grim.

"God, we have a stinker!" one producer wailed.

"What are you talking about?" snapped Thalberg. "It's great! This is going to make a marvelous picture. The second reel, the third reel, the sixth reel, and the eighth reel are wonderful. We have to fix up the beginning a little, the middle a little, and the end a little, and we'll have a great picture." Was it solely the box office that motivated him? Colleagues could recite his aphorisms for years after working with him.

"An audience will reach for quality. Don't make them stoop for it."

"Always remember there's nothing too good for our audience."

"Never let your standards be less than great."

Back at the studio, Thalberg would repair to the screening room, reviewing the film and dictating changes. He supervised at least three such sessions for *Grand Hotel*, including two after a tiring airplane trip to a preview in Monterey, California. He was not happy with the love scene between Grusinskaya and the Baron. It is a morning-after scene. Grusinskaya, who was suicidal the night before, is shocked to learn that the Baron broke into her room not because he was in love with her but to steal her pearls. He is repentant. "I never knew love like this— until now," he says. "Don't you believe me? Don't you?" Grusinskaya, awakened from years of abstinence, decides to believe him. The Monterey audience did not, according to their preview cards.

"I think it's because it's badly done," Thalberg told Goulding and Bern. "You must have the audience see the Baron's necessity of getting money. The scene is a great scene until the camera starts floating all over the place and following Gru with her pearls. Get a closeup of her. Cut to the place where she throws them down. Then a closeup of him while she is saying, 'That's horrible. You may keep the pearls.' You need to show shame, pity, and a little sweetness in his face. Then he should say: 'I was desperate.' That's never established as his breaking point. It's never clear. And it was never clear to me that she would forgive him. A closeup of her holding him in her arms would get that across. You need that beautiful transition." Thalberg then authorized Goulding to bring Garbo, Barrymore, and cameraman William Daniels back to the bedroom set for retakes.

Another problem scene had Flaemmchen sitting in the hotel restaurant with Preysing. "The scene should be concluded, and it isn't," said Thalberg. "It needs something to tell us that Flaemmchen has agreed to Preysing's getting her a room next to his in the hotel that night. Instead the Baron comes into the scene for no good reason and the camera follows him. So you don't know until too late in the picture what Flaemmchen has decided to do." Because of the censor's admonition, Goulding suggested that they not be explicit about Flaemmchen's decision to prostitute herself. Joy had already cautioned Thalberg that "great care ought to be taken not to have Preysing register too much anticipation" at the prospect of an assignation. Thalberg's solution to the problem was to end the scene with a closeup of Flaemmchen, "a rather sad one," in which she remarks that the Baron (unlike Preysing) is a gentleman. Crawford, too, was called back for retakes.

In these conferences, Thalberg often asked Bern for input, but usually over-ruled him. When he asked Goulding for ideas, he usually incorporated them. *Grand Hotel*'s credit sequence, with its trumpet fanfare and sparkling star montage, was Goulding's brainstorm. For the most part, though, Thalberg kept his own counsel, and when M-G-M rolled toward a profit of $8 million in the worst year of the depression, no one deserved credit as much as he did—for pursuing literary excellence, for cultivating theatrical talent, and for trusting Americans to accept adult themes. The diversity of M-G-M's 1932 schedule brought Thalberg a unique place in the history of Hollywood. No producer had made so many innovative films, so many quality films, or so many hits in one year as he had in 1932, and although he steadfastly refused to put his name on them, there was no question as to who was responsible. The only question was how long Thalberg could continue his superhuman pace.

No one is infallible, not even a Boy Wonder. While Irving Thalberg was creating a catalogue of hits, he took several false steps. The first was *Letty Lynton*. *Grand Hotel* had just elevated Joan Crawford to the level of Garbo, Shearer, and Dressler, so Crawford was understandably miffed at losing *Red-Headed Woman*, and she began to watch Jean Harlow with no small interest. "To her tactlessly open jealousy of Norma Shearer, Joan added a rivalry with Jean Harlow, for whom she developed a controlled detestation," wrote her then-husband Douglas Fairbanks Jr. Harlow added fuel to the fire by telling an interviewer which star she would most like to be.

"Honestly, I *could* say anyone else, but I mean Norma," said Harlow. "Every woman would like to be like her, I believe, but very few are. She pursues one line of thought and . . . doesn't clutter up her life with a lot of nonessentials." Shearer rarely had to deal with nonessentials; hers was a regal position.

On Friday, July 15, while all of M-G-M prepared for the premiere of *Strange Interlude*, George Hurrell quit the studio in a huff. He was immediately blackballed by Louis B. Mayer. When the photographer calmed down and realized what he had done, he remembered who had brought him to Metro. He sent a telegram to Shearer.

"I have left M-G-M," wrote Hurrell, "to open my own studio again. I feel that I cannot do justice to my subjects or to myself when sittings are made under the pressure of mass production. You as an artist must understand this. To me you will always be the loveliest and greatest. I hope I may still regard you as a friend and patron." Shearer appealed to Thalberg on Hurrell's behalf, and he was gradually reinstated. No one but Shearer could have effected such a pardon. She was the queen of the lot, not by virtue of her marriage to a vice-president, but by virtue of box office. The unlikely star had overcome self-doubt, corporate indifference, and invidious comparisons to become a top-ten attraction.

Much of Shearer's accomplishment was due to a studied objectivity about her limitations and an unending regimen of self-improvement. In addition to Hurrell, she cultivated the industry's greatest cinematographers. In *Strange Interlude*, she was photographed by both William Daniels ("Garbo's cameraman") and Lee Garmes ("Dietrich's cameraman"). "I can't do the Garbo or Dietrich thing," Shearer said. "I admire them both greatly and wish that I could play such characters as they interpret, but I have to go through a transition to become worldly. I begin by being very nice, and then, about the middle of the picture, I go haywire. That's when things really grow interesting. But if I just stayed sweet and appealing, the roles I played would be very dull."

Crawford's resentment of Shearer was also due to Shearer's new contract: six films at $110,000 each. Thalberg negotiated the contract with Nick Schenck only a few weeks before submitting to an adjustment of his own salary. On July 13, 1932, Thalberg, Louis B. Mayer, and J. Robert Rubin each took a pay cut of 35 percent. The cut was due to depressed business conditions and was to remain in effect for a year. Shearer's raise was not affected, even though Schenck tried to deny it. Crawford told Fairbanks that Shearer and Harlow were in some way "part of a conspiracy" to hold her back. When the gossip got back to Shearer, she decided to speak out.

> I admire and like Joan. And I believe she feels the same way about me. I hope so. I think both of us have been hurt and embarrassed by the persistent stories of our rivalry and hatred. . . . How could I hate Joan? She is so much like me. We have been through so many of the same painful but invaluable molding processes. We have both had to fight desperately to overcome self-consciousness. We have both made ourselves over, both struggled to create an illusion of glamour and beauty. . . .
>
> People think that because Irving Thalberg is my husband all I have to do is ask for any role I want. They think it's been easy sledding for me. What they don't realize is that I've had to work twice as hard to secure any recognition because Irving *is* my husband. I have to be twice as good in order to get half as much credit. Furthermore, the very fact that I am Irving's wife keeps me from

going out and fighting for rôles. I know just how busy and harassed he is. And I know that it is just as important to him that Joan Crawford should have good pictures. It is his job to see that all M-G-M films are excellent, not just Norma Shearer's.

To avoid charges of favoritism, Thalberg gave Crawford a role that few stars could have tackled, that of a dazzling, jaded sophisticate. Thalberg had seen *Dishonored Lady*, the hit play by Edward Sheldon and Margaret Ayer Barnes about the so-called "Edinburgh poisoner," Madeleine Smith, and offered the playwrights $30,000 if they could write an adaptation that would pass the SRC. Will Hays surprised them by declaring their treatment "obscene" and promptly put *Dishonored Lady* on his list of proscribed properties.

Thalberg was not easily blocked. He went around the SRC and purchased the Marie Belloc Lowndes novel *Letty Lynton*, which was based on the same 1857 murder trial—and cost only $3,500. As Hunt Stromberg and his team of writers adapted the novel to suit Thalberg's tastes, their script increasingly mirrored the structure of *Dishonored Lady*. They would later claim that they had never seen the play, but the SRC was not fooled. "*Letty Lynton* is with all intents and purpose the same story as *Dishonored Lady*," Jason Joy wrote Hays, who threw up his hands and let Thalberg make the film. Its script would eventually cause M-G-M to be sued for plagiarism, but at its release the film looked like another Thalberg triumph. Its half-million-dollar profit confirmed Crawford as a top-ranking star and Robert Montgomery as a star in his own right. Nonetheless, it was Thalberg who was responsible when M-G-M had to pay $100,000 in damages and permanently remove *Letty Lynton* from circulation.

Thalberg's treatment of Upton Sinclair did not qualify as a false step, but it showed his colleagues another side of him. Sinclair had gained renown twenty-five years earlier with *The Jungle*, an exposé of the meatpacking industry. An avowed Socialist, Sinclair used fiction to show how capitalism was destroying America. That his novels led to industrial reform was less important to him than his failure to win political office and institute socialist reforms. When Sam Marx heard from Sinclair, he had written more than thirty books and was living in Pasadena. Would M-G-M be interested in his latest? *The Wet Parade* was a sprawling story of the damage done to one family by the Eighteenth Amendment and the Volstead Act, which were collectively known as Prohibition.

Marx was thrilled at the prospect of meeting the famed muckraker. Thalberg was frankly hostile. "Don't let that Bolshevik inside this studio!" he said. Only

Marx knew the reason for Thalberg's attitude. When he was a teenager in Brooklyn—between bouts of illness—Thalberg had made pro-Socialist speeches, literally standing on soapboxes. He admitted this only in the course of a counseling session he was giving Maurice Rapf and Budd Schulberg. The young sons of Harry Rapf and B. P. Schulberg had recently been to Russia and were impressed with communism. "Every man is a socialist when he is young," Thalberg told them. "I was full of idealism as a boy and wanted to change the social order. . . . As we mature, we see things in a different light. We become more conservative. Keep your wits about you. Don't be overly swayed by what you saw in Russia."

While negotiating *The Wet Parade* contract, Marx and his wife, Marie, began to visit Sinclair and his wife, Mary Craig Sinclair, who was also a writer. It was at a congenial tea that Sinclair was about to sign a $25,000 contract. Mary Sinclair interrupted to ask if an amendment could be written in the margin to ensure that the film would respect the integrity of the novel. Marx agreed. A few days later, the intercom on his desk buzzed, and Thalberg's voice cut through its speaker. "Come up here!" said Thalberg. Marx hurried to Thalberg's office. Thalberg was in a rage. "Since when do you have the power to alter our contracts?" he demanded of Marx. "I'm a vice-president of this company and I haven't the temerity to do a thing like this!"

Marx could not excuse himself by saying that the Sinclairs had plied him with liquor; he liked them and trusted them. This meant nothing to Thalberg. "We can spend a million dollars," he said, "follow Sinclair's book word for word, and—thanks to you, Sam—he can still say that we didn't maintain its integrity. He can take us to court and prevent our showing the film. He's just the type to do it, too. The man's a Bolshevik!" Thalberg's tirade continued for so long that Marx feared that he was about to be sacked. "I won't make this picture!" said Thalberg finally, tossing the contract into the wastebasket, whereupon his secretary interrupted with a call from Pasadena.

The Sinclairs were calling to assure Thalberg that they had meant no harm by asking for the notations in the margin and would be happy to send a letter agreeing to the restoration of the contract to its previous form. Thalberg hung up the phone, but did not fire Marx. He merely said in a calm tone of voice: "Don't you *ever* do that again."

The Wet Parade was filmed with force and insight by Victor Fleming, who had been a race car driver, a flier, and cameraman before he became a director (and romanced both Clara Bow and Thalberg's future wife). Thalberg sensed a problem at the film's first preview: it showed the evils of drink but did not take sides, either for or against Prohibition. "If we support enforcement," he reasoned, "the public won't go. If we support bootlegging, we won't get by the SRC. We have got to be able to take a stand." At a later preview, he told its writer, John Lee Mahin, that it made Prohibition agents look ineffectual and might offend the Hoover administration or, worse yet, encourage federal censorship advocates. *The Wet Parade* was released as filmed, but its depressing story, not its politics, caused it to fail at the box office; it showed Jimmy Durante dying in a shootout. A short while later, Marx hesitantly brought the Sinclairs to Thalberg's office. "Aren't you the one they call the Boy Wonder?" Mary Sinclair asked.

"If they do, I've never heard it," Thalberg answered coolly.

Thalberg got the cold shoulder himself when William Randolph Hearst came to M-G-M to see the first cut of *Blondie of the Follies*. Goulding had made Billie Dove's scenes with Marion Davies good—too good. After the lights came up, Hearst turned to Thalberg and raised his high-pitched voice so that the entire room could hear: "Well, Irving, it's a nice *Billie Dove* picture." Thalberg put the film back into production and reshot it so that Dove would not steal the film from Davies. Four award-worthy scenes hit the cutting-room floor, and Dove angrily left Hollywood. *Blondie of the Follies* was prevented from being a great film by its backer.

Thalberg could not blame Hearst or anyone else for the false step he took with *Freaks*. It began when he authorized Tod Browning to adapt the Tod Robbins novel *Spurs*. At first glance, this made sense. A Browning film of a Robbins book had made Lon Chaney a star. This time the ingredients were stronger. *Spurs* was the love story of a midget named Hans and a tightrope walker named Cleopatra. When Cleopatra tries to poison Hans so she can share his money with her strongman lover, Hercules, angry sideshow freaks take the law into their own hands—if they have hands. Some of them are armless, legless, or both.

Thalberg had recently seen Universal saved from bankruptcy by horror films. He reasoned that *Spurs* could be a breakthrough for M-G-M. "I want you to write me something even more horrible than *Dracula* or *Frankenstein*," he told Willis Goldbeck. After story conferences with the eccentric Browning, Goldbeck brought Thalberg a script titled *Freaks*. "I asked for something horrifying," Thalberg said, shaking his head and putting his face in his hands. "Well, I got it." But he did not cancel the project, despite opposition from Mayer, Mannix, and Rapf. Instead, he allowed Browning to cast real-life sideshow "freaks" in the film. M-G-M employees were accustomed to seeing odd people on the lot, but pinheads, hermaphrodites, and Siamese twins were a bit much. "People run out of the commissary and throw up," Rapf told Mayer, but Thalberg would not stop filming. "If it's a mistake, I'll take the blame," he said, and Jack Conway defended him. "Irving's right so often, he's earned the right to be wrong," said Conway. The first preview told the tale.

Art director Merrill Pye was with Thalberg at a Huntington Park theater. "Halfway through the preview," recalled Pye, "a lot of people got up and ran out. They didn't walk out. They *ran* out." Thalberg had never seen such a reaction. He cut *Freaks* from ninety minutes to sixty-three minutes and released it without publicity. The film didn't need publicity; it achieved instant notoriety. "Well, I have seen that picture *Freaks*," wrote a San Diego reader of *Photoplay*, "and I certainly think that whoever directed it should be ashamed to have put his name to it." Another reader wrote: "I didn't mind its gruesomeness so much, but its cheap vulgarity is something that left a bad taste in my mouth. I am not easily shocked and do not hold with rigid censor laws. What amazes me is its frightfully bad taste."

Many exhibitors, although cash-strapped by the depression, were afraid to book *Freaks*. Exhibitors in San Francisco and Atlanta were prevented from booking it by local officials. Los Angeles exhibitors were forced to close it, even after two weeks of strong box office. The threat of federal censorship was again invoked, and when Great Britain banned the film altogether, it looked as if the threat might not be imaginary. Thalberg pulled *Freaks* from circulation, the first time he had done so since the 1927 scandal of *The Callahans and the Murphys*. Oddly enough, Thalberg's other horror films (*The Mask of Fu Manchu* and *Kongo*) made money.

Thalberg's love affair with "highbrow theater" continued to bloom. He and Shearer were avid first-nighters when Katharine Cornell brought her tours of *The Green Hat* and *The Barretts of Wimpole Street* to Los Angeles. Thalberg thought Cornell should come to Culver City. Cornell thought otherwise. "I know the theater," she told an interviewer. "I don't know pictures. Each time I am here, I promise Irving Thalberg to make a screen test. But I never do. I just go away and send a wire filled with regrets." If Cornell was not willing to essay classical roles for M-G-M, Shearer was. The industry looked askance at Thalberg when he announced her for Eugene O'Neill's controversial *Strange Interlude*. The five-hour play was so advanced in technique that O'Neill had its characters turn to the audience and speak "asides," a device that drew praise—and sometimes giggles. Thalberg cut O'Neill's text to two hours and Douglas Shearer made the asides plausible with a "voice-over" technique; a prerecorded disk was played on the set so that the actors could adjust their facial expressions to their audible thoughts.

The asides were plausible, perhaps, but not what movie audiences expected of Clark Gable and Norma Shearer. "There was nothing exactly normal about *Strange Interlude*," recalled Shearer. "How could there be with neurotic people going around talking to themselves all the time?" With so many static closeups, it was vital that Shearer be properly lit. She got the coveted William Daniels for her cameraman, but had no choice but to release him after two weeks of shooting when Garbo demanded him for *As You Desire Me*. "It's taken me three years to discover why I can't have Bill Daniels whenever I want him," Shearer lamented. "That's because Garbo is clever enough to have first choice. I can have him only when she isn't working."

Thalberg shut down *Strange Interlude* for several weeks to find a replacement. He and Shearer had seen what Lee Garmes did for Marlene Dietrich in Josef von Sternberg's *Shanghai Express*, so they brought Garmes to M-G-M. After a few lighting tests, Garmes gave Shearer as dramatic a makeover as Hurrell had given her two years earlier. Her eyes were suddenly larger and more expressive, and her bone structure looked chiseled. "Norma missed Bill at first," recalled Garmes, "but when she saw what I could do for her, she came to like me. I made a special key light for her. It was a double-broad [floodlight] with a white flap on each side. It made her eyelids look heavier and her cheekbones stronger." Shearer appreciated Garmes's sensitivity. "Norma had that cast in one of her eyes," said Garmes. "She'd whisper: 'Lee, if you see that I'm looking cross-eyed, signal me!' So I'd see her eye wandering and I'd say to the crew, but loud: 'A light went out up there.' This gave her time to do her Dr. Bates exercises or whatever while we were rigging another light overhead. That way if Louella Parsons or some writer was on the set, she wouldn't know about Norma's eye. Then Norma would wink me a signal and we'd go on."

If Shearer was unduly concerned about her closeups, it was because *Strange Interlude* required her to age onscreen. Makeup artist Cecil Holland gave her a striking middle-aged look, but his convincing old-age makeup was questioned by fans. Nina's son was only college age; why did she look eighty? Inconsistencies notwithstanding, *Strange Interlude* justified Thalberg's judgment both critically and financially, and, even though Mayer's yes-men continued saying nay to Thalberg's theater-derived projects, he persisted with them. Hoping that Fontanne would return and Cornell would relent, he purchased the best Broadway had to offer: *When Ladies Meet, Reunion in Vienna*, and *Biography*. On March 28, 1932, Thalberg escorted Shearer and Louella Parsons to the Angelus Temple in Los Angeles to see the flamboyant evangelist Aimee Semple McPherson debate Walter

Huston on the topic "Is Prohibition a Success?" McPherson won the debate but Thalberg did not invite her to M-G-M.

Thalberg did invite stage star Tallulah Bankhead, whose luster had been dimmed by five Paramount flops, to try her luck at M-G-M, but not in a classical role. He cast her as the heroine of Mildred Cram's novel *Tinfoil*, playing a spoiled rich girl who becomes one of the streetwalkers she scorns. This role gave Bankhead what her previous films had not, a setting for her showy personality and a chance to do some real acting. Thalberg changed the title to *Faithless* and costarred Robert Montgomery; Bankhead had her first hit. Her belated stardom was due in part to the M-G-M treatment—Holland's makeup, Adrian's gowns, and Oliver Marsh's creamy lighting. Bankhead's uneven features were far from camera-proof, a concern that may have kept the large-boned Cornell away from the movie camera. There was another great lady on Broadway, and Thalberg began to woo her, not seeing where his biggest misstep would take him.

Ethel Barrymore had been a revered Broadway star for thirty years. If she would consent to join her brothers John and Lionel at M-G-M, Thalberg could accomplish the greatest casting coup of the talkies: three Barrymores in one film. "The three Barrymores would have some box-office value," said John, "like a circus with three white whales." As it happened, the theater was feeling the depression, and even Ethel had been affected. Owing back taxes, she was tempted by Thalberg's offer. "I don't give a hang about the movies," she told Thalberg in a transcontinental call, "but I suppose playing with Lionel and Jack would be amusing." Thalberg assured her that she would complete the film in time to start September rehearsals for her next play. In February 1932 Ethel accepted an offer of $3,000 a week for a projected ten weeks, and the press went wild.

"Ethel Barrymore, the superwoman of the stage, has taken the great leap," wrote Edwin Schallert in the *Los Angeles Times*. On May 26 Ethel stepped off a train in Pasadena to much fanfare and John's embrace. "All the reporters and photographers thought he was telling me how wonderful it was to see me again," wrote Ethel. "What he was really muttering into my hair was 'For God's sake, get Bill Daniels!'" On her first visit to Thalberg's office, Ethel told him that she must have Daniels as her cameraman. Garbo was on her way to Sweden, so Thalberg could grant Ethel's request. It was not as easy to come up with a vehicle for the "Three Bs." Since they were siblings, Ethel could not be a romantic interest. Thalberg rooted around the studio's properties and discovered that he owned Alfred Klabund's 1927 novel *Rasputin*. In mid-June, M-G-M announced that the three Barrymores would star in *Rasputin*—Ethel as the Czarina, Lionel as

Rasputin, and John as Prince Felix Youssoupoff, the assassin; using his real name in the press release apparently worried no one. Ethel asked for top billing, which Thalberg denied her because John was earning $6,000 a week and had to be top-billed. Lionel, who was getting the showy role that John had wanted, requested Charles Brabin as director because he had liked working with him in *Washington Masquerade* and because Ethel had known him on Broadway years earlier. Bernard Hyman, flush with *Tarzan*'s success, was producing. The only thing missing was a script.

"Do you mean to tell me that they haven't got a story?" Ethel asked John after spending a few idle days in the Laurel Canyon home she was renting from P. G. Wodehouse.

"They have six and don't think any of them is good enough," answered John, referring to the collective labors of Bess Meredyth, C. Gardner Sullivan, John Meehan, and Lenore Coffee.

Ethel visited Thalberg and learned that he had been unable to secure the services of Charles MacArthur, the one writer who could do justice to the fall of the Romanoffs. "He's just the man," said Thalberg, "but he won't do it." Ethel stormed over to the Culver City avocado ranch MacArthur and Helen Hayes were renting. "You're going to write *Rasputin*," Ethel informed MacArthur.

"Nope," replied MacArthur. "Not me."

"You lazy, cowardly, incompetent, loafing, good-for-nothing ass!" said Ethel, knocking aside magazines, books, and lamps as she advanced on MacArthur. "Do you want me to tear down this house?"

MacArthur, hiding behind the diminutive Hayes, finally surrendered to the force of Ethel's will. "All right, I'll do your damned scenario," he said. "What's it about?" This was a fair question. None of the scripts had yet caught the essence of the Romanoff saga. Lenore Coffee had come the closest. "Rasputin didn't succeed because he was so clever," said Coffee to Thalberg. "It was because the Romanoffs were so damned stupid." Coffee's insight was not enough to make a compelling vehicle for the three Barrymores, and as it turned out, neither was MacArthur's. Ben Hecht (uncredited) blocked out the action, Ethel supplied reminiscences of her encounters with the royals, and Laurence Stallings wrote additional dialogue, all of which took until mid-July. The film was scheduled to start shooting on July 21. Confident that MacArthur could finish the script in time, Hyman ordered filming to commence. MacArthur was having trouble with Thalberg's slant on the story. "The Romanoffs kicked your people around for three hundred years," said MacArthur. "Now you're trying to make a hero out of that stupid Nicholas."

"The Czarina was the granddaughter of Queen Victoria," replied Thalberg. "Fifty percent of our foreign receipts come from England. I am not going to risk harming our foreign market because I'm a Jew. It wouldn't be fair to the stockholders." Furthermore, the royalty who had entertained Thalberg and Shearer a year earlier were cousins of the late czar and czarina. "Nicholas and Alexandra were rewritten as Mr. and Mrs. Hoover," recalled MacArthur years later.

Early on the morning of Friday, July 22, the three Barrymores reported to Stage 22, the set for the bedchamber and anteroom of the Czarevitch. "It was eerie huddling with three Barrymores at six A.M.," wrote Tallulah Bankhead, who was working on an adjacent soundstage. "I had often been up that late in pursuit of my craft, but never that early." The first scenes to be filmed were those in which Alexandra (Ethel) kneels with Czar Nicholas II (Ralph Morgan) to pray for their gravely ill son Aloysha (Tad Alexander), and then meets Rasputin (Lionel), who is ushered in by Prince Chegodieff (John) and lady-in-waiting Natasha (Diana Wynyard). Ethel had been warned by Lionel about the adjustment she would have to make to film acting. "The first thing to remember," Lionel said, holding his hand over his head, "is that the microphone is right *here*." When she saw the real thing, she was duly impressed; the black globe looked like an anarchist's bomb. The camera was formidable, too, its massive silver "blimp" remodeled to look like an Art Deco dragon. Daniels's crew had nicknamed the blimp "Grandma." Ethel was awaiting her cue when she heard one of the camera crew yell: "Is Grandma ready?" Thinking this moniker referred to her, she drew herself up to her full imperial height and glared at the offending crew member.

Thalberg's enthusiasm for the Royal Family of Broadway survived the first weeks of filming, but barely. John was drinking. Lionel was upstaging him. Ethel was slow to comprehend the camera's tendency to enlarge. "I'm moaning and flailing my arms and touching curtains all over the set," she told Ina Claire after viewing the rushes.

"What the hell are you doing?" John asked his sister.

"Jack, I haven't the faintest idea," she answered, and then found a scapegoat. Brabin was having a hard time keeping up with the demands of three Barrymores, let alone an unfinished script. On July 30, after watching Brabin put her brothers through some uninspired paces, Ethel marched to a telephone on the wall of the soundstage and in front of the entire company raised her stentorian voice to say: "See here, Mayer. Let's get rid of this Brahbin or Braybin or whatever his name is." The scandalized director picked up his coat, walked off the set, and went home to his wife, Theda Bara. At Ethel's urging, Thalberg replaced Brabin with Richard Boleslavsky, a former Polish lancer and Stanislavski alumnus. Boleslavsky started shooting on August 1. He picked up the pace but could not overcome the basic problem, an unfocused script. *Rasputin* became an unremitting headache for Thalberg, requiring his presence at more than fifteen story conferences.

At the end of August, Thalberg and Hyman reviewed the *Rasputin* footage. The expository scenes were didactic and unconvincing. Thalberg's pet project was in crisis, so he shut it down. Ethel Barrymore was placated with a $3,000 advance, and she adjusted her New York plans. Thalberg left MacArthur alone to rewrite the beginning of the film and then met with Bernie Hyman, Al Lewin, and Carey Wilson to decide what was missing from the rest. According to Mercedes de Acosta, this did not take long. Thalberg called her into his office and instructed her to contrive a scene in which Rasputin would seduce Natasha, the character based on Felix Youssoupoff's wife, Irina. "It must be a very violent and terrific scene," said Thalberg.

"But Irina Youssoupoff never even met Rasputin," said Acosta.

"Who cares?" said Thalberg. "Putting this scene in gives strength to the plot."

"But this is history," Acosta objected. "History in our own time. Such a sequence would be absolutely unauthentic and probably libelous."

"I don't need you to tell me a lot of nonsense about what is libelous and what is not," Thalberg said, rising from his chair to bid her good day. "I want this sequence in and that is all there is to it." Believing that she was right and that her friendship with Garbo would protect her job, Acosta went behind Thalberg's back and contacted Felix Youssoupoff. The exiled prince cabled Acosta that he "forbade any mention of Irina whatsoever." Acosta returned to Thalberg with the news. "How dare you consult anyone about this?" he snapped at her. "You had absolutely no right to do such a thing without my permission!"

Unaware of these intrigues, the *Rasputin* company ended a twelve-day hiatus. MacArthur wrote rapidly, striving to maintain a one-day lead. "The script was written day by day on the set, sometimes on the backs of old envelopes," recalled Ethel. She would typically be handed a carbon copy of revised dialogue. "And would you like me to recite it backwards too?" she asked. This happened no less than ten days in a row, pushing Ethel's stint into October. She became peevish, causing M-G-M's legal department to issue a series of reports to Thalberg. "I am at home listening to the World Series," she told one assistant director. "It's far more interesting than anything M-G-M ever did. And I am not coming down until I'm good and ready." She told another: "They needn't call me for nine A.M. tomorrow. I will *not* be called on the set and kept waiting." The crew had taken to calling Ethel the "Empress of all the Rushes," especially after she contradicted Hyman on the set one day. "You forget," she said, dismissing her producer, "I knew Her Majesty personally."

On October 21, in preparation for an "Emergency Conference," Wilson wrote a progress report. Ethel's salary had surpassed $45,000, and the project was in danger of being shut down if she exercised her right to leave for New York. MacArthur squeezed her remaining scenes into three days of shooting so that she could be removed from the payroll. As of October 26 Ethel had worked a total of fifteen weeks and earned $57,500. Unfortunately she had spent $65,000 on herself, her family, and her retinue of hangers-on.

The great lady finally returned to Broadway. Before falling ill with pneumonia, she told Sidney Skolsky what she thought of Hollywood. "The people are unreal," she sniffed. "The flowers are unreal. They don't smell. The fruit is unreal. It doesn't taste of anything. The place hasn't been thought in. There is no sediment of thought there. The whole place is a glaring, gaudy, nightmarish set, built up in the desert. It looks, it feels, as though it had been invented by a Sixth Avenue peep-show man."

Ethel's departure served as a cue for John and Lionel to misbehave in earnest. John took to arriving late, hung over, or not at all. When he was present, Lionel complained that he was "wriggling his ears, pursing his lips, flicking dust from his larcenous backside, and stealing whole scenes from me!" The film was now referred to as *Disputin*. MacArthur was still averaging only a scene a day, delivered barely a day in advance, yet Loew's had booked the film for a Christmas opening at the Astor Theatre. It looked as if Thalberg was barely in control; true, he spent much of the fall coping with a series of crises and was absent for weeks (as the following chapter relates). His most dramatic contribution to *Rasputin* became his biggest misstep of the year.

Against the advice of Mercedes de Acosta, Ethel Barrymore, and Helen Hayes, Thalberg insisted that MacArthur write the scene in which Rasputin rapes Natasha. "But their paths never crossed," MacArthur protested. He was overruled. As shot on November 12, Natasha comes to warn Rasputin that Paul wants to kill him. When Paul tries and fails, Rasputin finds Natasha alone in a darkened room, grabs her, and says: "We're going to punish Paul. You and I." He carries her to a couch and she faints into a knowing Fade Out.

By the time *Rasputin* finished shooting on December 12, it had been in production 104 days. Its editing crew began working double shifts to make the premiere. Anyone who had been involved with the production could see that the film was a patchwork quilt; scenes were composed of shots made months apart. Even so, Hyman managed to conceal the seams. At this point he decided that the opening credits needed a preface card. "This story concerns the destruction of an Empire," wrote Hyman, "brought about by the mad ambition of one man. A few of the characters are still alive. The rest met death by violence."

On December 23, the finished film, retitled *Rasputin and the Empress*, was premiered. Responding to the optimism of president-elect Franklin D. Roosevelt, New Yorkers mobbed the Astor Theatre to see the Royal Siblings of Broadway. The film garnered generally favorable reviews and, even in the depths of the Great Depression, it grossed over $1 million. Unfortunately, its $1.1 million–dollar cost precluded a profit. Thalberg had no regrets about his Barrymore epic. The few sour notes on *Rasputin and the Empress* were sounded by critics. "It achieves one feat that is not inconsiderable," wrote Richard Watts in the *New York Herald Tribune*. "It manages to libel even the despised Rasputin."

Taking liberties with history was not unknown in Hollywood, but the Russian Revolution was recent history. A few of the characters were indeed "still alive," and they found a sympathetic attorney in Fanny Holtzmann, whose friendship with Louis B. Mayer did not prevent her from preparing a lawsuit. Holtzmann contended that her clients Prince Felix Youssoupoff and Princess Irina Youssoupoff, exiled White Russians living in London, had been libeled by *Rasputin and the Empress* (shown in England under the title *Rasputin, the Mad Monk*). After Prince Felix testified in court that he had killed Rasputin in 1916, his attorney Sir Patrick Hastings argued that the film's character of Prince Paul (John Barrymore) could be no one else. Likewise Paul's onscreen fiancée, Natasha (Diana Wynyard), could be no one but Princess Irina, who had never met Rasputin, much less been raped by him.

On March 5, 1934, the jury found M-G-M guilty of libel. The studio ultimately paid more than $700,000 to the Youssoupoffs (and Holtzmann). The money restored the couple to their czarist standard of living, which had been the primary motivation of the lawsuit. In truth, London society was more interested in trumping a Jewish-owned studio than in the Youssoupoffs' reputations. Their rich friends had never believed M-G-M's version of Irina, and in 1916 Felix had not been the dashing hero portrayed by Barrymore, but a cross-dressing party boy.

The court's judgment also required that libelous scenes—and any reference to them—be cut from the negative of the film. Eleven cuts were made, starting with Hyman's preface. In its place was a disclaimer that immediately became an industry standard: "The events and characters in this film are fictional and any resemblance to characters living or dead is purely coincidental." Hyman's career continued unabated, and no one pointed a finger at Thalberg for the misstep. The only criticism had come from a brilliant but drunk comedian. "I'd rather be Buster Keaton in comedy," said Keaton while staggering by Stage 22, "than all the Barrymores in *Rasputin*." His remark made the rounds, and Mayer, fed up with Keaton's alcoholic misbehavior, abrogated his contract. Ironically, it was Thalberg who called Keaton and offered him one more chance. Keaton refused.

CHAPTER 15 · Hollywood Icarus

Like the mythical Icarus, who ignored his father's warnings and flew too close to the sun, Irving Thalberg was tempting fate. He was thirty-three, still a young man, but he continued to test his constitution by working seven days a week. He often brought Irving Jr. to work because there was no time to play with him at home. The reason for his schedule was obvious. M-G-M was straining to resist the depression. Because Louis B. Mayer was managing the Republican National Convention, Thalberg was forced to assume managerial duties. No one who had seen Thalberg in a hospital bed in 1925 could deny that he was working at a "killing pace," but in 1932 he looked invincible, and his work stood out in bold relief from the rest of the industry's. *Screenland* magazine catalogued his accomplishments in an article called "Hit-maker." *Fortune* magazine approached him for a December article that would explain why only M-G-M was making a profit in beleaguered Hollywood. As the interviews proceeded, it became obvious that every story pointed to Thalberg. The hit-maker was sharing both the limelight and the stress.

Thalberg's associates bore their own kind of stress. The fear of failure was not as compelling as the need to please the Little Boss. "All of us got sort of a father feeling about Irving," recalled Donald Ogden Stewart. "It was a real father-and-son relationship, and you wanted to please father." This was odd, because Stewart was a sophisticated New York playwright and five years older than Thalberg. Nonetheless, Stewart fell into role-playing. It was not always fun. "You'd write a love scene and you'd take it to him," said Stewart. "It was like going to a computer. You put your script into Irving and the wheels went around and out came 'yes' or 'no.' And he never praised you. The best you ever got was, 'That's not bad. That's *not* bad.' And that was—God Almighty—that was like being patted by an angel."

Stewart's work on *Smilin' Through* elevated him to the level of Thalberg's favorite writers, Anita Loos, Charles MacArthur, Frances Marion, and Carey Wilson; and to that of his fiercely loyal producers, Al Lewin, Hunt Stromberg, Harry Rapf, Bernie Hyman, and last but not least, Paul Bern, his trusted adviser. Bern's opinion was so valued that he sometimes flew across the country to preview plays for Thalberg. Without complaint, Bern would ride as a passenger in an open-cockpit biplane, sitting on stacks of canvas mailbags. His reward was the same as Stewart's—inclusion in the inner circle. "I'm one of half a dozen who are referred to as 'Irving's Boys,'" Bern told Samuel Marx. "I wouldn't trade that for all the screen credits in Hollywood." For Stewart, the rewards went beyond the obvious. "It wasn't just the salary," he recalled. "It was that you were a good craftsman. You took a great deal of pride in that. Irving taught me an awful lot about script construction. He didn't usually create scenes himself, but he had a memory of every scene that had worked. And from his criticisms of my scenes I really learned an awful lot about writing."

Bern was unabashedly grateful to Thalberg. "Irving humors my taste in material," said Bern. "I'm not inclined toward violence." Bern's 1932 projects were brittle, witty, sexy films: *Arsene Lupin*, *As You Desire Me*, and *Grand Hotel*. As with his previous year's films (*Politics*, *Susan Lenox*, and *West of Broadway*), their plausibility was directly proportionate to Thalberg's involvement in their story conferences. Bern was erudite, but he was not a storyteller. With Thalberg looking over his shoulder, that was unimportant. As Stewart said: "I never had any feeling about Irving—except that he was right."

Thalberg's omniscience was more intimidating than the spur of the depression. Constantly having to please him was nerve-wracking. Howard Strickling stammered. Hunt Stromberg developed a facial tic. Harry Rapf suffered a nervous breakdown while producing the 1932 film *Flesh;* the combined temperaments of Wallace Beery and John Ford had proven too much for him. He was temporarily replaced by studio manager Eddie Mannix, who answered only to Mayer. Al Lewin and Bernie Hyman communicated well enough with Thalberg to avoid these occupational hazards. It was his right-hand man who began to crack.

Bern's behavior first became suspect when he campaigned to have Jean Harlow cast in *Red-Headed Woman*. "You're behaving like I did with Norma," Thalberg chided him. "I knew positively that she could play anything. It's a kind of romantic astigmatism that attacks producers when they fall for an actress." Bern was barely through the mammoth exercise of *Grand Hotel* when he began to obsess over Harlow. Lewin and Wilson shook their heads when they saw the forty-two-year-old Bern escorting the twenty-year-old Harlow to the *Grand Hotel* premiere. "He's got that goddamned Pygmalion complex," remarked Lewin. "He's hellbent on finding someone to make over and fall in love with."

Bern's previous obsessions had been with damsels in distress. "Bern loved to take out sexy broads," recalled Strickling, "but it wasn't enough for them to be gorgeous dishes. They had to be in trouble." His acts of altruism included casting and directing the unpopular actress Jedda Goudal; buying a wardrobe for actress Olive Borden, who was going to lose a job because she could not afford clothes; grooming and squiring the unlettered Joan Crawford so that Thalberg would notice her, and helping her buy a home after her patron Harry Rapf had dropped her. Bern's most storied charities were deathbed visits to the spectacularly self-destructive stars Barbara LaMarr and Mabel Normand.

Bern's benevolence occasionally benefited men and children. He cast the unknown Lew Ayres in Greta Garbo's last silent, *The Kiss*. He championed John Gilbert after his fall from grace (but failed to make *West of Broadway* a decent film for him). He paid the hospital bills and funeral expenses of tubercular teenaged actress Lucille Ricksen (after her sister committed suicide). Most recently, Bern had learned that the depression was causing Los Angeles schoolchildren to go without lunch, so he subsidized a relief program at the studio, raising $14,000. What caused gossip was his moth-to-flame attraction to troubled beauties.

While working for Cecil B. DeMille in 1928, Bern had bailed out starlet Jeanne Williams, the victim of a failed publicity stunt. After confiding details of his lonely history over dinner, he returned her to the hotel room for which he was paying. "I felt there was only one way I could repay his kindness," Williams later told Sam Marx. "Paul turned red and ran out. I was stunned! I ran after him, calling to him that I only meant it as a gesture of thanks, and begging him to come back. But he wouldn't." When W. S. Van Dyke or Cedric Gibbons escorted a starlet to a premiere, it was rightly assumed that the date did not end at her door. When Bern escorted a starlet, her morning-after reports were neither glowing nor lurid. Bern was unique in a community obsessed with sex. "Dear Paul is the only man I have ever known who has permitted me to love him as a friend," said LaMarr before her untimely death in 1926. Although Bern was unmarried, he was not a known homosexual, and his treatment of single, available women was respectful, not fraternal.

Harlow did not fit the profile of Bern's charity cases. To all appearances, she was well bred, well off, and well adjusted. Her career was slightly stalled, but Thalberg was attending to that. She was essentially a happy person—an uncomplicated, uninhibited, fun-loving child. After the *Grand Hotel* premiere, Bern invited her to his new home at 9820 Easton Drive, which he had built in the style of a Bavarian hunting lodge. (Its concession to Hollywood was a set of famous faces carved onto the end of supporting beams: Mary Pickford, Douglas Fairbanks, Rudolph Valentino, and Barbara LaMarr). Few of Bern's celebrated confreres had seen his Benedict Canyon hideaway. "I love solitude," he told Marx. "I've always been self-sufficient, you know. And when a man isn't married at forty, well, he isn't likely to be."

Bern ushered Harlow into his lantern-lit patio and poured her a glass of wine. Just when she expected him to make advances, he proceeded to hold forth on the origins of the wine, "down to the last grape," said Harlow. "He's different. He explains things. He lets me know I have a brain." Stories like this made the rounds, but Bern's well-publicized kindnesses kept them from sounding nasty.

"Paul is for the downtrodden," said Hedda Hopper. "He is for the oppressed and for those in trouble, whether they are young or old, black or white, male or female. You hear of the sensational and exotic women he has befriended because naturally you would hear about them anyway. But you never hear of the dozens of obscure and humble persons he befriends, gives money to, gives time to." John Gilbert, who had earlier described Bern's "Magdalen complex," now amended it to a "Christ complex." There were few M-G-M actors or executives who did not respect Bern. Marx found Bern resourceful and patient. Thalberg was in awe of Bern's quiet intellectualism and listened at length as Bern held forth on Schopenhauer, Freud, and Nietzsche in his soft German accent. Thalberg regarded Bern as a mentor, showing him a respect that was almost filial. "Paul is the only individual in Hollywood about whom no one ever says an unkind thing," said actress Estelle Taylor. She might have added that no one dared to; he stood in the shadow of Hollywood's most powerful production head. The only film folk who found Bern's sanctity suspect were M-G-M's female writers.

When Lenore Coffee married director William Cowen in 1926, Bern magnanimously offered them the use of his auto, not stopping to think that Cowen, a decorated war hero, might take umbrage. "Thank you, Paul," said Cowen. "But when we own Cadillacs, we will drive Cadillacs."

Frances Marion worked with Bern on the 1930 Lawrence Tibbett flop, *The*

Rogue Song. One fanciful scene had Tibbett singing operetta while being whipped. Sitting in a script conference, Marion noted Bern's analysis of the scene. "The whip," said Bern. "That's very significant. Do you see it motivated by sadism or masochism?"

"Neither," replied Marion. "I merely thought of it as a gimmick. Nothing looks more vapid than a singer, backed by a full orchestra, with his arms dangling at his sides or suddenly thrusting one arm forward as if he were about to shake hands with a ghost."

"You're a clever woman. You assume naïveté, but it's obvious that you're a student of the psychology of sex, as I am."

"I don't know a damn thing about the psychology of sex and probably never will," snapped Marion.

In 1931, when Lenore Coffee and Bayard Veiller had just written *Arsene Lupin*, Bern approached them. "I know you two dear people won't mind," he said, "but I'm giving Carey Wilson some credit on this film."

"For what?" demanded Veiller. "We've done all the work—and done it damn well, too."

"Well, you see, my dears, Carey needs the credit."

"That's a nice warm overcoat you're wearing, Paul, and my chauffeur badly needs one," said Coffee. "Would you mind taking it off and giving it to me?"

Bern backed down. "He was kind, but weak as water," wrote Coffee. "That is why he clung to Thalberg. He needed his strength."

Salka Viertel was known as an actress in the German-language version of *Anna Christie* until her friend Garbo told Thalberg to add her to the writing staff. She met Bern at an April 1932 story conference for the film then titled *Christina*. She found Bern "a short, restless man, obviously devoted to Thalberg, but arrogant and pretentious with me. . . . I listened to what could almost be called a lecture from Thalberg, interrupted now and then by Bern's exclamations: 'Marvelous, Irving,' 'I see! Now it certainly makes sense! *Now* it becomes an important film . . .' etc., etc."

Anita Loos saw Bern frequently on the *Red-Headed Woman* set and at first thought him "good and kind and gentle; Jean [Harlow] had had too many experiences with men who were weak, selfish, or evil." Even so, and perhaps because she herself was married to a difficult older man, Loos began to feel that Bern and Harlow made an odd match. The startlingly beautiful girl who had just turned twenty-one was sexually aware yet emotionally immature, so she was intrigued by her soft-spoken mentor. "Expecting no return of his ardor, [Bern] had to woo her with arguments unrelated to sex," wrote Loos. "He maintained that as a producer he'd devote all his talents to her career." Harlow was ambitious, but not as ambitious as her mother, who was living a failed acting career through her daughter. Harlow's mother was married to a combination gigolo and con man named Marino Bello, so she was wary of Bern. Bello saw a golden goose and encouraged Harlow to accept Bern's attentions. Bewildered by a swirl of contradictions, Harlow wanted to believe the best. "Paul Bern is the sweetest man in the world," she told a columnist. "He is the only man I have ever met who seems to like me as a girl and a person, rather than as the vampy jazz baby that I have been made to appear on the screen."

"Jean was always lonely," wrote Loos, "and she longed to find companionship in a lover, one with wit enough to respond to her compulsive wisecracks. But very early in life she realized she was doomed to failure. Irving, for instance, found her nothing more than a booby trap for male stupidity." Strickling overheard Thalberg advising Bern against marrying Harlow. "Thalberg never accepted Harlow," recalled Strickling. "He didn't approve of that marriage."

Also dead set against it was Adela Rogers St. Johns, who knew more about Bern than even Thalberg did. She knew that while studying acting at the American Academy of Dramatic Art in 1920, Bern had become involved with a woman named Dorothy Millette who was both unstable and Gentile. He soon found himself torn between two neurotics: the clinging Millette and his domineering mother, who was unnaturally dependent on him. His mother threatened to commit suicide if he married Millette. Before he had time to respond, his mother assumed that he had eloped. She jumped off an embankment and drowned herself. Bern moved in with Millette at the Algonquin Hotel, but she soon had a total breakdown. He left her there when he went to Hollywood, but sent regular checks to support her, even when she was institutionalized for long periods.

More damaging than this history was what St. Johns had heard from Barbara LaMarr ten years earlier. "Paul has no right to marry any woman," declared LaMarr. "This I *know*." Why not? Was Bern already married? Was he a pervert? An invert? St. Johns wanted to know, and LaMarr, with "the direct, uninhibited honesty of a child, had been graphic, technical and explicit." She told St. Johns that Bern had sadly undersized genitals. Now the naïve daughter of a pushy mother and shady stepfather was about to marry a middle-aged eunuch, the so-called "Father Confessor of Hollywood." St. Johns felt it her duty to set Harlow straight.

"You mean Paul loves me for something else?" Harlow asked. "Then it's true. He loves me as he says he does, for my mind, my spirit, my companionship—for *me*. He's paid me the highest compliment I've ever had. Thank God! I'm sick of sex!"

The ripe young actress may have been sick of sex, but it was not sick of her.

It was at a spring 1932 party that Irene Selznick witnessed a disturbing scene. Harlow, draped in a clinging bias-cut gown, was enjoying a glass of gin and the advances of millionaire Cornelius Vanderbilt Whitney. Bern was unfazed by the scene, but Selznick was so embarrassed that she started to leave the room. With a melodramatic flair, Bern seized Selznick and declared: "Look at her! Look at her! She is an angel from heaven. I want you to remember and never forget it. No matter what happens, you are to remember that she is an angel from heaven!" Douglas Fairbanks Jr. had an equally weird experience when Bern invited him to meet Harlow. Bern had introduced Fairbanks to Joan Crawford years earlier and was now proudly telling Fairbanks over dinner that he was engaged. What Bern could not see was that Harlow was trying to fondle Fairbanks under the table. The disgusted Fairbanks avoided Harlow thereafter.

On July 2, 1932, Harlow and Bern were married in the living room of 1353 Club View Drive, the West Los Angeles home occupied by the Bellos (but supported by Harlow). John Gilbert was best man, and Irene Selznick was a witness. Thalberg and Shearer were also in attendance. The reception was held the next day at Bern's home. Marx overheard Shearer talking to Harlow in the garden. "When your producer-husband should be in bed with you," said Shearer, "he'll be in the living room reading a script. Or worse yet, at one of those story conferences, wherever they hold them!"

At one of "those story conferences" that same week, Thalberg joked to a writer that Bern was "obsessed with sex." At another conference, Bern said, "You can't mix sex with comedy," a strange statement after the successful premiere of *Red-Headed Woman*. On July 6 the newspapers carried a portentous item, the North Carolina suicide of Smith Reynolds, the twenty-year-old Winston-Salem tobacco heir who had recently married Broadway "torch singer" Libby Holman. The item had two connections to Thalberg and Bern. An important witness at the inquest was stage actress Blanche Yurka, whose ex-husband Ian Keith had been cast by Bern in *Susan Lenox*; and Holman had shot to fame in *The Little Show*, singing lyrics by M-G-M publicist Howard Dietz. As the southern scandal played itself out with items about Reynolds's alleged impotence, Bern began to show symptoms of depression. He even began to talk of suicide. Thalberg had been only half right; Bern was obsessed with both sex and suicide. "If the time comes when I'm no longer useful," Bern told M-G-M writer Willis Goldbeck, "I'd do it."

One night in August, columnist Sidney Skolsky and his wife joined Chico Marx and the newlywed Berns at the home of Samuel Marx and his wife, where dinner was followed by Broadway gossip. Bern held forth on theatrical trends with his usual acuity. "He was obviously an intelligent and extremely articulate person," wrote Skolsky later. "He seemed very attentive to Jean. Yet I had the feeling there was something strange about this man. He was a very gentle man, perhaps too gentle, too effeminate." Skolsky was taken aback, then, to see that Bern carried a pistol. "Oh, that's a new gun I got," Bern said. "You never can tell when you'll need a gun." He took the pistol from his coat pocket, regarded it sagely for a moment, and then put it away. "I intend using it someday," he said cryptically.

When Loos heard a similar story from actress Colleen Moore, she began avoiding Bern and referring to him as a "German psycho." St. Johns thought him "interested in abnormality and complexes, in inhibitions, perversions, suicide, and death." This was the side that Harlow began to see as Bern "educated" her to the level of an M-G-M star, which was silly since few of them had finished high school. At first she was flattered, professing a desire to sit at his knee and learn. Before long, though, the Father Confessor became a humorless pedant. "Honest, Paul makes me feel like I'm sitting at a desk in a classroom," Harlow told Marion. "Or on a stool with a dunce cap on my head!" At parties, Loos and St. Johns both saw Bern repeatedly belittle Harlow to the point of tears. With her concept of marriage in tatters, Harlow tried to escape, finding a dubious refuge in her mother's bossy company. Even there she could not relax. She confided to Loos and St. Johns that Bello sometimes made passes at her. Like Garbo, Shearer, and Crawford, Harlow felt most secure in front of a camera.

Harlow's marriage had admitted her to M-G-M's highest echelon. If she doubted it, she had only to look at her living room wall, where Bern commissioned a mural of a Renaissance-era banquet. On close inspection, the richly garbed nobility could be recognized as Bern's colleagues, including David and Irene Selznick, Edmund Goulding, John Gilbert, Norma Shearer, Douglas Fairbanks Jr., and Joan Crawford. Harlow was seated near the center of the painting. The only figure standing was Thalberg, who, unlike the others, was serious and slightly aloof, a Machiavellian prince observing his court.

The other new face in the inner circle was Mayer's twenty-nine-year-old son-in-law, David Selznick, who was upgrading RKO Radio Pictures with quality films such as *King Kong*. In mid-August Thalberg invited the Selznicks to 707 Ocean Front for a private preview of Selznick's *A Bill of Divorcement*. "We were one of the first in Hollywood to have a projection booth in our home," recalled Shearer, "including an eight-by-ten-foot screen which came up from the living-room floor. The first time we tried our equipment, we had a group of producers assembled. Irving picked up the phone and told the operator to go ahead. Well, the screen came up, the lights went out—and nothing happened. No picture, no sound. Just dead silence. He'd blown the main fuse. There we sat in total darkness and utter humiliation." Fortunately, the Selznick screening had no such problems. "That evening had a lot of meaning for me," wrote Irene Selznick. "I had never contemplated sitting in Irving's living room watching my husband's latest film and listening to Irving's praise. All things considered, it was a lovely moment." Less lovely was Irene's opinion of Harlow; she thought her unworthy of Bern.

Thalberg at least thought Harlow was talented. He allowed Bern to transform *Red Dust* from a Garbo-and-Gilbert project into a Harlow-and-Gilbert project. Gilbert's latest film, *Downstairs*, had flopped, and he was in desperate need of a hit. "Harlow was supposed to help Gilbert's fading image," recalled screenwriter John Lee Mahin. "He was too thin from drinking and everything else, and nervous because he was unsure of himself. If she liked him, maybe it would help." Mahin had come to know Gilbert through Hecht and MacArthur when the garrulous actor was interrupting their labors on various Thalberg scripts. "Get this man off our backs!" pleaded MacArthur. Mahin spent hours with Gilbert, drinking, womanizing, and listening to tales of bygone days at the Ince Studios, of daredevil slides down plaster pyramids overlooking the sea. Thalberg hoped that Mahin's rapport with Gilbert would inform the *Red Dust* script.

The script's evolution was typical of the Thalberg system. Playwright Wilson Collison worked at M-G-M for seven months in 1927 and then walked out when it appeared that none of his writing would be filmed. Assuming that he had been fired, he returned to Broadway and wrote a melodrama about a rubber plantation foreman and a Saigon prostitute. *Red Dust* lasted for eight performances in January 1928. A few months later, Collison discovered that his bank account balance was not $3,000 but $31,500; M-G-M had never stopped depositing checks to his account. He tried to return the money, but the accounting department could not absorb it without justification. Thalberg asked if Collison had an unsold property. He offered *Red Dust*. After M-G-M bought it, the play sat on a shelf until jungle films and the fallen woman cycle made it worth a second look. In July 1932 M-G-M announced *Red Dust* for Harlow and Gilbert, to be produced by Hunt Stromberg and directed by Jacques Feyder.

Mahin was working on the script when he happened to see Clark Gable in *Hell Divers*. Mahin immediately accosted Stromberg. "You're crazy if you use Gilbert with Harlow," said Mahin. "I just saw this new boy." Mahin described Gable as having the odd combination of a child's eyes and a man's body. "Hunt just looked at me," recalled Mahin. "I guess he thought I was queer or something. I was raving!

I told him that Gable and Harlow would be a natural." Stromberg screened some Gable footage, decided that Mahin was right, and went to Thalberg. For the second time in a year, Thalberg was faced with the prospect of hurting John Gilbert. "It was awfully hard," said Mahin, "but he did it." Virginia Bruce, who was engaged to Gilbert at the time, recalled: "I was working on another picture *[Kongo]* when Thalberg took Jack off *Red Dust*. It nearly killed him." Stromberg dictated notes for the new casting of *Red Dust:* "Gable as 'Dennis' is played as a heavy. Much the same characterization as in *A Free Soul* and *Dance, Fools, Dance*. He is ruthless—brutal—unbending—ruling this private situation with the same cruelty and brutality as in the operation of the plantation." Thalberg could not see Feyder directing this material, and he replaced him with the rugged Victor Fleming. It was Fleming and Mahin who created the masculine image that Gable would henceforth project.

Red Dust began production on Monday, August 22, with scenes of Gable roughing up "coolies" and a drunken coworker. Next to be shot were scenes of him ordering the scantily clad Harlow out of a plantation bedroom. Even Gable was surprised at the rawness of the language and the immodesty of Harlow's brassiere. These scenes, which had Harlow tussling not only with Gable but also with aging Donald Crisp and aged Tully Marshall, might not pass the SRC. Ralph Graves, a sometimes actor who specialized in military screenplays, was assigned to rework the script. He was meeting with Stromberg and Mahin when the Labor Day weekend arrived.

Saturday, September 3, was a workday.* Fleming directed Gable and Harlow in their morning-after farewell scene on the dock and then directed Harlow and Mary Astor in the scene where the prostitute Vantine (Harlow) tells Barbara (Mary Astor) that her sick husband, Gary (Gene Raymond), should not expect much from French doctors in Indochina. "Oh, these frog doctors!" sneers Vantine. "Even if you did get one, all they do is sit by the side of the bed and start crabbing at the government for not stamping out fever. And then they prescribe brandy and have to sample it themselves to see if it's any good. And by the time you're deciding whether to live or die, they're under the bed, singing the Marseillaise."

While Harlow honed her comedic skills, her husband sat alone in his office, completing a treatment for a film to be called *China Seas*. The climax of the film had its British sea captain give himself up to torture so that his American girlfriend can be saved from Malay pirates. He dies in the arms of his Chinese mistress. The

---

*This account of the events surrounding Paul Bern's death is based on the chronology established by David Stenn in his 1993 book, *Bombshell*. This includes conjectures about Bern's sexuality made to Stenn by primary reference sources.

theme of a double life often appeared in Bern's work. "I'm sure you know films like *The Cabinet of Dr. Caligari* and *The Unholy Three*," he said to Marx. "They deal with characters who use deception to hide their true identities. Masquerade is a fascinating theme. Very little in this world is what it seems." After two months of marriage to Bern, Harlow might have agreed. Her maid, Blanche Williams, would later relate how both Harlow and Bern seemed nonchalant about their unconsummated union. "The Baby's still a virgin," Bern told Williams in a feeble attempt at humor. Harlow's family pretended all was well, and her friends tried to. "Harlow admitted there had been conflict on their wedding night," wrote Marion, "but this was not unusual in Hollywood, so we passed it by." When Bern tired of reading the works of Josef Stalin to Harlow, he would turn to darker stuff, his own psyche. He told her that his efforts to cope with his physical deficiency had led to sexual experimentation with a male M-G-M bit player.* Harlow had been in show business long enough to cope with sexual deviance, but Bern's revelation of a demented common-law wife in New York was harder to take.

Harlow was spending Saturday night at Club View Drive while Bern was dining with Bernie Hyman and Barbara Barondess at the Cocoanut Grove so that the married producer would have a cover for his tryst with the young actress. The favor was typical of Bern. He was more concerned with the good it would do his image than with the harm it would do Hyman's wife. Bern was not spending Saturday evening with his own wife because she was supposedly working late at the studio. The sad fact was that she was avoiding him—and the scenes he was frequently making. "I stopped to sign an autograph for a young man in front of the house," Harlow confided to St. Johns. "And I smiled at him, of course. When I came inside, Paul hit me." If Thalberg had been aware of Bern's crisis, he could have sent him to a psychiatrist. But Bern was adept at dissimulation. No one realized how sick he was.

In 1991 Marx wrote that on Tuesday, August 30, Bern had told him a troubling story. Dorothy Millette, the incurably ill woman he had left in New York, had recently regained her faculties and was on her way to see him. Bern was hoping to keep Millette away from Harlow, who, he insisted, was unaware of her existence. In truth, he was terrified that she would come to the studio or go to the newspapers. Harlow and her mother had gone to San Francisco in mid-August, where Millette was coincidentally staying. There is no way of knowing whether they tried to pressure Millette to leave California, but surviving records do illuminate

---

*This may have been the epicene actor Douglas Walton, who began work at M-G-M under Bern's watch and whose filmography coincides with the recollections of Harlow intimate Ted Tetrick.

another aspect of Bern's life: he was on the verge of bankruptcy. This time, Bern was the one in distress, and he had nowhere to turn. He could not take this to Thalberg. He confided in Marx, but protocol dictated that Marx forget about it. When Bern lunched with Lewin on Friday, Lewin found him morbid. "Jean has been so wonderful," said Bern. "I didn't think it was possible that this could happen to a man my age with such a lovely girl." Then he added: "I couldn't be any happier, not even if I died tomorrow."

On the morning of Sunday, September 4, Harlow went from Club View Drive to the *Red Dust* soundstage. Bern stayed in bed reading *The Biological Tragedy of Woman*, *The Glands Regulating Personality*, and *Discourse on the Worship of Priapus*. When Harlow came home from work, accompanied by her maid, she was surprised to see a limousine parked in the driveway. Bern hesitantly introduced her to the woman about whom he had recently told her. Dorothy Millette was polite but vague. Harlow gave Bern an ultimatum. "When you find out who you're married to," she said, "let me know." Bern indignantly ordered Harlow to leave. She departed in tears. Millette stayed for another few hours. When she left, her limousine roared down the hill, skidding one hundred feet at its base. In the wee hours of the morning, Bern wrote a conciliatory note to Harlow, intending to attach it to a bouquet that could be delivered early to Club View Drive. Perhaps he hoped that she would understand and forgive him, as she had when he told her about his sexual experimentation.

Around 9 A.M. on the morning of Monday, September 5—Labor Day—a woman, possibly Harlow herself, returned to Easton Drive. She entered the quiet house and went upstairs to the bedroom, where she saw the apology note written in a guest book. Next to it was a gun. She heard Bern in the dressing room that adjoined their bedroom. He was standing naked in front of a mirror and holding another gun.

Howard Strickling's phone often rang early in the morning and sometimes on holidays, but this call was not from Louis B. Mayer. It was from a hysterical woman. "Paul just killed himself!"

Thalberg was hosting a Labor Day luncheon for Samuel and Frances Goldwyn when he was called from the table. Mayer's wife, Margaret, was telephoning him. When she told him that Bern was dead, he turned white and slumped into a chair. Shearer at first thought he was having a seizure. When he regained his breath, he said he felt strong enough to go to Easton Drive. Shearer insisted on going with him. They were followed by their neighbor David Selznick.

When they arrived, M-G-M security chief Whitey Hendry and photographer Virgil Apger were present, along with Bern's servants, Clifton Davis and John and

Winifred Carmichael. Carmichael had gone to Bern's room at 11:30 to serve him breakfast and found Bern lying on the dressing room floor. "It was quite pitiful," Carmichael later said. "He was lying in a pool of blood." Carmichael had fainted and been found by Davis, who had then called Hendry. Strickling and Mayer were also present, arguing about what was now being described as a suicide note:

Dearest dear,

Unfortunately this is the only way to make good the frightful wrong I have done you and to wipe out my abject humiliation. I love you.

Paul

You understand last night was only a comedy.

Mayer had already pocketed the note, intending to destroy it. Strickling pleaded that he leave it intact. After a brief look at his friend's body, Thalberg went outside and sat with Shearer on a stone bench in the eighty-degree heat. An hour elapsed before he called the police. In that time, reporters were free to come and go, and M-G-M executives were free to tamper with evidence. There was not much they could do. Bern's naked corpse was lying crumpled against the wall of the dressing room. Part of his head had been shot onto the wall. The gun was still in his right hand, but wedged between his body and the floor. Rigor mortis was setting in. Thalberg went back inside and pulled Strickling away from the dressing room. "Paul can't be helped now," said Thalberg. "The girl is the one who needs protection."

The police arrived at 2:30, at which time Thalberg and Shearer drove (without Selznick) to Club View Drive. Shearer sat in the living room while Thalberg went upstairs to tell Jean of Bern's death. He waited on the landing for Mrs. Bello to bring Harlow out of her bedroom. In 1974 Shearer remembered looking up and being able to see "his shoes and the cuffs of his trousers, as if one were looking at a low camera setup. He paced back and forth until Jean came out. I could see her slippers and the hem of her negligee.* They stood facing each other a minute.

*Norma Shearer told Samuel Marx (when he was interviewing her for his book *Mayer and Thalberg*) that she sat in the car below the house on Club View Drive and looked up to see Thalberg meeting Harlow on the balcony outside her bedroom. Photographs taken by Virgil Apger in 1932 and by Darrell Rooney in 2005 show that there was no balcony anywhere on the house. A landing above the living room afforded the kind of "low camera setup" that Shearer described to Marx.

Then she seemed to wilt." Harlow was in a state of shock, unable to tell Thalberg what she knew.

Thalberg and Shearer returned to their car. "He looked kind of strange," recalled Shearer. "He slumped down in the seat next to me. Then I found out that he'd gone there to tell Jean that the studio had everything under control. 'She claims that she doesn't understand what I mean,' was all he said. Then he burst into tears. It was a terrible, terrible day for us."

Part of the terror of that day came from the realization that no one at M-G-M would ever be able to talk about Bern without being coached by Mayer or Strickling. Mayer called a meeting at which he set forth the official version: Bern committed suicide because he was impotent. Thalberg bridled at the idea of slurring his friend. He told Mayer to shut up. "Everyone's talking too much!" snapped Thalberg. "Let Howard do the talking!" Yet Strickling decided to support Mayer's version. For once, Thalberg's authority meant nothing.

The coroner's inquest was held at the Price-Daniel Mortuary in West Los Angeles on Thursday, September 8. Harlow was too ill to attend, but Thalberg, looking tired and drawn, took the stand, answering every question as Strickling had instructed him.

Q: *[You had not] been upstairs to see the body before you called the police? Who did you call?*

A: I tried to get Chief of Police Steckel, and I was held up on the line several times. They finally told me he wasn't in, and they asked me to talk to the chief of detectives. I spoke to him and told him where I was and what I knew had happened and asked him to please send someone right up and do it as quickly and quietly as possible, and he said he would.

Q: *So you didn't lose any time in calling the officers, Mr. Thalberg. You are well acquainted with Mr. Bern and knew him a long time? . . . Did you know of any reason why he should take his life?*

A: Well, that is not for me to say. I don't know of any . . .

Q: *Was he working under severe strain at times, at any rate?*

A: Yes, he was.

Q: *Did you notice that he had been nervous at times?*

A: Yes, he had been nervous at times, and he would get better.

Q: *Did he ever discuss the suicide problem with you as a scientific fact or in any way?*

A: Yes, he did.

Q: *Do you know anything about his family history? Did he ever mention that some of them had ever taken their lives?*

A: He might have.

Q: *Did he ever mention that he might do that some time?*

A: Yes, he did.

Q: *So far as the domestic relations between Mr. Bern and his wife are concerned, do you know of anything in that that would constitute a reason for him wanting to take his life?*

A: I don't know of anything directly. I have heard of lots of things but I don't know of anything.

Dr. Frank Webb, who had performed the autopsy, testified that Bern's reproductive organs were "developed normally but undersized." Bern may—or may not—have been able to engage in sexual intercourse. The press had meanwhile been alerted of the existence of Dorothy Millette by Bern's brother Henry and had tracked her to San Francisco, where she disappeared after boarding a ferryboat. The coroner's inquest ruled Bern's death a suicide.

The funeral took place in the Grace Chapel at the Inglewood Park Cemetery on Friday, September 9. Conrad Nagel, a Christian Scientist, delivered a eulogy that denied the possibility of suicide. Harlow and Bern's sister Frederike both wept openly. More affecting than this was Thalberg's display of grief. After a week of almost unnatural poise, he could not control his emotions. Marx saw his boss sitting in the front of the chapel, his "shoulders hunched, weeping bitterly." Lewin was seated directly behind Thalberg. "Irving loved Paul," recalled Lewin. "He sobbed through the whole ceremony."

Outside the chapel, Harlow was mobbed by fans. "There were ghastly words and demands for autographs," she said. "They seemed heartless. To them I was not a person. I was an institution. I had no more personality than a corporation." Not only Harlow's fans had dehumanized her; Mayer had, too. Judging from his behavior, he was more worried about the money he had paid for her contract than he was about the human being behind it. Mayer could be crass. When Lon Chaney died in August 1930, Mayer tried to get back the $50,000 bonus Thalberg had negotiated for Chaney eight months earlier. Now Mayer was afraid that the public might turn against Harlow and render her worthless. He offered Tallulah Bankhead a contract if she would replace Harlow in *Red Dust*. Bankhead thought the idea treacherous and declined.

On Sunday, September 11, Harlow telephoned Thalberg. "This staying home is driving me crazy," she said. "I've got to get busy—to forget." She returned to M-G-M the next day by a side entrance. The *Red Dust* company had been shooting around her since September 7. "The day she came back, she was really subdued," recalled sound technician Bill Edmondson, "and for the Baby to be subdued was something." Fleming and the crew tiptoed around her. "How are we going to get a sexy performance out of her with *that* look in her eyes?" Fleming asked Mary Astor. The recovery of Dorothy Millette's body in the Sacramento River on September 14 did not help matters, but as Edmondson said, "Harlow was a trouper."

Thalberg was concerned that Harlow not appear too sluttish in *Red Dust*, so Stromberg had Mahin rewrite her early scenes. As he was completing them, the studio mail room was swamped with letters of sympathy and support for Harlow. She filmed the rewritten scenes the last week of September, wearing a less revealing negligee. Jason Joy attended the October 9 preview.

"Remembering the doubts amidst which this production was conceived," Joy wrote Thalberg, "and the extremely harassing circumstances which attended its delivery, we feel that you and your organization can take a special bow for the results." There were, however, two lines that Joy wanted Thalberg to remove from the negative. "The first is the derogatory speech by Harlow concerning the French doctors in which she refers to them as 'Frogs,' and goes on to make some crack about them hiding under the bed and singing the 'Marseillaise.' The second is Harlow's line, spoken to the parrot when she is cleaning its cage, to the effect that it must have been eating cement." Thalberg agreed to have Harlow "loop" the words "Sweet Adeline" onto the sound track over "the 'Marseillaise,'" but persuaded Joy to leave "Frog doctors" because it passed by so quickly. The birdcage line remained because she was crying when she said it, as suggested by Mahin. *Red Dust* opened October 22 without further incident. Rave reviews, box-office receipts, and fan mail justified Bern's faith in Harlow.

As Shearer and Marx later related, the Bern tragedy touched Thalberg on many levels—professional, philosophical, personal. He had fully expected Bern to tend the Thalberg legacy; he had never dreamed that Bern would predecease him. For several days after the funeral, Thalberg secluded himself in his home. When he returned to M-G-M, he was somber and withdrawn. Within a few days he was visibly depressed. Eddie Mannix grew concerned and urged Mayer to speak with him. Mayer, who was given to gushes of sentiment, became distant and brusque, unwilling to extend sympathy to Thalberg or to honor Bern's memory.

When Mayer had been away politicking, Thalberg had been able to ignore the truth. Now it was here and had to be faced. The bond that had tied him to Mayer no longer existed. Thalberg was grieving for Bern. He could not grieve for Mayer's friendship. He began to internalize the anger he felt at Mayer for vilifying Bern after his death, and the guilt he felt for allowing it. Thalberg grew curt and sarcastic with his colleagues. He tried to throw himself into his work, but he found it unsatisfying. He had seen death in person; on film it looked false. Straining to create illusions felt futile. For the first time, he lost his connection to his work. He had long since lost his connection to Mayer. Now he lost patience.

"What's it all for?" he asked Albert Lewin. "Why the hell am I killing myself? Just so Mayer and Schenck can get rich and fat?"

In the third week of September, Thalberg confronted Mayer. According to Bob Thomas, "He told Mayer he was sick and wanted to be relieved of his position as head of production. He wanted to be released from his contract so he could go away for a year and contemplate his future." For once, Mayer was unable to formulate a response. He was stunned. The best he could do was promise Thalberg that he would convey his message to Schenck. "You'd better come out here as soon as you can," Mayer told Schenck over long distance.

Schenck checked into the Ambassador Hotel on September 20. Mayer brought J. Robert Rubin to see him. "Thalberg claims he isn't well," said Mayer. "He's asking to be relieved of his contract." Schenck was skeptical. Thalberg had shown no signs of illness for seven years. On the other hand, he had more than once used threats of resignation to get a raise. Schenck asked Mayer what he thought was behind Thalberg's demands. "I think the boy is getting spoiled," answered Mayer. "People are telling him how good he is. I believe it's turning his head a little. There are all kinds of offers." Schenck knew that his brother at United Artists would love to sign both Garbo and Thalberg. It was also true that Paramount wanted Mayer to replace the recently ousted Jesse Lasky. And Sam Goldwyn had been pitching the Goldwyn studio to Thalberg at the interrupted Labor Day luncheon. Schenck quickly scheduled a meeting with Thalberg.

Thalberg came alone to Schenck's hotel room. Mayer and Rubin were already there. Thalberg wasted no time. He told Schenck that he wanted to break his contract, effective immediately.

"Irving, that is silly," snorted Schenck. "You have a contract up 'til 1937. And besides, I have no right to release you. I don't own the company. And you're a very valuable man."

"I don't feel well," Thalberg insisted. "The responsibility is too great. I work sixteen hours a day. I work weekends. I never see my son. It's too much. I'd like to go away for a while, think about all of this, and then come back and see what I want to do." When Schenck dismissed this out of hand, Thalberg rose from his seat in a cold fury and left the hotel. Mayer and Rubin called him when he got home and persuaded him to return the next day. And the next. He returned for a series of meetings but could not be moved from his purpose. Schenck reminded him that the New York office had indulged uncommercial whims such as *Strange Interlude*. Thalberg produced proof that it was turning a profit. Schenck reminded him that Loew's had granted him a raise only last April. Thalberg pointed to the multimillion-dollar profit that he was bringing Loew's. Paramount, RKO, and Warners were in the red. Schenck became surly. Thalberg would not yield.

"Now, Irving," said Schenck impatiently, "you're just a youngster after all. You're not prepared to retire. You will have to work somewhere else, do something else. No matter what you do, the government will tax you."

Thalberg countered that taxes were already eating up his income. He was under a terrific strain and had been for three years. He was not strong. He had made millions for the company. He was prepared to sit out his time, and it was better to be taxed for that than for working himself to death and not leaving his family provided for.

"What in the hell do you do with your money anyway?" Schenck snarled. "This is 1932, young man. People are living in boxes, but you get $400,000 per *and* bonuses!" Thalberg reminded Schenck that he had pocketed millions for selling Loew's to Fox.

Mayer and Rubin exchanged nervous glances as the argument escalated. "Oh, it was hell," recalled Mayer. "I was watching Schenck. His fingernails were purple as he held onto the side of his chair. Irving was riding him terribly hard, driving him. He told Schenck that he didn't give a damn, that he was cold as ice, that he wasn't even human just as long as we made lots of money for the company. Oh, it was just fierce! And Schenck kept yelling back at him: 'Damn it, Irving! I've been decent and right with you! This is a corporation! I've got legal responsibilities!'"

Thalberg said through clenched teeth that he was not going to work himself to death for Loew's.

"Fine!" yelled Schenck. "We'll sue you for breach of contract!"

Thalberg laughed in his face. Then he paused and said quietly, "We'll meet that later." With that he stood up and walked out of the room, slamming the door.

It may have been Thalberg's icy rage. It may have been rumors of an interest in Goldwyn. It may have been M-G-M's profits in the midst of the most serious economic crisis America had ever known. Whatever it was, it threw a scare into Nicholas Schenck. He hastened to New York and secured the approval of a special deal to appease Thalberg. It would not require the company to increase Thalberg's salary nor would it require Mayer to surrender more percentage points. According to Bosley Crowther, who interviewed most of the principals in the early 1950s and was shown what documents remained, the deal was as follows.

Thalberg would be permitted to buy up to 100,000 shares of Loew's common stock, between December 1, 1934, and March 1, 1939, at thirty to forty dollars a share, no matter what the market price. [It was then selling for sixty.] The shares would be automatically issued out of the surplus authorized by the corporation's charter and the purchase price would be paid to Loew's, Inc. Mayer would be permitted to buy up to 80,000 shares on the same terms, and Rubin 50,000. The contract with the "Mayer group" was extended to December 3, 1938.

Thalberg's loss of Paul Bern was also acknowledged. In late September, Howard Hawks and Sidney Franklin became associate producers under Thalberg. Working closely with him, they would supervise a total of eight films a year, as well as directing their own projects. On October 8, Thalberg and Shearer left for New York, where Thalberg signed his new contract. He appeared to be pleased with the concessions he had gained. Mayer, on the other hand, was stung. Why was he offered only 80,000 shares when Thalberg was offered 100,000? His question was a fair one. But corporate politics are not necessarily fair. If he wanted better terms, it was up to him to get them—by whatever means he could.

Mayer began consolidating power. He brought directors Mervyn LeRoy and Frank Capra to M-G-M and made them report directly to him. Thalberg had hired producer Walter Wanger on December 21 and cautioned Wanger to ignore Mayer's effusive, manipulative overtures. "Don't pay any attention to him," said Thalberg, but Wanger found himself working directly under Mayer in the last week of the year. Mayer's long-range plan was to groom a replacement for Thalberg. This would not be easy. Mayer did not know that each new man was conferring privately with Thalberg. There existed a "Thalberg cult," a coterie of intensely loyal executives. "M-G-M was a closely knit society as put together by

Thalberg," recalled producer Gottfried Reinhardt. Mayer would need to win over "Irving's boys" if he wanted to install a production head who would respect him as much as Thalberg initially had. Just when Mayer was wondering how to do this, he saw the galleys of the *Fortune* article.

The unsigned fifteen-page feature portrayed M-G-M as an impregnable citadel. Mayer was described as "the commercial diplomat, the man of connections," whose efforts encompassed "personal connections, intrigues, and affiliations." The article's faint praise was that he kept the powerful Hearst happy by making unprofitable Marion Davies movies. The patronizing, anti-Semitic tone of the piece was not limited to Mayer. It characterized Thalberg as brilliant and effective, even if he did happen to be a Jew. Bigotry aside, the article did more than any previous item of journalism or publicity to crystallize the legend of the Boy Wonder. Pushing Mayer to the sidelines, the article gave Thalberg most of the credit for M-G-M's preeminence:

> Tutored by a sharper master than adversity—success—he is now called a genius more often than anyone else in Hollywood, which means that the word is practically his nickname. . . . His brain is the camera which photographs dozens of scripts in a week and decides which of them, if any, shall be turned over to M-G-M's twenty-seven departments to be made into a moving picture. It is also the recording apparatus which converts the squealing friction of 2,200 erratic underlings into the more than normally coherent chatter of an M-G-M talkie.
>
> The kinds of pictures M-G-M makes and the ways it makes them are Irving Thalberg's problems.
>
> All the Associates . . . are just so many extensions of Irving Thalberg's personality.
>
> He is what Hollywood means by M-G-M.
>
> *His brain is the camera.*

According to Frances Marion, when Mayer read the article, he responded as if he were an "injured lion, lashing out blindly and furiously." Less than a week later, he made private overtures to his son-in-law.

David Selznick had his own concerns. He had improved RKO's product, but the studio was still in the red. It was owned by RCA, and Selznick resented having to ask permission for every expenditure from radio executives in New York. Even so, he could not see himself working for his father-in-law or, more to the point, for Thalberg. "I have the most enormous respect for Irving Thalberg," Selznick wrote Mayer on November 12. "I regard him as the greatest producer the industry has yet developed. I intend to try goddam hard to equal his achievements, and I hope one day to surpass them. I cannot do this at M-G-M . . . with the assets and the facilities that he has been so largely responsible for developing." Selznick felt that he could do better by developing his own stars, as he was doing with Katharine Hepburn. There was also his need to be top dog. "I could not help but be subordinate to Irving—and much as I respect him, I do not want, in my own field, to be subordinate to anybody . . . working for M-G-M, I would expect to be. His record is too excellent for me not to regard him as the master of that particular situation; and I should think very little indeed of his organization if they did not regard him as their master."

As 1932 drew to a close, Selznick found himself clashing more frequently with RCA. Thalberg, meanwhile, had regained his creative momentum and was soaring higher and higher, managing a multiplicity of projects. Anita Loos was writing *Nora* for Harlow and Helen Hayes. Frances Marion was writing *The Prizefighter and the Lady* for Gable and Shearer. Howard Hawks was directing Crawford and Gary Cooper in William Faulkner's script of his own novel, *Turn About*. Donald Ogden Stewart was preparing *Reunion in Vienna*, but not for Shearer; Thalberg was giving it to Diana Wynyard. He was also helping Frank Capra develop *Soviet* for Gable, Crawford, and Beery. He bought the novel *Presenting Lily Mars* for Marion Davies and was shooting makeup and wig tests for her film *Peg o' My Heart*. All of these projects were subsidized by the phenomenal autumn success of *Smilin' Through*. The studio Christmas party was a well-deserved celebration.

On Christmas Eve, most of the studio's employees reported to its largest sound-stage for turkey dinner and a speech by Mayer. "I say the country has emerged from the depression," he declared from the podium, "and so we have!" After he left the lot, work ceased. M-G-M's most strenuous, stressful year could not wait another week to be feted. "Suddenly bacchanalia reigned," wrote Marx. "Men and women poured in and out of offices, stages, and backlot sets. There was no shortage of alcohol, just glasses. . . . Stars and laborers, executives and secretaries shared drinks, paraded the streets, singing, embracing, kissing."

Thalberg did not venture into the carnival. He did not have to. All M-G-M came to his office. Hundreds of employees bypassed the "Million-Dollar Bench" and sauntered in. As Marx watched in amusement, the usually reserved Thalberg welcomed everyone. "They paraded past him," recalled Marx, "girls with kisses, men with handshakes. An office boy slapped him on the back and swore undying loyalty. Thalberg thanked him emotionally. He had taken more than his customary Scotch and soda. This was no time to be sober. For once, he, too, was one of the boys. He even left his office at times to embrace the girls he had missed."

The mindless revelry may have been Thalberg's attempt to cope with Paul Bern's absence. Bern deserved to celebrate that day as much as anyone did, yet less than four months after his death, he was forgotten. Thalberg may have felt guilty. Still, there was one reminder of the tragedy. Script clerk Willard Sheldon was leaving the party when he spied a girl lying on the ground. He looked more closely at the inert drunk and recognized Jean Harlow. "People were just passing by," recalled Sheldon, "so I picked her up and helped her inside."

Thalberg felt poorly the next day, but not because of a hangover. Shearer decided that it was the same thing that had happened a year earlier, another of those pesky colds. It continued for a second day, so Thalberg did not go back to work. Perhaps it was the flu. On the evening of December 28, he began to feel nauseated. He poured himself a glass of ginger ale, hoping to settle his stomach. Almost immediately after downing it, he felt pains in his chest and down his left arm. He managed to climb the stairs to the bedroom. Shearer checked the time. The pain continued for twenty minutes, then subsided.

Thalberg's regular physician was Dr. Philip Newmark, a resident of Lincoln Hospital in predominantly Jewish East Los Angeles. Shearer called him at his home. He arrived within the hour and performed an electrocardiogram in the bedroom. He then called in another specialist, Dr. Robert W. Langley. After several more tests, they were in agreement. Thalberg had suffered a heart attack. He was confined to his bed. When Henrietta came to the house, Shearer gently but firmly kept her from seeing her son. Shearer also prevented Mayer from entering the house. A few days later, he came back, accompanied by Nick Schenck. Again Shearer refused to admit them. She would admit no one until the doctors allowed it.

Mayer conferred with Schenck and again approached Selznick, who had quit RKO on December 17. Selznick was preoccupied with his father's health and could not consider Mayer's offer. Mayer was not discouraged. Thalberg had flown too high and too fast. He was grounded, perhaps permanently. With or without Selznick, Mayer was ready to take control.

The first weeks of 1933 were a tense time at Metro-Goldwyn-Mayer. Irving Thalberg was out of immediate danger, but whether he would resume his post was an open question. Unable to consult with him, Louis B. Mayer took charge of the studio. He could not be omniscient like Thalberg, but he could be omnipresent. He came to every production meeting for Walter Wanger's *Gabriel Over the White House*. In his diary Wanger recorded meetings with Mayer on January 3 (by telephone), January 4 (in his office), January 6 (a "long session" in his office), January 13 (a screening of five reels), and January 14 (a conference that included Harry Rapf). Wanger was one of five producers nervously dealing with Mayer while heart specialists monitored Thalberg's progress. At one point a doctor said that Thalberg should not be allowed to lift his arms for fear of another attack. The company was holding its breath. So was the country.

The Great Depression was not over, Mayer's pronouncement notwithstanding. Economists saw no sign of improvement. The gross national product had dropped by a record 13.4 percent. Bank failures had become commonplace; there were 1,493 in 1932 alone. They became newsworthy when they caused movie stars to lose huge sums of money. Marion Davies, John Gilbert, Jean Harlow, Greta Garbo, and Robert Montgomery were all hit by the insolvency of the First National Bank of Beverly Hills. Unemployment had risen to 23.6 percent, and fifteen million Americans were now out of work. These statistics could be verified in Hollywood, where more than 2,200 studio employees had been laid off. The film industry was in trouble. January saw Paramount and RKO in receivership, Universal half closed, and Warner Bros. reeling from a loss of $14.1 million. M-G-M's $8 million profit would tide it over, but if conditions did not improve, even it could be threatened. Thalberg had chosen the wrong time to fall ill.

Mayer was still burning from the stock deal he had gotten in September, and Nicholas Schenck was still smarting from Thalberg's tongue-lashing. While Mayer had not forgotten Schenck's 1929 maneuverings, he saw in him a potential ally. In early January, Mayer approached Schenck. He found that they were in agreement on basic issues. Before long, Mayer and Schenck were forging an alliance. The Hollywood studio system was barely twenty years old, but certain precepts were firmly in place. These unwritten rules were called "industry practice." "You're only as good as your last picture," was one of them. "You don't work for a studio other than your own without a loan-out arrangement," was another. Boardroom battles in Hollywood were different from their corporate counterparts. Part of the reason was that M-G-M's product was different from that of General Motors. Mayer liked to point out that a motion picture was the only product you could sell and yet own after you had sold it. More to the point, a motion picture was a product that did not really exist during its manufacture, and, although Thalberg's contribution to the finished product was pervasive, it was hard to isolate. This made him vulnerable to two resentful partners.

Thalberg had been away for four weeks, yet the studio was running smoothly. Mayer was even enjoying his newfound involvement in the creative process. He could not remember what Thalberg had spent all those hours contributing. Obviously it was not crucial, because M-G-M was doing fine without him. Mayer and Schenck began to formulate plans for a new production system. Never mind *Fortune* magazine's appraisal that M-G-M's system was the closest to perfection in Hollywood, and Thalberg its essential component. Never mind the $8 million profit. Mayer and Schenck wanted more films, more money, and no Thalberg. Mayer often claimed: "God is good to me." What happened next had to be an act of God.

On January 24, 1933, Lewis J. Selznick died. His son David was wild with grief. His mother tried to console him with his father's last words: "Tell David to stick to his own people. They're the men you can trust." Mayer interpreted this for his distraught son-in-law. It meant that he should never have trusted the executives at RKO, and that he should now trust his father-in-law, who wanted him to come to M-G-M. Even Irene later admitted that Lewis's deathbed words were "not a directive, but David took them to heart . . . [and] capitulated without warning."

When Selznick came to his senses a few days later and realized what he had done, Mayer was already on the doorstep of 707 Ocean Front.

Norma Shearer was once more her gracious self as she ushered Mayer to Thalberg's bedroom. Then she closed the door and left the partners alone. After a few minutes the sound of raised voices came through the door. Shearer was alarmed to hear her husband shouting. Mayer was shouting louder, of course, saying that he had "only hired Dave as a *replacement* producer!"

"*Replacement?*" yelled Thalberg. "Who will replace *you?*"

Before Shearer could intervene, the door flew open. She later told Bosley Crowther that "Irving virtually chased Mayer out of the house." After calming Thalberg, Shearer learned the reason for the argument. With Schenck's approval—and without Thalberg's—Mayer had signed David Selznick as an independent producer at $4,000 a week to supervise six pictures a year. That was more than twice what Paul Bern had been getting—and Selznick *would be answerable only to Mayer.* Thalberg was furious, but there was nothing he could do about it. Shearer tried to calm him. He kept saying how unfair it was that Schenck and Mayer had taken advantage of his illness. Thalberg liked and respected Selznick, which made the situation even more hurtful. But this was not all.

Included with the contract that Mayer had brought for Thalberg to sign (so that Selznick could be formally brought into the company) was a letter from Loew's, proposing that M-G-M be restructured. The production staff would be grouped in a "unit system" of six "executive producers," not including Thalberg, each of whom would head a unit responsible for ten films. Not coincidentally, this was the system that Selznick had implemented at RKO. The letter did not specify if the units would be answerable to him and Mayer, or only to him.

On February 2, Thalberg reluctantly signed the contract, the most important part of which read: "By consenting to the execution of such contract, you shall not be deemed to have approved the terms of the same nor the special conditions therein set forth . . . and you shall not be considered, by reason of such consent, as having acquiesced or approved of the policy which has been discussed of establishing the unit system of production, and, finally, it is agreed that no concessions similar to [those] made to Mr. Selznick shall be made in connection with any other contract or employment without your express consent." Once the contract had been ratified, Howard Strickling issued a formal announcement that Selznick had been hired.

Shortly thereafter, Frances Marion found herself in a story conference with Mayer for *The Prizefighter and the Lady*, which Mayer had changed from a Shearer-

Gable vehicle to a Myrna Loy–Max Baer vehicle. Before Marion could ask if the real-life pugilist Baer could act, Mayer explained that Shearer was out of the film because she would not be working while Thalberg was on sick leave. He also explained why Selznick was joining the M-G-M family. "I'm doing this," he told Marion, "not because David is married to my daughter, but to spare Irving, who is so dear to me."

Thalberg spent the next week at an unaccustomed task: writing. He composed a long, carefully worded letter to Schenck, addressing the proposed restructuring. The letter went through numerous drafts as Thalberg tried to balance logic and emotion.

> I felt it best to give you my conclusions in writing because in discussion the issues become confused and there is apt to be too much time spent on side-lights. As you have requested, I have been seriously considering your plan, in fact it has been in my thoughts day and night. Since you have had this plan in your mind for many years and since the majority of our partners are already in agreement on it . . . I shall make no attempt to dissuade you from it.
>
> I will admit that I was at first surprised and concerned from the sheer business end of it. After all, for nine and one-half years I have taken the major responsibility of the production end of our business. It has shown constantly increasing revenue from that end, and I believe it can safely be said that the gross percentage of Loew's, Inc., theater profits can be traced directly to M-G-M pictures; whereas, previous to the formation of M-G-M pictures that was not the case, as between Metro and Loew's. There has been assembled a vast array of talent, mostly of people who have never before been a success in pictures, or of people who had failed with other companies and under other policies. The supervisors are men, with the exception of one [Harry Rapf], who had not been successful prior to their coming with us, or had been given their first opportunity by me.

Thalberg's letter was not only a justification of his system but also a rebuttal to charges made by Schenck and others in New York. He reiterated his belief that the movie business was a business of stars, a business that he helped invent.

> Without stars a company is in the position of starting over each year. A star is not a matter of publicity. For example, Lilyan Tashman receives as much publicity as any of our stars. Nor is it a matter of playing in a great number of pictures; for she plays in from six to eight Warner Bros. or Paramount pictures

a year. Never have any of the pictures that she has been in been considered quite good or even had a fair box-office return. Yet she (along with the other girls like Lupe Velez and Lili Damita, who manage to keep in public print) draws quite well in personal appearances, but has no value as a star. Nor is it merely putting a star in good stories or fairly good stories. Otherwise how could we account for the drop in such splendid talking picture actors as Lew Ayres, Will Rogers, Janet Gaynor, Ruth Chatterton, William Powell, Richard Barthelmess, Chevalier, Colman, Jolson, and many others—some of whom were successful before a good picture and failures after.

The destruction of stars is a very subtle process. You scarcely notice that it is happening. . . . Sometimes what seems to be quite a good picture somehow tends to destroy the background of glamour and interest that has been built up in the star. Stars are not that much more beautiful or that much more talented than the ordinary player . . . as to account for the difference in box-office receipts. Certainly there is not that much difference between Joan Crawford and Claudette Colbert as to account for the difference in their actual value— or between Jean Harlow and Miriam Hopkins. Instead of capitalizing on the value in Hopkins created by "Dr. Jekyll and Mr. Hyde," [Jesse Lasky and Ben Schulberg of Paramount] put her in three or four ordinary pictures, which helped neither the pictures nor her.

Can it honestly be said that they were saving money by using Hopkins? In my opinion, they cost themselves a great deal more. Had they been able by real effort to . . . make an intensely interesting Hopkins story, they might have had a real asset instead of just an expensive leading woman. . . . I could cite many instances of similar "savings" made on the Famous Players [Paramount] lot which resulted in the complete annihilation of values accidentally or intention-ally created. They have never had any idealism in their organization. It has been a plant run for the purpose of making money, one year making expensive pictures and the next year making cheaper pictures. . . . I am personally and irrevocably opposed to any policy that may make a little money at the present time but which tends to destroy the industry and will leave us weakened when the destruction is complete.

Thalberg was especially irked by Schenck's contention that Warner Bros., with its assembly-line schedule, was an admirable business model. Unfortunately, Thalberg was unaware of and therefore could not cite Warners' huge deficit.

[Warners] have, since their gangster pictures, had only one picture, "I Am a Fugitive," in the big money class. Many of their pictures have been distasteful,

crude, a type of thing that only appeals in centers of large population, pos-
sesses very little entertainment value, and is very often in bad taste. Let every
company make this same kind of product and soon there will be no picture
business for the mass public. The picture business can only exist on the basis
of real entertainment, glamour, good taste, and stars. Without these it will
go the way of legitimate theater and vaudeville. The difference in receipts
between one picture and another shows why we must make great, not indifferent pictures. Indifferent pictures with a cheap sort of entertainment value
can draw audiences; but not fifty-cent audiences, nor forty-cent audiences, but
ten-cent audiences, and this type of product cannot be made for two hundred
fifty thousand as you intend, but for seventy-five thousand.

He then explained why the idea of squeezing more films out of the studio was
unrealistic. "We are geared to make a certain type of picture." M-G-M was known
for expensively mounted star vehicles. It might be possible to put a high-priced
star into an extra film per year if a cheap script and standing sets were available.
"However, this really only applies to Joan Crawford, as Beery and Dressler must
be handled with supreme care or there will be very little left to their value as stars.
As for Montgomery or Gable, they make an average of eight or nine pictures a
year, and I don't think even Columbia can do better than that. I think right now
that if we had kept Gable back and given him the right treatment, he would have
been another Valentino." Thalberg continued to chip away at Schenck's assertion
that M-G-M needed to make more films.

For fifteen years I have read bad scripts with good ideas that I have then
inspired the boys into making into good scripts with better ideas. I do not
believe that the boys could work any harder than they have been. No man
can conscientiously work until one and two in the morning (which is the kind
of concentration required on stories) and be expected to punch a time clock a
few hours later. What they require is not more scolding, but more inspiration,
more ideas, and more ideals. . . . I cannot concur with your theory that you are
going to get more pictures out of them. Each man you have is capable of only a
certain amount of worthwhile effort.

Thalberg's greatest objection was to Schenck's dual goals of more production
and less supervision. "The very fact that so frequently did one or the other [film]
need reconstructive work to change what might have been bad to good illustrates
the extreme need for this sort of supervision," wrote Thalberg. "Someone must

do it and do it well. Someone must do the job I have done in the past. . . . It has been proven that the successful lots are those dominated by a single idea." He predicted that decentralizing control—at least his control—during an economic depression would prove disastrous. "I would be derelict in my duty as a partner in this enterprise and as an official of this company if I did not point out to you in no uncertain terms the dangers that I see. I believe that the plan you have in contemplation will—in six months or a year and a half—result in the annihilation of our players, our prestige, and our profits."

Oddly, Thalberg felt it necessary to defend his record repeatedly during the letter. "I understand that it is your contention that we have slipped in the last nine months, or, rather that I have. I cite the following. Out of the entire industry we were considered by the critics to have made five of the ten best pictures of 1932. I defy anyone to show that the entire balance of the industry combined has released as many hits. Take any theater circuit, investigate its books, and then see whose product has grossed the most." That Hollywood's most gifted executive should have to defend himself after a banner year did not speak well for his partners; but neither did the surreptitious recruitment of Selznick.

> I do not wish to discuss in this letter the humiliation which I feel as a result of certain provisions in [David's] contract. I have the highest regard for Dave and am happy to have him associated with us, but I think the conditions of his employment are such that if they become known on the lot, a state of intrigue, politics, and hypocrisy will develop on the part of subordinates who will be anxious to ingratiate themselves either with Dave or myself, and that will spell disaster for the organization.

Thalberg's three drafts were for nothing. Mayer and Schenck had already made their decision. It was not only because Thalberg's contribution to each product could not be measured in concrete terms. It was also because his demands had begun to exceed the limits of what the film industry was able to understand. When an industry employee, no matter how valuable, became difficult, the standard practice was to throw money at him. That was thought to be the cure-all. The one who threw the money had control. The one who had complained and was accepting the money was being controlled. That was how it was supposed to work. Thalberg skewed the system by first having control and then wanting money, too. He did not fit the scheme. He was out of control. He had to be eliminated.

The tension eased slightly when Thalberg's doctor diagnosed tonsillitis and recommended a return visit to Dr. Franz Groedel in Bad Nauheim. Shearer assured Thalberg that his health was more important than her career, which she felt she owed him. She was willing to stay off the screen until he recovered. She agreed to a European vacation and then invited Helen Hayes and Charles MacArthur to accompany them. "My girlfriend is going along," Irving Jr. said upon hearing that the MacArthurs' young daughter, Mary, would be with them. The MacArthurs had become the Thalbergs' closest friends. "Irving fell for Charlie," wrote Hayes, "and Norma took to me. All four of us saw a lot of each other and spent weekends and holidays together." The MacArthurs planned the itinerary, only vaguely aware of the unrest in Germany since Adolf Hitler's January 30 inauguration as chancellor.

At M-G-M, meanwhile, Selznick moved into the bungalow recently vacated by John Gilbert, whose scandalous contract had come to a sad end with a mediocre film called *Fast Workers*. Gilbert was drinking even more heavily than before, so he had no offers from other studios. Selznick's first project would be an all-star production of the George S. Kaufman–Edna Ferber play *Dinner at Eight*, its casting of John Barrymore, Lionel Barrymore, and Wallace Beery an obvious bow to Thalberg's *Grand Hotel*, with Jean Harlow and Marie Dressler thrown in for good measure. Thalberg kept his distance from the studio. On February 23, he was surprised to receive a letter from Mayer.

> Dear Irving:
> I cannot permit you to go away to Europe without expressing to you my regret that our last conference had to end in a loss of temper, particularly on my part. It has always been my desire to make things as comfortable and pleasant for you as I knew how, and I stayed away from you while you were ill because I knew if I saw you it was inevitable that we would touch on business, and this I did not want to do until you were strong again. In fact I told Norma to discourage my coming to see you until you felt quite well.
>
> It is unfortunate that the so-called friends of yours and mine should be only too glad to create ill feeling, and attempt to disrupt a friendship and association that has existed for about ten years. Up to this time they have been unsuccessful, but they have always been envious of our close contact and regard for each other.
>
> If you will stop and think, you cannot mention a single motive or reason why I should cease to love you or entertain anything but a feeling of real sincerity and friendship for you. During your absence from the Studio, I was confronted with what seems to me to be a Herculean task, but the old

saying still goes—"The show must go on." Certainly we could not permit the Company to go out of existence just because the active head of production was taken ill and likely to be away from the business for a considerable length of time. I, being your partner, it fell to my lot, and I considered it my duty and legal obligation under our contract, to take up the burden anew where you left off, and to carry on to the best of my ability. . . .

I regret very much that when I last went to see you to talk things over I did not find you in a receptive mood to treat me as your loyal partner and friend. I felt an air of suspicion on your part towards me, and want you to know if I was correct in my interpretation of your feeling, that it was entirely undeserved. When I went to see you I was wearied down with the problems I have been carrying, which problems have been multiplied because of the fact that the partner who has borne the major portion of them on his shoulders, was not here. Instead of appreciating the fact that I have cheerfully taken on your work, as well as my own, and have carried on to the best of my ability, you chose to bitingly and sarcastically accuse me of many things, by innuendo, which I am supposed to have done to you and your friends. Being a man of temperament, I could not restrain myself any longer, and lost my temper. Even when I did so I regretted it, because I thought it might hurt you physically.

Regardless of how I felt, or what my nervous condition was, I am big enough to apologize to you, for you were ill and I should have controlled my feelings.

I am doing everything possible for the best interests of yourself, Bob, myself, and the Company, and I want you to know just how I feel towards you; and, if possible, I want you to divest yourself of all suspicion, and believe me to be your real friend, and to know that when I tell you I have the greatest possible affection and sincere friendship for you, I am telling the truth.

I hope this trip you are about to make will restore you to even greater vigor than you have ever before enjoyed, and will bring you back so that we may work together as we have done for the past ten years.

And now let me philosophize for a moment. Anyone who has said that I have a feeling of wrong towards you will eventually have cause to regret their treachery, because that is exactly what it would be, and what it would be on my part if I had any feeling other than what I have expressed in this letter towards you. I assure you I will go on loving you to the end.

I am going to take the liberty of quoting a bit of philosophy from Lincoln. This is a quotation I have on my desk, and one which I value highly:

"I do the very best I know how, and the very best I can, and I mean to keep doing so until the end. If the end brings me out right, what is said against me won't amount to anything. If the end brings me out wrong, ten angels swearing I was right, will make no difference."

I assure you, Irving, you will never have the opportunity of looking me in the eye and justly accusing me of disloyalty or of doing anything but what a good friend and an earnest associate would do for your interest, and for your comfort.

If this letter makes the impression on you that I hope it does, I should be awfully glad to see you before you go and to bid you Bon Voyage. If it does not, I shall be sorry, and will pray for your speedy recovery to strength and good health.

With love and regards, believe me,

Faithfully yours,

Louis

Two days later, Thalberg responded.

Dear Louis:

I was deeply and sincerely appreciative of the fact that you wrote me a letter, as I should have been very unhappy to have left the city without seeing you. I was indeed sorry that the words between us should have caused on your part a desire not to see me, as I assure you frankly and honestly they did not have that effect on me. We have debated and disagreed many times before, and I hope we shall many times again. For any words that I may have used that aroused bitterness in you, I am truly sorry and I apologize.

I'm very sorry that I have been unable to make clear that it has not been the actions or the words of any—as you so properly call them—so-called friends, whose libelous statements were bound to occur, that have in any way influenced me. If our friendship and association could be severed by so weak a force, I am sure it would long ago have been ruptured by that source. There are, however, loyalties that are greater than the loyalties of friendship. There are the loyalties to ideals, the loyalties to principles without which friendship loses character and real meaning, for a friend who deliberately permits the other to go wrong without sacrificing all—even friendship—has not reached the truest sense of that ideal. Furthermore, the ideals and principles were ones that we had all agreed upon again and again in our association, and every partner shared equally in the success that attended the carrying out of those principles.

I had hoped that the defense of those principles would be made by my three closest friends. I say this not in criticism, but in explanation of the depths of the emotions aroused in me, and in the hopes that you will understand.

I realize with deep appreciation the effort you have been making for the company and in my behalf, and no one more than myself understands the strain to which you are subjected.

Believe me, you have my sympathy, understanding and good wishes in the task you are undertaking; and no one more than myself would enjoy your success, for your own sake even more than for the sake of the company.

Please come to see me as soon as it is convenient for you to do so, as nothing would make me happier than to feel we had parted at least as good personal friends, if not better, than ever before.

Irving

Mayer came to say goodbye on the eve of Thalberg's departure but, conspicuously, did not allow Helen Hayes to leave the set of *The White Sister* early on her last day of shooting. She had to rush from the studio in a nun's habit and ride with a motorcycle escort to the dock at San Pedro in order to join the Thalbergs on the SS *California*. Three days later (on March 2), the ship docked in Panama. Thalberg was surprised that Hayes had brought $500 in cash. "It's not good form to be handing out currency all the time," he chided her. "You should pay with checks."

The roistering MacArthur wasted no time in finding out where the cash could be spent. "Someone told Charlie," wrote Hayes, "that some Panamanian prostitutes used the names of their favorite movie stars. The brothels displayed signs bearing these well-known names as a lure. Naturally, the men had to see that sight, and we ladies went along in a hired car through the heat and the dust to the red-light district. The driver knew where 'Norma Shearer' worked and took us to a ramshackle house. There, in bold letters, was Norma's name. We all thought it was very funny except Irving, who found it offensive. The madder he got, the more we laughed at him." Behind the laughter was the awareness that outside M-G-M, Thalberg was powerless.

One of Thalberg's best 1932 films, *Prosperity*, showed frightened depositors mobbing a neighborhood bank. As the Thalberg party made its way to New York, similar scenes were occurring all over America. A rash of bank failures had led to panic-stricken runs, and many banks were secretly exporting gold. In an effort to impose order, several states declared emergency bank holidays. Nevertheless, the banking system was on the verge of collapse.

The inauguration of Franklin D. Roosevelt on March 4, 1933, gave banks an excuse to shut their doors, if only for a day. Roosevelt took stock of the crisis and declared a three-day bank holiday effective Monday, March 6. While studio heads held an emergency meeting at the Hollywood Roosevelt, Thalberg was in Havana, unable to cash a traveler's check. "And how does my cash look to you now?" Hayes asked him. "You wouldn't be able to buy a postcard without it."

After two days of Hollywood meetings, a consensus was reached. On the morning of March 8, a select group of stars, producers, directors, writers, and department heads was summoned to an M-G-M screening room. Mayer shocked all present by appearing unshaven and red-eyed. "My friends," he began to speak, softly and hesitantly. Then he broke down. Apparently unable to speak, he extended his hands to his employees.

"We all know why we are here," drawled Lionel Barrymore. "Don't worry, L.B. We're with you." When Mayer announced that the industry needed to impose a 50 percent pay cut, there were groans of disbelief. A few sonorous words from Barrymore silenced them. A spiritless debate followed, and in a few minutes Mayer was able to dry his tears. The assembly voted to approve the salary cut. After the meeting, Sam Marx was walking behind Mayer on the way back to the executive building. He saw Mayer turn to talent scout Benjamin Thau. "How did I do?" asked Mayer.

He had done well enough with the employees who were told to support him, but the rest of the industry was not as compliant. Stagehands and other low-salaried staff went on strike. Meetings continued through the week. On Friday, March 10, at 5:55 P.M., nature provided a punctuation mark to Hollywood's tumult. "A strange rumbling sounded underneath the studio," recalled Marx. "Stages and offices began to shiver, arc lamps toppled off catwalks, and employees fled in panic." An earthquake of 6.4 magnitude, centered in Huntington Beach, was taking place. In Long Beach, terrified citizens dashed into the streets, only to be crushed by falling masonry. More than one hundred people were killed.

On Monday the 13th, strikes closed every studio in Hollywood. The deadlock ended when the Motion Picture Academy negotiated a sliding scale of cuts that would exempt employees making $50 or less per week. Thalberg arrived in New York the same day and wasted no time in calling Mayer to tell him what he thought of the salary cuts. He said that Mayer and Schenck were "destroying the loyalty and morale of my people" just to pacify stockholders. An argument ensued, and Thalberg left for Europe on bad terms with M-G-M, although he put on a brave front for the press. "Hollywood can never be doomed," he said at the dock on March 18, "except by producing bad pictures. These money troubles, I think, are only temporary. Art has never been fostered by finance."

The Thalbergs and MacArthurs arrived in Genoa on the SS *Conte di Savoia* a week later, then separated. The MacArthurs headed for the French Riviera, and the Thalbergs went to Germany. They found Bad Nauheim more tense than Hollywood had been. There were surprisingly few tourists at the resort, and Dr. Groedel's clinic had recently been smeared with anti-Semitic slogans. Hitler was blaming Jewish bankers for his country's problems and fomenting ill will against all Jews. Shop owners and pedestrians alike were fair game. On the evening of their arrival, the Thalbergs looked down from their hotel window and saw brown-shirted goons attack a Jewish couple in the street. When Thalberg tried to call the police, he was told to mind his own business. Dr. Groedel urged Thalberg to have his tonsillectomy performed elsewhere. "If anything happens to you while you are in my care," said Groedel, "I will be blamed. And my country. Everyone will say that a prominent American Jew has been murdered by Nazis." Thalberg would not be dissuaded, so Groedel performed the procedure. It was a success. After a short recuperation, Thalberg and Shearer joined the MacArthurs at the Hôtel du Cap, outside Antibes.

Paramount's soprano Jeanette MacDonald was also on the Riviera that April, relaxing after a Paris concert tour. When she lent her chauffeur-hairdresser to Shearer, the two stars became friendly. Shearer confided to MacDonald that although Thalberg was supposed to be relaxing, he was reviewing his Hollywood options. Among them was independent production. He was seriously thinking of leaving Metro to start the "I. G. Thalberg Corporation," a company similar to Goldwyn's. He would have stars under personal contract and would begin by remaking some of his silent hits. MacDonald would be perfect for *The Merry Widow*. MacDonald was accompanied by her manager (and boyfriend) Bob Ritchie, who liked the idea. MacDonald pressed Ritchie to make a formal proposal to Thalberg. Ritchie took the precaution of sending cables home. What he heard from some well-placed friends made him wait.

Schenck was in Culver City, calling "Irving's boys" into an office, one by one, to hear a carefully rehearsed speech. "We don't know when Irving is coming back—or even if he is," began the speech. "When he does come back, God will-ing, Louis and I want to conserve his health, to relieve him of the terrible burden of running all of the studio's production. So we are breaking the studio up into autonomous units, and we're asking you men to head the units. You will be full-fledged producers, and you will get screen credit for the films you produce. When Irving comes back, he will have his own unit, too."

Hyman, Rapf, Stromberg, Wanger, and Weingarten accepted Schenck's offer. Lewin declined. "I'm flattered, Nick," he answered, "but I can't make a decision without talking to Irving. Let me take a leave of absence. In fact, I'll do it without pay. I'll go to Europe, and when Irving and I both come back, I'll let you know." Schenck hired another producer, Lucien Hubbard, who had been in and out of M-G-M since the merger. With Mannix and Selznick, this made eight. Schenck and Mayer were ready to make their move.

Thalberg was still relaxing on the sunny terrace of the Hôtel du Cap, visiting with MacDonald, Ritchie, the MacArthurs, and the Basil Rathbones. He was excited about a new book, Stefan Zweig's *Marie Antoinette: The Portrait of an Average Woman*. He was not half as excited as Shearer was; she thought it could be the "part of a lifetime." Thalberg indulged her by cabling J. Robert Rubin to buy the book.

One quiet evening, the MacArthurs were alarmed to hear a frantic knocking at their hotel room. MacArthur opened the door to find Shearer standing there. "Charlie! Charlie!" she cried. "Come help! Irving's had another attack!"

"We all raced back to their room," recalled Hayes. Upon entering the room, they found Thalberg lying on his bed, holding a telegram in his hand. "There was that little, beautiful face," recalled Hayes, "ivory white, eyes closed." Thalberg handed MacArthur the telegram. It was from Mayer. Its terse message was that he and Schenck were reorganizing the studio and had eliminated the post of vice president in charge of production. Thalberg was hereby relieved of his duties. Mayer ended his missive with the phrase: "Am doing this for you." MacArthur handed the telegram to Hayes, who read it in disbelief. MacArthur moved closer to the bed. Thalberg reached for his hand and said weakly, "They knifed me, Charlie. They knifed me."

In Hollywood, meanwhile, the last of the films overseen by Thalberg in 1932 were ending their runs and the first of the new regime's films were beginning theirs. *The White Sister*, which Donald Ogden Stewart had adapted with Thalberg looking over his shoulder, was doing well. *Today We Live*, which had been tampered with during one of Thalberg's absences, was becoming Joan Crawford's second flop in a row. *Reunion in Vienna, The Prizefighter and the Lady*, and *When Ladies Meet*, all of which were planned as Shearer vehicles, were doing poorly, perhaps because of miscasting. It was too early to tell if David Selznick would justify Mayer's expecta-

Irving Thalberg and Carl Laemmle posed for this 1920 photograph at Universal City. Thalberg had recently been promoted to general manager.

In 1921 Louis B. Mayer used publicity photos like this to let the world know about his little studio at 3800 Mission Road; even a new generator was worthy of a press release. The photos did not show that the studio sat on the grounds of a zoo.

On April 26, 1924, Loew's, Inc., hosted a dedication ceremony on the lawn of the new Metro-Goldwyn studio. Pictured here are (right to left) Irving Thalberg, Louis B. Mayer, and Harry Rapf, a producer they brought from the Mission Road studio.

Irving Thalberg's office looked down from this façade, but he called it "that lousy little office on Washington Boulevard."

This production still from the 1926 production *La Bohème* shows (left to right) camera-man Hendrik Sartov, director King Vidor, Irving Thalberg, and Lillian Gish, who was the first established star signed to M-G-M by Mayer and Thalberg.

When Marcus Loew (center) visited M-G-M in December 1925, he was photographed with (left to right) Mike Gore, Boyle Workman (acting mayor of Los Angeles), Irving Thalberg, Frank Borzage, Erich von Stroheim, Victor Seastrom, Harry Rapf, Rupert Hughes, Robert Vignola, Marshall Neilan, Conrad Nagel, and King Vidor. Thalberg, only twenty-six, was recovering from a heart attack.

H. L. Mencken wrote: "No one in this world, so far as I know—and I have searched the records for years, and employed agents to help me—has ever lost money by underestimating the intelligence of the great masses of the plain people." As if to prove his point, he posed for a photo at M-G-M in 1927: (left to right) Paul Bern, Louis B. Mayer, Aileen Pringle, Mencken, Norma Shearer, Irving Thalberg, and Harry Rapf.

A 1925 group portrait shows most of the directors responsible for M-G-M's 1926 hits. From left: Victor Seastrom, Dmitri Buchowetski, Ernest Williamson, Monta Bell, Rupert Hughes (uncle of Howard Hughes), Josef von Sternberg, Erich von Stroheim (partially obscured), Jack Conway, Tod Browning, Hobart Henley, King Vidor, Fred Niblo, William Wellman, Reginald Barker, Marcel de Sano, Al Raboch, Christy Cabanne, and Benjamin Christensen.

A 1927 group shot at William Randolph Hearst's San Simeon castle shows (back row, left to right) King Vidor, Beatrice Lillie, Richard Barthelmess, Eleanor Boardman; (standing, middle row) Frank Orsatti, E. B. Harrick, Edmund Goulding, "Ma" Talmadge, Greta Garbo, Joseph Schenck, unidentified man, Harry Rapf, Aileen Pringle, J. Robert Rubin, Norma Shearer; (bottom row) Hal Roach, Natalie Talmadge, Eddie Mannix, Constance Talmadge, Buster Keaton, Paul Bern, Irving Thalberg; (lying down) John Gilbert.

Norma Shearer and Irving Thalberg were married by Rabbi Edgar F. Magnin on
September 29, 1927, in the garden of the Pauline Frederick mansion.

Thalberg posed with his parents, William and Henrietta Thalberg. Marriage did not materially affect their interdependence.

Thalberg and Shearer indulged in a showy kiss on their way to Europe in February 1928. Intimates maintained that the marriage was a happy one.

When Loew's president Nicholas Schenck visited Culver City in 1929, he posed for a photo with studio executives: (left to right) Buster Keaton, Harry Rapf, Thalberg, Schenck, Mrs. Schenck, L.B. Mayer, Eddie Mannix, and Hunt Stromberg.

The Thalbergs traveled to Europe again in 1931, meeting royalty and literati.

In June 1931 the Thalbergs moved into a home they had built at 707 Ocean Front in Santa Monica.

The Thalberg living room was a gathering place for the elite of Hollywood, but certain personalities were not welcome.

M-G-M's biggest hit of 1931 was a jungle epic called *Trader Horn*. Its success did little
for the career of Edwina Booth, shown here in the first polar bear portrait ever executed
by Hollywood portraitist George Hurrell.

M-G-M's biggest hit of 1932 was *Tarzan the Ape Man*. It almost didn't happen, thanks to a confused negotiation with author Edgar Rice Burroughs, shown here with director W. S. Van Dyke and Johnny Weissmuller.

The Wet Parade was one of numerous Thalberg films to deal with topical issues. In this production still are (left to right) director Victor Fleming; cameraman George Barnes; and novelist Upton Sinclair. Thalberg's dealings with Sinclair revealed an incipient conservatism.

Katharine Cornell, seen here with Norma Shearer, visited M-G-M, but declined Thalberg's invitations to join it.

In 1932 Thalberg's string of blockbuster films earned him the title of "Hit Maker," but he never entirely lost the tag of "Boy Wonder."

On Saturday, September 3, 1932, Jean Harlow and Clark Gable (center) posed on the Lot Three set of *Red Dust* with (left to right) Bolton Mallory, editor of the original *Life* magazine; Billy LaHiff, a New York restaurateur; and Sam Marx, M-G-M's story editor. Two days later, Marx would be called to Harlow's house to view her husband's corpse. Forty years later, Marx would write two books about the Thalberg era and an entire book about the tragic and unexplained events of that weekend.

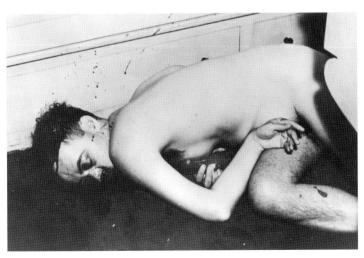

This is what Irving Thalberg saw when he went to the Bern house on Monday, September 5.

Thalberg endured the strain of the Bern inquest, but belated grief and a series of confrontations with his colleagues pushed his health to the breaking point. On December
28, 1932, he suffered a heart attack.

To restore his health, Thalberg traveled to Europe with Shearer in the midst of studio tumult, an economic crisis, and fascist uprisings.

The Thalbergs enjoyed visiting Santa Barbara, where they stayed at the Biltmore Hotel.

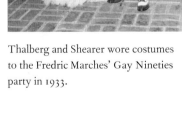

Thalberg and Shearer wore costumes to the Fredric Marches' Gay Nineties party in 1933.

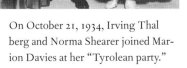

On October 21, 1934, Irving Thalberg and Norma Shearer joined Marion Davies at her "Tyrolean party."

Thalberg and his two-year-old son, Irving Jr., posed for George Hurrell in 1932. Thalberg's affection for his children is an overlooked facet of his legend. (Photo courtesy of Michael Hadley Epstein, HurrellPhotos.com)

The Thalbergs posed with Irving Jr. in front of Buckingham Palace in June 1933.

Photographer Tom Evans captured this image of Joan Crawford studying her lines for a day's work on *No More Ladies*, a 1935 film personally produced by Thalberg. After eighty years of reissues, television, video, cable, DVD, and Internet exposure, Crawford appears to be Thalberg's most enduring contribution to American culture.

Thalberg and Jean Harlow attended a banquet at Warner Bros. in January 1934. Harlow was not as well read as Thalberg, but her easy manner and intelligent conversation made her a frequent dinner guest. Harlow's popularity, like Crawford's, continues—a tribute to Thalberg's star-making system.

Negotiating with industry censor Joseph I. Breen was Thalberg's least favorite responsibility. His 1935 film *China Seas* was carefully monitored by the Production Code Administration, but, as this frame capture shows, not carefully enough. When pulling away from Wallace Beery, Jean Harlow felt her right breast suddenly exposed. In a few frames she corrected it. Surprisingly, no one in the PCA noticed.

Romeo and Juliet was Thalberg's last completed project. This production still shows some visitors to the filming of the fatal duel. Posed here (left to right) are John Masefield, England's then poet laureate; George Cukor (directing); Frances Marion, Hollywood's most respected screenwriter; Hugh Walpole, novelist and screenwriter; Lucy (Mrs. John) Masefield; Leslie Howard as Romeo; John Barrymore as Mercutio; Irving Thalberg; Constance (Mrs. James) Hilton; Basil Rathbone as Tybalt; James Hilton, novelist and screenwriter; and Reginald Denny as Benvolio.

Norma Shearer eschewed iambic pentameter but portrayed a believable Juliet in Thalberg's *Romeo and Juliet*.

The Thalbergs sat for a family portrait by D'Gaggeri in his Wilshire Boulevard studio in the spring of 1936. Irving Jr. was almost six; Katharine was a year old.

This pose of the Thalbergs by D'Gaggeri would be their last formal portrait.

Thalberg was visibly fatigued when he visited George Cukor on the set of *Camille* in late August of 1936.

A year after Thalberg's death, Norma Shearer had to exert her influence to ensure that *Marie Antoinette* would be made as he would have wanted it. She is seen here with producer Hunt Stromberg on the tense first day of shooting.

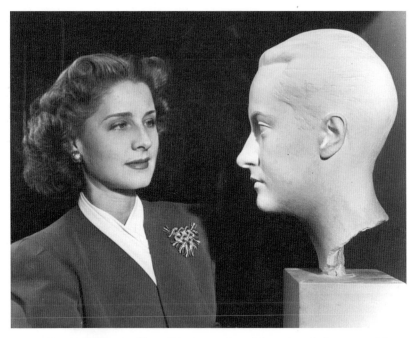

Norma Shearer also involved herself in the creation of the Irving Thalberg Award for
the Academy of Motion Picture Arts and Sciences. She disliked the first version of the
award, created in 1937 by Bernard Sopher. She commissioned Robert Ingersoll Aitken
to sculpt the second version, shown here. Shearer then paid for both the artist's work
and for statuettes to replace the first version. Darryl Zanuck and other previous award
recipients ended up with two Thalberg awards. In 1957 Shearer commissioned Gual-
berto Rocchi to sculpt a bust of Thalberg for the MGM building that bears his name.
Since 1966 this rendering has been used for the Thalberg Award. Shearer's devotion
to Thalberg's memory became the stuff of Hollywood legend.

tions, but he was getting preferential treatment. *Dinner at Eight* was given road show status, and Jean Harlow was being recalled for additional publicity photos. Selznick was already completing his second film, *Night Flight*, the drama of an air transport company. It starred John and Lionel Barrymore, Helen Hayes, Robert Montgomery, Clark Gable, and Myrna Loy. All this should have given Selznick satisfaction; it did not. Shamed by charges of nepotism ("The Son-in-Law Also Rises") and snubbed by Thalberg loyalists, he was morose and dispirited. "I feel like some sort of commercial pimp," he wrote Irene during the making of *Dinner at Eight*, "and my conviction that I'm about four times as valuable as most of the incompetents around here helps me only momentarily." He tried to find an escape in gambling, but he lost repeatedly to industry peers, which further depressed him.

"David told me he was 'wanting in moral courage,'" wrote Irene Selznick. "Late one morning I was heartsick to find him hunched in sobs on the daybed in his study, hat and briefcase by his side. 'I can't go on with it,' he told me. 'I can't face it. Not another day.'" Irene was able to rally her husband, but on June 14 he sent a letter to her father. "I am today regarded," wrote Selznick, "as the outstanding example of a nepotism that I must unfortunately agree is the curse of this business. . . . All past accomplishment is wiped out, because this is a business that forgets yesterday at dawn today; and any appreciation of future accomplishment is impossible because I am not an executive here, as I believe I am, by right of six or seven years of struggle, but by right of marriage." Selznick finished the letter by begging Mayer to release him from his contract. Mayer refused.

Darryl F. Zanuck, head of production at Warner Bros., was outraged when Jack Warner ignored his promise to restore salary cuts to employees. Zanuck wanted out, and Mayer knew it. "L.B. Mayer definitely wanted me to leave Warner Bros. and become an individual producer at M-G-M," Zanuck told Bob Thomas in 1968. "He made me many offers, as well as sending an elaborate piece of jewelry to Mrs. Zanuck." Seeing no point in competing with both Thalberg and Selznick, Zanuck declined Mayer's offer.

The Thalbergs spent June in Scotland and England, even photographing Irving Jr. with the Royal Guard at Buckingham Palace. Thalberg called MacDonald repeatedly at the Dorchester Hotel in London in hopes of securing a commitment. Ritchie told her not to answer; it would be impolitic not to give Mayer the right of first refusal. MacDonald complied, and then heard that the Thalbergs had sailed for New York on the White Star liner RMS *Majestic*. "That night I suffered my first asthma attack," recalled MacDonald. "The doctor called it psychosomatic. I called it hell."

Thalberg arrived in New York on July 15 and checked into the Waldorf Towers, where he received a call from Schenck inviting him to Long Island for a weekend visit. "The important thing is that Irving is in the best health he has ever enjoyed," Schenck told anyone who would listen. Thalberg brought his wife and son to Schenck's mansion, and while Shearer visited with Mrs. Schenck, the former vaudevillian Pansy Wilcox, Schenck brought Thalberg up to date.

According to Schenck, it was Mayer who had pressed for the reorganization, primarily out of fear that Thalberg might again fall ill and throw production into disarray. Thalberg allowed that this was not injudicious. It remained unspoken that Mayer's primary concern was neither production nor his partner's health; it was power. He felt that he was losing it to Thalberg. Mayer later said, "It got so bad that I couldn't hire an office boy without Irving's consent!" After suffering the indignities of the stock deal and the *Fortune* article, Mayer had used a health crisis to gain control of Thalberg's underlings. What Thalberg wanted to know was if Mayer would have control over *him*.

Schenck had read Thalberg's comments to the press about *Marie Antoinette* and felt that this was the type of film to which Thalberg should devote his energies. "As far as the company is concerned," said Schenck, "we will be better off, because we'll get more money out of that than we will if you spend your time on things on which you don't really have to." Apropos of that, Thalberg asked Schenck how he felt about his remaking *The Merry Widow* with the Paramount team of Maurice Chevalier, Jeanette MacDonald, and Ernst Lubitsch. Schenck said that he would see to it that Loew's approved both that and *Marie Antoinette*. "Isn't it better, Irving, that you make just the films you like to make?" asked Schenck. "You can do all of Norma's films, and five or six specials besides."

Thalberg knew what a prolonged absence from the screen could do to Shearer's career. It was up to him to keep her in the front ranks, if only for the sake of business. But he had a more heartfelt reason, and that was gratitude for the sacrifice she had made—and was making—on his behalf. "If it ever came to a choice between my career and Irving," Shearer had said, "I wouldn't hesitate for a moment. Not that work doesn't mean anything to me. But Irving means more."

It was Shearer's deportment that made Thalberg listen to Schenck. Four months had been sufficient time to weigh the options. Thalberg could not realistically consider going to work at another major studio, where he would be deprived of the stars he had cultivated—Harlow, Beery, Dressler, Gable, Crawford, Garbo. Nor did he believe that Sam Goldwyn would give him the power that Mayer had. Nor was there backing to start the I. G. Thalberg Corporation.

Thalberg looked Schenck in the eye and laid his cards on the table. He would return to M-G-M under the following conditions. His profit-sharing arrangement in the Mayer group would continue unchanged so that his value to the company would be acknowledged and his family would be provided for. He would make big-budget quality films. Most important, he would answer to Schenck, not to Mayer. Before the night was over, Schenck telephoned Mayer to say that there was good news. Thalberg was coming back, and on their terms.

Thalberg returned to the Culver City studio on August 19. A bungalow was being prepared for him alongside Selznick's, so he was temporarily installed in his old office. The anticipated parade of executives, stars, directors, and writers welcomed him back. Thalberg regaled them with European anecdotes, some more disturbing than charming. In Germany, he and Shearer had been awakened daily by the sound of Nazis marching under their hotel windows. At the mention of politics, the jovial mood dissipated. It disappeared completely when Thalberg voiced the opinion that fascism was better than communism. His former colleagues made a series of awkward exits, and Thalberg was left alone with Albert Lewin, the only "Thalberg man" who had chosen to wait for him. "Al, why didn't you accept Nick's offer?" Thalberg asked him.

"I didn't want to make a decision until I talked to you." said Lewin. "Either way it's all right with me—to have my own unit or to stay with you."

"Well," said Thalberg, "I think it would be better for you to have your own unit. But if you were to ask me what I'd prefer . . . I'd prefer that you remained."

"I was hoping you'd ask me," Lewin smiled modestly, and his modesty was genuine, as Thalberg discovered when he offered Lewin his first screen credit. "Thanks, anyway," responded Lewin, "but I couldn't take it. Everybody will know they're your pictures. I'd feel awfully foolish taking credit for them."

"Well, I'm not going to put my name on them," said Thalberg. "Suppose we call you an 'associate producer.' Would that be okay?"

Lewin agreed to that, and then began reviewing properties with Thalberg. Only later did it occur to him how odd it was to be working alone with Thalberg in the silence of a room that a year before had been buzzing with the voices of Paul Bern, Hunt Stromberg, and others. A few days later, Thalberg received a visit from David Selznick. "David was gratified to find that Thalberg, being intelligent and sensitive, bore him no ill will," recalled Irene. Thalberg even criticized the way his former disciples were slighting Selznick. Before long, Thalberg would learn how it felt.

In late 1932, Thalberg had been working with Columbia director Frank Capra on a story of the new Russia called *Soviet*. Beery was to have played a commissar, Crawford a worker, and Gable an American engineer, but Mayer had pulled the plug on it after Thalberg left for Europe. Thalberg could not revive the project; he was told that Crawford was tied up in films for Selznick and Hyman. When he asked for Beery, he was told that Beery had been loaned to Darryl F. Zanuck's new studio, Twentieth Century Pictures. "Not only must I contend with other producers here," Thalberg said angrily, "but now with Zanuck, too!" (Zanuck was not the issue; Thalberg knew that Mayer was helping Joseph Schenck finance Twentieth in order to make a place for his other son-in-law, William Goetz.) Gable was also unavailable; he was being loaned to Columbia for Capra's *Night Bus*.

Thalberg was scheduled to start producing in late October, so he needed writers. When he asked Donald Ogden Stewart to work on *Marie Antoinette*, Stewart turned him down, then showed up unexpectedly, and then left without a warning; the writer had become more interested in hosting drunken theme parties than in perfecting his craft. The same thing happened when Thalberg requested John Meehan for *The Green Hat*. Meehan said he was occupied with a play and would not be available for some time; then he showed up for a week, and then he called in sick. Thalberg suspected that his once-loyal writers were being manipulated by Mayer. Thalberg next hired the playwright Preston Sturges, whose screenplay for Fox Film's *The Power and the Glory* had been highly praised; after a month, Thalberg found Sturges intractable and fired him. The one project that had been steadily progressing, even in Thalberg's absence, was *Marie Antoinette*. Sidney Franklin had been preparing a treatment of the massive novel since June. By the time Thalberg settled into his new offices, he had junked the first draft and was overseeing a new continuity by Robert Sherwood.

Thalberg asked MacArthur to develop a story Edmund Goulding had thought up for Shearer, a trifle about an American girl who becomes a British noblewoman and then dallies with an American playboy. MacArthur tried his hand at it and then quit, warning Thalberg that depressed Americans would not care about the idle rich and that British audiences would find it insulting. "Fists across the seas," MacArthur called Goulding's story, which was then titled *Rip Tide*. Thalberg could not understand MacArthur's attitude. "Let's face it," Thalberg said privately to Lewin. "We win awards with crap like *The Sin of Madelon Claudet*."

The most ambitious of Thalberg's nine projects was *The Good Earth*. To film Pearl Buck's sprawling novel properly, he wanted Frances Marion and George Hill. They had divorced in 1931, but were willing to work together for Thalberg. In order to have first call on them, he needed new contracts drawn up. After waiting for an undue amount of time, Thalberg had to call the legal department, and then call again. When the contracts finally arrived, the availability clause was missing; other producers and studios—not Thalberg—would have first call on the artists. This also happened with contracts for actors Franchot Tone, Ian Wolfe, and Elissa Landi; denied access to Thalberg, Landi refused to sign with M-G-M.

After several incidents like this, Thalberg appealed to Schenck. "The utmost humiliation has attended the delay in the signing of the contracts with the few people that I have engaged," Thalberg wrote on October 13. "I regret this, as I believe Landi could have been developed into a real star." Thalberg did not come out and say it, but he knew he was being stonewalled by Mayer. "I made a request of Louis, inasmuch as Franchot Tone was dissatisfied with the treatment he had been receiving. . . . I believed I would be rendering the company a great service in taking over this man and making him into a star. Louis couldn't see it. Rather than press the matter further, I dropped it completely."

Thalberg had seen the films recently released by the studio—*Midnight Mary*, *Dinner at Eight*, *Penthouse*, *Beauty for Sale*, *Solitaire Man*, *Night Flight*, and *Bombshell*. With the exception of the two Selznick films and *Bombshell*, he thought them "juvenile, immature, uninspired, and lacking that finish that characterized our product for so many years." He felt that standards had slipped due to a lack of leadership. "I have never found the men in this institution so completely demoralized and uninspired." At a preview, one of Mayer's new producers was boasting how he had gotten his risqué film past the weak new administration at the SRC. "It's a smash!" he laughed.

"Yes," said Thalberg coolly. "A few more like it and we'll smash the company." For the most part, though, Thalberg kept quiet and stayed in his office. "I have expressed my opinions to no one," he told Schenck, "so as not to add to the discouragement that I see so much of. . . . I have, however, repeatedly assured Louis and Eddie [Mannix] and Dave that I am here to be of service, and the few times I have been called upon, I believe I have been helpful and constructive."

On November 9, Thalberg moved to his new office, the remodeled former bungalow of Cecil B. DeMille. Cedric Gibbons and his staff had converted the Spanish Revival interior into something resembling a gentlemen's club, complete with beamed ceilings, oak paneling, a large fireplace, red-leather armchairs, and an imposing glass-topped desk. "Thalberg's office was a long, wood-paneled room with a huge desk near the windows," recalled Salka Viertel. His office ran the entire length of the building, which was roughly forty feet. "Along the walls stood comfortable chairs and couches. One had to walk the full length of the room in order to reach the frail, small figure behind the desk, who was usually holding the telephone receiver in one hand and jingling coins in the other. After his long vacation trip to Europe, Thalberg had gained weight, looked healthier, and was in a much better mood than I had ever seen." Thalberg appeared to be pleased with the office, but Al Lewin sensed something. "Irving, you haven't deceived me," said Lewin one day. "You don't like this."

"To tell you the truth, Al, I'm superstitious," said Thalberg. "Every time you put on the dog, it's the beginning of the end. We had a lot of success in that lousy little office over there on Washington Boulevard."

Thalberg spent a great deal of time alone, ignored by the studio he had cofounded, but on November 14, he reminded Hollywood that he was back. *The Saturday Evening Post* of that week contained an article signed by Thalberg (and Hugh Weir, who had polished his prose). "Why Motion Pictures Cost So Much" was a critique of the industry that was treating him so indifferently. The article was not hostile, but it pulled no punches. Thalberg held that the studios were manufacturing more product than the distribution system could reasonably handle, and that much of that product was negligible. "Hollywood is extravagant," wrote Thalberg, "whether it spends $100,000 or only 100 cents, whenever it makes, in an effort to keep up with release demands, an ill-conceived, silly, inconsequential picture, for that picture will cost the exhibitors millions of dollars in losses . . . and the drain on creative talent attempting to make this vast supply of 500 or 700 pictures a year is dissipating the efforts of those capable of turning out a good product." Thalberg was not afraid to point the finger at the New York bosses of all the studios.

"The curse of this business is the mad effort to force more and more product on the public so as to hide the extravagant cost of the huge distribution machine and to avoid breaking up huge, unwieldy theater chains." This was a bold statement, considering the ongoing efforts of some politicians to institute antitrust suits against the film industry's monopolies, to break up its block-booking practices, and to subject it to federal censorship. Thalberg was apparently willing to risk these possibilities if he could make better films. "Nobody has ever been able to say definitely whether picture making is really a business or an art. Personally, I think it is both. It is a business in the sense that it must bring in money at the box office, but it is an art in that it involves, from its devotees, the inexorable demands of creative expression. In short, it is a creative business, dependent, as almost no other business is, on the emotional reaction of its customers." Significantly, for someone who spent so much time in darkened projection rooms and who had recently been anesthetized, Thalberg invoked the idea of a dreamlike state that films and film players should properly induce. "In pictures, the actor, even more than the play, is the thing," declared Thalberg. "He, more than the author, even more than the director, must hold the mirror up to life. By his ability to convey the author's and the director's ideas to the screen and to the people out front, he must transport his audience into a dream world."

In harsh contrast to this ideal of screen art, Thalberg described the conditions endured by many film artists:

> They cannot be forced to make hundreds of pictures rushed through on schedules—not because they are not trying to meet even that requirement, but because the human mind is incapable of doing creative work regularly under conditions that call for a time-table delivery of creative efforts.

> To continue the present destructive policy of rushing out pictures poorly made, of destroying stars by robbing them of their glamour and their ability to give distinguished performances, of bewildering the best creative efforts of the best writers through forcing them to work on silly material and rushing them on good material, of loading down good pictures with the production costs and selling expenses of pictures which nobody wants to see—to continue any such suicidal policy is to continue giving the one inescapable answer to the question of why pictures cost so much, and to invite a condition of public apathy in which there won't be any pictures at all.

Perhaps as a result of his article, Thalberg found M-G-M's resources even harder to tap in December. "The difficulties I encounter," he wrote Schenck, "are an inability to acquire talent and an inability to make that talent give its best efforts. The first is due to the fact that unless I wish to exercise the rights under my contract, I cannot get a first-class person who is employed on this lot." Thalberg explained that he had to address his grievances in writing because phone calls to Schenck usually resulted in antagonism due to Schenck's defensiveness. Thalberg's projects were coming along, but slowly; the only writers he could get were the "continuously-availables and the out-of-works." To calm him, Schenck called Mayer, and got an earful. "Thalberg wants first call on every artist on the lot!" cried Mayer. "I told him: 'Irving, I will have to throw up my hands! You ought to be fair! You are going to place me in a position where I will flop! You know that I will try to give you every darned thing that you want, as if you were my own son. But I have *got* to run this plant successfully!'"

Thalberg was not interested in being Mayer's son, any more than Mayer was interested in having Thalberg be the creative head that he used to be. Therein lay the problem. Mayer wanted deference. Thalberg wanted sovereignty. Neither man would acknowledge the other's needs, and the gulf between them was widening. In spite of that, and in spite of Thalberg's limited contribution to the 1933 release schedule, M-G-M posted year-end profits of $4 million. Stock dividends were paid. Salaries were restored to earlier levels, but no employee who took a salary cut was reimbursed. The Mayer group, however, did make up its losses. Even Thalberg banked profits, although he was not inclined to share them with underlings. In any event, both he and the studio had weathered the worst year of the Great Depression.

As his first film, now titled *Lady Mary's Lover*, neared its start date, the film community made bets on it. Thalberg described the film as "a story of the 'Divorcee,' 'Strangers May Kiss,' 'Free Soul' formula—gay, but with a strong dramatic undercurrent." Lilyan Tashman was playing Shearer's sister in *Lady Mary's Lover*, so the Thalbergs attended a New Year's Eve party at the Malibu home she shared with her husband, Edmund Lowe. Rather than dwell on the eventful year that was ending, Thalberg tried to think what kind of film Shearer could do next. She needed to recapture her earlier momentum. Howard Strickling was sure that *Lady Mary's Lover* would do well. "The money it makes won't help Norma's career," replied Thalberg. Sam Marx assured him that he could find a property for Shearer. "There's no shortage of stories," said Thalberg. "Just a shortage of people who can recognize them."

In early 1934 most Hollywood films had the logo of the National Recovery Administration superimposed over their credits. This was more than a nod to Franklin Roosevelt's New Deal; it was an affirmation of his success. In less than a year, the New Deal had slowed deflation and made it possible for almost every studio to stanch the flow of red ink. Film industry losses had totaled $55.7 million in 1932. In 1933—even with the severe March slump—losses were held at $4.9 million. The depression was not over, but fear was dissipating. At M-G-M, new policies were in force. Some, like B-picture units, were a response to economic concerns. Others were reactions to a shift in power. "Every son of a bitch in Hollywood is waiting for me to fall on my ass now that Irving has gone," Louis B. Mayer told Walter Wanger in mid-1933. "Well, I'm going to fool them. I'm going to build up the biggest collection of talent that Hollywood has ever seen. Then this studio can't fail." If at times it appeared that Mayer was building up the studio at Irving Thalberg's expense, that was something that Thalberg had to tolerate. Plenty of onlookers were waiting for him to fall, too. With his career on the line, he strode boldly into 1934.

Mayer's quest for talent netted a few fish: a gangly young man whose name was changed from Spangler Arlington Brugh to Robert Taylor; a blond baritone named Nelson Eddy, whom Ida Koverman had recommended after seeing his Shrine Auditorium concert; Maurice Chevalier, the charming refugee from Paramount; and the other half of his team, Jeanette MacDonald. Thalberg was also recruiting.

His complaints to Schenck had resulted in a sensational concession. Thalberg had permission from Loew's to sign talent exclusively to his production unit. He was the only M-G-M producer given the privilege of personal contracts. He began to exercise it. "The public is tired of ingénues," he declared, signing mature stage performers Mady Christians, Gladys George, and Lucile Watson. He then telephoned Gloria Swanson. The thirty-six-year-old superstar was momentarily without a studio, having burned bridges to Jesse Lasky, Joseph Kennedy, and Joseph Schenck. "I almost died of gratitude when Thalberg called," said Swanson. In February 1934 Thalberg signed her to a personal contract that called for three films a year and then assigned Frances Marion to adapt Elinor Glyn's *Three Weeks* for her. His plans were derailed by a tragedy.

Thalberg had contracted Marion and George Hill to prepare *The Good Earth*. Hill traveled to China to shoot background footage, but was unable to overcome the interference of the Chiang Kai-shek regime. Except for screen tests of Chinese actors and a boatload of props, the trip was a waste. When Hill came back, he learned that Thalberg had decided to make the film in California with Caucasian actors playing Chinese characters. Hill was at first dismayed, then depressed. On August 9, 1934, Thalberg held a *Good Earth* story conference. Marion hid her nervousness when Hill failed to show. Half an hour into the conference, Hill appeared, but barely. He was standing in the doorway of the conference room, almost too drunk to walk, but not too drunk to stare down Thalberg. After a few tense moments, Hill announced his resignation and staggered down the hallway.

The next morning, Thalberg was preparing to celebrate Norma Shearer's thirty-second birthday when he was notified that Hill had been found dead in his Venice home. He had apparently put a .45-caliber service revolver into his mouth and fired. The grim echo of Paul Bern's death cast a pall over the studio. Frances Marion was unable to work for a year, not only because of shock and grief but also because of a near-fatal automobile accident. Without Marion's skill and intuition, Thalberg failed to find a story for Swanson; she left M-G-M without making a film.

Another idol signed by Thalberg was Mrs. Patrick Campbell, the sleepy-eyed British star who had inspired G. B. Shaw to write *Pygmalion* twenty years earlier. At sixty-nine, the once-glamorous "hellcat" no longer evoked Eliza Doolittle, but Thalberg was so pleased to secure her services that he gave her Pekingese, "Moonbeam," a role in *Lady Mary's Lover*. The Thalbergs welcomed Campbell with a party and a screening of *Smilin' Through* at their home. After the lights came up, Thalberg asked Campbell what she thought of Shearer's performance. "Your wife is charming," replied Campbell. "Such a dainty little creature she is. Such a tiny waist, such tiny hands, and such tiny, tiny eyes."

Shearer started *Lady Mary's Lover* with some apprehension. She had not been on a soundstage for eighteen months. "I always dreaded the thought of having to start a new picture," wrote Shearer. "I guess it was a matter of not wanting to face up to the hazards. You have to be there day after day, delivering something very special. Each day is a new challenge. And after you've been away from it, even for a few months, you wonder if you've lost the touch—or if you ever had it." When Shearer sailed onto the soundstage in a new Adrian gown, she sensed something was wrong. The camera crew looked unfamiliar. These were not the men Lee Garmes used. Where was he? Assistant Director Joseph Newman informed Shearer that Garmes was unavailable and that Ray June had been hired in his place. Shearer did not wait to hear how qualified June was. She turned around and walked to her dressing room, whence a phone call soon emanated. "Norma was very unhappy that I wasn't there," recalled Garmes, who was finishing retakes on *George White's Scandals* at Fox Film before leaving for New York to shoot *Crime without Passion,* the first film both cowritten and codirected by Ben Hecht and Charles MacArthur. There was no way that Shearer could have Garmes for her film. It took the combined persuasiveness of Thalberg and Edmund Goulding to sell her the new cameraman.

In addition to Shearer's jitters and Thalberg's hopes for his first film as a unit producer, Goulding had problems. "We started without a finished script," recalled Newman in 1995. "Goulding was writing it every night, and in the morning he would give me the pages, and we'd have them copied and send them to the actors." Mrs. Pat was nervous, too, and Goulding tried to calm her. "I honestly urge you to dismiss from your mind the possibility of your name and appearance being ineffective photographically," Goulding wrote. "You are Mrs. Patrick Campbell. You are being put on the screen with all the charm and technique that made you that lady. Relax, trust, don't worry, sleep well, feel well, and give me your confidence." The veteran stage star became so relaxed that she forgot the basic rule of screen acting and looked directly into the camera lens during her first scene with Shearer. Moonbeam was equally troublesome; she barked during takes and had to be barred from the set. Mrs. Pat got even for this by badmouthing Shearer's requirement of a key light that was brighter than anyone else's. When asked what character she was playing in the film, Mrs. Pat replied, "I'm one of Norma Shearer's Nubian slaves."

Supporting Shearer, but not in the darkness Mrs. Pat described, were Herbert

Marshall and Robert Montgomery. Both of them had one-year-old children, so Shearer brought Irving Jr. to the set. One day he talked into the microphone after Goulding called "cut." Thalberg was so amused by the unexpected voice on the sound track that he began recording his son on a regular basis.

Thalberg knew that Marshall was carrying on an affair with Gloria Swanson in full view of the Hollywood press, but he did not censure him; Marshall had suffered the amputation of his left leg in the Great War and was stoically enduring phantom pain. Late in the filming, Goulding's wife, the dancer Marjorie Moss, fell ill with tuberculosis. Goulding absented himself from the film to place her in a sanatorium, and Robert Z. Leonard took over. By the time Goulding returned, Leonard had completed the film, which was now called *Riptide*. The first preview failed to engage the working-class audience in Huntington Park; the film was too "hoity-toity." Goulding responded by shooting retakes in which Shearer did one of her famous cartwheels, this time into a swimming pool.

Riptide was released in late March. Thalberg did not put his name in the credits, but he did allow it in full-page magazine ads: "An Irving Thalberg Production." Lured by this elegant ballyhoo, Shearer's fans gave *Riptide* a respectable profit of $333,000. Thalberg was disappointed, though. For all of Goulding's ingenuity, the film was little more than a "well-made play." *Time* magazine called it "an anecdote with elephantiasis, glossy but erroneous." The film had two basic problems: its early scenes did not establish the bond between the wife (Shearer) and the husband (Marshall); and the film lacked Thalberg's requisite "great scene." Shearer's acting had a newfound assurance, noticeably free of giggles and mannerisms, but it was wasted on scenes (and a story) that did not build to a climax. Most reviews praised her; all of them commented on the film's adult theme.

Thalberg had likened *Riptide* to Shearer's "daring" films of previous years, but there was a difference. In *Riptide*, she was far removed from the skittish Amanda of *Private Lives* and the neurotic Nina of *Strange Interlude;* she was playing a wife and mother, a character much like herself. Watching the sensible and dignified Lady Mary go astray was distasteful to many audience members. "It's a shame to ruin Shearer in this kind of story, regardless of how elaborate they produce it," wrote a Smithville, Texas, exhibitor. "It will draw plenty criticism from the church people."

Unlike *A Free Soul*, *Riptide* had no sensual episodes. Its adult content was woven into its fabric and could not be removed by cutting one sequence. In this regard *Riptide* was like many films released in early 1934; it violated the spirit of the law as much as the letter. *Men in White, The Affairs of Cellini, Search for Beauty,* and *Of Human Bondage* suffered cuts from censor boards, but their intrinsically adult content survived. "Filthy pictures are doing us a tremendous damage with the public," said Ed Kuykendall, president of the Motion-Picture Theater Owners, addressing a convention at the Ambassador Hotel on April 11. "It is not the function of the screen to moralize, but we must adhere to the fundamentals of common decency." Kuykendall reminded his audience that the Catholic Church had already launched a campaign against this type of film. An exhibitor who presented *Riptide* in Conway, New Hampshire, acknowledged this. "We hope that the churches," he wrote, "will make Hollywood producers understand that theaters want good clean pictures to show on our screens."

Two weeks later, on the eve of Metro-Goldwyn-Mayer's tenth anniversary, Thalberg spoke to the six hundred people who were gathered in the Biltmore ballroom to kick off the Chamber of Commerce's program, "Southern California Straight Ahead!" There was good reason for the optimistic tone of Thalberg's address. Weekly movie attendance had rebounded to almost 70 million. He reminded his listeners of the movies' curative power. "In these last four years," said Thalberg, "films have been one of the greatest elements in keeping peace and contentment in the American home. The quality and character of better screenplays have brought a message of hope into the lives of thousands. Persons who work in monotonous professions demand entertainment, and they will seek it, if not in the wholesome atmosphere of the theater, then in pool rooms and similar places." Thalberg criticized what he called "political censorship," claiming that out of 170 films submitted to unnamed censors, only seven "occasioned debate." What he failed to mention was that censors made no cuts in films like *Riptide* because the entire film was about adultery.

In the four years since Thalberg had coauthored the Production Code with Father Daniel Lord and Martin Quigley, the SRC had lost so many battles that the Code was more an annoyance than a policy. In late 1933, Will Hays removed the SRC's ineffectual director, James Wingate, and installed the militantly devout Catholic Joseph I. Breen, who promptly lost a dispute over a bedroom scene in *Queen Christina*. By the spring, however, Breen was a man on a mission, talking to producers in their own profane language, fighting over cuts, and winning small victories. In early April he forced M-G-M to withdraw *Tarzan and His Mate* and cut a nude swimming sequence from the camera negative, which was a major victory (even though a "protection fine grain positive" was first copied from the uncensored negative).

While Breen was becoming known as the first SRC boss who would not back down, he was secretly working with Quigley and a group of Catholic bishops called the Episcopal Committee. Their goal was to reconstitute the Code. Breen suggested that the committee take advantage of anti-Hollywood sentiment intensifying in the Midwest. There was already a grassroots movement against "sinful motion pictures." What the bishops needed was an organization that could mobilize Catholics against Hollywood. They found it on April 11, when the Catholic Legion of Decency was incorporated. The Legion was an organization whose members took a pledge to avoid any film on the Legion's "Condemned" list. America's Catholic population of 20 million was concentrated in the same cities as the industry's most profitable picture palaces. By late May the Legion of Decency had signed 300,000 members in Brooklyn, Los Angeles, and Philadelphia, 900,000 in Chicago, and 1 million in Boston. A crisis was brewing. The Legion's first Condemned list appeared in May. Among the films designated were *Queen Christina*, *Men in White*, and *Riptide*.

Writing in *The Queen's Work*, Father Lord took aim at Thalberg. "It seems typical of Hollywood morality that a husband as production manager should constantly cast his wife in the role of a loose and immoral woman," wrote Lord. "That the picture is beautifully mounted and the heroine elaborately gowned makes the plot that much more insidious. We advise strong guard over all pictures which feature Norma Shearer. They are doing more than almost any other type of picture to undermine the moral code and the Producers' Code." Thalberg complained angrily to Bishop Joseph Cantwell of Los Angeles, and Lord was reprimanded, but the damage was done. Thalberg's debut as a unit producer was only a qualified success.

Neither Greta Garbo nor Jean Harlow was available to him, so Thalberg's second independent project would also have to be a Shearer film. Before he could begin it, he almost lost it—twice. Rudolph Besier's play *The Barretts of Wimpole Street* had been a triumph for Katharine Cornell in 1931. Thalberg thought that the love story of poets Elizabeth Barrett and Robert Browning would be a natural for Shearer, but she could not see herself as a sickly Victorian. Her hesitation gave Joseph Schenck the opportunity to buy the play for Art Cinema Corporation, his subsidiary of United Artists. Over a card game, Thalberg learned that Schenck had paid $40,000 for it, but was contractually bound to both Besier and Cornell. When Thalberg offered Schenck $80,000, he signed full control of the play over to Thalberg, who was disappointed that Cornell was not included but pleased to have a Shearer vehicle.

Two years later, just as Shearer changed her mind about playing Elizabeth

Barrett, William Randolph Hearst decided that the "poetess" should be played by Marion Davies. "They'll laugh her off the screen," Thalberg told Sam Marx. In Thalberg's opinion, the only reason Hearst wanted Davies to play Barrett was because of the scene in which Browning rescues Barrett from her home; in order to steal through the night, she dresses in men's pants. Marx did not understand. Thalberg explained that Hearst required every Davies film to have a scene in which she wore pants. "It's a sexual thing, a fixation," said Thalberg.

A screen test was made in full costume, with Davies wearing a black Victorian wig that, according to Shearer, "hung shroudlike around her gamin face." Shearer saw Mayer wince at the test, and she urged Thalberg to get her the part. "Marion's a comedienne," Thalberg told Mayer. "She'll get laughs if she plays that part."

"Irving, it doesn't matter what you think of her," said Mayer. "Mr. Hearst believes she can do anything Norma can do."

"He's always been jealous of Norma's success," Thalberg added.

"Look, Irving, if you make a wrong move or say the wrong thing," continued Mayer, "he'll be insulted, and you'll never get it."

Thalberg had an idea. The studio owned a novel by Robert W. Chambers titled *Secret Service Operator 13*, a Civil War spy story in which the heroine disguises herself first as a slave and then as a soldier. Perhaps Hearst would lose interest in the play if baited with the novel. Thalberg assigned Marx to meet with the publisher, which meant traveling to Hearst's palatial headquarters in San Simeon, California. "Don't mention Norma," Thalberg told Marx. "Just point out that *Operator 13* will appeal to Marion's fans more than a starchy character like Elizabeth Browning. Be discreet, but see what you can do, and, of course, drop the fact that she'll be masquerading in a man's uniform."

Marx and his wife were thrilled to be visiting Hearst's famous "ranch," even if it was on business. Hearst had been entertaining Hollywood society at La Cuesta Encantada (The Enchanted Hill) since 1925. Film folk returned with breathless descriptions of the 40,000-acre estate, its private zoo, the lavishly furnished guesthouses, and the 115-room main house, La Casa Grande (The Great Home). "It was right out of a fairy story," wrote Cecil Beaton, "a vast, sparkling white castle in Spain." Frances Marion, who visited the estate numerous times, called it "a feudal castle right out of the Arabian nights." Even Davies, for whom Hearst had envisioned the unique setting, retained her initial thrill. "It was an awesome thing," she said in 1952. "I'd seen Versailles and palaces in Europe, but nothing could compare with this." Marx tried not to be overawed by the grand backdrop when he met with Hearst. The publisher recognized *Operator 13* from a preview chapter, "Blonde and Black," that had run in his *Cosmopolitan* magazine, but he took the bait. "Anyway," recalled Davies, "I didn't want a part where I was just going to sit on my tail and recite poetry." Thalberg pulled Sidney Franklin off the *Marie Antoinette* script and put him on *The Barretts of Wimpole Street*, where he quickly assembled a crack team.

"Irving was in need of an immediate script for *The Barretts*," wrote Donald Ogden Stewart. "Sidney's favorite writer was an extremely intelligent English woman named Claudine West, and, as it was a hurry-up job, a third writer was called in, the Hungarian playwright Ernst Vajda. We happened to hit it off very well and managed to get Irving's approval in almost record time." Thalberg's haste was due in part to the charged atmosphere at the SRC; Breen was often out of the office (conspiring with a group of militant clergy known as the Midwest Catholics), and Thalberg wanted to slip the film through without opposition. The unlikely love affair between the bedridden Barrett and the extroverted Browning offered no censorship problems, but the suffocating love of Barrett's father did. Besier's play had been a hit partly because its climax revealed that Edward Moulton-Barrett harbored incestuous desires for his daughter. Such a plot element was shocking on Broadway; it was impossible in Hollywood. Yet Thalberg was determined to make the film.

He signed the British actor Charles Laughton to a personal contract in the belief that Laughton could convey Papa Barrett's perversion without alarming censors or offending audiences. "They can't censor the gleam in my eye," Laughton assured Thalberg, but he was more discreet when interviewed by the *Los Angeles Times*. "Mr. Laughton was wearing the sideburns of Edward Moulton-Barrett when I talked with him," wrote Philip K. Scheuer, "Barrett being the unnatural parent of Elizabeth. The relationship, with its outré suggestion of irregularity . . . was largely discounted by Laughton. He described it as an affectionate bond often existing between father and child." Taking a cue from Breen's predecessor Jason Joy, Thalberg had Franklin shoot the key scene in an ambiguous fashion; the unknowing would see a domineering parent, but the cognoscenti would see attempted incest.

Franklin had attended the play eight times and wanted Cedric Hardwicke to reprise his Papa Barrett, but Thalberg said no. Thalberg approached Brian Aherne to reprise Browning, and he said no. As it turned out, casting Charles Laughton, Fredric March, and Norma Shearer in *The Barretts of Wimpole Street* made it the first film to star three Academy Award winners. The mood on the set fluctuated between extreme nervousness and manic silliness. Walking in Cornell's shoes gave Shearer stage fright. "Norma has found it a little difficult to get into the spirit of the picture," Franklin wrote to the semi-retired Fred Niblo, "as the speeches are very long and rather hard to say—in fact, you have to take two or three long breaths here and there, which she finds a bit of a problem, rather different from anything she's ever done." After making five films with Franklin, she had a rapport with him. "If I was having trouble with a scene," recalled Shearer, "I would go over to him just before the scene and hold his hand. Just this contact gave me what I needed. I had been 'emotionally sensitized.'" Laughton was not as open to direction. When Franklin asked the tense actor how he saw his character, Laughton snapped at him, "Like a monkey on a stick!"

During the scene in which Barrett forces a younger daughter, Henrietta (Maureen O'Sullivan), to swear on her dead mother's Bible, Laughton burst into giggles. O'Sullivan and Shearer caught them, too, as did Franklin, William Daniels, and finally the entire crew. The giggling fits caused so many tears to flow that the actors' makeup had to be redone. Laughton was giddy from a crash diet that had taken off more than forty pounds, and also from intense concentration. Holding the Bible transported him to a time when his uncle had forced him to memorize Scripture because he was a "hopeless sinner." Now he was making Barrett into his uncle. "I copied him," said Laughton. "He was both a magnificent prayer and a magnificent disciplinarian." Thalberg thought Laughton a magnificent actor and made him part of the social scene at 707 Ocean Front. They could be seen strolling on Santa Monica beach on Sunday mornings, deep in conversation.

Thalberg was regaining his status with *The Barretts of Wimpole Street*, and Shearer took full advantage. George Hurrell, who did an unprecedented three sittings for the film, remembered Shearer carrying herself as if she were indeed the "First Lady of M-G-M." O'Sullivan was with her almost every day of shooting. "Although she was definitely Queen of the Lot," recalled O'Sullivan, "she was so much fun. She created a very relaxed atmosphere, serving eggnog in her splendid trailer at four in the afternoon." Laughton envied her ability to pack away scrambled eggs and Canadian bacon, and to then turn cartwheels on the soundstage. She flirted with March and with Maurice Chevalier, whom she visited on an adjoining stage. She was, as always, gracious, except for one fateful occasion.

"I tried to visit Norma Shearer on the set of *The Barretts of Wimpole Street*," complained Marion Davies, "but I was shushed right off!" Davies angrily retreated to her own "trailer," a fourteen-room Italian-style bungalow. Thalberg spoke to Shearer, telling her that it was incumbent upon her to apologize to Davies. Shearer met with her and did her best to explain. "When you are meditating for a few precious moments before a scene," she rationalized, "it is devastating to have a voice suddenly say: 'Miss Shearer, I would like you to talk to so-and-so. Do you mind?' You mutter to yourself: 'Oh, God. Not *now!*' And you have to stop and be polite when all you want to do is commit murder. This sort of thing can affect you for hours!"

Davies was appeased, and she invited the Thalbergs to Hearst's birthday party at San Simeon on April 28; everyone was required to dress in Civil War costumes, in honor both of Hearst's birth year (1863) and the filming of *Operator 13*.* But Hearst was not as forgiving as Davies. When *The Barretts of Wimpole Street* made a profit of $668,000 and *Operator 13* lost $226,000, he blamed the Thalbergs. A showdown was coming.

Thalberg's next film was *The Green Hat*, which was to have been his return film and a Shearer vehicle. The story had served Garbo well as *A Woman of Affairs*. The excisions Thalberg made from its scandalous plot in 1928 should still have made it acceptable to the SRC in 1934. This was true, except that the world had changed in six years. No one cared about the seemingly wicked but actually martyred Iris March, especially if she was played by the coldly elegant Constance Bennett. This unlikely casting was a by-product of Thalberg's weekly card games with Joe Schenck, Darryl Zanuck, and other high rollers. Bennett was under contract to Schenck and Zanuck's Twentieth Century Pictures. At $30,000 a week, she was for a time the highest-paid actress in Hollywood. She was also the only woman allowed at the all-night games. Director Henry Hathaway was aghast when he saw her win a week's salary from her bosses.

"I don't understand," he said to Thalberg. "How can you do this?"

"You don't gamble unless you stand to win something or lose something," Thalberg answered. "If I can win $40,000 or $50,000 and buy a house at the beach and have Schenck pay for it—then I enjoy it. But if I go up there and bet only $400 or $500, for Christ's sake, it's like putting a dime in a slot machine, and I don't care whether I win or lose. You see, it's got to count. It's got to get to where you get hurt. You're either going to win something or get hurt. Really hurt." When Thalberg released *The Green Hat* as *Outcast Lady*, he got hurt, to the extent of $308,000. Unlike *Riptide*, it was an *un*qualified flop.

---

*W. R. Hearst's seventy-first birthday fell on Sunday, April 29, 1934, but the party took place the day before. Corroboration of this date and that of the Tyrolean party are courtesy of Taylor Coffman, author of *Building for Hearst and Morgan: Voices from the George Loorz Papers* (Berkeley: Berkeley Hills Books, 2003).

Part of the problem was censorship. Joe Breen's scheme had worked. In late May, Philadelphia's Denis Cardinal Dougherty, the same prelate who had banished *The Callahans and the Murphys* in 1927, ascended the pulpit and ordered his parishioners to boycott all movies under pain of mortal sin. Within a week, box-office receipts were down 40 percent. Within two weeks, the Stanley Theatre chain had lost $350,000. "You can fire a cannon down the aisle of any theater in Philadelphia without hitting anyone," Breen gloated. By mid-June, Hollywood had lost several million dollars. "Hollywood is in the most serious crisis of its history," declared Edwin Schallert in the *Los Angeles Times*. Only a year after the banking emergency, studios did not have the reserves to continue production for more than three weeks. Hollywood had no choice but to capitulate. When the smoke cleared, there was an enforceable Production Code, the Studio Relations Committee had become the Production Code Administration (PCA), and Joseph I. Breen was its boss.

The new office opened on July 11. Thus, *The Barretts of Wimpole Street*, released on July 25 but approved earlier, was not censored. *Outcast Lady*, which finished shooting on June 14, was caught in the teeth of the new Code. The sensational elements that had made Michael Arlen's book a best seller ten years earlier—homosexuality, venereal disease, and illegitimacy—while not specified in the first cut, were eliminated even by allusion in retakes. The film was released behind schedule, and its watered-down plot interested no one.

Thalberg's losing streak continued with his next film, in which he hoped to polish Helen Hayes's star and make Brian Aherne an M-G-M star. Hayes had been touring in *Mary of Scotland*. She returned to M-G-M only because Thalberg offered to film one of her Broadway hits, Sir James Barrie's *What Every Woman Knows*. Moviegoers who could not identify with the ultrachic Bennett would surely warm to a "spinster without charm" whose brothers dupe an unwilling student into marrying her. "I had high hopes for the movie," Hayes wrote in 1990, "but they were dashed when I read the script. Barrie's delicate comedy had been torn apart in the most insensitive way. In the play, Maggie is content to sit in a chair by the fire with her knitting. The movie script had her barging into 10 Downing Street and single-handedly saving the British Empire by taking England off the gold standard."

What Every Woman Knows and its gruff characters were inexplicably previewed to a Huntington Park audience that had just seen Jean Harlow in *The Girl from Missouri*. Hayes and Charles MacArthur sat uncomfortably with Thalberg and Shearer, who were trying to be "incognito" as children ran up and down the aisles, threw popcorn, and responded to the raucous mood occasioned by the first feature. Harlow would have been a tough act to follow for Shearer, but for a plain Scottish girl she spelled disaster. "It's so awful!" Hayes whispered to Thalberg. "I look like the devil. I change appearance three times." This had been caused by Bennett yanking cameraman Charles Rosher off Hayes's film to shoot retakes on *Outcast Lady.*

"Your change of appearance is no more important than a fly walking across the screen," Thalberg reassured Hayes. "The audience will never notice it." This was true, because most of the audience left before the film was over. Hayes was distraught. "It's all right," said Thalberg. "Fundamentally, it's a good picture. We'll do some retakes."

Hayes felt even worse when she read the new scenes. "Some stupid Scottish jokes had been added," wrote Hayes, "all about being a tightwad and trying to avoid paying bills, the most trite kind of attempts at humor. . . . It was wrong to put those awful jokes in a Barrie play." She appealed to the director, Gregory La Cava, who was an odd choice for this film, since he was known to improvise most of his scenes. "Oh, Greg, you can't do this!"

"Listen, baby," said La Cava. "Barrie laid an egg in Huntington Park. Forget Barrie."

Hayes did the scenes but complained to Thalberg.

"Helen," he said, "it isn't what you'd like or what I'd like. It's what will please those people in Huntington Park and get them to watch the rest of the picture, which we know is good. We've got to have something for everyone." *What Every Woman Knows* was released in October. What had been grafted onto Barrie's plot did not match the earlier scenes, and the film did not achieve the gentle whimsy of the play. Hayes made one more film, *Vanessa, Her Love Story,* with David Selznick; it also failed. The disenchanted star returned to Broadway.

Of all the projects in Thalberg's first year as an independent producer, none excited him as much as his remake of *The Merry Widow.* This was the project that he had carried in his head all through Europe. If "The Merry Widow Waltz" had been a showstopper in a silent film, how much more effective would it be in a talkie? Answering this question meant importing talent from Broadway and the ballet and assembling a cast that would do justice to a beloved operetta. Most significantly for Thalberg, it meant hiring a director who might want the final say. Many a director has maintained that a film is only as good as its casting; by the same token, casting the right director is crucial. Thalberg's concept of *The Merry Widow* required Ernst Lubitsch, whose wit could make the second *Merry Widow* as big a hit as Stroheim's irony had made the first. In 1934 Lubitsch was one of a handful of directors whose name and face meant something to the cinema addicts who thumbed through *Photoplay*. His jagged profile and jutting cigar were as singular as his use of a closed door to imply sex. Thalberg began negotiations with Lubitsch after first paying Stroheim a royalty; ironically, Stroheim had retained story rights to *The Merry Widow*.

Casting the widow was an even more delicate proposition. Mayer had hired Richard Rodgers and Lorenz Hart to adapt their musical comedy *I Married an Angel* for Jeanette MacDonald, but the SRC stopped the project; the plot implied that a human was having sex with an angel. While MacDonald was filming Jerome Kern's *The Cat and the Fiddle*, *Dancing Lady* pulled Crawford out of her slump, and she became a front-runner for *The Merry Widow*, even going so far as to take lessons from the famous voice coach Otto Morando. Yet Thalberg's choice was not an M-G-M star.

"Something has definitely happened to you and your voice," Thalberg said to Grace Moore at a party following her September 1933 Hollywood Bowl concert. What he meant was that she had improved her figure; she looked svelte. He was not the only executive to take notice of Moore. Columbia's Harry Cohn invited her to sign a contract, but had no project ready for her, so she stalled him. "I had one dominating ambition at that moment," wrote Moore. "I wanted to do *The Merry Widow* at M-G-M."

Meanwhile, Thalberg was enticing Maurice Chevalier. "Remember the last time we met and we were talking about a new kind of Chevalier on the screen?" asked Thalberg. Chevalier, who felt ill-used by Paramount, was only too happy to hear such blandishments. "You come over with me," said Thalberg, "and there'll be wonderful parts, and you'll make the kind of pictures you've wanted to. I will personally see to it." Chevalier's signing on September 12, 1933, was marked by a lavish soundstage party. Lubitsch had not been signed yet, but he met with Chevalier and Thalberg a few days later. Chevalier suggested Moore for the widow. "She's not right," decided Thalberg. "To make this a truly great film, we've got to find a girl to play the widow who's extraordinary and beautiful and dynamic—and unknown!"

Meanwhile, Moore was getting calls from Cohn asking "where in the hell" she was, and she knew she could not stall much longer. On the day he wanted her to sign, she rushed to Thalberg's office in a last-ditch effort. "We're probably going to sign another singer," Thalberg hedged. When Moore began to cry, he said that Lubitsch did not want her.

"I'll do it for nothing," wept Moore. "The role was made for me—the music for my voice. Cohn is waiting! He's given me until four thirty to make up my mind." Moore walked out to the Million-Dollar Bench. "I'll stay here until then and let you think over my offer!"

Thalberg did not relent. Moore signed with Columbia. Her first film, *One Night of Love*, did in 1934 what M-G-M had failed to do in 1930; it both made her a star and created a market for opera movies. After the preview, a triumphant Moore encountered Thalberg. "I bet this will top *The Merry Widow*," she smiled.

"Try and top it yourself," replied Thalberg.

"Has Columbia sent you a thank-you note for letting them have Grace?" Chevalier asked Thalberg later.

"Some days are just mistake days, Maurice," shrugged Thalberg. "I guess that was one of them."

Chevalier was less amused to hear that Thalberg was seriously considering MacDonald for *The Merry Widow*. "We had already done three pictures together," he wrote later. "Wasn't it time for each of us to have a new partner? Was this the 'change' Thalberg had so glowingly promised?" Thalberg got around Chevalier's objections but found Lubitsch more exigent.

"Mr. Lubitsch wants a contract with the exact terms and conditions of his present contract with Paramount," wrote studio lawyer M.E. Greenwood in a memo to Mayer. "Mr. Thalberg attempted to have Lubitsch agree to certain modifications, including the main modification that our decision would be final. . . . Mr. Thalberg's thought is that we should, if legally consistent, draft the provisions in such a way that [Lubitsch] will not lose face and yet we would have the control that we desire." Lubitsch held fast to his demands. Thalberg had resolved to make this *Merry Widow* better than Stroheim's. Lubitsch's contract was amended to read that "no changes, interpolations, modifications, additions or eliminations of any kind shall be made in the negatives or positive prints of the photoplay," other than censorship cuts, after Lubitsch had prepared his final cut of *The Merry Widow*.

As usual, Lubitsch prepared his shooting script with screenwriter Samson Raphaelson. Thalberg did, however, mandate minor revisions, first by Vajda and then by Anita Loos. "Although Ernst had none of the shortcomings of a Sidney Franklin," Loos wrote, "Irving was always worried about his tendency to neglect the human element in a story. Any love scene Ernst directed might just be warming up when his camera would zoom away from the sweethearts to focus on a pair of fancy bedroom slippers. . . . I was instructed to keep reminding Ernst that his plot concerned the human heart and not the prop department." Loos's appraisal was glib. Lubitsch's use of inanimate objects did not detract from the characters; it enhanced them cleverly and delightfully, in a purely cinematic manner. He even improved upon Thalberg's axiom that every film should have one great scene; *The Merry Widow* had one great scene after another. The only thing that Thalberg disliked when looking at the rough cut was a line: "I *had* hoped to bring a little moonlight into your life."

"There goes our love story," groaned Thalberg.

"I never told my boss that I was to blame for that phony line," wrote Loos forty years later.

The Merry Widow was one of the last M-G-M films to be shot in both an English- and a French-language version. Consequently, Lubitsch shot more angles than usual of sexy scenes such as the can-can at Maxim's restaurant. This served Thalberg when he needed to show Breen shots that could be cut in order to qualify for the newly required PCA seal. At an August 11, 1934, meeting with Lubitsch in Thalberg's office, censors Geoffrey Shurlock, Islin Auster, and Breen asked for a small number of cuts, including a shot in which a streetwalker leaves Maxim's on the arm of a policeman, saying, "You know, the trouble is—the policeman on my corner just doesn't understand me." On seeing the final cut in late September, Breen requested more cuts. Thalberg asked him to reconsider. The film was so heavily scored that the cuts would entail rerecording and remixing three entire reels. The film's budget had already crossed the million-dollar threshold, and Lubitsch was so enthusiastic about it that he had done his last week of work on it for free, an unheard-of thing in Hollywood. Breen grudgingly agreed.

The Merry Widow opened at the Astor Theatre on October 11 "amid the tumult and the shouting which befit important cinema openings and the coronation of emperors," wrote André Sennwald in the *New York Times*. "The overhead arc lamps threw a weird blue mist which was visible up and down Broadway. Mounted policemen clattered up on the sidewalk and gallantly beat back the surging proletariat. Miss MacDonald announced that her heart was full of gratitude. When Franz Lehar's name was flashed on the screen, everybody applauded." Thalberg could not have hoped for a better review—or reviewer—when Sennwald wrote that the film was "a good show in the excellent Lubitsch manner, as heady as the foam on champagne, fragile as mist and as delicately gay as a good-natured censor will permit." The censor reference was an unfortunate one, though not as unfortunate as the dour presence of Martin Quigley, who reacted to the masterly film as if it were pornography. He confronted Will Hays in the Astor lobby and denounced Breen for allowing an "industry double-cross."

Breen was summoned to New York and made to see how imperceptive he had been to let Thalberg introduce a "lot of filth" into a harmless musical. "If this picture goes out," said Quigley, "the jig is up; if M-G-M gets away with this, others will follow." A scant three months had passed since the PCA had opened. This was Breen's trial by fire. To survive it, he would have to bowdlerize the masterpiece created by Thalberg and Lubitsch. He demanded thirteen cuts. "It is going to embarrass us all seriously if the picture gets out as it now is," he told Thalberg. Hays called Thalberg to confirm his cooperation. Thalberg tried to reason with him, but failed. He then sent him a telegram.

> While I reiterate promises made to you over the telephone I again plead with you to help save this picture from being made jumpy and choppy wherever possible. It was made in the best of faith and $100,000 at least was spent in making retakes to avoid every possible expense [of local censor cuts]. If these men [Quigley, Lord, and Breen] are our friends, I am sure they would not use threats nor turn on us at the first opportunity. . . . In the long run, no one will be served by vicious attacks. The public today will certainly regard as completely unreasonable a war waged on any one picture out of a great group. Certainly the fact that so many agencies completely disassociated have passed the picture without even the usual minor cuts means that while their contentions may be right in certain small particulars such as a line here and there, still we couldn't have erred very far on the picture as a whole.

Thalberg's plea did not move Hays, whose reputation was also at stake. Thalberg reluctantly ordered the thirteen cuts made in the camera negative. He had, however, learned something from the *Tarzan and His Mate* controversy. Before sending *The Merry Widow* negative to the editing room, he had a fine-grain positive made from it so that a complete version would exist for posterity. Most of the censor's cuts were indeed abrupt and obvious. One eliminated a garter embroidered with sequins: "Many happy returns." Another abridged a message from an aging roué. "I know what to do but am too old to do it" was shortened to "I know what to do but—BUP!" Sad to say, the cuts became a moot point when lukewarm box office combined with Lubitsch's extravagance to effect a loss of $113,000. Thus, three out of five Thalberg films failed in 1934.

In early October, Thalberg was still working on the *Marie Antoinette* script, even meeting with Breen to secure his approval of key elements. On Sunday, October 21, the Thalbergs attended a Tyrolean-themed welcome-home party for Davies and Hearst in Santa Monica. At the party, Davies, who was slightly tipsy, told Thalberg how much she wanted to play *Marie Antoinette*. Thalberg smiled uneasily and said he would talk to Shearer. Nothing came of it until a disturbing call from the Hearst offices. Executive Edgar Hatrick told Thalberg that Hearst wanted *Marie Antoinette* for Davies. The showdown had commenced.

Another call came. This time it was so late that Thalberg and Shearer were already asleep. A groggy Thalberg realized that the drunken voice belonged to Davies. She again told him that she very much wanted to do *Marie Antoinette*. She had seen Versailles and was excited by the idea. "W.R. wanted me to do it," Davies later admitted. "I was going to try my best. I wasn't sure I could make the grade, but I'd read all the histories about Marie Antoinette and went through the whole routine, and I could visualize myself as Marie Antoinette with a big white wig and an upturned nose." Thalberg could not visualize her in his wife's dream role, and told her so. Shearer sensed a crisis. She took the phone from Thalberg and told Davies in a soothing voice: "Marion, I'll be delighted to give it to you if you want it."

The next day Mayer called Hearst, who immediately put Davies on. "Marion," said Mayer, 'Bob Rubin bought the book for Norma. And, Marion, I just can't visualize you as Marie Antoinette." Davies reminded him of all her costume films. "But certainly you are supposed to be a comedienne," he continued, "and I've no hopes of seeing a profit from a production of that size." Davies tried to talk over him, but he kept on. "I can't do it and I won't do it with you, Marion. I can't expend that much money on a grand production like that. With the idea that this would be for a comedienne? Strictly not. Forgive me, Marion, but you'd be no good as Marie Antoinette."

"Then I'll be no good for your studio, either," snapped Davies. She handed the receiver to Hearst.

"Louis! Louis, I—"

"Mr. Hearst, I don't say that Marion can't do it, but it *cannot* be made cheaply. Now I have been paying for all of Marion's pictures, up front and in back. You know that, and you know how grateful we are for your press. But this is different."

"Because Irving wants it for Norma?"

"No, Mr. Hearst. Because it will hurt Marion and you to do this picture." Mayer paused. "Tell you what I'll do. If you want to go ahead, I'll let you have this *Marie Antoinette*. But . . . you'll have to supply the full financing. I can't commit M-G-M to any share of the cost. You'll pay full cost of the production. And what's more, we'll distribute it free, until you've got back your money. Then you pay us double the usual distribution costs." There was silence at the other end of the line.

"However," Mayer resumed, "if you decide not to, I'll take it off your hands." Hearst quietly promised to think it over and call Mayer back in a few days.

Hearst did not require a few days. All Davies could think of that night was Mayer saying that he did not want to spend money on her. "That last part got me burned up," Davies recalled. "And W.R. was much more mad than I was. He said, 'I don't want you to ever have anything more to do with the M-G-M studio!'" Hearst immediately called Jack Warner to offer him Cosmopolitan Productions. A deal was signed on October 30. In the first week of November, crews began cutting Davies's Italian bungalow into sections. A young actor named David Niven almost drove his car into one of the sections when it was creeping across Sunset Boulevard at 5:00 in the morning. "Angry men with lanterns surrounded us," wrote Niven. "I inquired why a large building was crossing a main thoroughfare."

"It's Marion Davies' dressing room," came a reply that could only occur in Hollywood. A movie queen had been deposed. Even though Thalberg was carrying three flops, he and Shearer had more pull than Hearst and Davies. "I don't think Louis B. Mayer minded losing me so much," said Davies. "He did mind losing Mr. Hearst. . . . He had lost the power of the chess game—the visitors, and, of course, the press." Within a week, Howard Strickling noticed that the Hearst press was not printing items about Shearer. Louella Parsons denied that the omissions were intentional, but they continued, even when Strickling supplied exclusives. Once again Shearer had to bear the olive branch. Davies was more good-natured about her career than most. She accepted Shearer's overtures and asked Hearst to end the blackout. Ironically, after all the wrangling, Thalberg lost *Marie Antoinette*, too.

In November the Thalbergs were at dinner with the MacArthurs at a newly opened nightclub called the Trocadero Café. Shearer and Hayes repaired to the powder room. Once inside, Shearer assumed a conspiratorial air. "You know I'm pregnant again," she whispered to Hayes. "Irving is going to be furious with me. He's got *Marie Antoinette* all lined up. I'll never be able to finish it if I start now."

"What are you going to do?" asked Hayes.

"I know I'll have to tell him," replied Shearer. "But first I must tell Louella Parsons. I promised to let her know the minute I got pregnant again—that she would be the first to know." Even though Hearst had left M-G-M, the studio was still beholden to his correspondents. Shearer phoned her news to Parsons and then told Thalberg. When he showed more concern about a second child than about a postponed project, she was relieved. He had begun to entertain morbid thoughts since turning thirty-five the previous May. "I'm getting old," he said occasionally. The prospect of a second child stopped his brooding.

Mayer's loss of Hearst was in some measure compensated by a political favor from Thalberg. Upton Sinclair, whom Thalberg still called "that Bolshevik," was running as Democratic candidate for governor. Central to his platform was a Socialist reform program called End Poverty in California (EPIC). It proposed to guarantee employment by turning idle factories and farms into cooperatives. Sinclair's constituents were perceived, rightly or wrongly, as disenfranchised: poor, ethnic, or Communist. "Our plan does not propose to confiscate anything," said Sinclair. "We propose that the state shall tax the rich, whose money is lying unused in bank vaults." Statements like this frightened studio owners and their New York bosses. There was panicked talk of moving studios to Florida if Sinclair defeated the corrupt incumbent, Frank R. Merriam.

In September, polls showed Sinclair closing the gap between himself and Merriam. Mayer had been in Europe during the summer and missed the opportunity to rally his party against Sinclair. Thalberg offered to help. He put producer Felix Feist in charge of "California Election News," a series of one-reel films that were shot like newsreels but with actors. The films depicted "random" interviews with California voters who were asked whom they supported and why. Interview subjects who supported Merriam were clean-cut, well spoken, and respectable. Sinclair supporters were unkempt, unfriendly, and unemployed. One bewhiskered subject looked both fierce and foreign. The interviewer asked him his affiliation.

"I am voting for Saint Clair."

"Why are you voting for him?"

"Saint Clair is the author of the Russian government. It worked out well there. Why shouldn't it work out here?"

Some interviewees were not even Californians. "Why are you for Sinclair?" the offscreen interviewer asked a lean migrant worker.

"That's *my* business, pardner," snarled the worker.

How the films were made was also nobody's business. "Thalberg had the film processed at an independent laboratory," Carey Wilson admitted in a 1953 interview. "There was no way it could be traced to Metro."

"California Election News" was shipped with genuine Hearst newsreels to every Loew's theater and every independent theater showing M-G-M product. Even though the *New York Times* exposed the films for what they were during the campaign, they accomplished their goal. Merriam got 48 percent of the vote; Sinclair got 37 percent.

In mid-November, Thalberg attended a party hosted by Fredric March and his wife, Florence Eldridge. Thalberg was aware that the Marches were members of the new Screen Actors Guild, but he was not prepared for the liberal outrage they expressed at Sinclair's defeat by "fascist propaganda."

"I made those films," Thalberg said flatly.

"You did?" blurted March, staring in disbelief. "But that was a dirty trick. The damnedest unfair thing I've ever heard of."

"Nothing is unfair in politics," said Thalberg. "We could sit down here and figure dirty things all night, and every one of them would be all right in a political campaign. I used to be a boy orator for the Socialist party on the East Side in New York. Do you think Tammany ever gave me a chance to be heard? They broke up our meetings. If there had been any chance that we might beat them in our ward, they would simply have thrown the ballot boxes into the East River, as they did against Hearst."

"But that doesn't mean it's right," March shook his head. "There must be some place where they have honest elections."

"You mean England, I suppose," smiled Thalberg. "Well, don't kid yourself. Their heckling is just as bad as Tammany breaking up a meeting. But they have something even better up in the high places: the big lie. Do you remember the 'Hang the Kaiser' campaign after the war? And the fake Zinoviev letter that won another election? When an election comes up, all the nice English sportsmanship flies out the window. They take off their gloves and put on the brass knuckles, just as we do. A 'fair election' is a contradiction in terms. It just doesn't exist."

March mentioned that Robert Montgomery had recently been to Germany and been frightened by the virulent fascism he had seen. Thalberg had sponsored a Jewish defense group after his return, yet in private he appeared almost indifferent.

"You're a Jew yourself," said political writer Kyle Crichton. "You tell me you've seen something of what Hitler is doing to the Jews in Germany. It's plain he intends to wipe them out. Doesn't that mean anything to you?"

"A lot of Jews will lose their lives," said Thalberg unemotionally.

"A *lot* of them!" Crichton exclaimed. "Millions of them—maybe all of them!"

"No, not all of them," said Thalberg. "Hitler and Hitlerism will pass. The Jews will still be there."

To anyone at the party who had seen Thalberg unseated by Mayer and Schenck, his attitude was perplexing. Still, he had given them a clue. The attacks he suffered while espousing Socialism had left unhealed wounds. In the years since, he had found power in creativity; it had protected him from new attacks. Only his health left him vulnerable. After a year as an independent producer, it was obvious that creativity alone would not protect him. He needed power, even if he had to ally himself with his betrayers to get it. He hoped to gain enough power to leave Mayer and Schenck, but for the time being, he had to work with them. He would use their resources to make the greatest films in Hollywood—and the most profitable. He had done it ten years earlier, with his silent blockbusters, *Ben-Hur*, *The Merry Widow*, and *The Big Parade*. "But," he said to Sam Marx, "I don't expect it to be so easy this time."

Irving Thalberg needed to make big films in 1935. He was in the right place at the right time. M-G-M had ended 1934 with a profit of $7.5 million. The Great Depression was not over, but it was losing its grip on the cities where Loew's had most of its theaters. Unemployment was down to 20 percent, and movie attendance was hovering around 80 million a week. Paramount, RKO, and Warners had rebounded, but Universal was still in the red, trying to placate its creditors. The Fox Film Corporation was hemorrhaging money, even though it had three of *Film Daily*'s "Top Ten" movie stars—Will Rogers, Janet Gaynor, and Shirley Temple.* Weak management was to blame. Winfield Sheehan was no Louis B. Mayer, and Sol Wurtzel was no Thalberg. Fox's strategy was no strategy at all, just a mad scramble to supply product for its huge theater chain. The Production Code had stopped its run of racy films, so it was looking at literary classics. If Metro could put W. C. Fields in *David Copperfield*, Fox could put Spencer Tracy in *Dante's Inferno*. The million-dollar epic was the coming thing in 1935. Paramount was making Cecil B. DeMille's *The Crusades*. M-G-M was making David Selznick's *A Tale of Two Cities*. Even Darryl Zanuck's tiny Twentieth Century Pictures was making two epics, *Les Misérables* and *Clive of India*. The time was right for Thalberg to do something big. Eddie Mannix was singing his praises. "*The Barretts* is the best thing Norma's ever done," Mannix told Sam Marx one day. "Irving's

*According to a *Film Daily* exhibitors' poll, January 1935.

like his old self again." It was odd, then, that Thalberg's first film of 1935 was not an epic but an intimate comedy-drama.

S. N. Behrman's *Biography* was the story of an oft-loved portrait painter named Marion Froude. The witty and touching play had been one of Broadway's longest-running hits in the winter of 1932 and a scintillating success for Ina Claire. "Her readings were translucent, her stage presence encompassing," recalled Behrman. "She never missed a nuance." Thalberg knew Claire from her brief marriage to John Gilbert and from her contract with Pathé. Her films were well received, but she disliked the process of making them. After three years in Hollywood, she bought out her contract and made it clear that she had no intention of becoming the next Thalberg recruit. "I am through being stupid," she declared, then went on to triumph in *Biography*. When Thalberg decided to film it, Claire turned him down again. He then approached Katharine Cornell, who was at the Biltmore Theater in a new production of *Romeo and Juliet*. "No," responded Cornell. "Definitely no. At the present time I feel that I am suited for the stage rather than for pictures." Even when Thalberg broached the possibility of filming *Romeo and Juliet*, Cornell remained steadfast. "I am interested only in the stage," she said. "It is the medium best suited for whatever talent I may possess."

Of all the M-G-M stars available, Norma Shearer was the logical choice for *Biography*'s Marion, but she would have to go from *The Barretts* to *Biography* without a break, so she begged off. Thalberg opted for RKO's Ann Harding. A natural blonde, she was photographically lustrous and had a solid theatrical background. Most important, she could convey intelligence, which she had done in *The Animal Kingdom* and *When Ladies Meet*. This was necessary if Thalberg wanted to do *Biography* correctly. "Motion pictures have grown up—and so have the audiences," Thalberg told an interviewer. "Audiences are no longer made up of gullible babes, enthralled by the elementary. The man who puts gasoline in your car is a college man. You can't offer him a high-priced star and a glamorous publicity campaign and expect him to accept that as entertainment."

Not everyone agreed with Thalberg's notion of sophistication. To Joseph Breen, *Biography* was the scarlet saga of "a woman who has gained considerable notoriety through a succession of affairs." Thalberg promised to purify her character by adding lines in which "Marion regrets her loose life . . . and implies that the gossip about her is exaggerated." Even so, Breen found the first cut of the film in violation of the Code. Thalberg ordered a number of lines reshot, including a close-up of Robert Montgomery. When Montgomery reported to the soundstage, he thought he was wearing the same suit jacket that he had worn when first shooting the scene. He was wrong. Thalberg watched the reassembled scene and spotted a mismatch. It was too late to shoot it again. At the preview, he and his editors held their breaths when the shot appeared. "No one noticed," recalled assistant editor Chester Schaeffer.

With its main character renamed Marion Forsythe and its title changed to *Biography of a Bachelor Girl*, Thalberg's film opened in New York. The critics were quick to jump on it. "The elements that made *[Biography]* a success have been toned down," wrote Norbert Lusk. In cooperating with the censors, Thalberg had changed Marion from a droll connoisseur of life to a wistful observer. If the film had been made with Shearer in 1933, it could have honored its origins, but in the spring of 1935 it was a flop. Thalberg was disappointed, but not discouraged.

One day Sam Marx asked Thalberg what constituted box office. After a meaningful pause, Thalberg looked him in the eye. "Box office," he said, "is the combination of a star and a title that the public wants to see." Marx was one of the few who knew that Thalberg had put a scene from his own life into *Biography of a Bachelor Girl*. In the antechamber of his office one day in 1931, Thalberg had polled three secretaries on a "title that the public wants to see."

"Who is Susan Lenox?" Thalberg asked.

"Wasn't there a book about her?" offered Vivian Newcom, his secretary at the time.

"Yes, there was," said Mildred Kelly, Harry Rapf's secretary.

"It was something about her rise and fall, I think," said Stanley Partridge, Mannix's secretary. "Or maybe it was the other way around."

"That's enough," smiled Thalberg. "I'll buy the book." The scene was reproduced almost word for word in *Biography of a Bachelor Girl*. It was an object lesson for Thalberg's next film.

One of the 20,000 literary properties that passed through Marx's office in 1933 was a play by A. E. Thomas called *Home, James*. Its only public exposure had been an out-of-town tryout at Netcong, New Jersey. Marx liked it and offered Thomas $15,000 for it. Thomas agreed, but Thalberg countermanded Marx's offer. Thomas took his play to the Shuberts, who opened it in January 1934 as *No More Ladies*. The story of a socialite who punishes her philandering husband by throwing a party for his conquests became a Broadway hit. Only then did Thalberg authorize its purchase, at the cost of $65,000. According to Marx, Thalberg was "unperturbed by the additional $50,000 because he felt that the public approval of the story was worth the difference."

After the conspicuously expensive *Riptide* and *Barretts*, Hollywood gossip said that Thalberg was handing his best properties to his wife. The gossipmongers had to shut their mouths when he gave *No More Ladies* to Joan Crawford. No one was more surprised to be cast in a Thalberg production than Crawford, who had been in a series of hits with, respectively, Selznick, Hunt Stromberg, and Bernard Hyman. Since her divorce from Douglas Fairbanks Jr., she had been dating the wealthy Theatre Guild actor Franchot Tone, whom Thalberg also cast in *No More Ladies;* her costar would be Robert Montgomery, M-G-M's most versatile star. Crawford had invited the Thalbergs to her home and gotten a polite no. "I was much too easily hurt," recalled Crawford. "If I asked people to dinner and they couldn't come, I'd wonder if they liked me." Her question was answered when she received an invitation to 707 Ocean Front. "I don't know who was more frightened, Joan or me," wrote Shearer. "People said that I was inviting a friendly enemy to dinner. Joan proved them wrong by being a most delightful guest."

To adapt *No More Ladies* to Crawford's personality, Thalberg hired the renowned playwright Rachel Crothers, the author of *Let Us Be Gay* and *When Ladies Meet,* to the tune of $3,000 a week. She was not interested in viewing films or reading scripts at the studio, and she refused to work in a cubicle in the writers' building, so Thalberg allowed her to adapt the play in her hotel room. After twenty weeks, she had written an unusable script. "Even a first-rate playwright doesn't know as much about the picture business as we do," said Marx. "She should be willing to listen to people in the industry who want to help." Crothers expressed her gratitude by saying publicly that she wanted M-G-M to take her name off the script. "Hollywood's pious notion," she fumed, "is that producer and director come before the story, with every right to pull it to pieces and destroy it." Thalberg turned the original play script over to no fewer than six of his staff writers, who rushed to tailor it for Crawford.

"A Broadway producer," Thalberg told writer Gilbert Seldes, "with an investment of five hundred dollars in a dramatic script puts up another five hundred and tells the author to work on his second act for another couple of months. I can't do that. I've got a schedule to meet. If a man brings in a script, and it's got good characters and dialogue but no comedy, I get a man who can do comedy—and hope to God he won't spoil the characters. Some people are weak on character building, and I put them to work with a man who's first-rate that way. I know they don't like it. I don't like it. What else can I do?" Thalberg finally assigned *No More Ladies* to Donald Ogden Stewart, who was approaching burnout.

As Thalberg's most favored craftsman, Stewart was expected to contribute to each project in the Thalberg bungalow. The work was lucrative, and Stewart was in awe of Thalberg. "It was the most fortunate experience that a writer could have in the film world," wrote Stewart, "for Irving was the unrivaled Top. The effect on me, however, was not quite so fortunate. I became a commodity, a fairly valuable one, and I enjoyed the position tremendously." What he did not enjoy was losing the pride of authorship. No script that he began would bear his name. No script that he finished was completely his own. He hopped from *Biography* to *Marie Antoinette* to *No More Ladies* and back again. He was what Ethel Barrymore had called her brother, an "overpaid factory worker." While it was true that Thalberg had created the greatest stable of writers in history, none of them felt particularly respected, not even his favorite. "In trying to satisfy 'father,'" wrote Stewart, "I was responsible for making the best use of the material. I had little time to consider what that material was, or what its connection with truth might be. Little by little, as my salary rose, my image of the world became so blurred by Hollywood that truth came to resemble the celluloid interpretation. I was a better manipulator of my material, but I had lost sight of my own aims."

Stewart's scripts frequently included scenes of drunkenness and blackouts, episodes drawn from his own life. "I more or less succeeded in concealing from myself the fact that I was past thirty-nine and getting nowhere. Good old alcohol helped, of course." *No More Ladies* had several drunken characters, including a Park Avenue matron. "*No More Ladies* wasn't my picture," wrote Crawford. "It went strictly to Edna May Oliver as a highball-drinking grandmother." Crawford considered her previous two films "fashion layouts," but *No More Ladies* got especially dismissive reviews. "*No More Ladies*," wrote André Sennwald, "comes out of the same glamour factory as Miss Crawford's *Forsaking All Others*. If it is less furiously arch than that modern classic of sledgehammer whimsy, it is also somewhat less successful as entertainment.... Although Donald Ogden Stewart has contributed several really funny lines, the screen play is chiefly notable for its surface shimmer, the hollowness of its wit, and the insincerity of its emotions." The funny lines in question may have been the six lines that remained from Crothers's $60,000 script, and Thalberg was counting. *No More Ladies* made money, but not enough to justify the extra $50,000 he had paid for the play. Maybe it was time to forget about Broadway.

"To hell with art," said Thalberg. "This time I'm going to produce a picture that will make money." He grabbed a novel that had been banging around the story department for five years. It was called *China Seas*. He paged Stewart, who was engaged in an ongoing argument with his wife, Beatrice.

"Are you married to Irving or me?" Beatrice had asked him. To pacify her, Stewart agreed to go to London for the May 6 celebration of King George V's Silver Jubilee. But first he had to visit the Thalberg bungalow.

"I told Irving that I didn't want to be a screenwriter any more," said Stewart. "I wanted to write plays, my own plays. Father looked at me sadly, and made me feel that he hadn't heard what I'd said but that he'd forgive me if I'd sign for just one more year. I shook my head firmly, and went home to pack." Stewart's phone rang all evening with calls from his agent, from M-G-M, and finally from Thalberg. Stewart dodged them; he had to catch his train at 9:00 the next morning. At 7:00 A.M. there was a knock at the front door of the Stewart mansion. The butler had not been warned. "Don, are you upstairs?" came Thalberg's voice from the foyer. Stewart gritted his teeth, signed the contract, and left for Europe.

Some Stewart colleagues thought his corruption was due to changes in Thalberg. Charles MacArthur preferred to stay in New York, codirecting films with Ben Hecht and Lee Garmes, to sitting in Thalberg's bungalow, following five other writers on *Marie Antoinette*. Thalberg could not understand his attitude; he could barely believe it. Helen Hayes was in Pittsburgh on a tour of Maxwell Anderson's *Mary of Scotland*. She was awakened at 3:00 one morning in her hotel room, even though she had instructed the switchboard not to ring her. "It's a Mr. Thalberg from Hollywood," apologized the operator. "He says it's urgent."

"Helen, are you having another baby?" came the worried voice.

"No, Irving," she responded groggily. "What are you talking about?"

"Charlie left here a couple of days ago," said Thalberg. "He phoned me and said he was going to join you. I can't find him anywhere." There was a bewildered pause. "I never thought he would do this to me."

Hayes became worried that MacArthur was on a drinking binge until she reached him at their home in Nyack. He explained that he was fine; he just could not bear to watch Irving turn reactionary. He did not like the writers Irving was cultivating, right-wing Republicans like James Kevin McGuinness and John Lee Mahin. He did not want to see Irving any more, and that was that.

Maurice Chevalier also saw a change in Thalberg. When Chevalier asked about his long-overdue second film, Thalberg confirmed that he would be teamed with Grace Moore in *The Cardboard Lover*. Chevalier was exultant until Thalberg dropped a bomb. "Columbia insists on top billing for Grace."

"It's not possible, Irving," said Chevalier. "You know that. My contract with you says I get top billing over everyone, man or woman."

"The important thing is to make a good movie, Maurice," said Thalberg. "And earn money. Isn't that right?"

"No," Chevalier answered. "I'm sorry. It's not right. For almost twenty years I've been billed first, and I'd rather play that way in a cheap music hall than take second place at the Palace in New York." Chevalier sensed that Columbia's Harry Cohn was pressuring Thalberg. To get Grace Moore, Thalberg had to put the same pressure on Chevalier. "Suddenly I could see how precarious was one's position on the Hollywood ladder," wrote Chevalier in 1960, "how all must be governed by the law of business. If even Thalberg had to yield to that law, what could I hope for in dealings with lesser men?" Chevalier bought out his contract and returned to France.

Part of the change in Thalberg could be attributed to eighteen months of competing with men who had formerly been his disciples. Part of it could be the pressure of having to prove himself for the first time since Universal. And part of it was the icy divide that separated him from the formerly warm Louis B. Mayer. The two men appeared friendly when they attended B'nai B'rith Grand Lodge meetings and the Los Angeles Opera, but there was a studied formality to their interplay. Mayer lamented their lost confidence to Mannix.

"It was for Irving's sake that I took over the studio," he said. "That poor boy was working himself into the grave. I saved him so he can spend more years with Norma and his family. And these are the thanks I get! He rejects me. He fights me at every turn. He undermines me with Schenck. What have I done to deserve it?" Plant manager J. J. Cohn found himself stuck between Mayer and Thalberg, trying to arbitrate the use of facilities. "Thalberg was often unreasonable in his demands," recalled Cohn. "He wanted the best actors, the best writers, the best directors." Yet Mayer could be accommodating. "Schedules were rearranged and shooting dates were delayed or set ahead to give Thalberg what he wanted. But sometimes it just wasn't possible. After all, Mayer was running a studio, not a Thalberg operation."

It was no secret that Thalberg had recently exercised his option to purchase 10,000 shares of stock in Loew's, Inc., at $30 a share. There were also rumors that he was casting about for a company through which he could release his independent productions once his contract with Loew's expired. In early 1935, though, these were just rumors. Such a move was unlikely when he had a second child on the way. While he supervised the half-dozen projects that were gestating in his bungalow, his home life proceeded at a routine pace, belying talk that he had grown remote and steely. There were three constants: visits to his family, dinner parties, and bridge.

Thalberg's parents had moved into Larry and Sylvia Weingarten's Beverly Hills mansion. "We used to go there every Wednesday," recalled Shearer. "Henrietta prepared Irving's favorites, either pot roast and red cabbage or sweet-and-sour broiled tongue with raisins and almonds in cream sauce. He liked these with one glass of beer." The atmosphere made Thalberg as relaxed as he ever was, but Shearer saw family dynamics at work. When Thalberg's parents came to his home on Sunday afternoons, his mother would criticize him. Shearer took it in stride, but never forgot it. "Irving's mother had a habit of making observations that were accurate and amusing but not always kind." Shearer took care to stay on Henrietta's good side, even assuring her that the next child would be named after her. Thalberg was less diplomatic. "Although Henrietta had a lively mind and read everything in sight," said Shearer, "Irving told her that she remembered nothing of what she read, not even the titles. He delighted in teasing her, telling everyone that she couldn't stand not being in on everything, and that when he was a bachelor and used to come home late, she would always be up, prowling about in her dressing gown, hair disheveled, waiting to hear what she had missed at the Ambassador or the Montmartre."

The Weingartens got along with Henrietta in the same way they did with Thalberg, by being obsequious. Thalberg reproved Sylvia for not persevering at her writing. "Irving claimed his sister had talent but was lazy," said Shearer. Sylvia did manage to write one work without a collaborator—a novel called *Too Beautiful*—but by 1935, she had left M-G-M and was devoting her life to her mother, not to her husband. "Larry was patient—perhaps too patient," wrote Shearer. "His home life was dominated by Sylvia's mother, and he suffered from a lack of privacy. He never felt that he was the master of his home. His health began to show signs of nervous strain."

More put-upon than Weingarten was Thalberg's father, William; he had become a shadowy figure. "Irving and his mother called William 'impossible,' more often in front of him than behind his back," said Shearer. "He bore these affectionate insults with dignity." As Shearer wrote:

After thirty-five years of marriage, Henrietta treated William more like an uninvited guest she had to tolerate than like the head of the family. I could not imagine how they got together in the first place, the ambitious American girl and the solemn German boy. (His loyalty to the "Fatherland" drove Irving crazy.) Whatever romance had bloomed between them in Brooklyn had definitely lost its glow. He kept out of her way by going downtown to his real estate office early each morning. His only friend was a wire-haired terrier named Mickey, a feisty little creature who growled at everyone but him.

Shearer made certain that Thalberg was the master of his own home, presiding over the soirees that were essential to Hollywood society. Shearer's only concession to her pregnancy was to discontinue their Sunday afternoon teas. Dinner parties were de rigueur, regardless of her condition. "Thirty or forty guests meant a large buffet with a lot of little tables spread throughout the living room," said Shearer. "I found this form of entertaining difficult and untidy. Small sit-down dinners in the dining room were much more conducive to conversation. We felt that what we did for pleasure should not be a strain."

Shearer strove to keep the guest list intriguing. "I got away from the people Irving had been with all day at the studio because it would be refreshing for him to hear new ideas," said Shearer. "Irving sat at the head of the table. I sat at the other end, separated from him by lighted white tapers and silver bowls filled with white wax flowers. Removed from the studio, Irving was light-hearted and not above flirting. He loved to talk, about anything and everything, and as a listener he was superb, casting those enigmatic brown eyes at you, absorbing the meaning of your thoughts almost before you expressed them."

In 1935, guests to Thalberg dinners were most likely to include those working on current Thalberg projects (Robert Montgomery, Joan Crawford), those slated for upcoming projects (Gloria Swanson, Clark Gable, Jean Harlow, Basil Rathbone), those known from earlier projects (Edmund Goulding, Charles Laughton, Jeanette MacDonald, Leslie Howard, Ernst Lubitsch, Gary Cooper), and those who had survived Hollywood politics (William Haines, Joseph Breen, Sam Goldwyn, Grace Moore). Newly popular stars (Ginger Rogers, Charles Boyer, Merle Oberon, Oscar Levant, Kitty Carlisle) were also welcome. Those not invited included has-beens (Erich von Stroheim, B. P. Schulberg) and trouble-makers (John Barrymore, Herman Mankiewicz). Shearer found certain people too intimidating to invite: Katharine Cornell, Mary Pickford, Will Hays, L. B. Mayer, and Greta Garbo.

"As much as I adored Garbo," wrote Shearer, "we seldom if ever invited her. I found her superb isolationism admirable and I respected it. Perhaps she felt she had too much to live up to in the drawing room. She preferred to make an impromptu visit, like an enchanting urchin coming out of the fog. Irving and I were delighted by her impressions of Mr. Mayer." When Garbo did attend a dinner party in early 1935, she ignored the other guests and headed for the beach, first asking Maurice Chevalier to join her. He contemplated the cold salt water and politely declined. Garbo gave him an even colder stare and stalked off into the night.

Shearer never invited William Randolph Hearst to dinner, even though the immense beach house he had built for Marion Davies was two minutes away. "Marion had entertained us lavishly up the beach," wrote Shearer, "but I was reluctant to assume the task of beguiling her great and devoted friend. Although I'd always found Mr. Hearst gracious and as eager to please as a little boy, I knew that here was a will of steel, and the thought of it intimidated me. I'd never felt at ease in his presence."

Elsa Lanchester came to dinner on March 21 with her husband, Charles Laughton, because Thalberg had shown her a surprising degree of consideration. "I was not under personal contract to Thalberg as Charles was," wrote Lanchester, "but by advising me, he knew he was helping Charles. I used to walk into his office after being out on the beach with my hair all cockled up from the sea and wearing trousers. Once when I had to go to see another producer, Thalberg said: 'I must tell you that you cannot go and see other producers like this. You must wear a skirt.'" At the dinner party, Lanchester was so nervous sitting at the table with Clark Gable and Jean Harlow that she dropped her napkin on the floor and was then too self-conscious to retrieve it. After dinner, she was talking with Jeanette MacDonald, with whom she had just worked on *Naughty Marietta*. Harlow ran in from the beach, her skirt hiked up. Everyone looked at her as she put a wriggling fish into a flower bowl. Lanchester knew from the newspapers that the grunion were running that night. She pulled the saltwater fish from the freshwater bowl and dashed outside with it. The moonlit beach was iridescent with grunion. Lanchester pitched hers back in. To get to the beach, Thalberg's guests had to walk past his pool, which was divided into freshwater and saltwater halves. When someone complimented him on it, he said ruefully: "I've never been in it."

The third constant in Thalberg's personal life was a weekly bridge game. This took place in the living room on Thursday nights. Shearer welcomed the regulars, who included Sam Goldwyn, Constance Bennett, and Chico Marx. Before retiring to her bedroom, Shearer served refreshments. "None of them drank anything to speak of outside of a beer or a Coke or a ginger ale," she said. "Irving didn't smoke either. But there was plenty of fun, judging by the laughter that used to float upstairs. You can imagine what kind of humor there was with Sam Goldwyn and a Marx brother at the same card table." Only Thalberg was laughing the night he won $14,000 from his guests.

Shearer tried to insulate Thalberg's home life from M-G-M concerns, but she found it impossible. Thalberg was in thrall to the silver screen. "Irving would run rushes at home if he hadn't had time to see them at the studio," said Shearer, "or just look at a new picture from another studio. He was naturally eager to keep in touch with what was being produced at the other studios." There were constant appeals for money, too. "Although we were big earners we tried not to lose sight of our financial obligations," said Shearer. "We each supported various members of our families. We also donated to charities—the American Red Cross, the Community Chest, the Motion Picture Relief Fund, and the Jewish Welfare Fund." Rabbi Edgar F. Magnin, who had officiated at the Thalberg wedding, was a family friend and a frequent guest at the Thalberg home. According to Sam Marx, Thalberg underwrote a substantial part of the magnificent temple that Magnin built near the Ambassador Hotel when the B'nai B'rith outgrew its original location. Unlike Jack Warner, Thalberg took no credit for the Wilshire Temple.

"Irving said that generosity with money was the price one had to pay for success," wrote Shearer. "Of course we lived attractively. We worked to live, and at times it seemed that we lived to work. But we both loved to work." It was not surprising, then, that Thalberg would talk about work during a bridge game. In August 1934 he was playing with, among others, Chico Marx. "What are you fellows doing now?" asked Thalberg, referring to trade paper reports that the act was in trouble; one Marx brother, Zeppo, had left to become an agent.

"I'm loafing," replied Chico. "We're between pictures."

"Your contract's up, isn't it?" asked Thalberg, who was well aware that the last Marx Brothers film, *Duck Soup*, had flopped.

"Well," Chico said cagily, "we haven't signed our new one . . . yet."

"Look," said Thalberg. "Before you sign anything, I'd like to talk with you and Groucho and Harpo. Perhaps we could meet for lunch."

Lunch took place at the Beverly Wilshire Hotel. "I'm not very hungry," said Groucho as Thalberg sat down, "so if you're picking up the tab, I'll just order something small and expensive."

Thalberg did not respond to the joke. "I would like to make some pictures with you fellows," he said. "I mean *real* pictures."

"What was the matter with *The Cocoanuts?*" snapped Groucho. "And *Animal Crackers?* Are you going to sit there and tell me they weren't funny? Did you see them?"

"Of course," answered Thalberg. "They were funny. But they weren't movies. They weren't *about* anything."

"I thought they were pretty funny," said Groucho as his brothers sat in silence. "And I think I'm at least as good a judge of comedy as you are. What about *Horse Feathers* and *Duck Soup?*"

"Not bad," answered Thalberg. "Not good, either."

"People laughed, didn't they?" asked Harpo. "*Duck Soup* had as many laughs as any picture ever made—including Chaplin's."

"That's true," said Thalberg. "It was a very funny picture. But you don't need that many laughs in a picture. I can make a picture with you fellows that has half as many laughs. But I'll put in a legitimate story. And I bet it'll gross twice as much as *Duck Soup*. I don't agree with the principle of anything for a laugh. For my money, comedy scenes have to further the plot. It's more important to have a story that the audience is interested in than to have a laugh every other minute."

"So you didn't care for *Duck Soup* then," said Groucho.

"Women didn't. Your movies have strictly male appeal. Men like your comedy, but women don't. They don't understand your kind of humor. You have to start giving women what they want, a love interest, a romance they can become interested in."

"Well," said Groucho, "I didn't come here to be insulted. If you just want to knock our pictures, I'd rather have lunch by myself, somewhere else." He looked around. No one was getting up to leave. He paused. "If you want to talk a deal . . . well, that's something else, of course."

"No offense," said Thalberg. "I just thought it would be better for the four of us to understand each other. If you're willing to go along with my theories, I think it can be very profitable for all of us."

The brothers were poker-faced, but they promised to think over his offer of a personal contract. When Chico came home, he was anything but poker-faced. "Irving doesn't think we're has-beens!" he told his wife and daughter. "He wants to make a deal!" At Paramount the four brothers had gotten $200,000 per film plus 50 percent of the gross. The three remaining brothers asked Thalberg for $7,500 a week and 15 percent. He accepted, provided that he would have artistic control. The Marx Brothers agreed and signed. Hollywood was littered with has-beens too proud to accept a reasonable comeback offer. Sam Marx, who was a distant relative of the brothers, had seen the already legendary D. W. Griffith sitting alone and unwanted in the lobby of the Hollywood Knickerbocker Hotel. Thinking of Thalberg's gift for salvaging careers, he proposed a meeting. He was slightly taken aback when Thalberg refused. "I could never work with Griffith," said Thalberg, "nor he with me."

Getting along with the Marx Brothers was no easier than beating them at bridge. They didn't like James K. McGuinness, and not just because he was a Republican and they were Democrats. He could not formulate a workable concept for their first film. Their zaniness would not work in a vacuum. "Hit a fellow in old clothes with a snowball and it doesn't mean a thing," Thalberg told him. "Hit a fellow in a full dress suit and knock off his top hat. Then you get a laugh." McGuinness proposed that the Marxes be put in a very dignified setting. Thalberg was a patron of the Los Angeles Opera Company. That was it. The Marxes would demolish the opera. McGuinness wrote a step outline, enumerating the sequences of the film. The lyricist Bert Kalmar and composer Harry Ruby, who had written the screenplays for the last two Marx Brothers films, completed the first continuity.

"Listen, Irving," said Chico at the card table one night, "we've been looking over this script about the opera troupe. It's not funny." The Marxes wanted Thalberg to hire the high-priced playwrights who had crafted their template *The Cocoanuts*, so Thalberg sent word to Morrie Ryskind and George S. Kaufman. Ryskind welcomed the opportunity to work for Thalberg, but Kaufman was in the process of suing Samuel Goldwyn over a credit, so he was not eager to revisit Hollywood. He had to be coaxed. Thalberg offered him $5,000 a week and a guarantee of $100,000. Ryskind kept after him, and in January 1935 Kaufman finally agreed. "I'm going to Hollywood, God damn it," he wrote, "but only for a few weeks." Kaufman settled into the Garden of Allah, the exotic bungalow complex on Sunset Boulevard, and began the commute to Culver City. "On a clear day you can see Thalberg," quipped Kaufman as he waited outside Thalberg's office. Thalberg finally made time to see him and asked him if he had read McGuinness's treatment. Thalberg then proceeded to quiz Kaufman on plot points.

"Did you bring me out here to write or to play 'Twenty Questions'?" asked Kaufman.

"I brought you here—at considerable expense—to answer those and any other questions I might ask you," replied Thalberg.

"Very well, Mr. Thalberg. Ask away."

"Very well, Mr. Kaufman. I will. How soon can I have your improvements on Jim's outline?"

"Hmm . . . I can't say exactly."

"Wednesday?"

"Mr. Thalberg, do you want it Wednesday or do you want it good?"

Thalberg was no more amused by Kaufman than he was by the Marx Brothers' antics. When he kept them waiting for two days, Groucho growled: "Who does he think he is? Irving Thalberg?" When they were finally admitted to his office, he spoke with them for a few minutes, then suddenly walked out to consult with McGuinness, and did not return for an hour. The brothers reacted by pushing file cabinets against the doors. Thalberg could not get into his own office. "Save that kind of behavior for the soundstage," he said coldly.

Kaufman finished his first draft more quickly than expected. Thalberg listened to Kaufman while reading his mail, answering calls, and checking on writers in adjoining offices. Nevertheless, his critique was on target. "I feel like an idiot," Kaufman confided to Groucho by the Garden of Allah pool. "That man has never written a word, yet he can tell me exactly what to do with a story. He's another Sam Harris [their former Broadway producer]. I didn't know you had people like that out here."

The Marx Brothers grudgingly walked to the Thalberg bungalow again. "Thalberg was a difficult man to see," wrote Groucho. "Most everyone in his employ was afraid of him. Perhaps *afraid* is too strong a word. Let's say deeply respectful." Rosalind Russell was a newly signed player from Broadway when she visited Thalberg for the first time. "Thalberg's bungalow was the 'Holy of Holies,'" recalled Russell. "You passed it reverently. Going in was almost like going into church. There was an air of sanctity and mysticism. His desk was even raised a little bit, rather like an altar. When he looked at you, he did so with tremendous concentration. He had sad eyes, but they didn't pity you. They mesmerized you."

After less than two years, Thalberg's lair had acquired a mystique. "The atmosphere in the Thalberg bungalow was different from that in the rest of the M-G-M lot," wrote Salka Viertel, who relished the quiet she found within its oak-paneled walls. It had the stately air of a university library. "Downstairs was his office and a reception hall, where the secretaries ruled. Upstairs were offices for the writers. On the third floor was a kitchen, a pantry and Thalberg's dining room. In the afternoon a butler would knock at the doors to inquire if one wanted tea or a highball." Because Thalberg spent more time in the bungalow than at home, it had amenities. "Glass doors led to a walled patio which Irving never had time to enjoy," recalled Shearer.

The conference room was the creative hub, its long table reflecting a row of studious faces. "I heard the meetings at this table referred to as the Last Supper," wrote Shearer. "I never attended one. I thought I might have a hard time passing myself off as Jesus' wife." If Shearer was not admitted, she was at least acknowledged. "Irving would interrupt a story conference to blow a goodnight kiss to me over the telephone," said Shearer, "without an apology to his associates or even a blush." Thalberg was on edge about her pregnancy. He was hoping for a healthy child, but also hoping that her fans would not forget her. One night in May, as the Thalbergs were dressing for dinner, Shearer studied her swelling profile in the bedroom mirror.

"You're in a spot," said Thalberg. "What are we going to do for you?"

"I think I'd like to do Juliet," answered Shearer nonchalantly.

Thalberg stared at her for a moment and then rewarded her with one of his rarely heard guffaws. When he stopped laughing, he saw that she was looking at him with a half-smile. Within a few days, a variorum edition of Shakespeare's *Romeo and Juliet* had traveled from his library to his bungalow, and the scent of vellum hung in the air. Thalberg was meanwhile preparing two more films, *China Seas* and *Mutiny on the Bounty*. Clark Gable was second only to Will Rogers in box-office pull, and Thalberg had waited the requisite time for him, so he put him in a sure-fire three-star project: Gable, Harlow, and Wallace Beery in *China Seas*. To direct, he hired Tay Garnett, who had directed a popular tropical film, *One Way Passage*. Rosalind Russell was determined that Thalberg hire her, too. "I had made tests for the part of the British widow Sybil Barclay," recalled Russell. "I began to enumerate, somewhat truculently, the reasons why I should have the part of Sybil. Thalberg listened quietly, attentively. Finally I finished. He didn't say anything. I waited and then I said: 'Well?' There was another pause, and then he said, quite casually and simply: 'You may play the part.' That was all. No fuss. No feathers. He had made up his mind."

China Seas began to shape up as a million-dollar project, and not just because of the combined salaries of its stars. The story called for vistas of a full-sized ship in a harbor, a typhoon in which a steamroller breaks its cables and careens around the deck, and a pirate raid. Garnett began shooting scenes with the principals, while units headed by William Wellman, James McKay, and Harold S. Bucquet worked on crowd scenes, storm scenes, and pirate scenes. Garnett enjoyed working with Gable and Harlow and was getting authentic performances from both. His only problem with Harlow was that she tended to get carried away by her emotional speeches; she would sway out of camera range when the camera was shooting over Gable's shoulder. Garnett solved the problem by having Gable put his arm out below the frame line to hold Harlow to her marks. She had no such problem with Beery. The unpleasant actor refused to feed her lines or have his back to the camera during over-the-shoulder shots; his stand-in performed these chores.

This was Thalberg's most ambitious production to date, and he broke precedent by becoming a presence on the set. "When we had some trouble with the script on the set of *China Seas*, he would come down to the set," said assistant director Joe Newman. "Many times he would rewrite the scenes himself, right there on the set. Sometimes he'd dictate the changes so you could write them down. Sometimes he'd do it himself with a pencil." Thalberg's kibitzing eventually posed a problem.

While directing a scene, Garnett was told by Gable: "This is really Jean's scene, so let's play it a little more to her. You know, give it to her." Garnett told Gable that it was his scene and he should be favored. "That's not the way Irving wants it done," said Gable.

"Irving is not the director," said Garnett.

Because of the unusual number of units shooting *China Seas*, Thalberg was having the editor assemble scenes to ensure matches in continuity. Garnett viewed several scenes and saw that, contrary to what Thalberg had told him, his choice of angles was not being used. "Mr. Thalberg ordered it that way," the editor admitted. Garnett returned to the set, where he met with more resistance from his actors. When he pressed them, they admitted that they had been coached by Thalberg.

Garnett chose a Sunday morning for a visit to Thalberg's home. At first Thalberg tried to put him off, citing family obligations. "There's nothing more important than this," said Garnett over the phone, implying that he was about to walk off the film. Thalberg agreed to see him. Once in the door, Garnett doffed his hat and said: "I've heard stories that you were a son of a bitch where directors were concerned."

Thalberg was speechless. "Irving, you've hired me as director," said Garnett. "You've given me the best stars in the business and spent a million dollars—and now you won't let me direct the picture. I didn't come to Metro to be a stooge. Not for you. Not for anybody!"

"Is that all?" asked Thalberg.

"No, that isn't all," answered Garnett. "You've countermanded my instructions about the cutting—in violation of our agreement."

"Well, yes," Thalberg nodded. "You're right. All right, Tay. What do you want to do?"

"I'll help you find another director."

"No, wait a minute. You're absolutely right. I have behaved like a son of a bitch. But I'll make a deal with you. Henceforth I'll come on the set only for social purposes. I think I'm within my rights to visit the company now and then for morale. But I promise you that I won't interfere in the playing of scenes. As to the cutting, I'll not only let you assemble scenes, I'll let you prepare the rough cut as well. And I'll make no changes in the film without consulting you."

Garnett cooled down and went back to his work, which proceeded without further incident until Gable insisted on shooting the runaway steamroller scene himself, even though his stunt double had been injured. It was risky, but M-G-M's most valuable star completed the shot—being dragged across the set by the steamroller—without being harmed.

Gable's confidence in Thalberg was tested when the producer proposed that he star in another British sea epic, *Mutiny on the Bounty*. "You've guided me right many times, Irving," said Gable, "but not this time. I can't do this. The public will never believe me as a first mate in the British Navy. I'd be more believable as the first mate of a scow on the Puget Sound." *Mutiny on the Bounty* was shaping up as an even bigger project than *China Seas*. Director Frank Lloyd had purchased the rights to the novel by Charles Nordhoff and James Norman Hall for an economical $12,500. Lloyd fully expected that Fox Film would star him as Captain Bligh, the martinet against whom Fletcher Christian mutinied in 1789. Fox was in no position to make the project; it was on the verge of collapse. Lloyd approached Thalberg, who agreed to let him direct if Charles Laughton played Bligh. Mayer caught wind of this and told Nick Schenck not to underwrite the project; no one would want to see a film without women in it. More important, a mutineer could not be the hero of an M-G-M film. "People are fascinated with cruelty," Thalberg told Schenck. "*Mutiny on the Bounty* will have appeal." Thalberg further assured Schenck that the mutineer would be sympathetic because Clark Gable was playing him. Gable would have none of it. "Look, Irving," said Gable, "I'm a realistic kind of actor. I've never played in a costume picture in my life. Now you want me to wear a pig-tail and velvet knee pants and shoes with silver buckles! The audience will laugh me off the screen. And I'll be damned if I'll shave off my mustache just because the British Navy didn't allow them. This mustache has been damned lucky for me!"

Thalberg was also getting resistance from the Marx Brothers; they chafed at his story conferences. "We had been in vaudeville too long to be impressed by this cathedral atmosphere," said Groucho, "so we deliberately behaved like the Katzenjammer Kids in Thalberg's office. He wasn't accustomed to rowdy famil-iarity from his hirelings." The turning point in their relationship occurred when Thalberg repeatedly absented himself from meetings. "We weren't fooled," said Groucho. "We knew he was walking out to attend some other story conference." It was a cool January afternoon. The brothers glanced at the fireplace and got an idea. Harpo went to the commissary and returned with potatoes. A quarter of an hour elapsed. Thalberg came back to his office. The first thing he noticed was the smoke. Then he stopped and stared. "We were all of us sitting in front of a roaring fire—naked," said Groucho, "and roasting mickeys over the flames. Irving never walked out on us again."

As soon as Kaufman and Ryskind finished the script for *A Night at the Opera*, Thalberg put two more writers on it. "Thalberg was not satisfied with a couple of scenes," recalled George Seaton. "Robert Pirosh and I were called in to do a little patchwork. The funny thing about this is that Bert Kalmar and Harry Ruby were in the next office working on the same scenes and none of us knew the other. Eventually we found out and all four of us worked together." In addition to the six writers who had already labored on the Marx script, Thalberg hired Al Boasberg, an ebullient gag writer who did most of his typing in the bathtub. The pages were dry, though. So was the humor.

"You can't sit in an office in Culver City and know what they're going to laugh at in St. Louis," said the chronically insecure Groucho. "When we were on Broadway, we'd try a show out on the road for weeks before we'd bring it to New York." Thalberg cited his practice of previews; Groucho was not convinced. "Why do you think *The Cocoanuts* and *Animal Crackers* were such hits? They'd been broken in on the road—live—in front of audiences."

"Why can't we do the same?" asked Thalberg.

"How can you try a picture out on the road?" Groucho snorted.

"You don't have to take the *picture* on the road, Groucho!"

On April 13 the three Marx Brothers opened in Salt Lake City with a five-scene digest of *A Night at the Opera*. Appearing with them was one of the film's romantic leads, Allan Jones. He found their offscreen antics equally memorable. "I was scared to death we were going to be run in by the cops in Salt Lake City," recalled Jones. "Harpo would see pretty girls coming toward us and he'd run and jump and wrap his legs around their waists, and kiss them." In most cases, fortunately, Harpo's victims were flattered by the star's attentions, and they helped him let off steam after the rigors of the tour. "We gave four shows a day for twenty-five days," said Harpo. "Played Salt Lake City, Seattle, Portland, San Francisco, Santa Barbara, the old Pantages route. We made notes on every show. When a line didn't get the laugh we expected, we changed it or threw it out. Kept experimenting all the way. It was tough work."

Thalberg and Shearer took Joe Schenck's yacht to Santa Barbara to catch the end of the tour. Groucho was watching Thalberg from the stage during his performance. Thalberg was not smiling. "I was the most nervous I've ever been in my life," recalled Groucho. "Facing Thalberg was worse than going up against all the New York critics." After the curtain came down, Thalberg and Shearer came backstage to see Groucho. "We're going to have a great picture," said Thalberg.

"But you didn't laugh once," Groucho frowned.

"Well, this isn't the first time I've seen it. In fact, I've been out there watching you for the past four days. I didn't tell you because I thought it would make you nervous."

Groucho was skeptical until he heard from Ryskind that Thalberg had been similarly stone-faced while reading pages of funny scenes. "I never got so much as a chuckle out of him," said Ryskind. "He just flipped through the pages. I sat there thinking my stuff couldn't be *that* bad. He kept turning pages and he didn't laugh once. But when he finished, he looked at me and said: 'Morrie, this must be some of the funniest stuff I've ever read.'" Thalberg admitted to Groucho over cards that he had truly enjoyed the Santa Barbara shows. "This was his first experience in live show business," said Groucho. "Here he was sitting in a theater, watching the people in his employ. He was impressed by this and having a wonderful time."

Writer Allen Rivkin had the opposite experience with Thalberg, who had seen *The Lives of a Bengal Lancer* and wanted a comic scene like the one in which Franchot Tone tries to hypnotize a cobra with an off-key reed flute. Rivkin contrived a running gag for *Mutiny on the Bounty*: Herbert Mundin dumps the ship's garbage against the wind instead of with it. "Thalberg said it wouldn't play," wrote Rivkin. "I thought it would and I said so. Thalberg leaned far over the desk and tapped the following out slowly: 'Listen, young man, when I say a gag won't play, it won't play. I, more than any single person in Hollywood, have my finger on the pulse of America. I know what people will do and what they won't." When a preview test proved that the scene would play, Thalberg admitted that he had been wrong and used it. The willingness to concede was rare among Hollywood executives.

In February Frank Lloyd took a camera crew to Tahiti to shoot backgrounds for *Mutiny on the Bounty*, but the crew forgot to dehydrate the film before returning. Footage of natives running onto a palm-lined beach was ruined. Thalberg sent the crew back to Tahiti. On July 25 a camera crew had finished filming the *Pandora* shipwreck scene near San Miguel Island, off the coast of Santa Barbara, when a sudden wind capsized the barge dressed as the ship. An assistant cameraman named Glenn Strong tried to save his camera, but lost the camera, $50,000 worth of equipment, and his life. Two more employees were endangered when the twenty-seven-foot *Bounty* miniature they were piloting became separated from the camera barge and tug in heavy seas, even though radio stations had been installed on the barge and the tug. "I never should have done it," said Thalberg. "Two more men may be drowned—just to get one damned shot." He hired a fleet of boats to search for the little *Bounty*. After two fearful days, the craft was found.

Thalberg had gotten nowhere with Gable, so he enlisted the aid of Mayer's trusted story consultant, the grandmotherly-looking Stanford alumna Kate

Corbaley. "She was a wonderfully kind, white-haired, brilliant woman," recalled Gable. "She knew I was giving Irving a bad time."

"Don't be such a mule!" Corbaley told Gable. "Listen." As was her custom, she told the story in colorful, persuasive terms.

"Clark," added Thalberg, "if you play this part, I promise you that I will never again ask you to play a part that you don't want."

"Okay," said Gable reluctantly. "Let's go."

Where he went was Santa Catalina Island. *Mutiny on the Bounty* was too large a production to be shot on any of M-G-M's three lots. Cohn arranged to have a Tahitian village, complete with palm trees, built on the eastern side of the Catalina Isthmus. Portsmouth Harbor scenes, complete with six sailing ships, were shot on the other side of the isthmus. A full-sized replica of the *Bounty* was created from original British Admiralty plans by refitting a nineteenth-century schooner. M-G-M purchased the *Lily* for $10,000 and spent $50,000 to have a Wilmington shipyard attach a new hull to her. She was rechristened HMS *Bounty* by British actress Elizabeth Allan on August 14, 1934. Outdoor scenes were shot on this vessel. "Most of the time we had to stand on the deck," reported Laughton, "and the only seats were guns, anchors, chain cables and suchlike restful things." Scenes below decks were shot in the isthmus village's town hall, which M-G-M converted to a temporary soundstage; a second replica of the *Bounty* had been cut up, brought on barges, and reassembled there. The entire company was housed in barracks and bungalows constructed for a seven-week stay. In a situation reminiscent of *Ben-Hur* and *The Trail of '98*, the company was far from Thalberg's watchful eye. But Albert Lewin was on the island, coproducing the film, and telephone service had been installed.

"I can't do this Bligh fellow," said Laughton in a late-night call to Thalberg. "I don't understand him at all."

Thalberg was sufficiently acquainted with Laughton to know that he went through this process on every film. It was a ritual of self-torture. For almost ten days, Thalberg patiently went through the script with Laughton. Then, on schedule, the terrors subsided. Laughton had taken possession of the character; or vice versa.

The next problem came from Lloyd. He decided that he could not work with Lewin. "This picture isn't big enough for the two of us," Lloyd informed Thalberg. "You'll have to choose between us."

"I'm sorry to hear you say that," said Thalberg. "It will hurt me to have to take you off."

This conflict was barely resolved when Gable started to lose his self-assurance. The company was shooting on deck, a straightforward two-shot in which Christian tells Bligh: "These men aren't King-and-country volunteers, you know. They're from press gangs." When Lloyd ended the shot, Gable strode over to him. "Laughton's treating me like an extra," said Gable. "He doesn't even look at me when he addresses me! The audience won't see me in the shot! Laughton hogged it!" Lloyd halted production and took the principals below for a conference. Actor Ian Wolfe, who was playing Bligh's clerk, Maggs, could hear Gable yelling: "He doesn't play to me! He ignores me!" Lloyd put a call through to Thalberg. The situation was at an impasse. Gable refused to continue. Thalberg had no choice but to go to the island. He chartered a seaplane and then needed someone to accompany him, so he took one of his writers.

Talbot Jennings was a playwright with one success to his credit when Thalberg brought him to Hollywood. In a year and a half, he had been hired to work on *Marie Antoinette* (which was shelved because of Shearer's pregnancy), been loaned to Goldwyn, and then written *Mutiny on the Bounty* with Carey Wilson and Jules Furthman. Working in the insular bungalow, Jennings had gotten to know these writers—and Thalberg—better than writers who had been with M-G-M for ten years. "Story meetings on *The Bounty* went on almost every day for two months in Thalberg's office with me, Al Lewin, Wilson, and Furthman," said Jennings. "They usually started late in the day and continued until eight or nine. Thalberg was accustomed to a shave in the evening. I usually went with him to the barber shop, presumably to talk about the *Bounty* script, but it was seldom mentioned."

> A script was written in five parts, or "sequences." With the working script in hand, Thalberg went over the story with us, sequence by sequence, scene by scene. He never remained sitting. He used to walk about the room. He began by saying what he thought the sequence should be about, what should happen in it, and how it should affect the following sequence. Then he listened to anyone who had something to say. An opinion could be stubborn but at length an agreement would be reached. These meetings continued and the writing went on until Thalberg was satisfied that the continuity had become a shooting script. "It's like a string of sausages," he would say about the assembled scenes. "Each one is good, but the meal isn't satisfying. I'm left hungry. I want a big, thick steak."

Thalberg's approach led to a major alteration of the *Bounty* story. In the book, the ship *Pandora* sails to Tahiti and captures some of the mutineers. Bligh is not aboard. Thalberg thought that putting Bligh on the *Pandora* would give the third act a lift. The sequence was historically inaccurate, but it worked.

When Jennings sat next to Thalberg in the seaplane, it dawned on him that in spite of the hours they had spent together, he did not know Thalberg. And after a few remarks about the plane, the bay, and the weather, Thalberg had nothing to say. He was incapable of small talk.

Jennings tried to get him to open up. He was not intimidated by Thalberg, who was almost thirty-six. Jennings was forty-one, a decorated veteran of five Great War battles, and an alumnus of both Harvard and Yale. "Why did you buy that stage production of *Pride and Prejudice* for Miss Shearer?" asked Jennings. "You could have the book for free."

"Publicity value," answered Thalberg. "Every paper in the country will run a squib. You're English, of course."

"I am not. I was born in Shoshone, Idaho."

"That's funny," said Thalberg. "We've been working together almost every day for—what?—six months? I thought you were English. Tell me. Do you play bridge?"

"Yes. But, well—"

"What?"

"I've heard about your bridge games with Connie Bennett and that gang. What do you play for?"

"Twenty-five cents a point," answered Thalberg.

"I'm afraid that's twenty-four cents too much for me," said Jennings.

On the island, Thalberg met with Franchot Tone in an effort to get an impartial account of the crisis. It sounded as if both Laughton and Gable were guilty—and not guilty. Thalberg called a meeting and laid down the law. No more grousing. No more questioning Lloyd's direction. No more upstaging. No more averted eyes. Interestingly, this encouraged Laughton to do something that Gable found even more unnerving. In scenes shot in the town hall stage, Laughton looked Gable up and down as if he were the proverbial juicy steak. According to Anita Loos, Thalberg liked this. "The rivalry between Bligh and Christian was so bitter," said Loos, "that it could only be based on mutual fascination."

Gable was convinced that his performance was bad, especially alongside Laughton's, so he tried to make friends with the peculiar Briton. After work one day, they dressed up in tuxedos and took a launch to the Hotel St. Catherine on Avalon Bay. They relaxed over drinks and the ice was broken. Gable was surprised to hear that Laughton was depressed. "When I have a part like Captain Bligh or

Father Barrett," explained Laughton, "I hate the man's guts so much that I overact. Parts like this make me physically sick." The next day, after a confrontation scene on deck, Laughton broke into a soft-shoe routine and began reciting Shakespeare. Later, in an introspective moment, he pointed to a solitary Mexican fisherman and said to Gable: "I wish I were that man."

Jennings and Thalberg were alone again, this time in a car creeping along a mountain road on Catalina. "You know Larry Stallings?" Thalberg asked.

"The chap who wrote *Plumes?* And *Big Parade?* No. We've never met."

"He keeps after me to pack my mother on a train and take a trip back East like we did with Vidor that time we wrote the war picture. He says there are some little inns in New England where we could rent a room and hide out for a bit. Just get away." Thalberg regarded the island vegetation, and then spotted an M-G-M company incongruously perched on a bluff, shooting a Crawford film. "Sometimes I think I'll quit all this—get out of it," he said softly.

This was the last thing that Jennings had expected Thalberg to say. "But what would you do if you did get out of it?" he asked him.

Thalberg was silent, then breathed in through his nose. "I don't know," he answered.

"What you do know is that you never will."

Thalberg looked out at the ocean and made no reply. They finished their ride in silence.

Back in Los Angeles, Thalberg had new concerns. To celebrate his thirty-sixth birthday, he drove Shearer to the Oasis Hotel in Palm Springs. She was in her ninth month of pregnancy. While they were relaxing there, her water broke. Worried that a "dry birth" would endanger both mother and child, Thalberg hurried her into the car and drove at high speeds through the desert, headed for the Wilshire-district office of Dr. Verne Mason. During the three-hour drive, Shearer was hit with waves of nausea and pain. Added to her discomfort was the worry that this crisis might put a strain on her husband's heart. His mother and sister joined them at Dr. Mason's office. The doctor exhibited an air of nonchalance, and Thalberg grew angry. His family tried to calm him, but he was genuinely upset. A week passed. Thalberg had a new will drawn up. A week later, on June 12, he signed it.

On the morning of June 14, Shearer entered Cedars of Lebanon Hospital in Hollywood. Thalberg was so nervous that Shearer secured promises from his secretaries and the hospital staff to keep any news from him, for fear that inaccurate reports might trigger a heart attack. Then she went into a difficult labor.

After leaving the hospital, Thalberg was driven to the studio by Harold Garrison, who was now his chauffeur. He arrived at 10 A.M. to find dozens of people waiting for him. He made last-minute changes to *A Night at the Opera*, which was going into production that day. He authorized two uncredited New York singers to record the *Miserere* from *Il Trovatore* for the finale, even though the film's romantic leads, Kitty Carlisle and Allan Jones, were both classically trained and had already recorded the duet. (This would cause Carlisle and Jones to go on strike when they heard voices other than their own emanating from the playback horns on the set.)

Thalberg then held a story conference with Frances Marion for *Riffraff*, the script that Gloria Swanson had turned down. Thalberg's secretaries kept him busier than usual, confirming his attendance at a golf tournament at the El Rancho course, a speech at the B'nai B'rith Grand Lodge, and a cinema fashion show at the Trocadero. David Selznick called to discuss backing for his own company.

"Have you raised your money?" Thalberg asked.

"Not a dollar," Selznick answered.

"Well," said Thalberg, "I think you're doing the right thing. Norma and I would feel very pleased if you would let us be your first stockholders. Let's think about two hundred thousand. But in her name only."

Thalberg went to lunch in his dining room at 2 P.M. but did not eat. "I don't want to touch it," he joked to Lewin. "Maybe Louis has put poison in it."

After lunch he met with a young man Frances Marion was sponsoring, David Lewis. He had produced a number of films at RKO, but had quit. Marion and her children liked the attractive, ambitious young man, so she offered to introduce him to Thalberg, whom he knew only by reputation. "In an industry with a limited ambition to achieve real quality," Lewis recalled, "[Thalberg] stood out like a beacon." This was Lewis's second meeting with him. The first, six months earlier, had not gone well. Lewis had proposed a film about Gilbert and Sullivan that would use their songs to advance a story about their friendship.

"It sounds interesting," Thalberg had said. "Personally I know little about it, but I'll have it researched and get back to you." He had not. Lewis's pitch had been confident, perhaps overconfident. "That's an arrogant young man!" he had told Marion. "You and I are simple people. We have position in the industry. We've done a lot of things in pictures but we're not arrogant!" Marion prevailed upon Thalberg to give Lewis a second chance; this was it.

"I want to bring in a couple of young new associate producers," said Thalberg, leaning on a gold-tipped cane. "I've looked at a couple of your films. For what they are, they're pretty good." Lewis's last film at RKO, *Where Sinners Meet*, was the kind of literary adaptation that Thalberg liked. "I've decided to hire you." When Thalberg learned that Lewis had been paid $400 a week at RKO, he said: "I'll give you two hundred." Lewis took a quick breath. "Look," said Thalberg, "whenever I bring new people in, I cut their salary in half. I do at least half of their work for them. So I'll give you two hundred. I'm going to contribute so much to your education that you can pull in your belt a bit."

"Impossible," said Lewis.

Thalberg paused, looking Lewis in the eye. Lewis did not flinch. "All right. I'll give you two fifty, but if you ask me for a raise any time in the next two years, I'll fire you."

The rest of Thalberg's day was taken up with calls around the country in search of Chinese translators, French antiques, and opera experts because George S. Kaufman was doing "piece work" on—simultaneously—*The Good Earth*, *Marie Antoinette*, and *A Night at the Opera*. "Don't be surprised," Kaufman told Groucho Marx, "if you find yourself guillotined for not planting rice in China." Marx was surprised that Kaufman had stayed in Hollywood longer than his announced three weeks.

Thalberg next called publicist Ralph Wheelwright to confirm the San Bernardino preview of *China Seas*. By the time Wheelwright called back, Thalberg was eating his customary dinner—corn flakes. "We're going to San Berdoo with *China Seas* tomorrow," said Thalberg. "Don't tell anyone."

"We've got to call Harrison Carroll," said Wheelwright, referring to the aggressive columnist who would make trouble if not invited to the preview. Thalberg reluctantly agreed, as long as Carroll would delay the item for a few weeks. At 7:45 P.M. the laboratory called to say that dailies from *Mutiny on the Bounty* were ready to be looked at. Thalberg was preparing to walk to his screening room when the phone rang. The obstetrician was calling. Mrs. Thalberg had given birth to a girl. Thalberg paged Slickem and canceled the screening.

Seeing his newborn daughter had a profound effect on Thalberg. As recently as his last birthday he had been heard to say, "I'm getting old." He did not explain if he meant that he was surprised to have lived so long or that his time was running out. Whatever he meant, he did not sound happy. The birth of a second child changed that. His new refrain was "I want to see my children grow up." He was thinking of his legacy, of the continuity of his name, of his father's name.

What he and Norma chose to forget, unfortunately, was his mother's name. They named their daughter Katharine, after Katharine Cornell. A chill immediately descended on the elder Thalbergs' home. Sam Marx received a card from Shearer: "Father and child . . . doing well." Marx looked at Lewin and said gravely: "Henrietta has finally lost her hold on Irving." They both knew it was true. The silver cord had been severed.

Thalberg brought his son to the hospital to meet his new sister. The family gathering was interrupted by the arrival of a nervous Wheelwright. He reported that he had changed the *China Seas* preview to the next day, as Thalberg had asked, but he was still having trouble with Carroll. The columnist insisted on writing about the sneak preview in Sunday's edition of the *Los Angeles Evening Herald Express.*

"You're telling me this because you want me to call Harrison Carroll and kiss his ass?" asked Thalberg.

"Well, yes, sir," answered Wheelwright.

"Tell Harrison Carroll to go fuck himself."

The *China Seas* preview was an unmitigated wow. When Gable and Beery emerged from the theater, they were mobbed by an unruly crowd. Police moved in and stopped youths from ripping off Gable's clothes. As he was hustled into Thalberg's limousine, a child yelled at him, "You wrestled with a steam roller in there but you need the cops to help you out here!" Carroll printed the snide item, but Thalberg made him delay it for a month, and it did no harm to the steamroller of publicity that the film was generating. *China Seas* had been in production for fifty-three days and cost $1.1 million. It opened at the Capitol Theatre on Friday, August 9, 1935. By Monday morning, 53,181 tickets had been sold, breaking the house record held by Selznick's *David Copperfield. Mutiny on the Bounty* and *A Night at the Opera* both opened in early November. By the end of 1935, it was clear that Thalberg had made three of the biggest, most talked about, and most profitable films of the year.

PART SIX · THE CROWN PRINCE
OF HOLLYWOOD

Irving Thalberg and Norma Shearer resumed their social routine in late 1935. The term "brunch" had been coined only a few years earlier but was already popular in the mansions along Santa Monica Beach. Thalberg's schedule no longer required him to visit the studio on Sundays (much to the relief of his wife and mother), so he was able to enjoy brunch by his pool. When Sam Goldwyn or his next-door neighbor Douglas Fairbanks came to call, conversations did involve movies. When brunch was over and these friends had left, Thalberg would sit quietly under the striped awning at the back of the house, studying a script. "He just *lived* movies," said Howard Hawks. "Even his leisure time was given to them." While Thalberg read, Shearer swam in the pool with Irving Jr. Thalberg catered to his son but did not spoil him. When Irving Jr. asked for the model of the HMS *Bounty* that he saw in his father's bungalow, Irving Sr. told him he had to earn it by proving that he could swim across the pool. Irving Jr. did it.

When sea breezes kicked up in the afternoon, Thalberg moved indoors. The interior of his home was whisper-quiet. He had found the noise of the surf distracting when he and Shearer had first rented in Santa Monica, so he specified that their home be built with soundproof double-paned windows. Theirs was also the first beachfront home to have central air conditioning, a precaution against dampness. Thanks to such strictures, Thalberg's health remained stable. Albert Lewin complained that producing *The Bounty* was giving him palpitations and pains. Thalberg was not impressed. "Hell, I get those all the time," he laughed.

Goldwyn often complained of stomach problems, but his wife, Frances, was attentive to Thalberg, even to the extent of watching the veins on his temples.

Although Thalberg was no longer producing ten films and supervising forty others, his workload was no less heavy. A new literary agent, H. N. Swanson, wanted Thalberg to read a novel by his client Richard Sherman. Swanson thought *To Mary, with Love* would make a perfect Myrna Loy vehicle. Swanson was so eager that he bypassed Mayer, hand-carrying the galleys to the "thin, white-faced young man who was crouched behind a huge desk in an enormous office." Thalberg promised to read the novel over the weekend. On Monday Swanson received a summons from Mayer. "You did a terrible thing to Irving Thalberg," said Mayer. "He's not a well man. He sat up all night reading your book when he should have been in bed." Mayer began weeping. Swanson was incredulous and asked what he could do. "Just don't let it happen again," sniffed Mayer. The novel went to Darryl F. Zanuck.

At the gala premiere of Warner Bros.' *A Midsummer Night's Dream*, Mayer saw Shearer and Thalberg rushed by frenzied fans. Shearer calmly raised her arms. The fans stopped. "Thank you," said Shearer loudly, "but I'm afraid someone might be hurt. Won't you please step back?" The fans slowly complied. Mayer turned to Eddie Mannix and indicated Thalberg. "How can he live like this?" The question was disingenuous, coming from the executive who was known as "Trocadero Louis," but it was true that the Thalbergs were seldom at home in the evening. Thalberg accepted almost every filmland invitation because socializing greased the wheels of commerce. There were parties thrown by Charles Boyer, the Basil Rathbones, Grace Moore and Valentin Parera, Countess Dorothy DiFrasso, Kay Francis, and Joe Schenck. When Marion Davies and W. R. Hearst "forgot" to invite the Thalbergs to a big party at the beach house, Shearer's new friend Merle Oberon approached Davies, who agreed to have a talk with Shearer. Fences were mended and invitations were sent.

Thalberg had been living in the film capital for sixteen years. In that time, scores of small studios had given way to eight major studios. These majors had survived the talkies, the Crash, and the Production Code. Then, in April 1935, the Fox Film Corporation found itself sagging under its own weight, its grand plant imperiled by a bankrupt theater chain and mutton-headed managers. Casting about for a savior, Winfield Sheehan encountered the brash Nebraskan Darryl Zanuck, the only other studio boss who was not Jewish. On May 29, 1935, Zanuck's tiny Twentieth Century Pictures, which had been releasing through United Artists, pulled away from UA and merged with Fox to create a new "major," Twentieth Century–Fox.

Of significance to Thalberg was the company's financing: Mayer had underwritten the merger primarily to give a job to William Goetz—his daughter Edith's husband. No one was fooled into thinking that anyone but the savvy Zanuck (and Joe Schenck) would be running Twentieth.

The next change in the Hollywood landscape took place against Mayer's wishes. In October, David Selznick had sufficient capital ($3.1 million) to open Selznick International Pictures in a white colonial façade on Washington Boulevard, just a few blocks from M-G-M. Mayer was officially supportive of this son-in-law; in private, he said otherwise. In fact, he had tried to use Selznick's gambling debts as leverage to keep him at M-G-M, offering him a $1 million partnership. When Selznick refused it, Mayer railed at his daughter. "Don't be a fool, Irene!" he yelled at her in her home. "With Irving's health the way it is, Dave might have to step into his shoes." The Selznicks united to reject the notion.

"You'll fail!" Mayer told Selznick. "You'll fail!"

"I'm thirty-two," Selznick answered. "I can afford to fail."

Eddie Mannix suggested to Mayer that Selznick's departure gave him the opportunity to reinstate Thalberg as production head. Mayer would have none of it. "You think because Dave's gone I can't run my studio alone?" he blustered. "Let me tell you, Eddie, they love me here. Stars! Directors! Producers! I hear it every day!"

The one mogul who was truly loved by his employees (in part because so many were related to him) was Carl Laemmle. Thalberg had long forgotten the ill feeling that caused his departure from Universal and he now watched with interest as Laemmle's son, Carl Jr., tried to emulate Metro with ambitious projects such as *Magnificent Obsession* and *Show Boat*. While Thalberg's flops could be absorbed by M-G-M's hits, Junior Laemmle's could not be cushioned by Universal's modest income, and the company sank into a million-dollar hole. Laemmle put "The Big U" on the market for $9 million but found no takers. He chugged into 1936 with a $750,000 loan from Wall Street's Standard Capital Corporation. Laemmle was not unduly worried about Standard's ninety-day option to purchase Universal for $5.5 million.

On February 27, Thalberg was a guest speaker at Laemmle's thirtieth anniversary party. On March 15, a newspaper headline read "Carl Laemmle Out as Owner of Universal." By the time Thalberg acted as toastmaster for Laemmle's farewell dinner (on April 22), the "New Universal" was owned by a combine that included Eastman Kodak, J. Arthur Rank, Electrical Research Products, Inc. (ERPI), and Standard Capital. Thalberg's sentimental speech portrayed "Uncle Carl" as a high-principled businessman who "never stole a star, director or player from another company," at least while Thalberg had worked for him.

The success of Thalberg's production unit had not improved relations with Mayer. Their infrequent meetings revealed an undercurrent of hostility. What Mayer could not express to Thalberg he directed at Thalberg's colleagues. "How's your little communist friend?" Mayer asked Thalberg, referring to Albert Lewin, who was at worst a Democrat.

"Al's not a communist, Louis," smiled Thalberg. "He's got a hundred thousand in the bank." On another occasion, Thalberg came to Mayer's office with his new producer David Lewis in an attempt at cordiality. Mayer stepped between Thalberg and Lewis and closed the door in Lewis's face. Thalberg dropped his arms to his sides and faced Mayer. "Either he stays or I go," said Thalberg. Mayer backed down, but the visit was strained and pointless.

Thalberg did not expect the mood at the studio to improve. He began to make formal plans for the I. G. Thalberg Corporation. His existing contract would not expire until December 31, 1938, but he saw no reason not to prepare. In 1953 Bosley Crowther viewed documents confirming that in mid-1935 Thalberg took "legal steps to have his own company in January, 1939. He would release his films through Loew's, Inc., but otherwise he would be entirely separate from any association with Mayer. By the terms of his arrangement the contracts of several stars, including Norma Shearer and the Marx Brothers, would be assigned to his company, 'together with the contracts of any other artists, supervisors, directors, and writers who might be engaged' by Thalberg for work in his producing unit under his present contract."

Thalberg told David Lewis that he was included in the new company and would own a share of 7½ percent. "It was to be the first real production company financed by a major studio, yet totally independent," Lewis wrote in 1979. "It was really a fabulous contract for that time, and no one else in the industry could have commanded it. No one." Also included in the pioneering venture was Frances Marion. Since she was leaving for Europe, there was no time to draw up a formal contract. Thalberg composed an informal contract with his fountain pen, stipulating that she would "write, produce and direct as requested by Irving G. Thalberg," thus making her the first female auteur in 1930s Hollywood.

Predictably, when Mayer caught wind of Thalberg's plans, he roared like the Aesop's Fables lion that had a thorn stuck in his paw. No one sympathized with him, so he tried to block Thalberg from acquiring talent. When Mayer could not do this, he reverted to type and burst into Thalberg's bungalow, yelling. Thalberg was visiting with Lenore Coffee. He looked up at the red-faced Mayer and then said calmly to Coffee: "Would you mind leaving the room while I put Mr. Mayer in his place?"

Confrontations between Mayer and Thalberg began to occur on a regular basis. "I'm in a running battle with Louis," Thalberg told Jack Conway, "but I'm going to beat him." Both Thalberg's wife and his mother began to fret about his health. Before Shearer could appeal to Nick Schenck, help came from an unexpected quarter. Thalberg enjoyed a mutually respectful friendship with Sam Goldwyn. "Irving would come to see me once a week," recalled Goldwyn. Thalberg customarily attended previews at Goldwyn's studio on Santa Monica Boulevard in Hollywood. "Often Irving would come to our home for dinner after a preview to talk with Sam about ways to improve the picture," recalled Frances Goldwyn. "Irving had that same love and excitement for pictures that Selznick had," said Goldwyn. "You cannot succeed in this business unless you have that excitement." The only time that Thalberg was less than excited was when watching *Nana*, the much-publicized debut of Goldwyn's Russian discovery, Anna Sten. When Goldwyn asked Thalberg what he thought of the actress, Thalberg said: "Words fail me."

Goldwyn had a bitter history with Mayer. They had been feuding since 1914, when Mayer had shorted Goldwyn his rental fee on *The Squaw Man;* the breaking point came when Goldwyn obstructed the merger. Mayer was known to spread his arms and proclaim: "I love everybody!" Then his expression would darken. "Except Charles Chaplin, John Gilbert—and Sam Goldwyn." It was nothing short of amazing, then, when M-G-M employees saw Goldwyn's limousine come through the Washington Boulevard gates. A few minutes later, Mayer's secretary nervously ushered Goldwyn into Mayer's office. "It's like Mussolini's!" said Goldwyn to an unsmiling Mayer after a long stroll from the door. Then he came to the point. "I'm here to see you about Irving. I don't think you'll ever develop another talent like him. I think you have to ease up. Be a little more careful with him, a little more considerate. He is a sensitive boy—and he isn't at all strong."

Goldwyn was mildly surprised when Mayer agreed that Thalberg should be treated with respect and went so far as to promise Goldwyn that henceforth he would not interfere with Thalberg's plans. "Sam, you are a very brilliant fellow," said Mayer as Goldwyn started to leave. "What you did was kind and thoughtful. Why is it that people don't like you?"

"Louis," said Goldwyn in midstride, "if you knew what people here thought of you, you wouldn't come to work tomorrow."

The first week of 1936 saw Mayer in Panama and the Thalbergs at the La Quinta Resort in the Coachella Valley. Hollywood was still mourning the death of Thelma Todd in December when another star suffered an untimely end. On January 9, John Gilbert died of a heart attack. He was thirty-eight. Gilbert was arguably Thalberg's first star and the first to be a friend. Gilbert had been off the screen since making a minor Columbia film in 1934. His work with Garbo in *Queen Christina* had not resulted in a comeback; Mayer had removed his name from publicity and trapped him in a dead-end contract. Marlene Dietrich had tried to restore Gilbert's health, but she could not slow his tragic demise.

"Don't let them bury me like they did Thelma," Gilbert had told Cedric Gibbons, referring to Todd's tastelessly public funeral. "Don't let anyone see me after I'm dead." Gibbons arranged for a closed casket, one of the few dignified aspects of the services. Twenty-five policemen stood guard outside the mortuary to prevent any unseemly demonstration; that took place inside. Dietrich staggered down the aisle dressed in widow's weeds, passing two of Gilbert's ex-wives, Leatrice Joy and Virginia Bruce. "She behaves like she's his widow," Bruce whispered to Shearer as Dietrich sank to the chapel floor. Laurence Stallings, who had helped craft *The Big Parade* for Gilbert, eulogized him. "Jack was the perfect actor for our *Big Parade*," Stallings said. "He was feline, like a tomcat on an alley fence."

After the funeral, Leatrice Joy led her daughter, nine-year-old Leatrice Gilbert, to their car. A slim, dark figure startled them by running up from behind. It was Thalberg. "You know, Leatrice," said Thalberg, "Jack was on the verge of a real comeback. He had a contract waiting to be signed, but I honestly don't believe he wanted it any more." Fifty years later, Leatrice Gilbert Fountain was still trying to make some sense of Thalberg's statement and the "odd look" in his eyes. "Several people told me much later," wrote Fountain, "that Thalberg was tormented by his failure to stand up against Mayer for the man who had been his close friend." If Thalberg had hoped to sign Gilbert for the I. G. Thalberg Corporation, this was the only time anyone heard about it. A week later, he arranged for young Leatrice to see *The Big Parade* at the studio her father had helped create. The film was a sad reminder of the enthusiasm he had shown in 1924—and of the fragility of a film career. Marx, Lewin, and Conway remembered Thalberg's slump after Paul Bern's death and they watched him carefully. Though he had been a pallbearer at Gilbert's funeral, he showed no signs of depression. He had no time to dwell on the past. He was being confronted by the future.

In the years since Universal and the merger, Thalberg had seen his power challenged twice. Once the challenge came from outside, when William Fox tried to make him an employee. Then it came from his partners, when their hunger for power unseated him. Both times he had adapted and survived, even coming out ahead. These challenges were clear-cut compared to the ones he faced in 1936. Some involved governments and others involved employees. He found the intramural challenges harder to understand. He was sitting atop a pyramid of labor. This was the natural order of things. It was unnatural for the slaves who built the pyramid to question his right to order their work, their income, or their lives. Just as he brainstormed to make a scene work for an audience, he strategized to make politics work for him.

In 1934 Thalberg purchased *The Forty Days of Musa Dagh*, the best-selling Franz Werfel novel about an outpost of Armenians who resisted a siege by Turkish forces and survived the genocide of 1915. Thalberg conceived of the property as a vehicle for William Powell and Clark Gable. He was ignorant of the incident's resonance. Even twenty years after the massacre, the Turkish government wanted no reminder of it. A film about it would open old wounds and retard the government's efforts at democratic reform. As soon as the script reached the PCA, an alarm sounded. "While the Turkish market does not amount to much financially," warned Hays Office foreign liaison Frederick Herron, "our French [and French-colonial] market is a very important one." Without consulting Thalberg, J. Robert Rubin gave a copy of the script to the Turkish ambassador Mehmet Münir Ertegün. As might be expected, the Turks issued a warning. "We've run into some trouble with *Musa Dagh*," Thalberg informed director Rouben Mamoulian. "The Turkish government says if we make it, they will ban all M-G-M pictures from their country."

"That means?" asked Mamoulian, whose qualifications to direct *Musa Dagh* included several bona fide masterpieces—and Armenian blood.

"It means I'm going to make the picture anyway," said Thalberg. "There are thirty theaters in the entire country. To hell with the Turks." Thalberg assigned Frances Marion to work with Mamoulian on the script.

In September 1935 Will Hays received an ominous letter from Wallace Murray, the State Department head of Near Eastern Affairs. France might join the Turkish boycott. The 1934 Catholic boycott had been serious; to lose France—and all French territories—could be disastrous. Thalberg was at the Loew's office when Hays served notice on M-G-M. All that remained was for Thalberg to convey the news. "I'm afraid I'll have to postpone *Musa Dagh*," he told Mamoulian and Marion. "The Turks got the French to ban all M-G-M pictures. They may even go so far as to ban all movies from Hollywood."

Thalberg's next scuffle was over Mildred Cram's *Forever,* a novel he purchased for Shearer. Breen told him unequivocally that he could not film the novel; the story turned on an illicit romance, even though a fatal auto accident allowed the lovers to be united "forever." Thalberg appealed to Mayer, saying, "*Forever* can be the greatest prestige picture we ever made."

"When a producer tells me he has a prestige picture," Mayer answered, "I know we're going to lose money." *Forever* was not filmed.

Mayer got a taste of his own tartness when he bought *It Can't Happen Here,* Sinclair Lewis's number-one best seller. The controversial book told the story of a demagogue named Berzelius Windrip who becomes president by whipping the American people into a frenzy of fear, racism, and anti-Semitism. Once in power, he uses martial law to reinstate slavery and subjugate the country to a military-industrial complex. Lewis's novel could be a box-office blockbuster if directed by Vidor or Hawks, but Mayer assigned it to the B-picture team of producer Lucien Hubbard and director J. Walter Ruben. More encouraging were the casting of Walter Connolly as Windrip and the assignment of playwright Sidney Howard as screenwriter. Since working with Thalberg in 1930, Howard had won a Pulitzer Prize on Broadway; his script got no bouquets from Breen. In a solemn letter to Mayer, Breen warned that even though Howard had eliminated feminism, sex perversion, and adultery from the story, it was still "so inflammatory in nature, and so filled with dangerous material, that only the greatest possible care will save it from being rejected on all sides." Once again, M-G-M's foreign liaisons took an informal poll. Every fascist government promised to boycott *all* Hollywood films if *It Can't Happen Here* was made. Domestic movie attendance was estimated at 93 million weekly. Foreign countries accounted for another 41 million. M-G-M could offend no one, not even fascists.

On February 16, 1936, after consulting with Hays, Mayer contacted Sinclair Lewis and informed him that the film would not be made. Lewis issued a statement. "Is the American public," asked Lewis, "to be delivered over to a film industry whose every step must be governed by whether or not the film will please or displease some foreign power? I wrote that it can't happen here, but I am beginning to think that it most certainly can." Thalberg was no less perturbed at Mayer. "We've lost our guts," he told Sam Marx. "When that happens to a studio, you can kiss it goodbye!"

Losing the studio, or at least control of it, was on Thalberg's mind in early 1936. *Riffraff,* Thalberg's second Jean Harlow film, had just been released, and for once, her physique was not the hot topic. "*Riffraff* was so right wing, so anti-union, that

I was astonished," wrote David Lewis. Frances Marion had written the original story, but Thalberg had John Lee Mahin add a political subplot to a cannery row romance. Tay Garnett felt that Harlow would be ill-used. "You're making a terrible mistake to put Harlow in this," he said. "You're destroying a star."

"How?" asked Thalberg.

"Harlow is the most famous courtesan in the world. People know her as a lovable tramp. Now you're trying to put her in the role of a Madonna."

"I'm not destroying a star," Thalberg said. "I'm giving her a new dimension." Garnett refused to concede the point. Thalberg was not used to resistance. He became stern. "If you play on my team," he said, "you've got to play *with* the team."

"Look," said Garnett. "I'll put my shoulder to the wheel if I think there's gold in them thar hills. But I'm not going to dig holes in the backyard."

"Then I guess this is the end of the line."

Insubordination was one of the themes of *Riffraff,* although it was couched in terms of labor versus management. Thalberg would accept healthy debate, but he would not hear demands. As much as he knew what was right for a script, he knew what was best for his employees. They were well compensated, and if some were not, that was neither his fault nor his problem. The boy socialist had become a producer prince. He had a principality to protect. "We live in a paradise," said Thalberg indignantly. "Everyone has a good life, and it's going to be destroyed by organized labor." Hence he turned the union organizers in *Riffraff* into Communists.

The studio elite who worked in the Thalberg bungalow were increasingly aware of the Boss's leanings, which were far to the right of the average Hollywood worker. As accommodating and genteel as Thalberg could be in his dealings with assistant film editors, African American chauffeurs, and other lower-echelon employees, he was increasingly regarded as Hollywood royalty. Courtesy and favors were dispensed as noblesse oblige, not as tokens of appreciation. Some who labored for him were appropriately grateful. "I remember the feeling that was prevalent at M-G-M—carpenters, laborers, secretaries, script clerks, or whomever," recalled Goldie Appleby, his executive secretary. "We felt we were a cut above the other studios because M-G-M had Irving Thalberg. I worked very hard when I worked for Mr. Thalberg. There was something about him that kept you on your toes. He was never sharp with anyone. If we made mistakes, we felt worse about it than he did." Lawrence Weingarten was a part of Thalberg's family and a part of M-G-M. "It was a big family," said Weingarten in 1974. "If we had a success, everybody—every carpenter, every plasterer—was excited about it, was abuzz, was in a tizzy about the whole idea of picture making. This was the esprit de corps that was there." This was Mayer's concept of the corporation as family. To a great extent, Thalberg subscribed to it. It never occurred to them that their "children" might feel deprived.

"Irving Thalberg considered actors to be charming, vital, and beautiful children," wrote Bob Thomas in 1968 after interviewing more than sixty Thalberg colleagues. "Like children, they were to be enjoyed and admired for their ingenuous qualities and tolerated when their behavior seemed abnormal. . . . They were to be forgiven their tantrums, their erratic behavior as long as they caused no unreasonable interruption of the making of movies, which was Thalberg's all-consuming occupation." It was rare when an actor had either the intellect or the nerve to confront Thalberg as an adult.

Brian Aherne was under personal contract to Thalberg to make two films a year for two years. After making *What Every Woman Knows,* the thirty-three-year-old star of numerous London and New York stage hits found himself idle for eight months. He met with Thalberg to see what could be done. Thalberg suggested abrogating his contract and replacing it with a standard long-term contract so that he could play Charles Darnay in Selznick's *A Tale of Two Cities.* Aherne said he would think about it, and then fired off a letter.

> I am not a young man, anxious to get a break in pictures, Irving. I am a very successful actor whose position in the theatre is at least as promising as that of any actor today. . . . Do you seriously suppose that I would be willing at this stage to throw up a fine career to become a stock player in the M-G-M picture factory? .
>
> You have a fine reputation in this industry and your company undoubtedly does the best pictures. Beyond this you have a persuasive tongue and you convey the impression of integrity. A series of long talks began to plant in me the conviction that you were genuinely interested in me and were both anxious and able to handle my career in pictures. . . .
>
> Well, it is eight months since my last picture and you have done *literally* nothing for me. When Mr. Hyman suggested *Strauss* for me, I asked my agent to ask your opinion. He replied that you had not even heard of it. When Mr. Selznick suggested the wretched Charles Darnay, you, my "handler," knew nothing of it, and, when you did, thought it was a good part and I ought to do it. I should construe these things as due to the complete end of your interest in me if it were not for your talk of yesterday. As it is, I am both bewildered and disappointed.

Thalberg immediately responded to Aherne's letter, reminding him that he had been warned that his contract—which would allow him time off to do plays—would entail long periods during which Thalberg would try to find the right role for him but during which Thalberg would also be prevented from grooming him for stardom.

You state—and quite rightly—your experience and standing, and it perhaps permits me to point out my own experience and standing. For a great many years my position has been the handling of artists of world-wide renown, some of whom were very important before they came to me, and others of whom were quite unknown but all of whom over a period of a great many years have felt that the efforts I have made in their behalf have been productive of good results. In every instance, with every one of these people, they have signed long term contracts and permitted the usual relationship of producer and artist to exist. During the time that I was in active control of the entire studio, I look back with considerable satisfaction on the care and discrimination with which these people were handled. Their tremendous earning power and great popularity testify to this. Since I have reduced my activities to my unit, the people I have signed have accepted contracts similar to the ones made in the past with the exception of demanding my exclusive supervision. . . .

You finally worked out with Mr. Rubin in New York a contract for a very short period with the restriction that you could at any time refuse to play a role. That restriction made it impossible for me as an individual producer to work with these restrictions; no unit such as my own could afford to put the time and effort into the making of a picture . . . wherein the artist (after three or four additional pictures) would be completely free to go where he chooses. It was only because of my great respect for you as an artist that I urged the company to accept a contract of this kind, which I assure you is the only one of such a nature that we have. . . .

If it is not yet clear to you that the making of pictures is a career just as honorable, just as exciting, and a good deal more profitable than the stage, I hope for your own sake that you will soon come to this conclusion. You have been on the stage for a great many years, yet to my knowledge you have had only two really exciting roles, the lead in the *Barretts* and Mercutio in *Romeo and Juliet*. . . . I have the utmost confidence that you have in you that spark of personality that makes for public acceptance of a player and that I can guide your career to success as I have others. In that way, matters are not left to chance but to a definite plan of campaign which assures me, if I am right, of a future gain, even if at the moment immediate returns appear diminished. There is no use of either of us pretending that the arrangement we now have in any way contemplates this.

I am afraid you will find it a rather useless and quixotic task to attempt to gain for yourself concessions that practically everyone in the picture business has neither wanted nor needed. Sometimes in the gaining of these concessions much more is lost than established. . . . In my many years of experience with artists of importance, they have had a great deal more success in the roles that they objected to than in the roles that they desired. This may be only a coincidence, but I am afraid a close scrutiny would reveal that it was not.

Aherne served out his contract with one Joan Crawford film and several loan-outs. The intelligence and charm that had made him a stage star failed to make him a film star. Thalberg may not have been able to do better for him, but he did not like having his judgment questioned, no matter how well reasoned and articulate the question. After twelve years of running the most successful company in America's sixth-largest industry, he carried himself with the authority of an autocrat. A student of history, he had filmed *Rasputin and the Empress* and was about to film *Marie Antoinette*. It was no wonder that he saw the conflict between labor and management as a prelude to revolution.

The salary cuts of March 1933 had never been reimbursed. Employees who were accustomed to working six days a week in rotating shifts, often for as long as four-teen hours a day, were stung by the indifference that greeted their requests for full compensation. They began to feel that their hard-won positions were not terribly secure and that they were doing a lot of backbreaking work with few guarantees, little protection, and no rights. This feeling led to the Hollywood labor movement. First came a Screen Writers Guild (the SWG), then a Screen Actors Guild, and finally a Screen Directors Guild, all in defiance of the Academy of Motion Picture Arts and Sciences, which was in essence a company-controlled union. By early 1936 the SWG's nine hundred members included top-notch writers such as James Cain, Dashiel Hammett, Lillian Hellman, Nunnally Johnson, John Howard Lawson, Dudley Nichols, Laurence Stallings, Donald Ogden Stewart, Anita Loos, Bess Meredyth, and Frances Marion. "Anita, Bess, and I drew into these meetings other writers who had long-term contracts like ours," wrote Marion, "and they felt as we did toward the newcomers who had been fighting for credits on movies to which they had contributed, and for protection against being dismissed without cause. The contracts given to these potential scenarists abounded in clauses, and many of them had been let go before they had had an opportunity to prove their worth."

SWG grievances were many, and they included practices that Thalberg held dear: writers were lent from studio to studio without consent; writers were made to write on speculation; writers were suspended or laid off without written notice; writers were arbitrarily denied screen credit, regardless of their contribution; writers were made to work simultaneously on the same material without being informed of this by the producer; and writers who complained about any of these practices were blacklisted.* At one point, director George Cukor appealed to Thalberg to remove a talented artist from an intercompany blacklist. "There is no such thing as an industry blacklist," Thalberg said firmly. Then he paused and gave Cukor his famously enigmatic smile. "But I'll see to it that your young friend is taken off it."

A *Los Angeles Times* article, "Authors by Hundreds Meet Tragic Defeat in Films," described the plight of the average screenwriter. "One recent estimate placed the number of working Hollywood writers at 150, out of a possible 1000. . . . The studios' standards for hiring are 'What was his last film credit?' and 'The hottest credits get the job.'"

"M-G-M was a strange place for a new writer in those days," recalled Catherine Turney. "Thalberg was genuinely interested in getting new writers into the studio. But there was an entrenched group of writers there. And his policy kept the new writer from getting a fair share of the credits. The older writers would be put onto a script after you'd done most of the work—broken the back of the story. This tried-and-true writer would put the finishing touches on the thing, and then he or she would end up getting the main credit."

On the third floor of Thalberg's bungalow, Don Stewart and Salka Viertel were working on a screenplay for Greta Garbo about Napoleon's mistress, Marie Walewska. This meant that Stewart was doing the writing and Viertel was getting a credit in exchange for acting as a liaison to the elusive Garbo. Viertel, whose Santa Monica living room was a salon for every talented refugee from Hitler's Germany, was well aware of the SWG, but Thalberg still had to make his point during a February story conference. "These writers are living like kings," he declared. "Why on earth would they want to join a union, like coal miners or plumbers?" Viertel was fortunate to have Stewart in the room that day.

"Salka joined forces with me against Napoleon Thalberg," wrote Stewart. "This was a drawn battle in which Irving disclosed that in his Brooklyn high

*For a comprehensive history of the Screen Writers Guild, see Schwarz, *The Hollywood Writers' Wars*.

school days he had been a member of the Young Peoples' Socialist League and had made ardent street-corner speeches."

"What has a man of your talent and energy to fear from socialism?" asked Viertel. "With your organizational ability, your obsession for work, you would always be the head of production, making better and more artistic films, and you wouldn't have to worry about financing."

Thalberg took a deep breath and listed the demands of a typical day. "Rushes—story conferences—consultations with directors, the music department, set builders and costumers—telephone calls to China about the locust sequence in *The Good Earth*, talks with Paris to secure Charles Boyer for Napoleon. Now, children! All this I should do for five hundred dollars a week?" His punch line gave Viertel and Stewart a laugh, but Thalberg wanted the last word. When the meeting adjourned, Stewart caught Thalberg looking at him "with the sad, reproachful eyes of a betrayed parent."

The SWG situation escalated in early March when its leaders called for a boycott of the Academy Awards because they did not reflect the political makeup of the industry. The ceremony took place on March 5 at the Biltmore Hotel. SWG pickets lined the Fifth Street entrance. "Bea and I went to the banquet, crossed the picket line, and sat at Irving's table," wrote Stewart. "But I didn't sit there happily in my white tie and tails." Still dependent on "good old alcohol," Stewart drank too much and tried to show Thalberg that he was his own man by making jokes during the ceremony. He had to shut up, though, when Thalberg's *Mutiny on the Bounty* won the Best Picture award. And he kept quiet when it was announced that Dudley Nichols was refusing the award he had won for writing *The Informer*.

Faced with this defiance, Thalberg began to mobilize. He called Marion into his office and accused her of subscribing to communism. "That's nonsense," said Marion. "We're not flying a red banner. We're only asking help for a lot of helpless people."

"I thought you were my friend," said Thalberg, fixing Marion with a cold stare.

"I am your friend, Irving."

"Then promise me that you'll stop this agitation."

Marion left without promising anything. On March 9 the SWG board voted to stop signing contracts until the guild meeting on the evening of May 2, when the entire membership would vote whether to join with the Authors League and the Dramatists Guild in New York. The goal was to impose an embargo on contracts and literary sales until the major studios met their demands. The studios were being "asked" to refrain from, among other things, credit snatching and blacklisting. The ultimate goal, of course, was a guild shop and a minimum basic agreement. Thalberg was outraged by the potential of such an alliance—it could block him indefinitely from buying *any* book or play.

Donald Ogden Stewart was increasingly involved in the Hollywood Anti-Nazi League and related activities, some of which were openly Communist. One that was not was a well-publicized theatrical event on March 29, a staged reading by Fredric March and his wife, Florence Eldridge, of Irwin Shaw's antiwar play *Bury the Dead*. Stewart was preparing a speech for it when Sam Marx came to his cubicle in the writers' building. "How's the Napoleon script coming, Don? Now don't think anyone's pressing you. Irving's very pleased with what you've done. By the way, he wants to know if you and Mrs. Stewart can come to dinner Thursday."

"Mrs. Stewart's in Florida," said Stewart. "And, damn it, Thursday's no good this week."

"That's the night of that meeting, isn't it?" asked Marx. He was clearly ill at ease, but he continued. "Look, Don, Irving's been a very good friend of yours . . . and, well, he'll be hurt if you make a speech there."

The speech turned out to be more hurtful than Thalberg had expected. It made a snide reference to the centerpiece of M-G-M's three-hour production *The Great Ziegfeld*. "Let us," cried Stewart, "let us have no more million-dollar revolving staircases, no more star-filled symposiums of billion-dollar entertainment. Let us have some simple truths, as we have had tonight, some simple truths on a bare stage, against nothing but a plain background." The next time Stewart mounted an event, Thalberg attended. On April 28 the Stewarts hosted a $100-a-plate dinner to benefit the Anti-Nazi League. The guests of honor were the German Catholic prince Hubertus von und zu Loewenstein, who had escaped from the Gestapo after publishing an anti-Hitler newspaper, and Rudolph Breda, the refugee author of *The Brown Book of Germany*, an exposé of Nazi methods. Also in attendance were Sam and Frances Goldwyn, Mary Pickford, Norma Shearer, David and Irene Selznick, Walter Wanger, and John J. Cantwell, Archbishop of Los Angeles, who, when he realized that Herr Breda was a Communist, unceremoniously rose from the banquet table and departed. Given a choice between communism and fascism, many Americans—including Thalberg—would prefer the latter. After dinner, Thalberg sat down with the prince.

"When a dictator dies, his system dies, too," Thalberg told Loewenstein, "but if communism is allowed to spread, it will be harder to root out. What is at stake is our whole way of life, our freedom. They will have vanished forever."

Loewenstein reminded Thalberg that he had risked his life to criticize Hitler's tactics and had almost been captured by the Gestapo. And he was not even a Jew. "Mr. Thalberg, your own people are being systematically hunted down and rooted out of Germany." Thalberg nodded politely but maintained that the Jewish race would survive Hitler.

As May 2 approached, Thalberg confronted the sedition in his own principality, inviting comparisons with Machiavelli. Robert Montgomery bore a grudge against Thalberg for denying him a vacation between *No More Ladies* and *Mutiny on the Bounty*. Thalberg had then used his refusal to work as an excuse to take his role in *Bounty* away from him and give it to Franchot Tone. "Thalberg, not Mayer, was the toughest and most ruthless man in the industry," said Montgomery in 1953. "He was nothing of the dreamer. He was money-mad. He was a shrewd, tough, hard, cold operator, with a complete ruthlessness towards people."

In an April 30 *Los Angeles Times* article, Thalberg asked the Hollywood community of writers: "Why do you want to turn over your independence to a group of men who have continuously expressed nothing but contempt for you as artists and to whose dictation the producers would never and could never submit? Are there any principles at stake, in view of the fine consideration and generous salaries you have been receiving for years, that justify precipitating this business into strikes and confusion and disruption? This is a controversy that must be ended now. Otherwise writers, producers, and all others in the industry will have to pay a very heavy price."

Thalberg's methods included calling in favors from the conservatives to whom he had given coveted assignments. One was John Lee Mahin. SWG member John Bright had tried to convince Mahin to go on strike for a higher salary. Mahin was drunk, but obdurate. "Thalberg will take care of me," he kept repeating. Not until later did Bright understand the significance of this mantra. Other Thalberg loyalists (and hard-drinking Irish Catholics) included Howard Emmett Rogers and Patterson McNutt. Their leader was Thalberg's favorite story constructionist, James Kevin McGuinness, who was earning $1,500 a week but wanted to become a producer. He and his cohorts went from office to office, trying to persuade SWG members to abandon their agenda. "McGuinness was a very sharp, very personable guy," recalled Marx Brothers screenwriter Nat Perrin. "But he was a very dangerous man. They're the most dangerous—the genial, likable, smiling ones." McGuinness would sidle up to a young, impressionable writer and say with no little persuasiveness: "In this world, some people ride and some people walk. I'm gonna be one of the guys who rides. How about you?" Concurrent with this door-to-door technique was a gradual insinuation into the upper ranks of the guild. "It was hard to relate the charming, relaxed McGuinness to the fellow caught up in this extracurricular witch hunt," said Perrin, "but his was an extremely conservative, reactionary position. If it hadn't been for him and his crew when the writers' struggle began, unionism and communism would never have merged in producers' minds."

Even a hint of Communist influence in the SWG was enough to provoke Thalberg. He called a meeting of studio heads at the Beverly Hills Hotel on Friday, May 1. The three-hour convocation was less a round robin than a dictation of strategy. He instructed each studio head to call an emergency meeting the following day. At the meeting, the chief was to tell his writing staff in no uncertain terms that the SWG must not merge with the East Coast guilds. Jack Warner was mildly irritated because he would have to cut his Saturday-morning polo game short, but someone had to tell his writers what a soft job they had.

On the morning of May 2, Thalberg sent word to the writers' building, and the writers dutifully crowded into his private screening room, hoping to exchange views with the man they considered the most enlightened of the studio bosses. When Thalberg entered, he was not accompanied by David Lewis or "Professor" Lewin. An unsmiling Eddie Mannix walked in step with him, giving the impression of a body guard or a bouncer (which was how Mannix had entered show business). "I liked Thalberg very much," said Maurice Rapf, who was twenty-two at the time. "He was always nice to me. But the idea that he was a sweet, sensitive character was dispelled in five seconds when he came in with Mannix, the hard guy."

Thalberg began to speak, and he did not mince words. He was not going to acknowledge the Guild or its demands. He, and not any outside agency, had spent twelve years building the best writing staff in the world, had paid them handsomely, kept them on salary between assignments, treated them with loyalty and consideration, and given them a livelihood year after year. Now the same writers were contemplating action that would harm not only themselves but also thousands of studio employees with families to support.

"If you wish to put all these people out of work, they are your responsibility, as are the stockholders, some of whom are widows and orphans. Understand this. We will never allow a merger of the Screen Writers Guild and the Authors League. If you are foolhardy enough to proceed with this strike, I shall close down the entire plant, without a single exception." Any writer present who expected a discussion was quickly disabused of that notion by Thalberg's tone. "You've all gotten a great deal out of this industry. It's been good to you. What you are proposing is to turn it over to outside interests. You know who we mean, and we are not going to tolerate it. We want to be certain that you know what our stand, the studio's stand, is, and how we are going to feel about anybody who goes along with us, and how we are going to feel about those who don't. We have a lot to protect here, and we are going to protect it with everything we have." As he said "we," it was obvious that he was acting with the full support of Louis B. Mayer but that he felt personally affronted. The room was silent as Thalberg started to walk out. Then he stopped, turned, and said quietly: "Make no mistake. I mean precisely what I say. I shall close this studio, lock the gates, and there will be an end to Metro-Goldwyn-Mayer productions. And it will be you—the writers—who will have done it."

The SWG meeting took place that night. The outcome was described as a "love fest" between McGuinness and his crew and guild moderates. There was a unanimous vote to uphold the "principle of affiliation" until producers and writers would have the opportunity to negotiate a minimum basic agreement. The McGuinness contingent was elected to the board, and some radicals resigned in protest, presaging what would happen a few days later: a flurry of resignations, followed by a mass defection. On May 9 the decimated Screen Writers Guild was eclipsed by a new organization, the Screen Playwrights Guild (SP). Its president, not surprisingly, was John Lee Mahin. As it became obvious that the SP was a company union, totally beholden to the producers, his mantra was fulfilled: Thalberg had taken care of him. What Thalberg could not take care of was the lasting animosity between SWG diehards and SP reactionaries.

McGuinness's unsubtle recruitment spiel alienated as many writers as it seduced. For a while, the 156 Screen Playwrights got the plum assignments, sat at the better tables in the commissary, and sneered at SWG members. "At Metro," said Perrin, "the SP had the tables where conservatives like McGuinness and Mahin, Sam Marx, and occasionally actors like Tracy and Gable ate. The SWG had its one little table, a staunch island in the middle of a hostile sea." Thalberg may have wondered if the cure was worse than the disease. Under his control or not, the SP was still a union, and it was not about to go away. "Now what the hell is this?" he asked Mahin.

"The Federal Labor Relations Act is going to pass, so we do have a right to do this. Face it, Irving. You're going to have to recognize writers sooner or later, so you might as well recognize us—and not the SWG. You'll get in trouble with that bunch of communists." Thalberg signed with the Screen Playwrights, but before the summer was out, he was forced to troubleshoot. He heard that SP members were needling SWG members as they passed by the "elite" tables. "You still in the SWG?" came the taunt. "You better get out of that commie organization or you won't be here long!" Thalberg called two of the SWG victims to his office. George Seaton and Robert Pirosh, whom he had used on *A Night at the Opera* and was using on *A Day at the Races*, assumed the worst. "Better stock up on paper clips," Seaton said to Pirosh. "This is it."

"I understand you two are staying with the SWG," said Thalberg from behind his desk. "Why?"

"Because we don't believe in company unions and we do believe in the aims of the Guild."

"Well, I disagree with you about that," said Thalberg, shifting in his chair. "I understand you're being harassed in the commissary. If anybody tries to threaten you, to tell you your job is in danger, you come and tell me. You're entitled to your opinions." Thalberg rose, reached across his desk, and shook each writer's hand. "God bless you both," he said. Seaton and Pirosh were puzzled. So was David Lewis when Thalberg defended him against Edwin Loeb, the attorney who had originally brought Thalberg to Mayer. "Do you know you have a Democratic snake in your office, Irving?"

"Who might that be, Eddie?"

Loeb rudely pointed at Lewis. Thalberg frowned at Loeb and said: "He's entitled to his own opinions."

"Everybody had made Thalberg out a villain," said Seaton, but by the end of the summer, a number of reconciliations took place in the bungalow, including one with Frances Marion. Thalberg appeared to be heading in a different direction. McGuinness thought so. Whether Thalberg was fed up with McGuinness's scare tactics or just thought he was out of his league, McGuinness found himself demoted—and was loudly unhappy about it.

"Dick Maibaum and I had an office next to Jim McGuinness in a one-story building near the Motor Avenue gate at M-G-M," related Rapf. "Late one afternoon we heard muffled sounds of yelling from McGuinness's office. By putting my ear to a drinking glass pressed to the wall, it was possible to make out what the ruckus was about. He was plastered and was railing against Thalberg to Harry Edington, who was his agent."

"That son of a bitch!" came McGuinness's voice through the wall. "That dirty son of a bitch! He's got to learn that loyalty is not a one-way street!"

"Well, after all, Jim, you still have a great job," said Edington.

"I'll show that Jew bastard that loyalty is not a one-way street!"

"Now watch that, Jim," said Edington, who happened to be Jewish.

"God damn it, loyalty is not a one-way street!" came the drunken refrain.

Rapf and Maibaum finally deduced that Thalberg had decided against letting McGuinness produce *Maytime*; they laughed. "Still," said Rapf, "it was evident, whether Thalberg delivered or not, that the people who had led the union split had received contracts and promises as their part of the deal." Word came back to Thalberg that McGuinness was very upset, so Lewis was given the job of speaking to him. "Do the best you can," smiled Thalberg. "If he beats you up, I'll pay your expenses." Lewis returned unscathed, but except for some occasional work, McGuinness's career was over.

The union intrigue led to an incident unique to Thalberg's employees. One of Sam Marx's assistants took it upon himself to spy on a member of the SWG leadership. "I had this man trailed," the assistant story editor reported to Thalberg. "He was seen entering Paramount. I even have copies of the script he submitted to Manny Cohen." The assistant smugly dropped the manila envelope on Thalberg's desk. Thalberg seized the envelope and ripped right through it.

"I won't have it!" Thalberg shouted at his employee. "Any man who does this again will be fired! And I mean you!"

None of Thalberg's colleagues had ever seen him lose his temper. They were surprised, too, that he was more angry at the self-appointed spy than at the writer who was selling material out the back door. Neither employee was fired. The producer prince was both autocratic and enlightened.

Irving Thalberg was not one to do things by half measures. His successes of 1935 were big, complicated productions. Consequently, his 1936 projects would be bigger and more complicated. Their settings would include Renaissance Verona, Napoleon's Waterloo, and China's revolution. With Thalberg, of course, setting was secondary to story, and story to character. When there was a problem with a finished film, it was usually because his writers had been unable to resolve character. Tay Garnett refused *Riffraff* because he felt the heroine could never be reconciled with the actress who was playing her. "A lot of people thought Jean Harlow was way beyond her depth playing a dramatic part," wrote David Lewis. His housemate, director James Whale, had been Harlow's dialogue coach on *Hell's Angels* and could not believe that Paul Bern or George Cukor had improved her to that extent.

Riffraff was Lewis's first producing assignment for Thalberg. He expected Thalberg to keep a close watch, but Thalberg had politics, the Marx Brothers, and a Catalina mutiny; he did not visit the *Riffraff* set or look at rushes. *Riffraff* was directed by J. Walter Ruben without spawning a single backstage tale. Jean Harlow was a consummate professional, whether in satins on a soundstage or in cannery duds on a San Pedro pier. "She was always there on time, always prepared, always ready to work," wrote Lewis, who became friends with Harlow during the shooting. Harlow knew that Lewis was homosexual. "Often, in the evenings, Jean would telephone me at home and ask me to come and take a walk with her," he wrote. "She felt comfortable with me." Lewis would drive the six miles from Pacific Palisades to Beverly Glen to spend a platonic evening with the celebrity whom most American men thought the ultimate sex symbol. "Contrary to all the talk of the tough dame," wrote Lewis, "she spoke like the perfect lady. Her speech was good, her voice cultured and well modulated. She read a great deal, strange to report, and was intelligent about what she read." In the three years since Paul Bern's death, Harlow had been married (to cameraman Hal Rosson) and divorced, and was involved with the emotionally unavailable William Powell; she needed a confidant. "On these walks," said Lewis, "she told me of an unhappy childhood, of a frighteningly ambitious mother who was grooming Jean at any cost to become a picture star. . . . This woman was a fiend. She went through everything that Jean earned, giving much of it to Jean's stepfather [Marino Bello]. Although she was obviously being victimized, Jean never complained. I don't think she ever stood up for herself. She was struggling just to keep herself alive." Harlow's mother sensed Lewis's mistrust. "I found her mother cold and somewhat hostile," he remembered. Jeanette MacDonald was Harlow's next-door neighbor in the new M-G-M dressing-room building. "Harlow always played such sluts on the screen," said MacDonald. "At heart she was really a naïve, nice girl who was being exploited—and wanted just to be somebody's wife. She was a very unhappy young girl."

As in the case of many a film actor, inner conflict enhanced a performance, and Harlow's newfound depth saved *Riffraff*'s preview from being a disaster. It was held at the Golden Gate Theater, a Spanish Revival movie palace in East Los Angeles. Thalberg no longer traveled to previews on a special trolley; he made the fifteen-mile trip in a car caravan. With him on this occasion were his secretary Goldie Appleby, film editor Frank Sullivan, publicist Eddie Lawrence, Douglas Shearer, Lewis, Ruben, and various assistants. Sullivan's assistant brought the "work print," the separate picture and sound reels that would be run in "interlock" on twin projectors in the Golden Gate's specially equipped projection booth. The first cut of *Riffraff* had been accomplished in a three-day editing marathon.

"Because the assistant editor was so rushed," recalled Goldie Appleby Arthur in 1967, "he took a chance and left for the preview without numbering the separate picture and sound film edges. In the middle of the second reel, the film broke and the house went dark. We all waited a few minutes, and then the picture started again. But since they couldn't line it up exactly with those non-existent numbers on the edge, they could only guess. The picture was now ahead of the track." The audience laughed when Harlow's voice came out of Mickey Rooney. "So, the house went dark again," recalled Arthur. "In a few minutes, the film came on again. This time the track was ahead of the picture. Dark. Another try. This time it was worse than before." Lawrence glanced over at Thalberg. "He was out of his seat like a shot," recalled Lawrence. Doug followed him to the projection booth, where Sullivan was frantically trying to line up the two reels. Lewis remained in the roped-off section, sweating.

"The audience went outside to smoke," Lewis recalled, "but fortunately they all seemed to return. Just before the film broke, something had happened with Harlow that caught them." With his audience hooked, Thalberg dimmed the lights again. "There were two more tries," recalled Arthur. "Worse! Mr. Thalberg sent word to put the third reel on. More waiting. The house lights came on. People walked into the lobby for another smoke, but no one left. Then came the awful news that the sound track for the third reel was nowhere to be found. It was back in the cutting room at the studio."

Thalberg had no choice but to finish the preview with twenty minutes missing. "At the end of the film," wrote Lewis, "there was an ovation. But I don't think Thalberg was fooled." Outside the theater, Thalberg walked up to Sullivan, who was beside himself with distress. "Forget it, Frank," said Thalberg, patting him on the shoulder. "Go home and get some sleep." There was reason to be sanguine. In spite of everything, Harlow had touched the audience in a sensitive moment before the film broke. Thalberg believed that moments like this were the most important element of a film. In subsequent previews, Thalberg would indicate to Lewis that a scene was building in Harlow's favor and then going in the wrong direction. "It needs something," he would say softly. "It needs something . . . *here*." Lewis and the editor would take notes.

"Occasionally Thalberg would write a memo," recalled Lewis, "but he was not at his best with the written word. Sometimes he would even try to write a scene. But while the idea was generally excellent, the delivery was invariably disastrous. He wanted to be a writer more than anything in the world, but he just didn't have the flair for writing, and he was too stubborn to admit it. But the way his mind moved and the depth of his character understanding was magnificent." Albert Lewin saw a rare self-consciousness in Thalberg. "Irving always wanted me to correct the speeches he gave at luncheons and civic affairs," said Lewin. "He would give them to me and wait for me to comment. He was more widely read than some college professors I knew, but like many people with little formal education, he overestimated the value of higher education."

A few trims were made on *Riffraff;* Thalberg did not authorize retakes. This was highly unusual, but no one questioned him. "He felt that he had gotten the maximum," wrote Lewis. "To go further would be sheer vanity." The film opened to mixed reviews, not because of Harlow's acting but because of her new hair color. Her trademark platinum blonde had been replaced by a "brownette" wig, and people were undecided about it. Perhaps Garnett was right, but the "toning down" of Harlow was not Thalberg's idea; it had been imposed on M-G-M by the Production Code Administration. Audiences were also thrown by *Riffraff*'s anti-union stance. The film lost $60,000, the only instance of a Harlow film losing money for Metro. It was not a catastrophic loss, though, and for the most part, Thalberg was pleased. He made no particular comment to Lewis about his first project, but began to include him in story conferences on others.

One was the story of Napoleon and his Polish mistress, Marie Walewska, a project intended for Charles Boyer and Greta Garbo. Salka Viertel was helping Donald Ogden Stewart write it, but needed PCA approval. "Thalberg wanted me to tell the story to the censors," wrote Viertel. "We met in the Thalberg bungalow, and when I was halfway through, the two gentlemen began shaking their heads. There was not only an illegitimate child in it but also double adultery. Adultery was nothing new to the Breen Office. They had condoned it in other films. They also agreed that Thalberg had never offended 'good taste.' However, they would not okay a story with double adultery."

"Then I'll go ahead without your okay," said Thalberg. "This is a great love story and I am determined to produce it." The censors looked at each other, whispered a bit, and then made a decision.

"Only because it is you, Irving, we'll say go ahead—with this script," said the censors. "But that does not mean we will say yes to the picture."

As soon as Thalberg had cleared this hurdle, he lost both writers. "Donald Ogden Stewart was brilliant and delightfully amusing," wrote Viertel, "but he had a deep dislike for Napoleon and wriggled out of the assignment." Then Viertel begged Thalberg to let her go to Europe to see her husband. He passed the buck to Eddie Mannix, who, at Garbo's urging, let Viertel go. Thalberg replaced her with S. N. Behrman, who had written most of *Queen Christina* and *Anna Karenina*.

In addition to these projects, Thalberg had been announced as producing *Romeo and Juliet*, *Quo Vadis*, *Knights of the Round Table*, *The Prisoner of Zenda*, and *Goodbye, Mr. Chips*. None of these had gotten past the ditch-digging stage except *Romeo and Juliet*, which was in production from November 1935 through May 1936. Two projects had been developed and then delayed: *Marie Antoinette* and *San Francisco*. Anita Loos had come back to the Thalberg stable in order to support her erstwhile husband, John Emerson. Her regrettable practice was to write a script and then share credit with him so that his ego would not suffer. Thalberg would shake his head at her and then say, "Well, Anita, you shouldn't, but I understand." While the aging roué was blowing Loos's salary on gambling and prostitutes, she would be in the writers' building, matching wits with Robert ("Hoppy") Hopkins, M-G-M's famed "gag man." Both had lived in San Francisco, and both disdained Los Angeles.

"One day in 1935," wrote Loos, "when the two of us were pacing M-G-M's broad main alley, voicing our nostalgia for San Francisco, it crossed our minds to make its romantic charm the subject of a movie. It wasn't necessary to search for a character who might symbolize the spirit of our city." Wilson Mizner had been a gambler in San Francisco's bawdy Barbary Coast before the 1906 earthquake and fire. Hopkins had worked as a Western Union messenger and grown to idolize the dashing Mizner. Thirty years later, Hopkins had a brainstorm that he had to share with Thalberg. "Got a marvelous idea, Irving," said Hopkins, pointing a finger across Thalberg's desk. "Now listen: San Francisco. Gable. A rake. A pal that's a priest. A sweet young gal that's between them. Betrayal! Earthquake! Fire! Repentance! Get it? Get it? What? Grace Moore? Irving! Nobody will stand for that. Who in the hell do you think you are? It's for Jeanette MacDonald!"

Loos cringed at her friend's breach of etiquette, but the poker-faced Thalberg ignored it. He was used to Hopkins and made frequent use of his talent for one-liners. This was the first time Hopkins had come up with a concept. "Go ahead," Thalberg said to Loos and Hopkins. "Put something down on paper. We'll know if it's worth filming." A few weeks later, he reviewed their step outline. It was called simply *San Francisco*. "It's beginning to look like a natural for Clark Gable," he smiled, and then made arrangements to speak with Jeanette MacDonald. After the mixed success of *The Merry Widow*, Mayer had assigned her to Hunt Stromberg, who took a chance and teamed her with the unknown Nelson Eddy in *Naughty Marietta*. It was such a hit that Thalberg now had to wait for her to finish another Stromberg project, *Rose Marie*, before he could get her for *San Francisco*. The prospect of teaming her with Gable was exciting, both for her and for Thalberg. Unfortunately, when she was free to work with Gable, he was making *China Seas* back to back with *Mutiny on the Bounty*. Now MacDonald had to wait, which meant being taken off salary. "I'll wait," she told Thalberg. "I'll forfeit the pay. Just let it go, and I'll sit it out. Yes, I want Gable that badly." In the meantime, Thalberg got a *San Francisco* script from Herman J. Mankiewicz, but decided to let Loos bring the story to completion. By the time she did, her husband was clamoring to be credited as associate producer. This was where Thalberg drew the line. He would not give credit to the goldbricking Emerson, so he signed off on *San Francisco*. Bernie Hyman took over and used the script that Thalberg had prepared.

San Francisco was not the only blue-chip project that Thalberg declined in 1936. In mid-May, Albert Lewin came into Thalberg's office burdened with a fifty-page synopsis. "You've got to read this," said Lewin. "It's long, but it's great. The whole thing is surefire, laid out like a three-act play, and the main character is made to order for Gable." The synopsis was of a forthcoming Civil War novel called *Gone with the Wind*. Thalberg reminded Lewin that the Civil War films *Operator 13* and *So Red the Rose* had flopped. But Lewin had pulled strings with New York agents to get the synopsis, so Thalberg agreed to read it. A week later, David Selznick received galleys of *Gone with the Wind*. He was at first put off by the book's scale, but later found himself thinking about the characters. Word came through the grapevine that M-G-M might buy it. "I understand there is no executive there who has any particular interest in it," Selznick wrote an associate in late May, "but Thalberg is liable to take a gamble on it without reading it."

Lewin knew that interest was building. "Have you read the synopsis?" he asked Thalberg.

"Yes."

"And what did you think?"

"You're absolutely right," said Thalberg. "It's sensational. It will make a terrific picture, with a great role for Gable. Now get out of here with it." Lewin was puzzled. Why would his boss want to pass up a property like this? "Look," explained Thalberg. "I've just been to Verona and China. Now you want me to burn Atlanta. No, Al. It's out of the question. No more epics for me now. Just give me a little drawing-room piece. I'm tired. I'm just too tired."

Although he had acquired a streak of gray in his hair, Thalberg was not an éminence grise, but he was treated as one whenever an interstudio crisis arose. The competition for *Gone with the Wind* had grown so fierce that he was asked to arbitrate. A meeting was held in his office. Thalberg declared M-G-M out of the running; that left Selznick and Warners free to bid. "Thalberg was smiling like hell because Metro didn't get it," recalled Darryl Zanuck.

Thalberg was also asked to play King Solomon during Mary Astor's child custody trial. Her husband, Dr. Franklyn Thorpe, had named George S. Kaufman as co-respondent and purportedly had Astor's diary to prove it. Kaufman was with the Thalbergs on Joseph Schenck's yacht in early August. When he went ashore, a process server intercepted him. A few days later, Thalberg was asked to join Harry Cohn, Jack Warner, Jesse Lasky, and the Bank of America's A. H. Giannini in Sam Goldwyn's office. Speaking for the industry, Thalberg asked Astor and her lawyers to settle out of court so that her husband could not have her diary entered as evidence. Astor refused, but the diary turned out to be a hoax and was thrown out. Astor finished *Dodsworth* for Goldwyn; both she and the industry survived the scandal.

On another occasion in the spring of 1936, Thalberg was invited to Louis B. Mayer's office to hear songs being composed by Cole Porter for the John Considine production *Born to Dance*. Porter was the darling of Broadway and high society, but the thought of performing before Thalberg unnerved him. "After a stiff whisky and soda," wrote Porter, "and my arms full of books containing the lyrics in the order in which they come in the picture, I left for the studio."

All of the personnel involved with the film, including Eleanor Powell and Virginia Bruce, were seated expectantly in Mayer's office. But Porter was not given the signal to begin. "Suddenly the door opened," Porter wrote, "and in crept Thalberg, looking more dead than alive, and obviously angry at being disturbed to hear this score. I passed out the lyric books and began. By the time 'Rollin' Home' was over, I realized that the atmosphere was friendly. When I finished 'Hey, Babe, Hey!' there was wild applause, and L.B. began jumping around the room whispering to people. I attacked 'The Entrance of Lucy James' next, and it was during this that Thalberg suddenly became a different person and began smiling." When Porter reached the end of his concert, he was surprised. "Thalberg leaped out of his seat, rushed over to me, grabbed my hand and said, 'I want to congratulate you for a magnificent job. I think it's one of the finest scores I have ever heard.'" Porter could not have known that Thalberg had no ear for music and was most likely gauging the response around him. He admitted to Sam Marx that he had approved "Alone" for *A Night at the Opera* because he recognized it as "the kind of thing that Norma likes to hum."

Goodbye, Mr. Chips was an unusual subject for the self-educated Thalberg. The best seller by British novelist James Hilton tells the story of Mr. Charles Chipping, a colorless middle-aged teacher in an elite boys' school who finds personality and purpose through an inspiring wife. When she dies in childbirth, Chipping must find the strength to carry on without her. He fulfills his promise as "Mr. Chips," a beloved mentor to generations of schoolboys. The project looked uncomplicated, set primarily in a Cambridge-like school. "Thalberg did not think *Chips* would be an expensive picture," wrote Lewis, "but he did think it would be a very, very important picture." Thalberg told Lewis that he would not be supervising the production in Culver City. "I'm going to do something I've never done before," Thalberg said. "I'll make the picture in England with Charles Laughton. But I won't be in England with you. I'll be on the continent taking a vacation. You'll be in full charge. If you have any trouble or need me or need my backing in any way, I'll be available to you. My trips in Europe are short and I'll have none of the pressure of the studio. My only interest will be in *Goodbye, Mr. Chips*."

Thalberg began by dictating suggestions on how to set up the story. "Quite a bit of the first part of the story is taken up with mentions of various names and places which will be very vague to American audiences," Thalberg said. "We should eliminate the names of the other schools so that we will be conscious of only one name: Brookfield. And we must establish that 'Chips' is the biggest name in Brookfield's history." Thalberg was also mindful of the need to make his bookish hero a totally sympathetic character. "The story we should tell in our script," said Thalberg, "is that of a man who started his career as a failure and was bound to mediocrity. He never improved until he met a woman who gave him a viewpoint that turned his mediocrity into success."

To preserve the book's British flavor, Thalberg took Lewis's suggestion and hired R. C. Sherriff, the playwright of *Journey's End* and screenwriter of *The Invisible Man*. (Hilton was working at M-G-M but not interested in adapting his novel.) Thalberg granted Sherriff the surprising liberty of writing in England; the result was felicitous. "Thalberg was enchanted with the script," wrote Lewis. "He was not used to such a perfect job being done on a first writing." Thalberg was also open to Lewis's suggestion that the British James Whale should direct *Mr. Chips*. This may have raised some eyebrows in the Thalberg bungalow, since it was generally known that Lewis and Whale were living together as lovers. Thalberg was indifferent to gossip and eager to work with the director of *The Bride of Frankenstein*. He offered Universal's most valuable director a term contract for two films at $75,000 each, but with no time limit. This gave Whale pause; he knew Thalberg could take months to complete even a one-setting film like *China Seas*. Thalberg was willing to negotiate with Whale both on this and on the screen credit "A James Whale Production," but the management of the new Universal was unwilling to let Whale go.

These projects, slated for 1937 and 1938, held Thalberg's attention only when he had time to step away from his 1936 films: *Romeo and Juliet*, *The Good Earth*, *Camille*, *Maytime*, and *A Day at the Races*. That two large productions should originate from one unit was remarkable, but that all of them should come from

Thalberg was nothing short of astounding. *Romeo and Juliet* was a big project, and *The Good Earth* was bigger. Preproduction had already occasioned a trip to China, a Theatre Guild version starring Alla Nazimova, and a great deal of corporate resistance. "Irving, the public won't buy pictures about American farmers," said Mayer. "And you want to give them *Chinese* farmers?"

"The *Good Earth* isn't about farming," Thalberg countered. "It's the story of how a man marries a woman he has never seen before and how they live a life of intense loyalty. The public will be interested in such devotion."

Ironically, the husband and wife who had been with the project since its 1932 inception were no longer involved with it—or together. George Hill had committed suicide in August 1934, and Frances Marion had dropped out in November 1934. Thalberg had turned the project over to a tag team of writers—Jules Furthman, Marian Ainslee, Talbot Jennings, Tess Slesinger, *Porgy and Bess* librettist DuBose Heyward, and *Green Pastures* playwright Marc Connelly—but told them to work from the Owen Davis–Donald Davis play, not from Pearl Buck's novel. When Victor Fleming returned from a safari in October 1935, Thalberg assigned him to direct *The Good Earth* and Albert Lewin to associate-produce. Lewin and Jennings led Fleming to an office where the efforts of eleven writers were stacked knee-deep. "Throw 'em all out," said Fleming. "We'll start over—and we'll work from the book, not the play." In so doing, Fleming shifted the emphasis of the story from the stoic wife, O-Lan, to the impetuous husband, Wang Lung. Thalberg felt that *The Good Earth* would fail if it did not appeal to women. When Fleming was hospitalized with a kidney ailment, Thalberg removed him from the project.

Thalberg had at first toyed with the idea of an all-Chinese cast, but felt that starring Anna May Wong, who was not an actress of stature, was impractical. He decided to use Caucasian actors for the leads. He was warned that no one would accept this casting; this was not a Charlie Chan picture. "I'm in the business of creating illusions," Thalberg answered. Luise Rainer had come to M-G-M from Vienna eight months earlier and been cast in *Escapade* when Myrna Loy quit after a week. (Loy refused to imitate Paula Wessely's performance in the 1934 Austrian film *Maskerade*.) Rainer gave the part of a flighty Viennese such gusto that she became an overnight sensation. She was physically suited to play a Chinese girl—slight, angular, graceful—but she needed a director who could subdue her exuberance. George Cukor was ideal, but he was tied up with *Romeo and Juliet*.

Thalberg called Sidney Franklin to his office in January 1936. "How would you like to direct *The Good Earth*?" Thalberg asked. "It's a spectacle and it's tough, but it's a great story—and a great love story. It might be good for you."

"If it's a love story, I might like it," said Franklin. "I'm not crazy about spectacles per se."

"We're under pressure, Sidney. We've been waiting years to get this thing started."

One reason for the pressure was the casting of Wang Lung. Warner Bros. had agreed to the loan-out of Paul Muni, the chameleon-like star of *Scarface* and *The Story of Louis Pasteur*. Muni had not been easy to convince. "I'm about as Chinese as Herbert Hoover," Muni had protested over lunch in Thalberg's dining room in September. "I won't look Chinese, no matter how much makeup I use, and I won't sound it."

"You'll *be* it," said Thalberg. "Which is what I want." In fact, this exponent of the Yiddish theater had recently played Italian, Mexican American, and French.

"I'm too old for the part," continued Muni. "Wang Lung starts out as a kid—twenty years old—on his wedding day. A couple of days ago, Mr. Thalberg, I was forty years old. How do you tell a camera—and an audience—that an old character actor is a kid? Hell, I never played a twenty-year-old when I was twenty years old!"

"I've got an instinct about it," said Thalberg. "I'm convinced you can do it."

With Rainer and Muni set, Thalberg could get the massive project rolling. Franklin was willing to take it on, except for its script. "It's too Occidental," said Franklin. "I don't get the Oriental flavor at all." He offered to rewrite the entire screenplay. He said it would take three months. It was then mid-January.

"I can give you six weeks, tops," said Thalberg.

Six weeks later, on February 28, *The Good Earth* commenced shooting. Even for M-G-M, which was making two blockbusters (*San Francisco* and *The Great Ziegfeld*), this was a big one. The 380 shipping cases that Hill had brought from China three years earlier were finally being unpacked and organized. Eight thousand items emerged. Farmhouses that had been cut in pieces were now reassembled and copied by studio carpenters, plasterers, and painters in a bid to create the world's largest replica of China.

The hills of Mesmer City, a district near Culver City, became a background for the walled city where O-Lan lives at the beginning of the story. Studio technicians terraced the hills on each side of a canyon for two miles and planted them with wheat and rice—by hand. The valley floor was planted with Chinese radishes, cabbage, onions, and leeks. Modern irrigation was used, but Chinese water wheels were installed on an artificial river for photographic purposes, as were windmills and other ancient devices. The crops took eight months to cultivate, during which time Chinese flora and fauna were installed, including two water buffalo that had arrived with the shipping cases. Transplanted oaks took root and doves made homes in tiled roofs.

In addition to Mesmer City, four hundred acres of farmland in Chatsworth, twenty-five miles north, were converted into the wealthy Wang Lung farm of later scenes. When the sets were dressed with authentic farm implements and populated with Chinatown extras dressed in turn-of-the-century garb, the result was compellingly exotic. *Los Angeles Times* reporter John R. Woolfenden wrote:

> You turn off the highway, drive past an orange grove and suddenly come
> upon what looks like the winter quarters for a circus, with immense tents for
> commissary, dressing quarters, and makeup department. The location itself
> isn't visible until you walk up a dirt road, and then the thatched huts of Wang
> Lung's farm community come into view. Water buffalo get slowly to their feet
> from under the shade of a tree and stare with insolent indifference. They turn a
> water wheel which scoops up the water from the stream for irrigation. High on
> a hillside, above the thatch and bamboo, silhouetted against the sky, gleaming
> brown figures, stripped to the waist, work with real Chinese hoes.
>
> It's a lazy spring day, and the California hills are rapidly turning brown, but
> there's scarcely a sign that this might be anywhere but China until you turn
> around and gaze off across the San Fernando Valley and see telegraph wires in
> the distance. Here in the canyon, it's Wang's farm.

Accuracy was being observed, not only for aesthetics but also for politics. The Nationalist government of General Chiang Kai-Shek had approved an early script but took the precaution of sending an official observer, Major-General Ting-Hsui Tu. The general quickly ingratiated himself with the cast, crew, and musical director, Herbert Stothart, by filling the air with Chinese folk songs.

The immersion in Chinese culture had the desired effect on Paul Muni. "I forget the camera and think I am really on a farm on the other side of the world," he wrote. "The hundreds of Chinese extras. The water buffalo, my new friends, brought from China, and such actors! I hear the mournful call of doves and smell burning joss sticks in the air. It's all old and oriental. And just think—we are fifteen miles from the corner of Hollywood and Vine."

Rainer, who had just completed her role as the effervescent Anna Held in *The Great Ziegfeld*, was not having such a good time. She felt that Franklin was giving her too little to do and was allowing Muni to steal scenes. "I told her that was his character," wrote Franklin. "Her character was the quiet one. The less she did, the more she did. The less she said, the more she conveyed. And when she spoke, be it one line or two, everybody would listen."

Without warning, Major-General Tu and his family disappeared from Culver City. Before M-G-M could call the police, word came from the Chinese consul that Tu had been recalled to China for entertaining an out-of-favor official. Lewin stepped in and declared that he was bringing his own observers to the set, the Chinese writer Lin Yutang and the Chinese linguist Hu Shi. Thalberg enlisted the aid of Pearl Buck herself. All three assured the Nationalist government that the footage shot thus far was in no way detrimental to China's image and that Muni and Rainer were creating dignified characters.

Franklin's concern about the balance of human drama and spectacle was warranted. Ordinarily Thalberg strove to give each film one great scene. *The Good Earth* was trying for four: the birth of the farmer's first child during a storm; the death of another during a famine; the riotous looting of a palace that injures O-Lan but saves her family; and the farmers' fight against a locust swarm. Thalberg had Franklin direct the first two sequences. He assigned the looting sequence to Sam Wood, who created a terrifying set piece. The locust swarm worried production manager Joe Cohn. "The script doesn't show you the progression of events," he told Thalberg.

"Now, Joe, don't worry about it," Thalberg replied. "If it doesn't work, we'll fix it later."

"Maybe *you* can," said Cohn, "but I'll be the one who's blamed. The difference between us is that you can afford to make a quarter-million-dollar mistake. I can't."

Cohn's concern was valid, so Thalberg hired montage master Slavko Vorkapich (assisted by montage artists Peter Ballbusch and Charles Trego) to design and film the sequence. It eventually incorporated footage of a real swarm in Cedar City, Utah; "locusts" made with coffee grinds; macrolensed grasshoppers; and field footage shot by Fred Niblo. These elements were blended in the optical printer by disaster-scene wizards James Basevi and James Havens. The final editing of *The Good Earth* was done by Basil Wrangell, but the numerous montages that linked its scenes were given to Wrangell after Vorkapich had already edited them. This was an important step for Thalberg.

Since the advent of sound, he had depended on dialogue to advance a plot. In *Mutiny on the Bounty* he used montages composed of rhythmic, frenetic cuts to tell the story, an obvious bow to Sergei Eisenstein's "dialectical montage." Instead of trying to make film a stepchild of the theater, Thalberg was using film *as film*. No proscenium arch in the world could have contained the elemental forces that made *The Good Earth* so powerful.

Cohn's remark about money was appropriate, if not tactful. Thalberg was spending tremendous sums of money, mostly in drawn-out shooting schedules. While Stromberg was bringing elephantine projects like the three-hour *Great Ziegfeld* in on schedule, Thalberg was extending his schedules with both multiple previews and retakes. This could be excused with a modest film like *Riptide*, but when hundreds of extras were on location, repeated delays could raise a budget to a level at which a film could never break even. This had happened with *Rasputin and the Empress*. There were, after all, a finite number of theater seats in America. Spend too much on a movie and, even if all those seats were filled for two weeks, you could not make a profit. Thalberg was aware of this and needed to keep his production unit profitable. Mayer reminded him of this at the premiere of *San Francisco*. "This is *my* idea of a prestige picture," said Mayer, and, sure enough, the film (initially guided by Thalberg) made a whopping $2 million profit. Thalberg was not one to let a sensation slide by. He grabbed Jeanette MacDonald. But instead of putting her and Nelson Eddy into a modest romance with great songs, Thalberg put them into a big period musical based on Sigmund Romberg's 1917 operetta, *Maytime*—and decided to make it M-G-M's first Technicolor feature.

Since its introduction in 1935 with Pioneer Pictures' *Becky Sharp*, "three-strip" Technicolor had been utilized in only two features. Companies were wary of a process that required a tremendous amount of light, extensive color testing, processing off the lot, and a longer shooting schedule. The combination of these factors could raise a budget by 50 percent. Nonetheless, Thalberg got Nick Schenck's approval of a Technicolor *Maytime*. Edmund Goulding was still in Thalberg's orbit, having directed the "Alone" musical number in *A Night at the Opera*, so Thalberg gave him *Maytime*. Goulding started fiddling with the script. Color tests dragged on. On August 21, 1936, when the huge Technicolor camera rolled onto its fourth production, Goulding was still writing. As if using a new process was not enough, Thalberg was producing an unfinished script.

Thalberg was having *Maytime*'s composer write new songs for the film. Romberg was delighted to be working for Thalberg but could never find him. A secretary suggested that Romberg visit the office of Moss Hart, who was also writing for Thalberg. "I've been going crazy playing solitaire, waiting for Thalberg," Hart told Romberg. "At least with you around we can play some gin rummy." Romberg said he could play only until Thalberg called him back to the bungalow; they played for three and a half weeks.

"I can't tell you how embarrassed I am," said Thalberg finally. "I've been spending all my time on my wife's film. There's just so much involved. I couldn't get away."

Anyone observing Thalberg in 1936 saw him working harder and moving faster than ever before. For the most part he was energized by the work. But there were moments when he showed the strain. Cole Porter saw it. Frances Goldwyn saw it. When Frances Marion came to say goodbye on the eve of a trip, she saw it. "Irving looked so spent I could hardly conceal my alarm," wrote Marion. "He was underweight again and he walked with his head slightly tilted to one side, as if he were too frail to hold his head erect." Shearer confided to Merle Oberon that at the end of a workday, her husband had to lie down because of the throbbing in his head. His stillness and lack of color frightened her. "Irving seemed terribly fragile," recalled Sylvia Herscher, a friend of the Thalbergs' live-in nurse, Greta Morrison. "Norma was very protective of him. More so than of her children, it seemed." Adela Rogers St. Johns had not seen Thalberg in several years and was shocked at his appearance. "He looked like a little figure made of white ashes," she recalled. "He had that kind of frailness that you see in young people before death." Yet Thalberg pushed himself through each day, renewed by a late-afternoon nap, ready for *Anthony Adverse* at the Four Star or *Saint Joan* at the Biltmore.

A Night at the Opera had been a rewarding experience for everyone involved. Loath to lose momentum, Thalberg assigned George Seaton and Robert Pirosh to come up with another story for the Marx Brothers. At this point they were the only players for whom he was generating original stories. He would have preferred a literary source like *The Three Musketeers*, but their act was too specialized to be shoehorned into a classic, so Seaton and Pirosh looked for another institution to burlesque. "Bob and I had an idea which Groucho liked," recalled Seaton in 1975, "and that was to have him run a sanitarium. We thought it would be a funny idea, and Groucho agreed, but Thalberg thought it needed another element. After a few scripts, the racetrack idea came into it. And before you knew it, that aspect of the story evolved." The pace at which Thalberg worked the young writers made such progress possible. "In those days," said Seaton, "you had to be creative to the tune of twenty-five pages a week!"

The working title of the new film was *Peace and Quiet*. Before it became *A Day at the Races*, the Marxes' second Thalberg film went through more scripts than almost any of his previous. He encouraged this prolific pace with regular reviews of the material, more than he was giving his other writers. "I think this script is a good one, fellas," Thalberg would say. "Now, I'll tell you what to do. Start over again." The existing script would not be discarded, however. "He would instruct us to 'save this scene' or 'save that character,'" said Seaton, "and we worked and we worked. And we did eighteen complete scripts over a period of a year and a half."

Thalberg and the Marxes agreed that testing scenes before live audiences was essential, so "Scenes from *A Day at the Races*" spent six weeks on the road, two of which were with fill-in performers, so that the Marxes could sit in the audience and feel the ebb and flow of attention. More than five hundred jokes were tested. Seventy-five made the grade. Groucho was the show's harshest critic. He thought one line by Al Boasberg was not getting enough laughs. "Is he dead or is my watch stopped?" he asked while taking a patient's pulse. There were isolated chuckles and giggles. Groucho modified it. "Either he's dead or my watch has stopped." There were screams of laughter. Thalberg and Shearer were in San Francisco in mid-August to celebrate Shearer's thirty-fourth birthday. "Scenes" was playing the Golden Gate Theater there, so they caught one performance. The audience was thrilled when the usually mute Harpo broke precedent and introduced Shearer from the stage.

A Day at the Races commenced shooting on September 3. Observing the template established by the previous film, there was a romantic couple (Allan Jones and Maureen O'Sullivan), there were musical numbers, and Sam Wood was directing. The Marx Brothers found him no easier to work with than they had in *A Night at the Opera*. "Politically, Wood was impossible," recalled Groucho. "He was a fascist. We all disliked him intensely. But we respected Thalberg." Groucho once asked him why he was assigning them a director who had no feeling for comedy. "It suits my purpose," replied Thalberg. "If Wood shoots a scene and I don't like it, I can call him into my office and say, 'Sam, shoot that scene again. I didn't like the way you handled it.' And he will do it." Wood, along with the rest of the directors at M-G-M, accepted Thalberg's judgment as absolute. "If Thalberg said, 'Go back and do it over,' nobody complained," said Seaton. "Thalberg was astute enough in directorial matters to recognize when a scene was deficient." More important, he could justify the expense of the retake. "He was so highly respected that he could spend a lot of money on a film," Seaton said. "That was unusual in those days. Most pictures were produced in the $400,000 range. He would spend a million and a half on a film." Paramount had never spent that much on a Marx Brothers film, their salaries notwithstanding.

The Marxes, especially Groucho, felt privileged to have Thalberg for a producer. *A Day at the Races* was considered an important project, simply by virtue of

Thalberg's supervision. "He always hired the best," said Seaton. "He could lure the best people to his productions, because you knew that a Thalberg production was a class production."

If Thalberg's portfolio as a genius lacked one achievement, it was a transcendent vehicle for the singular conjunction of personality, beauty, talent, and skill that was Greta Garbo. He had found her formula in 1927, yet her career had been a series of imperfect films. The perfect vehicle, one that would allow the breadth and depth of her power, had never arrived. In 1934 he spoke to Mercedes de Acosta, whose obsession with the aloof Garbo had reduced her to a long-suffering acolyte. "Nature is Greta's element," said Acosta, "and in no picture had she been allowed to express it. I told Thalberg this. I also told him that I thought Greta should play the roles of saints."

"What saints?"

"Of course Jehanne d'Arc *[sic]*. She is a natural for this. All the scenes should be shot in France and in all the places where Jehanne d'Arc lived and fought."

Garbo was open to the idea, but, mercurial as ever, she suddenly called Thalberg to tell him that she would not play Joan of Arc. Thalberg had a hunch that the ideal vehicle for Garbo would be *The Lady of the Camellias,* the Alexandre Dumas fils story more popularly known as *Camille.* The story of Marguerite Gautier, a consumptive courtesan in 1847 Paris, would be far better for Garbo than the story of Marie Walewska. In mid-1935 Thalberg consulted Viertel, who informed him that Garbo would agree to play Marguerite only if she could play Marie too. Thalberg was more interested in *Camille.* He approached Selznick's favored director, George Cukor.

"Irving Thalberg was going to do two pictures with Garbo," recalled Cukor, "and he offered me the choice between them. One was *Marie Walewska,* with Napoleon as the leading man. . . . He's fascinating to read about, but he's a Great Man—and they all come out like waxworks in the movies, even American patriots. So I chose *Camille.* I'd seen the play, and I felt it would be the perfect meeting of the actress and the role." Though she was hoping for Clarence Brown, Garbo approved Cukor.

"I do not understand why they are not going to do Walewska first," Garbo wrote Viertel. "And are you not doing anything on *Camille?* God help me if Thalberg does it alone. Will you answer me on that? I could write Mayer otherwise and perhaps he could let Selznick do *Camille* instead of Thalberg." Garbo did not explain whether her objection to Thalberg was due to his independent producing status or to his exhausting schedule. In any case, she did not want him to know that she had doubts. "I shall write another sheet of paper, and, if you wish, you can show it to Thalberg. Please ask Thalberg to think very carefully about *Camille*. It's so like *Anna Karenina* that I am afraid. . . . It's devastating to do the same story again."

Thalberg asked Acosta what she thought of Garbo in *Camille*. "I answered that I thought she would be magnificent in the role, surpassed possibly only by [Eleanora] Duse," wrote Acosta. "He seemed pleased and relieved and asked me to reread the play in French and make notes." Acosta managed to get past the Cerberus-like Viertel and told Garbo about Duse, Bernhardt, and herself. Garbo's doubts were momentarily allayed.

In December 1935 Thalberg hired Frances Marion, and then at her urging, James Hilton, to transform *The Lady of the Camellias* into Garbo's *Camille*. Albert Lewin expected that Thalberg would assign the project to him. He was quietly angry when Thalberg decided to do the film himself but with David Lewis credited as associate producer. This was partly in retribution for a nasty stunt that Lewin had pulled on Lewis. The villain in *Riffraff* was originally called Nick Appopolis. Lewin came to Lewis's office and advised him that trouble loomed with Greek Americans if M-G-M portrayed a greasy gangster as a Greek; better to give him a neutral last name like, say, "Louis." Lewis chose not to take offense at the obvious resemblance to his own name; he could not see that he was being set up for something worse.

"My God!" Thalberg asked Lewis when he saw the cast list on the completed *Riffraff*. "How could you have done that? It looks like the villain is a combination of *Nick* Schenck and *Louis* Mayer!" A startled Lewis related Lewin's involvement. Thalberg was not amused. "That's just like the little bastard," he snapped. A few months later, Thalberg passed Lewin over and gave *Camille* to Lewis. In a few more months, after seeing Lewis pass Lewin in the bungalow numerous times, Thalberg could not resist a confidence in the car. "Do you like Al Lewin?" he asked Lewis.

"Well . . . yes," answered Lewis.

"He doesn't like you." Lewis became a little upset. Thalberg patted him on the knee. "It's only the old wife jealous of the new young mistress," Thalberg chuckled.

The production of *Camille* had a problem—the first draft script written by Marion and Hilton. "It was ludicrous—flowery, overblown, and just badly conceived and overwritten," wrote Lewis. "It was almost comic opera. I remember Armand's pet name for Marguerite was *ma petite choux* ("my little cabbage"). . . .

Frances thought it adorable, and the name was all through the script, even in the death scene." Lewis was reluctant to tell Thalberg what he thought, but Thalberg pressed him. "It's appalling," Lewis gulped.

"Now what do we do?" asked Thalberg; Garbo was impatient to start. He called Cukor to his office. The director also thought the script worthless. But he had a suggestion.

"I know who should write it," Cukor brightened. "Zoë Akins." Akins was a screenwriter of towering reputation with a penchant for younger men. She was, in fact, spending a great deal of money on one, so a deal was quickly made. Her script had the spice and sparkle that Marion's should have had, but it still lacked something. At a story conference, Thalberg searched for it, thinking aloud. "He did not relay his ideas through associate producers as did other executives," remembered Lewis. "His system was far more comprehensive; there were always open meetings, with everyone having his or her say." His 1931 Garbo film *Inspiration* had been spoiled by a young man's opprobrious attitude to an older woman's past; some critics had called it hopelessly old-fashioned. Yet here they were, trying to write a script from the old-fashioned story that had inspired *Inspiration*!

"We have a problem," Thalberg mused. "Audiences have to forget—within the first five minutes—that this is a costume picture. It has to be contemporary in its feeling. One thing mitigates against that: the idea that a girl's past can ruin her marriage. That problem doesn't exist nowadays. Men marry whores—and they make good wives. Look around this town. It's been proven." Thalberg was speaking from years of observing Hollywood mores. "Who would give a rip? Morality has changed since Dumas. The critics called André in *Inspiration* a prig. They'll do the same to Armand if he throws Marguerite over because of her past. This play is a museum piece. It's preposterous."

When Lewis was driving home from the studio one night, something occurred to him. He found a public telephone in a service station on Overland Avenue and dialed Thalberg's office. "Instead of the story being based only on the boy's life being ruined," he asked, "suppose we have a case of a very jealous boy? It isn't a question of his life being ruined by her past. It's a question of his *jealousy* ruining his life."

With the credibility problem licked and the character defined, *Camille* proceeded smoothly to Stage 23, where it began shooting on July 29. Playing opposite Garbo was Robert Taylor, M-G-M's newest sensation. "We can't miss with these two!" Thalberg enthused at a conference. Garbo's first day on the set was marked by an unaccustomed playfulness. Dressed in black silk pajamas and a pair of old bedroom slippers, she crept onto the set, tiptoed up to William Daniels, and poked him in the ribs. She also surprised coworkers by allowing dress extras who had not worked on her films before to share the set with her. "In an apparent effort to be like other stars," wrote Harrison Carroll in the *Evening Herald Express*, "the temperamental Swede started the picture minus the black screens that usually shield her from fellow players and set workers while she emotes before the camera. At the end of the day, though, La Garbo appealed to director George Cukor. 'I am so nervous seeing so many new faces.'" Cukor tactfully asked Garbo why she disliked people looking at her. "She said that when she was acting she had some kind of ideal picture in her mind, something she was creating," recalled Cukor. "She could imagine certain things [but] if she saw people off the set staring at her, she felt like an ass, like somebody with a lot of paint on her face making faces."

Thalberg preserved Garbo's ideal picture by surrounding her with superb character actors. The last part to be cast was Marguerite's friend, the parasitic Prudence. Lewis knew the veteran actress Laura Hope Crews from RKO, where she had delivered a bravura performance as the possessive mother in *The Silver Cord*. He was desperate for Thalberg to cast her as Prudence when he brought three screen tests to Thalberg's home. Thalberg was sitting at the dining room table in his bathrobe, sneezing into a handkerchief. Shearer brought in his one-year-old daughter, now called Katie, to greet him and Lewis. Then the curtains were drawn and the screen rose from the floor. Thalberg ran the tests, immediately disqualifying Mady Christians because she was obviously nasty. He said nothing about Crews. "You know," he said to Lewis, "that Fritzi Scheff is great."

"I thought Scheff was pale, a little bon bon," wrote Lewis. "Laura had guts and bite, vitality and humor and power."

Thalberg ran the tests again. When Scheff was on the screen, he said: "She's good!" The lights came up and then he signaled the projectionist. "I think I have to look at them once more." Lewis's heart sank. Then he noticed the twinkle in Thalberg's eye. He was giving the part to Laura Hope Crews.

After recovering from his head cold, Thalberg joined Cukor in his studio screening room to see what he had missed, a scene of Garbo at the theater with Crews and Lenore Ulric.

"George, she's awfully good," said Thalberg. "I don't think I've ever seen her so good."

"But Irving," said Cukor, "she's just sitting in an opera box."

"She's relaxed," said Thalberg. "She's open. She seems unguarded for once." Garbo's new attitude prompted Thalberg to rework the script with Akins. "She is a fascinating artist, but she is limited," Thalberg told Akins and Lewis. "She must never create situations. She must be thrust into them. The drama comes in how she rides them out."

Thalberg began visiting Stage 23 to watch Garbo work. He was entranced by the artistry he saw, both on the stage and in the rushes. "I think we have caught Garbo as she should be caught," he said to Lewis one day. "She will be the most memorable Camille of our time." Sam Marx asked Thalberg how the production was going. "If only they were all like this," replied Thalberg, alluding to thorny productions like *Mutiny on the Bounty*.

In the last week of August, a heat wave hit Los Angeles. Garbo's heavy costumes felt even heavier on a soundstage that registered ninety degrees. To make matters worse, she began to have symptoms of a recurring ovarian problem. Even in the best of times, Garbo was not a cheery person, but she could lose herself in the trance that attended her acting. This time, though, she was an unwell woman playing an unwell woman. She did not need distractions. Thalberg appeared on the set. Film editor Margaret Booth was also there, but Garbo singled out the thin figure in the shadows. She called Assistant Director Eddie Woehler over. Frowning, she whispered to him, and he had the unenviable job of asking Thalberg to leave his own production.

"I've been put off better sets than this one," Thalberg replied, but not loudly enough to be heard by Garbo. He was irritated with her, but in truth, his mind was elsewhere. As important as *Camille* was to him, there was something even more important. This was September 3. *Romeo and Juliet* was opening a limited engagement in thirteen theaters across the country. This was the project that Thalberg called "the fulfillment of a long-cherished dream."

CHAPTER 21 · A Labor of Love

The idea of selling Shakespeare to the masses was not predicated on Norma Shearer's whim. Since the advent of the Production Code, the public had been supporting films based on literary classics. Nostalgia for books read in school had made hits of *Treasure Island*, *The Count of Monte Cristo*, and *A Tale of Two Cities*. David Selznick was the most frequent purveyor of classics, and his were the most profitable; *David Copperfield* grossed $3 million. Of course Shakespeare was something else. Legend had it that *The Taming of the Shrew*, made in 1929 by Mary Pickford and Douglas Fairbanks, had flopped. It had, in fact, grossed twice its cost. It had not, however, flattered its stars; they sounded like students doing a first reading. As the sound film grew fluent, no one tried Shakespeare.

In December 1933 the newly formed Pioneer Pictures engaged Robert Edmond Jones and his wife, Margaret Carrington, to stage a screen test of John Barrymore in *Hamlet*. The couple had impeccable credentials. Jones had designed the famed 1922 production of *Hamlet*, and Carrington had coached Barrymore's landmark interpretation. Yet the test, shot in Technicolor, was a disappointment. Barrymore's reading had authority, but eleven years of debauchery could not be erased by lighting or filters. He looked as tired as he had playing the dissipated star in *Dinner at Eight*. He was unable to reach the peaks required of the role. Pioneer canceled its *Hamlet*, and the studios avoided Shakespeare.

On September 17, 1934, a local event changed Hollywood's attitude toward the Bard: an open-air performance of *A Midsummer Night's Dream*, directed by the

German impresario Max Reinhardt. Playing upon Los Angeles's ambition to be known as "a primary transept in the temple of cosmopolitan culture," Reinhardt brought his acclaimed production to the Hollywood Bowl. In one week, 149,000 people paid to see Shakespeare's fantasy performed by a cast of five hundred in the Hollywood hills. "The woods acted," wrote Gottfried Reinhardt, the director's son. "Trees, shrubbery, mist, moonlight intermingled with the lovers, the rehearsing artisans, the trolls, the elves, the spirits. The music, the running, the clowning, the fighting were all of one key and all came from one and the same source. So did the calm, the sweep, the dream, the poetry." Almost every movie executive saw the play. Forget that it was the most spectacular production of Shakespeare ever realized. This was the most spectacular show they had ever seen. Not even Ziegfeld could surpass the finale, a procession of torches through the hills. Still, there were philistines. "It's a swell spectacle," said one producer to another, "but it'll be forgotten in six months. It won't live on like *The Squaw Man* or *All Quiet on the Western Front*." These same executives were surprised when Jack Warner—not Irving Thalberg—signed Reinhardt to a three-film contract.

In the spring of 1935, Hollywood was guardedly curious as Reinhardt (in collaboration with his former pupil, William Dieterle) began shooting the first of his three contracted films, an all-star production of *A Midsummer Night's Dream*. It sounded like a costly long shot.* Then Pioneer Pictures announced a new *Hamlet* project, starring Fredric March instead of Barrymore. Twentieth Century–Fox announced that it was financing a British production of *As You Like It*, starring Elisabeth Bergner. Shakespeare was in the air. It was appropriate, then, that Shearer would look to Shakespeare rather than to Eugene O'Neill for her next film. Juliet was not an inapt choice. "Every actress has at one time or another wanted to play Juliet," said Shearer. "I saw Julia Marlowe play the part years ago. I determined then and there that someday I would play it too." The image of Shearer in Shakespeare fired Thalberg's imagination and gave him a heartfelt goal. On

---

***A Midsummer Night's Dream* was released in late 1935, too late to influence M-G-M's decision to film *Romeo and Juliet*. *A Midsummer Night's Dream* was not a box-office success, and critics were divided as to its efficacy. Seventy-four years later it has its supporters, the author among them. Reinhardt had shot some tests for his second film, which was tentatively titled *Danton*, when Jack Warner abrogated his contract. *A Midsummer Night's Dream* remains the primary token of Reinhardt's stage production. Contrary to what was written by Kenneth Anger in *Hollywood Babylon* (which was in fact ghostwritten by film critic Elliott Stein), Anger did not play the changeling prince in *A Midsummer Night's Dream*. According to call sheets from production records in the Warner Bros. Archives at the University of Southern California, the part was acted by a girl named Sheila Brown.

May 22, M-G-M announced a Thalberg production of *Romeo and Juliet*. Behind corporate doors, it was not so simple.

Louis B. Mayer chose his words carefully, having promised Sam Goldwyn (among others) that he would go easy on Thalberg, but he was appalled by the idea of such a project. He had not finished grade school, but he remembered that children groaned when teachers mentioned Shakespeare. Americans found Elizabethan English unintelligible. Trade publications such as *Harrison's Reports* were full of exhibitors' letters asking for snappy, modern fare. Mayer needed an answer to Shirley Temple, not another prestige picture. He predicted that *Romeo and Juliet* would fail. Thalberg politely but firmly insisted on doing the film and turned to Nick Schenck.

"It's a silly idea, Irving," said Schenck. He did not care if Warners was doing Shakespeare. He did not care that it could win an Academy Award. Loew's could not afford it. Thalberg wanted to hang up on him, but he knew better. He needed to present an irresistible package. He approached Clark Gable. "Irving," replied Gable, "I don't look Shakespeare, I don't talk Shakespeare, I don't like Shakespeare, and I won't do Shakespeare." In truth, Gable had played Mercutio in Jane Cowl's touring company ten years earlier and retained a deep respect for Shakespeare, but Thalberg had promised not to force any more unwanted projects on him, so he backed off.

The casting of Romeo was crucial, and the field was limited. March was already committed. That left Brian Aherne, Leslie Howard, and Robert Donat. The press was already speculating that Howard would get the part of the sixteen-year-old lover. Howard was forty-two, uninterested, and scornful of producers. "The trouble with Hollywood," said Howard, "is that the people above you don't belong there. Generally speaking, the higher you go, the lower the mentality." As if in fulfillment of Howard's statement, Warner refused to loan him. Thalberg approached John Masefield, the British poet laureate, to adapt *Romeo and Juliet*. Masefield was flattered and tentatively agreed. George Cukor agreed to direct. Thalberg still needed selling points.

At 3:30 P.M. on June 13, 1935, Thalberg had his secretary place a call to Howard Dietz, M-G-M's East Coast publicity director. Thalberg asked Dietz if he was alone. He was not. He had guests and they were waiting in a motor launch. This was the night of the hotly contested (and heavily wagered) championship bout between Max Baer and James J. Braddock. Dietz just had time to get to Madison Square Garden on Long Island. "I'll call you as soon as the fight is over," said Dietz.

"Do that," Thalberg said, somewhat distractedly. "I'm glad to see you're having a little recreation. You've been working too hard. Well, okay. Call me after the fight is over."

"I'll call you at the first opportunity," said Dietz, as his guests yelled from the pier. Still, Thalberg had not come to the point.

"Howard," said Thalberg abruptly, "there is one consideration before you hang up. Just answer me yes or no. Do you think we should make *Romeo and Juliet?*"

"Offhand, Irving, I'd say no. But look, can we discuss this after the fight?"

"What do you mean, 'no'? It's the greatest love story ever told. It's a work of art."

"Who'll play Juliet?" asked Dietz. "I heard that Kit Cornell turned you down." The yelling outside had stopped. "Who can you get to play a fourteen-year-old?"

"Norma," said Thalberg blithely.

"I doubt she'd be right for it," said Dietz, glancing at the clock and listening for the sound of the motor. "She's not that young."

"Juliet can be any age."

"Irving, I really don't think *Romeo and Juliet* is box office."

"With Norma, it will be a cinch."

While Thalberg enumerated the ways in which Dietz could huckster Shakespeare, Dietz heard the boat revving up. He strained the telephone cord to peer outside.

"But you'd better go to your fight," said Thalberg finally.

"Thanks," said Dietz, but he had just missed the boat. He knew there was no point arguing with Thalberg, or in trying to avoid the call. "He would track me down at Madison Square Garden and have me paged during the last round anyway," recalled Dietz. "If you objected, he would grow testy. You felt he was trying to spoil your day. The next time he called, he would pick up the conversation where he left it. As if nothing had happened. Frankly, the only thing that saved him from being the usual Hollywood monstrosity was his lack of interest in personal publicity. I told him that he ought to get some. All he would say was 'I'm thinking it over.' He didn't care about himself. Norma was his obsession."

Sam Marx was in Thalberg's office when he called Schenck again and presented the lineup, including Dietz's promise to push the picture. Schenck was impressed, but maintained that the company did not have $1.5 million to spend on Shakespeare. He would have to say no.

"Nick, I've never had any picture closer to my heart," Thalberg said.

"But Irving, a million and a half!"

"Nick, listen. I believe that I can bring it in for nine. The script won't need all that much work."

"Eight hundred thousand, Irving. That's the best I can do for you."

Thalberg hung up and smiled at Marx. The deal was set.

A few days later, Marx was meeting with Kate Corbaley, who was reading a memo from Thalberg. Masefield had decided not to work for M-G-M. Thalberg had to find another expert. This would be the most lavish, the most distinguished, the most authentic version of *Romeo and Juliet* ever filmed.

"Authentic!" laughed Corbaley. "How can a thirtyish wife play a fourteen-year-old virgin? 'Authentic'? Ha ha ha!"

Marx spent a couple of days trying to defend Thalberg's plan with quotes from the play. "Love is a smoke raised with the fume of sighs," he told Corbaley.

"There are quotations to fit any argument," Corbaley shook her head. "But you needn't worry. I know better than to tell Irving what I think about this."

Corbaley was not the only one in the industry who thought Thalberg misguided. "Jesse Lasky deprecated Norma's ability," recalled Howard Hawks. "I thought she had great skill. I had faith in her." Some of this talk reached Thalberg; he grew defensive. "I believe Norma can play anything—and do it better than anyone else," Thalberg responded.

Thalberg sent Marx to dicker with Cornell University's William Strunk Jr., the renowned Shakespeare expert. Strunk was asking $400. Albert Lewin, a former professor himself, told Thalberg that $150 a week was more appropriate for a technical adviser. "If necessary, offer Strunk two hundred," Thalberg told Marx. "After all, he is special."

Marx was brought up short when the dean of Cornell University stepped in to act as Strunk's agent. He refused even $200. "I assure you many professors are paid four hundred dollars a month," the dean said frostily.

Marx was too embarrassed to admit that he had been negotiating in industry terms (a weekly paycheck) instead of in academic terms (a monthly paycheck). After a decent interval, he called the dean and said: "Mr. Thalberg thinks Professor Strunk will find it difficult to live in Hollywood on four hundred a month. He wants him to have six hundred, so he'll be comfortable."

Cukor was committed to *Romeo and Juliet,* and he wanted it to have, according to his biographer Gavin Lambert, "a fresh, lightly baroque look." He urged Thalberg to consider the British designer Oliver Messel, who had done sets and costumes for Reinhardt's other great success, *The Miracle,* and more recently, for Leslie Howard's film *The Scarlet Pimpernel*. Thalberg signed Messel without consulting either Cedric Gibbons or Gilbert Adrian. Gibbons took the unexpected collaborator in stride, but Adrian made a beeline for Mayer's office. "Don't think that I'm just the M-G-M workhorse," he told Mayer, "because I am not. I'm the M-G-M designer. And if *Romeo and Juliet* is an M-G-M picture, I am designing it." Thalberg met with both Adrian and Gibbons and arrived at an agreement that Adrian would do one half of the women's costumes and Messel would do the other half. Messel would do all the men's costumes and Adrian would do all of Shearer's gowns. Gibbons and Messel would divide the sets between them. Upon Messel's arrival in late July, he was feted by Shearer's pal Merle Oberon and then sent to Italy with a camera crew to buy every Renaissance relic that was not nailed down and to photograph every one that was.

Cukor, meanwhile, was shooting tests of possible Romeos. One was Brian Aherne, who found veteran actress Constance Collier teaching Shearer iambic pentameter in her living room. Shearer had also been reading books on famous Juliets such as Sarah Siddons and Ellen Terry. She told Aherne that she wanted to sound as if she were speaking, not reciting. "Only a month or so earlier, Katharine had been born," recalled Aherne. "Norma was worried about maternal traces, but I didn't see any." Aherne rehearsed with Shearer and Collier for a week, and then shot the test at the studio. He asked to see the edited test. "I thought she could probably bring off the part," said Aherne, "but there was no chance for me." Shearer and he were both thirty-three, but he was wearing a toupee onscreen.

Professor Strunk arrived at M-G-M, and Marx could not believe that the little man with the thick glasses and toothbrush moustache was the pedant who drilled his students with the dictum "Omit needless words! Omit needless words! Omit needless words!" Strunk was a charming conversationalist. "Your job is to protect Shakespeare from us," Thalberg said with mock seriousness. In truth, he was enamored of the play. "What Shakespeare did with that potion scene," marveled Thalberg. "With his own imagination, poetry and vitality, he had Juliet describe what the potion was going to do to her. It's brilliant."

"*Romeo and Juliet* is one of the world's great plots," Strunk agreed. "Before Shakespeare tackled it, the story had been related in one form or another for one hundred fifty years. It was even written into the chronicles of Verona by the city fathers. But Will told it better, faster, more compactly." Strunk made points with Thalberg by likening him and his writing staff to Shakespeare and his cronies at the Mermaid Tavern. "Shakespeare was part owner of the Globe Theatre," said Strunk. "He had to have plays to keep the place going, in much the same way you have to supply your theaters. He cultivated the intellectuals who came in. They knew the plots of the old Italian novellas. He worked with them to embellish story lines and he rewrote their stuff to make it work for the Globe." Thalberg listened, enraptured.

"These fellows didn't have agents or a writer's guild," said Strunk. "There were no royalties to be paid, and besides, they were well off, so they didn't care about taking credit for authorship. They were simply there to drink and pass the time. Will would buy them another round. So they let him take the writing credit." The professor smiled at Thalberg and said, "Shakespeare would have made the best movie producer in history." Thalberg took the invidious comparison gracefully.

Talbot Jennings was the only M-G-M staff writer working on the script with Strunk. Jennings had grown used to hearing Thalberg say: "Put that scene through the typewriter again—just once more. You might come up with something better." But with Strunk on board, Thalberg held back. His major contribution was to open the film in front of the Church of San Zeno in order to establish the rivalry between the Montagues and Capulets. By having them arrive in parallel procession, he created a visual analogue to their enmity. True to Thalberg's prediction, Jennings completed the script in record time, delivering the final continuity in five months. In November 1935 the script was in Joseph Breen's office, and Messel was in Italy photographing Veronese frescoes by Pisanello and Venetian paintings by Bellini.

Shearer, meanwhile, was growing anxious. She had rehearsed ancient dances for three weeks with choreographer Agnes de Mille. She had been coached in Shakespeare for four months by Collier and her fellow veterans Rollo Peters and Mrs. Frances Robinson Duff. Still, Shearer could not forget that she was the only cast member who had no Shakespeare experience—or stage experience. She was intimidated by talents like Basil Rathbone and Edna May Oliver. "I was having moments of agonizing doubt," Shearer recalled. "You can risk failure when you haven't tasted success. You can have courage when you're unknown. But God help you when you have a reputation. You'd better be good. It's too easy to slip on those upper rungs and come sliding down." Thalberg shored her up by having Margaret Carrington come from her home in Santa Barbara. Carrington was Walter Huston's older sister. In addition to coaching him and John Barrymore, she had trained Alfred Lunt, Lillian Gish, and more recently, the young Orson Welles. "She had come to believe," said Robert Edmond Jones, "that it was possible to free the speaking voice to such an extent that she could hear, not the speaker's intention or his personality, but his inner essence, the self, the soul speaking through him." Carrington began a training program for Shearer. The first thing she did was tell Shearer to forget about the iambic pentameter; she could speak her couplets conversationally.

"Mrs. Carrington taught me not how to act but how to read any text with a richness of both tone and meaning," recalled Shearer. "She helped me make my voice flexible, widen its range, and sharpen my diction. She used a clever system that she called 'the litany of vowels.' I was made to repeat a silly sentence over and over: 'Who knows aught of art must learn and then take his ease.' I then had to apply these tones to a book of prose for an hour and to a book of poetry for fifteen minutes."

Shearer began to gain confidence. Thalberg had Joan Crawford's self-described "hair designer," Sydney Guilaroff, create a style based on Fra Angelico's *The Annunciation*. Thalberg also commissioned Renaissance-style gowns from Adrian. Then he had George Hurrell make portraits of Shearer in this "Juliet look." The strategy worked. Shearer began wearing the sleekly classic look to parties, wowing celebrities such as H. G. Wells and Lady Mendl. She was greatly relieved when the formerly indifferent Leslie Howard suddenly did an about-face and challenged Warner. Interstudio negotiations led to a four-way trade: Leslie Howard and Paul Muni for Clark Gable and Robert Montgomery. The talks had another benefit for Shearer, a future loan-out to Warners if a suitable property could be found.

The casting continued. Frank Lawton of *David Copperfield* fame was cast as Benvolio, but he made Howard look too tall (and too old), so Reginald Denny got the part. The last role to be cast was the quicksilver Mercutio. Cukor wanted John Barrymore, but Thalberg worried about Barrymore's unstable health and erratic behavior. During the past year the Great Profile had been involved in a scandalous affair with a gold digger named Elaine Jacobs. The aggressive nineteen-year-old had changed her name to Barrie in his honor and then pestered, seduced, and chased the fifty-three-year-old from New York to Hollywood, where he drunkenly quarreled his way through a series of restaurants, nightclubs, and hospitals. Yet there was no denying his greatness. Cukor had an idea. Why not intern Barrymore in the Kelley Sanitarium in Culver City for the duration of the filming? A burly male nurse could escort him to and from the studio and keep him from drinking during off hours. Barrymore reluctantly agreed.

Rehearsals began in earnest in early December, followed by an unusual procedure. The entire film was shot as a play, in ten-minute takes against blank backgrounds. Thalberg was leaving nothing to chance. Then, after four months,

Messel returned from Italy, bearing 2,769 photographs. He began conferring about balconies with Gibbons and about gowns with Adrian. It became obvious that M-G-M's workshops, already overworked with *The Great Ziegfeld*, could not accommodate a thousand Renaissance costumes. Producers of period films often rented garments for extras from a company called Western Costume. *Romeo and Juliet* was unique in that every costume for every extra would be individually designed and executed. Tights were subcontracted to two New York mills, and silks to three new looms in Los Angeles. Shearer's costumes alone consumed one hundred yards of fabric, which were finished with hand painting, embroidery, and the application of thousands of brilliants, beads, and pearls.

The question was how to integrate Adrian's designs for Shearer with Messel's designs for Howard. "The studio was very successful at this time and had its own way of doing things," recalled Cukor. "They bullied Messel and said he didn't know anything about pictures." This was hardly true, given his work on *The Scarlet Pimpernel*. The real reason was that Messel's designs were bizarre and homoerotic; Adrian feared he would be credited for them. The two designers were at odds. Cukor sought Thalberg's help. "Irving sat like Solomon and never committed himself," recalled Cukor. One reason was that he had no point of reference. Professor Strunk could help with language, not costumes, and Thalberg was too fascinated by the art to give it what a director is supposed to: the interpretation that sticks. He was so enchanted by the magical world he was creating that for the first time in his career, he lost objectivity. As a result, the film was inconsistent. Some of it looked like a literal re-creation of Verona, some of it looked like an Elizabethan conception of the Renaissance, and some of it looked like a dream ballet.

Thalberg considered the style of cinematography that would best capture these images. William Daniels was slightly baffled. "I went to Thalberg's office," recalled Daniels, "to talk with him about how I would treat the photography compared to what I had done earlier, in *A Free Soul*, for example." There was no comparison between the two projects. Daniels suggested using sharp focus for scenes involving Messel's contrasty costumes, soft focus for the lovers' scenes, and smoke machines to suggest a hazy Mediterranean summer. "There was also the problem of the long classical speeches," said Daniels. "Shearer was worried about the blank verse, about being interrupted. How would we capture them without changing angles? With several cameras?" The solution for the balcony scene was to build, in addition to a full-sized balcony on Stage 15, two smaller sections so that Shearer's closeups could be shot without a camera crane. There was the question of how to use lights and filters to make Shearer look younger. "I suggested taking off all her makeup," said Daniels. "Of course that went over like a lead balloon. She had to have that dead white makeup that she was accustomed to. So she decided to pitch her voice differently. And I sat there wondering, how can this mature, sophisticated woman think like a little girl?"

Joseph Breen wanted to protect audiences from mature, sophisticated thought; that meant keeping his eye on both Shakespeare and Thalberg. "Any attempt to inject anything approaching a 'hot' bedroom scene into a Shakespeare classic would be a serious mistake," Breen wrote Thalberg, urging him to "omit the actions of them [Romeo and Juliet] lying on the bed, fondling one another in a horizontal position, and pulling one another down." Against his better judgment, Thalberg agreed to a lukewarm bedroom scene. Breen approved the project.

Filming commenced on December 27 with the wedding scene in Friar Laurence's cell. The cell, with Messel's dreamy design and Daniels's caressing spotlights, looked more like the swank La Quinta Resort than a Franciscan rectory. Shearer settled in for a long stretch. "When I was on a picture," she said, "Irving used to go to previews without me, as I had to get to bed early. On these occasions, or when Irving was working late, I would have dinner alone, sometimes on a tray in bed, depending on how tired I was, but I was never too tired to have a romp and a hug with our little boy and girl before tucking them in."

Three weeks into the shooting, John Gilbert died. Shearer had made her first M-G-M film with him and had enacted the *Romeo and Juliet* balcony scene with him in *The Hollywood Revue of 1929*. Several days after his funeral, she was shooting a farewell scene. She burst into tears. Cukor began to see the human being behind the satin and silk. "Gracious" Norma Shearer, the First Lady of M-G-M, was in reality "a nervous, highly self-critical woman who has schooled herself to give an impression of self-confidence," Cukor decided. "She becomes so keyed up with a kind of taut, nervous energy that she will play a long, exhausting scene over and over again without appearing to lose an atom of her freshness. When it's over, she will tell you she feels fine—and believe it. Then she will go to her dressing room and collapse."

Shearer's tears did not move Thalberg. He thought the farewell scene was all wrong. "It's overdone," he said to Cukor and to David Lewis, who was sitting in. "It's too glum."

"But, Irving," said Cukor, "they're parting in the morning."

"It's beautiful, but if the parting were done, in a sense, with a smile, it would be more . . . more *poignant*." He pronounced the word "poigg-nent." David Lewis stared at him for a moment, and then caught himself. Thalberg realized that he had mispronounced the word. "He looked at me as if he was daring me to correct him," said Lewis. "I didn't." Still looking at Lewis, Thalberg continued. "As I was saying, it's better to underplay a scene than to act as they did at Jack's funeral."

There was no underplaying when John Barrymore was on the set—if he showed up. In late January, Cukor was shooting the duel between him and Basil Rathbone. The two actors shared the same dressing room. "I arrived at 7:30 A.M. to find Jack asleep on the couch, with a heavy growth of beard," wrote Rathbone. After being attended to by a makeup artist who had drunk Bourbon for breakfast, Rathbone was driven to Lot Three in a limousine. "We waited all morning, but no Jack." While Rathbone, Howard, Denny, Cukor, Daniels, and a score of extras and crew members waited, the makeup man and three assistants shaved, applied makeup to, and dressed Barrymore. "At about noon a studio car containing Jack and his dresser drove onto the lot," recalled Rathbone. "Jack looked breathtakingly beautiful as he got out of the car, walked over to Mr. Cukor, and said in a rasping whisper, 'Sorry, old boy, lost me voice. Can't speak a bloody word.'" Cukor opted to shoot close angles of the duel, which would not require dialogue. Wide angles would be shot with Rathbone and, doubling for Barrymore, Fred Cavens, the fencing instructor; Barrymore was not up to the exertion. Daniels lined up the shot for Barrymore's over-the-shoulder closeup with Howard. "Jack Barrymore suddenly drew his sword with a tremendous flourish and hit Leslie a violent and accidental blow on the head. In a matter of seconds an enormous pigeon's egg appeared on Leslie's head and we were all dismissed for the day."

Thalberg asked Carrington to take Barrymore in hand. She chided him; he thanked her by addressing her as "Christ's elder sister" in front of the company. "If only drink would finally kill the Barrymores, what a better world this would be!" she said, smiling. "Margaret Carrington was marvelous with him," recalled Cukor. "She behaved toward him like an older sister. He remembered incidents from the more distant past, but was rather helpless with his lines and business. He was on the defensive and would say to her, 'Where do I go?' in a snappish way." As Barrymore grew recalcitrant, another cast member grew grandiose.

On January 25, 1936, Shearer and Thalberg double-dated with Merle Oberon and David Niven. The event was the exclusive Mayfair Ball. Thalberg was still a sponsor, but this year's host was Carole Lombard, who decreed that only white gowns could be worn to the elegant event, which was held at the Victor Hugo restaurant. Shearer caused a mild scandal when she entered in a flaming red gown. Perhaps she thought that her husband's eminence exempted her from social obligations, or perhaps she was feeling the stress of a million-dollar production. "She might have had a little quirk in the back of her head," conjectured Marion Davies. "Irving always said she had a little something that was funny back there." Whatever the case, Howard Strickling had a job keeping the incident out of the press. He also had to work overtime a week later.

"One Sunday morning Irving called Howard and me," recalled Ralph Wheelwright. "Jack Barrymore had gotten loose from the rest home at Culver and Overland." At first they suspected that his drinking buddies Gene Fowler and Charles MacArthur had gotten him out; they had been sneaking alcohol to him by means of a knotted bedsheet while distracting the male nurse. "Elaine Barrie got him out," said Wheelwright. She had seduced the nurse to give Barrymore enough time to lope down the street. Wheelwright and Strickling made a few well-placed calls. "A taxi driver admitted that he had taken Jack to his old Tower Road house." Barrymore's little castle stood empty and desolate. Dolores Costello had taken their two children and filed for divorce. A skeleton crew was feeding the three hundred rare birds who occupied an aviary there; the neglected structure stank of bird droppings and mildew. Wheelwright and Strickling entered cautiously, not knowing how they might find Barrymore. "We heard him before we saw him," said Wheelwright. "His heels were echoing through the place like it was a mausoleum." When they approached him, they could see that he was disoriented but harmless. They took him back to Kelley's.

Thalberg had had enough. He called William Powell to his office and asked him to take over the part of Mercutio. "Mr. Thalberg, that's very flattering," said Powell, "and under any other circumstances I would jump at the chance. But you see, Jack Barrymore gave me my start in pictures. I had been on the stage for ten years and I wanted very much to break into movies. Jack arranged for me to get a part [in the 1922 Sherlock Holmes]. So you can understand that it would make me very unhappy to replace him in a picture."

"Yes," Thalberg sighed, "I understand. Maybe we can nurse him through it."

During the week of February 17, while Barrymore was drying out, Cukor was shooting the balcony scene. Cedric Gibbons had transformed Stage 15, the largest on the M-G-M lot, into the Capulet gardens. Looking down on the walls, pool, and vegetation was the façade of the Capulet house and, of course, the balcony of Juliet's bedroom. The set was so vast that thirty arc lights were needed to illuminate it—at 10,000 watts each. One day a sudden cloudburst created the phenomenon of a cloud inside the soundstage; the well-known M-G-M wind machines had to blow the cloud outside.

In this distinctly unreal setting, Cukor sought to create a balcony scene that would make Thalberg's production bona fide Shakespeare. If there was any director in Hollywood who could elicit emotion from an actress, it was Cukor. Unfortunately, he had a limited sense of screen geography. "He didn't set camera," recalled assistant film editor Chester Schaeffer. "He had some boyfriend or somebody do it for him. Then he'd come into the cutting room to see if it cut together. He'd bless himself like a Catholic, which was strange, because he was not Catholic. But he was definitely praying—that the shots would cut together." In fact, the gifted director relied on anyone who could free him to concentrate on his performers. Margaret Booth steeled herself for the rough cut, and not just one. "I had to cut five versions of the balcony scene," she recalled. "One with tears, one without tears, one played with closeups only, another played with long shots only, and then one with long shots and closeups cut in."

Cukor took so long to set up the first shot of the balcony that the arc lights started flickering. "The set got smoky," recalled Daniels. "I finally suggested to him, 'Why not shoot now, George?' He did a terribly long take. Then another. And another. He got up to take twenty-eight. Somebody told Thalberg. He came down on the set. George had gone to the can or something. Thalberg said to the assistant director: 'If this starts to happen again, you call me. We can't afford this.' Then George walked up. 'Irving, I've got an idea.' He ended up making six more takes. It was too much."

"This can go on forever," griped Howard. "Norma is wonderful, but she's too serious about this part. The public won't mind whether she says 'Wherefore *art* thou, Romeo,' or '*Wherefore* art thou, Romeo,' and who cares, anyway?"

Wheelwright happened onto this set on another day. Cukor was filming the last passage of the balcony scene. Shearer was saying to Howard: "My bounty is as boundless as the sea. . . . The more I give to thee, the more I have, for both are infinite." Wheelwright noticed that off in the distance, at the edge of the vast soundstage, partially hidden by a hedge, was a dark, slight, solitary figure. "It was Thalberg," recalled Wheelwright. "Nobody knew he was there. Except me. I could see him. He was hiding in the shadows so that no one would notice him watching his wife. When she said her lines, his face mirrored the lines of that love scene better than Leslie Howard's did." After the shot had been made, the doors of the soundstage were opened. A limousine cruised in. Thalberg glanced into it, realized he was being watched, and quickly walked outside. Sitting inside the automobile was Joan Crawford, who had come to see how her rival was doing. She did not stay long.

John Barrymore returned to work a week later. He had been making regular appearances at Sardi's restaurant with Elaine Barrie and, more often than not, creating a disturbance. The line between propriety and performance was becoming blurred. One day he was consistently flubbing his conjuration speech. Instead of saying "He heareth not, he stirreth not, he moveth not," Barrymore was saying "He heareth not, he stirreth not, he pisseth not!" Cukor could not make him cooperate. In short order, Thalberg was standing on the sidelines. At the first sign of mischief, he signaled to Cukor to cut. The entire company watched as Thalberg strode over to Barrymore. There was a moment of whispering. "Very well, Irving," said Barrymore capriciously. "Just once will I say it—that thou mayest see how it stinketh." Barrymore said the line as it was written, the camera caught it, and Thalberg left, just as Barrymore began to throw a fit.

As the production lumbered on, a creeping fatigue numbed some crew members, and a painful impatience gnawed at others. In late March, Daniels disappeared for three days. It was generally known that he had surrendered to nervous tension and gone on a drinking binge.* He was forgiven when he returned, because the images of Shearer that he had created so far were the loveliest that Thalberg had ever seen. Shearer may not have looked fourteen, but she did not look thirty-four.

In early April Thalberg went to La Quinta for the weekend to work on a script with two writers. Cukor reported to the set on Saturday, and the assistant director informed him that the scheduled scene could not be shot because the set was not fully dressed. The only set available was Juliet's bedroom. "How would you like to try the potion scene?" Cukor asked Shearer in her dressing room. "Let's just knock it off and see what we get." Even though Thalberg was not there to approve the change, Shearer agreed, and the proper wardrobe was prepared. In the potion scene, Juliet drinks a sleep-inducing chemical so that she may escape marriage to Paris and join Romeo. A friend of Cukor's suggested shooting the entire speech in one take, using the camera to follow Shearer around the room. Daniels had to block all the action, because no one else knew which angles would make Shearer look perfect. After a couple of hours of rehearsal, Cukor decided not to shoot it. He needed Thalberg's approval. Then he changed his mind. "Just for luck, we did the shot," recalled Shearer. "We only did the one take."

---

*Daniels also suffered an episode during the making of *Camille*, but it was not due to his father's death, as stated in this author's book *Greta Garbo*. California records reveal that Daniels's father died on June 21, 1939, during the making of *Ninotchka*.

"Okay, print it!" said Cukor. "We'll let Irving see it on Monday. And we can redo it on Tuesday."

"No one moved or said anything," remembered Shearer. "Somehow we all knew that it wouldn't need to be redone. Strange, yes, but we knew we'd made something special."

Thalberg looked at the rushes on Monday with Cukor and Shearer. "When she sees the rushes," Cukor remarked to a journalist, "she looks at her work with the mind of a producer." Her brother had seen her develop this faculty. "Norma had a bent right knee," said Douglas Shearer. "She learned to always turn it out. By studying hundreds of photographs of herself, she learned how to present this idealized image." She liked what she had done on Saturday, even if the lighting was not entirely flattering and the sharp focus showed some spittle caught on her lower lip. Her acting was extraordinarily forceful. Thalberg feigned irritation at not being consulted before the making of such an important scene, but he knew it could hardly be improved.

Principal photography of Metro-Goldwyn-Mayer production no. 879, *Romeo and Juliet*, ended on April 15, 1936. It had logged a monumental 108 days, which was appropriate. Thalberg hoped it would be a monument—a monument to his wife's career, a monument to his independent production unit, and a monument to the nearly perfected talking picture. Even though he was plagued with *The Good Earth*, the Writers Guild, and *Camille*, he began spending time in *Romeo and Juliet* postproduction. Douglas Shearer was surprised to see him in recording sessions, watching a "consort" of studio musicians use serpents, viols, dulcimer, and lutes to play the pavane that Herbert Stothart had found in Thoinet Arbeau's 1589 dance treatise *Orchésographie*. Thalberg looked transfixed—or exhausted. He became a fixture in the editing building after Margaret Booth was taken to the hospital for an appendectomy. Her assistant, understandably nervous to have Thalberg looking over his shoulder, cut a shot too short. Thalberg snapped at him, then apologized. In any case, the work print was ready for the first sneak preview.

Thalberg carried the cans of film in his own limousine to the California Theater in Pomona. On arriving, he was disturbed to see that, except for clusters of the cannery workers who lived in the area, the eight-hundred-seat auditorium was empty. He asked the manager to delay the curtain and had his assistants join him at the row of telephone booths in the lobby. They scanned the telephone book for fraternities and sororities and then made calls to local college students to alert them to an important event, the studio screening of a modern classic. Within an hour, enough seats were filled to justify a preview.

Seeing the film for the first time in a large theater, Thalberg felt that the music track had been mixed too high. He hoped that it would not detract from Shearer's performance. Sam Marx was sitting with him. When *Romeo and Juliet* ended, they heard only scattered applause. The film had failed to engage its first audience. Thalberg was crestfallen. Marx knew why. "With a classic story, retakes could only be made to a certain degree," wrote Marx. "There was no way to alter the motivations, cut out characters and replace them with others, or change the climactic situation. Irving was trapped by the classic construction of the play, for changes in Shakespeare would be called sacrilege." At the last minute, Thalberg had decided not to cut the swordfight between Romeo and Paris in the tomb; fortunately so, for the fruit pickers liked the fight scenes. He had also added comedy bits involving Edna May Oliver and, of all people, the horse-faced, donkey-voiced Andy Devine. There was not much else he could do to attract a wide audience. Before he could give the order to marry the sound track and cut the negative, there was one more preview. It took place on July 15, at the Four Star Theater on Wilshire Boulevard in Los Angeles.

When Thalberg emerged from the theater with his wife after the preview, he was almost ignored. John Barrymore, recently released from a Santa Barbara sanitarium, was there with his "protégée" Elaine Barrie, and they were hamming it up for the photographers. Carole Lombard and Clark Gable tried to sneak past them. The photographers spotted them and rushed from Barrymore and Barrie to the more important quarry. After the dust had settled and the Thalbergs were on their way back to Santa Monica, all they could do was hope that the critics liked *Romeo and Juliet*.

The next day *Los Angeles Times* film critic Philip Scheuer wrote: "I hesitate to call the picture great in the transcendental sense yet there is fierce magic in it. . . . Perhaps because I am too close, too near the source, I missed the final, solid ring of authenticity that only England, after all, can evoke from England." Scheuer was qualified in his praise for Shearer's Juliet. "Miss Shearer does her finest work as Juliet. Her voice is not rich or melodic, but her reading is clear and understanding."

Louella Parsons gave her usual rubber stamp, for what it was worth, calling the film "a credit not only to M-G-M but also to the entire film industry." James Francis Crow of the *Hollywood Citizen News* thought Juliet's death scene too realistic (the sound of the knife entering her chest could be heard), and then wondered why the audience, mostly critics, had given the film such a brief ovation. Only the *Hollywood Reporter* showed honest enthusiasm. "Mr. Irving Thalberg, producer, showman, and visionary, has evolved a picture that should be timeless as the story it tells," wrote Helen Gwynn. "For once he deserves top billing. Truly everything about this production will make you proud to be a movie fan."

After the Pomona preview, the lackluster reviews constituted the second *Romeo and Juliet* disappointment, but Thalberg still had the New York premiere to look forward to. He was too busy with new projects to go, but he did take Norma to John Barrymore's party for Elaine Barrie the night after the critics' preview. It was Barrie's twenty-first birthday, and Barrymore hoped to use his participation in *Camille* as leverage to get the untalented girl an M-G-M contract. Shearer sat next to her Mercutio at dinner. "He was a great raconteur," recalled photographer Ted Allan. "Norma enjoyed his stories about his early days in the theater and his irreverent comments on movie producers." This night he was more than irreverent. "Tell me, Norma," said Barrymore, nodding to Barrie and her equally meretricious mother. "I'm curious. I can't stand whores. Can you? Especially these whores who are never seen in public without their lady mothers." Shearer put down her fork and proceeded to remind Barrymore of the time in 1923 when he had tried to rape her in a dressing room at the old Warners studio on Sunset. Then she rose from the table and collected her husband. Thalberg canceled Barrie's contract and removed Barrymore from *Camille*.

The gala New York premiere of *Romeo and Juliet* took place on August 20. Howard Dietz made sure that it sparkled with newsworthy Broadway celebrities: Libby Holman, Cole Porter, Neysa McMein, and Clifton Webb. The next morning's papers told the tale. "With rare good taste and surprising resourcefulness," wrote Howard Barnes in the *New York Herald Tribune*, "the screen has translated *Romeo and Juliet* into a distinguished and beautiful photoplay. The singing measures of the tragedy have been framed in sumptuous pageantry. The acting, always effective, rises at times to genuine brilliance." He was equally complimentary about Juliet. "Miss Shearer is remarkably good. She is inclined to coyness at the start, but from the balcony scene on she plays with simple intensity and profound assurance. In her most ambitious role she does the finest acting of her career."

Frank Nugent's *New York Times* review was, of course, the clincher. "Metro the magnificent has loosed its technical magic upon Will Shakespeare and has fashioned for his *Romeo and Juliet* a jeweled setting in which the deep beauty of his romance glows and sparkles and gleams with breathless radiance. Never before in all its centuries has the play received so handsome a production as that which was unveiled last night at the Astor Theatre. . . . It is a dignified, sensitive and entirely admirable Shakespearean—not Hollywoodian—production." But what of Norma? "Miss Shearer was not at her best in the balcony scene," wrote Nugent. "With more pleasure and with a sense that this memory will endure the longer, do we recall Miss Shearer's tender and womanly perverse Juliet during her farewell scene with Romeo. Bright, too, with recollection of her surrender to uncertainty, fear and suspicion before swallowing the potion, and of that scene in which she finds her lover dead. Miss Shearer has played these, whatever her earlier mistakes, with sincerity and effect." If Nugent was perplexing, *Time* magazine was impertinent. It ignored Shearer and patronized Thalberg. "To avoid any possible gaffes in this production," said the review, "Metro-Goldwyn-Mayer's star producer Irving Thalberg did everything except recall Shakespeare from the grave."

When all the reviews were tallied, what was their common theme? An appreciation of the effort, the craftsmanship, and, of course, the intention. There was little emotion expressed for the film. Here, they said, was proof that Hollywood could do Shakespeare without looking stupid. This was a virtue to be sure, but a minor one. No one dared ask the obvious. Why had Thalberg done *Romeo and Juliet?* Shearer did not know Shakespeare. Cukor did not know Shakespeare. Thalberg did not know Shakespeare. Most important, as Reinhardt had proven with *A Midsummer Night's Dream*, a successful interpretation of Shakespeare—or of any work—depended on the vision of one person, be it Reinhardt, Cukor, or Selznick. *Grand Hotel* had worked because everyone involved with it answered to Thalberg. He knew what he wanted to say. He was not overawed by the material or swayed by experts. His interpretation was not compromised by star values or by a misplaced respect for culture.

Almost as important as the unanimity of purpose was the producer's sympathy with his characters. Both Romeo and Juliet were desperately passionate. Thalberg had not been a passionate youth. Neither had Shearer. Illness had forced him, as improvidence had pushed her, into single-minded maturity. They had little understanding of, or sympathy with, people who were in love with love. Even if they had tried to depict adolescent passion, Breen's strictures would have stopped them. Shearer's most effective scenes—the soliloquy of longing, the realization of Tybalt's death, and the potion scene—showed a new depth and power, yet this in itself was a problem. A fourteen-year-old would be incapable of profound, articulate rage. Would the public know? Or care?

In its first week, the film drew well on both coasts. Dietz had carefully timed department store tie-ins aimed at female patrons. The "Juliet cap" was a popular item. Shearer's Juliet hairstyle was creating a trend. There was also a photoplay edition of *Romeo and Juliet*, published by Random House. In the second week of release, box office improved. In fact, the film was well attended. Schools were bringing entire classes to see it. Letters to fan magazines congratulated Shearer on her performance. But there was an error in Thalberg's equation. He was supposed to spend no more than $800,000. Instead, a corps of advisers, an Italian expedition, filmed rehearsals, twelve hundred costumes, outsized sets, multiple star salaries, a vigorous ad campaign, and last but not least, 108 days of shooting added up to the very thing for which he had once condemned Erich von Stroheim: extravagance. *Romeo and Juliet* ended up costing $2.96 million. With that price tag, it simply could not make a profit. True, *The Good Earth* had cost $2.8 million—but it had those locusts. *Romeo and Juliet* had no locusts, and it had a sad ending. Thalberg was sad, too. For perhaps the first time in his career, he had become emotionally involved with a project—and it had been rejected. For all the power he possessed, he could not make America embrace his child. He was deeply hurt.

In the weeks following the previews, premiere, and release, Thalberg's colleagues noticed a change. J. J. Cohn thought he looked depressed, and blamed it on the box office. Thalberg sensed that Cohn was watching him. "It's a little slow," Thalberg said hopefully, "but it'll build. You'll see." Lewis, Jennings, Lewin, and Cukor all noticed a flattening of his energy, but he admitted nothing. "Irving disliked any show of emotion," recalled Frances Marion.

On August 21, after putting aside the New York reviews, Thalberg called Shearer. "Let's get a gang together," he suggested, "and go up to Monterey for the Labor Day holiday." Shearer was scheduled to do a radio broadcast late in the afternoon on Friday, September 4, but they could fly up the coast that night. Sam Marx overheard the phone conversation. He was aware of the Del Monte Lodge, the resort hotel where the Thalbergs had honeymooned almost nine years earlier. After Thalberg hung up, he invited Marx to the party. Thalberg looked very tired. "Sam," he said, "I've decided to add another movie to Norma's schedule before she retires. I want her to do a modern story before she does *Marie Antoinette*. We were faithful to Shakespeare . . . and I still hope the public will appreciate it. But . . . just in case . . ." On September 4, after Thalberg read the first exhibitor reports, he was more honest with Wheelwright. "I am bitterly disappointed," he told the publicist. Disappointment turned into depression. And he still had work to do.

CHAPTER 22 · The Gods Are Jealous

On Friday, September 4, Norma Shearer and Ralph Forbes were scheduled to promote *Romeo and Juliet* on Louella Parsons's CBS radio show, *Hollywood Hotel*. The program would consist of two scenes between Shearer and Forbes (as Romeo), followed by the potion scene with Shearer, and concluding with scripted banter between the actors and Parsons. Irving Thalberg spent more than a week rehearsing the actors—even recording their rehearsals—so that the radio audience would hear a flawless performance. This was part of his quest for perfection. For the past twelve years, this quest had inspired, exhilarated, and rewarded him. In the summer of 1936 it was exhausting him.

In addition to long, intense workdays, Thalberg was pledged to a punishing social schedule. In the first three quarters of the year he clocked more than forty events.* These included Joan Crawford's reception for Leopold Stokowski, the

*Thalberg's 1936 social calendar included the opening of the Ballets Russes on January 24; the Mayfair Ball, January 25; a Carole Lombard party at the Vine Street Brown Derby, February 5; the Jewish Center Association banquet, February 10; the *Modern Times* premiere, February 12; the Santa Anita Racetrack Handicap Ball, February 22; Carl Laemmle's birthday party, February 27; Joan Crawford's reception for Leopold Stokowski at the Ambassador, March 1; the monthly meeting of the advisory committee for the Film Library of the Museum of Modern Art, March 27; Charles Boyer's party for Anatole Litvak, April 3; *The Great Ziegfeld* premiere, April 15; a Leopold Stokowski concert, April 20; the Carl Laemmle dinner, April 22; the von Loewenstein dinner, April 28; the opening of Katharine Cornell's *Saint Joan*, June 25; the Actors' Fund Benefit Ball, July 1; a trip to Catalina on Baron Long's yacht *Norab* on

Jewish Center Association banquet, and the Museum of Modern Art Film Library meeting (Thalberg was a pioneer in film preservation). In the midst of all this, Frances Marion stopped by Thalberg's office on her way to Europe. "Have you anything in mind for me when I return?" she asked him.

"Not at present," he said quietly. "I have too many problems to iron out. I've had no time for future plans." He brightened at the mention of a trip. "That's what Norma and I intend to do for our children," he said. "As soon as Katharine is old enough, I'll take a sabbatical and we'll travel all through Europe. But I'll never return to Germany. There's evil there. It's corrosive. It's destroying Germany's roots." There was a momentary silence. Thalberg gazed into the distance. Marion looked at him and for a moment saw the boy she had met outside Carl Laemmle's office seventeen years earlier. A question brought her back to the present.

"How long do you expect to be gone?" Thalberg asked.

"About three months."

"I'll miss you," he said.

"I'll miss you, Irving." Marion stood up. She felt her eyes welling up with tears, a sight she had to spare Thalberg. She made a hasty exit.

Thalberg was cultivating the same formal affection for David Lewis. Months before he assigned the thirty-two-year-old producer to *Camille*, he favored him with a private office. "Irving moved my office to his library," wrote Lewis. "It was across from his office and had always been sacrosanct. He had used it as a second office when he wanted to get away from his own. It had a marvelous table desk, which, like Irving, I much preferred. It was really the nicest office in the building." If the tall, good-looking Lewis could not tell that Thalberg respected him, he had only to look around him. Most M-G-M executives regarded Lewis as an ambitious interloper. Many Thalberg associates disliked his studied elegance. Mayer's men were less diplomatic; they tagged him a "fairy." Albert Lewin thought he was a poor substitute for Paul Bern. "Al was decidedly unhappy," recalled Lewis. "He sensed the growing feeling Thalberg had for me and resented it bitterly."

The diminutive "Professor" Lewin had little reason to be resentful. Because of *The Good Earth*, he was spending long hours in Thalberg's company. Thalberg had further honored him by assigning him both *The Prisoner of Zenda* and the long-awaited *Marie Antoinette*. Lewin and his wife, Mildred, lived up the coast in

---

August 2; the opening of Tallulah Bankhead's play *Reflected Glory* at the Belasco Theater, followed by George Cukor's party in a downtown restaurant, August 10; the trip to San Francisco, August 14; and a banquet for Johannes Poulsen on September 2.

Malibu, so he often visited Thalberg on weekends (when Lewis was at home with James Whale). On one Saturday afternoon, Lewin was engaged in a story conference with Thalberg. They were conducting it outside the house, next to the pool. "I was sitting in the sunshine," Lewin recalled in 1967. "Irving was in the shade of an umbrella. Norma was in the pool with Katharine, teaching her to dog paddle. Irving Jr. was practicing diving. Breakers were crashing on the beach a few feet away. It was an idyllic scene, to say the least." In much the same way that Frances Marion had, Lewin found himself looking at Thalberg from an odd perspective. It caused him to interrupt. "Irving," Lewin cut in.

"What?"

"If I were you, I'd be worried."

"About this dialogue?"

"No, no."

"About what, then?"

"I was looking at you and it occurred to me," said Lewin. "You've just turned thirty-seven, and you've got everything that a man could want. You've got millions. You're a captain of industry. You have a lovely, talented wife, and two beautiful, healthy children." Thalberg smiled and nodded in agreement. Lewin took a deep breath of sea air and exhaled slowly. "The gods hate people like you. They're probably hiding behind that wall with a great big bat."

"You're right," Thalberg laughed. "You're absolutely right." He glanced at the wall, which belonged to his neighbor Douglas Fairbanks, chuckled, and went back to the script in his hand.

Thalberg's life was, to all appearances, a fortunate one. His health had been stable for more than three years, thanks to regular checkups by Dr. Philip Newmark. Thalberg was also corresponding with Dr. David Perla and his wife, Dr. Jessie Marmorston. In addition, Thalberg maintained contact with Dr. Franz Groedel, who was practicing clinical cardiology on Park Avenue in New York. (He had been forced to leave Germany when the Nazis discovered that his mother was Jewish.) Other than contact with these specialists, Thalberg's only concession to the time bomb in his chest was the presence of a new "assistant." The man's primary function was to hand him mild stimulants: raisins, dried fruit, chocolate candy bars, and Coca-Cola. Thalberg still carried nitroglycerine tablets to put under his tongue in the event of palpitations, but no one had ever seen him use them. What they did see was a studied carelessness.

When Sidney Franklin went looking for Thalberg in his bungalow, he would often find him in the mezzanine dining room, wolfing down his dinner before a preview. "Irving, you'll kill yourself some day doing this," said Franklin. Thalberg's excuse was that they no longer enjoyed catered trips to previews in Big Red, so he had to eat when he could. Anita Loos saw him pushing himself to exhaustion. "Irving did nothing but work," recalled Loos. "He was warned—numerous times. Do you know what he said? He said he'd rather die than stop working." In jest or not, death was a topic in the Thalberg bungalow. A cursory glance at his projects would reveal a common theme. *Romeo and Juliet*, *The Good Earth*, *Camille*, *Goodbye, Mr. Chips*, and *Marie Antoinette* all lost a main character to death. Even if Thalberg's work had morbid undertones, he assumed a cheerful façade, both at the studio and at home. After spending a day trying to persuade Charles A. Lindbergh to sign a $500,000 movie contract, Thalberg would signal David Lewis to bring his car around. No one said it aloud, but Lewis was becoming as trusted a friend as Paul Bern had been.

"Bit by bit," wrote Lewis, "I got to know Thalberg better. And he began to feel more comfortable with me. Almost every night I would drive him home and he would unwind. He always talked a lot in the car, and he always asked me in when we arrived. Thalberg was not a particularly outgoing person. But there was always that underlying cordiality and warmth; it developed over time. He treated me as the young neophyte, and he was the man who'd 'been there.'"

Lewis was always surprised to see Thalberg greeted upon his arrival, not by his butler or maid, but by Shearer. Even when he came in at 2:00 in the morning, she was waiting. "He was usually a little hungry," recalled Lewis, "and she would go into the kitchen, although they had an enormous staff of help, and make her specialty, fried bread sandwiches. Irving loved sandwiches prepared that way. She would make him a weak Scotch and, since I liked it weak too, she would make one for me. Then, in her robe, she would come in and join the conversation." Unlike Lewin or Jean Harlow's mother, Shearer was not proprietary. "She was always nice to me," Lewis said. "She approved of his having someone who was not a chauffeur or driver, but one of his staff with whom he could unwind." Lewis was, like Bern before him, the sole bachelor on Thalberg's staff. Thalberg was hardly unaware of Lewis's relationship with Whale, but he gently and tactfully expressed a concern for his future. "Someday you will have a family," Thalberg said when Shearer was in the kitchen. "And a wonderful wife like Norma."

Family was increasingly important to Thalberg. "He adored those children," said Lewis. Even in this, the busiest year of his career, Thalberg never left for work without playing with his children. He brought them to the studio whenever possible, even onto soundstages. He would have a gaffer aim a small spotlight at a wall. Then he would entertain. "I couldn't believe it," recalled Ralph Wheelwright. "I walked onto the *Romeo and Juliet* stage one day, and there was Irving, making shadow pictures on the wall for his kids." Thalberg fully expected his son to become a moviemaker. When discussing *Romeo and Juliet*, Thalberg said, "If it doesn't do as well as we'd like, Irving Jr. can remake it in color when he grows up."

Thalberg became angry when the gossip columnist Walter Winchell, whose *New York Daily Mirror* column was syndicated to more than two thousand newspapers, printed an item that was brazen even for him. "Winchell asserted that Irving and Norma had separated because Norma was unfaithful," said Lewin. "Irving was extremely agitated, so much so that we were anxious."

"Norma has been such a wonderful wife," said Thalberg, leaning on the glass top of his desk. "I hate to have her hurt by this." After making calls to force a retraction from Winchell, Thalberg found himself feeling sick. He went home. David Lewis came to the house a few days later and found Thalberg suffering from a cold. He was still incensed about Winchell. "I don't mind so much," he told Lewis. "I can take it. But it's hard on Norma."

Thalberg had to deal with another scandal that summer, and it was not a trumped-up one. After completing *Romeo and Juliet* and before starting *Camille*, George Cukor was arrested for soliciting sex from a policeman; he was also known to have cast a cop in a recent film as payment for his tearing up a friend's speeding ticket. Whatever the circumstances, Cukor's career was in jeopardy, not to mention Thalberg's production. He appealed to Mayer, who in turn asked District Attorney Buron Fitts to drop the morals charge and have every reference to it expunged from city records.

Thalberg made very few calls to Mayer in the summer of 1936. Mayer had been re-elected president of the Motion Picture Producers Association and was traveling. He took a cruise to Panama, and then he made a triumphal return to St. John, New Brunswick. He was given the key to the city and encouraged to make speeches; in them he credited Nick Schenck for helping him become an American success story, but did not thank Thalberg. When Mayer was back in his office, Thalberg thought it best not to bother him. There was no hope of reconciliation. Their natures were too different. Mayer was hotheaded and he was cold. And yet, in quiet evenings at the beach, he tried to understand how the rift had widened to a chasm, necessitating plans for the I. G. Thalberg Corporation. He shared his thoughts with Shearer, asking her what she remembered. In time, both of them were taking stock of the past thirteen years, tracing the path from Mission Road.

Shearer asked Thalberg what he thought of all they had done together. He told her that he had been fortunate in most things and unfortunate in a few others, but that for the most part, his life with her had been "golden." He did have regrets. He regretted losing his friendship with Mayer. Far from being an isolated trauma, this was an ongoing hurt, but he would bear it. He had to.

Needless to say, Thalberg was grateful that Shearer had put his health ahead of her career. He felt lucky for the time they had shared. And, if by some chance, his health should fail . . . he watched her eyes widen. "When I'm gone, you'll probably go off and marry some guy who'll get all my money!" Shearer realized that she was being kidded. Thalberg smiled and wagged his finger at her. "Just don't marry an actor!" They bore the reality with humor, but the reality was there.

Thalberg worried that he had spent too little time with his son, who was almost six. He also worried about "Katie." The one-year-old was aware that Shearer was giving more time to Shakespeare than to her. Perla recommended that the Thalbergs hire a child-care specialist named Greta Morrison. The live-in nurse's attention soothed the child, and Thalberg resolved to spend more time with her and "Little Irving" once his projects were out the door. Labor Day would be the watershed. The Thalbergs would go to the Del Monte Lodge to celebrate their ninth wedding anniversary. Irving would rest, relax, and come back to a new program. But even before they had packed, he found a new project.

Thalberg saw a missed opportunity in Reinhardt's Hollywood Bowl spectacle. He was intrigued, then, when his new friends Baron Long, the millionaire owner of the Biltmore Hotel, and Gilbert "Icky" Outhwaite, its flamboyant manager, told him of a theatrical opportunity. The California Festival Association was seeking sponsors for the medieval play *Everyman*, to be staged outdoors by Dr. Johannes Poulsen, director of the Royal Theater of Copenhagen. In short order, Thalberg secured the backing of Dr. A. H. Giannini of the Bank of America and reserved the Hollywood Bowl—with the proviso that a sizable portion of the profits would benefit Jewish refugees from Germany.

The production of *Everyman* was pulled together in record time, and it bade fair to compete with Reinhardt's. It had bigger sets and a cast that included the venerable Mrs. Leslie Carter. The pageant was scheduled to open on September 10, three days after Labor Day. On Wednesday, September 2, Thalberg hosted a lavish banquet for Poulsen at the Biltmore. Mayer, just back from a token visit to Franklin D. Roosevelt's White House, sat a safe distance from Thalberg. Poulsen thanked Thalberg for all that he had done to promote the *Everyman* pageant. Thalberg looked tired.

On Friday, September 4, Thalberg and Shearer were packed for their trip to the lodge. Confirmed guests included Harpo Marx, the Mervyn LeRoys, the Sam Marxes, the Robert Z. Leonards, the Jack Conways, the Sam Woods, and the Chico Marxes. While Shearer prepared for her radio broadcast, Thalberg spent the day in conferences. He planned to discuss *A Day at the Races* with Wood and the two Marx Brothers at the lodge, so he consulted with David Lewis on *Pride and Prejudice*. A filmed record had been made of the stage performance in late 1935. They would need to view it in order to decide on casting. Thalberg was considering it for Shearer, but a modern story might be better. He instructed Sam Marx to bring a list of properties to the lodge. No matter who starred in *Pride and Prejudice*, Lewis would be producing. The conference got under way.

While Lewis presented his ideas, Thalberg flipped a coin in the air, trying to land it on the sprinkler system pipe. Predictably, he did not miss a word of Lewis's presentation. He began to make comments. His most often used phrase, according to Howard Strickling, was "What you have is good; here's how you can make it better." If a writer resisted, Thalberg did not force the issue. "He didn't demand obedience," wrote Lewis. "He always listened. In case of a disagreement he would say, 'We'll try it both ways. Mine first.'" Lewis did not argue with Thalberg. "He knew I was in a process of learning," Lewis said. "He loved to see me gobble it up. He was the best kind of teacher." Thalberg once told Lewis:

> Nobody can teach you anything from his own experience, but he can find a key to you and make you open yourself up to reach the highest power you can reach, to make you never stop thinking. Many people are willing to settle for seventy percent or eighty percent. As far as I'm concerned, I don't want to settle for anything less than one hundred percent. Now I don't mean a one hundred percent assurance that the audience will buy it, but the assurance that you have given a hundred percent of what's in *you*.

After more than a year, Lewis had watched Thalberg in conferences, screening rooms, and editing rooms. He did not settle for second best. "Films that anyone else would ship, Thalberg worked on, made retakes, and continued to improve, improve, improve," said Lewis. Thalberg made no claim to infallibility, nor did he exhibit false modesty. "I've made my share of stinkers," he admitted, "but even if you choose wrong at the beginning, you must give it the very best you have." Lewis never heard Thalberg explain what motivated this attitude. All he saw was a striving for quality. "He was the one with the dream," wrote Lewis, "and it was he who would not sell his dream short."

Lewis withdrew to his office when Al Lewin arrived for a *Good Earth* editing "confab." This meeting was taking place, according to Sidney Franklin, six years to the day after Thalberg had purchased Pearl Buck's novel. Franklin and Lewin filed into Thalberg's office, followed by Basil Wrangell, the film's editor, and Margaret Booth, the editing department head. Thalberg had a surprise for them. No more sitting around in easy chairs; there was a new mahogany conference table with three chairs on each side and a wingback chair at each end. Thalberg was quite pleased with himself. "This is our director's table," he announced. "In the future, we'll have our meetings here. This will bring us closer together." He ambled to the head of the table and pulled out the richly upholstered chair. Instead of seating himself, he turned to Franklin: "Sidney, you sit here." Franklin stared at him for a moment. "Come on, Sidney," said Thalberg. "You sit at the head of the table."

"Irving," said Franklin, "you're the chief. The chief always sits at the head of the table."

"Sidney, I explained that this is the director's table. You're the director. You sit here."

Franklin would not come to the head of the table. He said he would feel uncomfortable taking Thalberg's place there. Thalberg finally had to give in. He did so with a smile. The meeting commenced, and Thalberg reviewed the most recent cutting continuity. He was in a chipper mood. When he heard that Franklin wanted a few shots to be restored to their former length, he said to Booth: "Now, Maggie, don't you let him have all that footage!"

The meeting had been in session over an hour when Thalberg interrupted it to have a portable radio set brought in. At 5 P.M. they tuned to KHJ and listened to Shearer and Forbes reprise *Romeo and Juliet* for half an hour. At the program's conclusion, Bernie Hyman appeared at the door to report that everything was ready for the trip to Monterey. "It's getting late," he said. "You have a few calls to make before Norma gets here." Thalberg told his colleagues that he had been looking forward to this weekend. He planned nothing more ambitious than getting in a few holes of golf at Pebble Beach, which was adjacent to the lodge. Franklin and the others liked that idea. Thalberg needed to rest, not take work with him. The meeting adjourned and Lewis came out of his office, Zoë Akins at his side. Would there be time for a short session?

Thalberg sat down with Lewis and Akins to review their progress on *Camille*. After five weeks of shooting, the film was winding down. Thalberg wanted Akins to change a few lines before the cast memorized the pages. "We were waiting for Norma to come back from the radio station with Louella Parsons," recalled

Lewis. "While we were talking, I said something about 'ten years from now,' and Thalberg said, 'I'm not going to be here ten years from now.'"

"Irving!" exclaimed Lewis.

"I might not be here ten days from now," said Thalberg matter-of-factly. "He shot a mischievous little boy look at me," recalled Lewis. Thalberg realized that he had scared Lewis. "Pay no attention to my nonsense," Thalberg said quickly. Before Lewis could comment, he heard the sound of a hubbub outside. Shearer and Parsons were arriving. Thalberg adjourned the meeting and told Lewis that he need not bring his car. Shearer was taking him directly to Municipal Airport, where a chartered plane was waiting. And so the long weekend began.

The noise and vibration of the airplane did not allow for conversation, which was just as well. Shearer was upset about something that had occurred at the radio station. After she had completed her potion scene, she had had a strong sensation that someone—something—was speaking to her. Whoever or whatever it was, it said: "You will never act again." The experience had disturbed her. It was not something she wished to share with her husband.

The Del Monte Lodge, which was often confused with the large Hotel Del Monte, was an exclusive inn overlooking the Pebble Beach Golf Course on the Monterey Peninsula. All of Thalberg's invitees were able to join him there for the weekend. Sam Marx had followed his instructions. "I brought along a list of new books and plays," recalled Marx. Saturday passed, and Thalberg did not ask for them. He was enjoying the scenery, the company, and the time off.

On Sunday, September 6, Thalberg played golf. The weather was mild, but still summery for Monterey. After finishing his game, he came into the lodge and saw Harpo Marx, Sam Wood, and a few others playing bridge on the veranda overlooking the Pacific. He sat down with them and they quickly dealt him in. Late-afternoon winds were kicking up from the ocean. Thalberg had worked up a sweat golfing and had left his sweater on the course. He was wearing a short-sleeved shirt. It was still damp. Shearer, ever alert, walked briskly through the lobby and spied him sitting in cross-ventilation. She turned on her heel and disappeared upstairs. Thalberg's game was moving along when Shearer reappeared, carrying a sweater. "Irving," she said, trying not to attract attention, "you'd better put this on. It's dropping."

"What?"

"The temperature. Put this on, please."

"Do you see Sam wearing a sweater?" he asked, not looking up from his cards. "Or Harpo?"

Shearer knew better than to argue with her husband. "He was sensitive to her babying him," said Lewis. He did not want to be mothered in front of his buddies. Rather than make a scene, Shearer left the sweater with him and went to their room. When Thalberg began to shiver, it was not because he was catching a chill; it was because he was already ill.

The next morning, Sam Marx brought his literary list downstairs, hoping to get a little time with Thalberg; he could then contact authors' agents on Tuesday. But Thalberg was not in the lobby. Shearer came down alone. She told Marx that Thalberg was in bed with a cold. She appeared tense, but tried to downplay it. The weekend ended on an uncertain note.

On Tuesday, everyone was back at work; everyone except Thalberg. He was at home in bed. Shearer was talking to him about Dr. Groedel. The phone rang. It was Edmund Goulding, who was writing *Maytime* as he went along. He needed Thalberg's approval of the next day's scenes. They could not be put off any longer by shooting Technicolor tests; there were no more costumes to test. Thalberg told Goulding to send the pages over with assistant director Joe Newman. An hour later, Thalberg read the scene, okayed it, then spent the rest of the day sleeping. In the late afternoon, Shearer was surprised to see him up and dressed. He was going to the Hollywood Bowl to help Dr. Poulsen with the *Everyman* rehearsal. Shearer tried to reason with him. Yes, it was eighty-six degrees today, but this was September and the fog would roll in. He told her that he had sponsored this pageant and had an obligation to see it through—and that was that. After he left, Shearer picked up the telephone and dialed the bungalow. Fortunately, David Lewis was still there. "Would you be willing to fly east with Irving?" she asked him. She explained that Thalberg needed to see a specialist. Lewis was surprised to hear that Thalberg was ill. "It's necessary," Shearer said tersely. "He wants someone to fly with him. I know you fly. Nobody else I know does."

"Surely," Lewis said. "Of course."

"I'll let you know as soon as I know something," Shearer said in a distant tone of voice.

Thalberg, meanwhile, was sitting in the Hollywood Bowl, giving Poulsen an occasional suggestion on staging. The *Everyman* pageant was a morality play dating from the fifteenth century. It tells the story of an average man, the "Everyman," who is told by Death that his time is about to run out. Everyman begins to prepare a Book of Accounts, adding up the credits of his Beauty, Strength, and Intelligence. He is confident that his Book will get him into Heaven even when his family, his friends, and his possessions betray him. By the hour of his death, his

Book of Accounts has been emptied of everything but his Good Deeds. As it turns out, that is all he has ever needed. What he has gained on earth during his lifetime is unimportant. What is important—what opens the gates of Heaven—is what he has given. The *Everyman* pageant was a far cry from Thalberg's cinematic fare, but here he was, sitting in the wings, watching a Danish director yell at Hollywood stage hands: "Oil the hinges to the gates of Heaven!"

Thalberg's cold was better on Wednesday, but he stayed home again. Shearer watched hopefully. She tried to make him skip a gratuitous social engagement. Icky Outhwaite wanted the Thalbergs to make an appearance at a tea he was giving for Rose Bingham, the countess of Warwick. Thalberg was not thinking clearly. He insisted on going to both the pretentious party and the final dress rehearsal of *Everyman*. Shearer was anxious. The temperature outside was twelve degrees lower than the day before. She bundled up her husband and accompanied him to both events.

On Thursday, September 10, Thalberg stayed home from work again, but his cold appeared to be on the wane. Lewis was in the bungalow when his phone rang. It was Shearer, calling about the proposed flight. "It won't be necessary," she assured him. "Everything's fine now." Lewis hung up thinking that Thalberg had had a cold in mid-July and it had been nothing. Besides, it wasn't a cold he needed to worry about; it was strain on his heart. That evening, Thalberg, Shearer, and a bevy of movie stars graced the opening of the *Everyman* pageant. Master of ceremonies Conrad Nagel introduced Thalberg as the play's sponsor, and 12,000 people applauded the man they recognized from March's Academy Awards. The majestic play proved popular, but not as popular as *A Midsummer Night's Dream* had been. Once again, Thalberg had given his all for a qualified success.

On Friday, September 11, something happened. Thalberg's condition changed—suddenly and drastically. The common cold was gone. In its place was a complex of symptoms: a raw throat, fever, dehydration, aches, and nausea. Shearer called Dr. Newmark, who rushed to Santa Monica. His diagnosis was worrisome. Thalberg was suffering from "septic sore throat," the popular designation for a streptococcus infection. There was not much to do except keep him comfortable, hydrate him with nonacidic liquids, and hope that the stress would not impose on his heart.

At this point, Shearer began to wonder about the sixty-eight-year-old Dr. Newmark. Was he too conservative? He bridled when she asked about the Mayo Clinic and its use of the new sulfonamide drug Prontosil. He cut her off when she brought up the possibility of flying Thalberg there or of flying the medicine from there. He was the physician, not she. As the hours passed, Shearer saw Thalberg suffering—and not improving. She decided to challenge Dr. Newmark. But it was too late to call Dr. Groedel in New York for a second opinion. Instead, she called Dr. Newmark on her own. Predictably, he treated her as a meddlesome rich woman foolishly questioning a medical professional who had forty-five years of experience. She immediately regretted the call. But she had to do something. Thalberg was growing worse. She called Thalberg's mother and her own mother.

Early on the morning of Saturday, September 12, Henrietta arrived. She stood shocked at what she saw. Thalberg was feverish and weak. He was complaining of chest pains. Shearer was on the phone to New York. Dr. Groedel said that he would charter a plane and worry about the expense later. He could probably be there by Sunday morning. Shearer asked Thalberg about the chest pains. Were they like the ones before? Were they "radiating," as Dr. Newmark used to say? No, they were deep in his chest—when he inhaled. Shearer looked at Henrietta. "Pneumonia," said Henrietta with a look of dread. Edith Shearer arrived shortly after and took over the management of the house, directing the staff and keeping the children downstairs. Shearer and her mother-in-law sat by the bed, trying to get Thalberg to tell them what exactly he was feeling. He had trouble talking. He was beginning to cough.

Shearer called Dr. Newmark. Then she called her best friend, Merle Oberon. She tracked her down to Sam Goldwyn's lot, where she was shooting *Beloved Enemy* with Brian Aherne. Oberon said that she would come as soon as the day's work was done. Shearer told her that it was serious. Irving could not stop coughing. His mother thought it was pneumonia. The coughing alone could cause a heart attack. Between coughs, gasping for breath, Irving was saying that this was going to do him in. Shearer was frightened. Shearer called Sam Goldwyn, but Frances told her that he was seriously ill, too; she would come by herself.

Dr. Newmark returned. All that he needed to make the new diagnosis was a stethoscope, two tapping fingers, and a cotton swab. Thalberg had lobar pneumonia. By this time it was midday. He asked Shearer if she could charter a plane. She called Howard Strickling. While arrangements were being made, Dr. Newmark came to her and took her aside. Henrietta could not hear what he was saying, but she could see his posture, the slope of his shoulders, the way his hands opened and fell against his pant legs. To put a pneumonia patient in this stage of illness on an airplane would be fatal. It was too dangerous to try. And there was no way to get a new drug from a research clinic on an airplane on the weekend. Dr. Groedel was already on his way. Dr. Newmark called the hospital and had a nurse sent over. There was nothing to do but watch and wait.

More family members arrived: Douglas Shearer, Athole Shearer Hawks, Sylvia and Larry Weingarten, and William Thalberg. When they entered the bedroom, they saw Henrietta sitting in silence at her son's bedside, her dark eyes fixed and staring. Thalberg was having trouble breathing, and he periodically broke into coughing spasms. There was whispering by the bedroom door. Someone tiptoed in. It was Rosabelle Laemmle (who was now married to Universal producer Stanley Bergerman). She approached the bed. Thalberg blinked at her in grateful recognition, but could not speak. She sat with him for a while. Shearer called Albert Lewin and asked him to phone "Irving's boys." Lewin called everyone, even Eddie Mannix, but somehow neglected to call David Lewis. Merle Oberon arrived around 7:00 and made sure that Shearer ate dinner.

Early on the morning of Sunday, September 13, Dr. Groedel was brought from the airport in an M-G-M limousine. Dr. Newmark consulted with him. There was good news. Thalberg's heart was functioning perfectly; there were no signs of damage or weakening. If he could survive the pneumonia, his heart might defy the old predictions. Thalberg was able to hear and comprehend, but he continued coughing intermittently.

His colleagues began arriving around 9:00, when the rest of M-G-M's employees were driving to the company picnic at Clarence Brown's newly purchased ranch in Calabasas. Mannix showed up, as did Lewin, Jack Conway, and Bernie Hyman. They sat on the patio and discussed the picnic. Lewin wrote a message for Mannix to read over the public address system at the ranch: "Only illness prevents me from being with you today. Best wishes, Irving Thalberg." In spite of all that had occurred between Mayer and Thalberg, Mannix hoped for a rapprochement. What he saw upstairs appalled him. Thalberg, whom he had thought fairly robust in the past few months, was a shivering wraith lost in the expanses of a vast white bed. Mannix sat down and tried to communicate with him. Lewin, Conway, and Hyman waited downstairs.

It was the same for each visitor. Thalberg tried to speak. The exertion provoked a coughing fit. Thalberg's mother reached in to wipe away the mucus. When he breathed deeply, a rumbling, gurgling sound came from his chest. Hyman was the last to sit with him. For a while, the coughing subsided. Thalberg was able to formulate sentences while Shearer stroked his forehead. Hyman glanced at her and tried to say something optimistic. Thalberg would have none of it. "I'm not getting the right treatment," he whispered, pausing repeatedly to clear his throat.

"They don't know what they're doing. They're killing me." Hyman tried to be sanguine. Thalberg was grimly succinct. "No, Bernie," he said slowly, barely able to shake his head. "This time I'm not going to make it." Shearer lowered her head and bit her lip. "I'm not going to make it," he repeated, then managed a wan smile. "'Nearer my God to Thee . . .'" he whispered. Shearer rose from her seat by the bed and walked out of the room, a hand to her face.

For the rest of Sunday, Thalberg's condition remained grave, but both doctors expected him to pass the crisis. In such cases, the hours around dawn decide if the patient will live. The family planned a vigil. Meanwhile, Lewin called Strickling and the Goldwyns with progress reports. Douglas Fairbanks came over every few hours to offer help. Shearer's mother and Greta Morrison put the children to bed. In a calm moment, Thalberg asked Shearer if one of his secretaries could come to the house to tell him what was happening at the studio. Lewin called Margaret Webster and arranged for her to come at 7:00 the next morning. The elder Thalbergs, the Weingartens, and Athole set up watch in the bedroom. Henrietta knelt by her son's bedside and began to pray. Her husband joined her. Occasionally they would go into a guest bedroom to lie down. No one slept.

Mannix had approached Mayer after the company picnic and told him the truth about Thalberg's condition. He advised him not to go to the house. Mayer had planned to go dancing at the Trocadero that night. Instead, he stayed home. Not one to indulge in introspection, he nevertheless spent the night thinking about what had gone wrong since "the Mission Road days."

Thalberg's condition worsened around 11 P.M. The nurse noted that his temperature was rising. He was visibly distressed and restless because of the fever. The coughing spells became more severe. There was blood in the mucus. The nurse called Dr. Newmark. He said he would go to the hospital for an oxygen tent. Shearer maintained her watch.

In the early-morning hours, the nurse pointed out that the coughing had stopped. Thalberg appeared to be sleeping peacefully. As day broke, there was hope. Shearer could hear cars outside. Frances Goldwyn was arriving, followed by Margaret Webster. Then Dr. Newmark came in, followed by an orderly carrying metal frames and isinglass panels. Thalberg opened his eyes and looked around him. He saw Webster. "What are the grosses?" he asked.

"I beg your pardon, sir?"

"At the Astor," he whispered. *Romeo and Juliet*. What were the weekend grosses?"

She hurried out of the room to call Loew's. Dr. Newmark and his assistant began assembling the oxygen tent. Thalberg regarded it with a fatalistic smile. "Norma," he called in a voice clogged with phlegm. As the rest of the family watched, Shearer drew close to him. "The children," he whispered. "Don't let them forget me." Shearer gripped his hand, then looked over her shoulder at the half-finished tent. Thalberg saw what she was thinking, looked at her, and weakly shook his head. He was too racked with fever to do much more. But he did manage to communicate one thing: he was dying. He closed his eyes, and Shearer rose quickly, calling for Edith. In a few minutes, Irving Jr. and Katharine, barely awake, were carried into the room by the Weingartens. Shearer brought them to the bedside. Thalberg was asleep, she thought. He did not respond when they spoke to him. She asked that they be taken back to the nursery. Dr. Newmark informed Shearer that Thalberg had just slipped into a coma. He positioned the oxygen tent over the bed.

Lewin and Conway arrived at 9:00 A.M. on Monday, September 14. Thalberg had been in a coma for nearly two hours. Henrietta and William were kneeling by the bed, their heads bowed in prayer. Shearer was at the head of the bed, looking at her husband through the prismatic panels of the tent. He moved occasionally and looked around, but when he spoke, it was in an incoherent murmur. Dr. Groedel sat on the other side of the bed, monitoring Thalberg's heartbeat. Dr. Newmark was at the foot of the bed. Frances Goldwyn and Merle Oberon were downstairs in the living room. Greta Morrison was feeding the children breakfast. By 10:00, the sickroom vigil included Athole, Edith, the Weingartens, Shearer, Lewin, Conway, and Hyman.

At 10:16 A.M. something startled Shearer. Dr. Groedel leaned into the bed and then checked Thalberg's pulse. Dr. Newmark joined him. They exchanged glances. Irving Grant Thalberg was dead.

One by one, the witnesses filed out of the room, leaving Shearer with her husband's body.

Downstairs, Lewin was dialing Mayer's office. He heard Dr. Newmark talking to Dr. Groedel. "This was the heart that was supposed to fail before he was thirty," he said. "It was magnificent. Even when his temperature rose to 103 and 104, his heart stood up. Ironic."

"Tragic," said Groedel.

The telephone in Louis B. Mayer's office rang through a tense silence. His secretary announced a call from Mr. Lewin. Mayer answered, then grunted and hung up. Mannix and the other executives waiting in the office looked at Mayer. "Irving is dead," he told them. Then he rushed into his private chamber.

Lewin went back upstairs to join Conway outside the bedroom. They saw Shearer leave her husband's body and come to the door, where her mother and sister were waiting for her. "Norma," said her mother, "what about the children?"

"They mustn't be told," Shearer said, closing her eyes and shaking her head. "Not yet." Edith Shearer had her arm around her daughter when Sylvia Weingarten brought Greta Morrison up the stairs. Edith instructed Morrison to take the children outside to the beach and keep them there until the undertakers had come and gone. Shearer looked faint, so Athole pulled a chair from the guest room and pushed it next to the door of the bedroom. Shearer slumped into it. Lewin looked into the bedroom. Edith pushed past him and pulled the door closed.

Lewin and Conway were following Morrison down the stairs when Mayer arrived. Sitting quietly in the living room were J. J. Cohn, John Considine, Ben Goetz, Harry Rapf, and Hunt Stromberg. Mayer ignored them and bounded up the stairs. When Lewin reached the bottom of the stairs, he looked past the living room to the French doors that led to the patio. Katharine was playing on the floor in a square of sunlight that was streaming through a high window. Lewin set his jaw and left the house, unable to greet his colleagues. "After what I had seen upstairs," he recalled, "and then to see the baby gurgling on the floor. I was stunned."

Shearer rose to greet Mayer. They both began sobbing. When they were able to speak, Shearer tried to relate Thalberg's sadness about the estrangement and his wish for reconciliation. Mayer promised to help with the arrangements. He went into the living room and assembled a team to carry out Shearer's wishes. Considine, Conway, Mannix, Rapf, and Stromberg were dispatched.

In the early afternoon, a hearse arrived from the Malinow & Simons Mortuary on Venice Boulevard in downtown Los Angeles. After Thalberg's body had been removed, Shearer spent a few minutes alone in the bedroom and then went outside to find her children. She hugged them and held them, but she did not tell them what had happened. She was coming inside when she saw Weingarten admitting Rabbi Edgar F. Magnin. He had been a frequent visitor in years past, and Shearer was relieved to have him there. All other visitors—Fairbanks, Darryl Zanuck, Jesse Lasky—were met at the door by Weingarten, who explained that Shearer was unable to see anyone. After Rabbi Magnin departed, Dr. Newmark gave Shearer a mild sedative. Thalberg's parents were already asleep in a guest room. Then the two doctors left the house.

Mayer returned to the studio and authorized Strickling to make a formal announcement. M-G-M employees were notified first, starting with the Thalberg bungalow. David Lewis was in a meeting with a group of newly recruited writers when Bernie Hyman came in, unannounced, and told him to end the meeting. This took Lewis by surprise because Hyman was not a part of Thalberg's production unit. Once the writers had left, Hyman turned to Lewis and said: "Irving just died." Lewis was too shocked to speak. He just stared. "Yes," said Hyman calmly, "he died a little after ten." He started to leave and then turned to Lewis and said blankly: "You haven't got anybody to protect you now. I'm taking over." Lewis did not understand what Hyman was saying. Perhaps it was shock. Lewis took a minute to compose himself. "I went into the anteroom," he recalled. "Everyone there was weeping; nobody seemed to know what to do. It had hit the staff as hard as it had hit me."

Sam Marx was returning to his office from a meeting with Kate Corbaley. When he entered, his secretary looked at him in an odd way. "Did you hear about Mr. Thalberg?" she asked. He had not. "He's died," she said sadly.

"William Thalberg?" he asked, trying to think of the last time he had seen him.

"No," she said. "Irving."

On the *Day at the Races* set, Sam Wood walked in, his face streaked with tears, and said, "The little brown fellow just died." One by one, soundstage telephones rang. Filming stopped on *Maytime*, *Camille*, and *Born to Dance*. Cries of disbelief were heard. Lights were doused. Work was suspended. M-G-M was in a state of shock. The shock soon spread to all of Hollywood and then to New York, where Nick Schenck made the obligatory statement. "Thalberg was the most important man in the production end of the motion picture industry. He was important personally even more than officially. We all loved him. It is difficult to bear such a blow." Schenck chartered a plane and brought Joseph L. Mankiewicz, J. Robert Rubin, and Howard Dietz with him. "Enormous headlines," recalled Lewis, "not only in Los Angeles but all across the country, screamed THALBERG DEAD!"

.   .   .

Irving Thalberg's funeral was scheduled for Wednesday, September 16, at the Wilshire Boulevard Temple. Rabbi Magnin would conduct the services. Jewish law required that the ceremony take place within forty-eight hours of death; in addition, Rosh Hashanah was commencing at sunset on the 16th. Thalberg's family hoped that the funeral of an individual who valued his privacy so highly could be carried out with dignity. Mayer instructed Strickling and Whitey Hendry, head of his private police force, to enforce etiquette. Formal invitations were delivered by courier and checked outside the temple. A crowd estimated at eight thousand persons flanked the corridor from the sidewalk to the temple. A roster of the attendees conveyed the number of persons whose lives Thalberg had touched.

From his Universal days came Tod Browning, Erich von Stroheim, and William Wyler. From Mission Road came Maggie Booth, John Stahl, Reginald Barker, and Ben Schulberg. From the first days of the merger came Abe Lehr, Edwin Loeb, Joe Cohn, Bob Rubin, King Vidor, Fred Niblo, Conrad Nagel, Aileen Pringle, and Clarence Bull.

From the thriving days of M-G-M silents came Ralph Forbes, Joan Crawford, Dorothy Sebastian, Lionel Barrymore, Benjamin Glazer, Waldemar Young, Ernst Lubitsch, Hans Kraly, Edmund Goulding, David Selznick, Harry Beaumont, and Clarence Brown. From the days of the early talkies came Bayard Veiller, Oliver Hinsdell, Cecil B. DeMille, and Ruth Chatterton.

From the years of Thalberg's preeminence came Anita Loos and John Emerson, Virginia Bruce, Johnny Weissmuller, Jean Harlow, John Lee Mahin, Victor Fleming, George Fitzmaurice, John Barrymore, Franchot Tone, Richard Boleslavsky, Gary Cooper, and Ralph Morgan.

From years of Hollywood politicking came Jason Joy, Joe Breen, Will Hays, Sid Grauman, A. H. Giannini, Buron Fitts, Charles Chaplin, Walt Disney, Mary Pickford, Winfield Sheehan, Darryl Zanuck, Jack Warner, Harry Cohn, Joe Schenck, and Jesse Lasky.

From his last years at M-G-M came Lenore Ulric, Laura Hope Crews, Allan Jones, Gloria Swanson, Jeanette MacDonald, Jules Furthman, Constance Bennett, George Cukor, the Marx Brothers, Karl Freund, Frank Lloyd, Paul Muni, Rosalind Russell, Robert Taylor, and Spencer Tracy.

Those who did not attend (but sent flowers) included Greta Garbo, William Randolph Hearst, Marion Davies, Carl Laemmle, and Sam Goldwyn. Guests were led to seats in the temple by Douglas Fairbanks, Clark Gable, Moss Hart, Sidney Franklin, Cedric Gibbons, Robert Z. Leonard, Fredric March, W. S. Van Dyke, Carey Wilson, and Sam Wood. Pallbearers were chosen from family members only. The temple's capacity was more than a thousand, and it was nearly full. Shearer and the family members who had stood watch with her were secluded in a small curtained room to the side of the altar. As the last guests arrived, an organist played Cesar Franck's "Andante." Occasionally the sound of the crowd outside could be heard, as when Mary Pickford entered alone and her ex-husband Doug Fairbanks entered with his new love, Lady Sylvia Ashley. For the most part, though, the crowd of gawkers was orderly. It was hard to fault them. The funeral featured a greater array of stars than a movie premiere, and a corps of photographers was splayed over the temple's entrance, vying for coverage of the biggest story of the year. By coldhearted comparison, the funerals of Thelma Todd and John Gilbert were low budget.

Rabbi Magnin restored dignity to the event with a reading from Psalm 121. "I will lift up mine eyes unto the hills, from whence cometh my help," he read. "My help cometh even from the Lord: who hath made Heaven and earth." Magnin was known for a certain theatricality, but more for his ability to move his listeners. "The service was impressive," wrote Lewis. "I vaguely remember sitting next to Merle Oberon, whom I knew only slightly. We were both weeping." Thalberg's casket was a solid copper affair blanketed with lilies of the valley, white orchids, and white roses. The huge synagogue was filled with floral offerings; many were set outside for lack of space, tempting onlookers.

Grace Moore was in the choir loft, and she began to sing from the Psalm of David. "She was visibly nervous," reported the *Los Angeles Times*. "Tears welled in her eyes as she finished. She swayed and fell backward into the arms of a friend. Mourners, too, were affected. Handkerchiefs came from pockets to blot tears." Shearer could be heard sobbing.

Magnin's stirring voice echoed throughout the temple. "It is strange," said Magnin, "that Irving, who dedicated his life to inspiring entertainment, should have attended *Everyman*, the last vehicle of entertainment he was to see. There is a lesson there for many, but when the Grim Reaper came to Irving, he came to one who was not vain, not drunk with power or lusting for wealth, but to a man, as I knew him, who was sweet and kind and charming. . . . You loved Irving, but you are not alone. A world so large that many temples could not hold the mourners, bows in sorrow at his passing. The world knows his accomplishments but few know the real part he took in community life. You could always call on Irving. He would listen." Magnin referred to Thalberg's domestic life as "a demonstration to the world that Hollywood is not as careless in these matters as it is usually painted. His love for Norma was greater than that shown in his greatest motion picture, *Romeo and Juliet*. He was a grand husband and father. I knew when I married them in that beautiful garden some years ago that this marriage would be productive of all that was good." At this, Shearer could be heard sobbing again.

"And now we say 'Au revoir,' dear Irving," continued Rabbi Magnin. "You have been true and loyal to those closest to you. God be with you on the journey. Awake from your sleep, my dear boy. March up the hill to a life that is more peaceful and sweeter still. God bless you." Rabbi Magnin prayed again, first in Hebrew and ˎ in English. *"Adonoi nosan, Adonoi lokach, yehi shem adonai mevoroch."* "The Lord has given and the Lord has taken away. Praised be the name of the Lord."

After the temple was cleared of people, Rabbi Magnin performed a brief ceremony around the casket and then accompanied the family on the drive to Forest Lawn Memorial Park in Burbank. Louis B. Mayer, Eddie Mannix, and Nick Schenck met them at the Sanctuary of Benediction, a marble mausoleum not accessible to the public. As the casket slid into the wall, Rabbi Magnin prayed the words of the Kaddish. "Extolled and hallowed be the name of God throughout the world." The family slowly filed out of the crypt. Suddenly Henrietta grew faint and collapsed. Family members helped her up and into a limousine.

Shearer made two brief stops on her way home, accompanied by her brother Douglas. She thanked Grace Moore for singing, and she visited Sam Goldwyn to see how he was recovering from abdominal surgery. Then she rode to 707 Ocean Front, where her children awaited her. "Little Irving knew," recalled Shearer. "So I had to tell him. I sent him and Katharine to stay with my sister for ten days afterwards." There was nowhere for Shearer to stay. There was no one to send her. Irving was gone.

At Irving Thalberg's funeral, one studio executive whispered to another: "They won't miss him today or tomorrow or six months from now or a year from now. But two years from now they'll begin to feel the squeeze." It did not take two years. The squeeze was felt as soon as Louis B. Mayer reviewed Thalberg's projects.

Romeo and Juliet was completed, of course, but had not yet premiered in Los Angeles. In spite of the sadness permeating the studio, canceling or postponing the September 30 event was impossible. Stars arriving at the premiere were not asked to make a cheery speech at the radio microphone that night; Howard Strickling dispensed with the custom because no one wanted to burst into tears on a nationwide hookup. The premiere helped remind moviegoers of Thalberg's last release, and *Romeo and Juliet* continued to sell tickets, but it could not make a profit.

The Good Earth was nearly completed. Mayer had a title card inserted in the film after Leo the Lion and before the credits. It read: "To the Memory of Irving Grant Thalberg We Dedicate this Picture, His Last Great Achievement." The epic film required no retakes, but editing took so long that its premiere was delayed until January 1937. *The Good Earth* was indeed recognized as a great achievement and was voted one of the year's Ten Best by the *New York Times* and several trade papers. Box office was something else. Although *The Good Earth* grossed more than *Romeo and Juliet*, it had also cost more. Thalberg's last achievement was also his last prestige picture. It garnered great reviews and lost half a million.

Mayer's producers gathered in his office to decide the fate of Thalberg's projects. David Lewis read the list. *Marie Antoinette, Goodbye, Mr. Chips,* and *Pride and Prejudice* were still being written. George Cukor's *Camille* had nearly finished shooting. Sam Wood's *A Day at the Races* had just started. Edmund Goulding's *Maytime* was not doing well; he could not find the right tone for it, even though his delays were running up bills at both M-G-M and Technicolor.

A newly hired executive named Sam Katz jumped on this. "It's a good thing Irving died when he did," exclaimed Katz. "He would have ruined M-G-M!" Lewis was outraged by the crude outburst. Mayer rose and quietly led Lewis into the anteroom. "You wait right here," said Mayer. Then he went inside and chewed out Katz. He returned to Lewis and said: "Nobody will ever speak badly of Irving in your presence again. Never."

The incident exposed the corporate tension that followed Thalberg's death. Many executives sincerely wanted to finish his projects as he had envisioned them. Others simply wanted to take them. David Lewis and Albert Lewin, who had been closest to Thalberg, were suddenly in the way, either because they reminded various producers of the debt they owed Irving or because they were sitting on a desirable project. Lewin sensed this and resigned, even though he unwittingly offended Mayer. "What I thought and never got a chance to explain," Lewin recalled, "was that since I had worked so closely with Irving, it was not fair to compel them to keep me for the last two years of my contract with him. The honorable thing for me to do was quit, and if they wanted me, they could make a deal. Instead, Mr. Mayer was affronted." Lewin soon discovered that Thalberg had praised him to executives at other studios, and he was welcomed at Paramount.

Before Lewis could decide what to do, Mayer decided for him. "You will be my next Irving," said Mayer. This eventuality soured when Mayer lost interest in the young producer and let Bernard Hyman take *Camille* from him. (Mayer would repeat this ritual with a succession of young producers.) Hyman had done well under Thalberg, but was not as astute as Lewin. Lewis was left to sit alone in the empty Thalberg bungalow. After months of isolation, he managed to escape to Warner Bros.

Sam Marx, Thalberg's oldest friend in Hollywood, asked Mayer if he could quit the job of head story editor and become a producer. Mayer refused, so Marx left M-G-M, too. Also cut loose were exclusive contractees of the Thalberg stable, including Donald Ogden Stewart, Talbot Jennings, and Charles Laughton.

Marie Antoinette, Goodbye, Mr. Chips, and *Pride and Prejudice* were shelved, along with early drafts of Henryk Sienkiewicz's *Quo Vadis,* Anthony Hope's *The Prisoner of Zenda,* and Mary Roberts Rinehart's *Tish.* But what about the projects already in progress? "These are Irving's last pictures," Eddie Mannix told Hyman. "If anything can be done to make them better, do it, no matter what the expense." *A Day at the Races* was assigned to Lawrence Weingarten, who made sure that writers and director alike respected the template Thalberg had created in *A Night at the Opera*. The result was a slightly denatured version of the Marxes' humor, but it grossed $5 million, more than any of their other films. Yet something was missing. "After Thalberg's death," said Groucho, "my interest in the movies waned. I appeared in them, but my heart was in the Highlands. The fun had gone out of filmmaking."

Maytime became a conspicuous target. The erratic Goulding was yanked off the film, and Hunt Stromberg took over, creating an entirely new script, canceling the Technicolor contract, and assigning the dependable Robert Z. Leonard to direct Jeanette MacDonald and Nelson Eddy. The film's setting was changed from a music hall to the court of Louis Napoleon. Stromberg was, after Lewin, the most intelligent of the original "Irving's boys." He made *Maytime* a hugely popular hit.

The most important of Thalberg's unfinished projects was *Camille*. Determined to improve on perfection, Hyman had a new opening written and spent $100,000 filming new scenes. The subtlety of Thalberg's script was lost. Preview audiences laughed at the new dialogue and applauded when the Lady of the Camellias was slapped. Lewis, who was still at the studio, bypassed Hyman and appealed to Mannix. He made Hyman restore the film to Thalberg's version. *Camille* became Garbo's signature film.

Thalberg had told Sam Marx that Norma Shearer would bow out after *Romeo and Juliet* and *Marie Antoinette*, but had later asked him to find a modern vehicle for her, so perhaps he was having second thoughts. She could not think of work without him; in truth, she could not think at all. On the night after his death, she had gone onto the beach outside the house and taken a long, solitary walk. She later confided to David Lewis that she was "tortured with the thought that—had she made the right decision—Thalberg might have lived." Her walk on the beach was the expression of a death wish.

"Grief does very strange things to you," Shearer recalled. "I didn't seem to feel the shock for two weeks afterwards. . . . Then, at the end of those two weeks, I collapsed." On October 4, Shearer was diagnosed with pneumonia. In a week, she was so ill that her lawyer, Edwin Loeb, came to prepare a will. Fortunately, she regained her strength by early November. She would need it. Mayer sent word that he would proceed with *Marie Antoinette* whenever she was ready. She asked for sixty days in which to decide and also asked Lewis to keep her abreast of studio news; his reports were not encouraging.

The company that owed Thalberg so much was doing little to honor his memory. "Mayer was less involved in downgrading Thalberg," said Lewis, "than were the others—all his 'friends' who owed their careers to him. Eddie Mannix was the sole exception. He had been the closest to Thalberg of anyone in the studio. . . . He was the only one, apart from Mayer himself, in that whole goddamned crew that showed any respect. They wanted to denigrate the Thalberg image and put their own in its place." Credit was not the only thing they wanted to grab.

Irving Thalberg's last will and testament left a smaller bequest than was expected. The November probate revealed an estate of $4.47 million. This was reduced to $2.24 million by Internal Revenue Service obligations dating to 1932 and by probate costs. Edwin Loeb cashed the stock options that Thalberg had exercised in late 1934 and paid bequests to other Thalberg family members. Shearer and her two children received only a million apiece, much of it in trust. This would, however, suffice for retirement, an idea that Shearer found increasingly appealing. She discussed it with her agent, Charles Feldman, who also represented Garbo, Marlene Dietrich, and Claudette Colbert. Mayer was shocked when Feldman said that Shearer wanted to leave both the studio and the screen. Presumably out of consideration for her grief, Mayer acquiesced. He would cancel her contract two years early, but she would have to buy it out—at the price of $50,000. Speaking through Loeb (who, incidentally, represented Mayer), Shearer agreed.

Since April 1932, Thalberg had enjoyed a 37.5 percent share in Loew's profits. Now that he was gone, Mayer and J. Robert Rubin, the remaining members of the original Mayer group, saw no reason why they should not help themselves to Thalberg's share, and this they proceeded to do. Thalberg's contract, however, was not due to expire until December 31, 1938, a full two years away. When Shearer discovered that she was not receiving a check for Irving's share of profits for the third quarter of 1936, she consulted Loeb. He, of course, tried to placate her. She would have none of it. Nick Schenck rushed from New York to meet with Mayer and Rubin in mid-December. Loeb informed them that Shearer would sue if payments were not reinstated. At this point Mayer asked Loeb whose side he was on. Loeb said that he was Mayer's lawyer, but that he was also Shearer's lawyer. "Nick," said Mayer, "I think we should ask Edwin to tell us how much money he is getting to represent Irving's estate and then pay him that much and have him give it up." He did give it up, but not for a bribe; Shearer fired him. She engaged a new attorney and then began to wage a war of nerves against M-G-M, striking the studio where it was most vulnerable.

For the first time since her *Romeo and Juliet* broadcast, Shearer went on Louella Parsons's radio show. The upshot of the interview was that the studio to which Irving had devoted his life was not showing respect, either to his memory or to his widow. She had left because she was being deprived of Irving's share in his "last great achievements." She was being forced to look around Hollywood for a more hospitable studio. "I must go back to work or face the poorhouse," she said in a tone which said that this was no joke. The situation began to reflect on the management of M-G-M. Thalberg had been a vital force. Why was the company denying this? Were they that greedy? Power-hungry? Ungrateful? The studio attempted to save face by pretending that all was well and that Shearer was scheduled to do both *Marie Antoinette* and *Pride and Prejudice*. David Selznick called M-G-M's bluff by announcing that the front-runner for *Gone with the Wind* was Norma Shearer. The legal wrangling continued. Mayer and Rubin wanted Thalberg's share.

The situation came to a head in March 1937. Victor Fleming had never been close to Thalberg but had known Shearer since their location romance in 1924. Taking her part, the virile director berated Schenck for the way the company was treating her and warned that its image could be permanently sullied. Schenck called Mayer and told him to have his lawyers reach a compromise agreement immediately. According to the *New York Times* critic Bosley Crowther, who interviewed all parties (except Mayer) in the 1950s for his books on M-G-M, the agreement was as follows: "Thalberg's estate would receive his full share of all profits paid to the Mayer group up to the conclusion of its contract at the end of 1938. Thereafter it would receive 4 per cent of the net profits earned by pictures more than half completed in the period from April 1924 through December 1938."

Of minor import at the time but of great significance later was a clause that included profits from television and any medium not yet invented or known. No one (but the Museum of Modern Art Film Library, which Thalberg had helped launch) believed that feature films had lasting value. Reissues of talking films had begun only recently; silent films were thought to be worthless. The 4 percent was considered a small price to pay for the truly valuable commodity, Shearer's stardom. She was still in the Film Daily Top Ten, and the compromise agreement was contingent upon her signing an exclusive contract with M-G-M. Shearer wanted $200,000 for four films, but Feldman could not get around Mayer. The contract, signed in late April 1937, gave her $150,000 for six films, to be completed over a period of three years.

Mayer and Rubin appeared to be satisfied. Schenck, as usual, skimmed off the top. He got away with cashing options on the 48,492 shares of common stock that Thalberg had not exercised. No one found out until years later. Shearer was pleased that after four years of preparation, *Marie Antoinette* would finally be filmed. This had been Mayer's main bargaining chip. He knew that she wanted to play the part.

"Sidney Franklin came to talk to me about doing *Marie Antoinette*," said Shearer, "about all the work Irving had done on it, about Irving's ambition and hopes for it. I couldn't bear to do it without Irving. But then I couldn't bear to have someone else do it, or worst of all, not have it done at all. It was the last picture Irving worked on, the last picture plan he worked out for me. I couldn't let that be for nothing."

Mayer had to justify the $400,000 that the company had already spent on *Marie Antoinette:* a trip to France for photographic research and the purchase of fabrics, jewels, and hundreds of antiques. Indeed, the Port of Los Angeles had never cleared such a large shipment of imports. Now these relics would provide a backdrop for a performance. Shearer hoped it would be the greatest performance of her career and a tribute to her late husband. It was up to her to see it through.

Mounting an Irving Thalberg production without Irving Thalberg posed a challenge. When Norma Shearer signed her contract, *Marie Antoinette* was no more than a stack of scripts in the former Thalberg bungalow. Louis B. Mayer assigned it a temporary production number, 1185, so that it could take its place on the studio's schedule. Whatever costs it generated would be billed to that number, not to a production unit that no longer existed. In deference to both Thalberg and Shearer, Sidney Franklin was assigned to direct. Since Albert Lewin was gone and David Lewis was inexperienced, Mayer accepted Shearer's suggestion that Hunt Stromberg produce. Thalberg would have approved of the choice. Stromberg was brainy and attentive to detail. More than any other project spawned in the Thalberg bungalow, *Marie Antoinette* was fraught with significance.

In 1933, while the Thalbergs were in Europe contemplating their relationship with L.B. Mayer and Nick Schenck, Shearer had happened on a new book, Stefan Zweig's *Marie Antoinette: The Portrait of an Average Woman*. She was immediately taken with it, and envisioned the "part of a lifetime." Even though Thalberg's status was uncertain, J. Robert Rubin bought the book for him. When Schenck wanted Thalberg back, he used *Marie Antoinette* as bait. Zweig wrote an article for the *New York Times* on translating his book to film. "Here the tragedy of an unhappy marriage is allied with the tragedy of royalty," he wrote. "History has effected so natural and inevitable a drama out of these that no poet's imaginings could ever hope to exceed it." For Shearer, there were compelling parallels between Antoinette and herself. She was the "Queen of Metro," her husband deposed by an intrigue. The role of a glamorous, doomed monarch was tempting. Not even Katharine Cornell or Lynn Fontanne had played it. Thalberg supported the idea without qualification. As soon as it was announced, other stars began (in the words of the press) "queening it." There was Marlene Dietrich as Catherine the Great, Greta Garbo as Queen Christina, and Claudette Colbert as Cleopatra.

Even before Thalberg's return to M-G-M, Franklin and Lenore Coffee began drafting *Marie Antoinette*. Thalberg told them to consider "the tragedy of people who make mistakes in judgment but die nobly for them." On June 13, 1933, Franklin began dictating his own concept. "Fate is really the heavy in this plot," he said. "The audience should feel that the Queen would have been perfectly happy if she hadn't been Queen." Four days later he sent Thalberg a progress report. "We are treating the story purely from the woman's angle," wrote Franklin, "and trying to make it an intimate story. . . . For that reason we feel that it will not be a big picture in a pictorial sense but a picture that is big in the sense that it affords a wonderful role for Norma, a marvelous character with a wide range of emotion. You once said it would be an actress's dream."

Marie Antoinette was also Thalberg's dream. It was the most proudly announced of his projects—and the most often postponed. He could not get the script he wanted, even with Robert Sherwood, Donald Ogden Stewart, George S. Kaufman, and Talbot Jennings working on it. No fewer than eleven writers contributed to it. Then there was the tug of war with William Randolph Hearst. After Thalberg won that, Shearer became pregnant. By the time she was ready to work, *Romeo and Juliet* had moved into first place. By mid-1936 Thalberg was referring to *Marie Antoinette* as Shearer's farewell performance. "Juliet and Marie Antoinette will mark the end of Norma's acting career," Thalberg told Sam Marx. "Too many stars stay on camera too long. I want her to bow out at her highest point." *Marie Antoinette* was growing into Thalberg's—and M-G-M's—biggest production: four years of writing and preproduction costs of nearly half a million.

After Thalberg died, many assumed that the project had died with him. Surprisingly, it was Mayer who kept it alive; he never expected that letting Shearer "queen it" would cost him the coveted percentage points. The complex and sometimes self-contradictory Mayer could bear a grudge, but since Thalberg's death he had been urged to control his temper, and he was sincerely trying. Still, he was not happy that Shearer had gotten the better of him. After all, he had made her a star— at Mission Road. That was the party line since Thalberg's death. The late producer must never be spoken of disrespectfully, but, as David Lewis wrote later, "it was to be subtly understood that Thalberg had not built M-G-M, and that M-G-M would continue without him." Nevertheless, Mayer had to concede that *Marie Antoinette* was a Thalberg project. Who would see to it that Thalberg's vision was honored?

Franklin had been babysitting the script on and off for four years and had just directed most of *The Good Earth*, an achievement by any standard. That film ran two hours and eighteen minutes. Stromberg had just produced *The Great Ziegfeld*, a three-hour showbiz saga. Unlike the other producers elevated by Thalberg's demotion, Stromberg had continued to consult him; Thalberg had told him that *The Great Ziegfeld* needed a centerpiece, a show-stopping musical number, and Stromberg had come up with "A Pretty Girl Is Like a Melody." With both Stromberg and Franklin in her corner, Shearer was confident that *Marie Antoinette* would have the Thalberg quality. She was ready to step before a camera. It would be her first time in twenty months.

"I don't know what I did through all that time," she said. "It just slipped away. I was dazed. There was no time marked out into weeks, days, hours. In a state of trance there is no time. That's how I found it. Something just passes over you, and the first thing you know it's a year already. When Irving was here I was conscious of time because every minute was precious." Shearer saw few people during her mourning period, other than her family and her neighbors the Fairbankses. One exception was David Lewis. He later wrote:

Norma wanted to know if Thalberg had ever discussed *Marie Antoinette* with me. He had, telling me he thought it a classic tragedy. He believed that great tragedy was illuminated by characters who, through their own folly, brought themselves to ruin, but who, in the face of their enemies, rose to great dignity and honor and paid for their sins with true nobility of spirit. Norma's instant reaction was that she had no intention of playing Marie Antoinette as a foolish woman or as an unsympathetic character. She said no audience would accept a star in that kind of role.

To make Marie more like Norma, Stromberg assembled the same team that had done *The Barretts of Wimpole Street*. Ernest Vajda, Donald Ogden Stewart, and Claudine West wrote the final drafts of *Marie Antoinette*, which were sent to Shearer in late May 1937. She was vacationing at Lake Arrowhead for the first time since she had been there with Thalberg. "It is lovely up here," she wrote Stromberg. "The weather is divine and the kids are loving it. There are a few too many poignant memories, but they make life sweeter—if sadder. . . . I have read the script and I am crazy about it. You have made a wonderful combination of the West and Jennings scripts. I had already marked the parts of each that I liked best. Your selection is almost identical, line for line." Shearer was pleased to see that Marie had become a sympathetic character. "You have done some very careful work, Hunt, so absolutely in keeping with the feeling of the thing as a whole. Your script is a little longer at present, but there has always been a great deal of bulk in the descriptive matter whereas I don't think the action and dialogue are overly long for a story of this importance and size."

The ongoing communication between star and producer should have alerted Franklin. Even though he was working with Adrian, Cedric Gibbons, J. J. Cohn, and William Daniels on the physical production, he was slowly and subtly being overruled. Shearer was determined that the film be a fitting vehicle for the widowed First Lady of M-G-M. Stromberg was determined that the project not turn into a money sponge like *Romeo and Juliet*. In mid-October, Mayer, assured that Stromberg was in control, approved the work order that gave *Marie Antoinette* an official production number, 1030. Production began in earnest.

"I had never worked on the M-G-M lot with anyone but Irving as my producer," wrote Franklin. "Claudine and I had put a great deal of time and effort into our script. Irving had liked it. We could only hope that Mr. Stromberg would like it. We were hoping for too much." Stromberg, acting on Shearer's behalf, continued to cut scenes that made Marie look vain or unfeeling. In addition, there was disagreement over the question of Technicolor. Franklin had seen *A Star Is Born* and been impressed by the film's subdued palette. Stromberg knew that Franklin was a meticulous craftsman who worked at an unhurried pace. The script promised to run nearly three hours. It contained no less than 192 speaking parts. Already drafted were ninety-eight sets, including a ballroom larger than the original at Versailles. Already designed—in color—were 2,500 costumes. Already on order from Max Factor were 903 wigs, 20 of which were for Shearer. In spite of precautions, this was becoming a bigger production than *Romeo and Juliet*, *The Good Earth*, or *The Great Ziegfeld*. Even if the actors and extras were to wear rags, Technicolor would inflate the cost to $4 million. With the extravagance of Versailles being matched, nay, surpassed by M-G-M, *Marie Antoinette* could end up costing $7 million. "Color would add a tremendous cost," Stromberg wrote Franklin. "I don't think that this additional burden would bring sufficient returns to justify it. We have a great story—and a great star—and we do not, in this instance, need whatever incentive color might offer."

Stromberg was not the only one undercutting Franklin. In the fall of 1937,

Franklin began shooting wig and costume tests for Shearer. Daniels was required, but on the day of the tests, he was shooting retakes on Joan Crawford's film *Mannequin*. Franklin sent assistant director Hugh Boswell to the *Mannequin* stage to ask if he could borrow Daniels for the afternoon. Producer Joseph Mankiewicz told Boswell to knock on the door of Crawford's trailer. With some trepidation, he did so, and was admitted. Shortly thereafter, he emerged from the trailer and hurried off the stage. Crawford appeared in the doorway of her trailer, dressed only in her underwear, and shouted after him: "And you can tell Miss Shearer that *I* didn't get where I am on my ass!" Shearer had to wait for Daniels, but the important thing was that she got him, and that she got him for *Marie Antoinette*. No other cinematographer—in black-and-white or color—could do better with this overwhelmingly opulent production, and no one could make a thirty-five-year-old woman look better on a thirty-foot screen.

Shearer was happy with the screen tests of her wigs, jewels, and gowns. As she had in *Romeo and Juliet*, she brought them home and practiced walking in them, perfecting a regal bearing. She had to be happy with casting, too. Thalberg had wanted Charles Laughton to play the phlegmatic Louis XVI, but he was unavailable, working in England for tax reasons. Screen tests were shot of other actors. Shearer passed on Emlyn Williams, Peter Lorre, and Roger Livesey in favor of the British stage actor Robert Morley, who had never made a film, but who looked remarkably like the eighteenth-century monarch. Franklin was not pleased that Shearer insisted on building up the romance between Marie and the Swedish diplomat Count Axel Fersen, but having Gary Cooper play him might sell enough tickets to offset the cost of a three-hour epic. Sam Goldwyn, who had been a vocal friend of Thalberg, offered to loan Cooper. Shearer was uninterested. She wanted Hollywood's newest heartthrob, Tyrone Power. She had met him at a party and saw why he was doing so well for Twentieth Century–Fox. He was beautiful but unaffected. She prevailed upon Stromberg to get him. Stromberg signed a conspiratorial letter to Shearer, "Yours for a bigger and better Tyrone Power!" Again, Shearer got her way. Darryl Zanuck okayed the loan of Power in exchange for M-G-M's loan of Spencer Tracy.

Shooting was scheduled to begin on January 4, 1938. Shearer confided to Merle Oberon that she was attracted to Power, but he was married, so she put the emotion into her performance. "I fell in love with every co-star I had," Shearer recalled in 1958. "I almost had to." Two years had passed since Thalberg's death, and Shearer was still a healthy, beautiful woman. She began dating stars such as James Stewart and George Brent. She was pursued—rather ludicrously—by seventeen-year-old Mickey Rooney. She and her assistant made sure that he was never admitted to the stages where she was shooting tests or scenes, much less to her dressing room; nevertheless the peculiar actor spread a rumor that Shearer had seduced him in her dressing room. Shearer appealed to Mayer, who summoned Rooney to his office for a dressing-down that was so loud it could be heard by writer Billy Wilder in an adjoining office.

In mid-December, Shearer took a last-minute vacation at the Desert Inn in Palm Springs. While there, she approved the final continuity. Based on this script, Franklin submitted a shooting schedule of eighty-eight days. Before long, he began to hear rumblings. Franklin took too long over details. He was indecisive. Another director could bring the film in more quickly. But who? Shearer would only work with an actor's director like Edmund Goulding or George Cukor, both of whom were out of favor since Thalberg's death. Who else was there? Robert Z. Leonard? Sam Wood? Victor Fleming? The name Franklin heard mentioned was that of W. S. Van Dyke, the "one-take director" of *Tarzan the Ape Man*, *The Thin Man*, and *Naughty Marietta*. But that was preposterous. "I was known as a slow director," recalled Franklin, "but I also knew that this was not exactly Van's type of picture. It was a love story, which was my cup of tea, not Van's." Franklin tried to dismiss the rumors. It would be years before he understood that he had been caught in the cross-fire as Mayer delivered the final payback to Shearer and Thalberg.

On December 31, while Franklin's wife prepared a New Year's Eve party, he was called to an emergency meeting with Schenck, Stromberg, Mayer, and Mannix. Mayer told Franklin that his schedule was impractical. "It was four against one," recalled Franklin. "They said I should cut my schedule to sixty days, thereby saving the studio many [hundreds of] thousands of dollars. It was monstrous to try to squeeze this film into a sixty-day schedule." Franklin assumed Shearer knew about this—had perhaps approved it. He did not bring up her name. He decided that the deck was stacked against him and that he had nothing to lose.

"Gentlemen," he said, "I will not be hurt if you think you can bring it in faster. I know you have spoken to Van Dyke. If he says he can shoot this picture in sixty days, well, then you give it to him. I could never do that without ruining it." Franklin's resignation was accepted. "If Irving had been there," wrote Franklin, "such an action would never have been taken, nor would they have submitted me to a situation of this kind. For well over a year we [he, West, Vajda, and Stewart] had labored for a near-perfect job. Our hearts and blood were in that script." He went home to a miserable New Year's Eve.

Mayer next summoned Shearer to his office, so quickly that she had no chance to compare notes with Franklin. She was told that he had resigned and that "Woody" Van Dyke was replacing him. "Put Van Dyke—or anyone you want—on it," said the disheartened star. She, too, went home to a sad New Year's Eve. "If only I had had the courage to say I wouldn't accept a compromise," she wrote Franklin years later. "But no, I thought I had to conform. Because there were so many skeptics waiting for me to be difficult, but principally because the subtle impression had been conveyed that you didn't want to direct me. Perhaps this doubt was placed in my mind to suit their purpose. I was vaguely aware that they had created an impasse to accomplish their ends."

There were two ironies to this story of manipulation and revenge. First, Stromberg had already hired not one, but two second-unit directors. The more prominent was the French director Julien Duvivier. He would come onto the set when Van Dyke left for the day, complete scenes in progress with the principals, and then shoot scenes with supporting characters. Jacques Tourneur, who had done the revolution scenes in *A Tale of Two Cities*, would do the same for this film. With this backup, Franklin could conceivably have shot the film in fewer than eighty-eight days. Mayer knew this. He deliberately unseated Franklin in order to pay back Shearer for her legal resistance eight months earlier. He knew that she relied on Franklin's soothing manner and articulate direction. Without him, she would not be sure how well she was doing. She had trusted Stromberg to stand behind her, but his loyalty was to Mayer, not her. The Thalberg era was over.

The second irony was that Van Dyke was not the insensitive speed demon described to Shearer. He was known for pushing actors to get the scene right on the first take, in part because he felt the first take had a spontaneity that was lost in repeated takes. This was important when dealing with wooden actors like Nelson Eddy or affected actors like Joan Crawford. As cameraman Hal Rosson attested, Van Dyke did not waste time on unnecessary things, but he did allow time to tell the story. "His thinking," said Rosson, "was to emphasize certain things in a picture. The girl in his picture had to look beautiful. So Van would permit you to take as much time as needed—within reason, of course—to get a good result of the girl. All these stories about Van Dyke as a one-take, hurry-up man were false, unless you were shooting some silly thing. But he never hurried me up on the girl! 'Let me know when you're ready,' he'd say."

Film editors who had to cut Van Dyke's footage did not agree. Chester Schaeffer worked on *Forsaking All Others* and several others. "Van Dyke could be careless," recalled Schaeffer. "He would shoot the master shot and then skip the over-the-shoulders. George Folsey and Richard Boleslavsky almost had a second career following Van Dyke, shooting closeups of Joan Crawford he had skipped." There were rumors that Van Dyke got a bonus of $1,000 for every day that he came in ahead of schedule. If that sounded far-fetched, there were witnesses to other idiosyncrasies. "The water cooler in his office was filled with gin," said Schaeffer. "He would tell you to have a drink of water and then break up when you choked on the gin." Just as Garbo quit promptly at 5:00, signaled by her maid's flashing a makeup mirror, Van Dyke called it a day when a Lilly cup of gin was brought to him by an assistant. On more stressful days, he would repair to a bar across from the studio and drink until he passed out. His chauffeur would then take him home to his wife, who was Mannix's niece. Shearer was aware of these stories as she reported for work on *Marie Antoinette* on Tuesday, January 4. She also knew that Van Dyke had read the script for the first time the previous weekend.

"Hi, honey," said Van Dyke to Shearer as she sailed onto the set, half an hour early, dressed in the dazzling "fireworks" dress. She was pleasant to him, but reserved and on edge. In her first take, she moved so quickly that she lost her balance on a smooth staircase and had to grab the imitation marble banister. She lurched to a halt, dislocating her heavy wig. "Say, what's all the rush?" Van Dyke asked her. "We don't have to finish this tomorrow." Slightly reassured, Shearer continued. It was not until her big fall that she felt she could trust him. She was making a grand entrance in front of dozens of extras when the metal hoop of her voluminous skirt broke loose and fell in front of her foot. She tripped on it and fell head over heels. She looked up from beneath layers of fabric, surprised but unhurt. The stage grew silent. Van Dyke stared at her but did not laugh. She did— uproariously. He joined in. The ice was broken.

At this point Shearer realized that if *Marie Antoinette* was to conform to her late husband's vision, she would have to play the game. She would have to win over both Stromberg and Van Dyke, in spite of their allegiance to Mayer. This is what she proceeded to do. She matched them at their own strength—hard work. Stromberg was known for fifteen-hour editing sessions. Van Dyke was known for covering five pages of script a day. Shearer began to show them what stamina was. Confounding the critics who said that she was always late on the set, she was always on time. Only in her still photography sessions with Laszlo Willinger was she tardy. "But once she arrived," said Willinger, "she worked. And she worked hard."

Years before, Shearer had complained to Thalberg about a difficult scene. "And you wanted to be a *star?*" he asked her. Now she had to answer that question, but not to him or Franklin. "And so *Marie Antoinette* was made," she wrote Franklin in 1955. "I was going to say without you or Irving, but as far as I was concerned, you were both there, tapping me on the shoulder." Shearer got through the film by recalling the lessons she had learned from Thalberg, both about filmmaking and corporate politics. And she did some tapping of her own.

She made sure that Mannix and Mayer knew that Van Dyke was rushing. They in turn told Stromberg to watch him closely. The reports were not complimentary. "The scene in the casino is without any fine points," Stromberg wrote in a memo after watching the rushes of a gaming house sequence. "Marie's closeup over the balcony is lacking. Fersen's closeup looking up is also lacking. The scene outside the salon is blunt and heavy-handed, with no particular thrill when Fersen sees this magnificent creature. The scene is very badly timed. Cues are missed. There is a very awkward moment when he begins to speak Swedish, and what could have been a delightful moment at this point is merely glossed over." This was the pivotal scene of Marie's first encounter with the young Swedish nobleman who has been in love with her "from a respectful distance" since hearing about her from the governess who was formerly hers. The entire romance depends on this scene. Fortunately, Stromberg was proving that he had been as well trained by Thalberg as Shearer had. He had Van Dyke remake the scenes, adding closeups.

At one point, Shearer considered agitating for Van Dyke's replacement. Stromberg was not opposed to the idea, but he did not tell her. "It's not that he isn't perfectly sincere in wanting to do a good job," Stromberg wrote to Mannix. "But I don't think that he is mentally or emotionally big enough for this story. I think he's overconfident, occupied mainly with speed. He has a tendency to hurry everything that he does, even conversations about scenes, as I have experienced. You feel he's always wanting to go, to get along."

Then why not replace him?

"If we took Van off," reasoned Stromberg, "we would be the laughingstock of the industry. Such a precedent would react against us with directors. I don't think any amount of money would be worth it." The huge amounts of money being spent on production forced Stromberg to keep a close watch on Van Dyke; in addition, both Mannix and Mayer spoke to the director.

Even after Van Dyke improved, Shearer saw that she would get little, if any, coaching from him. He was not in the same league as Goulding or Cukor. Like DeMille, he believed in painting with bold strokes. He helped with blocking and business, but his actors had to supply their own motivation. Neither Constance Collier nor Margaret Carrington was available to coach Shearer, so she had to apply the stylization she had learned from them. In her romantic scenes with Power, it worked. In her scenes with Morley, who was giving a subtly shaded performance, she reverted to the underplaying she had used in *The Barretts*. Her performance was not entirely consistent, but against a broad and multicolored canvas, it was skillful, inventive, and graceful. She accomplished it by doing what Thalberg had taught her. She attended the screenings of rushes during her daily lunch break and studied herself with the eye of a drama critic.

She also studied herself with the eye of a photographer. "She could leaf through a hundred photographs of herself in a couple of minutes and know exactly which should be passed for publication and which destroyed," wrote Robert Morley. One day a new publicity department employee found some of the "killed" proofs in a drawer. Even though the proofs had the corners torn off, he thought that one of them was worth saving. He went to Shearer's dressing room and presented it to her for an autograph. She studied it for a moment, stared at him, and then, without a word, went to her telephone and called Howard Strickling. Then she hung up. "You're very lucky," she told the young man. "Your boss is out of town." Then she tore up the proof. "Remember this," she said in an icy tone of voice. "When I kill a still, it stays killed."

On the set she was equally critical, not hesitating to correct Daniels. "Her knowledge of lighting was as great as the cameraman's," wrote Morley. "She could tell from a dozen lights bearing down on her which one was likely to cast the wrong shadow." One day there was a problem that could not be corrected with lighting. Shearer had to walk down a flight of stairs and speak to the actor Henry Kolker. The camera would crane in for a closeup. After three months of nonstop shooting, Shearer was tired. Her eye muscles were also tired. When the camera came in, her right eye rolled inward. Daniels told her. Van Dyke was forced to do a second take of an otherwise acceptable shot. Her eye rolled in again. Van Dyke finally had to break his precedent and do an unheard of twenty-eight takes; even then, Shearer's eye was not cooperating. Stromberg promised her that they would redo it later.

On April 15, when her scenes had been completed, Shearer submitted a list of twenty that she wanted reshot, ostensibly because they "could be improved photographically." Her eye problem was one reason, but in most cases, she was not pleased with her acting. She also proposed that her last scene in the film be changed. As shot, it showed the brutalized, prematurely aged queen looking up as the guillotine blade ascends. Shearer wanted "a superimposure of the young face of Marie Antoinette over the closeup at the guillotine, in which the knife in rising will erase the young face." Film editor Robert Kern asked Stromberg to approve a $400 expenditure for the "traveling matte" that would accomplish the special effect. Shearer did not want her last image in the film to be a sad, unflattering one. Because her idea was both cosmetically and dramatically effective, it was approved. The reshoots were made from May 17 to 19.

The first cut of *Marie Antoinette* ran over 170 minutes. The preview was held on June 1 at the California Theater in Pomona, the same theater where *Romeo and Juliet* had gotten a lukewarm response. This preview was very different, judging from the preview cards.

"A truly magnificent picture in all aspects."

"One of the finest productions I have ever witnessed. It's grand to see Norma Shearer again."

"Nothing could be taken away."

"Historically sound and directed with rare taste."

"I'm wondering if it wouldn't be just as great without that last ascending guillotine blade."

"The most beautiful production that has ever come out of Hollywood. Mr. Thalberg would be happy with the outcome of his dream. Congratulations to Miss Shearer."

In deference to Thalberg's methods, a few shots were retaken two weeks later. The running time was reduced to 160 minutes. Then, on July 8, *Marie Antoinette* had its gala premiere at the Fox Carthay Circle Theater in Los Angeles. The *Los Angeles Times* reported:

> Those associated with the motion-picture industry agree that this opening was the most spectacular in its history, even climaxing that of *Hell's Angels* at the Chinese Theater eight years ago. Traffic was tied up on Wilshire Boulevard for miles. San Vicente Boulevard was festooned with banners and dignified with French statues. Lights played into the sky. A thirty-piece orchestra directed by Frank Hodek, and accompanied by a chorus of twenty-four voices, entertained the 25,000 spectators seated in grandstands. The forecourt had been transformed into a veritable bower of flowers, shrubs, and fountains, a replica of the famous garden of Versailles. A battery of 265 sun arcs shone into the crowd of beautifully gowned and bejeweled stars and their escorts: Helen Hayes and Charles MacArthur, Carole Lombard and Clark Gable, Florence Rice and Gilbert Adrian. Wild cheers came from the stands when Norma Shearer arrived on the arm of her co-star Tyrone Power.

Although Shearer would at times express regret for the loss of Sidney Franklin, and wish that her late husband had been sitting with her in the Carthay, it was unquestionably one of the greatest nights of her life. At the conclusion of the magnificent scene in which she enters the French court, the audience burst into applause. There was also applause at the fadeout of the tastefully handled scene in which her husband informs her—on their wedding night—that he is impotent.

Trade paper reviews were as enthusiastic as the premiere audience, calling the film "a lavish, spectacular triumph" (the *Hollywood Reporter*), and "a pride to the entire industry" *(Variety)*. Van Dyke was credited with scenes he had not shot, but he redeemed himself in Franklin's eyes when he sent him a telegram saying: "A lot of people who have seen it say that it is good, but I will not be satisfied unless you think so too. Commercialism, playing the role of commissar, took your child and put it to work. My only hope is that the adult product measures somewhere near your expectations or somewhat near to what I know it would have been had your fine Italian hand not been amputated on the altar of greed."

For his part, Stromberg made a radio speech in which he said: "It has been a privilege to carry out the dreams of Irving Thalberg. *Marie Antoinette* was his dream, the picture he planned for Norma Shearer, and to which he devoted the full measure of his genius. As Irving Thalberg's friend and fellow worker, I am proud to have had a part in seeing that his dream reached fulfillment." To Shearer's and Stromberg's surprise, Mayer expressed genuine emotion for the film. He cried at Marie's death scene. But he would also have the last laugh. *Marie Antoinette* was Thalberg's very last "prestige picture." It opened exceptionally well in its urban engagements, but started to fall off before completing them. Stromberg wired the Astor Theater management, asking them if they thought that the brutal events in the second half of the film made it "too heavy or tragic for popular consumption." He was advised to shorten it. On September 2, he ordered twenty-one minutes' worth of cuts, averaging two minutes apiece. *Marie Antoinette* then went into general release, where it grossed almost $3 million, but, inevitably, lost $590,000. For her pains, Shearer received her sixth Academy Award nomination, but lost to Bette Davis's *Jezebel*.

In 1938, M-G-M mounted one other tribute to Irving Thalberg, a sleek white administration building bearing his name. And the Motion Picture Academy initiated the Irving G. Thalberg Memorial Award. Its first recipient was Darryl F. Zanuck. Shearer's second film under her new contract was a project of which Thalberg would have undoubtedly approved, an adaptation of Robert Sherwood's *Idiot's Delight*, the Broadway hit starring Alfred Lunt and Lynn Fontanne. Mayer was not paying attention. He had achieved his own goal. He had come up with an answer to Shirley Temple—in fact two answers: Judy Garland and Mickey Rooney. Who knows what Thalberg would have thought of the Andy Hardy films.

Epilogue

No two films better show the difference between Irving Thalberg's M-G-M and L.B. Mayer's M-G-M than *Marie Antoinette* and *Love Finds Andy Hardy*. Both were released in July 1938. *Marie Antoinette* was a painstakingly prepared star vehicle. It used character to create drama, and although it dealt in universal themes, its situations were unique to its story and too specific for a sequel. *Love Finds Andy Hardy* was the fourth entry in a series that began with the 1937 B picture *A Family Affair*. The series consisted of a small-town family's adventures, most of which centered on a rambunctious adolescent. Andy Hardy was played by Mickey Rooney and his eminently wise father by Lewis Stone, one of the few contract players left from the M-G-M merger. The simple plots of the Andy Hardy series affirmed Mayer's idealized notion of American life, and the rapport between Judge Hardy and Andy echoed Mayer's oft-expressed feeling that he was the father of the studio family. The films were cheap to make, and they grossed millions. While M-G-M continued to be the biggest, the glossiest, the most glamorous studio, its big films were underwritten by series like Andy Hardy, Maisie, and Dr. Kildare. Thalberg had never sneered at Westerns or comedies, and even though he used a highly methodical system, his films were not made with a cookie cutter. Mayer did not share Thalberg's creative vision, but he had the ability to both anticipate and shape the market. After Thalberg's death, Mayer brought M-G-M ten supremely prosperous years, but the studio's output became predictable. The thoughtful, quirky, innovative cinema of Irving Thalberg died with him.

This is not to say that every film made under Mayer's watch was, as sloppy scholarship would have it, saccharine and intellectually lacking. He was the great respecter of talent, the consummate showman, and the most accomplished, complex manager in the film industry. But he was not Thalberg and he knew it. When he saw "a new Irving" in RKO producer Dore Schary, he sowed the seeds of his own demise. In 1948, M-G-M was weakened by the loss of its theater chain and threatened by the advent of television. Mayer hired Schary to revitalize production and then promptly opposed his ideas. By 1951, the studio was in turmoil. Mayer dared anyone to unseat him. The challenge was taken up by the executive with whom he had unseated Thalberg. Nicholas Schenck demanded that Mayer resign from M-G-M. On August 31, 1951, Mayer, aged sixty-nine, left the company that he and Thalberg had founded.

.   .   .

In 1936, after Thalberg's demise, Albert Lewin, David Lewis, and Samuel Marx left M-G-M. The Thalberg Boys who stayed did so with varying degrees of success. Bernard Hyman never repeated the impact of *San Francisco*. Although he was the only producer who cared about Greta Garbo, he was unable to find a project to prolong her career. When he died of a heart attack in 1942, he had produced only four films since *San Francisco*.

Harry Rapf slid into B pictures and series. *Lassie, Come Home* was his only breakout, and it too became a series. He died in 1949, the year of M-G-M's twenty-fifth anniversary, a Mayer loyalist.

Hunt Stromberg became the preeminent producer at M-G-M (if not of the entire industry) after Thalberg, giving Norma Shearer and Joan Crawford their most intelligent projects, notably *The Women* and *Susan and God*. He eventually succumbed to the pressure of having to find the next Jeanette MacDonald–Nelson Eddy vehicle and the next Thin Man film. His nervous ailments became more severe and he lost patience with Mayer. He left the studio in 1942 to become an independent producer, releasing through United Artists, but he never equaled the success of films such as *The Great Ziegfeld*. He retired prematurely in 1950.

Lawrence Weingarten divorced Sylvia Thalberg in 1939, and, after the death of Dr. David Perla in 1941, married his widow, Dr. Jessie Marmorston, who became Mayer's personal physician and consultant. Weingarten was the Thalberg Boy with the longest M-G-M career; it included *I'll Cry Tomorrow* and *Cat on a Hot Tin Roof*. His last production was 1968's *The Impossible Years*, for which he hired William Daniels as director of photography. During its production both veterans were interviewed by Bob Thomas, and on the same lot where they had worked with Thalberg.

Sidney Franklin retained a lifelong reverence for Thalberg, but, at Mayer's behest, he moved from directing to producing in 1938. He was responsible for quality productions like *Ninotchka, Mrs. Miniver,* and *The Yearling.*

Albert Lewin did the opposite; he went from producing to directing. While preparing Somerset Maugham's *The Moon and Sixpence* for United Artists with Marcus Loew's son David, Lewin decided that it would be cheaper to direct than to hire a director. Thus began a career phase that would have pleased his friend Irving. Lewin's remarkable films included *The Picture of Dorian Gray, The Private Affairs of Bel Ami,* and *Pandora and the Flying Dutchman.*

David Lewis went to Warner Bros. in 1938, where he produced star vehicles like *Dark Victory* and *King's Row.* He returned to M-G-M in the mid-1950s to produce the epic *Raintree County.* Like Franklin and Shearer, he set fond, respectful memories of Thalberg to paper, but only his were published, albeit posthumously.

Samuel Marx left M-G-M when Mayer refused to let him produce. He went to work for Sam Goldwyn, who also refused him. When he returned to M-G-M six years later, he established a new relationship with Mayer and coproduced *Lassie, Come Home,* which made a star of Elizabeth Taylor. Marx had a happy tenure with Mayer, whom he came to respect almost as much as he had Thalberg. In the early 1970s Marx wrote the first of several books about the Thalberg era. For the next twenty years, he was the Boy Wonder's Boswell. Like Bob Thomas, he was scrupulously fair in his accounts of life in Culver City.

Norma Shearer cooperated with Marx to the extent of reviewing his manuscripts and contributing an account of the Paul Bern tragedy. She refused to be interviewed at length. More than any of the Thalberg loyalists, her career suffered from his absence. Although *Marie Antoinette* confirmed her stardom, and her subsequent films were successful, she—like Garbo, Crawford, MacDonald, and Myrna Loy—was denied guidance in the 1940s. The reason was obvious. Mayer was more interested in Judy Garland, Greer Garson, Hedy Lamarr, and Lana Turner. The M-G-M goddesses of the 1930s should not have been put out to pasture in 1942. If Thalberg had lived, they would not have been.

After two flops, Shearer surrendered to what she considered the inevitable. It was easier to leave M-G-M than to fight with Mayer over each new project. She received offers from Warner Bros. and Twentieth Century–Fox, but she took her cue from Garbo. "A great star should always leave them laughing—or crying for more," was Shearer's refrain. In 1942 she married a younger man named Martin

Arrouge; he was not an actor and not in the industry. Shearer devoted herself to her children and to helping Arrouge develop Squaw Valley. He in turn helped her tend the legend of Irving Thalberg, particularly by supporting her autobiography.

Shearer maintained Thalberg's memory through screenings of his films in her home and at the studio, well into the 1970s. She died in 1983. Irving Jr. chose a career in education, becoming a professor of philosophy and a published poet; he died in 1987. Katharine also made a life away from Hollywood, becoming a beloved bookstore owner and animal rights activist; she died in 2007. The six Thalberg grandchildren contributed to this biography in numerous ways. They, of course, are his true legacy.

The other legacy of Irving G. Thalberg is the body of work that he accomplished in his short lifetime. Fortunately, most of it exists. It is fine, uncompromising, and enjoyable because of the work he did while munching cereal in his screening room seventy-five years ago.

These films were listed in studio financial records as having been personally supervised by Thalberg.

Title	Profit (Loss)	Director
1924		
He Who Gets Slapped	$349,000	Victor Seastrom
His Hour	$159,000	King Vidor
Wife of the Centaur	$104,000	King Vidor
Married Flirts	$62,000	Robert Vignola
1925		
The Big Parade	$3,485,000	King Vidor
The Merry Widow	$758,000	Erich von Stroheim
The Unholy Three	$328,000	Tod Browning
The Tower of Lies	$271,000	Victor Seastrom
Confessions of a Queen	$122,000	Victor Seastrom
The Great Divide	$115,000	Reginald Barker
The Dixie Handicap	$114,000	Reginald Barker, John M. Stahl

(continued)

Title	Profit (Loss)	Director
1925 *(continued)*		
Lights of Old Broadway	$109,000	Monta Bell
Soul Mates	$97,000	Jack Conway
Excuse Me	$83,000	Alf Goulding
The White Desert	$77,000	Reginald Barker
Man and Maid	$62,000	Victor Schertzinger
The Mystic	$52,000	Tod Browning
Proud Flesh	$46,000	King Vidor
The Sporting Venus	$42,000	Marshall Neilan
Sun-Up	$37,000	Edmund Goulding
Don't	($52,000)	Alf Goulding
The Only Thing	($80,000)	Jack Conway
The Great Love	($161,000)	Marshall Neilan
1926		
La Bohème	$377,000	King Vidor
The Scarlet Letter	$296,000	Victor Seastrom
The Road to Mandalay	$267,000	Tod Browning
Mike	$213,000	Marshall Neilan
Beverly of Graustark	$180,000	Sidney Franklin
Bardelys the Magnificent	$135,000	King Vidor
The Torrent	$126,000	Monta Bell
Valencia	$101,000	Dmitri Buchowetzski
The Blackbird	$63,000	Tod Browning
Paris	$33,000	Edmund Goulding
Lovey Mary	$22,000	King Baggot
Exquisite Sinner	($26,000)	Phil Rosen
The Temptress	($43,000)	Fred Niblo
1927		
Tell It to the Marines	$664,000	Jack Conway
Love	$571,000	Edmund Goulding
London after Midnight	$540,000	Tod Browning
Flesh and the Devil	$466,000	Clarence Brown

Title	Profit (Loss)	Director
1927 *(continued)*		
The Unknown	$362,000	Tod Browning
Man, Woman, and Sin	$329,000	Monta Bell
The Show	$178,000	Tod Browning
The Fair Coed	$131,000	Sam Wood
Lovers?	$104,000	John M. Stahl
Slide, Kelly, Slide	$98,000	Edward Sedgwick
The Understanding Heart	$70,000	Jack Conway
Women Love Diamonds	($30,000)	Edmund Goulding
Callahans and Murphys	($44,000)	George Hill
The Red Mill	($50,000)	William Goodrich, King Vidor
Tillie the Toiler	($64,000)	Hobart Henley
Quality Street	($188,000)	Sidney Franklin
Annie Laurie	($264,000)	John S. Robertson
The Student Prince in Old Heidelberg	($307,000)	Ernst Lubitsch
1928		
Laugh Clown Laugh	$450,000	Herbert Brenon
The Big City	$387,000	Tod Browning
The Divine Woman	$354,000	Victor Seastrom
West of Zanzibar	$337,000	Tod Browning
The Masks of the Devil	$248,000	Victor Seastrom
Show People	$176,000	King Vidor
The Patsy	$155,000	King Vidor
Dream of Love	$138,000	Fred Niblo
The Enemy	$96,000	Fred Niblo
Bringing Up Father	$83,000	Jack Conway
The Crowd	$69,000	King Vidor
The Actress	$14,000	Sidney Franklin
The Wind	($87,000)	Victor Seastrom
The Trail of '98	($756,000)	Clarence Brown
1929		
The Broadway Melody	$1,604,000	Harry Beaumont

(continued)

Title	Profit (Loss)	Director

1929 *(continued)*

Title	Profit (Loss)	Director
Madame X	$586,000	Lionel Barrymore
The Pagan	$562,000	W. S. Van Dyke
The Trial of Mary Dugan	$421,000	Bayard Veiller
A Woman of Affairs	$417,000	Clarence Brown
Wild Orchids	$380,000	Sidney Franklin
The Idle Rich	$346,000	William de Mille
Where East Is East	$283,000	Tod Browning
Voice of the City	$241,000	Willard Mack
His Glorious Night	$202,000	Lionel Barrymore
Their Own Desire	$188,000	E. Mason Hopper
So This Is College	$157,000	Sam Wood
The Thirteenth Chair	$148,000	Tod Browning
The Last of Mrs. Cheyney	$128,000	Sidney Franklin
A Lady of Chance	($9,000)	Robert Z. Leonard
Wonder of Women	($86,000)	Clarence Brown
Hallelujah!	($120,000)	King Vidor

1930

Title	Profit (Loss)	Director
Anna Christie	$576,000	Clarence Brown
Let Us Be Gay	$527,000	Robert Z. Leonard
The Big House	$462,000	George Hill
The Unholy Three	$375,000	Jack Conway
The Bishop Murder Case	$138,000	Nick Grindé
War Nurse	$19,000	Edgar Selwyn
A Lady to Love	($104,000)	Victor Seastrom
Billy the Kid	($119,000)	King Vidor
This Mad World	($128,000)	William de Mille
Redemption	($215,000)	Fred Niblo
A Lady's Morals	($284,000)	Sidney Franklin
Way for a Sailor	($606,000)	Sam Wood

Title	Profit (Loss)	Director
1931		
Inspiration	$286,000	Clarence Brown
Private Lives	$256,000	Sidney Franklin
1932		
Divorce in the Family	$92,000	Charles F. Reisner
Strange Interlude	$90,000	Robert Z. Leonard
Lovers Courageous	$30,000	Robert Z. Leonard
Blondie of the Follies	($141,000)	Edmund Goulding
1934		
The Barretts of Wimpole Street	$668,000	Sidney Franklin
Riptide	$333,000	Edmund Goulding
The Merry Widow	($113,000)	Ernst Lubitsch
What Every Woman Knows	($140,000)	Gregory La Cava
Outcast Lady	($308,000)	Robert Z. Leonard
1935		
Mutiny on the Bounty	$909,000	Frank Lloyd
China Seas	$653,000	Tay Garnett
No More Ladies	$166,000	Edward H. Griffith
A Night at the Opera	$90,000	Sam Wood
Biography of a Bachelor Girl	($197,000)	Edward H. Griffith
1936		
Romeo and Juliet	($922,000)	George Cukor
1937		
Camille	$388,000	George Cukor
The Good Earth	($496,000)	Sidney Franklin

NOTES

PREFACE

Page xiv   *"Credit you give"*   Marx, *Mayer and Thalberg*, 49.

Page xvi   *"bland and romanticized"*   Lambert, *Norma Shearer*, 329.

CHAPTER 1

Page 3   *"dark and menacing"*   Lambert, *Norma Shearer*, 67.

Page 3   *"Henrietta got revenge"*   "Interview with Irene Selznick, Hotel Pierre, April 20, 1953," Bosley Crowther Papers, Brigham Young University (hereafter Crowther/BYU).

Page 4   *"What does that"*   "David Lewis Interview, September 20, 1967," Bob Thomas Collection, University of California, Los Angeles (hereafter Thomas/UCLA).

Page 4   *"turns away from"*   James, *Writings, 1902–1920*, 47.

Page 4   *"Never hold an"*   Boylan, "Great Executive Job Held by a Boy of 22."

Page 5   *"You've been sick"*   Marx, *Mayer and Thalberg*, 9.

Page 6   *"But it has Corbett!"*   Edmonds, *Big U*, 16.

Page 6   *"It changes so fast"*   Marx, *Mayer and Thalberg*, 18.

Page 6   *"The people have to take"*   Ibid.

Page 6   *"Our comedies"*   "Interview with Robert H. Cochrane," n.d., Crowther/BYU.

Page 7   *"When Laemmle brought"*   Ibid.

Page 7   *"While I was sitting"*   Marion, "Hollywood," 281.

Page 7   "I need someone"   Thomas, *Thalberg*, 46.

Page 7   "It was one of those"   "Thalberg's Rise to Fame Won Title of 'Boy Wonder.'"

Page 8   "In a business where"   Marx, *Mayer and Thalberg*, 28.

Page 8   "The first thing you should"   Thomas, *Thalberg*, 46.

Page 8   "Irving fought his way"   "Norma Shearer Arrouge Memoir Notes," unpublished typescript (hereafter NSA), 147.

Page 8   "$450 a week"   To account (approximately) for eighty-five years of inflation, multiply by twenty-five.

Page 8   "In those days it"   Rosenberg and Silverstein, *The Real Tinsel*, 177.

Page 9   "When I first arrived"   Davies and Marx, *The Times We Had*, 40.

Page 9   "We were all young"   Dardis, *Keaton*, 45.

Page 9   "Thalberg liked to"   Marx, *Mayer and Thalberg*, 36.

Page 9   "I had fancied"   Ferber, *A Peculiar Treasure*, 84.

Page 9   "it was no boy's mind"   Flamini, *Thalberg*, 37.

Page 9   "Although I had seen"   Coffee, *Storyline*, 64.

Page 10   "Cut it all from"   Marx, *Mayer and Thalberg*, 35.

Page 10   "Irving was that way"   Lambert, *Norma Shearer*, 71.

Page 10   "He understood stories"   NSA, 149.

Page 11   "Your father fell"   Marx, *Mayer and Thalberg*, 31.

Page 12   "I am freeing"   Kingsley, "Julius Stern Tells Conditions Abroad."

Page 12   "I have seen all the film"   Thomas, *Thalberg*, 50.

Page 13   "You will have to fire me"   Samuel Marx to the author, January 16, 1990.

Page 13   "If you were not"   Thomas, *Thalberg*, 50.

Page 13   "Since when does"   Marx, *Mayer and Thalberg*, 33.

Page 13   "I got a car"   Higham, *Hollywood Cameramen*, 61.

Page 13   "Got an idea"   Curtiss, *Von Stroheim*, 139.

Page 13   "watched Mr. von Stroheim"   NSA, 119.

Page 13   "Stroheim served real"   Higham, *Hollywood Cameramen*, 63.

Page 14   "That is impossible"   Thomas, *Thalberg*, 51.

Page 14   "You have time and"   Irving G. Thalberg to Erich von Stroheim, October 6, 1922, courtesy of the Photoplay Productions Collection.

Page 14   "This was the first"   Brownlow, *The Parade's Gone By*, 424.

Page 15   "Never remain"   Samuel Marx to the author, January 16, 1990.

Page 16   "We can't do it"   DeMille, *Autobiography of Cecil B. DeMille*, 100.

CHAPTER 2

Page 18   "My unchanging policy"   Crowther, *Hollywood Rajah*, 69.

Page 18   "Not a picture that"   Marion, *Off with Their Heads!* 99.

Page 18   *"If a story makes me cry"*   Marx, *Mayer and Thalberg,* 32.

Page 18   *"more puritanical about sex"*   Marion, *Off with Their Heads!* 99.

Page 18   *"I will make only"*   Crowther, *Hollywood Rajah,* 83.

Page 19   *"cheapest place in town"*   Hopper, *From under My Hat,* 112.

Page 19   *"That was a funny"*   Hopper, "And We're Still Friends."

Page 19   *"My mother doesn't"*   "Margaret Booth Oral History," p. 9, Special Collections, Fairbanks Center for Motion Picture Study, Beverly Hills (hereafter FCMPS).

Page 19   *"down on my knees to talent"*   Thomas, *Thalberg,* 63.

Page 19   *"only temporary quarters"*   Marion, *Off with Their Heads!* 99.

Page 19   *"funny little man"*   "Interview with Florence Browning," n.d., Crowther/BYU.

Page 19   *"So it costs"*   Marx, *Mayer and Thalberg,* 4.

Page 20   *"He's a good boy"*   Ibid.

Page 20   *"For God's sake"*   Crowther, *Hollywood Rajah,* 87.

Page 20   *"I'll pick the people"*   Ibid.

Page 20   *"one of the proudest moments"*   Marion, "Hollywood," 280.

Page 20   *"So Irving Thalberg joined"*   Selznick, *A Private View,* 49.

Page 21   *"Find your way"*   Marx, *Mayer and Thalberg,* 42.

Page 21   *"No one met us"*   NSA, 135.

Page 21   *"Mission Road was"*   Schulberg, *Moving Pictures,* 114.

Page 22   *"We were sitting"*   NSA, 137.

Page 22   *"I bet you'd be surprised"*   Marx, *Mayer and Thalberg,* 23.

Page 22   *"Just wait a year"*   Selznick, *A Private View,* 54.

CHAPTER 3

Page 25   *"I take lovers like roses"*   Bangley, "The Legendary Barbara La Marr," 71.

Page 25   *"He has a Magdalene complex"*   Marx, *Mayer and Thalberg,* 47.

Page 25   *"Paul has no right"*   St. Johns, *Love, Laughter, and Tears,* 272.

Page 25   *"We will have"*   "Adela Rogers St. Johns Interview," n.d., Thomas/UCLA.

Page 25   *"We fought all the time"*   Ibid.

Page 25   *"Mr. Thalberg"*   NSA, 138.

Page 26   *"The custom then"*   Lambert, *Norma Shearer,* 43.

Page 27   *"You can hardly"*   Marx, *Mayer and Thalberg,* 44.

Page 27   *"exchanged opinions and ideas"*   Selznick, *A Private View,* 48.

Page 27   *"[Barker] didn't like me"*   NSA, 140.

Page 27   *"You don't seem"*   Thomas, *Thalberg,* 67.

Page 28   *"The trouble is you're"*   Crowther, *Hollywood Rajah,* 91.

Page 28   *"This young man"* NSA, 142.

Page 28   *"My father's pride"* Selznick, *A Private View*, 49.

Page 29   *"Think big"* Carey, *All the Stars in Heaven*, 61.

Page 30   *"When you stop to think"* Marx, *Mayer and Thalberg*, 46.

Page 30   *"Thalberg can do"* Ibid., 48.

Page 30   *"Don't worry"* Ibid., 47.

Page 31   *"Two old companies"* Schulberg, *Moving Pictures*, 148.

Page 31   *"Ladies and gentlemen"* Thomas, *Thalberg*, 69.

Page 31   *"From my new dressing room"* NSA, 144.

CHAPTER 4

Page 35   *"Unbeknownst to anyone"* "J. J. Cohn Oral History," 25, FCMPS.

Page 35   *"Strangely enough"* Selznick, *A Private View*, 55.

Page 36   *"I'm telling you!"* Rosenberg and Silverstein, *The Real Tinsel*, 381.

Page 36   *"I just got back"* Thomas, *Thalberg*, 96.

Page 37   *"enthusiasm everywhere"* Eyman, *Lion of Hollywood*, 94.

Page 37   *"everything was very exciting"* Coffee, *Storyline*, 96.

Page 37   *"Thalberg was at first concerned"* Irene Selznick interview, Crowther/BYU.

Page 37   *"Every great film"* Chester W. Schaeffer to author, October 9, 1971.

Page 37   *"I could make"* Marx, *Mayer and Thalberg*, 54.

Page 37   *"the most imposing array"* "Harry Carr's Page," December 3, 1924.

Page 37   *"I don't want to impose"* Marion, "Hollywood," 282.

Page 38   *"high priestess"* NSA, 171.

Page 38   *"Miss Glyn was quite weird"* Vidor, *A Tree Is a Tree*, 107.

Page 38   *"Ahhh, behold the black stallion!"* Fountain and Maxim, *Dark Star*, 93.

Page 38   *"self-consciousness and scorn"* "Jack Gilbert Writes His Own Story, Part Four."

Page 38   *"Of course it's trash"* Fountain and Maxim, *Dark Star*, 93.

Page 38   *"acted like the little boy"* "Interview with King Vidor," n.d., Thomas/UCLA.

Page 39   *"What are you"* Fountain and Maxim, *Dark Star*, 90.

Page 39   *"You've got a beautiful wife"* Thomas, *Thalberg*, 91.

Page 39   *"I was cold sober"* Maas, *The Shocking Miss Pilgrim*, 71.

Page 39   *"These bums!"* Irene Selznick interview, Crowther/BYU.

Page 40   *"She scintillated"* Selznick, *A Private View*, 78.

Page 40   *"Often Irving would leave"* Loos, *Kiss Hollywood Good-by*, 32.

Page 40   *"There are twenty-two companies"* Fragmentary clipping, author's collection.

Page 41   *"There is that something"*   Forslund, *Victor Sjöström*, 199.

Page 41   *"Besides being a master"*   NSA, 193.

Page 42   *"Norma Shearer was determined"*   Interview with Florence Browning, Crowther/BYU.

Page 42   *"Mr. Thalberg, . . . will you please"*   NSA, 193.

Page 42   *"She makes me feel paternal."*   Thomas, *Thalberg*, 118.

Page 42   *"Look here."*   "Jack Gilbert Writes His Own Story, Part Four," 103.

Page 42   *"It was like making"*   Pensel, *Seastrom and Stiller in Hollywood*, 33.

Page 42   *"When Thalberg saw"*   Amory and Bradlee, *Cavalcade of the 1920s and 1930s*, 129.

Page 43   *"he disappeared into"*   Day, *This Was Hollywood*, 214.

Page 43   *"This immense theater"*   Klumph, *"He Who Gets Slapped* Is Triumph of Week."

Page 43   *"Norma, this is"*   Thomas, *Thalberg*, 99.

CHAPTER 5

Page 44   *"The author and the play"*   Stroheim, *Greed*, 28.

Page 44   *"I had graduated"*   Ibid., 7.

Page 45   *"The room into which"*   Schallert, "Stark Realism—At Last!" 47.

Page 45   *"There were no roads"*   Noble, *Hollywood Scapegoat*, 53.

Page 45   *"The paint on the cars"*   Koszarski, *The Man You Loved to Hate*, 137.

Page 46   *"Every day"*   Ibid.

Page 46   *"The picture was like the book"*   Curtiss, *Von Stroheim*, 340.

Page 46   *"We went to the studio"*   Selznick, *A Private View*, 56.

Page 46   *"When I arrived"*   Stroheim, *Greed*, 28.

Page 47   *"spectators laughed"*   Hall, "The Screen," 28.

Page 47   *"This whole story"*   "Harry Carr's Page."

Page 47   *"If a contest"*   Koszarski, *The Man You Loved to Hate*, 146.

Page 47   *"the most important picture"*   Ibid., 147.

Page 48   *"Mr. von Stroheim has"*   Stroheim, *Greed*, 32.

Page 48   *"It is a contract"*   Crowther, *The Lion's Share*, 93.

Page 48   *"a baby, in its teething stage"*   NSA, 164.

Page 48   *"I could make the whole thing"*   Crowther, *The Lion's Share*, 97.

Page 49   *"That Sunday noon"*   "Interview with Ramon Novarro."

Page 49   *"It is almost beyond"*   Irving Thalberg to Fred Niblo, September 23, 1924, *Ben-Hur* file, MGM story file collection, Cinematic Arts Library, University of Southern California (hereafter MGM-USC).

Page 49   *"The audience is going to think"*   Thomas, *Thalberg*, 72.

Page 50   *"Everyone in the picture business"*   NSA, 166.

Page 50   *"How many people"*   Thomas, *Thalberg*, 74.

Page 50   *"So it'll look like"*   Ibid.

Page 50   *"What about the people?"*   "Interview with J. J. Cohn," Thomas/UCLA.

CHAPTER 6

Page 52   *"The average theater patron"*   "Millions for Film Program."

Page 53   *"Mr. Mayer has put under contract"*   Klumph, "Many Producers Sail to Sign New Talent," C27.

Page 53   *"[Harry] agreed"*   Dietz, *Dancing in the Dark*, 176.

Page 53   *"Irving felt that"*   NSA, 124.

Page 53   *"Henrietta always entered"*   "Lucien Hubbard Interview," Thomas/UCLA.

Page 54   *"Mr. Thalberg writes"*   "Harry Carr's Page," January 7, 1925, C2.

Page 54   *"Irving loved parties"*   Davies and Marx, *The Times We Had*, 105.

Page 54   *"I always feel a fine ironical disdain"*   "Harry Carr's Page," January 7, 1925, C2.

Page 54   *"They are so frightfully wrapped up"*   Pizzitola, *Hearst over Hollywood*, 227.

Page 54   *"Mayer would sometimes"*   "Conrad Nagel Interview," n.d., Thomas/UCLA.

Page 54   *"That Gilbert"*   Fountain and Maxim, *Dark Star*, 123.

Page 55   *"I lost my grip"*   Marx, *Mayer and Thalberg*, 59.

Page 55   *"Irving was not one"*   NSA, 168.

Page 55   *"Stroheim would watch"*   "Harry Carr's Page," June 3, 1925, C1.

Page 55   *"I called them"*   "Studio Row Terminated by Scolding."

Page 55   *"This is filth"*   Ardmore, *The Self-Enchanted*, 128.

Page 55   *"The old man"*   Samuel Marx to the author, January 16, 1990.

Page 55   *"No matter how late"*   "Conrad Nagel Interview," Thomas/UCLA.

Page 56   *"Irving loved to debate"*   "Albert Lewin Interview, September 9, 1967," Thomas/UCLA.

Page 56   *"I was weary"*   Vidor, *A Tree Is a Tree*, 112.

Page 56   *"Irving was still too weak"*   "Lucien Hubbard Interview," n.d., Thomas/UCLA.

Page 57   *"The cutter was there"*   Davies and Marx, *The Times We Had*, 105.

Page 57   *"Well, kid, you were repaid"*   Flamini, *Thalberg*, 68.

Page 57   *"I cannot tell you"*   Ibid.

Page 57   *"That glorious night"*   NSA, 168.

Page 57   *"Others are ready"*   Marx, *Mayer and Thalberg*, 75.

Page 58   *"In fact, the Metro-Goldwyn"*   Howe, "Who Will Be the Next Great Star?" 13.

CHAPTER 7

Page 59   *"Leo, our gentle friend"*   NSA, 170.

Page 59   *"old head on young shoulders"*   Hall, "Fads of Stars Seen in Coast Tour," X2.

Page 60   *"Most films . . . would just"*   Vidor, *A Tree Is a Tree*, 111.

Page 60   *"The Capitol"*   Klumph, "Holiday Fare Receipts Low."

Page 60   *"I thought about how"*   Vidor, *A Tree Is a Tree*, 112.

Page 60   *"the skilled surgeon"*   Whitaker, "New Contract Awes Her."

Page 61   *"The purchase of a book"*   "A Producing Executive Describes the Gamut Run by Book or Play."

Page 62   *"I have a compartmentalized mind"*   Thomas, *Thalberg*, 74.

Page 63   *"When a production is finished"*   Woolridge, "How Pictures Are Tried Out."

Page 63   *"We were always previewing"*   "Margaret Booth Oral History," 12, FCMPS.

Page 63   *"Sometimes three or four days"*   Rosenberg and Silverstein, *The Real Tinsel*, 113.

Page 63   *"The difference between"*   Samuel Marx to the author, January 16, 1990.

Page 63   *"Movies aren't made"*   Chester W. Schaeffer to the author, October 9, 1971.

Page 63   *"Henrietta was a battle-ax"*   Irene Selznick interview, Crowther/BYU.

Page 64   *"When Rosabelle or Constance"*   Selznick, *A Private View*, 79.

Page 64   *"That won't do"*   Thomas, *Thalberg*, 116.

Page 64   *"Norma told me"*   "Interview with Florence Browning," Crowther/BYU.

Page 64   *"This ugly duckling"*   NSA, 222.

Page 64   *"They just seem"*   Kingsley, "What Ho at Lila Lee's."

Page 64   *At a Harry Rapf party*   Kingsley, "Star-Partying."

Page 64   *"I'm going to marry"*   Lambert, *Norma Shearer*, 66.

Page 65   *"Tell me if and when"*   Whitaker, "Norma, Are You Upstage?"

Page 65   *"Metro-Goldwyn-Mayer welcomed me"*   Gish, *The Movies, Mr. Griffith, and Me*, 283.

Page 65   *"We frequently found ourselves"*   Vidor, *A Tree Is a Tree*, 131.

Page 65   *"Where are the love scenes?"*   Fountain and Maxim, *Dark Star*, 119.

Page 65   *"It seemed to me"*   Affron, *Lillian Gish*, 209.

Page 65   *"Oh, dear, I've got to go through"*   Oderman, *Lillian Gish*, 145.

Page 65   *"Jack Gilbert fell in love"*   Davies and Marx, *The Times We Had*, 53.

Page 66   *"The Gish can do no wrong."*   Gish and Pinchot, *The Movies, Mr. Griffith, and Me*, 284.

Page 66   *"I consider the acquisition"*   Moulton, "Frances Marion Joins M-G-M."

Page 66   *"Irving asked me"*   Gish and Pinchot, *The Movies, Mr. Griffith, and Me*, 292.

Page 66   *"Miss Gish reveals"*   Forslund, *Victor Sjöström*, 209.

Page 66   *"Is the man mad?"*   Bainbridge, *Garbo,* 100.

Page 67   *"My father was tortured"*   Paris, *Garbo,* 108.

Page 67   *"They brought me here"*   Bainbridge, *Garbo,* 100.

Page 67   *"I couldn't hear"*   Ibid., 101.

CHAPTER 8

Page 68   *"hated M-G-M"*   Behlmer, *Memo from: David O. Selznick,* 43.

Page 68   *"The last thing"*   Marx, *Mayer and Thalberg,* 83.

Page 69   *"At first Gilbert didn't know"*   Clarence Brown, interview with Susan Edwards Harvith and John Harvith, September 17, 1975 (hereinafter Brown/Harvith interview).

Page 69   *"It was the damnedest thing"*   Fountain and Maxim, *Dark Star,* 126.

Page 69   *"I don't know where"*   Brown/Harvith interview.

Page 70   *"Jack lived like a prince"*   NSA, 237.

Page 70   *"Miss Garbo at first"*   Ibid., 236.

Page 70   *"She could hop a boat"*   Marx, *Mayer and Thalberg,* 87.

Page 71   *"I guess we'll have to"*   Marion, "Hollywood," 284.

Page 72   *"Any special actresses"*   Marion, *Off with Their Heads!* 154.

Page 72   *"That hard-boiled audience!"*   Dressler, *My Own Story,* 237.

Page 72   *"Films are more accurate"*   Schallert, "Features Fashion to Pattern."

Page 73   *"He's so marvelous"*   Brownlow, *The Parade's Gone By,* 394.

Page 73   *"This was the country's"*   "Conrad Nagel Interview," Thomas/UCLA.

Page 73   *"Unless Paramount can curb"*   R. H. Cochrane to Will H. Hays, April 5, 1927, on microfilm of selected Hays Papers at the Library of Cinematic Arts, University of Southern California (hereafter WHH-USC).

Page 73   *"Thalberg never raised his voice"*   "Conrad Nagel Interview," Thomas/UCLA.

Page 74   *"The real foundation"*   "Edwin Loeb Interview," Crowther/BYU.

Page 74   *"He wants pictures"*   Brownlow, *The Parade's Gone By,* 394.

Page 74   *"Most people sleep too much"*   Ibid.

Page 74   *"They stimulate me"*   Amory and Bradlee, *Cavalcade of the 1920s and 1930s,* 129.

Page 74   *"You wouldn't think so"*   NSA, 272.

Page 74   *"Mr. Thalberg, . . . I realize that"*   Amory and Bradlee, *Cavalcade of the 1920s and 1930s,* 129.

Page 75   *"In the cinema world"*   Ibid.

Page 75   *"You're the only producer"*   Marx, *Mayer and Thalberg,* 97.

Page 76   *"'Yes, sir!'"*   NSA, 268.

Page 76   *"There is no question"*   "Film Match Admitted by Mother."

Page 76   *"Well, don't you think"*   NSA, 269.

Page 76   *"But you told me"*   Thomas, *Thalberg*, 118.

Page 76   *"I had been privileged"*   Maas, *The Shocking Miss Pilgrim*, 94.

Page 77   *"Why don't you pick"*   Marx, *Mayer and Thalberg*, 93.

Page 77   *"Irving's decided"*   Selznick, *A Private View*, 79.

Page 77   *"Irving never knew"*   Florence Browning interview, Crowther/BYU.

Page 77   *"I want to talk to you"*   Thomas, *Thalberg*, 119.

Page 78   *"Finally we decided"*   NSA, 270.

Page 78   *"Novelty is always welcome"*   Thomas, *Thalberg*, 100.

CHAPTER 9

Page 81   *"After the first musical number"*   Wallis and Higham, *Star Maker*, 19.

Page 81   *"When Jolson ad libbed"*   Morris, "Opening Night," 32.

Page 81   *"You could hear the crowd"*   Wallis and Higham, *Star Maker*, 19.

Page 81   *"refused to believe"*   "Skeptic Asks Al to 'Quit His Kidding.'"

Page 81   *"The Jazz Singer is credited"*   Smith, "The Movies Speak Out," 1270.

Page 81   *"The film coined money"*   Sisk, "The Movies Try to Talk," 493.

Page 81   *"Theater records were broken"*   MacAlarney, "The Noise Movie Revolution," 50.

Page 82   *"The talking motion picture"*   Crowther, *The Lion's Share*, 145.

Page 82   *"It was certainly the opinion"*   Mann, *Wisecracker*, 144.

Page 82   *"Knowing that Irving"*   NSA, 274.

Page 82   *"Norma became a live-in wife"*   Selznick, *A Private View*, 49.

Page 82   *"Not the kind"*   Lambert, *Norma Shearer*, 43.

Page 82   *"It's my duty"*   Marx, *Mayer and Thalberg*, 110.

Page 83   *"This hardly held the privacy"*   NSA, 198.

Page 83   *"Don't do it"*   Blesh, *Keaton*, 298.

Page 83   *"Thalberg was in charge"*   Dardis, *Keaton*, 163.

Page 83   *"For God's sake"*   Blesh, *Keaton*, 303.

Page 83   *"Often a situation arises"*   Dardis, *Keaton*, 162.

Page 83   *"Buster had his own fun factory"*   Ibid., 169.

Page 83   *"I was madly in love"*   Behlmer, *Memo from: David O. Selznick*, 43.

Page 84   *"Tits and sand"*   Marx, *Mayer and Thalberg*, 100.

Page 84   *"I told Thalberg"*   Behlmer, *Memo from: David O. Selznick*, 43.

Page 84   *"If you don't apologize"*   Marx, *Mayer and Thalberg*, 104.

Page 84   *"Thalberg gave me a chance"*   Behlmer, *Memo from: David O. Selznick*, 43.

Page 84   *"Why do you save all the good roles"*   Thomas, *Joan Crawford*, 56.

Page 84   *"I stole the script"*   Crawford and Ardmore, *A Portrait of Joan*, 62.

Page 84   *"We've got ourselves another star."*   Marx, *Mayer and Thalberg*, 69.

Page 85   *"We were greeted"*   NSA, 283.

Page 85   *"You see, I did not believe you"*   Ibid., 313.

Page 85   *"He is now generally known"*   "Mr. Thalberg Returns from Europe."

Page 86   *"Motion pictures are not shoes"*   "Screen Pair Back from Honeymoon."

Page 86   *"Has Metro reached the point"*   Affron, *Lillian Gish*, 223.

Page 86   *"It's pretty gloomy"*   Marion, *Off with Their Heads!* 159.

Page 86   *"I worked on the script"*   Brownlow, *The Parade's Gone By*, 152.

Page 86   *"I don't mind the heat so much"*   "Trials of an Actress."

Page 86   *"Never again!"*   Albert, "A Picture That Was No Picnic," 33.

Page 86   *"All of us, including Thalberg"*   Gish and Pinchot, *The Movies, Mr. Griffith, and Me*, 301.

Page 86   *"Miss Gish"*   Affron, *Lillian Gish*, 231.

Page 86   *"I hardly think"*   Ibid., 234.

Page 87   *"the supreme emotional actress"*   Ibid., 237.

Page 87   *"It was a tough picture"*   Brownlow, *The Parade's Gone By*, 149.

Page 87   *"People just didn't care for the picture"*   Ibid., 304.

Page 87   *"The Smell of the Yukon"*   "Olive Carey Interview, 1/22/67," Thomas/UCLA.

Page 87   *"It's the story"*   "Peace-Time 'Big Parade.'"

Page 87   *"I can certainly afford"*   Vidor, *A Tree Is a Tree*, 153.

Page 87   *"Just as these stories"*   "Radical Picturization Due in New Film Tales."

Page 88   *"This 100 percent talkie"*   Crafton, *The Talkies*, 117.

Page 88   *"The screen appeared"*   "King Vidor Speaks of Sound."

Page 88   *"Suddenly I was asked"*   "Douglas Shearer Interview," n.d., Thomas/UCLA.

Page 88   *"After all, Doug"*   Crowther, *Hollywood Rajah*, 83.

CHAPTER 10

Page 89   *"It was the flaming youth period"*   Crawford and Ardmore, *A Portrait of Joan*, 32.

Page 89   *"The gigantic edifice"*   Allen, *Only Yesterday*, 271.

Page 90   *"There never was a silent film."*   Punter, "The New Sounds of Silence."

Page 90   *"Eddie was terribly inventive"*   Marx, *Mayer and Thalberg*, 112.

Page 90   *"I knew Broadway."*   "Goulding Most Versatile."

Page 90   *"The girls were easy to cast."*   Marx, *Mayer and Thalberg*, 112.

Page 91   *"Somebody at M-G-M"*   Kobal, *Gotta Sing, Gotta Dance*, 31.

Page 91   *"I don't want to decide"*   Thomas, *Thalberg*, 124.

Page 91   *"This is an experiment"*   Ibid., 125.

Page 91   *"Musical comedy will prove"*   Whitaker, "Beaumont Talkie Veteran," C13.

Page 91   *"We have a lot of problems"*   Thomas, *Thalberg,* 125.

Page 92   *"We were on stepladders"*   Kobal, *People Will Talk,* 637.

Page 92   *"Word had come down"*   Kobal, *Gotta Sing, Gotta Dance,* 32.

Page 92   *"We just went along"*   Kobal, *People Will Talk,* 638.

Page 92   *"That's not a motion picture."*   Thomas, *Thalberg,* 126.

Page 92   *"We've got a perfectly good recording"*   Ibid.

Page 93   *"When the picture"*   Eyman, *The Speed of Sound,* 311.

Page 93   *"the initial onscreen musical"*   "Broadway Melody."

Page 93   *"When I started out at Metro"*   Kobal, *People Will Talk,* 638.

Page 94   *"I learned of the Mayer-Rubin-Thalberg rift"*   Interview with Florence Browning, Crowther/BYU.

Page 94   *"Mayer adored Rubin."*   Ibid.

Page 94   *"Wait a minute"*   Thomas, *Thalberg,* 155.

Page 95   *"Mr. Mayer, what's the matter?"*   Crowther, *Hollywood Rajah,* 139.

Page 95   *"Florence, . . . they're over at the bank"*   Florence Browning interview, Crowther/BYU.

Page 96   *"Then in the small watch pocket"*   Allvine, *The Greatest Fox of Them All,* 126.

Page 96   *"I always bragged"*   Sinclair, *Upton Sinclair Presents William Fox,* 5.

Page 96   *"Now Fox had Leo the Lion's tail"*   Allvine, *The Greatest Fox of Them All,* 126.

Page 96   *"No one knew"*   Florence Browning interview, Crowther/BYU.

Page 96   *"an unprincipled sell-out"*   Marx, *Mayer and Thalberg,* 116.

Page 96   *"You haven't heard the last"*   Thomas, *Thalberg,* 156.

Page 97   *"The integrity"*   "Thalberg Tells M-G-M Plans for Operation."

Page 97   *"Where a story lends itself"*   "Plan Silent Versions of Metro Talkies."

Page 97   *"People ask me"*   NSA, 325.

Page 97   *"The talking picture"*   Crafton, *The Talkies,* 485.

Page 97   *"The synchronization gives signs"*   Scheuer, "Haines Acts Fighter in Ring Story."

Page 98   *"If they want me to talk"*   Hall, "The Hollywood Hermit."

Page 98   *"Sounds are sounds"*   "Nils Asther."

Page 98   *"In the silent movies"*   "Speakers Not Appreciated."

Page 98   *"the passing of the inaudible drama"*   "Talkies to Belong to Actors."

Page 98   *"The great quality"*   "Irving Thalberg."

Page 98   *"I talked with Thalberg"*   Veiller, *The Fun I've Had,* 287.

Page 99   *"Irving said that the change"*   Ramsey, "The Trial of Norma Shearer," 33.

Page 99   *"She was coming along"*   Veiller, *The Fun I've Had,* 287.

Page 99   *"During these sessions"*   NSA, 344.

Page 99   *"That's a man!"*   Dore Freeman to author, December 1, 1975.

Page 99   *"I was scared"*   Davies and Marx, *The Times We Had,* 100.

Page 100   *"Irving believed in training"*   NSA, 198.

Page 100   *"If you want her to play it"*   Veiller, *The Fun I've Had*, 287.

Page 100   *"They'll be the jury"*   Crowther, *The Lion's Share*, 153.

Page 101   *"Even the whir"*   Veiller, *The Fun I've Had*, 287.

Page 101   *"The inside of the booth"*   Ramsey, "The Trial of Norma Shearer," 100.

Page 101   *"For Norma Shearer"*   Lusk, *"Mary Dugan* Brilliant Hit," C14.

Page 101   *"Irving was informed"*   Marx, *Mayer and Thalberg*, 123.

Page 102   *"The first few years"*   Ibid., 127.

Page 102   *"Mr. President, the boy did wrong."*   Thomas, *Thalberg*, 226.

Page 102   *"I'm twenty-five"*   Ibid., 135.

Page 102   *"Oh, excuse me, Irving!"*   Kingsley, "Bal Masque."

Page 102   *"It was the height"*   Mann, *Wisecracker*, 144.

Page 103   *"The talkies had already arrived"*   Brownlow, *The Parade's Gone By*, 152.

Page 103   *"The audience fairly howled"*   Eyman, *The Speed of Sound*, 302.

Page 103   *"Seems the only type of love stuff"*   Walker, *The Shattered Silents*, 171.

Page 103   *"As an old and experienced hand"*   Barrymore, *We Barrymores*, 236.

Page 104   *"I watched Jack Gilbert"*   Hopper, *From under My Hat*, 164.

Page 104   *"Gilbert has not as yet"*   Schallert, "Gilbert Is Hero in Gay Intrigue," 11.

Page 104   *"A few more talker productions"*   "His Glorious Night."

Page 104   *"White-hot love speeches"*   Walker, *The Shattered Silents*, 172.

Page 104   *"That should take care of* Mr. *Gilbert."*   Fountain and Maxim, *Dark Star*, 186.

Page 105   *"I doubt that it will make a dollar"*   Vidor, *A Tree Is a Tree*, 153.

Page 105   *"Let the other fellows"*   Marx, *Mayer and Thalberg*, 104.

Page 105   *"It's not practical."*   Thomas, *Thalberg*, 163.

Page 105   *"It took me longer"*   Dowd and Shepard, *King Vidor*, 99.

Page 105   *"Terribly disappointed"*   Eyman, *The Speed of Sound*, 223.

Page 105   *"Nina was full of life"*   Dowd and Shepard, *King Vidor*, 102.

Page 105   *"All the incidents in* Hallelujah!*"*   Greenberg and Higham, *The Celluloid Muse*, 66.

Page 105   *"The big Chicago theater owners"*   Ibid., 67.

Page 106   *"There is nothing in it to attract"*   "Hallelujah."

Page 106   *"Vidor has poured himself"*   Morris, "Hallelujah."

Page 106   *"We guess it's a moving picture"*   "The Trial of Mary Dugan."

Page 106   *"One saw men looking defeat in the face."*   Allen, *Only Yesterday*, 273.

Page 107   *"L.B. was sure"*   Marx, *Mayer and Thalberg*, 125.

Page 107   *"Irving locked horns with Nick"*   Selznick, *A Private View*, 62.

Page 107   *"He got a quarter of a million"*   Marx, *Mayer and Thalberg*, 126.

Page 108   *"His only weakness"*   Crowther, *Hollywood Rajah*, 149.

Page 108   *"[Irving] wanted as much"*   Marx, *Mayer and Thalberg*, 126.

Page 108   *"I found Irving's demands"*   Selznick, *A Private View*, 62.

Page 108   *"Their marriage worked."*   Rosenberg and Silverstein, *The Real Tinsel*, 381.

Page 108   *"I knew that M-G-M owned the story"*   Parsons, "Norma Talks about Joan," 13.

Page 108   *"I was the one person"*   Crawford and Ardmore, *A Portrait of Joan*, 32.

Page 109   *"My first appearance"*   Ibid., 13.

Page 109   *"I found myself sitting"*   NSA, 214.

Page 109   *"I saw her crying"*   Ibid.

Page 109   *"I tried to watch everything"*   Crawford and Ardmore, *A Portrait of Joan*, 12.

Page 109   *"They were complete opposites."*   Maas, *The Shocking Miss Pilgrim*, 72.

Page 109   *"She blamed her overwhelming sense"*   Selznick, *A Private View*, 62.

Page 109   *"Certainly Norma had an advantage"*   "Joan Crawford, January 24, 1968, Cock and Bull," Thomas/UCLA.

Page 109   *"Irving laughed at me"*   Parsons, "Norma Talks about Joan," 13.

Page 109   *"Oh, Miss Shearer"*   "The Norma Shearer Irving Thalberg Loves."

Page 109   *"I had to prove"*   "What's Ahead for Norma Shearer?"

Page 110   *"Why, Ramon, . . . you've never"*   Stine, *The Hurrell Style*, 7.

Page 110   *"Norma planned her campaign"*   "The Norma Shearer Irving Thalberg Loves."

Page 110   *"a tough little gal"*   Kapitanoff, "Sixty-three Years of Shooting the Legends."

Page 110   *"I loved your photographs"*   Stine, *The Hurrell Style*, 7.

Page 110   *"A great deal depended"*   Busby, "The Camera Does Lie," 74.

Page 110   *"She was like an excited child"*   "The Norma Shearer Irving Thalberg Loves."

Page 110   *"Why, I believe you can"*   Parsons, "Norma Talks about Joan," 13.

CHAPTER 11

Page 111   *"I'd settle for another ten years."*   Thomas, *Thalberg*, 135.

Page 111   *"Why don't you try screenwriting?"*   Marx, *Mayer and Thalberg*, ix.

Page 112   *"I'll give you the same money"*   Marx, *A Gaudy Spree*, 5.

Page 112   *"They'll go see anything!"*   Marx, *Mayer and Thalberg*, 153.

Page 112   *"Each employee thrown out of work"*   Allen, *Only Yesterday*, 285.

Page 112   *"Irving had French doors"*   "Howard Dietz Interview, Port Washington, October 14, 1967," Thomas/UCLA.

Page 112   *"If I leave it there long enough"*   Thomas, *Thalberg*, 135.

Page 112   *"How'd you like"*   Marion, *Off with Their Heads!* 191.

Page 113   *"Irving was the only one"*   Marion, "Hollywood," 418a.

Page 114   *"Plots had narrowed down"*   Lord, *Played by Ear*, 295.

Page 114   *"No picture shall be produced"*   Vieira, *Sin in Soft Focus*, 214.

Page 114　*"We do not create these types"*　Maltby, "The Genesis of the Production Code," 19.

Page 114　*"That the Code will actually be applied"*　"Morals for Profit."

Page 115　*"Will you accept three hundred"*　Meryman, *Mank*, 133.

Page 115　*"Thalberg read every word slowly"*　Lawson, *Film, the Creative Process*, 104.

Page 116　*"Look! What a difference!"*　Moore, *You're Only Human Once*, 171.

Page 116　*"A lot of people"*　"The Rogue Song."

Page 116　*"Nothing would do"*　DeMille, *Autobiography of Cecil B. DeMille*, 301.

Page 116　*"It contains no semblance of reality."*　Marx, *Mayer and Thalberg*, 132.

Page 116　*"Why spend money"*　Chester W. Schaeffer to author, October 9, 1971.

Page 117　*"Well, I'm dreadful"*　Crawford and Ardmore, *A Portrait of Joan*, 69.

Page 117　*"You control the artistic side."*　Marx, *Mayer and Thalberg*, 120.

Page 117　*"When it came to musicals"*　Kobal, *People Will Talk*, 639.

Page 117　*"Arthur, you can be here"*　Ibid., 637.

Page 117　*"Why are there so many writers"*　Lawson, *Film, the Creative Process*, 104.

Page 117　*"What brings you to California?"*　Marx, *A Gaudy Spree*, 5.

Page 118　*"Thalberg wanted superior writing"*　Ibid., 20.

Page 118　*"Irving Thalberg was a fine boss"*　Hecht, *Charlie*, 171.

Page 118　*"I know less about writing"*　Ibid., 160.

Page 118　*"What's all this crap"*　Marx, *A Gaudy Spree*, 67.

Page 119　*"I was ready to read"*　Robinson and Spigelgass, *All My Yesterdays*, 104.

Page 119　*"Look, Mr. Thalberg"*　Thomas, *Thalberg*, 201.

Page 119　*"He assured me"*　Robinson and Spigelgass, *All My Yesterdays*, 105.

Page 119　*"Irving Thalberg seemed a bit"*　Bickford, *Bulls, Balls, Bicycles & Actors*, 218.

Page 120　*"She says it portrays Swedes"*　Marx, *Mayer and Thalberg*, 123.

Page 120　*"You don't suppose"*　Marion, *Off with Their Heads!* 196.

Page 120　*"What if Miss Garbo refuses"*　Marx, *Mayer and Thalberg*, 123.

Page 120　*"It's bad enough"*　Bickford, *Bulls, Balls, Bicycles & Actors*, 218.

Page 120　*"With blood in my eye"*　Ibid., 257.

Page 121　*"I don't want to talk"*　Nelson, "Chaney Comes Back," 33.

Page 121　*"Hyman kept talking"*　Maltin, *Hollywood, the Movie Factory*, 151.

Page 121　*"Dull, sluggish, agonizing."*　"Redemption."

Page 121　*"several tones higher"*　Fountain and Maxim, *Dark Star*, 190.

Page 122　*"This can't be considered"*　"Way for a Sailor."

Page 122　*"Just before Gilbert"*　Fountain and Maxim, *Dark Star*, 192.

Page 122　*"Once a star"*　Marx, *Mayer and Thalberg*, 138.

Page 123　*"The records kept going."*　Moore, *You're Only Human Once*, 174.

Page 123　*"This is a rip-roaring comedy"*　Marion, *Off with Their Heads!* 206.

Page 124　*"It was not until Frances"*　Dressler, *My Own Story*, 253.

Page 124   *"The best tunes"*   Hamann, *On the Sets in the 30s,* 6.

Page 124   *"The play was a showcase"*   Knight, "Oral Interview with Lawrence Weingarten."

Page 124   *"It's a good campaign"*   Day, *This Was Hollywood,* 99.

Page 125   *"'Garbo Talks' is, beyond quarrel, an event"*   "Anna Christie."

Page 125   *"She had to fight"*   "The Norma Shearer Irving Thalberg Loves," 71.

Page 125   *"Norma is a very . . ."*   Thomas, *Thalberg,* 164.

Page 125   *"presents divorce"*   Maltby, "The Genesis of the Production Code," 20.

Page 125   *"We had lots of fun"*   NSA, 364.

Page 126   *"I'm having a baby"*   Marx, *Mayer and Thalberg,* 143.

Page 126   *"She allowed nothing to interfere"*   Hall, "A Heroine to Other Stars," 66.

Page 126   *"She affects a laugh"*   Hamann, *Norma Shearer in the 30s,* 8.

Page 126   *"It was a tremendous gamble"*   Parsons, "Norma Talks about Joan," 13.

Page 126   *"Alas, . . . we just can't"*   Selznick, *A Private View,* 79.

Page 126   *"If I have to do any more"*   Hamann, *Joan Crawford in the 30s,* 8.

Page 127   *"My son has"*   Marx, *Mayer and Thalberg,* 144.

Page 127   *"Great not only because"*   Thomas, "A Gallery of Grotesques."

Page 127   *"Too many murders."*   Marx, *Mayer and Thalberg,* 153.

Page 127   *"Norma Shearer was Big Queen then"*   Moore, *You're Only Human Once,* 173.

CHAPTER 12

Page 131   *"After abusing his health"*   NSA, 372.

Page 131   *"We haven't been allowed"*   Hamann, *Norma Shearer in the 30s,* 15.

Page 132   *"No, . . . I won't go"*   Thomas, *Thalberg,* 174.

Page 132   *"Charlie and Irving had hit it off"*   Hayes and Hatch, *Helen Hayes,* 65.

Page 132   *"God damn it, Irving!"*   Thomas, *Thalberg,* 174.

Page 132   *"It was rancid"*   Carey, *All the Stars in Heaven,* 149.

Page 133   *"Is that a breadline"*   Allen, *Only Yesterday,* 287.

Page 133   *"Make lots of pictures."*   Marx, *Mayer and Thalberg,* 138.

Page 133   *"Now, more than ever"*   Ibid., 153.

Page 134   *"The front office wanted"*   Carey, *All the Stars in Heaven,* 144

Page 134   *"You know damned well"*   Thomas, *Thalberg,* 159.

Page 134   *"Oh, it was tough."*   Brownlow, *The War, the West, and the Wilderness,* 562.

Page 134   *"I learned about 'doo-doos'"*   Babcock, "Safari Scenes Grip Memory."

Page 134   *"She was always ripped to pieces."*   Riggan, "Damn the Crocodiles— Keep the Cameras Rolling!" 91.

Page 135   *"We had insects in our eyebrows"*   Ibid.

Page 135   *"They decided they would send over"*   Brownlow, *The War, the West, and the Wilderness,* 564.

Page 135   *"Africa just pours into one."*   Babcock, "Safari Scenes Grip Memory."

Page 135   *"In order to live in Africa"*   Riggan, "Damn the Crocodiles—Keep the Cameras Rolling!" 41.

Page 135   *"What are we going to do with this?"*   Crowther, *The Lion's Share,* 168.

Page 135   *"The picture must go on"*   Riggan, "Damn the Crocodiles—Keep the Cameras Rolling!" 41.

Page 136   *"We're not getting anywhere."*   Brownlow, *The War, the West, and the Wilderness,* 566.

Page 136   *"Hyman and Hume were weeping"*   Marx, *Mayer and Thalberg,* 151.

Page 136   *"Listen, Carey"*   Thomas, *Thalberg,* 161.

Page 136   *"We can't use it in Africa."*   Hamann, *W. S. Van Dyke in the 30s,* 8.

Page 136   *"In their village"*   Crowther, *The Lion's Share,* 169.

Page 137   *"Boss keep Slickem away"*   Day, *This Was Hollywood,* 61.

Page 138   *"Take the nipple out"*   Thomas, *Thalberg,* 135.

Page 138   *"He was a great, great fellow"*   Mann, *Wisecracker,* 160.

Page 138   *"self-appointed pariah"*   Carr, "The Story of Hollywood's Unhappiest Man," B5.

Page 139   *"I'm going to miss you terribly"*   "Ina Claire Divorces John Gilbert."

Page 139   *"He is a great actor."*   "Ina Claire in Reno to Get Divorce."

Page 139   *"Jack was very much distressed"*   "Ina Claire Divorces John Gilbert."

Page 139   *"Jack had a good friend"*   Fountain and Maxim, *Dark Star,* 219.

Page 139   *"When anyone can stir"*   Ibid.

Page 139   *"Jack told me"*   Ibid.

Page 139   *"If it was the purpose"*   Ibid.

Page 140   *"People—just people"*   NSA, 241.

Page 140   *"There's a part"*   Marx, *Mayer and Thalberg,* 156.

Page 140   *"Look, Buster"*   Blesh, *Keaton,* 299.

Page 140   *"There was only one thing"*   Dardis, *Keaton,* 190.

Page 140   *"Thalberg, as well as being a fine judge"*   Keaton and Samuels, *My Wonderful World of Slapstick,* 207.

Page 140   *"We were desperate."*   Dardis, *Keaton,* 190.

Page 141   *"It's a farce."*   Blesh, *Keaton,* 317.

Page 141   *"There were too many cooks"*   Dardis, *Keaton,* 188.

Page 141   *"Larry likes it."*   Keaton and Samuels, *My Wonderful World of Slapstick,* 239.

Page 141   *"such a complete stinker"*   Blesh, *Keaton,* 324.

Page 141   *"They would be given a script"*   "Letter from Lenore Coffee, January 21, 1968," Thomas/UCLA.

Page 142   *"Actors are like children."*   Marion, *Off with Their Heads!* 211.

Page 142 *"Irving would always give a script"* "Frances Marion Telephone Interview, August 28, 1967," Thomas/UCLA.

Page 142 *"Wives and shopgirls"* Marx, *A Gaudy Spree*, 31.

Page 142 *"A silent film"* McGilligan, *Backstory 1*, 143.

Page 142 *"That's not a motion picture."* Gussow, *Don't Say Yes until I Finish Talking*, 46.

Page 143 *"Irving was giving Johnny"* "Frances Marion telephone interview," Thomas/UCLA.

Page 143 *"How did you like the fellow"* Marx, *Mayer and Thalberg*, 157.

Page 143 *"What's going on?"* "Howard Strickling Interview, Beverly Wilshire Hotel, February 22, 1968," Thomas/UCLA.

Page 143 *"I tried to interest Irving"* "Frances Marion telephone interview," Thomas/UCLA.

Page 143 *"I'd like to star Beery"* Marion, *Off with Their Heads!* 225.

Page 144 *"He sat on a short, carpeted stairway"* Coffee, *Storyline*, 99.

Page 144 *"Thalberg sat in a large chair"* Acosta, *Here Lies the Heart*, 231.

Page 144 *"We are picking up your option"* Coffee, *Storyline*, 174.

Page 146 *"It reads funny"* Marx, *Mayer and Thalberg*, 152.

Page 146 *"The motion-picture business"* Whitaker, "Wodehouse Out and Still Dazed."

Page 146 *"You silly boys out there!"* Marx, *Mayer and Thalberg*, 153.

Page 146 *"Irving had a most practical awareness"* NSA, 203.

Page 147 *"Oh, these writers!"* McGilligan, *Backstory 1*, 250.

Page 147 *"If it isn't for the writing"* Samuel Marx to the author, January 16, 1990.

Page 147 *"He had the gift"* Coffee, *Storyline*, 99.

Page 147 *"Supervisor has become"* Marx, *Mayer and Thalberg*, 162.

Page 147 *"My dear, I have something"* Thomas, *Thalberg*, 179.

Page 147 *"Miss Fontanne, . . . I can assure you"* Zolotow, *Stagestruck*, 182.

Page 148 *"Why was that?"* Marx, *Mayer and Thalberg*, 162.

Page 148 *"Not another thing"* "The Norma Shearer Irving Thalberg Loves," 33.

Page 148 *"Yes, we all have those"* NSA, 380.

Page 149 *"We reached for"* Ibid., 395.

Page 149 *"acting strangely"* "Mrs. Shearer Kills Self before Crowd on Pier."

Page 150 *"Helen has been a star"* Marx, *Mayer and Thalberg*, 169.

Page 150 *"Helen is fine."* Thomas, *Thalberg*, 174.

Page 150 *"Irving had Charlie write a scene"* "Helen Hayes Interview, August 10, 1967," Thomas/UCLA.

Page 150 *"He lived two thirds of his time"* "Ben Hecht, June 1959," p. 723, Columbia University Oral History Collection (hereinafter CUOHC).

Page 150 *"Say, mister, . . . if you don't"* Crowther, *The Lion's Share*, 186.

Page 151   *"Don't be nervous."*   Ibid., 187.

Page 151   *"Well?"*   Zolotow, "The Facts about Alfred Lunt's Lips."

Page 151   *"Cut! Cut!"*   Thomas, *Thalberg*, 180.

Page 152   *"Don't read any more"*   Zolotow, *Stagestruck*, 184.

Page 152   *"But that's entirely out of keeping"*   Thomas, *Thalberg*, 180.

Page 152   *"Your wife will get all my stage roles"*   Haber, "Small Dinner Party for Alfred Lunts."

Page 152   *"enjoying the just reward"*   Hall, "Molnar's 'Guardsman,'" X5.

Page 153   *"Now and again"*   Marshall, "On the London Screen," 98.

Page 153   *"The 'lowly' movies"*   Scheuer, "An Old Story."

Page 153   *"ten important pictures a year"*   Jason Joy, "Résumé of Activities," February 4, 1931, *Strangers May Kiss* file, Production Code Administration papers, MPAA Collection, Margaret Herrick Library, Fairbanks Center for Motion Picture Study (hereafter PCA).

Page 153   *"this medium of entertainment"*   Hall, "The Actor's Experiment," 22.

Page 153   *"Studios are accused of imitation"*   Scheuer, "An Old Story."

Page 154   *"wholly objectionable"*   Lamar Trotti to Jason Joy, August 12, 1930, *Strangers May Kiss* file, PCA.

Page 154   *"Thalberg was inconsiderate."*   "Howard Dietz," Thomas/UCLA.

Page 154   *"Only small minds"*   NSA, 380.

Page 155   *"Is this entirely your thought?"*   Davies and Marx, *The Times We Had*, 104.

Page 155   *"Audiences like to see me"*   Hamann, *Norma Shearer in the 30s*, 16.

Page 155   *"Typecasting is slow death"*   Marx, *Mayer and Thalberg*, 156.

Page 155   *"How much do you want"*   Thomas, *Thalberg*, 184.

Page 156   *"There were several roles"*   "Joan Crawford," Thomas/UCLA.

Page 156   *"Norma was the Queen"*   Stine, *The Hurrell Style*, 25.

Page 156   *"She looked like her own grandmother."*   "Adela Rogers St. Johns Interview," Thomas/UCLA.

Page 156   *"I bit like a carp"*   Barrymore, *We Barrymores*, 241.

Page 156   *"He was shy"*   NSA, 354.

Page 157   *"Will they accept me"*   Coffee, *Storyline*, 174.

Page 157   *"The only trouble is"*   McGilligan, *Backstory 1*, 144.

Page 157   *"I fear that we have"*   Lamar Trotti to Jason Joy, October 21, 1931, *Possessed* file, PCA.

Page 157   *"In the picture"*   Crawford and Ardmore, *A Portrait of Joan*, 90.

Page 157   *"He would have ended my career"*   Considine, *Bette and Joan*, 51.

Page 158   *"If you were ever here"*   Marx, *Mayer and Thalberg*, 158.

Page 158   *"I'm being shortchanged."*   Ibid., 160.

CHAPTER 13

Page 161   *"The fog of despair"*   Schlesinger, *The Age of Roosevelt,* 5.

Page 161   *"Those who had survived"*   Marion, *Off with Their Heads!* 211.

Page 162   *"The onlookers on the sidewalks"*   Barrymore, *Memories,* 272.

Page 162   *"I had long believed"*   Behlmer, *Memo from: David O. Selznick,* 72.

Page 162   *"But will they lend us Thalberg?"*   Marx, *Mayer and Thalberg,* 161.

Page 162   *"We were making pictures"*   "D. A. Doran Interview, November 13, 1967," Thomas/UCLA.

Page 162   *"Get to Hillcrest right away!"*   "Howard Strickling Interview," Thomas/UCLA.

Page 163   *"Scottie, supposing"*   Fitzgerald, *The Last Tycoon,* 134.

Page 163   *"much more polite"*   Babcock, "Flaming Youth Called Feeble," B9.

Page 164   *"Poor Scott had quit drinking"*   Loos, *Kiss Hollywood Good-by,* 122.

Page 164   *"You don't really have time"*   Samuel Marx to the author, January 16, 1990.

Page 164   *"the man who had"*   "Anita Loos Interview, no date," Thomas/UCLA.

Page 164   *"Almost at the first sip"*   Marx, *Mayer and Thalberg,* 183.

Page 164   *"He was worried"*   Taylor, *Joyride,* 239.

Page 164   *"Novelists and playwrights"*   "Producer Discusses Pictures."

Page 164   *"There was a rankling indignity"*   Dardis, *Some Time in the Sun,* 29.

Page 164   *"I want to show Hays"*   Samuel Marx to the author, January 16, 1990.

Page 164   *"I have never seen a film"*   "Conference Notes, December 9, 1931," *Grand Hotel* file, MGM-USC.

Page 165   *"Irving was a realist."*   NSA, 221.

Page 165   *"Irving was tough and discerning"*   Walter Wanger to Bob Thomas, November 29, 1967, Thomas/UCLA.

Page 165   *"I couldn't get him"*   Carey, *Anita Loos,* 147.

Page 165   *"Far from approaching it"*   Turnbull, *The Letters of F. Scott Fitzgerald,* 29.

Page 165   *"We found ourselves standing"*   Taylor, *Joyride,* 239.

Page 165   *"take-a-chance affairs"*   "The Norma Shearer Irving Thalberg Loves," 33.

Page 166   *"Why didn't you bring your horse in too?"*   Latham, *Crazy Sundays,* 71.

Page 166   *"Scott tried to turn"*   Loos, *Kiss Hollywood Good-by,* 34.

Page 166   *"You've been tricked."*   Marx, *Mayer and Thalberg,* 184.

Page 167   *"Under the law of averages"*   Thomas, *Thalberg,* 146.

Page 167   *"The swift-moving, episodic character"*   "Producer Discusses Pictures."

Page 167   *"His confidence had been eaten away."*   Fountain and Maxim, *Dark Star,* 222.

Page 168   *"You studio people warp my character."*   Marx, *Mayer and Thalberg,* 122.

Page 168   *"Thalberg decided that he had no choice"*   Ibid., 188.

Page 168   *"People go to the movies"*   Thomas, *Thalberg,* 218.

Page 169   *"Don't lose it."*   Marx, *Mayer and Thalberg,* 177.

Page 169   *"We were so anxious"*   Marx, *A Gaudy Spree,* 41.

Page 169   *"It's good discipline"*   Ibid., 40.

Page 169   *"I think it would be very nice"*   Behlmer, *W. S. Van Dyke's Journal,* 80.

Page 169   *"Joe, we can't spend that much money."*   "J. J. Cohn Oral History," 143, FCMPS.

Page 170   *"A successful picture"*   Samuel Marx to the author, January 16, 1990.

Page 170   *"This man looks almost frail."*   Whitaker, "Hit-Maker," 19.

Page 170   *"I'd get sore"*   "Lawrence Weingarten Interview, MGM, August 21, 1967," Thomas/UCLA.

Page 170   *"Irving was invariably impersonal"*   "Albert Lewin Interview, September 9, 1967," Thomas/UCLA.

Page 170   *"You're asking four hundred"*   "John Lee Mahin Interview, Columbia Pictures, September 12, 1967," Thomas/UCLA.

Page 171   *"He was an amazingly attractive man."*   Walter Wanger to Bob Thomas, November 29, 1967, Thomas/UCLA.

Page 171   *"Freud has helped me"*   Flamini, *Thalberg,* 113.

Page 171   *"His head would vibrate"*   "Frances (Mrs. Samuel) Goldwyn Interview, September 12, 1967," Thomas/UCLA.

Page 171   *"Irving was still a rather pathetic figure."*   Loos, *Kiss Hollywood Good-by,* 32.

Page 172   *"Although his shoulders hunched forward"*   Kotsilibas-Davis and Loy, *Being and Becoming,* 79.

Page 172   *"I can keep tabs"*   Loos, *Kiss Hollywood Good-by,* 119.

Page 172   *"I wrote Red-Headed Woman"*   Kobal, *People Will Talk,* 173.

Page 172   *"I somewhat condescendingly agreed"*   Wilk, "Donald Ogden Stewart Oral History," p. 3, American Film Institute (hereinafter Stewart/AFI).

Page 173   *"He had an endless capacity"*   Veiller, *The Fun I've Had,* 292.

Page 173   *"Oh, Irving, . . . not in there!"*   Thomas, *Thalberg,* 219.

Page 173   *"You have three days"*   Veiller, *The Fun I've Had,* 293.

Page 173   *"Irving was a natural-born storyteller."*   "Ben Hecht, June 1959," p. 723, CUOHC.

Page 174   *"Wine, wine"*   Pirandello, *As You Desire Me,* 61.

Page 174   *"The girl in the play"*   "Conference Notes, May 12, 1932," *As You Desire Me* file, MGM-USC.

Page 174   *"I put into my original"*   Marion, *Off with Their Heads!* 232.

Page 174   *"I want to soft-pedal"*   "Conference Notes, May 6, 1932," *Blondie of the Follies* file, MGM-USC.

Page 175   *"People around here treat failure"*   Marx, *Mayer and Thalberg,* 187.

Page 175   *"To me the play was far better"*   "Conference Notes, November 17, 1931," *Grand Hotel* file, MGM-USC.

Page 176   *"I miss the increasing tempo"*   "Conference Notes, December 9, 1931,"
       ibid.

Page 177   *"I think Kringelein's speech"*   "Conference Notes, December 26, 1931,"
       ibid.

Page 177   *"How could you do this to me?"*   Hecht, *Charlie*, 161.

Page 177   *"Scott should have gone on drinking."*   "Anita Loos Interview, no date,"
       Thomas/UCLA.

Page 177   *"Let's first of all decide"*   Loos, *Kiss Hollywood Good-by*, 39.

Page 178   *"Do you think you can"*   Ibid., 40.

Page 178   *"utterly impossible"*   Trotti to McKenzie, April 27, 1932, *Red-Headed
       Woman* file, PCA.

Page 179   *"It was not any particular scene"*   Maltin, *Hollywood, the Movie Factory*, 188.

Page 179   *"This is in my mind"*   Trotti to McKenzie, April 27, 1932, *Red-Headed
       Woman* file, PCA.

Page 179   *"He and I went into a session"*   Trotti to Hays, April 30, 1932, ibid.

Page 179   *"The newspapers have got a nerve"*   Marion, *Off with Their Heads!* 227.

Page 179   *"He had a fanatic fondness"*   Veiller, *The Fun I've Had*, 289.

Page 180   *"To Irving Thalberg every film"*   Loos, *Kiss Hollywood Good-by*, 36.

Page 180   *"I want the audience to see"*   Marx, *Mayer and Thalberg*, 84.

Page 180   *"It wasn't at all necessary"*   Loos, *Kiss Hollywood Good-by*, 36.

Page 180   *"Why should producers"*   "What the Audience Thinks (3)."

Page 180   *"Thalberg said that Huntington Park"*   Chester W. Schaeffer to the
       author, October 9, 1971.

Page 180   *"The snub-nosed Interurban"*   Marx, *Mayer and Thalberg*, 136.

Page 181   *"Sometimes he would be right up there"*   Chester W. Schaeffer to the
       author, October 9, 1971.

Page 181   *"Well, you know"*   Thomas, *Thalberg*, 210.

Page 181   *"My feeling"*   Joy to Hays, June 17, 1932, *Red-Headed Woman* file, PCA.

Page 181   *"I'd like you to contrive"*   Loos, *Kiss Hollywood Good-by*, 43.

Page 182   *"They laughed because"*   Marx, *Mayer and Thalberg*, 138.

Page 182   *"Thalberg's idea"*   Walter Wanger to Bob Thomas, December 15, 1967,
       Thomas/UCLA.

Page 182   *"Thalberg caused M-G-M"*   "Howard Strickling Interview," Thomas/
       UCLA.

Page 182   *"He didn't go to previews just"*   Walter Wanger to Bob Thomas, Decem-
       ber 15, 1967, Thomas/UCLA.

Page 182   *"You work for Thalberg."*   Johnson, *Flashback*, 125.

Page 182   *"An audience will reach for quality."*   Chester W. Schaeffer to the author,
       October 9, 1971; Basil Wrangell to the author, November 23, 1975;
       Samuel Marx to the author, January 16, 1990.

Page 183   *"I think it's because it's badly done."*   "Conference Notes, March 18, 1932," *Grand Hotel* file, MGM-USC.

Page 183   *"great care ought to be taken"*   Joy to Thalberg, January 5, 1932, *Grand Hotel* file, PCA.

Page 183   *"a rather sad one"*   "Conference Notes, March 18, 1932," *Grand Hotel* file, MGM-USC.

CHAPTER 14

Page 185   *"To her tactlessly"*   Fairbanks, *The Salad Days,* 168.

Page 185   *"Honestly, I could say"*   Hall, "A Heroine to Other Stars," 27.

Page 185   *"I have left M-G-M"*   George Hurrell to Norma Shearer, July 16, 1932, Norma Shearer Collection, USC Library of Cinematic Arts.

Page 186   *"I can't do the Garbo or Dietrich thing."*   Schallert, "Norma Shearer Reveals Why She Went Wrong."

Page 186   *"I admire and like Joan."*   Parsons, "Norma Talks about Joan," 13.

Page 187   "Letty Lynton *is with all intents and purpose"*   Joy to Hays, January 11, 1932, *Letty Lynton* file, PCA.

Page 187   *"Don't let that Bolshevik inside"*   Marx, *A Gaudy Spree,* 68.

Page 188   *"Every man is a socialist when"*   Thomas, *Thalberg,* 216.

Page 188   *"Come up here!"*   Marx, *Mayer and Thalberg,* 179.

Page 189   *"If we support"*   Ibid., 180.

Page 189   *"Aren't you the one"*   Ibid., 179.

Page 189   *"Well, Irving, it's a nice* Billie Dove *picture."*   Rob McKay to the author, September 6, 1990.

Page 189   *"I want you to write"*   "Willis Goldbeck Interview, Bel Air Hotel, February 29, 1968," Thomas/UCLA.

Page 189   *"People run out of the commissary"*   Marx, *Mayer and Thalberg,* 180.

Page 190   *"If it's a mistake"*   Ibid.

Page 190   *"Irving's right so often"*   Marx, *A Gaudy Spree,* 132.

Page 190   *"Halfway through the preview"*   Skal and Savada, *Dark Carnival,* 174.

Page 190   *"Well, I have seen that picture"*   "The Audience Talks Back," 10.

Page 190   *"I know the theater."*   Scheuer, "Barretts Lead Drama Crusade," 18.

Page 191   *"There was nothing exactly normal"*   NSA, 404.

Page 191   *"It's taken me three years"*   Lee, "Norma Fights Back," 63.

Page 191   *"Norma missed Bill at first"*   Lee Garmes to the author, March 5, 1972.

Page 192   *"The three Barrymores"*   Barrymore, *We Three,* 87.

Page 192   *"I don't give a hang"*   Ibid., 88.

Page 192   *"Ethel Barrymore, the superwoman"*   Schallert, "Ethel Barrymore Takes Greatest Leap of Career," B11.

Page 192 *"All the reporters and photographers"* Barrymore, *Memories*, 271.

Page 193 *"Do you mean to tell me"* Barrymore, *We Three*, 89.

Page 193 *"Rasputin didn't succeed"* McGilligan, *Backstory 1*, 142.

Page 193 *"The Romanoffs kicked your people around"* Thomas, *Thalberg*, 228.

Page 194 *"Nicholas and Alexandra"* Samuel Marx to the author, January 16, 1990.

Page 194 *"It was eerie"* Bankhead, *Tallulah*, 198.

Page 194 *"The first thing to remember"* Barrymore, *Memories*, 272.

Page 194 *"Is Grandma ready?"* Fowler, *Good Night, Sweet Prince*, 343.

Page 194 *"I'm moaning and flailing my arms"* Kotsilibas-Davis, *The Barrymores*, 135.

Page 194 *"See here, Mayer"* Marx, *Mayer and Thalberg*, 212.

Page 195 *"It must be a very violent"* Acosta, *Here Lies the Heart*, 245.

Page 195 *"The script was written"* Barrymore, *Memories*, 273.

Page 195 *"I am at home"* Peters, *The House of Barrymore*, 584.

Page 196 *"You forget"* Biery, "Refereeing the Royal Family," 105.

Page 196 *"The people are unreal."* Peters, *The House of Barrymore*, 271.

Page 196 *"wriggling his ears"* Fowler, *Good Night, Sweet Prince*, 344.

Page 196 *"But their paths never crossed."* Hayes and Hatch, *Helen Hayes*, 77.

Page 196 *"We're going to punish Paul."* "Cutting Continuity, December 21, 1932," *Rasputin and the Empress* file, MGM-USC.

Page 197 *"It achieves one feat"* Crowther, *The Lion's Share*, 227.

Page 198 *"I'd rather be Buster Keaton"* Samuel Marx to the author, January 16, 1990.

CHAPTER 15

Page 199 *"All of us got"* Stewart/AFI, 17.

Page 200 *"I'm one of half a dozen"* Marx and Vanderveen, *Deadly Illusions*, 12.

Page 200 *"It wasn't just the salary."* Stewart/AFI, 18.

Page 200 *"Irving humors my taste"* Marx and Vanderveen, *Deadly Illusions*, 13.

Page 200 *"I never had any feeling"* Stewart/AFI, 20.

Page 201 *"You're behaving like I did"* Marx and Vanderveen, *Deadly Illusions*, 24.

Page 201 *"He's got that goddamned Pygmalion complex."* Marx, *Mayer and Thalberg*, 189.

Page 201 *"Bern loved to take out"* "Howard Strickling Interview," Thomas/UCLA.

Page 201 *"I felt there was only one way"* Marx, *Mayer and Thalberg*, 82.

Page 201 *"Dear Paul is the only man"* Fragmented clipping from *Modern Screen* (September 1932), Darrell Rooney Archives.

Page 202 *"I love solitude."* Marx, *Mayer and Thalberg*, 189.

Page 202 *"down to the last grape"* Ibid.

Page 202 *"Paul is for the downtrodden."* Fragmented clipping, *Modern Screen* (September 1932).

Page 202 *"Paul is the only individual"* Service, "The Man Jean Harlow Has Married—Paul Bern," undated fragmented clipping, Darrell Rooney Archives.

Page 202 *"Thank you, Paul."* Coffee, *Storyline*, 101.

Page 203 *"The whip."* Marion, *Off with Their Heads!* 213.

Page 203 *"I know you two"* Coffee, *Storyline*, 186.

Page 203 *"a short, restless man"* Viertel, *The Kindness of Strangers*, 174.

Page 203 *"good and kind and gentle"* Loos, *Kiss Hollywood Good-by*, 36.

Page 204 *"Paul Bern is the sweetest man"* Service, "The Man Jean Harlow Has Married—Paul Bern."

Page 204 *"Jean was always lonely"* Loos, *Kiss Hollywood Good-by*, 36.

Page 204 *"Thalberg never accepted Harlow."* "Howard Strickling Interview," Thomas/UCLA.

Page 204 *"Paul has no right"* St. Johns, *Love, Laughter, and Tears*, 272.

Page 204 *"You mean Paul"* "Adela Rogers St. Johns Interview," Thomas/UCLA.

Page 205 *"Look at her!"* Selznick, *A Private View*, 179.

Page 205 *"When your producer-husband"* Marx and Vanderveen, *Deadly Illusions*, 34.

Page 205 *"If the time comes"* Thomas, *Thalberg*, 232.

Page 206 *"He was obviously"* Skolsky, *Don't Get Me Wrong*, 80.

Page 206 *"interested in abnormality"* Stenn, *Bombshell*, 91.

Page 206 *"Honest, Paul makes me feel"* Marion, *Off with Their Heads!* 230.

Page 206 *"We were one of the first"* NSA, 417.

Page 207 *"That evening had a lot of meaning"* Selznick, *A Private View*, 180.

Page 207 *"Harlow was supposed to help"* Tornabene, *Long Live the King*, 150.

Page 207 *"Get this man off our backs!"* "John Lee Mahin Interview," Thomas/UCLA.

Page 207 *"You're crazy if you use Gilbert"* Samuels, *The King*, 170.

Page 207 *"Hunt just looked at me."* Tornabene, *Long Live the King*, 150.

Page 208 *"It was awfully hard"* Fountain and Maxim, *Dark Star*, 226.

Page 208 *"Gable as 'Dennis' is played"* "Conference Notes, July 21, 1932," *Red Dust* file, MGM-USC.

Page 209 *"I'm sure you know films"* Marx and Vanderveen, *Deadly Illusions*, 13.

Page 209 *"The Baby's still a virgin."* Stenn, *Bombshell*, 93.

Page 209 *"Harlow admitted"* Marion, "Hollywood," 405.

Page 209 *"I stopped to sign an autograph"* St. Johns, *Love, Laughter, and Tears*, 271.

Page 210 *"Jean has been so wonderful."* "Albert Lewin Interview, Part II, 880 Fifth Avenue," n.d., Thomas/UCLA.

Page 210   *"When you find out"*   Stenn, *Bombshell*, 126.

Page 211   *"It was quite pitiful."*   Ibid., 105.

Page 211   *"Dearest dear"*   Marx and Vanderveen, *Deadly Illusions*, 37.

Page 211   *"Paul can't be helped now."*   Thomas, *Thalberg*, 233.

Page 211   *"his shoes and the cuffs"*   Marx, *Mayer and Thalberg*, 192.

Page 212   *"He looked kind of strange."*   Marx and Vanderveen, *Deadly Illusions*, 62.

Page 212   *"Everyone's talking too much!"*   Thomas, *Thalberg*, 234.

Page 212   *Coroner's inquest transcription*   Marx and Vanderveen, *Deadly Illusions*, 137.

Page 213   *"shoulders hunched, weeping bitterly"*   Marx, *Mayer and Thalberg*, 194.

Page 213   *"Irving loved Paul."*   "Albert Lewin Interview, Part II," Thomas/UCLA.

Page 213   *"There were ghastly words"*   Churchill, "Hollywood Magic Revealed Again, XI."

Page 214   *"This staying home"*   "Jean Harlow Resumes Work to Forget Grief."

Page 214   *"The day she came back"*   Stenn, *Bombshell*, 123.

Page 214   *"How are we going to get"*   Astor, *A Life on Film*, 95.

Page 214   *"Remembering the doubts"*   Jason Joy to Irving Thalberg, October 10, 1932, *Red Dust* file, PCA.

Page 215   *"What's it all for?"*   Thomas, *Thalberg*, 236.

Page 215   *"He told Mayer he was sick"*   Ibid.

Page 215   *"You'd better come out here"*   Crowther, *The Lion's Share*, 192.

Page 216   *"Oh, it was hell."*   Thomas, *Thalberg*, 237.

Page 217   *"Thalberg would be permitted"*   Crowther, *The Lion's Share*, 195.

Page 217   *"Don't pay any attention to him."*   Bernstein, *Walter Wanger*, 83.

Page 217   *"M-G-M was a closely knit society"*   Ibid., 90.

Page 218   *"the commercial diplomat"*   "Metro-Goldwyn-Mayer."

Page 218   *"injured lion"*   Beauchamp, *Without Lying Down*, 301.

Page 218   *"I have the most enormous respect"*   Behlmer, *Memo from: David O. Selznick*, 80.

Page 219   *"I say the country has emerged"*   Marx, *Mayer and Thalberg*, 201.

Page 219   *"Suddenly bacchanalia reigned"*   Ibid., 202.

Page 220   *"People were just passing by"*   Stenn, *Bombshell*, 134.

CHAPTER 16

Page 223   *In his diary Wanger recorded meetings*   Walter Wanger Diaries, State Historical Society of Wisconsin.

Page 224   *"Tell David"*   Thomson, *Showman*, 150.

Page 224   *"not a directive"*   Selznick, *A Private View*, 189.

Page 225   *"only hired Dave"*   Marx, *Mayer and Thalberg*, 205.

Page 225   *"Irving virtually chased Mayer"*   Crowther, *The Lion's Share*, 196.

Page 225 *"By consenting to the execution"* Thomson, *Showman*, 151.

Page 226 *"I'm doing this"* Marion, "Hollywood," 449.

Page 226 *Irving Thalberg to Nicholas Schenck, February 1933 drafts* Author's collection.

Page 230 *"My girlfriend is going along."* Kingsley, "Hobnobbing in Hollywood."

Page 230 *"Irving fell for Charlie"* Hayes and Hatch, *Helen Hayes*, 66.

Page 230 *"Dear Irving"* Crowther, *Hollywood Rajah*, 167.

Page 232 *"Dear Louis"* Ibid., 169.

Page 233 *"It's not good form"* Thomas, *Thalberg*, 242.

Page 233 *"Someone told Charlie"* Hayes, *Helen Hayes*, 75.

Page 234 *"And how does my cash look"* Thomas, *Thalberg*, 242.

Page 234 *"My friends"* Marx, *Mayer and Thalberg*, 206.

Page 234 *"A strange rumbling"* Ibid.

Page 234 *"destroying the loyalty and morale"* Ibid., 207.

Page 235 *"Hollywood can never be doomed"* Crowther, *The Lion's Share*, 198.

Page 235 *"If anything happens"* Marx, *Mayer and Thalberg*, 209.

Page 235 *"We don't know when"* Thomas, *Thalberg*, 250.

Page 236 *"part of a lifetime"* Lambert, *Norma Shearer*, 195.

Page 236 *"Charlie! Charlie! . . . Come help!"* M-G-M: *When the Lion Roars.*

Page 237 *"I feel like"* Behlmer, *Memo from: David O. Selznick*, 93.

Page 237 *"David told me"* Selznick, *A Private View*, 190.

Page 237 *"I am today regarded"* Behlmer, *Memo from: David O. Selznick*, 93.

Page 237 *"L.B. Mayer definitely"* Darryl F. Zanuck to Bob Thomas, February 26, 1968, Thomas/UCLA.

Page 237 *"That night I suffered"* Turk, *Hollywood Diva*, 129.

Page 238 *"The important thing"* Crowther, *The Lion's Share*, 207.

Page 238 *"It got so bad"* Eyman, *Lion of Hollywood*, 181.

Page 238 *"As far as the company is concerned"* Crowther, *Hollywood Rajah*, 181.

Page 238 *"Isn't it better"* Marx, *Mayer and Thalberg*, 210.

Page 238 *"If it ever came to a choice"* Lee, "Norma Fights Back," 63.

Page 239 *"Al, why didn't you accept"* Thomas, *Thalberg*, 250.

Page 239 *"David was gratified"* Haver, *David O. Selznick's Hollywood*, 132.

Page 240 *"Not only must I contend"* Marx, *Mayer and Thalberg*, 220.

Page 240 *"Fists across the seas"* Crowther, *Hollywood Rajah*, 212.

Page 240 *"Let's face it."* Thomas, *Thalberg*, 219.

Page 241 *"The utmost humiliation"* Author's collection.

Page 241 *"It's a smash!"* Marx, *Mayer and Thalberg*, 243.

Page 241 *"I have expressed my opinions"* Thalberg to Schenck, October 13, 1933, author's collection.

Page 241 *"Thalberg's office was a long, wood-paneled room"* Viertel, *The Kindness of Strangers*, 199.

Page 242 *"Irving, you haven't deceived me."* Thomas, *Thalberg*, 250.

Page 244 *"The money it makes"* Marx, *Mayer and Thalberg*, 222.

CHAPTER 17

Page 245 *"Every son of a bitch"* Thomas, *Thalberg*, 271.

Page 246 *"The public is tired"* Merrick, "New Gossip of Filmland Is Told," 10.

Page 246 *"I almost died of gratitude"* Swanson, *Swanson on Swanson*, 434.

Page 246 *"Your wife is charming"* Hayes and Hatch, *Helen Hayes*, 109.

Page 247 *"I always dreaded the thought"* NSA, 403.

Page 247 *"Norma was very unhappy"* Lee Garmes to the author, October 2, 1971.

Page 247 *"We started without a finished script."* Kennedy, *Edmund Goulding's Dark Victory*, 146.

Page 247 *"I honestly urge you"* Ibid., 147.

Page 247 *"I'm one of Norma Shearer's"* Kanin, *Hollywood*, 144.

Page 248 *"an anecdote with elephantiasis"* "The New Pictures."

Page 248 *"It's a shame"* Hamann, *Norma Shearer in the 30s*, 60.

Page 249 *"Filthy pictures are doing us"* "Film Vulgarity Assailed by Theater Owners Head."

Page 249 *"We hope that the churches"* Hamann, *Norma Shearer in the 30s*, 60.

Page 249 *"In these last four years"* "All Southland Rallies under Chamber Banner," A1.

Page 250 *"It seems typical"* Lord, "Code Violators," 1.

Page 251 *"They'll laugh her off the screen."* Marx, *A Gaudy Spree*, 106.

Page 251 *"hung shroudlike"* Crowther, *Hollywood Rajah*, 214.

Page 251 *"Marion's a comedienne."* Marx, *Mayer and Thalberg*, 223.

Page 251 *"Don't mention Norma."* Marx, *A Gaudy Spree*, 106.

Page 251 *"It was right out of a fairy story"* Beaton, *The Wandering Years*, 206.

Page 251 *"a feudal castle"* Marion, *Off with Their Heads!* 136.

Page 251 *"It was an awesome thing."* Davies and Marx, *The Times We Had*, 133.

Page 252 *"Anyway, . . . I didn't want a part"* Marion, "Hollywood," 450.

Page 252 *"Irving was in need"* Stewart, *By a Stroke of Luck!* 204.

Page 252 *"They can't censor the gleam"* Thomas, *Thalberg*, 260.

Page 252 *"Mr. Laughton was wearing"* Scheuer, "Charles Laughton Never Through," A1.

Page 253 *"Norma has found it a little difficult"* Lambert, *Norma Shearer*, 206.

Page 253 *"If I was having trouble"* NSA, 428.

Page 253 *"Like a monkey on a stick!"* Higham, *Charles Laughton*, 42.

Page 253   *"I copied him."*   Singer, *The Laughton Story,* 145.

Page 253   *"First Lady of M-G-M"*   George Hurrell to the author, December 1, 1975.

Page 253   *"Although she was definitely Queen"*   Lambert, *Norma Shearer,* 207.

Page 253   *"I tried to visit Norma Shearer"*   Davies and Marx, *The Times We Had,* 134.

Page 254   *"When you are meditating"*   NSA, 498.

Page 254   *"I don't understand."*   Behlmer, *Henry Hathaway,* 46.

Page 255   *"You can fire a cannon"*   Jack Vizzard to the author, January 31, 1998.

Page 255   *"Hollywood is in the most serious crisis"*   Schallert, "Film Producers Shaken by Clean-up Campaign," 1.

Page 255   *"I had high hopes"*   Hayes and Hatch, *Helen Hayes,* 121.

Page 256   *"It's so awful!"*   Thomas, *Thalberg,* 178.

Page 257   *"Something has definitely happened"*   Moore, *You're Only Human Once,* 199.

Page 257   *"Remember the last time we met"*   Chevalier, *With Love,* 262.

Page 257   *"She's not right."*   Ibid., 266.

Page 257   *"We're probably going"*   Moore, *You're Only Human Once,* 200.

Page 258   *"I bet this will top* The Merry Widow."   Ibid., 204.

Page 258   *"Has Columbia sent you a thank-you note"*   Chevalier, *With Love,* 267.

Page 258   *"We had already done three pictures"*   Ibid., 266.

Page 258   *"Mr. Lubitsch wants a contract"*   Eyman, *Ernst Lubitsch,* 216.

Page 258   *"Although Ernst had none of the shortcomings"*   Loos, *Kiss Hollywood Good-by,* 166.

Page 259   *"You know, the trouble is"*   Joseph I. Breen, "Memo," August 13, 1934, *The Merry Widow* file, PCA.

Page 259   *"amid the tumult"*   Sennwald, "A Lubitsch Production of *The Merry Widow.*"

Page 259   *"industry double-cross"*   Black, *Hollywood Censored,* 201.

Page 260   *"lot of filth"*   Ibid.

Page 260   *"If this picture goes out"*   Walsh, *Sin and Censorship,* 109.

Page 260   *"While I reiterate promises"*   Thalberg to Hays, October 26, 1934, *The Merry Widow* file, PCA.

Page 261   *"W.R. wanted me to do it."*   Davies and Marx, *The Times We Had,* 253.

Page 261   *"Marion, I'll be delighted"*   Pizzitola, *Hearst over Hollywood,* 331.

Page 261   Mayer conversation with Davies and Hearst as recounted in, respectively, Crowther, *The Lion's Share,* 224; Marx, *Mayer and Thalberg,* 223; Pizzitola, *Hearst over Hollywood,* 331.

Page 262   *"That last part"*   Marx, *Mayer and Thalberg,* 236.

Page 262   *"Angry men with lanterns"*   Niven, *Bring On the Empty Horses,* 272.

Page 262   *"I don't think Louis B. Mayer minded"*   Davies and Marx, *The Times We Had,* 254.

Page 262   *"You know I'm pregnant"*   Hayes and Hatch, *Helen Hayes,* 72.

Page 263 *"I'm getting old."* "Benjamin Thau Interview," Thomas/UCLA.

Page 263 *"Our plan does not propose"* "Sinclair Alters Meaning of EPIC Scheme Slogan."

Page 263 *"I am voting for Saint Clair."* Mitchell, "Thalberg: Father of the Attack Ad," 22.

Page 263 *"Thalberg had the film processed"* "Carey Wilson, April 28, 1958," Crowther/BYU.

Page 264 *"I made those films."* Thomas, *Thalberg*, 269.

Page 265 *"But . . . I don't expect"* Marx, *Mayer and Thalberg*, 243.

CHAPTER 18

Page 266 "The Barretts *is the best thing"* Samuel Marx to the author, January 16, 1990.

Page 267 *"Her readings were translucent"* Behrman, *People in a Diary*, 196.

Page 267 *"I am through being stupid."* Babcock, "Star Declares for Stage," A5.

Page 267 *"No. . . . Definitely no."* Schallert, "Katharine Cornell Refuses New Movie Offer."

Page 267 *"Motion pictures have grown up"* Hays, "'Good' Film Now Not Good Enough for Moviegoers."

Page 267 *"a woman who has gained"* Joseph I. Breen to Irving G. Thalberg, July 19, 1934, *Biography of a Bachelor Girl* file, PCA.

Page 267 *"Marion regrets her loose life"* Joseph I. Breen, Memo, July 27, 1934, ibid.

Page 268 *"No one noticed."* Chester W. Schaeffer to the author, July 3, 1988.

Page 268 *"The elements that"* Lusk, "News and Gossip of Stage and Screen."

Page 268 *"Box office . . . is the combination"* Marx, *Mayer and Thalberg*, 217.

Page 268 *"Who is Susan Lenox?"* Ibid., 154.

Page 268 *"unperturbed by the additional $50,000"* Naumburg, *We Make the Movies*, 27.

Page 269 *"I was much too easily hurt."* Crawford, *A Portrait of Joan*, 107.

Page 269 *"I don't know who"* NSA, 418.

Page 269 *"Even a first-rate playwright"* "Meet the Story Editor."

Page 269 *"Hollywood's pious notion"* "Rachel Crothers and the Movies."

Page 269 *"A Broadway producer"* Seldes, *The Great Audience*, 56.

Page 269 *"It was the most fortunate experience"* Stewart, *By a Stroke of Luck!* 196.

Page 270 "No More Ladies *wasn't my picture."* Crawford, *A Portrait of Joan*, 107.

Page 270 "No More Ladies . . . *comes out of the same"* Sennwald, "No More Ladies," 18.

Page 270 *"To hell with art."* Thomas, *Thalberg*, 257.

Page 270 *"Are you married to Irving"* Stewart, *By a Stroke of Luck!* 211.

Page 271 *"It's a Mr. Thalberg"* "Helen Hayes Interview," Thomas/UCLA.

Page 271 *"Columbia insists"* Chevalier, *With Love*, 267.

Page 272 *"It was for Irving's sake"* Thomas, *Thalberg*, 295.

Page 272 *"Thalberg was often unreasonable"* Ibid.

Page 272 *"Schedules were rearranged"* Carey, *All the Stars in Heaven*, 192.

Page 272 *"We used to go there"* NSA, 439.

Page 274 *"Thirty or forty guests"* Ibid., 422.

Page 275 *"I was not under personal contract"* Lanchester, *Charles Laughton and I*, 142.

Page 275 *"I've never been in it."* "Talbot Jennings Notes," Thomas/UCLA.

Page 275 *"None of them drank anything"* NSA, 412.

Page 275 *"Irving would run rushes"* Ibid., 411.

Page 276 *"What are you fellows doing now?"* "Groucho Marx Interview," n.d., Thomas/UCLA.

Page 277 *"Irving doesn't think we're has-beens!"* Marx, *Growing Up with Chico*, 85.

Page 277 *"I could never work with Griffith"* Marx, *Mayer and Thalberg*, 96.

Page 277 *"Hit a fellow in old clothes"* Marx, *My Life with Groucho*, 134.

Page 278 *"Listen, Irving"* Marx, *Growing Up with Chico*, 86.

Page 278 *"I'm going to Hollywood"* Goldstein, *George S. Kaufman*, 243.

Page 278 *"On a clear day"* Meredith, *George S. Kaufman and His Friends*, 525.

Page 278 *"Who does he think he is?"* Marx, *My Life with Groucho*, 133.

Page 278 *"Save that kind of behavior"* "Eddie Lawrence Interview, MGM, August 21, 1967," Thomas/UCLA.

Page 279 *"I feel like an idiot."* Thomas, *Thalberg*, 183.

Page 279 *"Thalberg was a difficult man to see."* Marx, *Groucho and Me*, 235.

Page 279 *"Thalberg's bungalow was the 'Holy of Holies'"* "Interview with Rosalind Russell," n.d., Crowther/BYU.

Page 279 *"The atmosphere in the Thalberg bungalow"* Viertel, *The Kindness of Strangers*, 199.

Page 279 *"Glass doors led"* NSA, 433.

Page 279 *"I heard the meetings"* Ibid.

Page 279 *"You're in a spot."* Crowther, *The Lion's Share*, 232.

Page 280 *"I had made tests"* "Interview with Rosalind Russell," Crowther/BYU.

Page 280 *"When we had some trouble"* Eyman, *Lion of Hollywood*, 229.

Page 280 *"This is really Jean's scene"* Hamann, *Jean Harlow in the 30s*, 79.

Page 281 *"That's not the way"* Thomas, *Thalberg*, 257.

Page 282 *"You've guided me right"* Martin, "I Call on Clark Gable," 64.

Page 282 *"People are fascinated with cruelty."* Thomas, *Thalberg*, 274.

Page 282 *"Look, Irving, . . . I'm a realistic kind of actor."* Ibid., 276.

Page 282 *"We had been in Vaudeville"* Marx, *Groucho and Me*, 235.

Page 282 *"Thalberg was not satisfied"* Anobile, *The Marx Bros. Scrapbook*, 209.

Page 283 *"You can't sit in an office"* Marx, *My Life with Groucho*, 136.

Page 283 *"I was scared to death"* Arce, *Groucho*, 229.

Page 283 *"We gave four shows a day"* "Plucking a Few Notes from Harpo."

Page 283 *"I was the most nervous"* Marx, *My Life with Groucho*, 138.

Page 284 *"I never got so much as a chuckle"* Anobile, *The Marx Bros. Scrapbook*, 81.

Page 284 *"This was his first experience"* Kanfer, *Groucho*, 191.

Page 284 *"Thalberg said it wouldn't play."* Rivkin and Kerr, *Hello, Hollywood!* 74.

Page 284 *"I never should have done it."* Thomas, *Thalberg*, 278.

Page 285 *"She was a wonderfully kind"* Martin, "I Call on Clark Gable," 64.

Page 285 *"Most of the time"* Singer, *The Laughton Story*, 158.

Page 285 *"I can't do this Bligh fellow."* Thomas, *Thalberg*, 277.

Page 285 *"This picture isn't big enough"* Marx, *Mayer and Thalberg*, 243.

Page 286 *"Laughton's treating me like an extra!"* Dockter, "Interview with Ian Wolfe," December 30, 1985.

Page 286 *"Story meetings on* The Bounty*"* "Talbot Jennings Notes," Thomas/UCLA.

Page 287 *"The rivalry between Bligh and Christian"* Loos, *A Cast of Thousands*, 113.

Page 287 *"When I have a part"* Singer, *The Laughton Story*, 158.

Page 288 *"You know Larry Stallings?"* "Talbot Jennings Notes," Thomas/UCLA.

Page 288 *"dry birth"* Samuel Marx to the author, January 16, 1990.

Page 289 *"Have you raised your money?"* Behlmer, *Memo from: David O. Selznick*, 131.

Page 289 *"I don't want to touch it."* "Goldie Arthur Interview," n.d., Thomas/UCLA.

Page 289 *"In an industry"* Lewis, *The Creative Producer*, 59.

Page 289 *"That's an arrogant young man!"* Ibid., 63.

Page 290 *"Don't be surprised"* Arce, *Groucho*, 233.

Page 290 *"We're going to San Berdoo"* "Ralph Wheelwright Interview, August 28, 1967," Thomas/UCLA.

Page 290 *"I'm getting old."* "Benjamin Thau Interview," Thomas/UCLA.

Page 290 *"I want to see my children grow up."* Samuel Marx to the author, January 16, 1990.

Page 291 *"You're telling me this"* "Ralph Wheelwright Interview," Thomas/UCLA.

Page 291 *"You wrestled with a steam roller"* Hamann, *Clark Gable in the 30s*, 63.

CHAPTER 19

Page 295 *"He just lived movies"* "Howard Hawks Interview," n.d., Thomas/UCLA.

Page 295 *"Hell, I get those all the time."* Thomas, *Thalberg*, 297.

Page 296 *"thin, white-faced young man"* Swanson, *Sprinkled with Ruby Dust*, 69.

Page 296   *"Thank you, . . . but I'm afraid"*   Hamann, *Norma Shearer in the 30s,* 71.

Page 296   *"How can he live like this?"*   Marx, *Mayer and Thalberg,* 239.

Page 297   *"Don't be a fool, Irene!"*   Selznick, *A Private View,* 201.

Page 297   *"You'll fail! . . . You'll fail!"*   Thomas, *Selznick,* 95.

Page 297   *"You think because Dave's gone"*   Marx, *Mayer and Thalberg,* 245.

Page 298   *"never stole a star"*   Dick, *City of Dreams,* 101.

Page 298   *"Al's not a communist, Louis."*   "Arthur Freed Interview, MGM, August 18, 1967," Thomas/UCLA.

Page 298   *"Either he stays or I go."*   Thomas, *Thalberg,* 295.

Page 298   *"legal steps to have his own company"*   Crowther, *Hollywood Rajah,* 203.

Page 298   *"It was to be the first"*   Lewis and Curtis, *The Creative Producer,* 91.

Page 298   *"write, produce and direct"*   Beauchamp, *Without Lying Down,* 333.

Page 299   *"Would you mind leaving the room"*   Thomas, *Thalberg,* 295.

Page 299   *"I'm in a running battle"*   Marx, *Mayer and Thalberg,* 246.

Page 299   *"Irving would come to see me"*   "Samuel Goldwyn Interview, November 27, 1967," Thomas/UCLA.

Page 299   *"Often Irving would come to our home"*   "Mrs. Samuel Goldwyn Interview, September 12, 1967," Thomas/UCLA.

Page 299   *"Irving had that same love"*   "Goldwyn Notes," Thomas/UCLA.

Page 299   *"I love everybody!"*   Samuel Marx to the author, January 16, 1990.

Page 299   *"It's like Mussolini's!"*   Thomas, *Thalberg,* 312.

Page 300   *"Don't let them bury me"*   "Last Honors Paid Gilbert."

Page 300   *"She behaves like she's his widow."*   Marx, *Mayer and Thalberg,* 246.

Page 300   *"Jack was the perfect actor"*   "Laurence Stallings Interview, September 15, 1967," Thomas/UCLA.

Page 300   *"You know, Leatrice"*   Fountain and Maxim, *Dark Star,* 256.

Page 301   *"While the Turkish market"*   Frederick Herron to Joseph I. Breen, July 18, 1934, *The Forty Days of Musa Dagh* file, PCA.

Page 301   *"We've run into some trouble"*   Thomas, *Thalberg,* 310.

Page 301   *"I'm afraid I'll have to postpone"*   Marion, *Off with Their Heads!* 266.

Page 302   "Forever *can be the greatest prestige picture"*   Marx, *Mayer and Thalberg,* 246.

Page 302   *"so inflammatory in nature"*   Joseph I. Breen to Louis B. Mayer, January 31, 1936, *It Can't Happen Here* file, PCA.

Page 302   *"Is the American public"*   Black, *Hollywood Censored,* 263.

Page 302   *"We've lost our guts."*   Marx, *Mayer and Thalberg,* 246.

Page 302   "Riffraff *was so right wing"*   Lewis, *The Creative Producer,* 69.

Page 303   *"You're making a terrible mistake"*   Thomas, *Thalberg,* 289.

Page 303   *"We live in a paradise."*   Lewis, *The Creative Producer,* 69.

Page 303 *"I remember the feeling"* "Goldie Arthur Interview, September 21, 1967," Thomas/UCLA.

Page 303 *"It was a big family."* Knight, "Oral Interview with Lawrence Weingarten," March 5, 1974.

Page 304 *"Irving Thalberg considered actors"* Thomas, *Thalberg*, 196.

Page 304 *"I am not a young man"* Brian Aherne to Irving Thalberg, April 28, 1935, Special Collections, USC.

Page 305 *"You state—and quite rightly"* Irving Thalberg to Brian Aherne, April 30, 1935, ibid.

Page 306 *"Anita, Bess, and I"* Marion, *Off with Their Heads!* 240.

Page 307 *"There is no such thing"* Thomas, *Thalberg*, 271.

Page 307 *"One recent estimate"* "Authors by Hundreds Meet Tragic Defeat in Films."

Page 307 *"M-G-M was a strange place"* Server, *Screenwriter*, 231.

Page 307 *"These writers are living like kings."* Thomas, *Thalberg*, 267.

Page 307 *"Salka joined forces"* Stewart, *By a Stroke of Luck!* 227.

Page 308 *"What has a man"* Viertel, *The Kindness of Strangers*, 206.

Page 308 *"with the sad, reproachful eyes"* Stewart, *By a Stroke of Luck!* 227.

Page 308 *"Bea and I went"* Ibid., 211.

Page 308 *"That's nonsense."* Marion, *Off with Their Heads!* 240.

Page 309 *"How's the Napoleon script"* Stewart, *By a Stroke of Luck!* 224.

Page 309 *"Let us, . . . let us have no more"* Ibid.

Page 309 *"When a dictator dies"* Flamini, *Thalberg*, 258.

Page 310 *"Thalberg, not Mayer"* Eyman, *Lion of Hollywood*, 204.

Page 310 *"Why do you want"* "Screen Head Sounds Plea."

Page 310 *"Thalberg will take care of me."* Server, *Screenwriter*, 83.

Page 310 *"McGuinness was a very sharp"* Ibid., 149.

Page 311 *"I liked Thalberg very much."* Schwartz and Schwartz, *The Hollywood Writers' Wars*, 67.

Page 311 *Thalberg began to speak* Samuel Marx to the author, January 16, 1990; Marion, *Off with Their Heads!* 239; Maurice Rapf, Richard Maibaum, and James M. Cain in Schwartz and Schwartz, *The Hollywood Writers' Wars*, 67.

Page 312 *"At Metro, . . . the SP had the tables"* Schwartz and Schwartz, *The Hollywood Writers' Wars*, 76.

Page 312 *"Now what the hell is this?"* McGilligan, *Backstory 1*, 259.

Page 313 *"You still in the SWG?"* Schwartz and Schwartz, *The Hollywood Writers' Wars*, 76.

Page 313 *"Do you know"* Lewis and Curtis, *The Creative Producer*, 69.

Page 313   *"Everybody had made Thalberg"*   Schwartz and Schwartz, *The Hollywood Writers' Wars*, 75.

Page 314   *"Do the best you can."*   Lewis and Curtis, *The Creative Producer*, 69.

Page 314   *"I had this man trailed."*   Thomas, *Thalberg*, 271.

CHAPTER 20

Page 315   *"A lot of people"*   Lewis, *The Creative Producer*, 69.

Page 315   *"She was always there on time"*   Ibid., 71.

Page 316   *"Harlow always played such sluts"*   "Jeanette MacDonald, June 1959," p. 1563, CUOHC.

Page 316   *"Because the assistant editor was so rushed"*   "Goldie Arthur Interview," Thomas/UCLA.

Page 317   *"He was out of his seat"*   "Eddie Lawrence Interview," Thomas/UCLA.

Page 317   *"The audience went outside"*   Lewis, *The Creative Producer*, 69.

Page 317   *"There were two more tries."*   "Goldie Arthur Interview," Thomas/UCLA.

Page 317   *"At the end of the film"*   Lewis, *The Creative Producer*, 70.

Page 317   *"Forget it, Frank."*   Thomas, *Thalberg*, 271.

Page 317   *"It needs something"*   Lewis, *The Creative Producer*, 70.

Page 317   *"Irving always wanted me"*   "Albert Lewin Interview," Thomas/UCLA.

Page 318   *"He felt that he had gotten"*   Lewis, *The Creative Producer*, 67.

Page 318   *"Thalberg wanted me to tell the story"*   Viertel, *The Kindness of Strangers*, 206.

Page 319   *"Well, Anita, you shouldn't"*   Samuel Marx to the author, January 16, 1990.

Page 319   *"One day in 1935"*   Loos, *San Francisco*, 193.

Page 319   *"I'll wait."*   "Jeanette MacDonald, June 1959," p. 1570, CUOHC.

Page 320   *"You've got to read this."*   Thomas, *Thalberg*, 315.

Page 320   *"I understand there is no executive there"*   Thomson, *Showman*, 150.

Page 320   *"Have you read the synopsis?"*   Thomas, *Thalberg*, 315.

Page 320   *"Thalberg was smiling like hell"*   Gussow, *Don't Say Yes until I Finish Talking*, 70.

Page 321   *"After a stiff whisky and soda"*   Eels, *The Life That Late He Led*, 150.

Page 321   *"the kind of thing"*   Samuel Marx to the author, January 16, 1990.

Page 321   *"Thalberg did not think Chips"*   Lewis, *The Creative Producer*, 93.

Page 322   *"Quite a bit of the first part"*   "Notes dictated by Mr. Thalberg, July 16, 1936," *Goodbye, Mr. Chips* file, MGM-USC.

Page 322   *"Thalberg was enchanted"*   Lewis, *The Creative Producer*, 94.

Page 323   *"Irving, the public won't buy pictures"*   Thomas, *Thalberg*, 303.

Page 323   *"Throw 'em all out."*   "Talbot Jennings Notes," Thomas/UCLA.

Page 323   *"I'm in the business"*   Marx, *Mayer and Thalberg*, 247.

Page 323   *"How would you like"*   Franklin, "We Laughed and We Cried," 233.

Page 324   *"I'm about as Chinese"*   Lawrence, *Actor*, 225.

Page 324   *"It's too Occidental."*   Thomas, *Thalberg*, 303.

Page 325   *"You turn off the highway"*   Woolfenden, "Location Sets So Realistic Swallows Build Nests There."

Page 325   *"I forget the camera"*   Lawrence, *Actor*, 226.

Page 325   *"I told her that was his character."*   Franklin, "We Laughed and We Cried," 237.

Page 326   *"The script doesn't show you"*   Thomas, *Thalberg*, 303.

Page 327   *"This is my idea of a prestige picture."*   Marx, *Mayer and Thalberg*, 246.

Page 327   *"I've been going crazy"*   Arnold, *Deep in My Heart*, 406.

Page 328   *"Irving looked so spent"*   Marion, "Hollywood," 281.

Page 328   *"Irving seemed terribly fragile."*   Lambert, *Norma Shearer*, 227.

Page 328   *"He looked like a little figure"*   Thomas, *Thalberg*, 311.

Page 328   *"Bob and I had an idea"*   Anobile, *The Marx Bros. Scrapbook*, 211.

Page 329   *"Is he dead"*   Kanfer, *Groucho*, 212.

Page 329   *"Politically, Wood was impossible."*   Anobile, *The Marx Bros. Scrapbook*, 203.

Page 329   *"If Thalberg said, 'Go back'"*   Ibid., 209.

Page 330   *"Nature is Greta's element"*   Acosta, *Here Lies the Heart*, 258.

Page 330   *"Irving Thalberg was going to do"*   Lambert, *On Cukor*, 108.

Page 330   *"I do not understand why"*   Greta Garbo to Salka Viertel, November 22, 1935 (courtesy Kevin Brownlow, Photoplay Productions).

Page 331   *"I answered that I thought"*   Acosta, *Here Lies the Heart*, 273.

Page 331   *"My God!"*   Lewis and Curtis, *The Creative Producer*, 76.

Page 331   *"Do you like Al Lewin?"*   Ibid.

Page 331   *"It was ludicrous"*   Ibid., 83.

Page 332   *"He did not relay his ideas"*   Ibid., 89.

Page 332   *"We have a problem."*   Thomas, *Thalberg*, 306; Lewis, *The Creative Producer*, 84.

Page 332   *"We can't miss with these two!"*   Marion, *Off with Their Heads!* 265.

Page 333   *"In an apparent"*   Hamann, *Greta Garbo in the 30s*, 67.

Page 333   *"She said that when she was acting"*   McGilligan, *George Cukor*, 109.

Page 333   *"You know, . . . that Fritzi Scheff is great."*   Lewis, *The Creative Producer*, 90.

Page 333   *"George, she's awfully good."*   Thomas, *Thalberg*, 308.

Page 334   *"If only they were all like this."*   Marx, *Mayer and Thalberg*, 247.

Page 334   *"I've been put off"*   Thomas, *Thalberg*, 308.

Page 334   *"the fulfillment of a long-cherished dream"*   Shakespeare, *Romeo and Juliet*, 13.

CHAPTER 21

Page 336   *"a primary transept"*   "A Significant Event."

Page 336   *"The woods acted."*   Reinhardt, *The Genius,* 280.

Page 336   *"It's a swell spectacle"*   Shippey, "The Lee Side o' L. A."

Page 336   *"Every actress has at one time"*   Fragmentary clipping, author's collection.

Page 337   *"It's a silly idea, Irving."*   Marx, *Mayer and Thalberg,* 248.

Page 337   *"Irving, I don't look Shakespeare"*   Ibid.

Page 337   *"The trouble with Hollywood"*   Nugent, "Mr. Howard Casts a Stone."

Page 337   *"I'll call you as soon"*   Dietz, *Dancing in the Dark,* 159; Samuel Marx to the author, January 16, 1990.

Page 338   *"He would track me down"*   "Howard Dietz Interview," Thomas/UCLA.

Page 338   *"Nick, I've never had any picture closer"*   Samuel Marx to the author, January 16, 1990.

Page 339   *"Authentic!"*   Marx, *A Gaudy Spree,* 132.

Page 339   *"Jesse Lasky deprecated Norma's ability."*   "Howard Hawks Interview," Thomas/UCLA.

Page 339   *"I believe Norma can play anything"*   Marx, *Mayer and Thalberg,* 248.

Page 339   *"If necessary, offer Strunk two hundred"*   Marx, *A Gaudy Spree,* 133.

Page 339   *"a fresh, lightly baroque look"*   Lambert, *Norma Shearer,* 223.

Page 340   *"Don't think that I'm just"*   Gutner, *Gowns by Adrian,* 156.

Page 340   *"Only a month or so earlier"*   Lambert, *Norma Shearer,* 222.

Page 340   *"Omit needless words!"*   Strunk and White, *The Elements of Style,* viii.

Page 340   *"Your job is to protect Shakespeare"*   Thomas, *Thalberg,* 298.

Page 340   *"What Shakespeare did"*   Ibid., 299.

Page 340   *"Romeo and Juliet is one"*   Scheuer, "Hollywood Imports College Professors," A1.

Page 340   *"Shakespeare was part owner"*   Marx, *A Gaudy Spree,* 134; Samuel Marx to the author, January 16, 1990.

Page 341   *"Put that scene"*   Thomas, *Thalberg,* 277.

Page 341   *"I was having moments"*   NSA, 460.

Page 341   *"She had come to believe"*   Kobler, *Damned in Paradise,* 135.

Page 342   *"Mrs. Carrington taught me"*   NSA, 461.

Page 343   *"The studio was very successful"*   Lambert, *On Cukor,* 103.

Page 343   *"I went to Thalberg's office"*   "William Daniels Interview, September 11, 1967," Thomas/UCLA.

Page 344   *"Any attempt to inject"*   Joseph I. Breen to Irving G. Thalberg, December 20, 1935, *Romeo and Juliet* file, PCA.

Page 344   *"When I was on a picture"*   NSA, 461.

Page 344   *"a nervous, highly self-critical"*   Watts, *Behind the Screen,* 22.

Page 344   *"It's overdone."*   "David Lewis Interview, September 20, 1967," Thomas/UCLA.

Page 345   *"I arrived at 7:30 A.M."*   Rathbone, *In and Out of Character*, 133.

Page 345   *"Christ's elder sister"*   Thomas, *Thalberg*, 299.

Page 345   *"Margaret Carrington was marvelous"*   Alpert, *The Barrymores*, 345.

Page 346   *"She might have had a little quirk"*   Davies, *The Times We Had*, 220.

Page 346   *"One Sunday morning Irving called"*   "Ralph Wheelwright Interview," Thomas/UCLA.

Page 346   *"Mr. Thalberg, that's very flattering"*   Thomas, *Thalberg*, 297.

Page 347   *"He didn't set camera."*   Chester W. Schaeffer to author, October 9, 1971.

Page 347   *"I had to cut five versions"*   Brownlow, *The Parade's Gone By*, 302.

Page 347   *"The set got smoky."*   "William Daniels Interview," Thomas/UCLA.

Page 347   *"This can go on forever."*   Howard, *A Quite Remarkable Father*, 229.

Page 347   *"It was Thalberg."*   "Ralph Wheelwright Interview," Thomas/UCLA.

Page 348   *"He heareth not"*   Rathbone, *In and Out of Character*, 133.

Page 348   *"How would you like"*   Crowther, *The Lion's Share*, 232.

Page 349   *"When she sees the rushes"*   Watts, *Behind the Screen*, 22.

Page 349   *"Norma had a bent right knee."*   "Douglas Shearer Interview," Thomas/UCLA.

Page 350   *"With a classic story"*   Marx, *Mayer and Thalberg*, 250.

Page 350   *"I hesitate to call the picture great"*   Scheuer, "A Town Called Hollywood."

Page 350   *"a credit not only to M-G-M"*   Hamann, *Norma Shearer in the 30s*, 78.

Page 350   *"Mr. Irving Thalberg, producer"*   Jacobs and Braum, *The Films of Norma Shearer*, 210.

Page 351   *"He was a great raconteur."*   Lambert, *Norma Shearer*, 229.

Page 351   *"Tell me, Norma."*   Peters, *The House of Barrymore*, 389.

Page 351   *"With rare good taste"*   Jacobs and Braum, *The Films of Norma Shearer*, 210.

Page 351   *"Metro the magnificent"*   Ibid.

Page 352   *"To avoid any possible gaffes"*   "Cinema," 30.

Page 353   *"It's a little slow"*   "J. J. Cohn Interview," Thomas/UCLA.

Page 353   *"Irving disliked any show"*   Marion, "Hollywood," 461.

Page 353   *"I've decided to add another movie"*   Samuel Marx to the author, January 16, 1990.

Page 353   *"I am bitterly disappointed."*   "Ralph Wheelwright Interview," Thomas/UCLA.

CHAPTER 22

Page 355   *"Have you anything in mind"*   Marion, *Off with Their Heads!* 267.

Page 355   *"Irving moved my office"*   Lewis and Curtis, *The Creative Producer*, 76.

Page 356 *"I was sitting in the sunshine."* "Albert Lewin Interview," Thomas/ UCLA.

Page 357 *"Irving, you'll kill yourself"* "Sidney Franklin Interview, Trancas Beach, September 18, 1967," Thomas/UCLA.

Page 357 *"Irving did nothing but work."* "Anita Loos Interview," Thomas/UCLA.

Page 357 *"Bit by bit"* Lewis, *The Creative Producer*, 76.

Page 358 *"I couldn't believe it."* "Ralph Wheelwright Interview," Thomas/ UCLA.

Page 358 *"If it doesn't do as well"* Samuel Marx to the author, January 16, 1990.

Page 358 *"Winchell asserted that Irving and Norma"* "Albert Lewin Interview," Thomas/UCLA.

Page 358 *"I don't mind so much"* Lewis and Curtis, *The Creative Producer*, 90.

Page 359 *"golden"* Gavin Lambert to the author, January 23, 1996.

Page 359 *"When I'm gone"* Crowther, *The Lion's Share*, 232.

Page 360 *"What you have is good"* "Howard Strickling Interview," Thomas/ UCLA.

Page 360 *"He didn't demand"* Lewis and Curtis, *The Creative Producer*, 73.

Page 360 *"Nobody can teach you"* Ibid., 78.

Page 360 *"He was the one with"* Ibid., 89.

Page 361 *"This is our director's table."* "Sidney Franklin Interview," Thomas/ UCLA; Franklin, "We Laughed and We Cried," 239.

Page 361 *"It's getting late."* Lewis and Curtis, *The Creative Producer*, 96.

Page 362 *"You will never act again."* Gavin Lambert to the author, January 23, 1996; Parsons, "Norma Shearer Reveals Plans," 12.

Page 362 *"I brought along a list"* Marx, *A Gaudy Spree*, 138.

Page 362 *On Sunday, September 6* Lewis and Curtis, *The Creative Producer*, 99; Gavin Lambert to the author, January 23, 1996; "Sidney Franklin Interview," Thomas/UCLA.

Page 363 *"Would you be willing to fly east"* Lewis, *The Creative Producer*, 99.

Page 364 *"Oil the hinges"* *"Everyman* in Final Stages."

Page 364 *"It won't be necessary."* Lewis and Curtis, *The Creative Producer*, 100.

Page 364 *On Friday, September 11* and following account of Thalberg's last days Private and published interviews with Norma Shearer Arrouge, Frances Goldwyn, Sylvia Herscher, Gavin Lambert, Albert Lewin, Samuel Marx, Suzanne McCormick, Norma Pisar, Howard Strickling, Lawrence Weingarten, and Basil Wrangell.

Page 366 *"Only illness prevents me"* Thomas, *Thalberg*, 317.

Page 366 *"I'm not getting the right treatment."* Marx, *Mayer and Thalberg*, 251.

Page 369 *"They mustn't be told."* "Pneumonia Kills Noted Producer," 9.

Page 370 *"Irving just died."* Lewis and Curtis, *The Creative Producer*, 100.

Page 370   *"Did you hear about Mr. Thalberg?"*   Marx, *A Gaudy Spree*, 139.

Page 370   *"The little brown fellow just died."*   "Groucho Marx Interview," Thomas/ UCLA.

Page 370   *"Thalberg was the most important man"*   Thomas, *Thalberg*, 318.

Page 370   *"Enormous headlines"*   Lewis and Curtis, *The Creative Producer*, 101.

Page 372   *"I will lift up mine eyes"*   "Tribute Paid to Thalberg."

Page 372   *"The service was impressive."*   Lewis and Curtis, *The Creative Producer*, 101.

Page 372   *"She was visibly nervous."*   "Tribute Paid to Thalberg."

Page 372   *"It is strange . . . that Irving"*   "Films to Pay Homage to Thalberg Today."

Page 373   *"Little Irving knew."*   Hall, "Love Comes Once," 34.

CHAPTER 23

Page 377   *"They won't miss him today"*   "Trust Everyone but Cut the Cards."

Page 378   *"It's a good thing"*   Lewis and Curtis, *The Creative Producer*, 102.

Page 378   *"What I thought"*   Rosenberg and Silverstein, *The Real Tinsel*, 113.

Page 378   *"You will be my next Irving."*   Lewis and Curtis, *The Creative Producer*, 103.

Page 379   *"These are Irving's last pictures."*   Thomas, *Thalberg*, 322.

Page 379   *"After Thalberg's death"*   Kanfer, *Groucho*, 213.

Page 379   *"tortured with the thought"*   Lewis and Curtis, *The Creative Producer*, 112.

Page 379   *"Grief does very strange things"*   Hall, "Love Comes Once," 34.

Page 380   *"Mayer was less involved"*   Lewis and Curtis, *The Creative Producer*, 105.

Page 380   *"Nick, . . . I think we should"*   Eyman, *Lion of Hollywood*, 250.

Page 381   *"I must go back to work"*   Lambert, *Norma Shearer*, 244.

Page 381   *"Thalberg's estate would receive"*   Crowther, *The Lion's Share*, 240.

Page 382   *"Sidney Franklin came to talk to me"*   Hall, "Love Comes Once," 72.

CHAPTER 24

Page 383   *"Here the tragedy"*   Zweig, "History and the Screen," X4.

Page 384   *"the tragedy of people"*   "Interview with Lenore Coffee, n. d.," Thomas/ UCLA.

Page 384   *"Fate is really the heavy"*   "Sidney Franklin Dictated Notes, Tuesday, June 13, 1933," MGM-USC.

Page 384   *"We are treating the story"*   Franklin, "We Laughed and We Cried," 245.

Page 384   *"Juliet and Marie Antoinette"*   Marx, *Mayer and Thalberg*, 248.

Page 384   *"it was to be subtly understood"*   Lewis and Curtis, *The Creative Producer*, 105.

Page 385   *"I don't know what I did"*   Hall, "Love Comes Once," 34.

Page 385   *"Norma wanted to know"*   Lewis and Curtis, *The Creative Producer*, 111.

Page 385　*"It is lovely up here."*　Norma Shearer to Hunt Stromberg, May 17, 1937, *Marie Antoinette* story files, MGM-USC.

Page 386　*"I had never worked"*　Franklin, "We Laughed and We Cried," 247.

Page 386　*"Color would add a tremendous cost."*　Hunt Stromberg to Sidney Franklin, June 29, 1937, *Marie Antoinette* story files, MGM-USC.

Page 387　*"And you can tell Miss Shearer"*　Thomas, *Joan Crawford*, 122.

Page 387　*"Yours for a bigger and better"*　Hunt Stromberg to Norma Shearer, December 3, 1937, *Marie Antoinette* story files, MGM-USC.

Page 387　*"I fell in love"*　Norma Shearer Arrouge to Fred Watkins, unpublished 1958 interview in the collection of the author.

Page 388　*"I was known as a slow director"*　Franklin, "We Laughed and We Cried," 256.

Page 388　*"It was four against one."*　Ibid.

Page 388　*"Gentlemen, . . . I will not be hurt"*　Ibid.

Page 389　*"Put Van Dyke—or anyone"*　Crowther, *The Lion's Share*, 245.

Page 389　*"If only I had had the courage"*　Franklin, "We Laughed and We Cried," 267.

Page 389　*"His thinking . . . was to emphasize"*　Maltin, *Behind the Camera*, 152.

Page 389　*"Van Dyke could be careless."*　Chester W. Schaeffer to author, October 9, 1971.

Page 390　*"Hi, honey."*　Cannom, *Van Dyke and the Mythical City, Hollywood*, 381.

Page 390　*"But once she arrived"*　Kobal, *The Art of the Great Hollywood Portrait Photographers*, 257.

Page 390　*"And you wanted to be a star?"*　NSA, 324.

Page 390　*"And so* Marie Antoinette *was made."*　Franklin, "We Laughed and We Cried," 267.

Page 391　*"The scene in the casino"*　Hunt Stromberg, notes dictated January 13, 1938, *Marie Antoinette* story files, MGM-USC.

Page 391　*"It's not that he isn't perfectly sincere"*　Ibid.

Page 392　*"She could leaf through"*　Morley and Stokes, *Robert Morley*, 127.

Page 392　*"You're very lucky."*　Dore Freeman to author, December 1, 1975.

Page 392　*"Her knowledge of lighting"*　Morley and Stokes, *Robert Morley*, 127.

Page 392　*"could be improved photographically"*　"Suggestions by Miss Shearer," April 15, 1938, *Marie Antoinette* story files, MGM-USC.

Page 392　*"a superimposure of the young face"*　Robert Kern, memo to Hunt Stromberg, May 14, 1938, *Marie Antoinette* story files, MGM-USC.

Page 393　*"A truly magnificent picture"*　"Pomona Preview Notes," June 1, 1938, *Marie Antoinette* story files, MGM-USC.

Page 393　*"Those associated with the motion-picture industry"*　Kendall, "Crowd of 25,000 Views Arrival of Screen Celebrities."

Page 394   *"a lavish, spectacular triumph"*   "Marie Antoinette a Triumph," *Hollywood Reporter,* July 9, 1938, fragmentary clipping, *Marie Antoinette* story files, MGM-USC.

Page 394   *"a pride to the entire industry"*   "Marie Antoinette," *Daily Variety,* July 9, 1938, fragmentary clipping, ibid.

Page 394   *"A lot of people"*   Franklin, "We Laughed and We Cried," 270.

Page 394   *"It has been a privilege"*   Hunt Stromberg, memo to Ralph Wheelwright, July 6, 1938, *Marie Antoinette* story files, MGM-USC.

Page 394   *"too heavy or tragic"*   Hunt Stromberg, telegram draft, September 1, 1938, ibid.

EPILOGUE

Page 397   *"A great star"*   Dore Freeman to author, December 1, 1975.

SELECT BIBLIOGRAPHY

BOOKS

Acosta, Mercedes de. *Here Lies the Heart*. North Stratford, N.H.: Ayer, 2003.

Affron, Charles. *Lillian Gish: Her Legend, Her Life*. New York: Scribner, 2001.

Allen, Frederick Lewis. *Only Yesterday: An Informal History of the Nineteen-Twenties*. New York: Harper and Row, 1964.

Allvine, Glendon. *The Greatest Fox of Them All*. New York: Lyle Stuart, 1969.

Alpert, Hollis. *The Barrymores*. New York: Dial Press, 1964.

American Film Institute Catalog of Motion Pictures Produced in the United States, 1931–1940, The. Berkeley: University of California Press, 1993.

Amory, Cleveland, and Frederick Bradlee. *Cavalcade of the 1920s and 1930s*. New York: Viking Press, 1960.

Ankerich, Michael G. *The Sound of Silence*. Jefferson, N.C.: McFarland, 1998.

Anobile, Richard J. *The Marx Bros. Scrapbook*. New York: Darien House, 1973.

Arce, Hector. *Groucho*. New York: G. P. Putnam's Sons, 1979.

Ardmore, Jane Kesner. *The Self-Enchanted*. New York: McGraw-Hill, 1959.

Arnold, Elliott. *Deep in My Heart*. New York: Duell, Sloan and Pearce, 1949.

Astor, Mary. *A Life on Film*. New York: Delacorte Press, 1967.

Bainbridge, John. *Garbo*. New York: Holt, Rinehart, and Winston, 1971.

Bankhead, Tallulah. *Tallulah: My Autobiography*. New York: Harper, 1952.

Barrymore, Ethel. *Memories*. New York: Harper, 1955.

Barrymore, John. *We Three: Ethel, Lionel, John.* New York: Saalfield, 1935.

Barrymore, Lionel. *We Barrymores.* New York: Appleton-Century-Croft, 1951.

Beaton, Cecil. *The Wandering Years: Diaries, 1922–1939.* Boston: Little, Brown, 1961.

Beauchamp, Cari. *Without Lying Down: Frances Marion and the Powerful Women of Early Hollywood.* New York: Scribner, 1997.

Behlmer, Rudy. *Henry Hathaway.* Lanham, Md.: Rowman and Littlefield, 2001.

———. *Memo from: David O. Selznick.* New York: Avon Books, 1972.

———. *W. S. Van Dyke's Journal: White Shadows in the South Seas, 1927–1928: And Other Van Dyke on Van Dyke.* Lanham, Md.: Scarecrow Press, 1996.

Behr, Edward. *The Good Frenchman.* New York: Villard Books, 1993.

Behrman, S. N. *People in a Diary: A Memoir.* Boston: Little, Brown, 1972.

Bernstein, Matthew. *Walter Wanger: Hollywood Independent.* Berkeley: University of California Press, 1994.

Bickford, Charles. *Bulls, Balls, Bicycles & Actors.* New York: Paul Eriksson, 1965.

Black, Gregory D. *Hollywood Censored: Morality Codes, Catholics, and the Movies.* Cambridge: Cambridge University Press, 1994.

Blake, Michael. *Lon Chaney: The Man behind the Thousand Faces.* Lanham, Md.: Vestal Press, 1990.

———. *A Thousand Faces: Lon Chaney's Unique Artistry in Motion Pictures.* Lanham, Md.: Vestal Press, 1995.

Blesh, Rudi. *Keaton.* New York: MacMillan, 1966.

Brown, Jared. *The Fabulous Lunts: A Biography of Alfred Lunt and Lynn Fontanne.* New York: Atheneum, 1986.

Brownlow, Kevin. *The Parade's Gone By.* New York: Ballantine Books, 1969.

———. *The War, the West, and the Wilderness.* New York: Alfred A. Knopf, 1979.

Cannom, Robert W. *Van Dyke and the Mythical City, Hollywood.* Culver City, Calif.: Murray and Gee, 1948.

Carey, Gary. *All the Stars in Heaven: Louis B. Mayer's M-G-M.* New York: E. P. Dutton, 1981.

———. *Anita Loos: A Biography.* New York: Alfred A. Knopf, 1988.

Chevalier, Maurice. *With Love.* Boston: Little, Brown, 1960.

Coffee, Lenore. *Storyline: Recollections of a Hollywood Screenwriter.* London: Cassell, 1973.

Coffman, Taylor. *Building for Hearst and Morgan: Voices from the George Loorz Papers.* Berkeley: Berkeley Hills Books, 2003.

Considine, Shaun. *Bette and Joan: The Divine Feud.* New York: E. P. Dutton, 1989.

Crafton, Donald. *The Talkies: American Cinema's Transition to Sound, 1926–1931.* Berkeley: University of California Press, 1999.

Crawford, Joan, with Jane Kesner Ardmore. *A Portrait of Joan.* Garden City, N.Y.: Doubleday, 1962.

Crowther, Bosley. *Hollywood Rajah.* New York: Holt, Rinehart, and Winston, 1960.

———. *The Lion's Share.* New York: E. P. Dutton, 1957.

Curtiss, Thomas Quinn. *Von Stroheim.* New York: Farrar, Straus, and Giroux, 1971.

Dardis, Tom. *Keaton: The Man Who Wouldn't Lie Down.* London: André Deutsch, 1996.

———. *Some Time in the Sun.* New York: Scribner, 1976.

Davies, Marion, and Kenneth Marx. *The Times We Had.* New York: Ballantine Books, 1990.

Day, Beth. *This Was Hollywood.* Garden City, N.Y.: Doubleday, 1960.

DeMille, Cecil Blount. *The Autobiography of Cecil B. DeMille.* Englewood Cliffs, N.J.: Prentice-Hall, 1959.

de Mille, William C. *Hollywood Saga.* New York: E. P. Dutton, 1939.

Dick, Bernard F. *City of Dreams: The Making and Remaking of Universal Pictures.* Lexington: University of Kentucky Press, 1997.

Dietz, Howard. *Dancing in the Dark.* New York: Quadrangle/New York Times Book Co., 1974.

Dowd, Nancy, and David Shepard. *King Vidor: Interviewed by Nancy Dowd and David Shepard.* Metuchen, N.J.: Scarecrow Press, 1988.

Dressler, Marie. *My Own Story.* Boston: Little, Brown, 1934.

Eames, John Douglas. *The MGM Story: The Complete History of Fifty Roaring Years.* New York: Crown Publishers, 1975.

Edmonds, I. G. *Big U: Universal in the Silent Days.* South Brunswick, N.J.: A. S. Barnes, 1977.

Eels, George. *The Life That Late He Led.* London: W. H. Allen, 1967.

Eyman, Scott. *Ernst Lubitsch: Laughter in Paradise.* New York: Simon and Schuster, 1993.

———. *Five American Cinematographers.* Metuchen, N.J.: Scarecrow Press, 1987.

———. *Lion of Hollywood: The Life and Legend of Louis B. Mayer.* New York: Simon and Schuster, 2005.

———. *The Speed of Sound: Hollywood and the Talkie Revolution, 1926–1930.* New York: Simon and Schuster, 1997.

Fairbanks, Douglas Jr. *The Salad Days.* New York: Doubleday, 1988.

Ferber, Edna. *A Peculiar Treasure.* New York: Reprint Press, 1991.

Fitzgerald, F. Scott. *The Last Tycoon.* New York: Collier Books/MacMillan, 1986.

Flamini, Roland. *Thalberg: The Last Tycoon and the World of M-G-M.* New York: Crown Publishers, 1994.

Forslund, Bengt. *Victor Sjöström.* New York: New York Zoetrope, 1988.

Fountain, Leatrice Gilbert, with John R. Maxim. *Dark Star.* New York: St. Martin's Press, 1985.

Fowler, Gene. *Good Night, Sweet Prince.* New York: Viking Press, 1944.

France, Anatole. *The Crime of Sylvestre Bonnard.* New York: John Lane, 1920.

Gish, Lillian. *Dorothy and Lillian Gish.* New York: Scribner, 1973.

———, with Ann Pinchot. *The Movies, Mr. Griffith, and Me.* Englewood Cliffs, N.J.: Prentice-Hall, 1969.

Goldstein, Malcolm. *George S. Kaufman: His Life, His Theater.* New York: Oxford University Press, 1979.

Greenberg, Joel, and Charles Higham. *The Celluloid Muse.* New York: Signet Books, 1972.

Griffith, Richard, and Arthur Mayer. *The Movies.* New York: Simon and Schuster, 1957.

Gussow, Mel. *Don't Say Yes Until I Finish Talking.* New York: Doubleday, 1971.

Gutner, Howard. *Gowns by Adrian.* New York: Harry N. Abrams, 2001.

Hamann, G. D. *Clark Gable in the 30s.* Los Angeles: Filming Today Press, 2004.

———. *Greta Garbo in the 30s.* Los Angeles: Filming Today Press, 2003.

———. *Jean Harlow in the 30s.* Los Angeles: Filming Today Press, 2004.

———. *Joan Crawford in the 30s.* Los Angeles: Filming Today Press, 1999.

———. *Norma Shearer in the 30s.* Los Angeles: Filming Today Press, 2002.

———. *On the Sets in the 30s.* Los Angeles: Filming Today Press, 2002.

———. *W. S. Van Dyke in the 30s.* Los Angeles: Filming Today Press, 2003.

Haver, Ronald. *David O. Selznick's Hollywood.* New York: Alfred A. Knopf, 1980.

Hayes, Helen, with Katherine Hatch. *Helen Hayes: My Life in Three Acts.* New York: Harcourt, Brace, Jovanovich, 1990.

Hecht, Ben. *Charlie: The Improbable Life and Times of Charles MacArthur.* New York: Harper and Row, 1957.

Higham, Charles. *Charles Laughton: An Intimate Biography.* Garden City, N.Y.: Doubleday, 1976.

———. *Hollywood Cameramen.* Bloomington: Indiana University Press, 1970.

Hopper, Hedda. *From under My Hat*. New York: McFadden-Bartell, 1964.

―――, and James Brough. *The Whole Truth and Nothing But*. New York: Pyramid Books, 1963.

Howard, Leslie Ruth. *A Quite Remarkable Father*. New York: Harcourt, Brace and Company, 1959.

Jacobs, Jack, and Myron Braum. *The Films of Norma Shearer*. Secaucus, N.J.: Citadel Press, 1977.

James, William. *William James: Writings 1902–1920*. New York: Library of America, 1906.

Johnson, Nora. *Flashback: Nora Johnson on Nunnally Johnson*. New York: Doubleday, 1979.

Kanfer, Stefan. *Groucho: The Life and Times of Julius Henry Marx*. New York: Vintage Books, 2001.

Kanin, Garson. *Hollywood: Stars and Starlets, Tycoons and Flesh-Peddlers, Moviemakers and Moneymakers, Frauds and Geniuses, Hopefuls and Has-Beens, Great Lovers and Sex Symbols*. New York: Viking Press, 1967.

Keaton, Buster, with Charles Samuels. *My Wonderful World of Slapstick*. Garden City, N.Y.: Doubleday, 1960.

Kennedy, Matthew. *Edmund Goulding's Dark Victory: Hollywood's Genius Bad Boy*. Madison: University of Wisconsin Press, 2004.

Kobal, John. *The Art of the Great Hollywood Portrait Photographers*. New York: Alfred A. Knopf, 1980.

―――. *Gotta Sing, Gotta Dance: A History of Movie Musicals*. New York: Exeter Press, 1987.

―――. *People Will Talk*. New York: Alfred A. Knopf, 1985.

Kobler, John. *Damned in Paradise: The Life of John Barrymore*. New York: Atheneum, 1977.

Koszarski, Richard. *The Man You Loved to Hate: Erich von Stroheim and Hollywood*. New York: Oxford University Press, 1983.

Kotsilibas-Davis, James. *The Barrymores: The Royal Family in Hollywood*. New York: Crown Publishers, 1981.

―――, and Myrna Loy. *Being and Becoming*. New York: Alfred A. Knopf, 1987.

Lambert, Gavin. *Norma Shearer: A Life*. New York: Alfred A. Knopf, 1990.

―――. *On Cukor*. New York: G. P. Putnam's Sons, 1972.

Lanchester, Elsa. *Charles Laughton and I*. New York: Harcourt, Brace, 1938.

―――. *Elsa Lanchester, Herself*. New York: St. Martin's Press, 1983.

Latham, Aaron. *Crazy Sundays*. New York: Pocket Books, 1972.

Lawrence, Jerome. *Actor: The Life and Times of Paul Muni*. New York: G. P. Putnam's Sons, 1975.

Lawson, John Howard. *Film, the Creative Process: The Search for an Audio-Visual Language and Structure*. New York: Hill and Wang, 1968.

Lee, Betty. *Marie Dressler: The Unlikeliest Star*. Lexington: University Press of Kentucky, 1997.

Lennig, Arthur. *Stroheim*. Lexington: University Press of Kentucky, 1997.

Levy, Emanuel. *George Cukor, Master of Elegance*. New York: William Morrow, 1994.

Lewis, David, with James Curtis. *The Creative Producer: A Memoir of the Studio System*. Metuchen, N.J.: Scarecrow Press, 1993.

Long, Robert Emmett. *George Cukor: Interviews*. Jackson: University of Mississippi Press, 2001.

Loos, Anita. *A Cast of Thousands*. New York: Grosset and Dunlap, 1977.

———. *Kiss Hollywood Good-by*. New York: Viking Press, 1974.

———. *San Francisco: A Screenplay*. Carbondale: Southern Illinois University Press, 1978.

Lord, Daniel A., S.J. *Played by Ear*. Chicago: Loyola University Press, 1956.

Maas, Frederica Sagor. *The Shocking Miss Pilgrim: A Writer in Early Hollywood*. Lexington: University Press of Kentucky, 1999.

Maltin, Leonard. *Behind the Camera: The Cinematographer's Art*. New York: Signet Books, 1971.

———. *Hollywood, the Movie Factory*. New York: Popular Library, 1976.

Mann, William J. *Wisecracker: The Life and Times of William Haines, America's First Openly Gay Star*. New York: Viking Press, 1998.

Marion, Frances. *Off with Their Heads!* New York: MacMillan, 1972.

Marx, Arthur. *My Life with Groucho*. Fort Lee, N.J.: Barricade Books, 1988.

Marx, Groucho. *Groucho and Me*. New York: Bernard Geis Associates, 1959.

Marx, Maxine. *Growing Up with Chico*. Englewood Cliffs, N.J.: Prentice-Hall, 1980.

Marx, Samuel. *A Gaudy Spree*. New York: Franklin Watts, 1987.

———. *Mayer and Thalberg, the Make-Believe Saints*. New York: Random House, 1975.

———, and Joyce Vanderveen. *Deadly Illusions*. New York: Random House, 1990.

Maxwell, Elsa. *R. S. V. P.: Elsa Maxwell's Own Story*. Boston: Little, Brown, 1964.

McGilligan, Patrick. *Backstory 1: Interviews with Screenwriters of Hollywood's Golden Age*. Berkeley: University of California Press, 1986.

———. *George Cukor: A Double Life*. New York: St. Martin's Press, 1991.

Menjou, Adolphe, and M. M. Musselman. *It Took Nine Tailors*. New York: McGraw-Hill, 1948.

Meredith, Scott. *George S. Kaufman and His Friends*. New York: Doubleday, 1974.

Meryman, Richard. *Mank: The Wit, World, and Life of Herman J. Mankiewicz*. New York: William Morrow, 1978.

Moore, Grace. *You're Only Human Once*. Garden City, N.Y.: Doubleday, Doran, 1944.

Morley, Robert, and Sewell Stokes. *Robert Morley: A Reluctant Autobiography*. New York: Simon and Schuster, 1966.

Naumburg, Nancy. *We Make the Movies*. New York: W. W. Norton, 1937.

Niven, David. *Bring On the Empty Horses*. New York: Dell, 1976.

Noble, Peter. *Hollywood Scapegoat*. London: Fortune Press, 1950.

Oderman, Stuart. *Lillian Gish: A Life on Stage and Screen*. Jefferson, N.C.: McFarland, 2000.

Paris, Barry. *Garbo: A Biography*. New York: Alfred A. Knopf, 1995.

Parish, James Robert, and Gregory W. Mank. *The Best of MGM: The Golden Years (1928–59)*. Westport, Conn.: Arlington House, 1981.

Pensel, Hans. *Seastrom and Stiller in Hollywood: Two Swedish Directors in Silent American Films, 1923–1930*. New York: Vantage Press, 1969.

Peters, Margot. *The House of Barrymore*. New York: Alfred A. Knopf, 1991.

Pirandello, Luigi. *As You Desire Me*. Translated by Samuel Putnam. New York: E. P. Dutton, 1931.

Pizzitola, Louis. *Hearst over Hollywood: Power, Passion, and Propaganda in the Movies*. New York: Columbia University Press, 2002.

Rapf, Maurice. *Back Lot*. Lanham, Md.: Scarecrow Press, 1999.

Rathbone, Basil. *In and Out of Character*. New York: Limelight Editions, 1997.

Reinhardt, Gottfried. *The Genius: A Memoir of Max Reinhardt by His Son*. New York: Alfred A. Knopf, 1979.

Rivkin, Allen, and Laura Kerr. *Hello, Hollywood!* New York: Doubleday, 1962.

Robinson, Edward G., and Leonard Spigelgass. *All My Yesterdays*. New York: Hawthorn Press, 1973.

Rosenberg, Bernard, and Harry Silverstein. *The Real Tinsel*. New York: MacMillan, 1970.

Samuels, Charles. *The King: A Biography of Clark Gable*. New York: Coward-McCann, 1961.

Schlesinger, Arthur M., Jr. *The Age of Roosevelt, Volume I: Crisis of the Old Order, 1919–1933*. New York: Houghton and Mifflin, 1957.

Schulberg, Budd. *Moving Pictures: Memoirs of a Hollywood Prince*. London: Allison and Busby, 1993.

Schwartz, Nancy Lynn, and Sheila Schwartz. *The Hollywood Writers' Wars*. New York: Alfred A. Knopf, 1982.

Seldes, Gilbert. *The Great Audience*. New York: Viking Press, 1950.

Selznick, Irene. *A Private View*. New York: Alfred A. Knopf, 1983.

Server, Lee. *Screenwriter: Words Become Pictures*. Pittstown, N.J.: Main Street Press, 1987.

Shakespeare, William. *Romeo and Juliet: A Motion Picture Edition*. New York: Random House, 1936.

Sinclair, Upton. *Upton Sinclair Presents William Fox*. Los Angeles: Sinclair Press, 1933.

Singer, Kurt. *The Laughton Story: An Intimate Story of Charles Laughton*. Philadelphia: John C. Winston, 1954.

Skal, David J., and Elias Savada. *Dark Carnival: The Secret World of Tod Browning*. New York: Anchor Books, 1995.

Skolsky, Sidney. *Don't Get Me Wrong—I Love Hollywood*. New York: G. P. Putnam's Sons, 1975.

Soares, Andre. *Beyond Paradise*. New York: St. Martin's Press, 2002.

Spicer, Chrystopher J. *Clark Gable: Biography, Filmography, Bibliography*. Jefferson, N.C.: McFarland, 2002.

Stenn, David. *Bombshell: The Life and Death of Jean Harlow*. New York: Doubleday, 1993.

Stewart, Donald Ogden. *By a Stroke of Luck! An Autobiography*. New York: Paddington Press, 1975.

Stine, Whitney. *The Hurrell Style: Photographs by George Hurrell*. New York: John Day, 1976.

St. Johns, Adela Rogers. *The Honeycomb*. Garden City, N.Y.: Doubleday, 1969.

———. *Love, Laughter, and Tears: My Hollywood Story*. Garden City, N.Y.: Doubleday, 1978.

Stroheim, Erich von. *Greed*. London: Faber and Faber, 1989.

Strunk, William Jr., and E. B. White. *The Elements of Style*. New York: MacMillan, 1959.

Swanson, Gloria. *Swanson on Swanson*. New York: Random House, 1980.

Swanson, H. N. *Sprinkled with Ruby Dust*. New York: Warner Books, 1989.

Taylor, Dwight. *Joyride*. New York: G. P. Putnam's Sons, 1959.

Thomas, Bob. *Joan Crawford: A Biography*. New York: Bantam Books, 1978.

————. *Selznick*. Garden City, N.Y.: Doubleday, 1969.

————. *Thalberg: Life and Legend*. Garden City, N.Y.: Doubleday, 1969.

Thomson, David. *Showman: The Life of David O. Selznick*. New York: Alfred A. Knopf, 1992.

Tibbetts, John C. *Introduction to the Photoplay, 1929: A Contemporary Account of the Transition to Sound in Film*. Shawnee Mission, Kans.: National Film Society, 1977.

Tornabene, Lyn. *Long Live the King: A Biography of Clark Gable*. New York: Pocket Books, 1978.

Turk, Edward Baron. *Hollywood Diva: A Biography of Jeanette MacDonald*. Berkeley: University of California Press, 1998.

Turnbull, Andrew. *The Letters of F. Scott Fitzgerald*. New York: Scribner, 1962.

Veiller, Bayard. *The Fun I've Had*. New York: Reynal and Hitchcock, 1941.

Vidor, King. *A Tree Is a Tree*. Hollywood, Calif.: Samuel French, 1989.

Vieira, Mark A. *Sin in Soft Focus: Pre-Code Hollywood*. New York: Harry N. Abrams, 1999.

Viertel, Salka. *The Kindness of Strangers*. New York: Holt, Rinehart, and Winston, 1969.

Wagner, Walter. *You Must Remember This*. New York: G. P. Putnam's Sons, 1975.

Walker, Alexander. *The Shattered Silents: How the Talkies Came to Stay*. New York: William Morrow, 1979.

Wallis, Hal, and Charles Higham. *Star Maker*. New York: Berkley Books, 1981.

Walsh, Frank. *Sin and Censorship: The Catholic Church and the Motion Picture Industry*. New Haven, Conn.: Yale University Press, 1996.

Watts, Stephen. *Behind the Screen: How Films Are Made*. London: Arthur Barker, 1938.

Winters, Ralph E. *Some Cutting Remarks: Seventy Years a Film Editor*. Lanham, Md.: Scarecrow Press, 2001.

Zolotow, Maurice. *Stagestruck: The Romance of Alfred Lunt and Lynn Fontanne*. New York: Harcourt, Brace, and World, 1964.

SIGNED ARTICLES

Albert, Katherine. "A Picture That Was No Picnic." *Motion Picture* 34, no. 3 (October 1927): 32–33, 97.

————. "Did Garbo and Brown Fight?" *Photoplay* (March 1931): 33, 130–131.

Babcock, Muriel. "Flaming Youth Called Feeble." *Los Angeles Times*, December 27, 1931, B9.

————. "Safari Scenes Grip Memory." *Los Angeles Times*, December 15, 1929, B13.

————. "Star Declares for Stage." *Los Angeles Times*, January 4, 1932, A5.

Bangley, Jimmy. "The Legendary Barbara La Marr." *Classic Images*, no. 251 (May 1996): 16–18, 71.

Biery, Ruth. "Refereeing the Royal Family." *Photoplay* 42, no. 5 (December 1932): 28–29, 104–105.

Boylan, Malcolm Stuart. "Great Executive Job Held by a Boy of 22." *Los Angeles Times*, October 15, 1922, p. 37.

Busby, Marquis. "The Camera Does Lie." *Movie Mirror* 5, no. 1 (December 1933): 46–48, 74.

Carr, Harry. "Harry Carr's Page." *Los Angeles Times*, December 3, 1924

————. "Harry Carr's Page." *Los Angeles Times*, January 7, 1925, C2.

————. "Harry Carr's Page." *Los Angeles Times*, June 3, 1925, D2.

————. "The Story of Hollywood's Unhappiest Man." *Los Angeles Times*, August 9, 1931, B5.

Churchill, Douglas W. "Hollywood Magic Revealed Again." *New York Times*, June 13, 1937, X1.

————. "Out of the Golden West." *New York Times*, November 11, 1934, X5.

Haber, Joyce. "Small Dinner Party for Alfred Lunts." February 25, 1970. Unsourced clipping, Fairbanks Center for Motion Picture Study, Academy of Motion Picture Arts and Sciences, Beverly Hills (hereafter FCMPS).

Hall, Gladys. "A Heroine to Other Stars." *Motion Picture* (January 1933): 26–27, 66–67.

————. "Love Comes Once." *Modern Screen* (November 1938): 34, 72.

Hall, Mordaunt. "The Actor's Experiment." *New York Times*, September 10, 1931, p. 22.

————. "Fads of Stars Seen in Coast Tour." *New York Times*, August 2, 1925, X2.

————. "The Hollywood Hermit." *New York Times*, March 24, 1929, X1.

————. "Molnar's 'Guardsman.'" *New York Times*, September 20, 1931, X5.

————. "The Screen." *New York Times*, December 5, 1924, p. 28.

Hays, Richard. "'Good' Film Now Not Good Enough for Moviegoers." Unsourced clipping on microfilm in Irving Thalberg core collection, FCMPS.

Herzog, Dorothy. "How to Be a Producer." *Photoplay* 29, no. 5 (April 1926): 66, 130.

Hopper, Hedda. "And We're Still Friends." Unsourced clipping on microfilm in Greta Garbo core collection, FCMPS.

Howe, Herbert. "Who Will Be the Next Great Star?" *Los Angeles Times*, December 27, 1925, p. 13.

Kapitanoff, Nancy. "Sixty-three Years of Shooting the Legends." *Los Angeles Times* Calendar, December 15, 1991.

Kendall, Read. "Crowd of 25,000 Views Arrival of Screen Celebrities." *Los Angeles Times*, July 8, 1938, A7.

Kingsley, Grace. "Bal Masque." *Los Angeles Times*, June 2, 1929, G4.

———. "Hobnobbing in Hollywood." *Los Angeles Times*, May 23, 1933, A5.

———. "Julius Stern Tells Conditions Abroad." *Los Angeles Times*, November 5, 1920, I-14.

———. "Star-Partying." *Los Angeles Times*, August 22, 1926, p. 15.

———. "What Ho at Lila Lee's." *Los Angeles Times*, August 15, 1926, p. 15.

Klumph, Helen. "*He Who Gets Slapped* Is Triumph of Week." *Los Angeles Times*, November 16, 1924, C27.

———. "Holiday Fare Receipts Low." *Los Angeles Times*, December 27, 1925, C27.

———. "Many Producers Sail to Sign New Talent." *Los Angeles Times*, December 21, 1924, C27.

Lee, Sonia. "Norma Fights Back." *Hollywood* 22, no. 6 (March 1933): 29, 63.

Lord, Daniel A., S.J. "Code Violators." *The Queen's Work* 26, no. 9 (June 1934): 1.

Lusk, Norbert. "*Mary Dugan* Brilliant Hit." *New York Times*, April 7, 1929, C14.

———. "News and Gossip of Stage and Screen." *Los Angeles Times*, March 10, 1935, A3.

MacAlarney, Robert E. "The Noise Movie Revolution." *World's Work* (April 1929): 50.

Maltby, Richard. "The Genesis of the Production Code." *Quarterly Review of Film and Video* 15, no. 4 (March 1995): 5–57.

Marshall, Ernest. "On the London Screen." *New York Times*, August 16, 1931, p. 98.

Martin, Pete. "I Call on Clark Gable." *Saturday Evening Post*, October 5, 1957, pp. 24–25, 64, 66, 68.

Merrick, Mollie. "New Gossip of Filmland Is Told." *Los Angeles Times*, June 7, 1934, p. 10.

Mitchell, Greg. "Thalberg: Father of the Attack Ad." *New York Times*, April 19, 1992, pp. 21–23.

Morris, George. "Opening Night: A Memoir from the Only Warner Who Was There." *Take One* (January 1978): 30–32, 55–56.

Morris, Ruth. "Hallelujah." *Variety*, August 25, 1929, p. 21.

———. "Sinful Girls Lead in 1931." *Variety*, December 29, 1931, p. 37.

Moulton, Herbert. "Frances Marion Joins M-G-M." *Los Angeles Times*, August 25, 1926, A8.

Nelson, Bradford. "Chaney Comes Back." *Screenland* (May 1930): 32–33, 116–17.

Nugent, Frank S. "Mr. Howard Casts a Stone." *New York Times*, January 3, 1935, X1.

Parsons, Harriet. "Norma Talks about Joan." *Picturegoer Weekly*, March 25, 1933, pp. 12–13.

Parsons, Louella. "Norma Shearer Reveals Plans." *Los Angeles Examiner*, October 18, 1936, p. 12.

Punter, Jennie. "The New Sounds of Silence." *Toronto Globe and Mail*, July 4, 2003, p. 4.

Ramsey, Walter. "The Trial of Norma Shearer." *Motion Picture* 38, no. 4 (May 1929): 33, 100–101.

Riggan, Byron. "Damn the Crocodiles—Keep the Cameras Rolling!" *American Heritage* 19, no. 4 (June 1968): 40–41, 89–92.

Schallert, Edwin. "Clever Character Study." *Los Angeles Times*, November 12, 1924, C12.

———. "Ethel Barrymore Takes Greatest Leap of Career." *Los Angeles Times*, June 12, 1932, B11, B13.

———. "Features Fashion to Pattern." *Los Angeles Times*, November 6, 1927, C13.

———. "Film Producers Shaken by Clean-up Campaign." *Los Angeles Times*, June 10, 1934, p. 1.

———. "Gilbert Is Hero in Gay Intrigue." *Los Angeles Times*, October 19, 1929, p. 11.

———. "Katharine Cornell Refuses New Movie Offer." *Los Angeles Times*, March 2, 1935, p. 5.

———. "Norma Shearer Reveals Why She Went Wrong." *Los Angeles Times*, July 10, 1932, B17.

———. "Stark Realism—At Last!" *Picture Play* (October 1923): 46–47, 104.

Scheuer, Philip K. "Barretts Lead Drama Crusade." *Los Angeles Times*, June 5, 1932, B13, B18.

———. "Charles Laughton Never Through." *Los Angeles Times*, May 27, 1934, A1, A2.

———. "Haines Acts Fighter in Ring Story." *Los Angeles Times*, April 6, 1929, A11.

———. "Hollywood Imports College Professors." *Los Angeles Times*, August 4, 1935, A1.

———. "An Old Story." *Los Angeles Times*, September 6, 1931, p. 11.

———. "A Town Called Hollywood." *Los Angeles Times*, July 19, 1936, C1.

Sennwald, André. "A Lubitsch Production of *The Merry Widow*." *New York Times*, October 12, 1934, X1.

———. "No More Ladies." *New York Times*, June 22, 1935, p. 18.

Shippey, Lee. "The Lee Side o' L. A." *Los Angeles Times*, September 26, 1934, A4.

Sisk, Robert. "The Movies Try to Talk." *American Mercury* (August 1928): 492–93.

Smith, Helena Huntington. "The Movies Speak Out." *Outlook and Independent*. December 5, 1928, 1270.

Thomas, Kevin. "A Gallery of Grotesques." *Los Angeles Times*, June 26, 1983.

Whitaker, Alma. "Beaumont Talkie Veteran." *Los Angeles Times*, January 27, 1929, C13.

———. "Hit-Maker." *Screenland* Magazine 25, no. 4 (August 1932): 19.

———. "New Contract Awes Her." *Los Angeles Times*, November 7, 1926, C19.

———. "Norma, Are You Upstage?" *Los Angeles Times*, May 2, 1926, C27.

———. "Wodehouse Out and Still Dazed." *Los Angeles Times*, June 7, 1931, C9.

Woolfenden, John R. "Location Sets So Realistic Swallows Build Nests There." *Los Angeles Times*, June 7, 1936, C1.

Woolridge, A. L. "How Pictures Are Tried Out." *Los Angeles Times*, March 18, 1925, C7.

Zolotow, Maurice. "The Facts about Alfred Lunt's Lips." *Variety*, January 6, 1965. Fragmentary clipping, FCMPS.

Zweig, Stefan. "History and the Screen." *New York Times*, April 1, 1934, X4.

ANONYMOUS ARTICLES

"Actors Fill Unexpected Film Roles." *Los Angeles Times*, June 27, 1926, C26.

"All Southland Rallies under Chamber Banner." *Los Angeles Times*, April 25, 1934, A1, A2.

"Anna Christie." *Variety*, March 19, 1930.

"The Audience Talks Back." *Photoplay* 41, no. 6 (May 1932): 6, 10–11, 12.

"Authors by Hundreds Meet Tragic Defeat in Films." *Los Angeles Times*, October 7, 1934, B1, B2.

"Bank Failure Hits Screen Players." *Hollywood Citizen-News*, June 6, 1932.

"Broadway Melody." *Variety*, February 11, 1929.

"The Callahans and the Murphys." *Variety*, July 13, 1927.

"Cinema." *Time*, August 24, 1936, pp. 30–32.

"*Everyman* in Final Stages." *Los Angeles Times*, September 9, 1936, A1.

"Film Match Admitted by Mother." *Los Angeles Times*, August 2, 1927, A1.

"Films to Pay Homage to Thalberg Today." *Los Angeles Times*, September 16, 1936, A1.

"Film Vulgarity Assailed by Theater Owners Head." *Los Angeles Times*, April 11, 1934, A1, A2.

"Foreign Language Films." *New York Times*, November 17, 1929, X5.

"Goulding Most Versatile." *New York Times*, February 24, 1929, C14.

"Hallelujah." *Variety*, August 20, 1929.

"His Glorious Night." *Variety*, October 9, 1929.

"Hollywood Cleans House." *New York Times*, July 15, 1934, X3.

"Hollywood Revue." *Variety*, June 2, 1929.

"In Studios and Theatres." *New York Times*, November 9, 1930, X5.

"Ina Claire Divorces John Gilbert." *Los Angeles Times*, August 5, 1931, A1.

"Ina Claire in Reno to Get Divorce." *Los Angeles Times*, March 12, 1931, p. 1.

"In Studios and Theatres." *New York Times*, November 9, 1930, X5.

"Irish Film Causes Another Disturbance." *New York Times*, August 26, 1927, p. 5.

"Irving Thalberg." *Los Angeles Times*, April 23, 1929, C6.

"Jack Gilbert Writes His Own Story, Part Four." *Photoplay*, September 1926.

"Jean Harlow Resumes Work to Forget Grief." *Los Angeles Times*, September 13, 1932, p. 1.

"King Vidor Speaks of Sound." *New York Times*, July 8, 1928, p. 94.

"Last Honors Paid Gilbert." *Los Angeles Times*, January 12, 1936, p. 1.

"Let Us Be Gay." *Variety*, July 16, 1930.

"Letters to the Editor." *Motion Picture* 33, no. 4 (May 1927): 96–98.

"Mata Hari in a Film." *New York Times*, December 20, 1931, X5.

"Meet the Story Editor." *New York Times*, May 19, 1935, X3.

"Metro-Goldwyn-Mayer." *Fortune* 6, no. 6 (December 1932): 60–74.

"Millions for Film Program." *Los Angeles Times*, June 2, 1924, A1.

"Morals for Profit." *New York World*, April 1, 1930.

"Mr. Thalberg Returns from Europe." *New York Times*, May 13, 1928, p. 112.

"Mrs. Shearer Kills Self before Crowd on Pier." *Los Angeles Times*, June 7, 1931, B1.

"The New Pictures." *Time*, April 9, 1934.

"Nils Asther." *Screenland* (February 1929): 83, 112.

"The Norma Shearer Irving Thalberg Loves." *New Movie Magazine* 9, no. 5 (May 1934): 32–33, 70–71.

"Peace Sought in Film Row." *Los Angeles Times*, October 16, 1933, A2.

"Peace-Time 'Big Parade.'" *New York Times*, May 22, 1927, X5.

"Plan Silent Versions of Metro Talkies." *New York Times*, April 18, 1929, p. 37.

"Plucking a Few Notes from Harpo." *New York Times*, November 17, 1935, X4.

"Pneumonia Kills Noted Producer." *Los Angeles Examiner*, September 15, 1936, pp. 1, 8–9.

"Producer Discusses Pictures." *New York Times*, May 3, 1931, X6.

"A Producing Executive Describes the Gamut Run by Book or Play." *New York Times*, December 20, 1925, X7.

"Rachel Crothers and the Movies." *New York Times*, April 28, 1935, X3.

"Radical Picturization Due in New Film Tales." *Los Angeles Times*, July 8, 1928, C33.

"Redemption." *Variety*, May 7, 1930.

"The Rogue Song." *Variety*, February 5, 1930.

"Screen Head Sounds Plea." *Los Angeles Times*, April 30, 1936, A1.

"Screen Pair Back from Honeymoon." *Los Angeles Times*, May 20, 1928, B3.

"A Significant Event." *Los Angeles Times*, September 16, 1934, p. 12.

"Sinclair Alters Meaning of EPIC Scheme Slogan." *Los Angeles Times*, September 18, 1934, p. 4.

"Skeptic Asks Al to 'Quit His Kidding.'" *Los Angeles Times*, February 2, 1928, A9.

"Speakers Not Appreciated." *Film Daily*, September 29, 1929, p. 10.

"Studio Row Terminated by Scolding." *Los Angeles Times*, January 30, 1925, A2.

"Talkies to Belong to Actors." *Los Angeles Times*, September 23, 1928, C13.

"Thalberg's Rise to Fame Won Title of 'Boy Wonder.'" *Los Angeles Times*, September 15, 1936.

"Thalberg Silent on 'Wedding.'" *Los Angeles Times*, June 2, 1927, A1.

"Thalberg Tells M-G-M Plans for Operation." *Los Angeles Times*, March 19, 1929, p. 13.

"Thunder." *Variety*, July 10, 1929.

"The Trial of Mary Dugan." *Variety*, April 3, 1929.

"Trials of an Actress." *New York Times*, July 3, 1927, C7.

"Tribute Paid to Thalberg." *Los Angeles Times*, September 17, 1936, A1.

"Trust Everyone but Cut the Cards." *Fortune* (August 1939): 104.

"Way for a Sailor." *Variety*, December 17, 1930.

"What's Ahead for Norma Shearer?" *Modern Screen* 14 (December–May 1936–37): 40–41, 97–99.

"What the Audience Thinks." *Photoplay* 41, no. 3 (March 1932): 6, 10, 112–15.

"What the Audience Thinks (2)." *Photoplay* 41, no. 4 (April 1932): 6, 14, 16, 121.

"What the Audience Thinks (3)." *Photoplay* 41, no. 5 (May 1932): 6, 7, 18, 120–21.

"With Brickbats and Bouquets." *Photoplay* 41, no. 8 (August 1932): 7, 16, 17.

UNPUBLISHED DOCUMENTS

Arrouge, Norma Shearer. "Norma Shearer Arrouge Memoir Notes." Unpublished document, private collection.

Dockter, Phil. "Interview with Ian Wolfe." Glendale, California, December 30, 1985. Unpublished audio tape in author's collection.

Franklin, Sidney. "We Laughed and We Cried." Photoplay Collection, used by permission of Carole K. Johnston, the Sidney Franklin Estate.

Knight, Arthur. "Oral Interview with Lawrence Weingarten." Recorded March 5, 1974, in Knight's Cinema 305 class, History of American Sound Film, University of Southern California, Los Angeles.

Marion, Frances. "Hollywood." Frances Marion Collection, Cinema-Television Library, University of Southern California.

Wilk, Max. "Donald Ogden Stewart Oral History." American Film Institute, Los Angeles.

DOCUMENTARY FILM

M-G-M: When the Lion Roars. Turner Entertainment, 1992.

ACKNOWLEDGMENTS

Irving Thalberg: Boy Wonder to Producer Prince has traveled eighteen years to completion. In 1990 the retired film editor Chester W. Schaeffer introduced me to Samuel Marx, whom he knew from M-G-M in the 1930s. Sam could trace his memories of Irving Thalberg all the way back to 1919, when they worked together as teenagers in Universal's New York offices. At the time of our introduction, Sam was writing his third book about the Thalberg era. I assisted Sam with photo research and even made a publicity portrait of him. In the course of working with him, I expressed an interest in writing my own book about Thalberg. Sam agreed to help me. He shared detailed reminiscences of M-G-M and reviewed my early progress on the project. He passed away in 1992, but he continues to inspire me. I trust that this book would have met with his approval. He loved Thalberg, and was always proud of it.

For helping me research *Irving Thalberg: Boy Wonder to Producer Prince*, I wish to thank the following institutions, archives, and individuals: the library at California State University, Hayward; the Beverly Hills Public Library; and the Los Angeles Public Library. My thanks go to Nancy and Eddie of Columbia Printing in Los Angeles for helping me copy so many book proposals. I thank Caroline Sisneros of the American Film Institute for access to Donald Ogden Stewart's oral history. I thank Courtney Smith at the Oral History Research Office of Columbia University for access to the histories of Lee Garmes, Ben Hecht, and Jeanette MacDonald.

After more than thirty-five years of research in the Cinema-Television Library of the University of Southern California, I am further indebted to Ned Comstock. He never fails to illuminate the unexpected corner of an archive, whether it be his own or a distant one. He administers, among others, the M-G-M Script Collection; in it I made discoveries about Thalberg's working methods that I have shared here.

I wish to thank Bob Thomas for access to the interview notes he transcribed for his 1969 book on Thalberg. When I contacted him, I spared him the gooey reminiscence of my reading his book as a college freshman, but I still have a great fondness—and respect—for that groundbreaking work. Mr. Thomas deserves praise as the first M-G-M historian who did not approach his subject with either reverence or skepticism. It is obvious from the forthright interviews he gathered that his subjects trusted him, and with good reason. He is a journalist of integrity.

The following memorabilia dealers and photographic agencies helped me illustrate this volume: Marc Wanamaker of the Bison Archives and Howard Mandelbaum of Photofest.

Many collector friends helped me with the loan of rare production stills. I thank Robert S. Birchard, Philip Dockter, Jim Kaufmann, Connie Parker, Karl Ruddy, Harvey Stewart, and Jack Tillmany.

I thank Ben Carbonetto for being a modern de Medici.

I thank the following for advice, assistance, and referrals: Gregory Byberg; Frank Coiro and Roseanna Giordano Coiro; Robert L. Hillmann; Jann Hoffman; and Norma Pisar.

I am grateful to Kurt Bier, Jonathan Quiej, and Bronni Stein for helping me accomplish research in various archives; thanks to them, I was able to work around my disability.

I wish to thank the following scholars, not only for sharing the knowledge gained in years of diligent research but also for taking the time to keep me on the path of accuracy: Cari Beauchamp; Taylor Coffman; John Connolly, Executive Director of Actors Equity; Lee Cozad of the Lake Arrowhead Historical Society; James Curtis; Scott Eyman; Matthew Kennedy; Emily Leider, and Mick La Salle.

I owe special thanks to the following for bringing me closer to Irving Thalberg than would otherwise have been possible: to Darin Barnes for every fact about Norma Shearer that exists in two dimensions; to Browne Greene for the privilege of visiting a former Thalberg home; to Suzanne McCormick for sharing memories that helped me paint truthful portraits of both Thalberg and Shearer; to Christina

Rice for utterly invaluable help with a treasure trove of history; to Darrell Rooney for access to his Jean Harlow research library; to David Stenn for help with the most obscure aspects of Paul Bern's life; and to Deborah Thalberg for support of yet another project.

For giving me access to documents without which this book and its companion volume would have been exercises in vanity, I sincerely thank the Reverend John Lea McDaniels; Bobby Litts; and Kevin Brownlow of Photoplay Productions. I owe a special thank you to the Estate of Howard Strickling.

I wish to thank the following individuals for taking the time to review and critique the manuscript. It has benefited greatly from their insight and candor: Cari Beauchamp, Jacinto Guevara, Kim Hill, Emily Leider, Howard Mandelbaum, Suzanne McCormick, André Soares, P. R. Tooke, and Charles Ziarko.

I again acknowledge George Feltenstein at Warner Bros.; Roger L. Mayer, President and Chief Operating Officer of the Turner Entertainment Company; and Richard P. May, former Vice President in Charge of Preservation at Warner Bros. Because of these dedicated individuals and the farseeing patronage of Ted Turner, we can enjoy the Thalberg legacy. No company has done as much for our American film heritage.

I thank my literary agent, Alan Nevins of Firm Books, for his ongoing work on my behalf. I thank Mary Francis, Suzanne Knott, and Kalicia Pivirotto of the University of California Press.

Finally, I want to acknowledge the part that my parents played in helping me write my books. *Irving Thalberg: Boy Wonder to Producer Prince* is the second book I have completed without their active encouragement and support.

INDEX

Bellamy, Ralph, 139
Bell Laboratories, 88
Bello, Marino, 204, 205, 206, 316
Beloved Enemy, 365
Ben-Hur, 56, 285; censored, 73; economics, 48, 49, 51, 60, 71, 93; Goldwyn companies, 30, 44, 48; Metro-Goldwyn, 30, 44, 48–51, 54; premiere, 57
Bennett, Constance, 180; card games, 147, 275, 287; *The Easiest Way*, 143; *Ex-Wife*, 108; *Outcast Lady*, 254, 255, 256; Thalberg funeral, 371
Bennett, Richard, 13
Berg, Phil, 95, 145
Bergere, Ouida, 102
Bergerman, Stanley, 366
Bergner, Elisabeth, 336
Bern, Paul, 25, 62, 82, 164–65, 200–213; *Blondie of the Follies*, 174; *Captain Applejack*, 31; *China Seas*, 208–9; and credits, 147; death, 208–15, 246, 300, 397; economics, 107, 210, 225; and Gilbert, 139, 201, 202; *Grand Hotel*, 175, 177, 183, 200, 201, 202; and Harlow, 178, 200–214, 315, 316; and LaMarr, 25, 201–2, 204; Paramount, 68; Pathé, 93–94; *Red-Headed Woman*, 163, 166, 178, 200–201, 203, 205; *Susan Lenox*, 200, 205; Thalberg friendship and mourning, 200, 202, 203, 210–15, 217, 220, 300, 357; Thalberg's awe of education, 171
Bernstein, Isadore, 6, 7
Besier, Rudolph, 250, 252
Bickford, Charles, 119–21, 123, 169
Big House, The, 113
Big Parade, The, 265; censored, 73; economics, 60, 71, 93; Gilbert, 60, 62, 63, 300; Loew's, Inc., 60, 63; Stallings, 56, 62, 288, 300; Vidor, 56, 60, 62
Big Red, 180–81, 357
Bill of Divorcement, A, 206

Billy the Kid, 127
Bingham, Rose, 364
Biography, 191, 267–68
Biography of a Bachelor Girl, 268
Birth of a Nation, The, 18
Bishop Murder Case, The, 142
Blackbirds of 1928, 105
Blind Husbands, 12, 13
Bloch, Bertram, 148
Blondie of the Follies, 174–75, 189
Boardman, Eleanor, 42, 52, 69–70
Boasberg, Al, 118, 283, 328
Bohème, La, 65–66
Boleslavsky, Richard, 195, 371, 389–90
Bombshell, 208n, 241
Booth, Edwina, 134–37
Booth, Margaret: appendectomy, 349; *Camille*, 334; *The Good Earth*, 361; Mission Road studio, 19; previews, 63, 87; *Romeo and Juliet*, 347, 349; Thalberg funeral, 371
Borden, Olive, 201
Born to Dance, 321, 370
Boswell, Hugh, 387
Bow, Clara, 72, 178, 188
Bowes, Edward, 90, 92, 93
Boyer, Charles, 274, 297, 318
Boy Friend, The, 60
B pictures, 245, 302, 395, 396
Brabin, Charles, 24; *Ben-Hur*, 30, 44, 48, 49; *Rasputin*, 193, 194–95
Braddock, James J., 337–38
Bread, 36, 52
Breda, Rudolph, 309
Breen, Joseph I., 249–50, 255; *The Barretts of Wimpole Street*, 252; *Biography*, 267; guest at Thalberg dinners, 274; *It Can't Happen Here*, 302; *Marie Antoinette*, 260; *The Merry Widow*, 259–60; *Romeo and Juliet*, 341, 344, 352; Thalberg funeral, 371
Brent, Evelyn, 56
Brent, George, 387

Episcopal Committee and, 250; fan mail vs., 180; *Freaks*, 190; *The Merry Widow*, 257, 258, 259–60; *Outcast Lady*, 255; and profits, 114; Stroheim and, 14; talkies, 98–99, 113–14; Thalberg and, 73, 113–15, 125, 128, 153–57, 164–65, 177–83, 189, 249–60, 302, 318, 344. *See also* morality; Production Code; sexuality

Chambers, Robert W., 251

Champ, The, 143–44, 180

Chaney, Lon, 60, 68, 69, 71, 97, 136; Browning film of a Robbins book, 189; death, 127; *He Who Gets Slapped*, 42–43; *The Hunchback of Notre Dame*, 14–15, 42; pay, 121, 213–14; talkies, 121, 127; *Tell It to the Marines*, 71; *The Unholy Three*, 121, 127

Channing of the Northwest, 21

Chaplin, Charlie, 83, 276; audience value, 61; *City Lights*, 133; Mayer and, 299; Thalberg funeral, 371; United Artists, 52

Chase, Charley, 133

Chatterton, Ruth, 103, 108, 227, 371

Cheri-Bibi, 139

Chevalier, Maurice, 227, 245; *The Cardboard Lover*, 271–72; Garbo and, 274; *The Merry Widow*, 238, 257–58; screen test, 85; Shearer and, 253; top billing, 271–72

Chiang Kai-shek, 246, 325

China, *The Good Earth*, 246, 324–26

China Seas, 208–9, 270, 280–81, 290, 291, 319

Christians, Mady, 246, 333

Christina, 203

Churchill, Winston, 148

cinematography: *Marie Antoinette*, 392–93; moving pictures, 106; multiple-camera, 115–16, 143; one-camera setups, 116; *Romeo and Juliet*, 343–44; zoom lens, 115. *See also* cameramen; Technicolor

Circe the Enchantress, 37

City Lights, 133

Claire, Ina, 102, 104, 139, 194, 267

Clive of India, 266

Cochrane, Robert H., 7, 10, 73

Cocoanuts, The, 276, 278, 283

Code. *See* Production Code

Cody, Lew, 60, 68, 127

Coffee, Lenore: *Arsene Lupin*, 203; and Bern, 202, 203, 206; *Captain Applejack*, 31; and Gable as Harvard guy, 157; *Marie Antoinette*, 384; marriage, 202; Metro-Goldwyn merger, 37; *Rasputin*, 193; on Thalberg, 9–10, 42, 71–72, 102, 141, 142, 144–46, 147, 299

Cohn, Harry, 257–58, 272, 321, 371

Cohn, Joe/J.J., 24, 35, 36, 50, 272; Africa shoot, 134; *The Good Earth*, 326–27; *Marie Antoinette*, 386; *Mutiny on the Bounty*, 285; *Tarzan*, 169–70; Thalberg death, 369, 371; Thalberg depressed, 353

Colbert, Claudette, 227, 380, 384

Collier, Buster, 83

Collier, Constance, 340, 341, 391

Collison, Wilson, 207

Colton, John, 38–39, 112, 159

Columbia, 228; Capra, 239–40; *The Cardboard Lover*, 271–72; Harry Cohn, 257–58, 272; Gilbert, 300

communism: Mayer and, 298; Upton Sinclair's constituents, 263; SWG and, 308, 309, 311, 313; Thalberg and, 88, 239, 303

Connelly, Marc, 323

Connolly, Walter, 302

Considine, John, 321, 369

Conway, Jack, 38–39; Astor child custody trial, 321; bridge, 95; Del Monte Lodge gathering, 360; and Harlow, 178–79; talkies, 98; Thalberg death, 366, 368, 369; Thalberg-Mayer conflict, 299; Thalberg right to be wrong,

Thalberg funeral, 371. *See also* Studio
Relations Committee (SRC)
Joy, Leatrice, 39, 300
Joyce, Peggy Hopkins, 40, 75
June, Ray, 247
Jungle, The, 187–88

Kalmar, Bert, 278, 283
Katz, Sam, 278
Kaufman, George S., 230, 278–79, 290,
320–21, 384
Keaton, Buster, 41; alcoholic misbehav-
ior, 141, 198; decline, 166–67; *Grand
Hotel,* 167–68; Hollywood adjustment,
9; Metro-Goldwyn used by, 52, 53;
M-G-M, 60, 69, 83, 103, 126, 132,
140–41, 166–68; talkies, 103, 140;
The Three Ages, 24
Keenan, Frank, 21
Keith, Ian, 139, 205
Kelly, Mildred, 268
Kennedy, Joseph, 246
Kern, Jerome, 257, 392
King Kong, 206
Kiss, The, 106, 124, 201
Klabund, Alfred, 192–93
Klaw, Marc, 48
Klumph, Helen, 43
Knights of the Round Table, 318
Knoblock, Edward, 132
Kolker, Henry, 392
Kongo, 165, 190, 208
Koverman, Ida, 82, 245
Kraft-Ebbing, Richard, 179
Kraly, Hans, 371
Kuykendall, Ed, 249

labor: Hollywood labor movement,
306–14; *Riffraff* stance, 318; strikes,
234–35, 308–12; Thalberg vs. insubordination in, 301, 303, 304–14
La Cava, Gregory, 256
Lady Mary's Lover, 240, 244

Lady's Morals, A, 116
Lady of the Night, 43, 109
Lady to Love, A, 118–19
Laemmle, Carl: celebrations of, 133, 297–
98; Thalberg funeral, 371; Thalberg
introduction and job, 5–8, 10–12, 15–
16, 20; Thalberg meeting Marion, 7, 66
Laemmle, Carl Jr., 10, 297
Laemmle, Rosabelle, 10–11, 15, 40, 64,
366
LaMarr, Barbara, 25, 30, 201–2, 204
Lamarr, Hedy, 397
Lambert, Gavin, 339
Lanchester, Elsa, 274
Landi, Elissa, 241
Lang, Fritz, 85
Langdon, Harry, 104
Langley, Robert W., 220
Lasky, Jesse, 58; Astor child custody
trial, 321; Chevalier, 85; Famous
Players–Lasky, 23, 29, 227; Hayes,
132; Hopkins, 227; Mankiewicz, 115;
not invited to Thalberg dinners, 274;
Paramount ousting, 215; Shearer abil-
ity deprecated by, 339; Swanson and,
246; Thalberg death/funeral, 369,
371; Thalberg job search, 16
Lassie, Come Home, 396
Last Laugh, The, 61
Laughton, Charles, 252–53; *Goodbye,
Mr. Chips,* 322; *Marie Antoinette,* 387;
Mutiny on the Bounty, 282, 285–88;
after Thalberg death, 378; Thalberg
dinner guest, 274, 275
Laurel, Stan, 133
Lawrence, Eddie, 316–17
Lawson, John Howard, 115, 306
Lawton, Frank, 342
Lederman, D. B., 5
Lehar, Franz, 259
Lehr, Abraham, 24, 35, 44, 371
Leonard, Robert Z., 10, 36–37, 125, 248,
360, 371, 379

Marlowe, Julia, 336
Marmorston, Jessie, 171, 356, 396
Marsh, Oliver, 192
Marshall, Herbert, 247–48
Marshall, Tully, 208
Marx, Chico, 205–6, 275, 276–78
Marx, Groucho, 276–79, 282, 283, 290, 328–29, 379
Marx, Harpo, 276–77, 283, 328, 360, 362
Marx, Samuel, 107, 265, 266–67; *Amusements*, 111; assistant spying on SWG writers, 314; *The Barretts of Wimpole Street*, 251; Bern, 201, 202, 205–6, 209, 210, 211n, 213–15, 300; on box office, 268; *Camille*, 334; Christmas Eve celebration, 219; Del Monte Lodge gatherings, 353, 360, 362, 363; double-star films, 167–68; earthquake, 234; and Fitzgerald, 164, 165; *A Free Soul*, 155; Gilbert restoration, 122, 123; Griffith comeback, 277; Hearst's La Cuesta Encantada, 251–52; Henrietta's hold on Irving, 291; *Home, James*, 268; and "Irving's Boys," 147, 200; *It Can't Happen Here*, 302; labor politics, 309, 312; leaving M-G-M, 396, 397; and Marx Brothers, 277; Mayer's announcement of pay cuts, 234; *Operator 13*, 251; on playwrights, 269; previews, 181; *Red-Headed Woman*, 163; *Romeo and Juliet*, 338–39, 350; Shearer bowing out, 379; Upton Sinclair, 187–88; *Tarzan of the Apes*, 169; Thalberg charitable contributions, 276; Thalberg death, 370, 378; Thalberg era in books by, 397; Thalberg-Gilbert friendship, 168; Thalberg meeting, 6; Thalberg and music, 321; Thalberg screenwriting offer, 111–12, 117–18; Thalberg and Shearer property, 244; Thalberg taxes, 101–2; *Trader Horn*,

135, 136; Universal, 9, 10, 21, 111; wife Marie, 188, 251
Marx, Zeppo, 276
Marx Brothers, 276–79, 282–84, 298, 310; *A Day at the Races*, 313, 322, 327–30, 360, 370; Thalberg funeral, 371. See also *A Night at the Opera*
Mary Dugan, 98–99, 100–101, 106, 115
Mary of Scotland, 255, 271
Masefield, John, 337, 339
Maskerade, 323
Mask of Fu Manchu, The, 172, 190
Masks of the Devil, The, 87
Mason, Verne, 287
Mata Hari, 138, 154, 158–59, 167
Mathis, June, 44, 48, 49, 53
Mayer, Edith. *See* Goetz, Edith (Mayer's daughter)
Mayer, Irene. *See* Selznick, Irene Mayer (Mayer's daughter)
Mayer, Louis Burt, 17–20, 111; assistant Mannix, 75, 83, 200, 297; and *Ben-Hur*, 48–49; birth, 17; and Chevalier, 85; childhood, 17; depression economics, 133, 162, 219, 234; Dr. Marmorston, 396; Fox purchase and ownership of Loew's, 95, 96–97, 102, 107; and Gable-Crawford affair, 157–58; vs. Gilbert, 54–55, 94, 104, 121, 122, 299, 300; and Goldwyn, 24–25, 299; and *Great Day*, 117; and *Greed*, 46–47; and Haines, 138; and *Hallelujah!*, 105; Louis B. Mayer Productions, 18–31, 35–36; Metro-Goldwyn, 30–31, 35–36, 41, 46–47, 52–55; office at Goldwyn, 35; Orpheum, 18; president of Motion Picture Producers Association, 358; Republican politics, 82, 88, 94, 96, 111, 199, 215, 263; self-doubt, 19; and sexuality, 18, 19–20, 27, 39, 55; and Shearer, 22, 26–28, 36, 77, 379–80, 384–85, 388; and Thalberg's shares of Loew's after death, 380–82, 384,

317. *See also* Thalberg, Irving Grant, and Norma Shearer—marriage and family; Thalberg, Irving Grant, and Norma Shearer—social life

Thalberg, Irving Grant—finances: card game, 275, 287; charitable contributions, 275–76; generosity, 276; investments, 89–90, 102, 107, 217, 272, 289, 380; Loew's shares, 59–60, 107, 217, 272, 380–82, 384, 388–89; pay before M-G-M, 15–16, 20, 57; pay from M-G-M, 59–60, 107–8, 158–59, 160, 186, 216–17, 239, 308; Selznick company backing, 289; Shearer buying out contract, 380; will, 288, 380

Thalberg, Irving Grant—health, 199, 264–65; Bickford on, 120; congenital heart defect, 3, 15, 368; Dr. Groedel, 148–49, 230, 235, 356, 363, 365–66, 368; Dr. Marmorston, 171, 356; Dr. Newmark, 220, 356, 364–66, 367–68; Dr. Perla, 171, 356, 359; dying, 364–68; expected life span, 3, 5, 14, 20, 28–29, 111, 171, 359, 362; heart attacks, 56, 63, 220, 223–26; Henrietta and, 3, 5, 15, 20–21, 56, 57, 82–83, 126, 147, 171, 220, 299, 365–68; home protections for, 295; hydrotherapeutic treatment, 148–49; illnesses, 4, 56–57, 60–61, 131, 220, 333, 362–68; insurance premiums, 102; Mayer absences and, 94, 111; and M-G-M contract, 215–17; and M-G-M reorganization, 224–29, 235–36, 238; newborn daughter's effect, 290–91; palpitations and pains, 295–96, 356; Roaring Twenties, 89; and second child, 262–63; and Selznick International Pictures, 297; Shearer and, 57, 147, 148–49, 171, 220, 225–26, 230, 238, 288, 299, 327, 359, 362–68; stable, 356–57; strain showing, 328; and Thalberg-Mayer

confrontations, 299; tonsillitis, 229–30, 235; Winchell column and, 358; and workload, 61, 94, 199, 295, 297

Thalberg, Irving Grant—Mayer relationship: bonding, 27, 28–29, 56; Henrietta and, 20–21; independent Thalberg corporation, 298–99, 358–59; letter exchange, 230–33; Mayer absences, 94, 111, 157–58, 215; Mayer hostility, 298; Mayer not invited to Thalberg dinners, 274; Mayer stonewalling, 241; meeting, 16, 18, 19–20, 313; power struggle, 215–20, 243–44; at public events, 272; schism, 93–96; and Selznick joining M-G-M, 226; Thalberg death, 366, 367, 368, 369–70; Thalberg desire to leave M-G-M, 215–17, 265, 298; Thalberg funeral, 370–71, 373; after Thalberg heart attack, 220, 223–32, 235–36; Thalberg men friends, 147; Thalberg pay, 108, 216–17; Thalberg theater-derived projects, 191; Thalberg wedding, 77; Thalberg workload, 297

Thalberg, Irving Grant—M-G-M, 54, 59–76, 86–88, 90–128, 131–68; and actors, 119–21, 128, 131–33, 142, 147–51, 304–6; administration building named after, 394; adventurous filmmaking, 168–69; aphorisms, 182; Bern friendship and death, 200, 202, 203, 210–15, 217, 220, 300, 357; on box office, 268; and censorship, 73, 113–15, 125, 128, 153–57, 164–65, 177–83, 189, 249–60, 302, 318, 344; change in, 271–72; Christmas Eve celebration, 219–20; contracts, 57, 59–60, 75, 140, 186, 216–17; corporation as family, 304; death, 370; depression economics, 133, 162, 166–67, 182, 183–84, 186, 199, 200, 217, 244; desire to leave M-G-M, 215–17, 265; difference between Mayer M-G-M and, 395–96;

and Niven double-dating with, 345–
46; projection booth in home, 206–7;
Schenck yacht, 110, 283, 320–21; soirees at home, 162–63, 274–75; trips to
Europe, 84–86, 147–49, 230, 233–39,
242, 322, 355, 383

Thalberg, Irving, Jr. (son), 131, 398;
birth, 127; Europe trip, 147–48, 230,
237; father's death, 368, 373; father-
son relation, 199, 216, 295, 357–58,
359; father's will, 380; *Lady Mary's
Lover* set, 248; and Mary MacArthur,
230; pool, 295, 356; sister's birth, 291

Thalberg, Katharine (daughter), 333;
birth, 288, 290–91, 340; death, 398;
father's death, 368, 369, 373; father's
relationship with, 357–58, 359; father's
will, 380; pool, 356; travel plans, 355

Thalberg Weingarten, Sylvia (sister), 3,
20, 90, 272–73; divorce, 396; Irving's
death, 366, 367–68, 369

Thalberg, William (father), 3, 20; at
home, 3, 53–54, 82, 272–73; Irving's
death, 366, 368, 369, 370

Thau, Benjamin, 143, 234

theater. *See* Broadway

theaters. *See* movie theaters

Their Own Desire, 109, 110

Thérèse Raquin, 85

There You Are! 60

They Knew What They Wanted, 118

Thin Man films, 388, 396

Thomas, A. E., 268

Thomas, Bob, 109, 215, 237, 304, 397

Thorpe, Franklyn, 320–21

Those Three French Girls, 146

Three Ages, The, 24

Three Weeks, 37–38, 246

Thy Name Is Woman, 30

Tibbett, Lawrence, 116, 123, 202–3

Tiffany Productions, 24

Time magazine, 248, 352

Time, the Comedian, 60

Tinfoil, 181, 192

Tish, 378

Today We Live, 236

Todd, Thelma, 133, 300, 372

Tolstoy, Leo, 71

To Mary, with Love, 297

Tone, Franchot, 241; Crawford dating,
269; *Mutiny on the Bounty,* 284, 287,
310; Thalberg funeral, 371

Too Beautiful, 273

Torrent, The, 66, 69

Tourneur, Jacques, 389

Tracy, Spencer, 266, 371, 387

Trader Horn, 87, 133–37, 169

Trail of '98, The, 86, 87, 285

Treasure Island, 335

Trego, Charles, 326

Trial of Mary Dugan, The, 98–99, 100–
101, 106, 115

Triangle Films, 23

Trotti, Lamar, 157, 178–79

Tu, Ting-Hsui, 325–26

Tucker, George Loane, 18

Tully, Jim, 41, 42, 75

Turkey, Armenian genocide, 301

Turn About, 219

Turner, Lana, 397

Turney, Catherine, 307

Twentieth Century–Fox, 297–98, 336,
387

Twentieth Century Pictures, 240, 254,
266; Twentieth Century–Fox, 297–
98, 336, 387

Two Worlds/Lady of the Night, 43, 109

Ulric, Lenore, 333, 371

Unashamed, 165

Unholy Night, The, 106

Unholy Three, The, 121, 127, 209

United Artists (UA), 52; Art Cinema
Corporation, 250; Lewin, 397; Joseph
Schenck, 83, 140, 215, 250; Stromberg,
396; Twentieth Century Pictures, 297

Universal City, founded, 6
Universal Film Manufacturing Company, 5–16, 20; Bickford, 120; celebrations of Laemmle, 133, 297–98; Cochrane, 7, 10, 73; economics, 161, 224, 266, 297; horror films saving from bankruptcy, 189; Laemmle's son Carl Jr., 297; Samuel Marx, 9, 10, 21, 111; name, 23; New, 297, 322; Stroheim, 12–14, 44, 46, 133; Thalberg, 5–16, 21, 25, 39, 46; Thalberg funeral, 371; Whale, 322. *See also* Laemmle, Carl
Upright, Blanche, 27

Vajda, Ernst, 252, 258, 385, 388
Valentino, Rudolph, 24, 44, 48, 52, 53, 202
Van Dyke, Woodbridge Strong ("W.S."/Woody), 201; *Marie Antoinette*, 388–92, 394; *Tarzan*, 169; Thalberg funeral, 371; *Trader Horn*, 134–35, 136, 169
Vanessa, Her Love Story, 256
Vanity Fair, 75
Van Runkle, Samuel, 7
Van Vechten, Carl, 74
Variety: The Broadway Melody, 93; Gilbert in talkies, 104; *Grand Hotel*, 168; *The Lights of New York*, 88; *Marie Antoinette*, 394; *Mary Dugan*, 106; *Redemption*, 121; on Tibbett in talkies, 116; *The Wind*, 86
Veiller, Bayard: *Arsene Lupin*, 203; Coffee and, 142, 145; *Mary Dugan*, 98, 99, 100–101; *Mata Hari*, 159; on Thalberg, 172–73, 179; Thalberg funeral, 371; *Within the Law*, 126
Velez, Lupe, 166, 227
Vidor, Doris Warner, 81
Vidor, King, 36, 61–62, 288; *The Big Parade*, 56, 60, 62; *The Crowd*, 87; and Fitzgerald, 164; Gilbert's parties,

69–70; and Gish, 65; and Glyn, 38; Goldwyn Company, 24; *Hallelujah!*, 105–6; Normand funeral, 127; and talkies, 88; Thalberg funeral, 371; Thalberg social scene, 38
Viertel, Salka, 203, 241, 279, 307–8, 318, 330–31
Virtuous Wives, 18
Vitaphone, 78, 81–82, 87–88, 112, 113
Voice of the City, 118
voice training, 100, 341–42
Vorkapich, Slavko, 326

Wallace, Lew, 48
Wallis, Hal, 81
Walsh, George, 48, 49
Walton, Douglas, 209n
Wanger, Walter, 245; Anti-Nazi League dinner, 309; *Gabriel Over the White House*, 223; and Mayer, 217; on Thalberg, 165, 171, 182; "unit system," 236
Wanters, The, 27
Warner, Harry, 81
Warner, Jack, 276; Astor child custody trial, 321; Cosmopolitan Productions, 262; Max Reinhardt signed by, 336; and salary cuts, 237; and SRC, 157; Thalberg funeral, 371; and writers, 147, 311
Warner Bros.: business model, 227–28; Code, 114; Cosmopolitan Productions, 262; economics, 161, 216, 224, 227, 237, 266; *Gone with the Wind*, 320; Leslie Howard, 337, 342; *The Jazz Singer*, 78, 81–82, 88; David Lewis, 378, 397; *Little Caesar*, 121, 139, 142; M-G-M trailing, 112, 115; *A Midsummer Night's Dream*, 297, 336, 337; Muni, 324; Robinson, 121; Shearer loan-out films, 36; talkies, 78, 81–82, 87–88, 90, 121; Tashman, 226; Zanuck, 142, 237. *See also* Warner, Jack

Text: 10.25/14 Fournier

Display: Fournier

Indexer: Barbara Roos

Compositor: BookMatters, Berkeley

Printer and binder: Sheridan Books, Inc.